HANDBOOK OF ASIAN MANAGEMENT

HANDBOOK OF ASIAN MANAGEMENT

Edited by

Kwok Leung

City University of Hong Kong

And

Steven White

INSEAD, France and Singapore

KLUWER ACADEMIC PUBLISHERS
Boston / Dordrecht / London

Distributors for North, Central and South America:
Kluwer Academic Publishers
101 Philip Drive
Assinippi Park
Norwell, Massachusetts 02061 USA
Telephone (781) 871-6600
Fax (781) 681-9045
E-Mail <kluwer@wkap.com>
Distributors for all other countries:
Kluwer Academic Publishers Group
Post Office Box 17
3300 AH Dordrecht, THE NETHERLANDS
Tel: +31 (0) 78 657 60 00
Fax: +31 (0) 78 657 64 74

E-Mail <services@wkap.nl>

   Electronic Services <http://www.wkap.nl>

Handbook of Asian Management / edited by Kwok Leung and Steven White.
    p.cm.
    Includes bibliographical references and index.
ISBN HB: 1-4020-7754-8 (alk.paper)
ISBN E-book: 1-4020-7932-X
    1. Management—Asia. 2. Organizational behavior—Asia. 3. Strategic planning—Asia. 4. Personnel management—Asia. I. Leung, Kwok, 1958-II. White, Steven, 1963-

HD70.A7H365 2004
658'.0095—dc22   **2004044052**

TABLE OF CONTENTS

FOREWORD

John Child
Birmingham Business School
University of Birmingham

No one can afford to ignore Asia. This is not just because of its past, as the cradle of great civilizations and religions. Nor is it just because of its present, as the largest landmass on earth, the home to more people than any other continent, and the greatest aggregation of economic activity. The significance of Asia lies as much as anything in the way its future is emerging as a steadily developing force in the world economy. The newly industrialized Asian nations located in the East and South of the continent are, in most cases, maintaining high rates of growth and combining these with current account surpluses. They are becoming increasingly integrated into the global economic system, and some are playing a major role in the global redistribution of employment as companies outsource their manufacturing to countries like China, and their service support activities, notably to India. Although Japan's economy has been stalled for a long time, even this is showing signs of recovery at the time of writing, and many Japanese companies remain highly successful competitors in the world market. As Asia's economic power grows, so too will its political influence in the world's affairs.

The significance and relative success of many Asian countries requires that the ways in which they manage their business and other organizations be given much more careful and considered attention than has generally been the case to date. Many of the contributions to this wide-ranging Handbook justifiably complain that the wrong assumptions have been made, and the wrong questions therefore asked, about Asian management. Among the commonly made but incorrect assumptions are that Asia is sufficiently homogeneous to be treated as one region or cultural area, and that the study of Asian management can unproblematically be fitted into "Western" theoretical frameworks, usually those emanating from North America. On the contrary, Asian management needs to be studied with sensitivity to its special features. Only then can conclusions be drawn as to how far existing concepts and theories are adequate to account for its characteristics. In turn, we may expect Asian management research to contribute importantly to further theoretical development. This is partly because management in Asian countries has its own distinct features, and partly because the rapid rate of change being experienced in many parts of Asia can bring to light the dynamic processes that inform theoretical understanding. The subject therefore presents all the opportunities of what is still a new research frontier. This is a further, and arguably more important, reason to grant Asian management priority in our research agendas, over and above the continent's economic standing.

The study of Asian management has, with few exceptions, suffered from several limitations. The first is that there are large areas of Asia in which management has been barely studied, if at all. This applies to much of the Middle East, Central Asia and Indonesia. The cultural, economic, and social heterogeneity of the continent means that conclusions cannot be drawn from just some countries, albeit that they are influential ones, and then applied to the others. Management scholars have so far given most of their attention to only a limited number of Asian countries. These are the industrialized or industrializing societies – notably China, India and Japan, and the four so-called little dragons of Hong Kong, Korea, Singapore and Taiwan. A further, related limitation is the tendency to intimate a false homogeneity to certain regions of Asia, usually by focusing on one of their common characteristics at the expense of others. For example, the East Asian countries have often been classified in terms of their common Confucian heritage, ignoring the substantial political and institutional differences between them.

Another problem arises from intellectual arrogance. This is an unwillingness to accept the possibility that research in Asia may require a substantial revision of our existing theories, if they are to be generally applicable. Rather than dismissing results from Asia as an aberration that does not "fit" a theory to which we remain committed – the exception that is assumed to prove the rule – we need to remain open to the likelihood of having to develop and validate new models and theories that can accommodate what is found in Asia. This is a fundamental issue, on which a number of chapters in this Handbook elaborate.

One of the prime contributions of this Handbook derives from the editors' requirement that each author should contribute to a broadening of the reader's perspective on Asian management. Each chapter not only offers a review or critique of research on an aspect of Asian management, but also signposts avenues for further research, suggesting questions that need to be addressed. In addition, some chapters discuss methodological procedures that can be followed in order to enhance the validity of such research. In the present underdeveloped state of research in this field, it is important to explore the intrinsic qualities of Asian management and organization with interpretative sensitivity, as well as undertaking larger-scale comparisons that aim to examine the limits of generalization. The problem is that Asia is hugely diverse, and so are some of its large constituent countries. Given this diversity, it is not usually feasible to pursue both kinds of study at the same time, even though they need to inform each other continuously.

Two fundamental questions remain unresolved in Asian management research. The first is whether an understanding of Asian management requires its own idiosyncratic concepts or whether we can achieve sufficient equivalence between western and Asian concepts to permit valid comparative studies. For instance, is there sufficient overlap in their indexicality between a western concept such as "old-boy network" and the Chinese term "guanxi" such that both can be subsumed within the notion of "reciprocal relationship"? I have argued elsewhere that it should be possible to go beyond the inconsistency imposed by different formal definitions of culturally specific, yet similar, concepts to look for their constituent categories or dimensions (Child, 2000). The intention here is to arrive at a multidimensional operationalization of the concepts that not only takes into account those aspects supposed to be prominent within a given culture but that also permits an exploration of the possible overlap and similarities between dimensions emphasized by different cultures. The question is whether this procedure offers the prospect of a common operational basis for making comparisons within the space denoted by each concept. If it does, then we can progress along the road to conceptual equivalence.

The second question is whether we shall have to develop distinct theories for Asian management. Some years ago, I concluded from an analysis of management in China that we could, on the whole, find sufficient conceptual equivalence to deploy the same key terms in China as are used in the West – such as authority and control – but that China's unique situation required that the relationships between the variables identified by these concepts had to be modelled differently (Child, 1994). While I remain optimistic about conceptual equivalence, we have not advanced far enough to reach a clear conclusion on the extent to which our present theories would retain interpretative and predictive power if applied to Asian situations.

In any case, so many of these existing theories are inadequate even for the contexts in which they were formulated. Indeed, it may be that one contribution of research into Asian management will be to indicate theoretical refinements that can be applied to non-Asian contexts. Take, for example, the issue of international diversification. Studies of East Asian companies may serve to refine our general understanding of the role that social networks can play in the internationalisation of firms. State sponsorship, as illustrated by the experience of many Asian countries, may need to be added to the list of "ownership" advantages open to firms diversifying abroad. Examples of Chinese and Indian emigration may indicate how diasporas can also confer internationalisation advantages, perhaps through reducing the psychic distance of potential overseas investment locations where emigrants have settled. More broadly, research into the paths taken by Asian countries towards economic development can be expected to illuminate our existing development theories with respect to issues such as stages, modes and convergent versus non-convergent trajectories.

Despite the huge challenge that it presents, there is no question that research into Asian management needs to be given priority. Our professional pursuit of scholarship cannot allow us to rest content with simply assuming that conclusions drawn from another part of the world will necessarily apply to Asia. As Singh states in concluding his chapter in the Handbook, the conduct of contextually sensitive comparative research within Asia "is essential to allow consideration of whether there is value and validity in seeking to establish a theory applicable across a region that has some features in common but few that are shared." Whether the result is the formulation of new theories, the modification of existing theories to fit Asia, or an endorsement that existing theories are sufficiently comprehensive to encompass Asia, research that clarifies these possibilities would be highly valuable. To make the point in somewhat populist language, research on Asian management is an essential step towards the globalisation of management and organizational theory.

Such a large undertaking must in practice be broken down into manageable projects. These in turn require a focus around specific issues and an identification of theoretical perspectives that are sufficiently broad as not to be restrictive, yet sufficiently defined in order to offer some guidance. The wide scope of the contributions to this Handbook, which together articulate a range of potentially relevant perspectives and cover many topics at both a macro and micro organizational level, makes the book a valuable resource for the formulation of future projects.

A lesson that can be learned from this Handbook is that there is virtue in applying a range of theoretical perspectives to the study of Asian management, and of exploring the potential combinations or configurations between the variables they identify. For instance, there is a hiatus between the subject of comparative management, which primarily adopts a cross-cultural perspective, and the broader purview of international business and management research, which more readily takes into account the impact of institutional and political factors as well. The study of Asian management has for too long relied unduly upon a cross-cultural perspective, and many of the chapters in this Handbook illustrate the value of broadening beyond this. For example, it has become clear that the difficulties entrepreneurs from Hong Kong often encounter when operating in Mainland China are attributable mainly to institutional differences between the "two systems" of the "one country" rather than to cultural differences which are extremely low in the case of Guangdong Province. Attention to the institutional context draws attention to its level of maturity as a facet of economic and social development. It also points to the role of the state, which is often very active and extensive in Asian countries. Scholars such as Hall and Soskice (2001) and Whitley (1999) have drawn attention to the critical part that institutional differences play in giving rise to varieties of capitalism. Such differences are not only of obvious practical significance for the managers who work within them, but they also bear upon very large issues, such as the debate about whether economic development, transition and reform are accompanied by convergence.

Similarly, given the "high context" nature of most Asian cultures and institutional regimes, studies in the region need to take account of socio-institutional as well as economic explanations for phenomena such as firms' diversification strategies, as Lu and his colleagues argue in their chapter. At the same time, the retention of a strategic choice perspective in combination with a recognition of institutional constraints, as recommended by Carney and Gedajlovic, should enlighten our understanding of how Asian managers can through their own volition develop competitive strategies, including those that enable their firms to advance from the vulnerability of cost-leadership towards a differentiation strategy.

The Handbook of Asian Management brings together scholarly treatments of more issues and topics than any other single source on the subject. While the focus of its chapters broadly divides into "macro" and "micro" level subjects, it is a virtue of most contributors that they express an awareness of the interdependencies between the two levels of inquiry. This is evident, for example, in the way that several of the micro chapters draw attention to the sensitivity of managerial and organizational processes to their wider Asian contexts. A combination of the many macro and micro insights contained in the Handbook encourages a balanced view of the field, by indicating ways through which managerial action, organization, and environment interact and co-evolve.

The richness and quality of this Handbook will mark it out as a major source of reference for many years to come. It is a tribute to the foresight and determination of the editors that they have brought it to fruition.

REFERENCES

Child, J. 1994. *Management in China During the Age of Reform*. Cambridge: Cambridge University Press.

Child, J. 2000. Theorizing about organization cross-nationally. *Advances in Comparative International Management*, 13: 27-75.

Hall, P.A. and Soskice, D. 2001. *Varieties of Capitalism: The Institutional Foundations of Comparative Advantage*. Oxford: Oxford University Press.

Whitley, R. 1999. *Divergent Capitalisms: The Social Structuring and Change of Business Systems*. Oxford: Oxford University Press.

PREFACE

When Kluwer approached us with the idea of editing a handbook of Asian management, we hesitated. Would there be sufficient material for such a handbook, and could we recruit a slate of dedicated and high-calibre contributors who could make a valuable collective contribution? Eventually, we helped each other look at these questions as challenges instead of obstacles and, more importantly, as an opportunity to make a broad contribution to understanding what we do and do not know about management in this region. This project became the best way to take stock of research in this area and, perhaps even more importantly, identify what we do not know. After some scouting around, we were also encouraged by the large pool of academic talent that we could tap to realize such a project.

The "go" decision resulted in a three-year journey of virtual and face-to-face collaboration among authors, us and, at a symposium on the same theme at the Asian Academy of Management Conference in Bangkok in 2002, some of the growing number of academics with an interest in this region. Like any such project, ours had its ups and downs; frustration from delays, withdrawals, and heated debate around conceptual issues and interpretation of empirical data, balanced by many inspirational exchanges and pleasant gatherings. With the goodwill and hard work of everyone involved, however, the problems encountered were no more than typical bumps in an off-road rally, and well worth the bother given what we have found at the end of this journey. Nor was it all drudgery; working on this handbook gave the two editors a legitimate reason to hold long discussions over fine wine in Fontainebleau, seafood in Hong Kong, and amid the warm smiles of the Thai people. We can now see that this journey was less risk and offered more return than perhaps any of us—editors or contributors—may have expected. It has shown that a broadly dispersed "invisible college" has made great progress in furthering our understanding about management in Asia. Our contributors have also shown that there are large, numerous and critical blind spots in our understanding. Rather than a reason for despair, however, we see this situation as offering vast opportunities for current and future scholars to pursue exciting and meaningful lines of inquiry.

We are extremely glad that we have been involved in this soul-searching, path-finding effort. Of course, only time will tell whether our optimistic conclusions and outlook are justified, and whether we have collectively provided a spirit and direction for management research in Asia. We are confident, however, that this handbook represents an important stride in the right direction.

We would like to take this opportunity to thank the contributors for their sustained interest and commitment to this project, reflecting their personal dedication to developing Asian management research. We would also like to thank Crystal Farh for her meticulous work in formatting and copy-editing the drafts, as well as the staff at Kluwer for their professionalism in the production of the Handbook. Colleagues in INSEAD's Asian Business and Comparative Management Area have also provided useful feedback and, more importantly, moral support for pursuing rigorous and relevant research focused on this region. Last but not least, we would like to thank our families for their unfailing support and care, which has cushioned us against the bumps and jerks along this three-year journey.

Kwok Leung
Hong Kong

Steven White
Fontainebleau

PART I

INTRODUCTION

Chapter 1

TAKING STOCK AND CHARTING A PATH FOR ASIAN MANAGEMENT RESEARCH

Kwok Leung
City University of Hong Kong

Steven White
INSEAD, France and Singapore

INTRODUCTION

No other region compares to Asia in terms of mid- and long-term growth trends or prospects for the future. China has continued to record consistently high growth rates, despite zigzagging reforms in its business and political systems. Even the most pessimistic observers recognize China's eventual role as a major economic competitor to the United States, Western Europe and Japan. While Japan's economy has stagnated for more than a decade, it is still the second largest economy in the world, and firms in certain industries—autos and consumer electronics, for example—continue to be global leaders. The four dragons and other ASEAN states, after having sustained phenomenal growth for decades, were in temporary shock after the 1997 Asian financial crisis. Although some argue that many of the fundamental problems that led to that crisis—at both the national, institutional and corporate levels—have survived reform efforts, most of those economies and surviving firms seem to be emerging with stronger fundamentals and improving performance. In summary, despite misgivings in particular areas, overall the region is one of the most dynamic and promising in the world.

Our understanding of management in this increasingly important region, however, is fragmented and lags too far behind its significance in the world economy. In a recent review of twenty years of management research in the region, White (2002) concludes that the focus of Asian management research has been limited to a small number of countries, primarily Japan and more recently China. Cross-country comparisons within the region are rare, with most scholars focusing on how management phenomena in Asia differ from those in the US. The development of new constructs and theory drawing on Asian contexts has been a relatively rare pursuit, and even rarer are the export and testing of such conceptual results outside of the region.

In many ways, White's conclusions simply confirmed what many scholars had realized themselves within their more restricted areas of management research. Too often, however, those conclusions were ignored in otherwise standard journal articles that perpetuated rather than challenged the pattern of restricted inquiry. "Suggestions for future research" to correct these problems have hardly been followed up, while research on topics considered "legitimate" continues to flourish within accepted paradigms. The result has been a stock of research that is often intellectually unadventurous and uncritical of its fundamental (usually US-based) theoretical assumptions and epistemology.

In this respect, this *Handbook of Asian Management* represents much more than the most comprehensive set of critical reviews of major areas in organizational behavior and strategic management. The volume is also a call to arms for researchers who investigate management issues in Asia to show the confidence to challenge "legitimate" theories, exposing implicit assumptions and establishing boundary conditions underlying constructs, frameworks and theory developed in other contexts. It is also a call for researchers to shrug off the self-perpetuating image of either "Asia hands" or eccentrics who drift into "fringe" areas, and to play a central role in theory building and "mainstream" intellectual debate. To this end, the authors of each chapter provide a map of research and findings conducted so far, and also point the way towards research that will be rigorous, relevant and influential in Asia and in the rest of the world.

Without repeating the specific findings and recommendations of the authors of the chapters, we present in the following a number of significant themes that run through many of their analyses, conclusions and recommendations. We hope that our discussion of these themes will provide a roadmap for our individual and collective pursuits of more rewarding research in the region and become the basis for moving it to a central position in management discourse.

WHAT DOES RESEARCH IN ASIA OFFER?

Asia represents one and many different management contexts, but differences alone need not be the only justification for funding, conducting or publishing research on the region. Nor will the justifications be the same for all researchers concerned; for example, we may reasonably expect Asians, or scholars based in the region, to have different motivations than "outsiders". However, the researchers contributing to this handbook have shown that research in this region is important beyond parochial concerns, and not just because it is "different" from a Western context. Below, we consolidate the reasons that emerge from the chapters in this volume.

Asia as a source of problems and phenomena

For researchers driven by an interest in understanding empirical phenomena, Asian contexts offer a broad range of problems and phenomena that are unique or relatively rare in other contexts. Particular problems and behaviors may be more common in the cultural, social, political, and economic contexts in or across Asia than in Western contexts usually studied. For example, China—not the US or Western Europe—is an ideal context to study the process and impact at all levels of analysis of a business system's transition from central planning to a more decentralized (even if not pure "market") system. The particular configuration of cultural dimensions will make the specific dynamics and process in China different from that of Russia or other Eastern European business systems undergoing a similar transition (Child, 1994). The role, dynamics and relative importance of family businesses similarly reflect the particular social and economic features in the region (Redding, 2001), thus sharing some but not all characteristics with family enterprises in other regions (e.g., Khanna and Palepu, 1997; Fukuyama, 1995; Carney and Gedajlovic, this volume).

The region also offers an important context for empirical research and theory development related to international joint ventures as firms and managers based in very different business systems are coming together. Research on Sino-foreign joint ventures, for example, has highlighted the relatively greater importance of the state in their formation and evolution, as well as cross-cultural dynamics, and has lead to considerable progress in our understanding of international joint ventures in general (e.g., Kotabe and Zhao, 2002; Leung, Smith, Wang, and Sun, 1996; Yan, 2000).

The various configurations of cultural features and societal characteristics of Asian countries give rise to differences in observed behaviors and outcomes at all levels of analysis. In some cases, as Singh (this volume) points out, the difference may not involve "new" variables, but a difference in the salience of particular variables in the Asian context. In other cases, observed differences may be the result of alternative causal chains; i.e., a similar set of antecedents is related to different outcomes. Heracleous' (2001) finding of the relatively high performance of state-owned enterprises in Singapore, for example, calls into question simple conclusions regarding the link between state-ownership and low performance found in other contexts. Along the same line of enquiry, Lu, Bruton, and Lan (this volume) have found important differences in the diversification strategies of Asian and Western firms, while Xiao and Su (this volume) find significant differences in decision-making processes.

Finally, Asia offers a wide variety of contexts in which the process and outcomes of change can be studied. Many of the countries and firms in the region have grown and evolved dramatically in a relatively short time frame. It is possible to track such changes and draw comparisons with other countries or firms that have chosen alternative paths. Descriptive comparisons can reveal alternative trajectories of change and highlight key contingencies in the process. For example, the 1997 financial crisis in Asia represents an environmental jolt of a much greater magnitude and impact than found in today's developed market economies, and provides a golden opportunity for studying how drastic environmental changes impact organizational restructuring. Again, a comparison of the antecedents of and responses to the crisis in Asian contexts with the antecedents and responses in similar crises in other contexts—Russia and South America, for example—represents an unexploited opportunity for practice and theory development.

Asia as a theory-testing ground

If local research focusing explicitly on local problems and phenomena (often reported in local outlets) is discounted, by far the most common use of Asian contexts is to "test" theory and hypotheses developed in, primarily, the US. This is where the bulk of OB research incorporating the region falls, often through explicit comparisons of Asian and non-Asian samples. In strategy, this takes the form of including country dummy variables in regression models when Asian (usually Japanese) firms are included in a broader sample. In other cases, the generality of Western theories is tested through implicit comparison, with findings from Western studies compared to those of studies collecting data on (supposedly) the same variables in an Asian context.

While the evaluation of Western theories in Asia is useful, this type of research can easily fall prey to a common trap in cross-cultural research; namely, there is usually insufficient recognition that key variables or relationships may have very different meanings, or a different range of meanings and implications, than in the original setting. "Conceptual equivalence" is often elusive in cross-cultural research (van de Vijver and Leung, 1997), and it cannot be ascertained by simple methodological safeguards such as translation/back-translation. For example, interorganizational relationships in Asia may represent more than simply an economic or task-defined solution to the problem of accessing or acquiring resources. To the extent that the firm represents an organ and instrument of a founder or founding family, the decision to form, terminate or introduce changes to an alliance may depend more on variables not usually incorporated into "mainstream" studies of alliances. Similarly, studies of conflict resolution generally conclude that conflict avoidance is an unproductive strategy for handling a conflict in the West. In Asia, however, this strategy occurs more frequently because of its overtone of harmony, which is a central Asian value (Tinsley and Brodt, this volume). If such differences in the Asian context are recognized and incorporated into the research design (a "value-added" replication), results from such studies can further our understanding of both the Asian context and the original context on which the study was based.

Asia as a source of constructs and theory

It would be self-handicapping if Asian management research were only concerned with validating Western constructs and theories. Original constructs, relationships and findings from research in Asian contexts holds considerable promise to inform, refine, and extend research conducted elsewhere. Indeed, this is one of the most common justifications that scholars offer for conducting Asian-based research and presenting results based on Asian samples (e.g., Shenkar and von Glinow, 1994; Biggart and Hamilton, 1992; Boyacigiller and Adler, 1991).

Unfortunately, the feedback from Asia-focused research and scholars to "mainstream" theories has been minimal. Perhaps the strongest impact has been the steady stream of management research in Asia in which the nature of relationships among individual or organizational actors is a central issue (e.g., work on firm-supplier relationships by Bensaou and Venkatraman (1995), or Ouchi's (1981) Theory Z). This focus on the nature and implications of relationships is common to much of the research in the region and across levels of analysis, reflected in the dominant themes and associated phenomena of networks, in/out-groups, trust, cooperation and collectivism. Ng and Ang (this volume) provide an insightful analysis of how relationalism in Asia gives rise to some distinct features of human resource management practices in this region. As we have argued, concern with one's interconnections and dependence on others, often associated with collectivism or allocentricism, is part of the configuration defining the region (Hofstede, 1980).

It is not a coincidence that interest in relational and network phenomena among mainstream researchers and managers gained momentum during the 1980s as Japanese firms seemed able to gain competitive advantage through relationships among employees as well as between organizations. This relational perspective presented a contrast and challenge to Western assumptions that individuals and organizations should be viewed as atomistic economic actors. At a more general level, one may even argue that relational issues are also important in the West, but they have been ignored because of an individualist bias among Western researchers. The emphasis on relationalism thus can shed light on a blind spot in Western management research, which is exactly the kind of contribution that Asian management research must continue to make.

In more specific topical areas of management research, however, Asian research does not seem to have realized its promise in terms of refining Western theories or developing new ones. One reason mentioned is that the bulk of researchers and studies have been focused on a relatively unambitious goal—testing Western theories. Another reason may be due to the entrenched research paradigms in the West, which have a tendency to relegate Asian findings that identify boundary conditions, additional moderating variables, or alternative processes and relationships to the fringe of research findings. Kuhn (1970) has shown how strong paradigms may develop a life of their own and become self-perpetuating, even in the face of mounting contradictory findings. Some important Asian findings have fallen victim to such an exclusionary tendency in the face of dominant Western paradigms (see Shenkar, this volume, for an in-depth discussion of this issue).

We expect the particular cultural configuration that characterizes Asia to give rise to some novel constructs and theory that are relatively unexplored in the West. Furthermore, these constructs and theory may have relevance in the West as well as in other regions that share some of the cultural and structural characteristics of Asia. For example, the dynamics and implications of "guanxi" relationships may be key to understanding managerially relevant phenomena in Latin countries. Hitt, Lee, and Yucel (2002) even argue that guanxi and related notions from East Asia could provide a model for Western firms to emulate to enhance their global competitiveness. Similarly, unraveling the dynamics underlying the acceptance of logical contradictions (Nisbett, 2003) and the avoidance of disagreements (Leung and Tjosvold, 1998) in East Asia may be important for understanding conflict resolution, problem-solving, or organizational design in other collectivist contexts.

Asia as an alternative cluster of management systems

One of the most compelling reasons to study management issues in Asian contexts—and beyond the reasons discussed above—is that it is the most promising source of alternative systems of organizing human endeavor that is both (1) broadly different from the cluster based on the American model that currently dominates management theory and practice, and (2) economically competitive with the American model. The Western European model represents one alternative in which economic efficiency and competition are tempered by more humanist performance criteria and in which corporations are governed differently (e.g., O'Sullivan, 2000), but it is not yet clear whether these alternative configurations will survive the American challenge.

Besides Western Europe, however, no other region outside of Asia promises to offer broadly different and competitive alternatives. Continental Africa and the Middle East certainly have systems that differ significantly from that of the US, but they show no signs of giving rise in the future to systems that are competitive on a global scale. Central Europe, after a brief interlude of central planning and communist ideology, is rapidly regaining its "European" identity while simultaneously incorporating more and more elements of American management ideology and practice. Central and South America, also with distinctive local socioeconomic features, are similarly strongly influenced by the American system through their closer proximity and integration with the American economy.

In none of these cases are we arguing that the American socioeconomic system—a complex of values, behaviors and institutions—has been or will be perfectly replicated in other regions. Each nation and subnational region has distinct features that will preclude a replication of an American model in total. Still, we see variation between these systems and the American model as narrowing, even if not destined to converge.

The cluster of socioeconomic systems found in Asia, in contrast, differs fundamentally from that of the US-styled system on a broad range of dimensions. And while some of these features match those found in other regions, it is the configuration that, taken as a whole, differs most substantially. These configurations of features have given rise to alternative organizational forms and subsystems. Moreover, as Carney and Gedajlovic (this volume) argue, a number of these are not only the most competitive structures in their particular environments, but also characterize the global competitors that have emerged from the region. In spite of recent drops in economic performance—lasting over a decade in Japan, and during the post-1997 crisis years in Southeast Asia—these alternative systems seem to offer the greatest likelihood for an alternative and competitive approach to business and management.

The practical value of having insights into the business systems that offer the greatest promise (or threat, depending on one's point of view) as competitive alternatives should be obvious. Firms and industries, emerging from systems fostering different means and ends, will be competing and bring to the competition different strengths and weaknesses. One implication will be the continued specialization by different regions and economies in particular industries or types of economic activity. Gereffi (1994) has shown that socioeconomic features of business and management in the region have contributed to local firm's increasing role in global commodity chains. Redding (2001) similarly argues that the structure, control and other dynamics of Chinese family-owned enterprises that dominate many of the economies of the region are particularly well-suited to dealing with volatile environments and grasping fleeting opportunities. Allen and Gale (2000) have also identified alternative transaction structures that are most efficient in particular environments.

In the increasingly lucrative Asian markets, local firms and managers will have an advantage over outsiders who are not willing or able to adapt strategically to important elements of the local socioeconomic system. Of course, Asian firms will face similar challenges when they attempt to compete directly in markets outside of Asia (discussed by Pangarkar and Carney and Gedajlovic in their contributions to this volume). The winners in cross-system competitions will be those who are either more similar or able to adapt to local imperatives. In these cases, success using an exported business model will be strongly affected by the ability of a firm to achieve fit in environments that are of varying degrees of unfamiliarity. For example, the success of Japanese auto makers in the US market testifies to the importance of agile local adaptation as well as effective leverage of their competitive advantages (Florida and Kenney, 1991; Fucini and Fucini, 1990).

The theoretical importance of studying management in Asia does not lie in its competitive implications (although such implications will certainly attract funding from governments and firms), but that so many of the elements of Asian business systems are different from those in American or Western European contexts. The wide range of differences and their configuration at and across levels of analysis extends the use of Asian management research beyond the disciplinary and topical focus (i.e., specific phenomena, constructs and theory) into the increasingly important area of comparative business systems (e.g., Whitley, 1992; Redding, 2002).

ISSUES FOR THE FUTURE

Asian management research is still in its take-off stage, and there are a number of challenges that need to be tackled for the field to continue to progress. In this section, we highlight several critical conceptual and methodological challenges.

Are all Asians Alike?

Although "Asia" and its variants (e.g., East Asia, Southeast Asia) refer to a geopolitical cluster of countries, its relevance for research and the challenges it presents to practice stem from what are considered its social and cultural rather than physical distance from other regions. Culture, and its manifestations in individual behavior and social dynamics, has been implicitly accepted as similar enough across the region to justify generalizations based on an otherwise vague list of features.

The common cultural thread that runs through the entire Asia is that it has been characterized as collectivistic and high in power distance (Hofstede,

1980). By far the strongest dimension associated with the entire region is collectivism, which is often used at all levels of analysis to justify comparative analyses of samples from one or a few groups from any Asian country and a Western, usually American, sample. The importance of hierarchy or, in Hofstede's terminology "power distance", is also used to justify comparisons between Asian and Western/US samples. Similarly, paternalism within both firm and political systems has been offered as a characteristic shared broadly across the region (Whitley, 1992; Redding, 2001, 1990). A few researchers have identified holism, particularism, and communication patterns as particularly strong points of difference between their Asian and Western samples.

There are at least three major problems with this cultural approach. First, Asia is the largest continent on Earth, and the variation across Asia is phenomenal. Some of the wealthiest countries (Japan and Singapore) are neighbors to some of the poorest (e.g., Cambodia and Bangladesh). All major religions are represented; for example, Indonesia and Malaysia are Islamic, Thailand and Japan are Buddhist, Philippines is Catholic, and India is Hindu. Some countries are extremely homogenous ethnically (e.g., Japan and South Korea), while some are very diverse (e.g., Malaysia). Some countries are huge in terms of land area and populations (China and India), while others are tiny (e.g., Maldives and Singapore).

Variations on these features—economic development patterns or stages, political systems, ethnic composition, absolute size—could be critical factors in particular research questions pursued in the region. None of them, however, may be used as defining criteria for the entire region. The variation also precludes the development of sweeping generalizations for the entirety of Asia.

The second problem with the cultural approach is that the Asian cultural context is not unique in its cultural characterization. For example, in Hofstede's (1984) results, Central and South American countries as well as some Southern European countries (e.g., Greece) share a number of cultural features. If collectivism and power distance were the two sole explanatory mechanisms underlying a phenomenon, we would not expect any differences between Asian and Central and South America! There is an obvious need to go beyond broad, abstract cultural constructs and develop mid-range constructs that can differentiate Asian countries. One example is provided by Tinsley and Brodt (this volume), who propose the use of cognitive constructs such as frames, scripts and schemas to understand cultural differences in conflict behavior.

Third, a methodological problem that is commonly associated with, but not an inherent problem of, the cultural approach is the negligence of within-nation variation across social groups (Au, 1997; Brockner, in press; White, 2002). Too few studies attempt to locate their particular sample (university students, manufacturing workers, local managers in multinationals, etc.) on the dimension relative to other groups in the same regional context to test their assumption that their particular sample is representative of a more broadly defined population. Instead, sampled populations are typically assumed to be representative of the entire society. Obviously, an easy remedy of this problem is to include measures of cultural orientation in future research to evaluate whether a sample is indeed representative of the general community.

Configurational Approaches

Meyer and Tsui (1993) have suggested that more management research should adopt the configuration as the unit of analysis. Applying their critique to Asian management researchers, it highlights the dominance of unidimensional characterizations of actors, rather than an actor as a configuration of states on a number of dimensions. The manifestation is that comparative management researchers will focus on a particular dimension of culture to contrast two sets of actors or define the degree of social distance between samples from "Asia" (or, more often, a particular Asian country or ethnic group, like the Chinese) and the West (usually US). The implicit assumptions in such studies—which dominate comparative research in Asian contexts—are that (a) differences on other cultural dimensions are unimportant as explanatory variables, and (b) the interaction among particular dimensions is unimportant.

The fundamental problem with this unidimensional approach is that behaviors—either at the individual, group or organization levels—are clearly not driven by cultural dimensions in isolation. They are the outcome of a complex process in which meanings, motivations and choices are all heavily influenced by a particular configuration of cultural dimensions. For this reason, conclusions drawn from the bulk of comparative research including Asian contexts that contrasts findings between Western (usually US) and Asian samples on a single dimension rest on questionable grounds. The attribution of observed behavioral differences to a particular cultural dimension may be unfounded, because the samples may differ on a range of interrelated dimensions. The observed differences may depend on cultural differences in the entire configuration, not differences on a single element within the configuration. In fact, Hofstede (1980) attempted to move away from a unidimensional focus in his now classic study, placing nations on two-dimensional axes to see what aggregations emerged. That approach—incorporating multidimensionality into analyses and conclusions—has regretfully been relatively unexplored.

If we adopt a configurational approach, i.e., capturing the characteristics of a country by the particular configuration on multiple dimensions, the term "Asian" may lose its currency. There may be several clusters of countries in Asia that are distinct from each other. In fact, East Asia (including Singapore, but excluding China) is often treated as a cluster because of its Confucian heritage, its similar level in economic development, and its adoption of a capitalist system. Of course, to what extent does China fit into this cluster is an important research question. In spite of its being the source of Confucian tradition, it represents a distinct combination of economic underdevelopment, hyper economic growth, a move from central planning to a market economy, and a communist government. In sum, while we do not argue that unidimensional comparative research is useless, we believe that a configurational approach presents a significant opportunity for researchers to break away from sweeping generalizations about Asia and to navigate into finer descriptions and distinctions of Asian cultural contexts. A new generation of constructs and theories are likely to emerge from this more fine-grained approach to understanding similarities and differences across diverse Asian contexts.

Interplay of Emic and Etic Traditions

There are two broad traditions in cross-cultural research, one focusing on culture-specific (emic) issues and processes and the other focusing on culture-general (etic) issues and processes. Sinha (this volume) has provided a succinct description of these two traditions, their strengths and weaknesses, and how they augment each other. In the context of Asian management research, we can also discern these two traditions. For example, Carney and Gedajlovic (this volume) provide a conceptual characterization of dominant categories of business groups in East Asia: Japanese *keiretsu*, Korean *chaebol*, and Chinese Business Groups. These business groups are indigenous to East Asia and their description and analysis fall into the emic tradition. In contrast, Olekalns (this volume) has provided an analysis of how culture shapes justice phenomena and processes in Asia, with an eye toward developing a universal theoretical framework. Her orientation is more in the etic tradition, as the goal of her analysis is to develop culture-free generalizations.

Sinha (this volume) suggests that there are multiple paths for fruitful research in cross-cultural contexts. First, researchers may orchestrate large-scale cross-cultural projects to develop etic concepts and frameworks, which is the standard etic approach. One example of this is the GLOBE project orchestrated by Robert House around the world to develop a general theory of leadership (House, Hanges, Javidan, Dorfman, and Gupta, 2003).

A significant weakness of etic concepts and frameworks, however, is that they are by nature abstract and do not provide "thick" descriptions of meanings and dynamics in a given culture. To overcome this weakness, a widely adopted strategy in current etic research actually follows a combined emic–etic design in that etic frameworks are substantiated by emic constructs. In other words, culture-general notions are enriched by different emic manifestations in different cultural contexts.

The problem for Asian management research to adopt an etic approach is that large-scale cross-cultural projects are resource-intensive, and only researchers from well-endowed institutions can attempt such undertakings. Unfortunately, while many Asian researchers follow the etic approach by validating Western concepts and theories, the first large-scale etic project originating in Asia has yet to emerge. Most Asian based academics simply do not have the resources to enter into this arena of research, which is dominated by American and European researchers. To overcome this hurdle, Asian researchers who are committed to the etic approach must develop their research networks and develop synergistic working relationships with other researchers to pool their resources.

Second, some researchers are intrigued by phenomena and processes unique to a particular culture, and their primary goal is to gain an in-depth understanding of these emic issues. This orientation represents the standard emic approach, and it is widely adopted by many Asian researchers. Chikudate (this volume) identifies studies that provide grounded insights into the "life worlds" and sensemaking within Japanese organizations. One problem with much emic research, however, is that it tends to be ignored by researchers who are not interested in the cultural contexts from which the emic findings emerge. In other words, emic research is unlikely to be influential or even noted unless it targets a popular cultural context, such as China, or is pushed further to develop more general constructs (discussed below). This explains why many emic studies in Asian contexts are ignored by those not concerned with that particular context. An important challenge for researchers working on these issues and contexts is to increase the visibility of their work and disseminate their findings more widely.

A third approach, involving a synergistic interplay between the emic and etic perspectives (Morris, Leung, Ames, and Lickel, 1999), may help overcome the respective weaknesses of both "pure" approaches. In the synergistic approach, both emic and etic research can be the starting point of a research program. Emic research can stimulate the development of etic frameworks, and etic research can point to interesting and novel emic phenomena and processes. The central premise is that the iteration between emic and etic research is mutually stimulating and can thereby lead to a more comprehensive knowledge base for understanding and managing organizations across different cultural contexts.

On the applied side, researchers who subscribe to this synergistic perspective can identify strategies and practices from a diverse range of cultural contexts and assimilate them into a new workable configuration. This is the focus of the "third culture" literature, which advocates the synergistic assimilation of practices and processes from two cultures to form a new culture that is more effective than either of the original ones alone (e.g., Graen and Wakabayashi, 1994). Unfortunately, such a synergistic perspective is relatively uncommon in Asian management research. Because of its theoretical and practical importance, however, it should be a high priority area for future development.

Interaction Processes

One growth area in Asian management is the study of what happens when groups differing on one or multiple dimensions interact, a logical but underdeveloped extension beyond comparative work. At the macro level, researchers can examine how, for example, the different cultural backgrounds of the partners of an international journal venture or alliance may shape the structure, processes, and outcomes of the collaboration. While the literature on international alliances is voluminous, the emphasis is mostly on structural issues, such as equity share and technology transfer. Cultural issues and interaction processes have been relatively unexplored. Rare exceptions including Asian actors are Brannen and Salk's (2000) study of negotiated culture in joint ventures, and Johnson et al.'s (1996) work on trust-building between US and Japanese firms. More studies on how culture shapes the way Asian firms form alliances among themselves and with non-Asian firms would have significant theoretical and applied implications.

At the micro level, management research in Asia (and more broadly, for that matter) has paid insufficient attention to the collaboration of people with different backgrounds. We cannot assume that Asians must work well with each other because they are from Asia. In fact, Leung, Wang, and Smith (2001) found that Chinese employees of international joint ventures in China reported higher job satisfaction working with Western mangers than with Japanese and overseas Chinese managers. Brislin and Mac Nab (this volume) provide an extensive discussion of the body of research investigating elements affecting the communication process and outcomes between Asians and Westerners.

The dearth of research on how culture shapes cross-boundary collaborations is disappointing from a practical perspective. The field has little to offer to individual managers or multinational firms who must deal with choices and processes at interfaces between different groups. For example, how do the norms, cultures, and other formal and informal processes change when people or groups with differing cultural backgrounds interact? Under what conditions is the interaction positive and constructive, and what sends it down a negative spiral? Current comparative methodologies have little to offer to the pursuit of interaction questions.

Fortunately, a new field of cross-cultural management has been emerging in recent years, one that views these issues as central to their enquiry (e.g., Tjosvold and Leung, in press). Research on Asian management should definitely venture into this relatively uncharted area and play a front-and-center role in the development of this exciting new field.

Methodological Rigor

One reason that the body of Asian management research has not realized its potential is due to general methodological weakness. By this, we do not mean a lack of technical expertise (although that, too, can be questioned in too many cases). Many researchers who have conducted management research in this region have developed skills in comparative study design, in addition to the human networks and logistic capabilities to carry out multi-sample studies. The more fundamental problem is that too many researchers have used only correlational techniques or simply compared two or more country samples on a set of measures. By limiting themselves to a particular quantitative methodology, they at the same time restrict the types of research questions they can investigate (Redding, 1994). Quantitative methods, however, still only lead to conclusions about cross-temporal correlation or, depending on the design, causation. They are inadequate in providing insight into the processes linking antecedents and outcomes. Too few studies probe further to ask why those differences exist or how a certain correlation pattern emerges (White, 2002).

To fulfill the promise the region offers, researchers must elevate the rigor and range of their methodologies. Simply documenting cultural differences is not very interesting or useful. Researchers should seek answers to why these differences occur, which typically calls for the analysis of complex and often endogenous interactions among variables, mutual causation and feedback loops. Additional methodologies and data are often needed to substantiate the context-dependent discussion of observed differences, and to answer the questions of process—emergence, interaction—and causality (van de Vijver and Leung, 1997; Leung and Su, in press). Such questions call for qualitative approaches—such as anthropologically-based observational and interpretive methods, or "ethno-science" (Redding, 1994)—in order to identify meanings and processes and shed light on the origins that lead to differences in behaviors and outcomes. Such methodologies, combined with the plethora of phenomena in Asia that represent alternative trajectories to those in other contexts, could help researchers realize the promise of the region's interesting and important research opportunities.

CONCLUSIONS

The practical relevance of having a better understanding of management in Asia—with its huge economic potential and growing competitive challenge—is clear. The contributions to this *Handbook of Asian Management* represent our collective prescription for how to achieve this. The authors of each chapter of the handbook not only consolidate prior research in organizational behavior and strategy focused on the region, but they also identify specific directions for further research that is relevant, theoretically innovative and methodologically rigorous. The potential contribution of such research also extends beyond the geographical borders of this region. Indeed, to realize its full potential, we urge researchers to draw on findings from the region and actively engage in "mainstream" management discourse and, thereby, enrich the field.

REFERENCES

Adler, N. 1983. Cross-cultural management: The ostrich and the trend. *Academy of Management Review*, 8: 226-232.

Allen, F. and Gale, D. 2000. *Comparing Financial Systems*. Cambridge, MA: MIT Press.

Au, K. 1997. Another consequence of culture: Intra-cultural variation. *International Journal of Human Resource Management*, 8: 743-755.

Bensaou, B. and Venkatraman, N. 1995. Configurations of interorganizational relationships: A comparison between U.S. and Japanese automakers. *Management Science*, 41: 1471-1492.

Biggart, N. and Hamilton, G. 1992. On the limits of a firm-based theory to explain business networks: The Western bias of neoclassical economics. In N. Nohria and R. Eccles (eds.), *Networks and Organizations: Structure, Form and Action*. Boston: Harvard Business School Press.

Boyacigiller, N.A. and Adler, N.J. 1991. The parochial dinosaur: Organizational science in a global context. *Academy of Management Review*, 16: 262-290.

Brannen, M.Y. and Salk, J.E. 2000. Partnering across borders: Negotiating organizational culture in a German-Japanese joint venture. *Human Relations*, 53: 451-487.

Brockner, J. (In press). Unpacking country effects: On the need to operationalize the psychological determinants of cross-national differences. In B.M. Staw and R.M. Kramer (eds.), *Research in Organizational Behavior* (Vol. 25). Greenwich, CT: JAI Press.

Child, J. 1994. *Management in China During the Age of Reform*. Cambridge, UK: Cambridge University Press.

Florida, R. and Kenney, M. 1991. Transplanted organizations: The transfer of Japanese industrial organization into the U.S. *American Sociological Review*, 56: 381-398.

Fucini, J.J. and Fucini, S. 1990. *Working for the Japanese - Inside Mazda's American Auto Plant*. New York: Free Press.

Fukuyama, F. 1995. *Trust: The Social Virtues and the Creation of Prosperity*. New York: Free Press.

Gereffi, G. 1994. The organization of buyer-driven global commodity chains: How US retailers shape overseas production networks. In G. Gereffi and M. Korzeniewicz (eds.), *Commodity Chains and Global Capitalism*. Westport, Connecticut: Greenwood Press.

Graen, G.B. and Wakabayashi, M. 1994. Cross-cultural leadership making: Bridging American and Japanese diversity for team advantage. In H.C. Triandis, M.D. Dunnette and L.M. Hough (eds.), *Handbook of Industrial and Organizational Psychology* (2nd edn, Vol. 4, pp. 415-446). Palo Alto, CA: Consulting Psychologists Press.

Heracleous, L. 2001. State ownership, privatization and performance in Singapore: An exploratory study from a strategic management perspective. *Asia Pacific Journal of Management*, 18: 69-81.

Hitt, M.A., Lee, H.U. and Yucel, E. 2002. The importance of social capital to the management of multinational enterprises: Relational networks among Asian and Western firms. *Asia Pacific Journal of Management*, 19: 353-372.

Hofstede, G. 1980. *Culture's Consequences: International Differences in Work-related Values*. Beverly Hills, CA: Sage.

Hofstede, G. 1984. *Culture's Consequences: International Differences in Work-related Values* (Abridged edn). Beverly Hills, CA: Sage.

House R.J., Hanges, P.J., Javidan, M., Dorfman, P. and Gupta, V. (eds.). 2003. *GLOBE, Cultures, Leadership, and Organizations: GLOBE Study of 62 Societies.* Newbury Park, CA: Sage.

Johnson, J., Cullen, J., Sakano, T. and Takenouchi, H. 1996. Setting the stage for trust and strategic integration in Japanese-U.S. cooperative alliances. *Journal of International Business Studies*, 27: 981-1004.

Khanna, T. and Palepu, K. 1997. Why focused strategies may be wrong for emerging markets. *Harvard Business Review*, 75(4): 41-51.

Kotabe, M. and Zhao, H. 2002. A taxonomy of sourcing strategic types for MNCs operating in China. *Asia Pacific Journal of Management*, 19: 11-27.

Kuhn, T.S. 1970. *The Structure of Scientific Revolutions* (2nd edn). Chicago: University of Chicago Press.

Leung, K., Smith, P.B., Wang. Z.M. and Sun, H.F. 1996. Job satisfaction in joint venture hotels in China: An organizational justice analysis. *Journal of International Business Studies*, 27: 947-962.

Leung, K. and Su, S.K. (In press) Experimental methods for research on culture and management. In B.J. Punnett and O. Shenkar (eds.), *Handbook for International Management Research* (2nd edn). Cambridge, MA: Blackwell.

Leung, K. and Tjosvold, D.W. (eds.) 1998. *Conflict Management in Asia Pacific Rim.* Wiley: Singapore.

Leung, K., Wang, Z.M. and Smith, P.B. 2001. Job Attitudes and Organizational Justice in Joint Venture Hotels in China: The Role of Expatriate Managers. *International Journal of Human Resource Management*, 12: 926-945.

Meyer, A.D. and Tsui, A.S. 1993. Configurational approaches to organizational analysis. *Academy of Management Journal*, 36: 1175-1195.

Morris, M.W., Leung, K., Ames, D. and Lickel, B. 1999. Incorporating perspectives from inside and outside: Synergy between emic and etic research on culture and justice. *Academy of Management Review*, 24: 781-796.

Nisbett, R.E. 2003. *The Geography of Thought.* New York: The Free Press.

O'Sullivan, M. 2000. *Contests for Corporate Control.* Oxford: Oxford University Press.

Ouchi, W. 1981. *Theory Z: How American Business Can Meet the Japanese Challenge.* New York: Addison Wesley.

Redding, G. 1990. *The Spirit of Chinese Capitalism.* New York: Walter de Gruyter.

Redding, G. 1994. Comparative management theory: Jungle, zoo or fossil bed? *Organization Studies*, 15: 323-359.

Redding, G. 2001. The smaller economies of Pacific Asia and their business systems. In A. Rugman and T. Brewer (eds.), *The Oxford Handbook of International Business* (pp. 760-781). Oxford: Oxford University Press.

Redding, G. 2002. The capitalist business system of China and its rationale. *Asia Pacific Journal of Management*, 19: 221-249.

Shenkar, O. and von Glinow, M. 1994. Paradoxes of organizational theory and research: Using the case of China to illustrate national contingency. *Management Science*, 40: 56-71.

Tjosvold D. and Leung, K. 2003. *Cross-Cultural Management: Foundations and Future.* Aldershot, UK: Ashgate.

Van de Vijver, F. and Leung, K. 1997. *Methods and Data Analysis for Cross-cultural Research.* California: Sage.

White, S. 2002. Rigor and relevance in Asian management research: Where are we and where can we go? *Asia Pacific Journal of Management*, 19: 287-352.

Whitley, R. 1992. *Business Systems in East Asia: Firms, Markets and Societies.* London: Sage.

Yan, Y. 2000. *International Joint Ventures in China: Ownership, Control and Performance.* London: MacMillan Press.

Chapter 2

ETIC AND EMIC APPROACHES TO ASIAN MANAGEMENT RESEARCH

Jai B. P. Sinha
ASSERT Institute of Management Studies, India

EMIC AND ETIC APPROACHES

The Concepts

Pike (1967) coined the words 'emic' and 'etic' from the linguistic terms 'phonemic' and 'phonetic' to describe behaviour from two different standpoints. He wrote: "The etic viewpoint studies behaviour from outside a particular system as an essential initial approach to an alien system. The emic viewpoint results from studying behaviour from inside the system" (p. 37). The terms, because of their wide applications, became very popular in the 1970s and 1980s in various social science disciplines such as education, medicine, anthropology, and so on. Headland, Pike, and Harris (1990) identified 262 references by the end of 1980s. By the same token, the terms suffered from surplus meanings. Of 262 references, 38 per cent did not define them precisely. Some scholars wrongly associated emic and etic with culture-specific and culture-general constructs or differences in their methods – sustained and wide ranging observations of a single culture (e.g., Geertz, 1983; Kondo, 1990) versus surveys (Hofstede, 1980) and quasi-experimental designs (Earley, 1989). In fact, some of the usages were apparently wrong. For example, authors equated emic and etic with verbal versus nonverbal, specific versus universal, subjective knowledge versus scientific knowledge, bad versus good, ideal versus actual behaviour, sloppy versus precise approach, and so on. Although the terms, emic and etic, were used with reference to a variety of systems, anthropologists used them for the study of cultures. Berry (1969) popularized them to signify within-culture versus between-cultures studies of behaviour that may eventually lead to near universal psychological laws.

Drawing on Pike, Berry (1990) delineated a number of distinguishing characteristics of etic and emic approaches that are relevant for determining cultural influences on management research. According to Berry, the etic approach is based on the assumption that there are universal features of cultures that exist either in reality or in the minds of the researcher. The researcher knows them in advance and, by using them as absolute criteria, simultaneously compares a number of cultures on those features. In other words, the features provide an external view of cultures. The etic approach is, thus, selective in the choice of cultural features, and yields only partial data that serve as a starting point for a more detailed analysis of cultures. The results of etic studies, therefore, are at best tentative, if not false.

On the other hand, the emic approach, according to Berry, is culture-specific and grounded in one culture. The emic ideas, concepts, or theories are not known in advance. They are discovered during research mostly on or by the members of that culture. Hence, emic is an internal view based on the cultural features that are relevant with reference to the internal functioning of the culture itself. The emic view insists that every feature of the culture must be related to the other relevant features of the culture by integrating findings from the emic studies. The integrated findings lead to a comprehensive understanding of the totality of the culture.

Pike (1967) emphasized that both emic and etic approaches are equally important. An etic approach is important because (a) there is "no other way to begin an analysis [of systems] than by starting with a rough, tentative (and inaccurate) etic description" (p. 40). Further, it provides a broad perspective for comparing systems around the world and enables to identify standard ways of managing them. An emic approach is important because it focuses on the way a system is actually constituted, "not as a series of miscellaneous parts, but as a working whole" (p. 41), helps understand individuals in their contexts including their attitudes, motives, interests, and personality, and "provides the only basis upon which a predictive science of behaviour can be expected to make some of its greatest progress ..." (p. 41). Furthermore, Pike contended that emic and etic approaches do not constitute a dichotomy. They only differ in having an insider's or outsider's views of a system and may be integrated to yield an in-depth understanding of a system: "Through the etic 'lens' the analyst views the data in tacit reference to a perspective oriented to all comparable events (whether sounds, ceremonies, activities), of all peoples, of all parts of the earth; through the other lens, the emic one, he views the same events, at the same time, in the same context, in reference to a perspective oriented to the particular function of those particular events in that particular culture, as it and it alone is structured. The result is 'tri-dimensional understanding' of human behaviour instead of a 'flat' etic one" (Pike, 1967, p. 41).

What is an inside or an outside view of a system depends on how the boundary lines of a system are drawn. Cultures have sub-cultures as systems that may have their own sub-systems. On the other hand, cultures are also clustered into regional sets (Ronen & Shenkar, 1985). Similarly, organizations within a culture are the systems on their own right. They too have their sub-systems. Pike (1990) went to the extent of identifying 'a set of games' versus 'a set of kinds of jobs' as emic units "to which individual native participants of a culture either implicitly or explicitly attribute the characteristics of appropriateness for its occurrence in a particular kind of context" (p. 28). Thus, it is possible to conceptualize emic–etic interface at different systemic levels such as organization, societal culture, or a universe of cultures. The *meso analysis* (Cappelli & Sherer, 1991; Rousseau & House, 1994), for example, aims to integrate micro level organizational behaviour with macro level socio-economic processes providing an emic view of an organization. One may also visualize clusters of cultures sharing emic features to the extent that some *mid-range etics* relevant to that specific universe of clusters may be derived. In other words, organizations, societal cultures, and the universe of all cultures constitute concentric circles of the systemic frames, the inner rims of which have the potential to provide emic views while the outer rims may allow etic comparisons. What is emic or etic is a matter of the vantage point that the researcher occupies with regard to a system or systems. For the present purpose, we take the societal culture as the systemic frame to examine etic and emic issues pertaining to work organizations.

The Etic–Emic Divide

Contrary to the preceding conceptualization and the Pike's emphasis on the complementary nature of emic and etic approaches, scholars across disciplines such as anthropology (between Geertz, 1983 and Munroe & Munroe, 1971), psychology (between Shweder, 1991 and Smith & Bond, 1998), organizational behaviour (between Rohlen, 1974 and Hofstede, 1980), organizational culture (between Gregory, 1983 and Schneider, 1990), and so on have been divided in their allegiance to either of the two manifesting a common tendency "to dismiss insights from the other perspective based on perceived conceptual or methodological weaknesses" (Morris, Leung, Ames, & Lickel, 1999, p. 782).

Those who are committed to an etic approach believe in the universality of basic human nature. If genetic structures of human beings and chimpanzees are 99 per cent the same (King & Wilson quoted by Triandis, 2000, p. 186), they argue, human beings across cultures must be basically the same, except that human behaviour takes unique culture-specific forms. The aim of a scientific enquiry is to search such universals and, as Pike suggested, the search has to start with a priory or pre-conceived framework, no matter how tentative or false it might be.

There are additional justifications in favour of an etic approach. Greenfield (2000, p. 233) believed that it is also likely that there are aspects of culture that are so deeply engrained in the minds of people that they take them for granted or they are repressed to the extent that only knowledgeable outsiders can notice them. Further, purely emic studies do not establish formal procedure of research and therefore lack validity (Brown, 1991). They deserve to be discounted because of the findings are often misconceptions from cultural insiders (Marano, 1982), inconsistent, (Kloos, 1988), and may not be representative of the whole culture (Triandis, 1999, p. 191). Above all, they do not lead to universal laws of behaviour (Berry, 1990) that is the ultimate aim of any scientific endeavour. Martin (1992) even took an extreme position that assimilation of non-western emics into well-established western etics would threaten the latter's conceptual and political integrity (p. 187).

On the contrary, those who subscribe to the emics are more interested in having a holistic and comprehensive view of culture. They believe that "the nature of things is emic not etic" (Levi-Strauss quoted by Berry, 1990, p. 87) and therefore, each system should be viewed in its own term and with respect to its context implying that cross-systems comparisons are essentially untenable and false (Malinowski, 1922). Nisbet (1971) commented that the comparative method itself is grossly ethnocentric. Boesch (1996) opined that valid information is obtainable only through emic methods.

It seems to me that Pike was wrong in arguing that a research has to start with an etic framework. In fact, the process of initiating a piece or research is more emic than etic in nature. An innovative research evolves through a process in which raw, intuitive, and naïve ideas about regularity in a set of behaviour converge in the mind of a researcher who describes, defines, operationalizes, and refines them over a period of time into a concept, a theory, or a framework that is made available for further research. As it gets sufficiently replicated within the culture of its origin, there develops a natural urge to take it beyond one's own cultural boundaries and get it established as an etic concept, theory, or framework. The studies that follow in other cultures validate, elaborate, modify, or reject it, although the implicit desire is to see it established as the etic. Many researchers in the host cultures resent this process of imposing an alien framework that may have built-in biases. They tend to counteract the imposed etics by advancing their own cultural emics that are claimed to provide a more appropriate perspective on the reality of the host culture. Still others see this etic–emic process as dialectics that have a better potential to advance our knowledge of management science.

DIALECTICS BETWEEN EMIC AND ETIC APPROACHES

The dialectics between etic and emic approaches in social sciences, particularly in cross-cultural psychology, have a parallel in management research including the research pertaining to Asian management. The dialectics have led to diverse ways of studying organizational behaviour that may be examined under broad groups of (a) Imposed etics, (b) Etics that aim to explain cultural differences, (c) Emics that stand out, and (d) Integration of etics and emics. Selective studies are reviewed under the four groups by way of illustrations.

Imposed Etics

Underlying the approach that imposed etics is the worldview that all societies, although located at different levels of economic development and modernization, are evolving to become alike. As the societies get modernized by the exposure to Western values, life styles, and industrialization, the people's values, attitudes, habits, and lifestyles converge into a single pattern characterized by the industrialized cultures of the West (Kerr, 1983; Meyer, 1970; Weinberg, 1969). The work organizations manifest a similar converging trend in their structures and functions. In fact, there seems to exist a belief that their structures and principles *should* converge in order to enable them to function efficiently.

This standpoint provided rationale for imposing etics from the industrialized West on other countries including those in Asia in order to show where the latter stood with reference to the former and how they have to change in order to catch up with the West. In the sixties and the seventies, the trend was to compare non-western countries on one cultural dimension that proved the superiority of the west. For example, in a study of six countries that included India and (now) Bangadesh, Inkeles and Smith (1975) took the position that "the man defined as 'modern' in one country will 'definitely' be defined modern in another country" (p. 109). The modern man is characterized by, among other qualities, openness to new experience, ability to learn how to exert considerable control over his environment, high aspirations, respect for personal dignity, and understanding the logic underlying decision making at the basic level of production. The factors that were reported to facilitate modernity were industrial experience, eroded respect for aged (including parents), political participation, and rights to women. The factors that inhibited modernity were family and kinship cohesiveness and religion. It was not realized at that time that family ties and filial piety can facilitate business activities and economic growth (Redding, 1990), and religion in countries like Indonesia (Ali, 1992), Pakistan (Dhakan, 1994), Iran (Habibi & Amirshahi, 2000), Mongolia (Shurchuluu, 2000), and Fiji (Merekula, 2000) can serve as a rallying ground for motivating people to work diligently often as a duty. Learner (1958) studied modernization in Turkey, Lebanon, Egypt, Syria, Jordan, and Iran to conclude that modernization is related to empathic capacity, although later on, Triandis (1995a, p. 168) listed empathy as a characteristic of interdependent self of collectivists while modern people are generally more self-focused and less empathetic to others.

McClelland (1961) propounded a theory that a country's economic growth depends on high need for achievement in its entrepreneurs. McClelland and Winter (1969) reported supportive evidence from India. House, Wright, and Aditya (1997) quoted seven studies by House and his associates indicating the predictive value of achievement motivation theory for managerial effectiveness or success. McClelland's conceptualization of achievement motivation, however, is strongly influenced by western cultural values (Kornadt, Eckensberger, & Emmingaus, 1980; Maehr, 1974; J.B.P. Sinha, 1968; J.B.P. Sinha & Pandey, 1970). J.B.P. Sinha and Pandey demonstrated that the individuals with high achievement motivation of course strive to maximize their achievement through their entrepreneurial behaviour. But in a resource-scarce country such as India, they also monopolize and hoard resources for future use thereby restricting others' access to them. This prevents others from utilizing the resources optimally and causes inter-personal conflicts among them. It is the social need for achievement – striving for group's excellence – that is likely to facilitate collectives' achievements leading to economic growth of the country (Mehta, 1991). Indian culture expects that the person must grow up with his social group and collectives rather striving for personal excellence that might alienate him from his in-group members (J.B.P. Sinha, 1984).

There were also efforts to conceptualize universal principles of management. Nagandhi (1986, p. 47) quoted Kootz and O'Donnell stating that: "The principles related to the task of managing apply to any kind of enterprise in any kind of culture". The classic Aston group conducted 30 separate studies of a wide range of manufacturing, service, government, and other organizations in fourteen countries (Pugh, 1976; Pugh & Hickson, 1976) to delineate two main dimensions along which organization's structures were reported to vary universally. They were concentration of authority including *centralization* and structuring of activities including *standardization, specialization*, and *formalization*. The structures, they argued, vary as a direct function of the contextual factors such as size, technology, nature of industry, and market condition, irrespective of the countries in which the organizations are located. Hickson, Hinnings, McMillan, and Schwitter (1974) observed, "simply stated, if Indian organizations were found to be less formalized than American ones, bigger Indian units would still be more formalized than smaller Indian units" (p. 59). Although Hickson et al. did refer to improving efficiency by putting in place the appropriate structure, their emphasis remained largely on the stability of relationship between the contextual factors and the structures of organizations across cultures.

Smith and Tayeb (1988) have reported two limitations of the Aston model. First, while the relationship between contextual factors and structures may hold cross-culturally, the meanings attached to the relationship may be different. For example, a study by Tayeb, having two matched samples of English and Indian organizations, revealed that while the extent of centralization was similar, the processes that lay behind this similarity were quite different. Senior managers made decisions in both cases, but the English managers consulted and delegated much more than their Indian counterparts (p. 157). Second, the stability of the relationships between contextual and structural variables has also been challenged. Redding and Wong (1986), for example, found substantial differences in organizational structure between firms of similar size in Hong Kong and England. The Hong Kong organizations had less precisely defined roles, fewer standardized procedures, fewer staff functions, and more centralization. Negandhi (1973) reported large differences in the structure of locally, Japanese, and American owned companies in Taiwan despite their being matched by size and market conditions. Smith and Tayeb (1988) observed that the case of Hong Kong shows that "cultural values may ensure that firms remain small, thus circumventing the imperative that large firms must employ formalization and functional specialization" (p. 160).

Haire, Ghiselli, and Porter (1966) conducted a large survey of managers in North American, European, and Asian countries (such as India and Japan) that led to identify universal managerial values and practices. They substantiated the convergence thesis by reporting that managers across all countries favour democratic style of management, endorse egalitarian organizational structure, and were concerned about their unsatisfied needs for autonomy and self-actualization (all western values!). The convergence thesis was, however, contradicted by another large sample study of a number of countries (again including India and Japan) that reported strong country effects on a variety of managerial practices (Bass, Berger, Doctor, & Barrett, 1979). Whiteley and England (1980) also reported that managers from the countries such as Japan, Korea, and India were largely moralists while their counterparts from Australia and the USA were pragmatists again negating the expectations that they all are becoming pragmatic.

Despite the evidence casting doubts on the validity of the etics of the sixties and seventies, the trend to impose such etics seems to continue in certain cases. What Jahoda (1977) observed about cross-cultural psychologists seemed to be true for management researchers: "When cross-cultural psychologists [read management researchers] are wearing their theoretical-methodological hats, they tend to make ritual emic–etic gestures; having discharged their duty in this manner, they turn to getting on with research and forget all about it" (p. 55). An example is the GLOBE (Global Leadership & Organizational Behaviour Effectiveness) project of House, Wright, and Aditya (1997). Although they found a strong empirical support for a cultural congruence thesis in the sense that leaders or managers must meet cultural expectations and norms in order to remain effective, they went on arguing that leaders must also introduce new values, techniques, and behavioural patterns that are culturally incongruent but proved to be effective in the west. Employing this logic, they launched the GLOBE project in over 50 countries imposing what they called "the near universal leader behaviours" – future-oriented and inspirational – that reflect charismatic style of leadership. They went on openly imposing what they believed to be universally applicable:

> "There is reason to suspect that several leadership behaviours that might be universally acceptable and effective have never been widely introduced to the members of many societies. When individuals have never experienced such leader behaviours, it may be difficult for them to express a preference for these behaviours and unrealistic of researchers to expect such preferences." (House, Wright, & Aditya, 1997, p. 593.)

Partial results have started appearing (Dastmalchian, Javidan, & Alam, 2001) that indicate that managers from some of the Middle East countries, despite their values of familism, paternalism, and so on, attributed universally desirable leadership characteristics like being supportive, visionary, and charismatic to their leaders. Smith (1997) alleged that the measures of the GLOBE project lacked emic validity (p. 637). It seems to me that findings reflect the demand characteristics of a highly prestigious project launched globally with lots of fanfare.

Etics That Aim to Explain Cultural Differences

A landmark in management research is the Hofstede's (1980) classic work, *Culture's Consequences*, identifying four bipolar dimensions of work values for comparing cultures. They were *individualism–collectivism, power distance, uncertainty avoidance, and masculinity–femininity*. Later on, Hofstede (1991) added the fifth dimension, *long-term orientation*. A major improvement by Hofstede over the single dimensional cross-cultural comparisons was that he derived the dimensions inductively from the responses of IBM managers from a large number of countries and put them into a theoretical framework that stimulated a lot of further research. Of 39 countries in his first survey (Hofstede, 1980), 10 were from Asia, and they all had above average scores on collectivism and power distance. Hofstede (1983) extended his values survey to other five Arab countries and found them high again on collectivism and power distance. The GLOBE research (Kabasakal & Dastmalchian, 2001) also indicated that four Arab countries were high on power distance and family collectivism. On the remaining dimensions, the Asian countries manifested varying positions.

Despite the critique that Hofstede's dimensions lack internal consistency (Spector, Cooper, Sparks et al., 2001) and that IBM managers do not necessarily represent their country's modal cultural values (Lytle, Brett, Barsness,

Tinsley, & Janssens, 1995, p. 196), the salience of the dimensions for studying cultural differences and investigating their impact on a wide range of organizational behaviour has been proved beyond doubt by the volume of work that has followed (Kim, Triandis, Kagitcibasi, Choi, & Yoon, 1994; Triandis, 1995b, among others). The impact is manifested in (a) the efforts to add, elaborate, or modify the dimensions, (b) strengthening the trend to examine the direct effects of etic dimensions on cultural differences, (c) investigating the moderating effects of etic dimensions on relationships between organizational behaviours, (d) conducting studies that add emic elaborations to the etic concepts and relationships.

The Cultural Dimensions

Combining power distance with collectivism, Triandis and Bhawuk (1997) conceptualized vertical and horizontal types of collectivism and individualism, the individual level parallels of which were termed as *allocentrism and idiocentrism* (Triandis, 1995b). Bond (Chinese Culture Connection, 1987) added *Confucian Work Dynamism* to the four dimensions of Hofstede. Smith, Dugan, and Trompenaars (1996) identified seven constructs on which individualist and collectivist societies were found to differ. They were integration, utilitarian versus affective commitment based on loyalty, Confucian work dynamism, status based versus earned achievement, particularism versus universalism, power distance, and collectivism. Hall (1981) found a parallel of collectivism–individualism in high (e.g., Asian) and low (western) context oriented cultures. Schwartz and his associate (Schwartz, 1992, 1994; Schwartz & Bilsky, 1987) identified collectivist and individualist clusters of values that he called *conservatism and harmony* versus *intellectual and affective autonomy* respectively. *Conservatism and harmony* included values regarding family security, social order, respect for tradition, honouring parents and elders, security, and politeness. *Intellectual and affective autonomy* consisted of the importance for being curious, broadminded, and creative, and having an exciting and varied life full of pleasure. Recently, Leung, Bond, Carrasqel, Munoz, Murakami, Yamaguchi, Bierbrauer, & Singelis (2002) have extracted five etic factors of beliefs, *Cynicism, Social Complexity, Reward for Application, Spirituality, and Fate Control*, that are being used to compare cultures.

Cultural Dimensions that Directly Affect Organizational Behaviour

Despite the Bond's (1997) review of studies showing that cultural values dimensions do not match with organizational values dimensions and that, in turn, do not predict organizational practices, there is plenty of evidence to show that cultural differences affect how organizations are managed, work is viewed, and relationships at work are handled. Hofstede (2001) has reviewed 877 publications after and 287 before the publication of *Cultures' Consequences* (1980) to show that his dimensions have consistent effects on, besides family and school related variables, work behaviour and organizations.

Despite this massive evidence that suggests that cultural dimensions consistently and coherently affect a wide range of organizational behaviour, there are doubts about the conceptual or metric equivalence that are necessary for establishing them as true etics. Triandis (1999, 2000), for example, observed that even widely used concepts such as self, control, intelligence, well-being, honour, anger, shame, happiness, and so on have different meaning in different cultures. The MOW (*Meaning Of Work*, 1987) research project in eight countries highlighted the different functional meanings attached to a construct, work, which is so familiar to us. According to Hulin (1987), a construct is equivalent across cultures when the construct and its measurement hold the same relationship in each cultural group. Similarly, a measuring instrument has metric equivalence when individuals having the same score on the measure, irrespective of the levels of cultures on the dimension, have the same probability of endorsing the cultural dimension. Such rigorous requirements are hardly met in cross-cultural comparisons.

Moderating Effect of Cultural Dimensions

The effects of culture have been refined to show that the cultural dimension differentially affects relationships between behavioural variables in the cultures that differ on that dimension. Earley (1989), for example, found that the more collectivist Chinese subjects did not engage in social loafing, especially under the condition of high-shared responsibility, the more individualized American subjects, on the contrary, manifested an opposite trend of strong social loafing under the conditions of high-shared responsibility and low accountability. Erez and Earley (1987) examined the differential impact of American individualism and Israeli collectivism on the relationships between the conditions of goal setting and performance. Goals were either assigned or set through subjects' participation. The results showed that the Israeli students had significantly lower performance score when goals were assigned to them than when goals were set in a participative way. Further, Israeli subjects under assigned goal conditions had poorer performance that American subjects. However, there was no significant difference in performance between the two groups when goals were set through participation. In other words, the collectivist Israelis reacted adversely to the goals that were assigned to them, instead of being set in a participative way.

Etics that Stimulate Emic Elaborations

There are instances in which an etic framework creates a basis for developing emic descriptions within a system. In such cases, the researcher may focus on an organization or a culture as an intact whole rather than a bundle of discrete dimensions for comparing organizations or cultures. Earley & Singh (2000, p. 5) labeled such research as the Gestalt Form. The gestalt form of research has three important features. First, relationships among variables are established within each of the sampled organizations or cultures separately. Second, the hypothesized relationships and the constructs involved, however, are derived from an etic framework rather than are inductively obtained emic characteristics. Third, findings from a given organization or culture are interpreted with reference to the specifics of that organization or culture. Thus, the concepts may be etic in nature, but the pattern of relationships among them is essentially culture specific and emic, and the comparisons across cultures are secondary in researcher's interest. For example, Erez (1986) studied three industrial sectors within Israel. She adopted an etic motivational model, goal setting, to compare the goal setting strategies and performance in Kibbutz, Hahistadrut, and private sector organizations. The findings were explained in terms of the ethos that was specific to the organizational settings: Group participation was most effective in Kibbutz, participation by a representative in Hahistadrut sector, and no participation in private sector organizations. It was of secondary interest to incorporate the findings into the theories of work motivation and goal setting (Erez & Earley, 1987).

There are also efforts to borrow etic dimensions and to elaborate them either by incorporating emic components, defining in emic ways, discovering emic meanings, or suggesting different configurations of the etic dimensions. Pandey (1986), for example, reported that the American construct of ingratiation includes Indian emics such as self-degradation, instrumental dependency, name-dropping, and changing positions with changing situations. Hofstede (1980) reported Japanese culture as quite high on masculinity. However, Hamada (1996) found that "Japanese prefer non-masculine managers" (p. 168) and quoted Japanese emic, *amae*, as a manifestation of Japanese femininity. According to Hofstede (2001), Hamada defined his etic measure of masculinity in an emic way (p. 314). Misumi's (1985) differentiated etic dimensions of leadership and their emic manifestations in various organizations within Japan. He borrowed the Initiating Structure and Consideration factors by labeling them as performance (P) and maintenance (M) functions of leadership. However, he found that P is further differentiated into *planning for performance* and *pressure for performance*. P is seen as pressure for performance when m (low salience of maintenance) is used, but P becomes emphasis on planning when *M* (high salience of maintenance) is present. In other words, when the interpersonal relationships in a group are satisfactory, the leader focuses on planning for future performance. But when they are problematic, the leader has to press for performance. Further, as Smith & Peterson (1988) reported, consideration in an individualist culture might mean the leader respecting subordinates' autonomy. But in a collectivist culture *M* means more interactions with one's subordinates. Similarly, a superior who talks to a colleague about a subordinate's personal difficulty is considered to be inconsiderate in the USA but considerate in Japan and Hong Kong. Ayman and Chemers (1983) reported that Initiating Structure and Consideration loaded on a single factor that was related to productivity in a factory in Iran. Hofstede (1988) conceptualized McGregor Theories X and Y as complementary rather than mutually exclusive in the Indonesian culture. Indonesian collectivism was found to be different from the collectivism in Hong Kong (Triandis, McCusker, Betancourt, Iwao, Leung, Salazar et al., 1993). In-group orientation in Hong Kong is blended with high need for mastery and task orientation while Indonesian culture is characterized by "affiliation without competition" expressing sociability and a need for maintaining good relationships.

Triandis (1994) suggested that while examining the impact of culture on behaviour, a distinction should be made between contents and process; the former could be emic in nature while the latter may be etic in function. He (p. 108) quoted a study by Haruki, Shigehisa, Nedate, Wajima, and Ogawa who showed that the learning process is the same in the USA and Japan, but what reinforces the learning process are different. Rewards to the learners facilitate learning in both countries, but the Japanese also learn significantly more when the experimenter is rewarded. Probably, the collectivist culture fosters an implicit bond between the learner and the experimenter that causes vicarious satisfaction of getting rewarded when the learner finds the experimenter being rewarded. Another example is performance management. Mendonca and Kanungo (1990) contended that employees can be motivated by giving them rewards that are made contingent on their performance. Thus, the process of rewarding good performance is universal and is rooted in the goal setting and reinforcement theories, but what constitute rewards in a country depend on what the people in a culture value. Earlier, participation in goal setting was reported to have a rewarding impact on performance in the collectivist low power distance culture of Israel (Erez & Earley, 1987). In collectivist high power distance cultures of Kuwait, Turkey, and Qatar, however, participation means only consultation and is employed either to induce feelings of belonging or to satisfy the ego needs of the group members (Kabasakal & Dastmalchian, 2001, p. 485).

Emics That Stand Out

Limitations of the Etic Approach

The etic approach arising from western social sciences, irrespective of whether it is imposed or solicited, is alleged to have serious limitations. Yang (1997), for example, complained that "...an imposed, 'soulless psychology' [that may also be true for management science] would not do much good in explaining, predicting, and understanding Chinese behaviour simply because the imported westernized [etic] concepts, theories, methods, and tools ... could not do justice to the complicated, unique aspects and patterns of Chinese people's psychological and behavioural characteristics" (p. 65). Redding (1990) shared Yang's views: "It is difficult at a practical level for western people to comprehend the way in which the power of Chinese tradition still permeates everyday life among the overseas Chinese..." (p. 41). Triandis (1993), too, admitted that the cultural influence on organizational behaviour "operates at such a deep level that people are not aware of its influence. It results in unexamined patterns of thought that seem so natural that most theories of social behaviour fail to take them in account. As a result, many aspects of organizational theories produced in one culture may be inadequate in other cultures" (p. 139).

In such a case, Berry's (1969) recommended sequence of research from western emics to non-western emic studies for deriving near universal etics is "little more than a pipe dream" (Jahoda, 1977, p. 61) primarily because it requires the researchers to get so fully immersed in the host culture that they can have a truly emic perspective. Shweder (2000, p. 213) wonders how many of them get so thoroughly immersed into the natural concrete details of the culture!

Supposing that researchers do get fully immersed, they are still handicapped by the etic baggage that they have been knowingly or unknowingly carrying. The baggage consisting of the concepts and theories developed in the industrialized West which, according to Azuma (1984, p. 84), may not have the schemata for describing and understanding the people in a very different culture. They may even include some concepts that are likely to distort perception and block a deep understanding when applied to another culture. Even the motives in extending the etic approach to Asian cultures have been suspected. D. Sinha (1997), for example, argued that the need of western researchers to prove universality of their theories predominates over the relevance of such attempts to the non-western cultures. Initially, many researchers in the host culture did not realize this hidden agenda and enthusiastically participated in substantiating imported theories and models. Many of them failed, only to be blamed for the flaws in their translation of instruments, lack of rigour in data collection, or use of inappropriate methodology (U. Kim, 2000; J.B.P. Sinha,

1984). Consequently, some became disenchanted and, fuelled by their national pride, started looking into their cultural roots to identify emic concepts that contrasted non-western and western cultures. D. Sinha (1997) described such efforts by Yamasoka (in Japan), Yang (in Taiwan), U. Kim (in South Korea), Samy (in Fiji), Enriquez (in Philippines), Al Faruqui (in Pakistan), himself and J.B.P. Sinha (in India) towards doing relevant research on vital issues for 'de-colonization of knowledge' and 'cultural empowerment'.

The researchers have drawn on religious, philosophical, and folk traditions to identify the emics that can put the Asian organizations into appropriate cultural contexts. The emics, thus discovered, manifest variations across Asian countries emanating from the diversity in geography, history, religion, economic and political systems, and the demography of people. Whitley (1995), for example, compared Korean *chaebol*, Japanese *kaisha*, and the Chinese family business. The Korean and the Chinese organizations have much more personalized managerial authority than Japan where managerial control has been separated from ownership. As a result, managerial style is facilitative in Japan, directive in Korea, and didactic in Chinese family business manifesting in emotional commitment of employees in Japanese organizations and conditional attachment in the organizations from the other two cultures. Alston (1989) made similar observations that business relations are guided by harmony and social cohesion (*wa*) in Japan, personal relations (*guanxi*) in China, and hierarchical orientation that fosters obedience to authority (p. 26) in Korea. Hong Kong managers held more western values than the main land Chinese managers (Ralston, Gustafson, Elsass, Cheung, & Terpstra, 1992).

Religiosity in Islamic cultures and spirituality in Philippines (Abella, 1995) and India (Roland, 1988) advance an emic perspective on work and organizations that is different from the one we find in cultures influenced by Confucian philosophy. Chakraborty (1993) advanced and Srinivas (2000) provided supportive evidence for a "giving" theory of motivation that negates the western principles of exchange and reinforcement. Unlike in the west where giving valuable resources to someone means obliging and, thereby, gaining power over the recipient (McClelland, 1975), giving in the traditional Indian worldview enriches both the giver and the recipient by establishing a bond between them. Similarly, yogic exercises and meditation may help managers purify their self (*chittashudhi*), cultivate spiritual orientation, and transform themselves to initiate the process transforming an effective and spiritually oriented work culture. Pande and Naidu (1992) identified a work orientation that does not follow the goal setting theory of the west. Instead of setting a high goal and striving to chase it, the model suggests 'effort orientation' without being overtly concerned about goal realization (*nishkam karm*), i.e. to focus on the process of realizing the goal rather than the goal itself by cultivating a mind-set of 'non-attachment'. D. Sinha (1987) described *ahinsak* (non-violent) approach through which interpersonal conflicts can be resolved in a win-win mode. The processes first involve reasoning with the adversary, failing that the person resorts to self-suffering in order to awake a moral responsibility the opponent's mind for the person's suffering. If that too fails then the person is entitled to resort to non-cooperation, polite disobedience, and stopping of interaction with the opponent. None of these measures either harms or causes the adversary lose face.

Towards Mid-range Etics

Despite these fine-grained variations, there are patches of similarities in cultural values and practices across Asian countries that seem to suggest Asian etics for cross-cultural comparisons with other collectivist societies. The Asian Productivity Organization sponsored three surveys of productivity related factors including values in its member countries (Hsu, 1994; Hwang, 1995; J.B.P. Sinha, 2000a). The reports of the country experts identified four values – familism, hierarchical orientation, personalized relationships, and paternalism – that are shared by almost all Asian countries included in the surveys. Although India stands alone independent of the Asian cluster (Ronen & Shenkar, 1985) because of her exposure to western influences and growing awareness of the cultural heritage, the Indian dominant social values overlap with the social values in many Asian cultures. The cultures under Confucian influence share the worldview that "individuals achieved their identity solely through family membership which carried with it not only the obligation of deferring to the collectivity in critical decision-making but of acknowledging that the mortal life of the individual was less important than the immortality of the ancestral family line" (Pye, 1985, p. 62). U. Kim (1995) and U. Kim and Yamaguchi (1995) observed that Korean concept of *chong* (affection and attachment for a person, place or thing) may be functional equivalent of *ren*. Familial piety can be interpreted as an example of *yi*. The concepts of loyalty and duty may also capture the essence of *yi*. Finally, the concept of 'face' parallels the concept of *li*. Indians have similar values and orientations (J.B.P. Sinha, 1990). The Japanese in-group (*miucht*) out-group (*nakamauchi*) distinction is similar to Indian concepts of *apane* (own) *paraye* (others) people and the Chinese concept of *guanxi* (Luo & Chen, 1997). The Indian *ahinsak* way of resolving conflicts through self-suffering and stopping of interaction (D. Sinha, 1987) is similar to the way the Japanese mother influences her misbehaving child (Azuma, 1988).

Leadership is another area where Asian emics seem to converge, although some variations are still noticed. Kabasakal and Dastmalchian (2001) reviewed the GLOBE project on leadership in four Arab countries. Apart from leaders having the hypothesized universal attributes, the respondents also perceived effective leaders as familial, humble, and faithful in Iran, traditional and tribalistic in Qatar, and paternalistic in Turkey. According to Dastmalchian, Javidan, and Alam (2001), the familial leader sacrifices personal gains for the sake of the family, enjoys home and family life, and remains devoted to the family; the humble leader presents oneself as modest and humble and employs soft ways of communication; the faithful leader beliefs in religion and acts according to religious doctrine; the receptive leader is benevolent, understands subordinates' feelings, and is conscious of status and class differentiations (p. 544). The ideal Thai leader has *baramee* (charisma, goodness, and loving kindness) that enables the leader to command respect, love, loyalty, and sacrifices from subordinates (Komin, 1999, p. 279). *Barame* is expressed, among other things, in benefiting subordinates who solicit leader's influence. The leader in India is expected to be warm, affectionate, and caring like a father who guides, directs, and makes the subordinates work hard (J.B.P. Sinha, 1980, 1995). Pye (1985) noted: "In most Asian cultures leaders are expected to be nurturing, benevolent, kind, sympathetic figure who inspires commitment and dedication" (p. 28). Redding (1990, p. 61) collaborated as follows: "The leader or manager, and certainly the owner of a business [in Hong Kong], can look to his workforce and to his immediate subordinates also for a degree of deference unusual when compared to that found in other [western] cultures" (p. 61).

There is also a trend towards convergence in values among Asian cultures. House, Wright, and Aditya (1997, p. 570) reviewed a number of studies to observe that global management practices may be converging but not necessarily towards American management styles. Maybe some Asian nuclei are emerging pushing and pulling management cultures towards each other. Historical analyses have shown that management practices in Korea (Amsden, 1989) and Taiwan (Wade, 1990) are becoming similar to Japanese practices in the preceding decade. Hong Kong managers, because of their exposure to American and Chinese cultural influences, held more western values than the main land Chinese managers and more eastern values than American managers (Ralston, Gustafson, Elsass, Cheung, & Terpstra, 1992). Malaysian values reflect a mix of Chinese and Islamic influences (Rahman, 1995) and Singapore is characterized by 'pragmatic acculturation' (Quah, 1995) because of its international business environment. In sum, Asian values and management practices display distinct configurations that look like Asian emics that pose a challenge to the western organization theories (Redding, Norman, & Schlander, 1994).

The reactions to these emerging Asian emics are varied. They range from a tendency to trivialize them, to show that they reflect varying shades of Asian collectivism, or to attempt to show that they are manifestations of western etics. Poortinga (1997), for example, questioned the utility of the emics by asking how do they fit in the well-established etic configurations, do they add another dimension, or provide a new perspective, or just stand alone without being able to develop into full blown conceptual or theoretical frameworks. Erez (1994, p. 590) felt that the emic researchers are probably carried away by their concern for the relevance of certain research questions to their immediate socio-cultural context and are not quite driven only by pure scientific curiosity; their concern for cultural relevance probably overtakes the need to maintain scientific rigour.

Instead of undermining the importance of emerging emics, a more promising approach may be to integrate the emerging emics and with the existing etics in order to realize a more comprehensive understanding of how etic principles might manifest in emic forms and how the latter might throw up new etics in Asian management research. We now turn to focus on the efforts towards this direction.

Integrative Approaches

There are strands of interactive approaches that either take a sequential route, propose to derive etics on the basis of simultaneously conducted emic studies, or search for etics in the available etic and emic literature.

Sequential Approach

Berry's (1969, 1990) sequential model suggests that researchers, while transporting their own cultural emic as imposed etic to other cultures, should solicit emic elaborations and refinements that may enable them to derive a true etic that would have universal validity. If the etic and emic concepts have equivalent meaning and serve the same functions in the sampled cultures, and the instruments are shown to have equivalent metric properties across cultures under study, the cultures can be justifiably compared with regards to the concepts. If such comparisons yield shared features and common behavioural processes, the resultant understanding of etic nature may be taken to approximate universals with reference to these features and processes to the extent that the cultures under the study represent the universe. While moving from imposed etic to emic research, Triandis (2000) recommends that the researchers may have an etic framework, but the items in the research instrument must be both emic and etic in nature allowing culture sensitive measurements as well as common ground for cultural comparisons (p. 192).

If conducted in the specified way, this approach is called a hybrid form of doing research (Earley & Singh, 2000). In the hybrid form, research questions are examined as a complete set to identify important aspects of each of the systems or cultures. But, "the hypothesized relationships are derived across systems, and they are not necessarily unique to a given system, Furthermore, constructs and relationships are assumed to be separable from the system in which they are embedded, but mapping back isolated relationships to an existing system might not be straightforward. Specific relationships are interpreted using reduced parts of the system but with reference to the general system. These interpretations can, in turn, lead to a further refinement of general principles" (Earley & Singh, 2000, p. 7). The approach by Schwartz and his associate (Schwartz, 1992, 1994; Schwartz & Bilsky, 1987) for mapping universal values structure approximates this form of research. They first conceptualized a set of universal values arising out of human being's need for survival and effective functioning, but took an emic approach to see whether the values interrelate with each other in the same way within each of the cultures that they sampled, although average values scores may be different. They did find a similar pattern of relationships in most of the sampled countries that confirmed a universal structure of values.

Synergetic Approach

Morris, Leung, Ames, and Lickel (1999) have advanced an interactive model in which both emics and etics can stimulate each other to help realize "several general forms of synergy that can occur between emic and etic research programs within a topic area" (p. 789). It is not necessary in Morris et al. model that the same researcher follows the Berry's sequence. Rather, researchers who are exposed to both traditions may inspire each other to create knowledge that enables them either to build on the previous base of knowledge or to create a new one. Leung (1997) showed how this model works. In contrast to the individualist culture that fosters equity rule in resource allocation, the Confucian collectivist cultural setting promotes the principle of harmony that is maintained by following the equality rule (Leung & Bond, 1984). However, the Chinese respondents did not always follow equality rule. Leung found that they differentiate between the core and the peripheral members of the in-group. While harmony is maintained with a peripheral member of the in-group by following the equality rule, the generosity rule is evoked for maintaining harmony with a core in-group member. The distinction illustrates the differential way of maintaining harmony with peripheral and core in-group members and can serve as an etic hypothesis for comparing other highly collectivist societies.

Another example is the formulation of the nurturant-task (*NT*) model of leadership (J.B.P. Sinha, 1980, 1995). Contrary to the western finding, Indian managers generally perceive participative leaders as weak because they abdicate their responsibility to take decisions and lead the group. Subordinates prefer those leaders who are, like a father figure, warm, affectionate, caring, and helping subordinates in their personal matters. However, such leaders are likely to create sycophants unless they are nurturant only to those subordinates who work hard and sincerely. Thus, while the concept of nurturance is emic, the process of rewarding subordinates follows the etic principle of reinforcement. Further, *NT* leaders are effective only with regard to the subordinates who value dependency and personalized relationships and look up to the leaders as the superior father figure. For those who value autonomy and prefer to work without being closely supervised, it is the participative leaders who prove to be more effective. Again the contingency principle is basically etic in nature. Finally, the effectiveness of leaders is contextualized in the dyadic interactive framework of relationships between leaders and subordinates. As NT leaders induce subordinates to work hard and sincerely, the latter gain work expertise and start looking for autonomy and independence. The changed expectations of the subordinates put the NT leaders under pressure to start behaving in a participative way, thus validating the etic finding regarding the effectiveness of participative leadership, but only for the subordinates who are either ready or are prepared to accept such style of leadership.

Assimilative synthesis is similar to the previous approach except that it accepts the predominant position of the existing principles and practices of management, but attempts to delineate only their relevant parts and integrates them with functional parts of traditional wisdom into research designs that may create a new hybrid knowledge base for meeting practical needs of organizations (D. Sinha, 1997). The existing principles and practices are largely western in origin. However, many new Japanese ideas and practices have been added to them. For example, added to the ideas of management by objectives, matrix structure, pay for performance, outsourcing, and downsizing are the salience of quality circles, total quality management, just-in-time, and so on. Thus, a triangular space has been created where western, Asian, and country-specific indigenous principles and practices of management interact and counteract posing a challenge to the researcher to find out how to integrate and assimilate some of the ideas for common organizational purposes, and allow different practices to serve separate functions. The central concern in the assimilative synthesis approach is to design studies that may deliver a package of principles and practices for understanding and managing organizations. An example of this approach is a description by Cole (Triandis, 1994, p. 107) of the Japanese delegations that visited the USA after the Second World War to learn about American productivity. The delegation met with American academics that shared with them about normative management principles such as participative management, cooperation, communication, and so on. Because they did not know English that well, they took them as operative principles and practices. Back to home they integrated them with their traditional cultural orientations that yielded remarkable results. Management research in Asian countries is replete with the instances where western, eastern, and indigenous concepts have been integrated with positive results. S.U. Kim (1999) reported that Korean organizational culture is shaped by the specific characteristics of the organizations (e.g., size, technology, capital structure, and organizational climate), business environment (e.g., labour market, government assistance, and consumers), and socio-cultural environment (consisting of institutions and cultural values).

Meso Level Integration

Assimilative synthesis comes handy at meso level for the practical reason that organizations can benefit by aligning their internal micro level processes with the external macro level socio-economic and cultural forces. The term 'meso' means 'middle' or 'intermediate'. Hence, meso level integrations refer to "an integration of micro and macro theory in the study of processes to specific to organizations which by their very nature are synthesis of psychological and socio-economic processes" (Rousseau & House, 1994, p. 14). Erez (1997, p. 196) quotes a number scholars who have adopted this focus turning individual level variables such as learning, goal setting, and self-efficacy into organizational leaning, goals and targets, and efficacy in specific socio-economic settings, market conditions, and governmental support (or lack of it). Earlier reported study by Erez (1986) of three industrial sectors within Israel showed how specific organizational settings in Kibbutz, Hahistadrut, and private sector organizations affect goal setting, participation, and performance. J.B.P. Sinha (in press) examined how five multinational companies in India (a Korean subsidiary, a Japanese joint venture, a Danish subsidiary, a Swedish subsidiary, and an Anglo-American subsidiary) managed the interfaces of the nature of industry, cultures of the home and host countries, and business practices that were claimed to be universally applicable. Each of the five organizations manifested some common and some unique configurations of these triangular influences.

Search for Deeper Structure

Greenfield (2000) suggested the need to search for "deep structure of culture" that is essentially etic and "generates behaviours and interpretations of behaviour in an infinite array of domains and situations" (p. 229). The conceptualization of deep structure entertains the possibility of intermediate levels of etics. For example, specific configurations of managerial practices and values are identified as collectivism or individualism that may themselves reflect the deep principle of how people relate to others by prioritizing either their self or group interests (Greenfield, 2000, p. 229). Earley (1997) searched the etic roots of the Chinese concept of *face* to conclude that: "Two forms of face, *lian* and *mianzi*, appear to be universal forms of self-presentation that manifest themselves in unique ways across particular cultures" (p. 253). Similarly, Triandis (1994), while conceding the western cultural construal of achievement motivation, quoted studies to conclude that there is a universal aspect of the concept of achievement motivation. That is, the arousal of this motive depends on uncertainty in attaining standards of excellence, affective reactions when these standards are reached or not reached, and a sense of responsibility to reach them. "Thus, a basic structure of motive arousal may be universal" (Triandis, 1994, p. 124) that manifests in culture specific ways, achievement motivation being one such manifestation.

Emics that May Create Overarching Etics

Yang (2000) took a more radical approach of deriving etics through simultaneously conducted emic studies. He questioned Berry's sequential model: "... how the researcher from culture A [western] is able to discover systematically and without bias the relevant emics in culture B [non-western], and then finds out whether or not some communalities (derived etics) really exit in the two cultures by transporting the same concept or instrument developed in culture A to culture B ..." (p. 256). A better approach, according to Yang, lies in adopting a three-phase sequence in which scholars located in different cultures (not the naturalized immigrants) would develop an overarching etic framework through working together as equal partners. The framework then would lead to conduct simultaneously emic studies in their cultural settings, the findings of which may be converged to yield true etics that all cultures participating in the research programme will own. Ng and Liu (2000) called this approach Olympian partly because researchers live in a world where material resources, infra-structural facilities, and growth of management science are asymmetrically distributed allowing the advantaged partner in an international project to set the tune of research.

SUGGESTIONS FOR RESEARCH

The preceding sections describe the diverse approaches to organizational behaviour some of which are dominated by etic traditions while others by emic concerns. Research in etic traditions was started earlier and as such, still enjoys advantages in terms of more precisely defined concepts and elaborately formulated theories. Emic studies are either instigated by the etics and are, thereby, bounded by the etic parameters or are conducted to discover indigenous concepts and relationships that are distinct in profiling specific cultures and hold potential to develop mid-range theories relevant for organizational behaviour. The dialectics between the two approaches have resulted into models of integrative strategies that are likely to attract researchers' attention in the coming years, although a tension between the two will most likely continue. It is by working out of this tension that more fruitful and scientifically sound research on Asian management can be conducted. Some of the suggestions may be the following:

Those who have adequate resources, a network of contacts across cultures, and interests in currently available etic concepts, theories, and methods will certainly conduct comparative studies of organizations across cultures. However, they need to realize that etics are essentially abstract principles and laws of organizational behaviour that must be elaborated into emic details in order to help understand the particular organizational reality and manage it effectively. Starting with an etic framework, the researcher has to think of culture-specific behaviours and episodes carrying same meanings that the underlying concepts have and yielding similar relationships with other concepts and behaviour. The measures may not be identical in terms of either the items or the procedures for collecting data, but should be culturally appropriate to generate findings that may allow the researchers to validate, modify, or reject the etic framework. This requires not only familiarity with the etics but sensitivity to the host culture.

On the other hand, there may be researchers who are intrigued by the interplay of the organizational, societal, and trans-cultural factors in a particular cultural setting, and may like to gain, first of all, an emic understanding that can be subsequently integrated into a larger cross-cultural etic mosaic. They should first define and operationalize the phenomena that interest them, develop emic measures, and adopt procedures that are culturally appropriate. While doing all theses, they should keep searching literature for relevant etic concepts, methods, and theories that may facilitate their efforts to align emic processes with the relevant etic ones. In sum, whether a research is initially an etic or an emic in nature, the process should involve both emic and etic approaches stimulating each other and creating a comprehensive knowledge base for understanding and managing organizations.

There may be researchers who are more concerned about enabling organizations to function effectively and less inclined to get stuck with the etic–emic debate. They may pick up principles and practices of management from any source (inside or outside the organization or the culture) and assimilate them into a synthetic research design that can yield a package of internally consistent and workable system of management without having a compulsion to take a side in the etic–emic debate. The assimilative synthesis process may also subsume a search for Asian etics of management in the existing culture-specific and even organization-specific emic managerial practices in Asian organizations with an aim to identify unifying systems for managing diverse organizations in different Asian cultures.

There may still be researchers whose primary allegiance lies in developing universally valid principles of management. For them, the strategy is to form a team of participants who jointly identify a broad and loosely defined etic framework that leads them to simultaneously conduct emic research in their respective cultural settings. The findings then are integrated to develop an overarching truly etic framework with emic manifestations for understanding and managing organizations. The essential requirement of such a research programme is an equal partnership of the researchers from the start to finish, their shared perspective, and the aim to advance the science of management. A major constraint in this approach is the disparity in resources available to researchers in the different parts of the world. Unequal resource condition creates power distance and deters equal partnership. One way out may be to separate ownership of resources from participation in conducting multi-cultural research programme. This may be attempted by approaching international management associations to solicit funds from different sources and sponsor multi-cultural projects in which researchers from the relevant cultural locations team up as equal partners.

In sum, a number of options are available to researchers who may choose a particular route depending on their interests and circumstances, but they must realize that all routes involve varying degrees of integration of etic and emic approaches to management in general and Asian management in particular.

PRACTICAL IMPLICATIONS

The etic–emic perspectives also have practical use for practicing managers. There are three considerations that are creating a need for having an integrative conceptual framework that managers must have in order to function effectively. First, the workforce is getting more diversified demographically, better educated, more demanding, and more conscious of their need to balance work roles with other life roles and goals (Triandis, Kurowski, & Gelfand, 1994). Second, Asian organizations, unlike the western ones that pursue their enlightened self-interests efficiently (Nord, 1986, p. 440), also have developmental roles and societal obligations that often interfere with their competitive orientation (J.B.P. Sinha, 1994). Third, Asian domestic companies are becoming multinational (MNCs), crossing boarders into the neighbouring countries, and competing or forming alliances with other Asian and western MNCs. Many of them are developing into transnational organizations (TNOs) that have changed the way they were working previously. While MNCs operated as de-centralized units that sensed and responded to diverse international needs and opportunities within a broad federal type of arrangements with the centre, TNOs tend to encourage local flexibility while achieving a tight global integration. This requires a distinct corporate identity, a global management perspective, and complex process of coordination and cooperation involving strong integrative devices for establishing interactive networking among local operations that are also linked to the center in a flexible way (Bartlett & Ghosal, 1988).

Asian managers need to have a radar-like sensitivity to all these forces in order to be able to identify policy options, formulate business and human relations strategies, and adopt effective ways of implementing their policies and strategies (Morris, Leung, Ames, & Lickel, 1999). However, the tendency is to stick to their home-grown etics, primarily because the etics are global, familiar and time tested. They are fewer in number to be evoked efficiently for leveraging managerial systems and practices such as equity rule (e.g., pay for performance only), participation (e.g., working through autonomous project teams that form, perform, and disband only to form again for another project), reengineering work process (through continuous downsizing, outsourcing, and shortening people's and product's life cycles), and so on (J.B.P. Sinha, 2000b). Following an etic approach, MNCs and TNOs tend to develop and standardize strategic human resource management packages that, they believe, can be used globally (Geringer & Frayne, 2000; Shenkar & Zeira, 1987; Taylor, Beechler, & Napier, 1996). The packages generally consist of (a) aligning human resource management to business strategies, (b) rotating managers across countries by creating a pool of portable managers who can use the standardized practices wherever they go, and (c) encouraging portable managers to cultivate sensitivity to local cultural imperatives by forming teams with host culture managers.

The evidence, however, indicates that the package has limited success. The cultural training guides do not incorporate Asian values and managerial practices (Morris, Leung, Ames, & Lickel, 1999) and expatriates learn about cultural sensitivities in a country-by-country fashion (Cushner & Brislin, 1996). Probably, there are differences in the way expatriates and local managers perceive management principles and practices, apply the abstract principles into practices, or both (Morris, Leung, Ames, & Lickel, 1999). One way that MNCs and TNOs try to cope the differences is to arrange massive training programme to change employees' perceptions, values, and work habits (Florida & Kenney, 1991; Wilms, Hardcastte, & Zell, 1994) for aligning them with their etics. Others compartmentalize technical operations and handle them etically leaving human resource management to be managed emically by local managers (J.B.P. Sinha, in press). In neither case global perspective seem to be integrated with local operations.

A more effective way may be to evoke one of the integrative approaches discussed earlier. Following the sequential model of Berry (1969, 1990), an organization may start with the etics but must look for its emic elaborations in the local units. For example, the equity rule that means that employees should be compensated in proportion to their contributions to the organization may be a valid etic principle. But its emic manifestation may be different; for contributions in Asian cultures also include the years of service and loyalty to the organization. Thus, pay for performance, if practiced strictly, is likely to get problematic. In fact a better way may be to approach management issues from both – etic and emic – ends in order to realize synergy (Morris, Leung, Ames, & Lickel, 1999). For example, pay for performance may be a valid principle, but performance in a collectivist culture might mean group performance and incentive, therefore, has to be based on equality rule irrespective of individuals' performance or seniority. Individual appraisals strictly on self-set targets without due consideration to the amounts of efforts that one puts in, 360-degree appraisal in a high power distance culture, and so on are often counterproductive. There are probably principles and practices of management of both western and Asian origin that can be assimilated to yield best results in the highly turbulent global business environment in Asia (D. Sinha, 1997).

In sum, Asian managers and their organizations have to adopt a strategy of integrating etic principles for maintaining a global perspective with emic sensitivity to manage diversified workforce in culturally embedded organizations.

REFERENCES

Abella, C.T. 1995. Socio-cultural factors influencing firm-level productivity in Philippines. In K.K. Hwang (ed.), *Easternization; Socio-cultural Impact on Productivity* (pp. 234-265). Tokyo: Asian Productivity Organization.

Ali, J. 1992. Islamic work ethic. *Journal of Psychology*, 126: 507-519.

Alston, J.P. 1989. *Wa, gunaxi*, and *inhwa*: Managerial principles in Japan, China, and Korea. *Business Horizon*, March-April, 26-31.

Amsden, A.H. 1989. *Asia's Next Giant: South Korea and Late Industrialization*. New York: Oxford University Press.

Ayman, R. and Chemers, M.M. 1983. Relationships of supervisory behaviour ratings to work group effectiveness and subordinate satisfaction among Iranian managers. *Journal of Applied Psychology*, 88: 338-341.

Azuma, J. 1984. Psychology in a non-western country. *International Journal of Psychology*, 19: 145-155.

Azuma, J. 1988. Are Japanese really that different? The concept of development as a key for transformation. Invited Address at the XXIV International Congress of Psychology, September, Sydney, Australia.

Bartlett, C.A. and Ghosal, S. 1988. Organizing for world-wide effectiveness: transnational solution. *California Management Review*, Fall: 54-74.

Bass, B.M., Berger, P.C., Doctor, R. and Barrett, G.V. 1979. *Assessment of Managers: An International Comparison*. New York: Free Press.

Berry, J.W. 1969. On cross-cultural comparability. *International Journal of Psychology*, 4: 119-128.

Berry, J.W. 1990. Imposed etics, emics, derived etics: Their conceptual and operational status in cross-cultural psychology. In T.N. Headland, K.L. Pike and M. Harris (eds.), *Emics and Etics: The Insider/Outsider Debate* (pp. 28-47). Newbury Park, CA: Sage.

Boesch, E.E. 1996. The seven flaws of cross-cultural psychology: The story of conversion. *Mind, Culture, and Activity*, 3: 2-10.

Bond, M.H. 1997. Adding value to the cross-cultural study of organizational behaviour: Reculer pour mieux sauter. In P.C. Earley and M. Erez (eds.), *New Perspectives on International Industrial/Organizational Psychology* (pp. 256-275). San Francisco: New Lexington Press.

Brown, D.E. 1991. *Human Universals*. Philadelphia: Temple University Press.

Cappelli, P. and Sherer, P.D. 1991. The missing role of context in OB: The need for a meso-level approach. In B. Shaw and L.I. Cummings (eds.), *Research in Organizational Behaviour* (Vol. 13, pp. 55-110). Greenwich, CT: Jai Press.

Chakraborty, S.K. 1993. *Managerial Transformation by Values: A Corporate Pilgrimage*. New Delhi: Sage.

Chinese Culture Connection. 1987. Chinese values and the research for culture-free dimensions of culture. *Journal of Cross-Cultural Psychology*, 18, 143-174.

Cushner, K. and Brislin, R.W. 1996. *Intercultural Interactions: A Practical Guide*. Thousand Oaks, CA: Sage.

Dastmalchian, A., Javidan, M. and Alam, K. 2001. Effective leadership and culture in Iran: An empirical study. *Applied Psychology: An International Review*, 50: 532-558.

Dhakan, A.A.M. 1994. Case Studies: Pakistan. In P.S.C. Hsu (ed.), *Corporate Culture and Productivity: Case Studies on Asia and the Pacific* (pp. 499-533). Tokyo: Asia Productivity Organization.

Earley, P.C. 1989. Social loafing and collectivism: A comparison of United States and Peoples Republic of China. *Administrative Science Quarterly*, 34: 385-581.

Earley, P.C. 1997. Doing an about face: Social motivation and cross-cultural currents. In P.C. Earley and M. Erez (eds.), *New Perspectives on International Industrial/Organizational Psychology* (pp. 243-255). San Francisco: New Lexington Press.

Earley, P.C. and Singh, H. 2000. *Innovations in International and Cross-national Management*. Thousand Oaks: Sage.

Erez, M. 1986. The congruence of goal-setting strategies with socio-cultural values and its effects on performance. *Journal of Management*, 12: 83-90.

Erez, M. 1994. Towards a model of cross-cultural industrial and organizational psychology. In H.C. Triandis, M.D. Dunnette and L.M. Hough (eds.), *Handbook of Industrial Organizational Psychology* (2nd edn, Vol. 4, pp. 559-608). Paulo Alto, CA: Consulting Psychology Press.

Erez, M. 1997. A culture-based model of work motivation. In P.C. Earley and M. Erez (eds.), *New Perspectives on International Industrial/Organizational Psychology* (pp. 193-242). San Francisco: New Lexington Press.

Erez, M. and Earley, P.C. 1987. Comparative analysis of goal setting strategies across cultures. *Journal of Applied Psychology*, 72: 658-665.

Florida, R. and Kenney, M. 1991. Transplanted organizations: The transfer of Japanese industrial organization into the U.S. *American Sociological Review*, 56: 381-399.

Geertz, C. 1983. *Local Knowledge: Further Essays in Interpretive Anthropology*. New York: Basic Books.

Geringer, J.M. and Frayne, C.A. 2000. Strategic human resource management in international joint ventures. In P.C. Earley and H. Singh (eds.), *Innovations in International and Cross-national Management* (pp. 107-128). Thousand Oaks: Sage.

Greenfield, P.M. 2000. Three approaches to the psychology of culture: Where do they come from? Where can they go? *Asian Journal of Social Psychology*, 3: 223-240.

Gregory, K. 1983. Native-view paradigms: Multiple cultures and culture conflicts in organizations. *Administrative Science Quarterly*, 28: 359-376.

Habibi, M. and Amirshahi, M. 2000. Key cultural factors in management and productivity: Case studies in the Islamic Republic of Iran. In J.B.P. Sinha (ed.), *Managing Cultural Diversity for Productivity: The Asian Ways* (pp. 152-181). Tokyo: Asian Productivity Organization.

Haire, M., Ghiselli, E.E. and Porter, L.W. 1966. *Managerial Thinking: An International Study*. New York: Wiley.

Hall, E.T. 1981. *Beyond Culture*. New York: Doubleday.

Hamada, T. 1996. Unwrapping Euro-American masculinity in a Japanese multinational corporation. In C. Cheng (ed.), *Masculinities in Organizations* (pp. 160-176). Thousand Oaks, CA:
Sage.

Headland, T.N., Pike, K.L. and Harris, M. 1990. Introduction. In T.N. Headland, K.L. Pike and
M. Harris (eds.), *Emics and Etics: The Insider/Outsider Debate.* Newbury Park, CA: Sage.

Hickson, D.J., Hinings, C.R., McMillan, C.J. and Schwitter, J.P. 1974. The culture-free context
of organizational structure. *Sociology*, 8: 59-80.

Hofstede, G. 1980. *Culture's Consequences: International Differences in Work-related Values.*
Beverly Hills, CA: Sage.

Hofstede, G. 1983. The cultural relativity of organizational practices and theories. *Journal of
International Business Studies*, 14: 75-89.

Hofstede, G. 1988. McGregor in South East Asia. In D. Sinha and H.R.S. Kao (eds.), *Social
Values and Development: Asian Perspectives* (pp. 304-314). New Delhi: Sage.

Hofstede, G. 1991. *Culture and Organizations.* Beverly Hills, CA: Sage.

Hofstede, G. 2001. *Culture's Consequences: Comparing Values, Behaviours, Institutions, and
Organizations Across Nations* (2nd edn). Thousand Oaks, CA: Sage.

House, R.J., Wright, N.S. and Aditya, R.N. 1997. Cross-cultural research on organizational
leadership: A critical analysis and a proposed theory. In P.C. Earley and M. Erez (eds.),
New Perspectives on International Industrial/Organizational Psychology (pp. 535-625). San
Francisco: New Lexington Press.

Hulin, C.L. 1987. A psychometric theory of evaluations of item and scale translations. *Journal
of Cross-Cultural Psychology*, 18: 115-142.

Hsu, F. 1953. *Americans and Chinese: Two Ways of Life.* New York: Abelard-Schuman.

Hsu, P.S.C. 1994 (ed.), *Corporate Culture and Productivity; Case Studies on Asia and The
Pacific.* Tokyo: Asia Productivity Organization.

Hwang, K.K. 1995 (ed.). *Easternization: Socio-cultural Impact on Productivity.* Tokyo: Asia
Productivity Organization.

Hwang, K.K. 1999. Filial piety and loyalty: Two types of social identification in Confucianism.
Asian Journal of Social Psychology, 2: 163-183.

Inkeles, A. and Smith, D.H. 1975. *Becoming Modern: Individual Change in Six Developing
Countries.* London: Heinemann Educational.

Jahoda, G. 1977. In pursuit of the emic–etic distinction: Can we overcome it? In Y.H. Poortinga
(ed.), *Basic Problems in Cross-cultural Psychology* (pp. 55-63). Lisse: Swets & Zettlinger.

Kabasakal, H. and Dastmalchian, A. 2001. Introduction to the special issue on leadership and
culture in the Middle East. *Applied Psychology: An International Review*, 50: 479-488.

Kerr, H.C. 1983. *The Future of Industrial Societies; Convergence or Continuing Diversity.* Cambridge, MA: Harvard university Press.

Kim, S.U. 1999. Determinants and characteristics of the corporate culture of Korean enterprises.
In H.S.R. Kao, D. Sinha and B. Wilpert (eds.), *Management and Cultural Values: The Indi-
genization of Organizations in Asia* (pp. 86-101). New Delhi: Sage.

Kim, U. 1995. Psychology, science, and culture: Cross-cultural analysis of national psychologies
in developing countries. *International Journal of Psychology*, 30: 663-679.

Kim, U. 2000. Indigenous, cultural, and cross-cultural psychology: A theoretical, conceptual,
and epistemological analysis. *Asian Journal of Social Psychology*, 3: 265-288.

Kim, U. and Yamaguchi, S. 1995. Conceptual and empirical analysis of *amae*: Exploration into
Japanese psycho-social space. In *Proceedings of the Japanese Group Dynamics Conference*,
Tokyo: Japanese Group Dynamics Association.

Kim, U., Triandis, H.C., Kagitcibasi, C., Choi, S.C. and Yoon, G. 1994 (eds.). *Individualism and
Collectivism: Theory, Method, and Applications.* Thousand Oaks, CA: Sage.

Kloos, P. 1988. *Door het oog van anthropolog (Through the Eyes of the Anthropologist).* Muider-
berg: The Netherlands.

Komin, S. 1999. The Thai concept of effective leadership. In H.S.R. Kao, D. Sinha and B. Wilpert (ed.), *Management and Cultural Values* (pp. 252-264). New Delhi: Sage.

Kondo, D.K. 1990. *Crafting Selves: Power, Gender, and Discourses of Identity in Japanese.*

Kornadt, H.J., Eckensberger, L.H. and Emmingaus, W.B. (1980). Cross-cultural research on motivation and its contribution to a general theory of motivation. In H.C. Triandis and W.W. Lonner (eds.), *Handbook of Cross-cultural Psychology* (Vol. 3, pp. 223-321). Boston: Allyn & Becon.

Learner, D. 1958. *The Passing of Traditional Society: Modernizing of the Middle East.* Glencoe, IL: Free Press.

Leung, K. 1997. Negotiation and reward allocations across cultures. In P.C. Earley and M. Erez (eds.), *New Perspectives on International Industrial/Organizational Psychology* (pp. 640-675). San Francisco: New Lexington Press.

Leung, K. and Bond, M.H. 1984. The impact of cultural collectivism on reward allocation. *Journal of Personality and Social Psychology*, 47: 793-804.

Leung, K., Bond, M.H., Carrasqel, S.R., Munoz, C., Murakami, F., Yamaguchi, S., Bierbrauer, G. and Singelis, T.M. 2002. Social axioms: The search for universal dimensions of general beliefs about how the world functions. *Journal of Cross-Cultural Psychology*, 33: 286-302.

Lytle, A.L., Brett, J., Barsness, Z.I., Tinsley, C.H. and Janssens, M. 1995. A paradigm for confirmatory cross-cultural research in organizational behaviour. In L.L. Cumming and B.M. Staw (eds.), *Research in Organizational Behaviour* (Vol. 17, pp. 167-214). Greenwich, CT: Jai Press.

Maehr, M.L. 1974. Culture and achievement motivation. *American Psychologist*, 29: 887-896.

Malinowski, B. 1922. *Argonauts of the Western Pacific.* London: Routledgo.

Marano, L. 1982. Windigo psychosis: The anatomy of an emic–etic confusion. *Current Anthropology*, 23: 385-412.

Martin, I. 1992. *Cultures in Organizations: Three Perspectives.* New York: Oxford University Press.

McClelland, D.C. 1961. *The Achieving Society.* New York: Van Nostrand.

McClelland, D.C. 1975. *Power: The Inner Experience.* New York: Free Press.

McClelland, D.C. 1985. *Human Motivation.* Glenview, IL, Scott, Foresman.

McClelland, D.C. and Winter, D.G. 1969. *Motivating Economic Development.* New York: Free Press.

Mehta, P. 1991. *People's Development, Motivation, and Work Organization.* New Delhi: Participation and Development Centre.

Mendonca, M. and Kanungo, R.N. 1990. Performance management in developing countries. In A.M. Jaeger and R.N. Kanungo (eds.), *Management in Developing Countries* (pp. 223-263). London: Routledge.

Merekula, J.R. 2000. Comparative study of Indo-Fijian and native Fijian cultural practices in managing business enterprises in Fiji. In J.B.P. Sinha (ed.), *Managing Cultural Diversity for Productivity: The Asian Ways* (pp. 68-93). Tokyo: Asian Productivity Organization.

Meyer, A.G. 1970. Theories of convergence. In C. Johnson (ed.), *Change in Communist Systems* (pp. 113-129). Stanford: Stanford University Press.

Misumi, J. 1985. *The Behavioural Science of Leadership.* Ann Arbor: University of Michigan Press.

Morris, M.W., Leung, K., Ames, D. and Lickel, B. 1999. Views from inside and outside: Integrating emic and etic insights about culture and justice judgement. *Academy of Management Review*, 24: 781-796.

MOW International Research Team. 1987. *The Meaning of Working.* London: Academic Press.

Munroe, R. and Munroe, R. 1971. Effects of environmental experience on spatial ability in East Africa. *Journal of Social Psychology*, 83: 15-22.

Negandhi, A.R. 1973. *Management and Economic Development: The Case of Taiwan.* The Hague: Nijhoff.

Nagandhi, A.R. 1986. Three decades of cross-cultural management research. In S.R. Clegg, D.C. Dunphy and S.G. Redding (eds.), *The Enterprise and Management in East Asia* (pp. 35-66). Hong Kong: Centre of Asian Studies, University of Hong Kong.

Ng, S.H. and Liu, J.H. 2000. Cultural revolution in psychology. *Asian Journal of Social Psychology*, 3: 289-293.

Nisbet, R. 1971. Ethnocentrism and the comparative method. In A. Desai (ed.), *Essays on Modernization of Underdeveloped Societies* (Vol. 1, pp. 95-114). Bombay: Thacker.

Nord, W.R. 1986. Continuity and change in industrial/organizational psychology: Learning from previous mistakes. In F.J. Landy (ed.), *Readings in Industrial and Organizational Psychology* (pp. 438-447). Chicago: Dorsey Press.

Pande, N. and Naidu, R.K. 1992. *Anasakti* and health: A study of non-attachment. *Psychology and Developing Societies*, 4: 89-104.

Pandey, J. 1986. Cross-cultural perspective on ingratiation. In B. Mahler and W. Mahler (eds.), *Progress in Experimental Personality Research* (pp.). New York: Academic Press.

Pareek, U. 1988. *Organizational Behaviour.* Jaipur, India: Rawat.

Pike, K.L. 1967. *Language in Relation to a Unified Theory of The Structure of Human Behaviour.* The Hague: Mouton.

Pike, K.L. 1990. On the emics and etics of Pike and Harris. In T.N. Headland, K.L. Pike and M. Harris (eds.), *Emics and Etics: The Insider/Outsider Debate* (pp. 28-36). Newbury park, CA: Sage.

Poortinga, Y.H. 1997. Towards convergence? In J.W. Berry, Y.H. Poortinga and J. Pandey (eds.), *Handbook of Cross-cultural Psychology, Vol. 1. Theory and Method* (2nd edn, pp. 347-387). MA: Allyn & Bacon.

Pugh, D.S. 1976. The Aston approach to the study of organizations. In G. Hofstede and M.S. Kassem (eds.), *European Contributions to Organizational Theory* (pp. 62-78). Assen, The Netherlands: Van Goreum.

Pugh, D.S. and Hickson, D.J. 1976. *Organizational Structure in Its Context: The Aston Programme.* London: Saxon House.

Pye, L.W. 1985. *Asian Power and Politics; The Cultural Dimension of Authority.* Cambridge, MA: Harvard University Press.

Quah, S.R. 1995. Socio-cultural factors and productivity: The case of Singapore. In K.K. Hwang (ed.), *Easternization; Socio-cultural Impact on Productivity* (pp. 266-333). Tokyo: Asian Productivity Organization.

Rahman, N. 1995. Socio-cultural factors influencing productivity in the Malaysian Malays. In K.K. Hwang (ed.), *Easternization; Socio-cultural Impact on Productivity* (pp. 177-200). Tokyo: Asian Productivity Organization.

Ralston, D.A., Gustafson, D.J., Elsass, P.M., Cheung, F. and Terpstra, R.H. 1992. Eastern values: A comparison of managers in the United States, Hong Kong, and the People's Republic of China. *Journal of Applied Psychology*, 77: 664-671.

Redding, S.G. 1990. *The Spirit of Chinese Capitalism.* New York: W. de Guyter.

Redding, S.G., Norman, A. and Schlander, A. 1994. The nature of individual attachment to the organization: A review of East Asian variations. In H.C. Triandis, M.D. Dunnette and L.M. Hough (eds.), *Handbook of Industrial Organizational Psychology* (2nd edn, Vol. 4, pp. 747-688). Paulo Alto, CA: Consulting Psychology Press.

Redding. S.G. and Wong. G.Y. 1986. The psychology of Chinese organizational behavior. In M.H. Bond (ed.), *The Psychology of the Chinese People.* New York: Oxford University Press.

Rohlen, T. 1974. *For Harmony and Strength: Japanese White-cellar Organization in Anthropological Perspective.* Berkeley: University of California Press.

Ronen, S. and Shenkar, O. 1985. Clustering countries on attitudinal dimensions: A review and synthesis. *Academy of Management Review*, 10: 435-454.

Rousseau, D.M. and House, R.J. 1994. Meso organizational behaviour: Avoiding three fundamental biases. In C.I. Cooper and D.M. Rousseau (eds.), *Trends in organizational behaviour* (Vol. 1, pp. 15-29). New York: Wiley.

Schneider, B. 1990. *Organizational Climate and Culture*. San Francisco: Jossey-Bass.

Schwartz, S.H. 1992. Universals in the content and structure of values: Theoretical advances and empirical tests in 20 countries. In M.P. Zanna (ed.), *Advances in Experimental Social Psychology* (Vol. 25, pp. 1-65). Orlando: Academic Press.

Schwartz, S.H. 1994. Beyond individualism and collectivism. In U. Kim, H.C. Triandis, C. Kagitcibasi, S.C. Choi and G. Yoon (ed.), *Individualism and Collectivism: Theory, Method, and Applications* (pp. 85-119). Thousand Oaks, CA: Sage.

Schwartz, S.H. and Bilsky, W. 1987. Toward a universal structure of human values. *Journal of Personality and Social Psychology*, 53: 550-562.

Shenkar, O. and Zeira, Y. 1987. Human resource management in international joint ventures: Directions for research. *Academy of Management Review*, 12: 546-557.

Shurchuluu, P.U. 2000. The preconditions for cross-cultural management of productivity in Mongolia. In J.B.P. Sinha (ed.), *Managing Cultural Diversity for Productivity: The Asian Ways* (pp. 245-294). Tokyo: Asian Productivity Organization.

Shweder, R.A. 1991. *Thinking Through Cultures: Expeditions in Cultural Psychology*. Cambridge, MA: Harvard University Press.

Shweder, R.A. 2000. The psychology of practice and the practice of the three psychologies. *Asian Journal of Social Psychology*, 3: 207-222.

Sinha, D. 1987. *Ahinsa* as conflict resolution technique and instrument of peace: A psychological appraisal. Paper presented at the seminar on Peace and Conflict Resolution in the World Community, New Delhi.

Sinha, D. 1997. Indigenizing psychology. In J.W. Berry, Y.H. Poortinga and J. Pandey (eds.), *Handbook of Cross-cultural Psychology, Vol. 1. Theory and method* (2nd edn, pp. 129-169). MA: Allyn & Bacon.

Sinha, J.B.P. 1968. The nAch/nCooperation under limited/unlimited resource conditions. *Journal of Experimental Social Psychology*, 4: 233-248.

Sinha, J.B.P. 1980. *The Nurturant Task Leader*. New Delhi: Concept.

Sinha, J.B.P. 1984. Towards partnership for relevant research in the Third World. *International Journal of Psychology*, 19: 169-178.

Sinha, J.B.P. 1990. The salient Indian values and their socio-ecological roots. *Indian Journal of Social Sciences*, 3: 477-488.

Sinha, J.B.P. 1994. Cultural embeddedness and developmental role of industrial organizations in India. In H.C. Triandis, M.D. Dunnette and L.M. Hough (eds.), *Handbook of Industrial Organizational Psychology* (2nd edn, Vol. 4, pp. 727-764). Paulo Alto, CA: Consulting Psychology Press.

Sinha, J.B.P. 1995. *The Cultural Context of Leadership and Power*. New Delhi: Sage.

Sinha, J.B.P. 1997. A cultural perspective on organizational behaviour in India. In P.C. Earley and M. Erez (eds.), *New Perspectives on International Industrial/Organizational Psychology* (pp. 53-74). San Francisco: New Lexington Press.

Sinha, J.B.P. 2000a. (Ed.). *Managing Cultural Diversity for Productivity: The Asian Ways*. Tokyo: Asian Productivity Organization.

Sinha, J.B.P. 2000b. Interface of foreign and Indian values in productive organizations. In J.B.P. Sinha (ed.), *Managing Cultural Diversity for Productivity: The Asian Ways* (pp. 94-126). Tokyo: Asian Productivity Organization.

Sinha, J.B.P. in press. Multinationals in India: Strategies for managing the interface of cultures. New Delhi: Sage.

Sinha, J.B.P. and Pandey, J. 1970. Strategies of high nAch persons. *Psychologia*, 13: 210-216.

Smith, P.B. 1997. Cross-cultural leadership: A path to goal? In P.C. Earley and M. Erez (eds.), *New Perspectives on International Industrial/Organizational Psychology* (pp. 626-639). San Francisco: New Lexington Press.

Smith, P.B. and Bond, M.H. 1998. *Social Psychology: Across Cultures* (2nd edn) Boston: Allyn & Bacon.

Smith, P.B., Dugan, S. and Trompenaars, F. 1996. National culture and values of organizational employees. *Journal of Cross-Cultural Psychology*, 27: 231-264.

Smith P.B. and Peterson, M. 1988. *Leadership in Context*. London: Sage.

Smith, P.B. and Tayeb, M. 1988. Organizational structure and process. In M.H. Bond (ed.), *The Cross-cultural Challenge to Social Psychology* (pp. 153-164). Newburry Park, CA: Sage.

Spector, P.E., Cooper, C.L., Sparks, K. et al. 2001. An international study of the psychometric properties of the Hofstede Values Survey module 1994: A comparison of individual and country/province level results. *Applied Psychology: An International Review*, 50: 269-281.

Srinivas, K.M. 2000. *Pilgrimage to Indian Ethos Management: A Look at Indigenous Approaches to Organizational Development*. Calcutta: Indian Institute of Management.

Taylor, S., Beechler, S. and Napier, N. 1996. Towards an integrative model of strategic international human resource management. *Academy of Management Review*, 2: 939-985.

Triandis, H.C. 1993. Dimensions of cultural variations as parameters of organizational theories. *International Studies of Management and Organizations*, 12: 139-169.

Triandis, H.C. 1994. Cross-cultural industrial and organizational psychology. In H.C. Triandis, M.D. Dunnette and L.M. Hough (eds.), *Handbook of Industrial Organizational Psychology* (2nd edn, Vol. 4, pp. 103-172). Paulo Alto, CA: Consulting Psychology Press.

Triandis, H.C. 1995a. *Culture and Social Behaviour*. New York: McGraw.

Triandis, H.C. 1995b. *Individualism and Collectivism*. Boulder, GO: Westview Press.

Triandis, H.C. 1999. Cross-cultural psychology. *Asian Journal of Social Psychology*, 2: 127-144.

Triandis, H.C. 2000. Dialectics between cultural and cross-cultural psychology. *Asian Journal of Social Psychology*, 3: 185-196.

Triandis, H.C. and Bhawuk, P.S. 1997. Culture theory and meaning of relatedness. In P.C. Earley and M. Erez (eds.), *New Perspectives on International Industrial/Organizational Psychology* (pp. 13-54). San Francisco: New Lexington Press.

Triandis, H.C., Kurowski, L.L. and Gelfand, M.J. 1994. Workplace diversity. In H.C. Triandis, M.D. Dunnette and L.M. Hough (eds.), *Handbook of Industrial Organizational Psychology* (2nd edn, Vol. 4, pp. 769-827). Paulo Alto, CA: Consulting Psychology Press.

Triandis, C.H., McCusker, C., Betancourt, H., Iwao, S., Leung, K., Salazar, J.M. et al. 1993. An etic–emic analysis of individualism–collectivism. *Journal of Cross-Cultural Psychology*, 24: 366-383.

Wade, R. 1990. *Governing The Market: The Role of Government in East Asian Industrialization*. Princeton, NJ: Princeton University Press.

Weinberg, I. 1969. The problems of convergence of industrialized societies: A critical look at the state of a theory. *Comparative Studies in Society and History*, 11: 1-15.

Whitley, R.D. 1995. The social construction of business systems in East Asia. In S.G. Redding (ed.), *International Cultural Differences*. Aldershot, England: Brookfield.

Whiteley, W. and England, G.W. 1980. Variability in common dimensions of managerial values due to value orientation and country difference. *Personnel Psychology*, 33: 77-89.

Wilms, W.W., Hardcastte, A.I. and Zell, D.M. 1994. Cultural transformation at NUMMI. *Sloan Management Review*, 38: 99-113.

Yang, K.S. 1997. Indigenizing westernized Chinese psychology. In M.H. Bond (ed.), *Working at The Interface of Culture: Eighteen Lives in Social Science* (pp. 62-75). London: Routledge.

Yang, K.S. 2000. Monocultural and cross-cultural indigenous approaches: The royal road to the development of a balanced global psychology. *Asian Journal of Social Psychology*, 3: 241-264.

PART II

STRATEGY

Chapter 3

TOWARDS THE DEVELOPMENT OF STRATEGY THEORY
Contributions from Asian Research

Kulwant Singh
National University of Singapore

INTRODUCTION

Research on strategy in Asia has the potential to make substantial contributions to strategy theory and research. Existing strategy theory and research is currently undersocialized and pays insufficient attention to the context within which firms and strategy are embedded. The complexity of the Asian context represents a considerable challenge to researchers, but also offers the opportunity for improving both empirical understanding and theoretical development of strategy in general. The plurality of environments in which firms operate suggests that firm strategies, behavior and performance will necessarily be varied, and that theories must account for such variation.

This chapter elaborates this argument by addressing three major themes. First, I discuss the question of why it is useful to examine the issue of strategy in Asia. Clearly specifying the importance of the question and the bounds of its possible answers represent substantial challenges, which may partially explain the lack of research on the issue. However, I suggest that it is beneficial to examine strategy in Asia because we have little extant knowledge, because such examination can correct this deficiency, and because resulting insights have the potential to contribute to the development of the broader theory of strategy.

This chapter's second theme is to identify variables that could potentially differentiate strategy theory in Asia from what has become received (or "mainstream") strategy theory. I identify two sets of factors, those that have relatively little influence and those that have significant influence in the Asian context. The more significant influences on strategy in Asia are specific to or more salient in Asia, though they are also likely to be significant elsewhere. These factors therefore should represent the focus of research seeking to develop strategy theory in Asia. The third theme is to outline briefly several ideas that can guide the search for "answers" to the core question this chapter addresses, how is strategy in Asia different?

I do not attempt to provide a comprehensive overview of research on strategy in Asia, nor even propose the need for a theory of strategy in Asia. Instead, this chapter has the limited objective of facilitating the development of the theory of strategy in Asia, on the presumption that this will contribute towards strategy theory generally. The approach will be pragmatic, with a focus on research in Asia that is most current and visible, on the assumption that this research reflects the current state of the art. A narrow view is adopted of strategy theory, as the set of theories that seek to explain the long-term performance of business organizations and which fall within the bounds of the academic field of strategy. Emphasis is placed on the content rather than the process of strategy. In line with its aims of facilitating theoretical development, this chapter focuses on strategy in Asia, irrespective of its origins. The coverage is not limited to strategy emerging from Asia or developed by Asians, nor its practice by Asian firms in Asia.[1]

Current State of Research

What does research tell us about strategy in Asia and the extent to which existing models of strategy are applicable in Asia?[2] I submit that the clearest answer is, very little. I believe we lack rigorous understanding of strategy in Asia, of whether it differs from strategy elsewhere, and if so, how it differs. It can be argued, though perhaps not established, that we have not yet demonstrated the validity of the key models, concepts and axioms of strategy theory in Asia.[3] A related critique of the state of strategy theory is that with the exception of a few research streams – examples may be business groups, supplier relationships and networks, and technology strategy – research on strategy in Asia has also failed to make substantial conceptual or theoretical contributions to the larger body of strategy theory (Hoskisson et al., 2000; White, 2002). This failure reflects inadequate rigorous and theoretically driven research aiming to establish theoretical models specific to Asia or to falsify models claiming such validity.

Firms in emerging markets face social, economic, political, institutional, and resource environments that are significantly different from those in other regions. Researchers have observed that some business practices (for example, ownership structures, interfirm relationships within group structures, and the general tendency to grow by diversifying) are different for firms in emerging markets in Asia, as compared to firms in North America. Firms in emerging markets sometimes pursue strategies that are inherently different, if not contradictory, from prescriptions for firms in advanced economies. However, extant theories of strategy do not offer sufficient explanations for differences in strategy and other characteristics observed between firms in advanced and emerging economies, and strategy researchers have only recently taken interest in issues relating to the external economic and institutional environments in emerging markets.

There are several reasons why strategy theory is inadequate for Asian contexts. First, in absolute and relative terms, the body of research of strategy in Asia is small (Hoskisson et al., 2000; White, 2002). As a result, relatively little research has examined most strategy related issues. In his overview of Asian management and strategy research, White (2002) provides a useful list of 840 papers on Asia published between 1980 and 2000 in 30 management journals. An overview of these papers suggests that about 150 papers (approximately 18%) are strategy related.

Second, the research that has been undertaken has not systematically tested the applicability of existing theories in the region, with few studies specifically seeking to replicate findings. Instead, most studies adopt the dominant theory and methodology to study country or cross country phenomena on the tacit or explicit assumption that established theory is valid and adequate across empirical contexts. Most of these studies appear to focus on establishing associations between variables, rather than on identifying antecedent conditions, explaining their manifestations, and their impact on performance (White, 2002). Alternatively, other studies assume that existing theory is not applicable, and propose context-specific ideas or models, often without adequate conceptual development. Consequently, strategy and management theory in Asia have been described as theoretically inadequate (Lau, 2002; White, 2002).

A related reason why existing research is not very illuminating, is that it has not been conducted programmatically. Studies have been structured by individual researchers' agendas, rather than by systematic attempt to establish the validity of theory. An added feature of these studies – their concentration within a single country or dispersion across different samples of countries – contributes to this problem. This has made knowledge accumulation and coherent theorizing even more challenging.

Third, as is common with empirical strategy research generally, results of studies done in the region typically explain a small proportion of the total variance in the phenomena studied. As an example, several of the most heavily cited empirical studies of management and organization in China identified by Li & Tsui (2002), have average explanatory powers below the levels necessary to offer comprehensive explanation of the phenomena studied. However, few of these studies aim to develop comprehensive models, with most papers aiming to test associations between phenomena. Consequently, it is not possible to refute the proposition that variables that are specific to the region, but

which have been excluded from existing models, significantly influence results. A pragmatic interpretation is that while current theories may be applicable, significant adaptation or addition to these theories to take into account
region-specific factors will improve explanatory power significantly.[4]

Finally, it is possible that theories of strategy in Asia have not emerged because Asia is not a meaningful context for the conduct of strategy research.
This argument questions the value of examining theories of strategy for a geographic region that is vast and diverse, and which at the level of business
strategy, may have little construct validity. No parsimonious sets of models or
theories may be able to incorporate meaningfully the variety of different organizations, institutions and contexts that Asia embodies. Relatedly, the relative
absence of equivalent questions, "how is strategy different in Europe?" or "in
South America?" is consistent with the view that efforts to develop strategy
theory in Asia are irrelevant. The issue therefore arises whether it is useful to
study strategy in Asia, and whether it is useful to do so at this particular point
in time.

How is Strategy Different?

The proposition that strategy in Asia should be studied can be justified on
the grounds that it should be intrinsically appealing to researchers interested
in Asia, to researchers seeking boundary conditions for theories of strategy,
and on the grounds that prima facie differences that support investigation exist. A grounded theory approach to testing the hypothesis that strategy in Asia
is different would focus on existing theoretical contributions made by research
on Asia. Identifying a significant body of theory would support the view that
knowledge and concepts from the region should be developed into unique theories or should be incorporated into mainstream strategy theory. I do not aim
to summarize these unique contributions, but instead identify several ideas that
should be central to theories of strategy in Asia. Interestingly, with two exceptions (business networks and corporate governance), the variables to be discussed have received relatively limited attention in mainstream strategy theory.

What are some of the differences that might warrant investigation? I first
argue that one commonly identified construct, society-level culture, does not
in fact substantially influence strategy theory. This is followed by discussing
variables that substantially influence strategy theory. The institutional environment, the roles and impact of governments, rates of change, regional diversity,
business networks, and corporate governance make strategy in Asia different.
The distinctiveness and significance of these factors will be indicative, though
not conclusive, of the need for new theories and of the potential for these theories to inform the wider body of strategy research.

Among the six factors listed above, the institutional environment and governments are variables, while business networks and corporate governance are phenomena that partially result from the first two variables. The other two factors identified as significant, regional diversity and rates of change, are environmental characteristics. These distinctions are important in some contexts but are not particularly useful for the purposes of this chapter. I therefore propose them as equally important influences on strategy in Asia, which warrant further investigation in strategy theory.

Limits of Cultural Impact

One of the attributes business research commonly assigns to Asia is its culture, which is typically described as being unique or being different from cultures elsewhere. It is clear that real cultural differences exist within many Asian countries, within Asia, and between Asia and other regions, and that these have significant influence on various aspects of personal exchanges, decision-making, management and organization (Chen, 2001; Fukuyama, 1995; Hamilton & Biggart, 1988; Luo, 2000; Redding, 1990; Westwood, 1997). Persuasive arguments have also been made for Asian cultures being fundamentally different from western cultures (e.g. Redding, 1990), not merely variants or developing versions of these cultures.

It is possible that culture influences how strategy is formulated and implemented through its impact on, for example, senior managers' beliefs and practices, authority relationships and trust, and firm characteristics. The collective impact of these influences may add up to a case for culture influencing strategy. In Asia, traditional texts such as Sun Tzu's Art of War and their modern interpreters (e.g. Chu, 1994; Wee, Lee & Bambang, 1991) are believed to have greater impact on Asian managers than the modern strategy theory and concepts that influence western managers. As a result, the argument is made that Asian firms and managers conceive of and implement strategy from more intuitive, tradition-based and informal perspectives than western managers, who are driven more by systematic, "scientific," and formal approaches (Chen, 2001).[5] In turn, the underlying influence of strong and different cultures leads to Asian strategy being presented as more calculating, emergent, risk-seeking and results-oriented, in contrast to western strategy, which is projected as more calculated, inflexible, risk-avoiding and process-driven.

These cultural differences have been extended to the widely made and popular argument that Asian culture was one of the key drivers of the economic and business success of Asia. The case was often made prior to the economic crisis of 1997–1999, that the success of countries such as South Korea, Taiwan, Hong Kong and Singapore, and of their firms and managers, was due to Confucian (or equivalently, "Asian") values and culture. Similarly, the emergence and success of disparate organizational forms such as the Korean conglomerate chaebol, or the small entrepreneurial Taiwanese firm, were attributed to the influence of culture.[6] This was despite the absence of rigorous evidence of national culture's influence on firm strategy and performance, and despite it being self-apparent that even the selected sample of the most successful Asian countries differed substantially on several dimensions of culture. Nevertheless, this position strongly influenced intellectual discourse and appears to have had substantial influence among researchers, practitioners and policy makers, until restrained by the economic difficulties of flagship countries and firms in the mid and late 1990s.

Another example of an argument for culture's influence is that the strong collectivist orientation of Asian culture, and therefore of Asian firms, makes them more trustworthy and cooperative. As business in Asia was thought to be conducted on the basis of trust, the argument has been made that Asian businesses enjoy lower transactions costs, which lead to more efficient markets (Dore, 1983; Hill, 1995). This suggests that markets and market mechanisms may be different in Asia (Hamilton & Biggart, 1988), being driven by trust, reputation and reliability, rather than by arms length contracting. Following similar arguments, firms in Asia are believed to be much more likely to establish and operate within trust based cooperative relationships. However, a contrary view is that Asians and Asian businesses do not operate on trust at all, but in fact distrust all individuals and organizations other than the ones with which they have developed relationships (Fukuyama, 1995; Redding, 1990). This suggests that transacting outside of the defined "in-group" is costly, and that markets and their clearing mechanisms are less efficient than elsewhere.

I believe that the impact of society-level culture on strategy in Asia and globally is relatively unimportant. Despite suggestions for culture's influence, it is difficult to conceive of specific models or theories of strategy whose explanatory power or validity would be substantially improved by the incorporation of culture ahead of alternate explanations. Though there may be preliminary evidence of the links between cultural values, particularly of "Confucian dynamism," with economic growth (Bond & Hofstede, 1990; Hofstede, 1980; World Bank, 1993), there is no convincing evidence that these values affect firm level performance.[7] Even if culture and related factors impact strategy, their influence is likely to be complex and indirect, and felt through impact on structures, authority relationships and managerial processes (Hofstede, 1984). This is likely to hold for both "high-context" Asian countries and in "low-context" Western countries.

Many of the influences attributed to culture can be explained more effectively by stage of development and related factors, such as socio-political, market and institutional development (Biggart & Hamilton, 1992; Clegg, Higgins & Spybey, 1990; Hamilton & Biggart, 1988; North, 1990; World Bank, 2001).

The following description (World Bank, 2001, citing Avnar Greif; for background see Grief, 1996) is typical of the business practices attributed to Asian firms, except that it describes practices in a context far removed in time, geography and culture, but possibly close in institutional makeup: "In the 11th century the Maghribi traders of North Africa had a problem. They wanted to expand across the Mediterranean, but uncertainties hindered their plans ... Over time, they came up with a solution. They set up a network of Maghribi agents in the major Mediterranean trading centers to represent their interests and exchange information about markets. Bound by social ties, they had information flowing freely among them. Theft and deceit were rare, because each member's interests were best served by staying in the network of traders. And membership was self enforcing, even though there were no rules ... The Maghribis lowered transactions costs among themselves but in so doing, excluded other communities."

It is not my position that culture has no impact on strategy. It is inconceivable that a force as prevalent as culture and within which all business activities are embedded, can be irrelevant, particularly with regards to issues such as leadership and strategy processes. But as (Hamilton & Biggart, 1988: S73) argue, the "... culture argument alone will not work well because ... culture is a broadly based underlying cognitive factor (Redding 1980) that affects the society in general and for that reason explains nothing in particular." Following Redding (2002), I view culture as being a prior or background institution which frames or moulds other institutions, which then impact strategy more directly. This makes culture an endogenous, though indirect factor, rather than an exogenous influence. In any case, efforts to incorporate culture should focus more on corporate or even industry culture, rather than on national or ethnic culture. My proposition of limited impact is also restricted to the narrowly defined field of business strategy, particularly to content related issues.

Although long-standing arguments (e.g. Hamilton & Biggart, 1988; Redding, 1990) have provided solid foundations for the evaluation of the relative impact of culture, specific hypotheses on how culture affects firm strategy and performance have not been made coherently or reliably. Instead, evidence is usually offered piecemeal, often without adequate conceptual development, skeptical review or academic publication. The case can also be made that the examination of culture's consequences has inadequately evaluated its impact at the firm or organizational levels of analysis and in terms of performance outcomes. These arguments have influenced academic research and thinking, and therefore merit examination and falsification.

Clearly, the argument that culture and related influences are less significant than alternate constructs in strategy theory must be held to the same standards of empirical and conceptual verification as the proposition that they are. As the validity of these alternate views has not been established, more conceptual and empirical evidence must be obtained on the impact of culture on firms.

Establishing either of these propositions conclusively will require more rigorous research than has been conducted to date. Asia provides sufficient variation on culture and performance dimensions to permit the conduct of such research.

SIGNIFICANT DIFFERENCES

Institutional Environment

The key challenges that firms face in internationalizing their operations can be summarized as those pertaining to dealing with different local characteristics (social customs, language, and other related features), managing operations across distances, and operating in different institutional environments. International business and, to a lesser extent, strategy research has focused more on the first of these three issues. Further, the difficulties posed by the first two challenges have been moderated by improved knowledge, greater experience and better technology. The challenges of operating across different institutional environments, in contrast, continue to be substantial but have not been adequately recognized and investigated by strategy researchers (Hoskisson et al., 2000; Kock & Guillen, 2001; Peng, 2002).

Institutions are the humanly devised constraints that structure human interaction (North, 1990; Alston et al., 1996). A particular institutional context is created by the combination of formal constraints (rules and constitutions), informal constraints (norms of behavior, conventions and self-imposed codes of conduct), and their enforcement characteristics. Institutions and their manifestation (e.g. property rights) determine the opportunity set, the basic system of incentives and the transaction costs associated with various actions (e.g. investment) and strongly influence individual and organizational activity (Aoki, 2001; Biggart & Hamilton, 1992; DiMaggio & Powell, 1991; Williamson, 1985). Business practices are therefore influenced by the institutional environment within which they are embedded.

Emerging markets, such as those in Asia, are characterized by varying degrees of underdevelopment in government, business and other forms of institutional development (Peng, 2000). The institutional environment in Asia is also substantially different from other regions, and is a key factor that makes strategy in Asia different (Whitley, 1992). The institutions in Asia have been created or have evolved differently from elsewhere, despite the important influence of western colonialism and the convergent forces of trade and globalization. Underdeveloped financial markets, inadequate financial intermediaries, poor corporate governance, and underdeveloped banks, in combination with poorly developed communications infrastructures and reporting requirements, restrict information flows and impede market efficiency. Stock exchanges may have lax disclosure and governance standards, while firms often have inadequate financial reporting capabilities. Other characteristics include inadequately trained, inflexible, and relatively unproductive labor; scarce management talent; unreliable property rights protection; few consumer organizations; inefficient and corrupt governments; inefficient judicial systems, and weak enforcement of laws and contracts (Johnson et al., 2000; Khanna & Palepu, 1997; La Porta et al., Lopez-de-Salines & Shleifer, 1999; World Bank, 2001). These and other weaknesses distort the efficient functioning of factor and product markets, limit opportunities, and inhibit firms from pursuing opportunities that firms in institutionally developed economies can appropriate. Clearly, institutional environments differ across countries, impact the organization and conduct of business activity, and are potentially important determinants of strategy.

It is a widely accepted proposition that institutions are important to the practice and theory of business. The issue is not whether the institutional environment affects firms, but rather how it does so. For example, greater diversification may not lead to poorer performance in emerging economies because of insufficient market and institutional development (Khanna & Palepu, 1997; Kock & Guillen, 2001; Singh et al., 2003). In such environments, internal factor markets are more effective in allocating resources than inefficient or non-existent external markets, supporting the emergence of business groups and of diversification (Ghemawat & Khanna, 1998; Khanna & Palepu, 1997, 2000). Therefore, profitable diversification is more likely in less developed than in more developed institutional contexts, indicating the need to examine the diversification-performance relationship across varying institutions environments.

Despite persuasive arguments for the impact of the institutional environment on strategy in Asia (e.g. Aoki, Kim & Okuno-Fujiwara, 1996; Biggart & Hamilton, 1992; Khanna & Palepu, 1997; Whitley, 1992) or more broadly (Lowe, 1998; Porter, 1990; Williamson, 1975, 1985), and the increasing influence of institutional research (Aoki, 2001; North, 1990) relatively little empirical research on Asia has adopted this approach. Empirical studies that have incorporated institutions have tended to view the institutional environment as a context to be controlled for. Others studies have equated institutional development with economic development. Though the rapidly growing Asian countries are economically progressive, they have often lagged in the development of institutions necessary for markets to function smoothly (Aoki, 2001; Alston, Eggerston & North, 1996; World Bank, 2001). Even when efficient, they may operate on different assumptions and fundamentals from western markets, because of their historical evolution and nature of participants (Biggart & Hamilton, 1992).

Institutions have not been adequately incorporated into strategy theory or operationalized in ways that capture their impact. In fact, institutions are striking for their absence in strategy research. Though more attention has been accorded to institutions in strategy research in Asia, more research that explores the richness and influences of institutions in the region is needed. Carney & Gedajlovic (2001), Nishida & Redding (1992) and Whitley (1992) represent examples of such work. Methodological development of how to measure institutions and their impact on strategy and firms outcomes in Asia will facilitate such research. More direct and comparative examination of the institutional environments across nations is also likely to provide greater insights for strategy theory than cross-cultural comparisons. Arguably, the "iron cage" of institutions constrains and drives firms and strategy more than the "collective programming" of culture, which acts on and guides individuals and their behavior.

The Role of Governments[8]

Though there has been some recognition of governments and their agencies as economic actors (e.g. Hillman, Zardkoohi & Bierman, 1999; Murtha & Lenway, 1994; Peng, 2000; Porter, 1990; Wade, 1990), they continue to attract relatively little attention in strategy research, which usually treats governments as part of the background institutional environment.[9] An overview of strategy research might conclude that governments are most notable for their irrelevance to strategy. Even when included in models or studies of strategy, governments are often restricted to regulatory roles, or are evaluated in terms of the social constraints or transfer costs they impose on business. This is probably inadequate in the U.S. and in many Western nations, where governments engage in business more than is commonly recognized (Nelson, 2002). However, a similar treatment of governments in Asia would seriously under-estimate one of the most significant influences on firms, their strategies and their success.

A prominent feature of the business environment in Asia is the significant role of governments, and their affiliated agencies and corporations. The importance and impact of governments both reflects and is a root cause of a key challenge firms face when operating in Asia, different economic systems and priorities. Governments in Asia have typically played more varied and significant roles in businesses than most western governments (Aoki et al., 1996; Hamilton & Biggart, 1988; Lasserre & Schutte, 1995; Wade, 1990; World Bank, 1993), while having varying degrees of free-market orientation. In essence, Asian governments have combined interventionist roles with support for free markets, so that their economic systems can broadly be classified as stronger combinations of both approaches than in most other regions. These governments therefore view open or free markets as being open and free for them to participate in and for their policies to take effect through. Most governments participate directly in business when necessary or profitable. As a result, Asian governments have been promoters, partners, regulators and actors in business, assisting firms in many areas, while also competing against them. While Asian governments have not been unique in their pursuit of the "combined" economic systems approach, they have probably been more active and effective than most countries at balancing the mix of approaches to support their economic systems.

Most Asian governments have placed strong emphasis on economic development and have actively guided and participated directly in this development. Though industrial policy has largely been discredited in the West as a development strategy, the success of most of the high growth Asian economies was importantly driven by successful industrial policies (see World Bank, 1993). Governments offered significant financial and other incentives in support of their development agendas. Most Asian governments have been far more supportive of businesses than governments in other regions, offering financial and other incentives, and being more willing to intervene (Amsden, 1994; Wade, 1990; World Bank, 1993) on their behalf. The direct impact of most Asian governments on business suggests that recognizing the endogeneity of governments to most competitive systems would help improve the explanatory power of many strategy theories. However, most strategy research not explicitly focused on governments treats them as exogenous and make little attempt to incorporate or explain their impact.

Another example of a government role that may be more prevalent in, if not unique to, Asia is that some governments have actively encouraged outward Foreign Direct Investment (FDI) even as their economies developed and while actively seeking inward FDI (Singh & Quek, 1999). This is uncommon, and raises questions for theories related to FDI, MNCs, and the competitiveness of nations. In general, the relationships between governments and businesses in Asia contrast greatly with the more arms-length or confrontational relationships common in North America, and represent an area that may yield theoretical insights into how public-private partnerships can improve firm performance and foster economic growth, or fail on both counts.

To the extent that existing strategy research incorporates aspects of the government, it often makes an implicit presumption that governments and their agents are inherently inefficient (Sikorski, 1993) and therefore necessarily detract from market efficiency. In striking contrast, Asian research often portrays governments as playing a diversity of roles with varying degrees of efficiency and effectiveness (Aoki et al., 1996; World Bank, 1993), and as suggesting that governments can and do succeed in business (Singh & Ang, 1999). Despite the economic crises of the late 1990s and recent uneven performance, governments in Asia can still claim credit for being important catalysts and drivers of their nation's rapid growth in recent decades (Weder, 1999). This influence was not entirely positive, such as when inefficiency, incompetence and corruption created market distortions that resulted in outcomes that would not have occurred in competitive contexts. Whether for positive effect or not, governments significantly impact businesses in Asia.

The influence of governments has important impact on strategy in Asia. The incentives offered can alter the efficacy of a strategy and can significantly influence business and industry outcomes. Governments' preferences for and policies in support of some industries, particularly technology-oriented industries, have greatly affected the viability, strategies and performance of many industries and businesses. Consideration of the possible impact of government objectives and policies is therefore far more important in Asia than in most other regions. Businesses in Asia often treat governments as a primary influence on business success, rather than one of the important background environmental factors. Recent questioning of the efficiency and roles of markets and of their status in theory (Nelson, 2002) supports long standing arguments (e.g. Hamilton & Biggart, 1988) that markets in emerging economies may be different. These arguments indicate the need to pay much closer attention to governments, the roles they play, and their impact on firms, competition and markets. This in turn suggests scope for theoretical development on the economic roles of governments, and of the efficiency and operation of emerging and non-traditional markets, at least from the business and strategy perspectives. This represents an area of strategy theory that can be informed by research from Asia.

Rate of Change

It is axiomatic in strategy research that environmental changes must be considered for its impact on strategy and performance. The important impact of economic and technological change, and less frequently, of political and social change, result in change being fundamental to the study and practice of strategy. Consequently, existing theory recognizes the importance of change at the firm and industry levels, and of external shocks to the system. However, there appears to be an implicit assumption of the absence of radical economy-wide shifts, such as the transformation of an economy from an agricultural to industrial base within the space of one or two decades, or from closed domestic economies to open, international economies. Following economic theory, most strategy research appears to regard radical change as exogenous, and thus excludes it from theory. However, radical change has characterized most economies of Asia in recent decades, and has been more than a background or contextual issue.

It is likely that rates of changes in Asia have eclipsed the rates of theoretical development, particularly with the belated start of the latter. For example, it is useful to note that in the late 1970s, some studies attributed the then economic failure of China to Confucian values, the same factor offered in the 1990s as the cause of its success. The rapid transformation of urban society in China is, for example, possibly even more striking than the changes in China's economy. Other examples of dramatic change in Asia include the rapid economic and technological upgrading of firms, industries and economies; increased regional and global integration through the entry of MNCs and large volumes of FDI; the emergence of world leading industry clusters; major increases in consumption and disposable incomes; shifts in consumer tastes; industrialization and urbanization; the increased competitiveness of Asian firms; and the rapid emergence of Asian MNCs and successful latecomer firms.

One major consequence of rapid change is the frequent displacement of industries. The hard disk drive industry is an example of an industry that has displaced rapidly to and within Asia. The industry was almost entirely located in the US, with a significant segment in Japan, up to the early 1980s. Noting the success of some of its suppliers in Singapore, Seagate moved some operations there in 1982. By the mid-1980s, Singapore was host to most of the major players in the industry and produced a majority of the world's non-captive output of drives. However, by the late 1980s labor shortages and a rising cost structure made Singapore unattractive for the industry. Starting from the late 1980s, several firms relocated their operations to Malaysia. Others from the US moved there directly. However, by the mid-1990s, Malaysia experienced its own labor shortages and rising costs, causing the industry to displace again, this time to China and Thailand. Meanwhile, most Japanese manufacturers moved their operations from Japan to the Philippines, and various suppliers dispersed operations throughout the region. The displacement of the industry from the US to Singapore, to Malaysia, and broadly within Asia in the space of less than 20 years is remarkable, and reflects the rate of technological, industrial, social and economic change within Asia.[10] Displacements of this type are not uncommon within Asia and are not restricted to technology-based industries.

Changes of this nature have directly impacted businesses but have not been adequately evaluated in theory. Industry and country exit strategies are examples of issues that have not received attention in the strategy and international business literatures. Extant theory implies, largely through lack of attention, that having made a country or industry entry decision, firms' commitment should be so strong as to make consideration of exit unnecessary. This is consistent with the perspective of advanced western MNCs entering relatively stable and emerging economic environments for market or resource exploitation. However, rapid development of the Asian countries demonstrates that even in the absence of external shocks, industry and country characteristics change rapidly, and can cause entry and investment decisions to be invalidated within the economic life of specific assets. The exit decision has only received attention in the context of socio-political threats, such as exit from South Africa during the Apartheid era or the introduction of the European Union free trade area.

In Asia, rapid industrial and economic changes have been much more important in causing firms and their complementary and supporting industries to displace. This has caused firms to be careful in undertaking long term specific investments whose value may be rapidly reduced by external changes. The relatively short horizon of these investment decisions stands in stark contrast to most theories, which suggest permanence in entry and investment decisions. In some respects, the typical MNC entry into Asia can be viewed as a phased entry, with initial investments into the most hospitable country followed by subsequent displacement into more favorable host environments. These examples suggest that traditional models of FDI, while appropriately emphasizing location choices and entry modes, miss the important issue of country or industry entry. Relatedly, the existence of industry clusters strongly suggests the existence of agglomeration economies, and the importance of geography in location decisions. The emergence of these greenfield clusters, and their subsequent displacement provides natural experiment opportunities for research that can contribute towards theoretical development.

Clearly, significant research opportunities exist in Asia for the examination of how firms adapt to sudden and radical, local and widespread, and economic and geopolitical change. The nature of the change also suggests that adequate understanding of strategy and firm processes must be based on longitudinal analysis. Change is a factor that should be endogenous to models of strategy in Asia, whose impact should be directly incorporated into theory.

Regional Diversity

Though most of Asia has enjoyed rapid economic growth for more than three decades up to the late 1990s, development was not uniform within or across countries. The countries of Asia differ substantially in their social, legal, regulatory, language, governance and business systems. The countries in the region also differ in respects that are unrelated to their stage of development, varying greatly in socio-cultural, political and technological sophistication. Though many Asian countries draw generally from the Confucianist tradition and are rooted in or have been influenced by Chinese culture, they differ significantly in their socio-cultural and political characteristics. Economic systems differ significantly, with some countries having relatively free markets that offer firms considerable flexibility, while others are much more restrictive, directly or indirectly imposing significant constraints on operations (Weder, 1999). These and other differences make the disparity in physical, human, institutional and public infrastructure in Asia much greater than in other regions.

Institutions across countries are based on very different traditions, colonial experiences, economic philosophies and political regimes. The variance in the nature and quality of institutions within Asia also appears to be greater than in other regions (PricewaterhouseCoopers, 2001; Weder, 1999), with institutions in some Asian countries approaching global standards of performance, while proximate neighbors have institutions of much lower quality. Though institutional development is often associated with the general wealth and development of countries (Aoki et al., 1996; Worldbank, 2001), this relationship does not necessarily hold in Asia. For example, the Opacity index (PricewaterhouseCoopers, 2001) rates relatively wealthy South Korea and Japan as having institutions of equal or lower quality than much poorer Asian countries. The variation in quality across countries is mirrored within countries, with significant variation in quality and wealth across geographic areas, and types of institutional infrastructure (World Economic Forum, 1999).

Firms that operate across Asian countries have to adapt to institutions that vary greatly in operating procedures and quality, and have to structure their operations accordingly. For example, cooperative relationships or family ties may be more important for operations in some countries because of the difficulty of enforcing contracts (Fukuyama, 1995), while other countries largely operate on contracts and strict legal enforcement. Though operating across cultures, geographic distance and institutional contexts is a normal aspect of multinational operations, the disparity within Asia on these dimensions is much greater than the disparity within Europe or in the US. In contrast with trends in Europe, and despite the impact of multilateral agencies such as the World Trade Organization, it is unlikely that there will be much convergence in these institutions in the short or medium term. There is no real desire to increase cooperation or integration and the people of Asia have little knowledge or interest in neighboring countries, or of their cultures and languages. Almost all countries in Asia currently have or have recently had strained relations with their neighbors. Though regional trade is increasingly important, and several overlapping trade and political groupings exist, the countries of Asia are not well integrated and have relatively few mechanisms to facilitate sharing or transfer of resources.

This disparity has important and strategic implications. Many MNCs locate their operations broadly across the region, attracted by incentives from host governments, actual or potential markets, and the operating and cost efficiencies of host countries. As a result, firms often disperse activities across the region to exploit the fit between country and business activity. However, these firms face substantial difficulty integrating their operations across the region, because physical, information and logistics links remain weak between most countries. The availability and level of competencies, particularly of managerial and technical talent, is vastly different across the region. Technological capabilities vary greatly across countries. Cultural and managerial barriers are significant, and often prevent the transfer of knowledge, technology, and importantly, managerial and technical staff. Differences in financial, accounting, taxation, governance, property rights and law significantly affect the conduct of operations.

For firms located in more than one country, the disparity and divergence of the region make issues related to location, geographical space, mode of entry, dispersion of operations, and supply chain decisions more challenging and potentially more rewarding. The principle of requisite variety (Ashby, 1969) dictates that firms embody at least as much complexity as the environment in which they operate. As firms have to adapt to divergent host country characteristics, they are likely to embody more variety within their Asian operations than elsewhere. As a result, these firms have to invest more heavily in structural and organization integration devices to ensure effective coordination of activities. Alternatively, these firms may adopt a very different approach, restricting activities within each country to relatively defined operational activities or to subsets of activities, to simplify interactions between country operations. For MNCs, this approach restricts most strategic decisions to regional, global or home HQs. Consequently, it is common to find large MNC operations within countries having little or no strategic responsibilities, and to have relatively small HQ, managerial and technology-capable staff. Other firms may have sophisticated operating and technical functions, but lack marketing and customer oriented functions and capabilities. Some firms and industries may develop to global standards while lacking fundamental capabilities in particular functions or technologies because these are conducted elsewhere. Though none of these descriptions are unique to Asia, their applicability to broad swathes of firms and industries, even in the wealthier Asian nations, is unusual.

Business Networks

Alliances, networks and other forms of inter-organizational cooperation are common in Asia, being driven by the similar resource and competence sharing, market access, and competitive considerations as in other regions. Though business networks or business groups exist in most countries and regions, the prominent business networks in Asia have significantly greater influence in Asia than equivalent organizations in other regions.[11] These networks include Keiretsu in Japan, Chaebol in South Korea, the Chinese family business groups across much of Asia, the government linked corporations in Singapore, the politically connected conglomerates in Malaysia and Indonesia, and other family businesses in most countries (East Asia Analytical Unit, 1995; Hamilton & Biggart, 1988; Lasserre & Schutte, 1995; Richter, 1999). Though not monolith organizations, the broad reach and size of these networks give them powerful presence, with the ability to undertake investments and acquisitions, transfer resources, overcome regulatory and political barriers, and enter markets in many countries. The Chaebol for example, continue to account for a majority share of Korea's GNP, despite having suffered severely during the Asian crisis. The Chinese business network, which loosely links ethnic Chinese business across the region, is viewed as having greater wealth and resources than all but the largest Asian countries (East Asia Analytical Unit, 1995). The power of the Chinese Business Network is illustrated by the estimate that it has undertaken a majority of the FDI into China since the 1980s, thereby playing a pivotal role in one of the major economic transformations in recent decades.[12] These networks also enjoy substantial market power and privileged access to political and other decision makers, which give them social and political capital (Richter, 1999).

The power and presence of these business networks has important strategic implications. First, firms entering the region often align themselves with local partners to facilitate entry into and across the region, a role that the Chinese business network has performed well. These networks have often been able to facilitate entry by overcoming competence, resource, regulatory and other barriers. The corollary position, in which these networks directly or indirectly prevent entry, is also a feature of business in Asia. Other characteristics, such as their apparent preference for growth over profitability, their ability to withstand persistent losses, and their strong alignment with selected shareholders, directly affect the strategies of competitors.

These networks also represent inherently interesting subjects for study, as they reflect a mix of institutional and cultural influences (Hamilton & Biggart, 1988; Lowe, 1998; Whitley, 1992). The apparent ability of many of these firms to achieve significant presence, scale, scope and flexibility while often having relatively parsimonious structures, unelaborated cultures and limited diversity (Pant and Singh, 2001), is a feature with implications for strategy theory. At the same time, business groups vary in their effectiveness and prospects, with Chinese business groups likely to have higher failure rates because of their family structures and weaker managerial capacities (Fukuyama, 1995; Carney, 1998). On the other hand, the technological, size and large resource strengths of Korean and Japanese business groups embody other weakness, such as financial and managerial complexity, and inflexibility. This indicates that the celebratory tone of research focusing on Asian business groups is perhaps misplaced, that more attention should be placed on contrasting business groups within Asia to identify their distinctive characteristics and similarities, and that business groups continue to represent an interesting area of research that can provide meaningful theoretical contributions.

Business group research is an example of how rigorous research undertaken on Asia (e.g. Hamilton & Biggard, 1988; Khanna & Palepu, 1997, 2000; Lincoln, Gerlach & Ahmadjian, 1996) has importantly influenced theoretical development, and is indicative of how strategy research in Asia can usefully contribute to theory development. The formal Japanese and Korean networks and the more informal Chinese business networks attracted significant popular attention, but had relatively limited impact on the largely US-based network literature until recently. It is possible that the network research stream would have emerged sooner and on stronger theoretical grounding, if it had taken earlier note of work on networks in Asia. Though their recent poor performance indicates that the Asian network models have fundamental weaknesses, their administrative, management and coordination systems, and stronger focus on cooperative rather than adversarial relationships, continue to offer ideas that may be valuable to network and strategy theories. These networks or groups merit special attention in theories of strategy in Asia.

Governance Systems

The dominant perspective of corporate governance is that of the Anglo-American "arms-length contracting within an agency relationship". This perspective has largely driven understanding of corporate governance, and of transactions and markets. It is not evident, however, that this model is applicable to or should be used in countries with different fundamentals or in different stages of development (Phan, 2001). Indeed, it is not obvious that the definition of good "corporate governance" is universal, or that all corporate governance systems should have the same objectives. Instead, the philosophical and economic bases for the organization of firms and their boards have to be re-examined in the context of the institutional and regulatory regimes within which they are embedded (Carney & Gedajlovic, 2001). Though the need for examination of governance and ownership issues in Asia has been recognized, these issues have only been partially examined in Asia (Claessens, Djankov & Lang, 2000; Johnson et al., 2000; Walker & Fox, 2002).

Khan (1999) argues that a combination of cultural, firm and institutional differences makes corporate governance in Asia different. Asian family-based corporate governance systems are believed to differ significantly from the equity market or bank-led governance systems that dominate elsewhere and which exist to lesser degrees in Asia. Recent studies report high levels of ownership concentration in most Asian firms, with families and government being prominent owners in several countries (Claessens et al., 2000). A particularly striking finding is the concentration of significant corporate ownership in the hands of a few families. These patterns of concentration and the specific identity of the major owners may result in different patterns in the exercise of control and ownership rights. The different composition, characteristics and interests of major owners in Asia, different legal and other traditions, and different environments dictate the need for modifications to accepted governance methods.

The underdeveloped environments in emerging economies directly affect governance regimes. Rules governing ownership and agency rights are often inadequate, uncertain, or unevenly enforced. These rules also differ significantly across countries, reflecting development patterns, legal and political traditions, and economic characteristics (La Porta et al. 1998; Carney & Gedajlovic, 2001; Gedajlovic & Shapiro, 2002). In general, owners and managers in Asia have faced fewer pressures and constraints to focus on shareholder returns, and greater latitude to pursue their private interests than their counterparts in more developed economies, as a result of inadequate governance systems (Johnson et al., 2000; Walker and Fox 2002).[13]

It is therefore essential to examine governance related issues within the context of the environment in which firms operate and governance is exercised (Carney & Gedajlovic, 2001). At the same time, it is difficult to envision situations in which fundamental principles of governance – such as protecting the interest of minority shareholders, or having independent directors to represent these shareholders – would not be applicable. This is one force behind efforts to define new and more effective governance systems in many countries in Asia. Specific measures include the introduction of independent external monitors, reduction in government oversight and increase in regulation by other agencies, the adoption of codes of practice, and the general introduction of western corporate governance systems. The imposition of these systems on family and business groups that have different ownership and organizational structures, different managerial philosophies, and that operate in relatively weak financial sectors, represents an interesting experiment in change. The transition in corporate governance systems, and the effectiveness and implication of this transition represents significant research issues and opportunities for the development of corporate governance models and theories set in the Asian context.

Explaining the Differences

Why are these factors – institutional environment, role of government, rates of change, regional diversity, business networks, and governance – different in Asia? Returning to the theme discussed at the beginning of this chapter, culture is often identified as a primary explanation. Therefore, an explanation for the different institutions, roles of governments, networks, etc. in Asia, would be that Asian culture or cultures cause them to be different. However, it is likely that these differences are better explained by Asia's current state of development and by its recent economic and social evolution. Most of the factors discussed above are associated with Asia's rapid development and the characteristics of its institutions. Comparisons with advanced economies when they were at equivalent stages of development are likely to demonstrate substantial similarity with phenomena currently observed in Asia (e.g. Piore & Sable, 1984).

The importance of business networks in Asia, for example, can primarily be attributed to the under-development of institutions and markets, rather than to cultural factors. Therefore, the strength of the Chinese business network is better explained by inadequate markets, the weakness of contractual enforcement, weak financial and banking sectors and the absence of reliable information providers and suppliers, rather than by cultural influences. The apparent uniqueness of Chinese family business practices is perhaps reduced by evaluating them in the contexts of the business group phenomena, of family businesses, and of institutional differences. Rather than being primarily driven by socio-cultural values such as trust and collectivist tendencies – Fukuyama (1995) argues that these networks operate within a low trust culture, while Redding (1990) believes their trust is limited to insiders – the network relies on its ability to enforce compliance through reputation effects and family links, and for its greater efficiency in locating and sharing financial, information and managerial resources.

In addition, many of the features of Asia identified as unique are so only in inappropriate comparisons. It is arguable that most of the "unique characteristics" of the region are found in other regions and within less developed countries, though perhaps in different combinations. Khanna & Palepu (1999), for example, find many similarities among business groups in India and Chile. Piore & Sable's (1984) description of the structuring of transactions among businesses and communities in Italy bears strong resemblance to the links between Asian family business groups, and ethnic or village-linked enterprises. The structure and management of family businesses in Britain in the first half of the 20th century, described by Chandler (1990) as "personal capitalism" overlaps that of many businesses in Asia. Carney (1998) uses Chandler's (1990) notion of personal management to provide a useful explanation of many characteristics of Chinese family businesses in Hong Kong. The obviously different cultures and the existence of some similarities in the state of institutions across these cultures, suggest the importance of alternate explanations.

It is likely that as Asian countries develop, they and their institutions will continue recent trends of convergence on western models of business. Therefore it is possible to predict that as Asia follows the path of development of the western countries, its institutions will also converge towards – though not necessarily arrive at or replicate – western models. As the economies of Asia develop, industrialize, modernize and mature, they will increasingly take on the characteristics of the more developed countries. Consequently, strategy in Asia will become increasingly like strategy in the West. A logical conclusion is that strategy theory will also move towards general strategy theory. This view suggests support for theories of convergence, though the slow pace of economic evolution can accommodate views of persistent heterogeneity at the firm and industry levels.

Research Implications

What outcomes can strategy research in Asia be reasonably expected to produce or seek to deliver? Will it lead to entirely new models and theories that are specific to Asia because it is different, or models and theories that are modified incrementally to incorporate the differences that exist in Asia? I believe that the latter case is more likely. It is important to note that both alternatives rely on the notion that Asia is different. Therefore, the most popularly offered justification for conducting research in Asia – that the region is visibly and importantly different – is irrelevant. Though epistemological questions arise, this is in some respects an empirical question, which can be answered at three overlapping levels: first, by verifying the applicability of existing theory through replications in Asia; second, by identifying and evaluating factors that may be distinct to Asia and which appear to impact strategy; and third, if necessary, by developing and validating new models and theory specific to Asia. Existing efforts have been scattered across all three levels, though most appear to have concentrated on the second level. Clearly, a more systematic approach to the study of strategy in Asia is required.

Strategy research's focus on firms and the determinants of their performance provides a consistent framework for the evaluation of broader variables such as national, institutional and cultural environments. Firm and networks of firms, rather than larger business systems, nations and regions, are therefore the most suitable level of analysis for such research. This approach will allow clearer understanding of the boundary conditions of extant theories, and through this process, facilitate the development of new theories.

There is also a need for researchers to undertake the fundamental task of establishing the validity of extant theory in Asia. Ideally, this would be undertaken as a deliberate program of systematic replications, to establish the validity of seminal strategy studies in Asia.[14] Most strategy studies have been conducted in North America, and have been accepted and applied in Asia, usually without adequate demonstration of applicability through replication. The mirror image problem is equally serious and in need of correction as a second order effort: research conducted in Asia is dismissed as irrelevant or inapplicable, or is simply ignored, often without attempts to refute results through replication. Increased replication would be also consistent with the falsificationist approach, and increase the rigor of strategy research generally.

It is likely that most replication efforts will support the applicability of existing theoretical models in Asia, if only through the detection of partial support for some measures or elements of models, or because these models are essentially generic. It is possible that most models of strategy are necessarily generic; these models become specific only through their application, in the process of which peculiar aspects are identified and assigned appropriate importance. This would suggest that the basic issue with the application of extant theory in Asia is that of incompleteness rather than irrelevance. The failure to undertake the baseline analysis of the applicability of received theory is a fundamental hurdle that must be overcome before the higher order challenges of assimilating findings of significance in Asia into coherent theory.

A related step would be to examine existing theory and models to evaluate the need for modification to increase applicability in Asia. The changes required may be fairly minor. As an example, one of the most visible models in strategy, Porter's "five forces" industry structure model does not incorporate the government as a distinct force impacting competition, on the grounds that governments are better evaluated through their impact on the other five forces. As discussed above, the role and importance of governments in Asia suggests that this position is not appropriate in Asia, and that the impact of governments may be better evaluated through direct incorporation into the model. A relatively minor modification of this model would suffice. Other changes to theory might be more significant, such as to models of internationalization and the development of multinationals, which are being challenged by, for example, work on Asian latecomer firms (Hobday, 1995; Mathews, 2002). Latecomer firms are those that have rapidly achieved multinational status despite starting much later, with fewer resources, and at greater distance from markets, than western multinationals. Emerging work suggests that these firms may have employed different strategies from those employed by Western firms in the areas of internationalization, technological innovation, organizational learning and leapfrogging, and in the structuring of organizations (Hobday, 1995; Mathews, 2002). These differences may impact theories on the emergence and growth of MNCs, and theories of FDI. The role of Asian governments in encouraging outward investments thus creating MNCs, while they concurrently sought inward FDI, may require interesting changes to models of FDI and MNCs. These issues may require fundamental theoretical modification.

From a process and methodological perspective, strategy research on Asia differs from and can inform the broader body of knowledge in several respects.[15] First, several phenomena may be more effectively studied in the region, as the recency of their emergence may permit study without significant "left censoring." One example is the emergence of multinational corporations, which is possible because several countries in the region have only recently seen the emergence of their first MNCs.[16] Another opportunity is to study reactions to a sudden external shock, such as in the context of the natural experiment that the recent Asian Economic Crisis represents. The relatively small size of many industries and economies in the region also permits the study of complete populations, an approach that may be much more difficult to undertake in large, developed economies.

If stage of development and institutional factors are more important determinants of strategy, it follows that rapid changes in these factors will influence the future directions of strategy in Asia much more than slow changing cultural influences. This proposition provides an opportunity to test the validity and importance of most of the factors identified above. The disparity within urban and rural communities and between rapidly growing economic zones and laggard regions within many countries, provide other opportunities to test this proposition. An examination of how strategy has evolved in recent years, and the comparison of these changes with cultural and alternate influences will establish their relative importance.

A pragmatic approach is to focus research efforts on theoretically driven issues within countries first. Subsequent research should then focus on examining these same issues within industries across countries. Relevant external factors and their impact are best identified and understood by varying the external context while retaining a strong focus on the firm within its industry. The conduct of research at this level will allow the subsequent emergence of theories generalizing findings across country and other contexts, and perhaps, theories of strategy in Asia. While there are obviously alternate research strategies, this grounded approach to theoretical development is consistent with the pragmatism that characterizes strategy research generally, and with the positivist-realist perspectives of most strategy researchers.[17] Recent efforts at developing frameworks to guide research in the broader organizational field (e.g. Whitley, 1992, 1999; Redding, 2002) may also help frame the "firm within industry across country" approach.

Rather than searching for what is merely Asian, researchers should focus on the investigation of phenomena that are different or unique from business and strategy perspectives. This should lead to conceptual models and theoretical development, which should then be tested and replicated across Asian countries and beyond, for generalizability. This suggests that strategy researchers should focus on underlying factors and conceptual variables, rather than on their country-specific manifestations.

The Way Forward

What is a reasonable approach to adopt, in light of the above discussion, to move towards a theory of strategy drawing on and relevant for Asia? Through their discussion of general management research, Earley and Singh (1995: 329) provide a possible direction forward for strategy research in Asia. Such research should focus on "... improving understanding of fundamental theories of management and a convergence with research on international management (that) has driven international and intercultural research. These studies are not necessarily sweeping or grand, nor do they necessarily propose universal laws of behavior, typologies of organizational form, and the like. What they attempt is something more difficult: to shift the motive of international and intercultural research from curiosity to achieving an enlightened understanding of how management and organizational phenomena relate to cultural and national characteristics. Is it useful to develop models that fail to generalize outside of the United States? Can researchers learn invaluable lessons by better understanding of the boundaries of our endogenous theories?"

The diversity of Asia questions the utility of generalizing research that is geographically bound, as the tenuous links between the major countries and cultures of the region make it unlikely that anything other than broad generalizations will emerge.[18] But the conduct of such studies and of multi-country studies is essential to allow consideration of whether there is value and validity in seeking to establish a theory applicable across a region that has some features in common but few that are shared. This process may result in new theories of strategy in Asia or in the modification of existing theories to fit Asia, as some have claimed necessary (e.g. Hamilton and Biggart, 1988). Equally likely, the conclusion may be that existing theories are not geographically constrained, and are comprehensive enough to encompass an Asia that occupies a different location within existing theories but does not lie outside them. Research that moves us toward either answer is valuable.

ACKNOWLEDGEMENTS

I thank Steven White and Gabriel Szulanski for their useful inputs.

NOTES

1. Restricting this chapter to only researchers within Asia would severely limit the validity of the discussion. Li and Tsui (2002) identify the 52 most cited papers on Management and Organization research on China. They find authors to be affiliated with 3 Asian, 15 US and 2 European universities. A more difficult to justify constraint but one convenient for focusing the chapter, is excluding research that are related to strategy but which lie outside its mainstream. Theories grounded in sociology, political science, and economics that address strategy related issues probably provide richer perspectives than mainstream strategy. Incorporating these perspectives would moderate some of the arguments made here. However, this chapter views these perspectives as external to mainstream strategy, while accepting their important influence on strategy theory and research.

2. It is necessary to limit the question by establishing its geographic scope. Specifically, the question is "what is Asia?" The obvious answer, Asia is the geographic continent Asia, is clearly wrong. A quick overview of academic, managerial and popular usage suggests convergence on limiting Asia to what was traditionally described as East Asia, or East and Southeast Asia, to the exclusion of South and Central Asia, and the Middle East. This narrow scope offers three advantages. First, it reduces an unmanageably diverse, vast and complex region to a more manageable but still diverse, vast and complex region. Southeast Asia and

East Asia collectively form a large region with diverse cultures, nation states, institutions, and economies. A second advantage is that this definition is consistent with business and economic usage and trends. Many MNCs organize their regional operations along the lines of this definition. Economic integration is stronger among the economies of the East and Southeast Asia, with greater trade, foreign investment, and business operations within the region, than with the countries of the rest of Asia. Third, several of the factors that I propose distinguish strategy in Asia, are different or have differential impact in East and Southeast Asia than in other parts of Asia. This region is also substantially different on other dimensions from much of the rest of Asia, so that it is best evaluated separately. As a result, the definition of Asia adopted in this chapter is East and Southeast Asia, comprising the countries within the broad triangle formed by the extremes of China, Myanmar and Indonesia. This region will henceforth be referred to as Asia.

The inadequacies of this definition are clear. First, it excludes South Asia, but includes Japan. India's exclusion is explained by the factors discussed above. Japan is included, though it is strikingly different from the rest of Asia in many respects. Its wealth – which is approximately equal to that of the rest of Asia – and stage of development makes it more appropriate to evaluate it with the US and Europe. Yet Australia is excluded. Though proximate and an important part of the region's political economy, it is often excluded because of its development and "Anglo-Saxon" culture.

Another anomaly in this definition and on research in Asia is also noteworthy: almost all discussions focus selectively on the rapidly growing countries of the region. Though clearly falling with the scope of even narrowly defined Asia, countries such as Laos, Cambodia, North Korea, Papua New Guinea and East Timor are rarely considered. Excluding these small and under-developed economies has little impact on business and strategy issues but is theoretical unjustifiable. An example is when the economic success of the richer Asian countries and of their firms, are attributed to culture that is common to poor countries. This in effect, amounts to sampling on the dependent variable.

It must be recognized that the term Asia is a used as a convenience, and that fundamentally, the complexities of the region make it futile for firms to actually develop a "strategy for Asia". This convenience is mirrored in the adoption of the terms "West" or "Western" which similarly encompass extremely diverse nations and cultures from Western Europe and North America. In essence, the comparison in this chapter is between two less than well-defined constructs, Asia and the West. Readers clearly should be cautious.

3. A similar case can probably be made for strategy theory and models in general. It would be useful to define the established strategy theory and models that should be evaluated in Asia. Critics of strategy research will argue that there is no coherent theory of strategy and no grand theory or model of strategy, making it futile to investigate theory of strategy in Asia. It is arguable that the problems associated with strategy theory in Asia are applicable to strategy theory in general. As a result, strategy theory will only be discussed in the abstract in this chapter, and reference will be made to *theories* and *models* of strategy.

4. The absence or relative lack of authority of Asian institutions such as research organizations, journals, and academic conferences, to motivate and structure research agendas partially explains the under-development of strategy theory in Asia. Reliance on US institutions has resulted in the adoption of mainstream perspectives and agendas, which have discouraged Asian research. Recent attempts to strengthen these institutions in Asia will therefore facilitate theoretical progress.

5. Studies of Asia often highlight the importance of personal relationships and social capital as necessary features and requirement for doing business in many parts of Asia (Chen, 2001; Lasserre & Schutte, 1995; Luo, 2000). These relationships are rooted in culture and tradition, and are often suggested to be unique to Asia. It is probably however, that that these relationships are variants of networks that also exist elsewhere among ethnic communities,

alumni of associations and members of social organizations (e.g. Tsui & Farh, 1997). These relationships are often most valuable when institutions are weak or markets fail.

6. Much of this attribution has taken place in political and popular circles within the debate on the extent to which "Asian values" were responsible for the growth of Asia. Proponents of Asian values attribute the growth of Asia to core cultural values, particularly Confucian beliefs. Others reject this view, citing the absence of evidence linking values and growth, and pointing out that Confucian values had been used to explain the failure and slow growth of the Asian economies until the 1960s. For an overview of related issues, see Huntington & Harrison (2000; particularly Chapters 17 to 19), and Subramaniam (2000).

7. The difficulties of extrapolating cultures' impact are illustrated by findings of higher levels of protestant work ethics in Malaysia than in Britain (Furnham & Muhiudeen, 1984) and of the relevance of Confucian values in the US (Robertson & Hoffman, 2000)! Nevertheless, Redding (2002) argues that there has been recent recognition of the importance of culture, including on economic growth.

8. As the rest of this section will argue, governments are an important element of the institutional environment. Governments will be evaluated directly as separate actors rather than as part of the institutional environment, to emphasize their importance in Asia.

9. An exception in the context of strategy in Asia is the attention placed on state owned enterprises in China, particularly with respect to their adaptation to the liberalization of the Chinese economy. However, most studies treat the government link as a context for the study and focus on the problems of transition rather than on the impact of governments on firms and their strategies.

10. For more details of the displacement of the HDD industry in Asia, see Wong (1999) and McKendrick, Doner & Haggard (2000).

11. Business groups and business networks will be used as synonymous terms, though they clearly differ. For example, Japanese Keiretsu tend to be organized horizontally and to accord member firms relatively high levels of autonomy. Many Asian family business groups and Chaebol, on the other hand, tend to be more closely integrated, and to provide firms much less autonomy. These differences have been explored elsewhere (e.g. Richter, 1999) and will not be elaborated on here.

12. The power of this network is illustrated by the relative impact of the Indian business network on India's growth. The Indian business network is smaller, less cohesive and comprises managers and professionals to a larger extent than it does entrepreneurs and businesses. It lacks the wealth and reach of its Chinese equivalent and has had much less impact on India's growth. One of the factors that will hinder India's economic growth is that the Chinese business network appears to have little understanding of India and little interest in investing there, depriving the country of access to a large pool of investments and business talent. Haley & Haley (1999) provide an overview of the similarities and differences of the Chinese and Indian business networks.

13. The spate of accounting, leadership and governance scandals that struck US firms in 2002 clearly indicates the existence of major institutional deficiencies in the US as well. Despite these problems, the institutional environment in most developed economies is significantly stronger than in most emerging economies. The existence of a poorer environment is not a requisite condition for the evaluation of the issues we focus on; instead, the existence of a different institutional environment is sufficient.

14. Singh, Ang & Leong (2003) argue for a reconceptualization of replication research, in favor or a pragmatic "good enough" standard. This approach recognizes the difficulty of conducting exact replications in social science and business research, and proposes the adoption of the good enough replication. The good-enough replication is one that conscientiously follows as closely as possible, the stated methodology of the original study pertaining to design, procedure, data collection, analysis, and reporting of results. If variations are made,

the replication should document departures, provide sound theoretical or methodological rationale for these departures, specify their likely impact on the research findings, and account for the affected outcomes arising from them. This definition encourages faithful adherence to original procedures so as to preserve methodological integrity, but allows for departures to be made, while keeping the onus on the replication researchers to furnish persuasive evidence permitting independent evaluation of their rationale and effects. It is likely that a significant amount of strategy research in Asia can be classified at being good enough replications of research conducted in the West. The adoption of this concept may permit more replication and more research to be recognised as replications. One suggestion is to identify the 25 most influential empirical studies in strategy and to replicate them in Asia.

15. Strategy research in Asia also faces significant methodological challenges. Large scale empirical studies are often more difficult to conduct in Asia because of the relative absence of public datasets and reliable archival data sources, and the greater difficulty of conducting mail surveys. Managers are not used to the tradition of research by outsiders and are reluctant to provide access to internal operations. A related problem is that many Asian industries are very small and cannot provide useful samples. It is often necessary to develop new measures and metrics for application in Asia and to have these translated, which raises the barriers for conducting research. Though these problems are obviously not unique, they represent real constraints that hinder empirical research in Asia.

16. On the other hand, the recency of the phenomena suggests substantial contextual differences that must be controlled for. For example, young Asian MNCs have emerged in an environment widely populated by MNCs, making their phenomena substantially different from the emergence of the first MNCs into a less global world.

17. In line with this pragmatism, the research effort should have both normative and prescriptive aims. It is likely though, that research in the past was too heavily influenced by the popular press, and has tended to be prescriptive and celebratory.

18. The same question is of course, applicable to this chapter.

REFERENCES

Academy of Management Journal. 2000. Special Research Forum on Emerging Economies. 43(3).

Alston L.J., Eggerston T. and North D.C. 1996. *Empirical Studies in Institutional Change.* Cambridge: Cambridge University Press.

Amsden, A.H. 1994. The specter of Anglo-Saxonization is haunting South Korea. In L.J. Cho and Y.H. Kim (eds.), *Korea's Political Economy: An Institutional Perspective.* Boulder, Colorado: Westview.

Aoki, M. 2001. *Towards a Comparative Institutional Analysis.* MIT Press: Cambridge, MA.

Aoki, M., Kim, H.K. and Okuno-Fujiwara. 1996. *The Role of Government in East Asian Economic Development.* Oxford: Clarendon.

Ashby, W.R. 1969. Self-regulation and Requisite Variety. In F.E. Emory (ed.), *Systems Thinking.* Middlesex, England: Penguin.

Asia Pacific Journal of Management. 2001. Special Issue: Corporate governance in the newly emerging economies. 18:2.

Biggart, N.W. and Hamilton, G.G. 1992. On the limits of a firm-based theory to explain business networks: The Western bias of neoclassical economics. In N. Noria and R.G. Eccles (eds.), *Networks and Organizations.* Boston: HBS Press.

Bond, M.H. and Hofstede, G. 1990. The cash value of confucian values. In S.R. Clegg and S.G. Redding (eds.), *Capitalism in Contrasting Cultures.* NY: de Gruyter.

Carney, M. 1998. A Management capacity constraint? Obstacles to the development of the over-
    seas Chinese family business. *Asia Pacific Journal of Management*, 15: 137-162.
Carney, M. and Gedajlovic, E. 2001. Corporate governance and firm capabilities. A comparison
    of Managerial, Alliance and Personal Capitalisms. *Asia Pacific Journal of Management*, 18:
    335-354.
Chandler, A. 1990. *Scale and Scope. The Dynamics of Industrial Capitalism*. Cambridge, MA:
    Harvard University Press.
Chen, M.J. 2001. *Inside Chinese Business: A Guide for Managers Worldwide*. Boston, MA:
    HBS Press.
Cheng, J.L.C. 1994. On the concept of universal knowledge in organization science: Implica-
    tions for cross cultural research. *Management Science*, 40: 162-168.
Chu, C.N. 1994. *Thick Face, Black Heart: The Path to Thriving, Winning & Succeeding*. NY:
    Warner Books.
Claessens, S., Djankov, S. and Lang, L.H.P. 2000. The separation of ownership and control in
    East Asian Corporations. *Journal of Financial Economics*, 58(1-2): 81-112.
Clegg, S., Higgins, W. and Spybey, T. 1990. 'Post-Confucianism', social democracy and eco-
    nomic culture. In S.R. Clegg and S.G. Redding (eds.), *Capitalism in Contrasting Cultures*.
    NY: de Gruyter.
Clegg, S.R. and Redding, S.G. 1990. *Capitalism in Contrasting Cultures*. NY: de Gruyter.
DiMaggio, P.J. and Powell, W.W. 1991. Introduction. In W.W. Powell and P.J. DiMaggio (eds.),
    The New Institutionalism in Organizational Analysis (pp. 1-38). Chicago: University of
    Chicago Press.
Dore, R. 1983. Goodwill and the spirit of market capitalism. *British Journal of Sociology*,
    XXXIV: 459-482.
Earley, C.P. and Singh, H. 1995. International and intercultural management research: What's
    next?, *Academy of Management Journal*, 38(2): 327-340.
East Asia Analytical Unit. 1995. Overseas Chinese Business Networks. Canberra, Australia:
    AGPS Press.
El Kahal, S. 2001. *Business in Asia Pacific: Text and Cases*. NY: Oxford University Press.
Fukuyama, F. 1995. *Trust: The Social Virtues and the Creation of Prosperity*. NY: Free Press.
Furnham, A. and Muhiudeen, C. 1984. The protestant work ethic in Britain and Malaysia. *The
    Journal of Social Psychology*, 122: 157-161.
Gedajlovic, E.R. and Shapiro, D.M. 2002. Ownership structure and firm profitability in Japan.
    Academy of Management Journal, 45: 565-575.
Ghemawat, P. and Khanna, T. 1998. The nature of diversified business groups: A research design
    and two case studies. *Journal of Industrial Economics*, 46 (1): 35-61.
Ghoshal, S. and Westney, E.D. 1993. Introduction and overview. In S. Ghoshal and E.D. Westney
    (eds.), *Organization Theory and the Multinational Corporation* (pp. 1-23). NY: St. Martin's
    Press.
Grief, A. 1996. The study of organizations and evolving organizational forms through history:
    Reflections from the late medieval family firm. *Industrial and Corporate Change*, 5: 473-
    501.
Hamilton, G.G. and Biggart, N.W. 1988. Market, culture and authority: A comparative analysis
    of management and organization in the far east. *American Journal of Sociology*, 94: S52-S94.
Haley, G.T. and Haley, U. 1999. Weaving opportunities: The influence of overseas Chinese and
    overseas Indian business networks on Asian business operations. In F.-J. Richter (ed.), *Busi-
    ness Networks in Asia. Promises, Doubts, and Perspectives* (pp. 149-170). London: Quorum
    Books.
Hill, C.W.L. 1995. National institutional structures, transaction costs economizing, and compet-
    itive advantage: The case of Japan. *Organization Science*, 6:119-131.

Hillman, A.J., Zardkoohi, A. and Bierman, L. 1999. Corporate political strategies and firm performance: Indications of firm-specific benefits from personal service in the US government. *Strategic Management Journal*, 20: 67-81.

Hobday, M. 1995. *Innovation in East Asia. The Challenge to Japan*. Aldershot, England: Edward Elgar.

Hofstede, G. 1980. *Culture's Consequences: International Differences in Work-related Values*. Beverly Hills, CA: Sage.

Hofstede, G. 1984. Cultural dimensions in management and planning, *Asia Pacific Journal of Management*, 1: 81-99.

Hoskisson, R.E., Eden, L., Lau, C.M. and Wright, M. 2000. Strategy in emerging economies. *Academy of Management Journal*, 43(3): 249-267.

Huntington, S.P. and Harrison, L.E. 2000. *Culture Matters: How Values Shape Human Progress*. NY: Basic Books.

Itami, H., Kagono, T., Yoshihara, H. and Sakuma, A. 1982. Diversification strategies and economic performance. *Japanese Economic Studies*, 11: 78-110.

Johnson, S., Boone, S., Breach, A. and Friedman, E. 2000. Corporate governance in the Asian financial crisis. *Journal of Financial Economics*, 3(4): 305-360.

Khan, H. 1999. Corporate governance of family businesses in Asia: What's right and what's wrong? ADBI Working Paper No. 3. Tokyo, Japan: ADB.

Khanna, T. and Palepu, K. 1997. Why focused strategies may be wrong for emerging markets. *Harvard Business Review*, July-August: 41-51.

Khanna, T. and Palepu, K. 1999. Policy shocks, market intermediaries, and corporate strategy: Evolution of business groups in Chile and India. *Journal of Economics and Management Strategy*, 8: 271-310.

Khanna, T. and Palepu, K. 2000. Is group affiliation profitable in emerging markets? An analysis of diversified Indian business groups. *Journal of Finance*, 55(2): 867-91.

Kock, C.J. and Guillen, M.F. 2001. Strategy and structure in developing countries: Business groups as an evolutionary response to opportunities for unrelated diversification. *Industrial and Corporate Change*, 10(1): 77-113.

La Porta, R., Lopez-de-Silanes, F. and Shleifer, A. 1999. Corporate ownership around the world. *Journal of Finance*, 54(2): 471-517.

Lasserre, P. and Schutte, H. 1995. *Strategies for Asia Pacific*. London: Macmillan.

Lau, C.M. 2002. Asian Management Research: Frontiers and Challenges. *Asia Pacific Journal of Management*, 19(2&3): 171-178.

Lau, C.M., Law, K.K.S., Tse, D.K.T. and Wong, C.S. 2000. *Asian Management Matters: Regional Relevance and Global Impact*. River Edge, NJ: Imperial College Press.

Li, J.T. and Tsui, A.S. 2002. A citation analysis of management and organization research in the Chinese context: 1984–1999. *Asia Pacific Journal of Management*, 19(1): 87-107.

Lincoln, J.R., Gerlach, M.L. and Ahmadjian, C.L. 1996. Keiretsu networks and corporate performance in Japan. *American Sociological Review*, 61: 67-88.

Lowe, S. 1998. Culture and network institutions in Hong Kong: A hierarchy of perspectives. *Organization Studies*, 19(2): 321-343.

Luo, Y. 2000. *Guanxi and Business*. River Edge, N.J.: World Scientific.

Mathews, J.A. 2002. *Dragon Multinationals. A New Model for Global Growth*. NY: Oxford University Press.

McKendrick, D.G., Doner, R.F. and Haggard, S. 2000. *From Silicon Valley to Singapore: Location and Competitive Advantage in the Hard Disk Drive Industry*. Stanford, CA: Stanford University Press.

Millar, C., Grant, R.M. and Choi, J.C. 2000. *International Business: Emerging Issues and Emerging Markets*. NY: St. Martin's Press.

Murtha, T.P. and Lenway, S.A. 1994. Country capabilities and the strategic state: How national political institutions affect multinational corporations' strategies. *Strategic Management Journal*, 15: 113-129.

Nelson, R. 2002. The problem of market bias in modern capitalist economies, *Industrial and Corporate Change*, 11: 207-244.

Nishida, J.M. and Redding, S.G. 1992. Firm development and diversification strategies as products of economic cultures: The Japanese and Hong Kong cotton textile industries. In R. Whitley (ed.), *European Business Systems. Firms and Markets in their National Contexts* (pp. 241-266). London: Sage.

North, D. 1990. *Institutions, Institutional Change, and Economic Performance*. NY: Cambridge University Press.

Pant, N. and Singh, K. 2001. Corporate culture and diversity: Strategic perspectives. In C. Cooper, S. Cartwright and P.C. Earley (eds.), *The International Handbook of Organizational Culture and Climate*. London: John Wiley.

Peng, M.W. 2000. *Business Strategies in Transition Economies*. Thousand Oaks, CA: Sage.

Peng, M.W. 2002. Towards an institution-based view of business strategy. *Asia Pacific Journal of Management* 19: 251-267.

Phan, P.H. 2001. Introduction: Corporate governance in the newly emerging economies. *Asia Pacific Journal of Management*, 18(2): 131-136.

Pfeffer, J. 1987. Bringing the environment back in: The social context of business strategy. In D. Teece (ed.), *The Competitive Challenge. Strategies for Industrial Innovation and Renewal*. Cambridge, MA: Balinger.

Piore, M.J. and Sable, C.F. 1984. *The Second Industrial Divide: Possibilities for Prosperity*. NY: Basic Books.

Porter, M. 1990. *The Competitive Advantage of Nations*. London: MacMillan.

PricewaterhouseCoopers. 2001. The Opacity Index. http://www.pwcglobal.com.

Redding, S.G. 1980. Cognition as an aspect of culture and its relation to management processes: An exploratory view of the Chinese case. *Journal of Management Studies*, 17: 127-148.

Redding, S.G. 1990. *The Spirit of Chinese Capitalism*. Berlin: Walter de Gruyter.

Redding, S.G. 2002. The capitalist business system of China and its rationale. *Asia Pacific Journal of Management*, 19: 221-249.

Richter, F.-J. 1999. *Business Networks in Asia. Promises, Doubts, and Perspectives*. London: Quorum Books.

Robertson, C.J. and Hoffman, J.J. 2002. How different are we? An investigation of confucian values in the United States. *Journal of Managerial Issues*, 12: 34-47.

Sikorski, D. 1993. A general critique of the theory on public enterprises: Part II. *The International Journal of Public Sector Management*, 6: 56-67.

Singh, K. and Ang, S.H. 1999. *Corporate Strategies of Singapore GLCs: An Exploratory Analysis*. Chicago, USA: Best Papers Proceedings, Academy of Management Conference.

Singh, K., Ang, S.H. and Leong, S.M. 2003. Increasing replication for knowledge accumulation in strategy research. *Journal of Management*, forthcoming.

Singh, K. and Quek, L.K. 1999. Regionalisation strategies of Singapore corporations. *Seoul National University-Organisation Science Conference*, Seoul, Korea.

Subramaniam, S. 2000. The Asian values debate: Implications for the spread of liberal democracy. *Asian Affairs, An American Review*, 27: 19-35.

Tsui, A. and Farh, J.L. 1997. Where guanxi matters: Relational demography and guanxi in the Chinese context. *Work and Occupations*, 24: 56-79.

Wade, R. 1990. *Governing the Market*. Princeton, NJ: Princeton University Press.

Walker, G. and Fox, M. 2002. Corporate governance reform in East Asia. *Corporate Governance*, 2 (1): 4-9.

Weder, B. 1999. *Model, Myth or Miracle. Reassessing the Role of Governments in the East Asian Experience*. NY: United Nations University Press.

Wee, C.H., Lee, K.S. and Bambang, W.H. 1991. *Sun Tzu: War and Management. Application to Strategic Management and Thinking*. Singapore: Addison Wesley.

Westwood, R. 1997. Harmony and patriarchy: The cultural basis for "Paternalistic Headship" among overseas Chinese. *Organization Studies*, 18: 445-480.

White, S. 2002. Rigor and relevance in Asian management research: Where are we and where can we go? *Asia Pacific Journal of Management*, 19(2&3): 287-352.

Whitley, R. 1992. *Business Systems in East Asia. Firms, Markets and Societies*. London: Sage.

Whitley, R. 1999. *Divergent Capitalisms: The Social Structuring and Change of Business Systems*. Oxford: Oxford University Press.

Williamson, O.E. 1975. *Markets and Hierarchies*. NY: Free Press.

Williamson, O.E. 1985. *The Economic Institutions of Capitalism*. NY: Free Press.

Wong, P.H. 1999. The dynamics of the HDD industry development in Singapore. Unpublished Report 99-03, Information Storage Industry Centre, University of California, La Jolla, CA.

World Bank. 1993. *The East Asian Miracle. Economic Growth and Public Policy*. NY: Oxford University Press.

World Bank. 2001. *Building Institutions for Markets. World Development Report*, 2002. Washington, D.C.: World Bank.

World Economic Forum. 1999. The Global Competitiveness Report. Geneva: World Economic Forum.

Chapter 4

CONTEXT, CONFIGURATION AND CAPABILITY
Organizational Design and Competitive Advantage in Asian Firms

Michael Carney
Concordia University

Eric Gedajlovic
University of Connecticut

THE CONCEPT OF ORGANIZATION DESIGN IN THE ASIAN CONTEXT

Strategic choice and contingency theories regard organization design as the process of choosing and implementing a structural configuration (Mintzberg, 1979). These perspectives suggest that organization structure should be designed to accommodate the firm's strategy (Chandler, 1962), environmental uncertainty, (Lawrence and Lorsch, 1967), technological interdependence (Thompson, 1967), size (Child and Mansfield, 1972), and informational complexity (Galbraith, 1977). Scholarly interest in the design concept reached its apex in the mid-1970s, but by the early 1980s organization theories emphasizing efficiency (transactions costs, agency theory), power (resource dependence) and environmental influences (population ecology, institutional theory) had become more influential.

With few exceptions (e.g. Azuni and McMillan, 1975; Redding, 1990), strategic choice, contingency theory and other theoretical accounts which emphasize the role played by human agents have been largely absent from the literature on asian industrial organization. Instead, most organizational theorizing about Asian firms more often portrays business structures and processes as the product of a particular culture (Hall and Xu, 1990; Hamilton, 2000), or institutional context (Hamilton and Biggart, 1988). In contrast to strategic choice approaches which emphasize managerial implications, the focus of much current research is theoretical, relating organizational characteristics to particular institutional structures and/or cultural phenomena. At the limit this reasoning appears to suggest that organizations are uniquely a product of their national business systems and that factors such as technology, efficiency, and managerial choice play little role in shaping organization structures.

Throughout East and Southeast Asia unique mosaics of business groups, government linked enterprises and small family businesses constitute the major forms of indigenous business enterprise in countries as culturally and socially diverse as Mainland China, Islamic Indonesia, Buddhist Thailand and Christian Philippines. Indeed, the emergence of business groups and small family businesses is not unique to East Asia; they constitute important forms of indigenous enterprise in other emerging and developed economies around the world (Khanna and Palepu, 1997; Fukuyama, 1995).

A central theme of this survey is that *structural configurations are neither unique to societies, nor are societies uniquely defined by a single structural configuration.* There are salient structural differences between Japanese *keiretsu*, Korean *chaebol*, and Chinese Business Groups and the institutional contexts in which they are embedded. At the same time, there are some striking similarities as well. This survey examines *both* differences and similarities in providing an overview of Asian organizational design. Rather than rely on either a purely functional approach that emphasizes techno-economic organizing imperatives, or an approach which focuses solely on socio-cultural factors, this survey considers insights from both schools of thought.

In this survey of organization designs in the Asian context, we discuss six organizational forms and describe their defining structural characteristics as well as the environmental circumstances that engendered them. Four forms are diversified business groups and are found in the national business systems literature, namely: Japanese *keiretsu*, Korean *chaebol*, and Chinese Business Groups and Overseas Chinese Family Business Groups. These forms have both structural differences as well as similarities. We also delineate the government-linked enterprise, a configuration about which little is written but whose economic importance is vital in a region where government-led industrialization was virtually universal. Finally, the region's myriad small family-owned enterprises are included in this survey under the rubric of global commodity chains (Gereffi, 1994), an important and common regional configuration that transcends the national business system stereotype. Subsequently, we examine how the structural attributes of each form engenders it with inclinations and disinclinations towards the development of particular organizational capabilities (Carney and Gedajlovic, 2002a). In concluding the survey we take stock of the existing inventory of Asian organizational structures and discuss their strengths, limitations and developmental trajectories.

INSTITUTIONAL CONTEXT AND ORGANIZATIONAL DESIGN: SIX CONFIGURATIONS

East and Southeast Asia is a culturally and physically diverse region that has produced distinct national business systems (Whitley, 1992) with organizing patterns that reflect prevailing traditions of authority in each society (Hamilton and Biggart, 1988). Major differences in basic factor endowments have shaped national industrial development strategies. For example, lacking significant natural resources the economies of Japan, Korea, and Taiwan embarked upon export oriented development industrialization (Deyo, 1987; World Bank, 1993). In contrast, the industrial policies of the resource rich economies of Southeast Asia were initially focused upon the exploitation of these resources combined with import-substitution based industrialization (McVey, 1992).

Socio-economic differences across Asian economies should not be understated. On the other hand, we should also be alert to important similarities across the region. Over the past fifty years, the general institutional context of the East and Southeast Asia region can be distinguished by two broad eras (McVey, 1992; Vogel, 1991). Each era engendered distinct organization forms. The first era, the nationalist, followed the watershed of World War II, and is marked by the introduction of post-colonial governments in the region that were essentially nationalist in orientation. Dominated by cold-war politics, almost every state in the region was mired in civil war or the threat of war or both. In this extremely turbulent environment the main concern for post-war governments was national security. There was a need to restore internal order or fend off external communist threats – a goal shared by US foreign policy. Consequently, these conditions legitimised the establishment of strong centralized states. In the interest of national security states were able, in the short term, to resist the demands of particular sectional interests and were endowed with the authority to direct industrial and economic policy (Stubbs, 1999). Through the early cold war era national economic agendas were commonly limited to managing strategic industries and rebuilding basic infrastructure. This period saw the emergence of Government Linked Enterprises (GLEs), Family Business Groups (FBGs), Keiretsu and Chaebol as major forms of business enterprise.

A second broad era which can be referred to as the Modern Era is marked by two epochal events. First, the adoption by China in 1978 of Deng Xiao Ping's four modernizations, which resulted in the gradual opening of China to foreign investment. China later became a major rival to Southeast Asia for FDI. China's open door also signaled a reduction in Cold War tensions and allowed states to focus upon trade issues and economic competitiveness. The second major event was the Plaza Accord of 1985, which led to the Japanese yen's appreciation against the U.S. dollar and stimulated a sudden increase in Japanese, and later Western, investment (Stubbs, 1999). Together these events accelerated the movement of capital into and within East and Southeast and further increased the already rapid pace of industrialization (Krugman, 1994). In this environment, we see the birth and growth of mainland Chinese Business Groups (CBGs), as well as the organization of the region's myriad of small-family businesses and China's township and village enterprises into global commodity chains.

Government Linked Enterprises (GLEs)

Context

As their name suggests, GLEs are Southeast and East Asian firms which are either fully or partially owned and managed by a national government, or are privately owned but maintain multiple and long lasting ties with a government. GLEs emerged during the post WWII Nationalist Era and continue to play an important role in the economies of many Asian economies. The GLE came into being to meet the economic development and infrastructural needs of Southeast Asian economies in the post WWII period.

To control their natural resources, infrastructure, and natural monopolies, governments created state owned enterprises or vigorously supported national champions (Williamson, 1997) to manage a particular portfolio of industrial assets such as energy, telecommunications and transportation. As part of industrial policies designed to establish manufacturing industries, the Taiwanese and Singapore governments created GLEs as vehicles for acquiring and developing strategic assets. Several writers (Lim, 1996; McVey, 1992) note that Singapore's state capitalism is a proactive response to a perceived lack of entrepreneurial acumen on the part of indigenous entrepreneurs. States in Malaysia and Indonesia have established and supported enterprises that are owned and managed by indigenous entrepreneurs called Bumiputera firms. Public policy goals of modernization and a desire to advance the social position of previously excluded ethnic groups were prominent features of the business environment that marked the emergence of Bumiputera GLEs in the early Nationalist Era (Robison, 1992; Lim, 1996).

Configuration

The core GLE mission is capacity building or the creation of capital-intensive industry and technological capability. Such capacity is often complimentary to the small firm size-structure that characterizes light engineering and consumer manufacturing sectors. Fukuyama (1995) suggests the need for state involvement in heavy and technologically complex industry results from small-firm dominated economies that are ill equipped to organize large-scale industry or bear the risk associated with technological uncertainty. Since much of the industrial capacity and infrastructure provided by GLEs has a significant public-good component, they are directly subsidized by the state or permitted to operate under a 'soft-budget' constraint. Where GLEs are substantially privately owned they operate under a relational contracting system (Rajan and Zingales, 1998) that provides the state with the means of disciplining opportunistic behavior. Relational contracting with GLEs has permitted policy makers to ration capital, set investment priorities, invest in human capital and reward export-oriented firms with preferential access to limited export quotas or other scarce resources (Lall, 1990; Singh, 1998).

There are several detailed accounts of the micro-management of GLEs by state agencies (Schein, 1996; Sikorski, 1996; Vogel, 1988; Wade, 1990; Zutschi and Gibbons, 1998); however, most focus upon the provision of multiple sources of support. There are few studies of GLE organization and management structure.

Southeast Asian countries with strong states strive to operate developmental or goal-oriented rational administrative structures. In these countries, GLE decision making is made consultatively by a small number of strong policy making agencies that are able to maintain investment and development priorities in the face of opposing interests (Stubbs, 1999). Decisions are implemented in the organization by an economic bureaucracy (Wade, 1990) or a cosmopolitan technocracy (Schein, 1996). An elite cadre of policy officials monitors GLE compliance with state goals. GLE organizational structures and management practices have often been based upon foreign models. For example, Schein (1996:187) describes the use of the Royal Dutch-Shell management development model used in Singapore's EDB. The adoption of alien but apparently modern organizational structures and processes, especially at lower hierarchical levels and within the organizational operating core, is an important source of legitimacy.

States have encouraged the adoption by GLEs of rational-formal organizational structures most suitable for their product market scope. Typically single-business GLEs are structured using a functional or U-form design (Williamson, 1985), while more diversified GLEs adopt an M-form structure. Figure 1 illustrates the organization structure of a typical U-form GLE, Singapore International Airlines. SIA's U-form is a classic functional organization appropriate for a single-business, medium technology business that operates in a highly regulated international business environment. GLEs adopted broadly meritocratic management development programs and rational-legal bureaucratic structures (Vogel, 1991). Indeed, GLEs have been used as instruments for the development of a managerial cadre that is viewed as necessary in the development of more technologically advanced industries.

As the vehicles for capacity building, GLEs are generally protected from competition and many have become inefficient. McVey (1992) suggests that

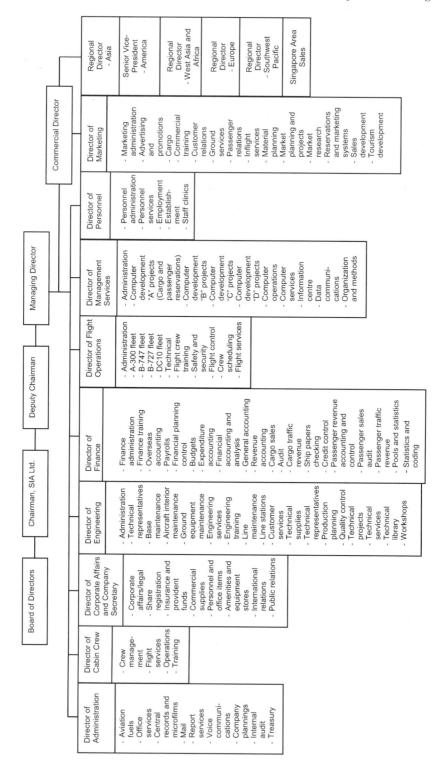

Figure 1. Singapore international airlines organizational structure. (Source: Chen, 1997.)

many have lapsed into 'bureaucratic inertia'. However, others have demonstrated superior performance. On the other hand, Laserre and Schutte suggest that GLEs such as Singapore Airlines and the China Steel Corporation of Taiwan are "managed by professional executives evaluated mainly on profitability criteria" (1999:266) and are excellent examples of well-managed government controlled firms.

Family Business Groups (FBGs)

Context

Most often identified with overseas Chinese entrepreneurs, FBGs emerged and developed in their modern configuration during the post WWII Nationalist Era in response to three sets of institutional forces diaspora, discrimination and nationalistic economic policy. The overseas Chinese in Asia are in many ways a product of turmoil in their home country. Successive rebellions, civil war and revolutions in China produced a steady flow of migration from China to Hong Kong, Taiwan, and countries in Southeast Asia (Fairbank, 1994). In their capacity as intermediaries, migrant Chinese entrepreneurs were exposed to a wide range of indigenous commercial activities in their adopted societies. As intermediaries, the Chinese immigrants learned techniques of both trade and basic manufacturing (McVey, 1992; Yoshihara, 1988). The value of skills and contacts developed by the immigrant Chinese in the Colonial Era made them vitally important during the subsequent Nationalist Era when indigenous entrepreneurial skills were in short supply (Twang, 1998).

Overseas Chinese entrepreneurs were well positioned for the changes in political power that occurred in Southeast Asia after WWII. The Chinese diaspora was widespread in the region and entrepreneurs maintained personal contacts among Chinese entrepreneurs from the same family or language group in many countries in the region. Geographically dispersed kin-networks provided secure channels for asset movements and for learning about profitable opportunities (Kao, 1993; Hodder, 1996). The diaspora produced an entrepreneurial class that was well placed to operate international networks and which was attuned to the behavior of a diverse group of key actors in Southeast Asia.

Despite their economic success, and indeed possibly because of it, Chinese entrepreneurs encountered discrimination and risked asset expropriation in their adopted societies (Hodder, 1996; Twang, 1998; Wu and Wu, 1980). Recent violence against Chinese property in Indonesia indicates that this hostility is both grave and enduring. Overseas Chinese entrepreneurs suffered official discrimination in Malaysia and Indonesia from nationalist policies intended to secure greater participation in the economy for ethnic nationals (Lim, 1996).

In Thailand, Indonesia and The Philippines, political corruption and bureaucratic 'rent-seeking' (McVey, 1992) produced wariness of the state. In Hong Kong, FBG entrepreneurs enjoyed a relatively laissez faire relationship with the Colonial state, but nevertheless, they were all but excluded from elite positions in Hong Kong society (Whitley, 1992). During their critical founding phase overseas Chinese entrepreneurs were in the paradoxical position of 'essential outsiders' (Chirot and Reid, 1997). They were essential to nationalist governments intent on developing their economic resources yet they were outsiders who did not always enjoy an equal status or the full protection of the state in often turbulent civil conditions.

Configuration

FBGs are not distinguished by the separation, but by the coupling of ownership and control (Carney and Gedajlovic, 2002b). In this regard, FBGs fit Chandler's (1990) depiction of personally managed enterprises, which he defines as "firms managed by individuals or by small numbers of associates, often members of founders' families, assisted by only a few salaried managers, or they (are) federations of such firms" (p. 236). The core strategic goal of FBGs is to enhance and protect the value of the family's communal fortune (Suehiro, 1993). In an often hostile operating environment the concerns of "wealth conservation and consolidation" (Wong, 1985) have important implications regarding organizational design.

Many scholars contend that, compared with managerial enterprise, kin-based organization is neither enduring nor conducive to large-scale capital accumulation (Redding, 1990; Fukuyama, 1995). Sociological studies of Chinese capitalism suggest that family businesses rarely span more than two or three generations of senior management before weakening and disintegrating (Kao, 1993; Yoshihara, 1988; Tam, 1990). Economic studies of risk bearing in family firms reach similar conclusions about strategic goals and firm longevity. Such economic analyses begin from the recognition that the family firm's assets account for a significant proportion of that family's wealth. This concentration of assets creates a significant risk that can be reduced by extracting capital from the business and allocating it to alternative, safer, sources. Fama and Jensen (1983) observe that families are inherently risk averse in their strategic behavior because their personal wealth is closely tied to the firm's fortunes. Such an analysis is consistent with studies which have found that FBGs tend to be generally risk averse (Kao, 1993) and to favor investments in generic rather than specialized assets (Redding, 1990).

Since the family has a direct claim on their firm's residual income (Alchian and Demsetz, 1972), owner/managers have a strong incentive to ensure that capital is deployed sparingly and used efficiently and that indirect production costs are tightly managed (Brickley and Dark, 1987). In addition, the incentive effects of direct ownership reduce the need for third party monitoring and supervision (Carney and Gedajlovic, 1991). On the other hand, the tight coupling of ownership and control allows owner/managers to exhibit the particularistic values of their owner/managers (Demsetz and Lehn, 1985; Fukuyama, 1995). The personalized character of family business is often manifested in terms of the selection of top management on the basis of family ties, rather than on the basis of professional expertise (Schulze, Lubatkin, Dino and Buchholtz, 2001).

Many researchers have described and documented these tendencies among Asian FBGs and have outlined their structural consequences (Redding, 1990; Westwood, 1997; Whitley, 1992; Wong, 1985). The basic structural configuration adopted by FBGs is the Holding Company or H-Form structure (Williamson, 1975). This structure facilitates the undiluted control of a diverse range of assets while requiring limited coordination, planning and auditing capacity (Carney, 1998a). The H-form permits a small management team to oversee heterogeneous businesses by focusing upon financial performance metrics such as ROI (Chandler, 1997; Goold and Campbell, 1987).

Management is exercised through a senior owner-manager who typically assumes the presidency of the core firm and concurrently holds the post of chairman in the major affiliated firms whose presidential posts are occupied by kin or close trusted associates (Koike, 1993). Top management in larger groups typically consist of two separate board levels: one exercises policy and auditing power while the second subordinate group consists of professional managers who have day to day operating responsibility (Numazaki, 1993). Figure 2A illustrates the Taiwanese variant of a federated or partnership form of the FBG. According to Numazaki (1993), the salient features of this corporate structure is a partnership consisting of overlapping-ownership and directorships. In Figure 2A each banana represents a group member corporation that is linked at the stem by senior owner-partners who direct the group as a whole. The partnership is hierarchical in the sense that some owners do not commit fully to overlapping ownership and directorship of the entire group but who concern themselves with a more limited range of enterprises.

Elsewhere in Asia, FBG ownership is ordinarily concentrated in the hands of a founding entrepreneur, the immediate family or ancestral trust depending upon the age of the firm (Wong, 1985). Greater unity of control is possible when a single family or entrepreneur controls the entire group through ownership of equity (Weidenbaum and Hughes, 1996). Control in the first generation typically rests with the founding entrepreneur and in later generations with a group of family members and trusted business associates. If successor family members' interests begin to diverge, then segmenting forces tend to reproduce the structure indicated in Figure 2A (Tam, 1990).

The senior management team tends to be small, and the limited numbers of non-kin professional managers are often excluded from strategic decision making processes (Kao, 1993; Redding, 1992). Where professional managers

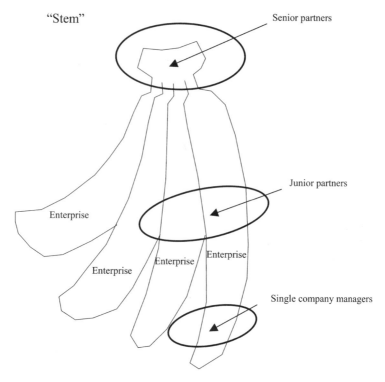

Figure 2A. Taiwanese business group (Tainanbang): The banana-bunch-shaped partnership of partners. (Source: Numazaki, 1993.)

are employed in senior positions, the roles are considered subordinate to entrepreneurial roles held by family members or trusted friends (Redding, 1990; Whitley, 1992). Non-kin professional managers from different group divisions rarely meet and the structural integration of group management is weak. On the whole, "groups look more like a collection of independent firms than an integrated business group" (Numazaki, 1993:502).

Figures 2B and 2C illustrate the corporate structure of Sahaviriya, a medium-sized Thai family business group. The majority of the firm's revenues and assets are concentrated in steel distribution and real estate businesses (Tanlamai and Chandrachi, 1994). However, the corporate structure emphasizes many of Sahaviriya's diverse technology affiliates and subsidiaries. The figure with its subsidiaries and different joint venture forms is indicative of a highly flexible 'deal' or 'project' based structure that allows financial assets to be easily shifted between separate legal entities (Carney and Gedajlovic, 2002b). Sahaviriya's organizational structure, depicted in Figure 2C, describes a simple product structure consisting of two support offices: an office of the executive and a financial and administrative group.

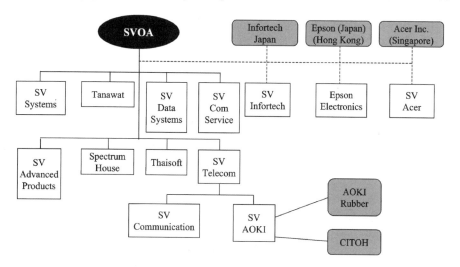

Figure 2B. Sahaviriya OA group of companies corporate structure.

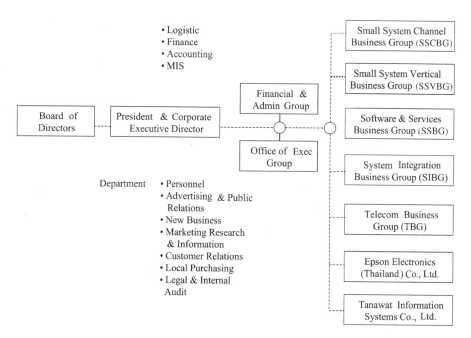

Figure 2C. Sahaviriya OA organizational structure. (Source: Tanlamai and Chandrachai, 1994.)

The structuring of the larger group's assets across smaller units with individual legal identities is a mechanism for asset mobilization and reduces the enterprise's visibility, which can be a crucial defense mechanism when operating in hostile environments (Hodder, 1996). Moreover, this structure provides for a means of achieving monitoring and feedback on unit performance when subsidiary managers are not trusted or when the organization has inadequate capacity to perform a thorough internal auditing function (Carney, 1998). Redding notes the avoidance of organizational complexity and the tendency to subdivide business units to maintain financial simplicity. This solution allows entrepreneurs to "carry the paper and pencil in the head" (Redding, 1990:181). Ampalavanar-Brown (1995:2) says "the financial structure, which might have held the structure together more firmly, did not play a large part in pulling the parts together into a cooperation. The purposes of the accounting system were to track sales and purchases and to prevent fraud."

The managerial style of FBG entrepreneurs is distinctly personalistic. Managerial processes are infused with leadership values that Westwood (1997) describes as 'paternalistic headship'. The structural consequences of paternalistic headship include high centralization, low or selective formalization, and noncomplex structural processes. FBGs make little use of formal organizational structure, rules or written procedures (Redding, 1990). Nor do they typically create indirect or direct service functions such as personnel offices or market research. All employees are expected to be directly involved in the main products or services of the company which directly create profits (Chen, 1995). Whitley (1992) suggests that FBG structures exhibit much lower degrees of role specialization and work standardization than comparable UK or Japanese firms.

The human resource implications of such structures are significant. Immediate and extended family and trusted quasi-family employees (Westwood, 1997) may be expected to be highly committed and motivated members of the management team (Whitley, 1999). On the other hand, for employees without any special relationship to the patriarchy, commitment is likely to be weak. Such employees are typically paid less and do not enjoy the protection of face (Chen, 1995). Consequently, employee turnover tends to be very high and exit decisions can be precipitated by marginal salary differences (Shieh, 1992). Nontrusted employees in the organization may be subject to a functional handicap because "didactic leadership emasculates subordinates by depriving them of the information necessary to have a clear idea of what is going on in the organization" (Westwood, 1997:469).

Chaebol

Context

Chaebol are the dominant enterprise form in Korea (Amsden, 1989) and are in some respects a hybrid of the GLE and FBG. Chaebol are diversified family owned business groups that are closely linked to the state. The multibusiness chaebol emerged following the Korean War in the 1950s to leverage

Korea's scarce pool of capital and management in order to create an industrial infrastructure and enter new export oriented industries (Amsden, 1989). The chaebol were the State's preferred vehicle for these tasks. Consequently, this configuration replaced the more specialized, single business firms that were an important part of Korea's pre-war economy (Amsden, 1997). Non-bank financial institutions were very undeveloped and the Korean Ministry of Finance effectively controlled all forms of debt and trade credit. Access to capital was subject to state determined priorities using a subsidy allocation principle that made diversification into new industries contingent on performance in old ones (Amsden, 1991).

Recently, the South Korean state has encouraged the chaebol to seek public listings on domestic stock markets. However, most of these listings float only a minority stake in a small number of constituent firms. Consequently stock markets are not a source of discipline and majority ownership remains in the direct hands of a dominant owner or indirectly, pyramid style, in the hands of a corporation concentrated in the hands of a majority owner (Gedajlovic and Shapiro, 2001; Claessens et al., 2000).

Configuration

Despite rapid growth and state pressure to sell public equity and become more widely held, chaebol remain private and family owned entities (Amsden, 1997). Rather, to avoid dilution of family shareholdings and in the absence of liquid equity markets, chaebol growth was funded largely through state-subsidized debt. Reinforced by state incentives, chaebol adopted strategic goals that favored growth and market share over profitability (Amsden, 1989:118). Chaebol have endured many years of profitless growth. Two factors have contributed to the lack of profits. First, state control of pricing in domestic markets has not permitted firms to generate excess returns in protected home markets. Secondly, chaebol compliance with state growth plans in targeted industries has frequently led to global overcapacity as investments were made without regard to cash flows. Long periods of depressed earnings have not provided many chaebol with much positive cash flow. This protracted indebtedness has reinforced a reliance on state mediated debt.

Chaebols are diversified business groups that are typically much larger than business groups elsewhere. At the macro-structural level, these diversified conglomerates resemble Western corporations with a vertically integrated set of economic activities operating under a unified, centralized management structure (Orru, Biggart and Hamilton, 1991). Figure 3A illustrates the corporate structure of a typical chaebol, the Hyundai Group, which indicates the breadth of diversification in the typical chaebol. Indeed, the larger chaebol are much more diversified and also more vertically integrated than the Japanese kaisha with whom they are frequently compared. Chaebol are also less reliant upon

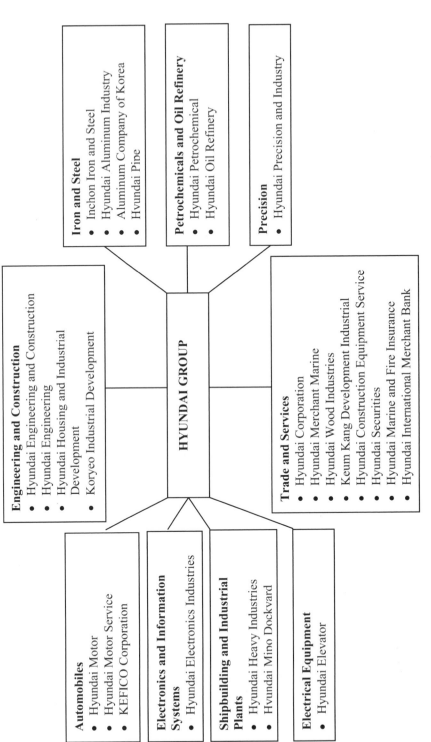

Figure 3A. Hyundai Group corporate structure. (Source: Ungson, Steers and Park, 1997.)

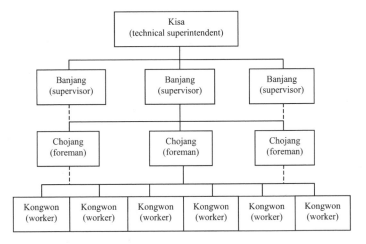

Figure 3B. Organization chart for production unit at Hyundai Motor unit. (Source: Ungson, Steers and Park, 1997.)

subcontracting (Whitley, 1992) and are less likely to enter into domestic strategic alliances (Bloom, 1994).

Chaebol organization structures possess two defining structural features: highly centralized decision making, planning and resource allocation and a pervasive paternalistic approach to labor management relations (Ungson, Steers and Park, 1998; Whitley, 1999; Wilkinson, 1996). At the peak of each chaebol is a planning and coordination group responsible for the collection, analysis and presentation of data for decision making. The main component in the planing group is a founder Chairman who assumes and exercises personal authority over every aspect of the firm's operations. This centralized and personalized authority structures facilitate negotiation and bargaining with governments and assures family oversight over strategic decisions.

Chaebol hierarchies are purposely tall so that differentiation between ranks is clear (Ungson, Steers and Park, 1997). There is minimal reliance on staff functions; rather, advisory roles are filled by deputies and assistants in line positions, which serves to further lengthen hierarchical chains of command (Chen, 1995). Figure 3A is indicative of long chains of command and narrow spans of control. Managerial and operational roles are rarely formalized; job descriptions are brief generalized role descriptions that specify broad job parameters. The absence of formal job descriptions facilitates paternalistic control and, while authority is typically centralized, responsibility for performance is often delegated (Ungson, Steers and Park, 1998:176). This authoritarian management style is also characterized by close supervision of task performance at the operational level. Plants and facilities are frequently designed to promote surveillance of work processes (Whitley, 1999). Close supervision is also allied with high role specialization among manual and craft workers.

Chaebol management is typically less committed to lifetime-employment and the generation of intense employee loyalty. In this regard, little attention is given to training and cross-training (Whitley, 1999). More often, management relies upon extrinsic rewards to motivate employees (Chen, 1995). The main thrust of labour management is the creation of a disciplined and obedient workforce. The outcome is a labor force that is industrious, but is lacking the commitment and discretion found on Japanese shopfloors (Fukuyama, 1995).

In marked contrast to their operational labor forces, chaebol have sought to develop a middle level managerial cadre with more valuable company specific skills. In their attempts to develop managerial resources, they have abandoned informal recruitment practices based upon nepotism and personal connections and have adopted more formalized, merit-based recruitment, selection and performance appraisal systems. Greater attention is given to formal training and managers are circulated across functions and divisions to ensure the production of well rounded general managers (Ungson, Steers and Park, 1997). However, while Chaebol attempt to develop their managerial capital, Fukuyama (1995) suggests that they are not well equipped to fully utilize it. Efforts to establish consensual decision making processes are frustrated because managers are reluctant to express their opinion. Ungson, Steers and Park (1997) suggest that consensual decision making systems are essentially designed to diffuse responsibility for decisions made elsewhere. Tsui-Auch and Lee (2001) suggest that Chaebol have adopted the bureaucratic form of professional management, but remain committed to a personalistic management style. They further suggest that the financial crisis of 1997 has reinforced such a dualistic approach to their internal organization.

Keiretsu & Kaisha

Context

Like GLEs in Taiwan and in Southeast Asia and the chaebol in Korea, large-scale industrial enterprise in Japan has historically worked closely with the state to create domestic industrial capacity in capital intensive industries. Unlike GLEs and Chaebol, where the state has been the dominant partner in directing the resource allocation process, Japan's state-business relations are characterized by consensus and mutual accommodation (Chalmers, 1982; Fukuyama, 1995). Beginning shortly after the Meiji Restoration in 1868, the Japanese State encouraged the development of modern industries as part of a concerted attempt to catch-up with the West. Prior to World War II, large enterprise was concentrated in the hands of family owned zaibatsu and their affiliated sogo-shosa, which managed Japan's international trade. These organizations bear many similarities to modern day Family Business Groups.

For example, zaibatsu did not consolidate production into large efficient scale plants nor did they employ significant numbers of professional managers (Best, 1990; Morikawa, 1992). However, Japan's firms had little need for complex organizational structures. Prior to the 1930's Japan's internationally competitive industries were limited to labour-intensive businesses such as paper-making and silk and cotton spinning (Morikawa, 1997).

The context for the nascence of Japan's modern corporate and organizational structures lay in her militarization, which precipitated a revolutionary change in Japan's corporate governance culminating in the separation of enterprise ownership and its control (Storry, 1982). After 1930, the military dominated government became increasingly dissatisfied with zaibatsu concern with short-term profits at the expense of building organizational capabilities (Morikawa, 1992, 1997). To build up civil and military infrastructure and weapons production, the state sought to expand the influence of full-time salaried managers in the commanding heights of the economy. The transition to professional management was completed during and immediately after World War II. Owner managers completely withdrew from management when the occupational authorities dissolved the zaibatsu and were replaced by non share-owning professional managers. Moreover, the major shareholders of non-zaibatsu, as well as zaibatsu, firms lost significant property following tax and land reforms enforced by the occupying authorities. While much has been made of the apparent reemergence of (some of) the zaibatsu in the guise of modern day keiretsu, and the organizational continuity that it represents, it is equally important to recognize that the corporate governance of these reconstituted organizations provided for a new managerial approach; namely, the creation of capital-intensive, vertically-integrated and geographically-diversified businesses (Carney and Gedajlovic, 2000).

Configuration

There are two basic forms of the keiretsu configuration. The first is the horizontal or conglomerate form centered on a major bank or holding company, such as Fuyo, Sanwa, and Mitsui. The second is the vertical form, which are quasi vertically integrated 'giant companies' or kaisha that focus upon two or three core industries such as Toyota, Matsushita, and Toshiba (Aoki, 1988). Figure 4A illustrates the corporate structure of a typical vertical keiretsu, Hitachi. This figure indicates Hitachi's historical ownership links with separately listed Hitachi Metals, Hitachi Chemical and Hitachi Chemical. Six other core divisions are listed under Hitachi wherein share ownership varies from a low of 12% for Nippon Columbia to full ownership for several other units.

The corporate structure provide stakeholders such as banks, affiliated companies and labour with both the capacity and means to reciprocally monitor

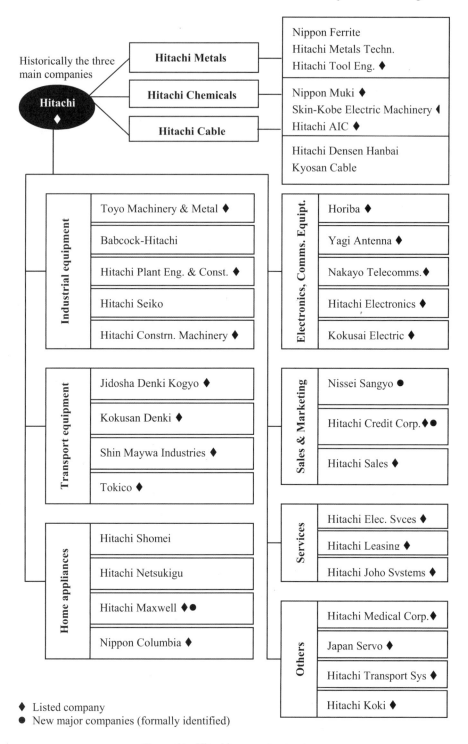

Figure 4A. Hitachi corporate structure.

each other through a multiplicity of equity, debt and commercial ties (Geda-jlovic and Shapiro, 2002). Banks which are often a firm's largest shareholder are more interested in the firm's financial stability, the sale of professional services and the continuation of debt-financed growth, rather than market re-turns (Gerlach, 1992). Similarly, affiliated firms which are shareholders are commonly more interested in mutual assistance and in cementing and expand-ing their range of commercial ties, such as the provision of complementary assets, access to superior technology, or an outlet for their products, rather re-turns on their equity investment. Above all, almost all stakeholders, including those who reciprocally hold each other's shares, are interested in preserving and growing relations with each other. Such shareholders are viewed as 'sta-ble' or relationship investors (Yoshikawa and Gedajlovic, 2002). The focus of much keiretsu analysis is the performance advantages of their corporate struc-ture and cooperative role in Japan's industrial policy (Lincoln, Gerlach, and Ahmadjian, 1996).

Japanese human resource and shop floor management practices involving intensive socialization, lifetime employment, group work-designs, job rotation, and concern for employee well-being have also received extensive attention (Abegglen and Stalk, 1985; Ouchi, 1981). Much less attention has been given to the formal and hierarchical nature of Japanese organizations. Beginning in 1950, Japanese enterprises embarked upon a sustained forty-year period of 'vigorous equipment investment' (Morikawa, 1997). Japanese firms, with state assistance, started *de novo* to create efficient scale plants, marketing and re-search organizations, and the bureaucratic and managerial apparatus to coordi-nate them that produced a diverse range of globally scaled organizations. By 1990, Japanese enterprises dominated every industrial sector in Asia except agriculture and forestry.

At the heart of this performance is a salaried upper and middle management class that created and implemented a series of organizational design innova-tions, such as layered production, TQM, JITI, and cooperative subcontracting (Best, 1990), comparable in scope and impact to American organizing innova-tions of an earlier era (Chandler, 1962). State support and complex corporate financial structures provided a nurturing environment for the development of an extensive managerial hierarchy that pioneered, perfected and deployed these capabilities (Carney and Gedajlovic, 2001).

Some indication of the extent of Japanese managerial hierarchies is indi-cated in Figure 4B. Early research on Japanese structures suggested high levels of formalization, task structuring, and the centralization of authority (Azuni and Macmillan, 1975). However, later research suggested that the apparent centralized coordination and task specialization evident in formal documents were less important than intense socialization, shared decision-making (Ouchi, 1981) and attention to management development through processes such as job rotation and work group evaluation (Aoki, 1988). More recently, these views

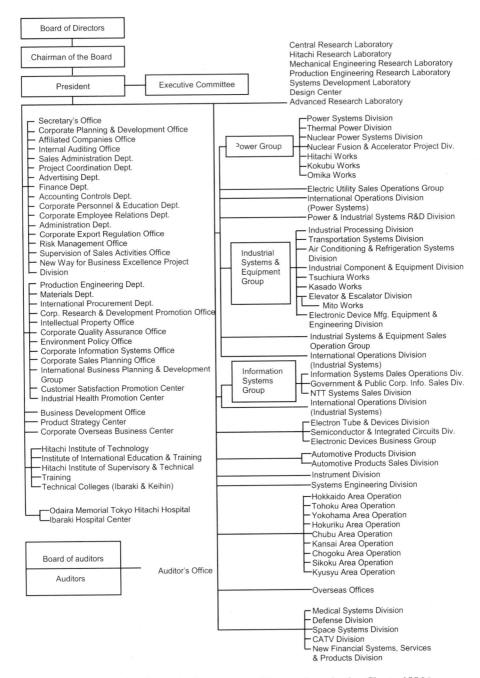

Figure 4B. Hitachi organization structure. (Source: Organization Charts, 1996.)

are being reevaluated. The suggestion is that much shared decision making is rather symbolic and ritualistic (Whitley, 1992) and is oriented toward the preservation of the status quo and rigid hierarchical relationships (Yoshimura and Anderson, 1997). While Japanese organizations are more centralized and bureaucratic than popularly portrayed, they have created structures that possess a range of formidable organizational capabilities.

Mainland China State-led Business Groups (CBGs)

Context

Beginning in 1978 with Deng Xiaoping's open-door economic policy, China has experimented with market-oriented reforms. A major contextual influence on the creation of corporate and organization forms is a politicized and circuitous reform process that leaves property rights in the wider economy ambiguous and ill-defined (Jefferson and Rawski, 1996). Formal ownership of public, private and joint venture enterprises often bears no clear relationship to rights of asset use and disposal or income streams derived from them (Child, 1994). Rather, enterprises are located in a 'system of dependencies' (Child, 1994) that includes the Communist Party, labour unions, Central and local government industrial bureaux, and a variety of functional agencies responsible for factors such as energy and telecommunications. Each of these actors has formal and informal means of intervening and influencing decision processes.

The creation of organizational configurations is a state policy goal of organizational experimentation. The objective is to "explore new ways of combining business autonomy with a changed role for government" (Child, 2000:42). Confronting a need to reconcile numerous social and economic dilemmas, policy makers encouraged the development a large variety of organizational forms. Some experiments were imitations of foreign corporate models, others hybrid arrangements of existing forms (Nee, 1992; Tseo, 1996). Perhaps the most decisive and dramatic recent trend is the formation of giant conglomerates from the myriad state-owned enterprises. As such, the emergent dominant organizational form in recent years is the diversified business group, similar in range and scope to both chaebol and FBGs (Child, 2000).

However, while the chaebol and FBGs developed their structures through internal or organic growth, China's business groups represent a regroupment of existing state-owned assets consisting of public research institutes, manufacturing enterprises and import-export trading organizations. CBGs are organized around a large core firm, such as Sinochem. They are widely diversified, multi-industry entities with strong State, but not familial, links. When a firm enters a group, partial ownership is transferred to the group's core firm. Ownership links are reinforced through a series interlocking directorates.

Configuration

Since property rights remain vaguely defined, it is far from clear who's interests and strategic goals prevail in any systematic way. However, CBGs have developed under a regime of state administrative guidance, which has encouraged the creation of several structural features and strategic goals (Keister, 1998). An overriding administrative goal is broader social system stability, and enterprises are expected to accommodate this aim through incremental restructuring and gradual change, especially in employment practice. At the same time, Child (2000) detects a trend in corporate governance towards control by insiders, managers and local state holding companies rather than by external stockholders and other providers of capital. Control by insiders exposes the enterprise to the risk of asset stripping and profit diversion (Claessens et al., 2000). On the other hand, given limited legal protection for property rights in China, an insider-dominated governance system may be well aligned with the broader institutional environment (Khanna and Palepu, 1997; Dyck, 2001). Despite the inherent risk with insider governed enterprises, policy makers in China were impressed by the capacity of keiretsu and chaebol to achieve scale economies, technological progress and favourable financial performance (Keister, 1998). The state has encouraged the formation of giant business groups, and these groups have much autonomy over managerial and organizational variables (Child, 1994). By 1997 the 97% of the firms reported in Child (2000) had full autonomy over internal organization issues.

Figure 5 illustrates the organizational structure of a typical Chinese business group. The core firm's president is responsible for the oversight of the group's management council or enterprise office, which comprises the vice presidents and general managers of the group's member firms. A senior role in the hierarchy is reserved for the president of the group's finance company or quasi-bank. Beginning in the late 1980s, CBGs created internal finance companies (caiwu gongsi) to collect and distribute group member funds and seek external funds from state banks. Early reforms in China produced sectoral or industry banks, but these institutions proved unable to allocate capital effectively. Consequently, CBGs began to embrace insider lending as a substitute for poorly organized financial markets. Also enjoying seniority in the hierarchy are the presidents of marketing or import–export trading companies.

Keister (1998) finds that there is much variation among CBGs in the degree to which authority is centralized in the enterprise office. While some enterprise offices attempt to involve themselves directly in day-to-day activities, others permit greater autonomy. Initial findings suggest that more decentralized groups perform better financially (Keister, 1998). The virtue of group

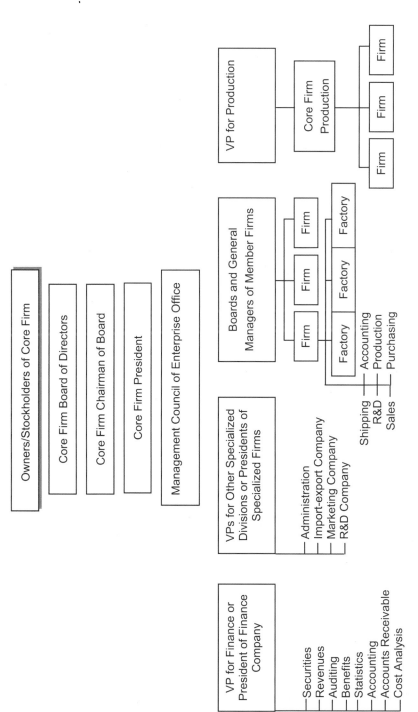

Figure 5. The organization of the typical Chinese business group. (Source: Keister, 1998.)

membership appears to stem from "group money and protection" (Keister, 1998:416). Due to imperfections in factor and intermediate product markets, business groups in China can provide access to scarce resources (Park and Luo, 2001). However, groups need not be highly centralized to accomplish these benefits. Keister (1998) finds that financially better performing groups achieve coordination through cross-membership of group member boards rather than through central planning.

Studies of micro-organizational processes in Chinese firms show a continuing state of flux (Shenkar, 1991; Child, 1994). Child adopts a cultural-insitutional perspective on continuing developments, concluding that "HRM practices amount to an institutionalization of cultural values and sociopolitical ideology" (2000:54). However, given the embedded, multi-layered quality of Chinese culture and the seemingly circuitous and often contradictory development of socio-political ideology (Jefferson and Rawski, 1996), there is an absence of a consensus regarding preferred organization organizational processes.

Production Networks and Global Commodity Chains

Context

Beginning in the mid-1960s, vertically integrated European and American firms confronting growing labor costs and increased Japanese competition in mature product markets such as textiles, garments and consumer durables began to outsource manufacturing. Asian economies that lacked substantial natural resources, such as Hong Kong, Singapore and Taiwan, began to establish export-led development programs to either attract foreign investment (Singapore) or to promote domestic entrepreneurship (Hong Kong and Taiwan). In the mid-1980s, following a global depression in commodity prices, resource rich economies of Southeast Asia switched their emphasis from the production of natural resources and began to pursue export-led development through manufacturing (Deyo, 1987). Falling commodity prices also triggered a major change in China's industrial policies toward export-oriented manufacturing (McNaughton, 1997). Following the Plaza Accord in 1985, Japanese investment in Southeast Asia began to increase rapidly. These factors created numerous market opportunities, which were quickly seized by the region's business groups (Carney and Gedajlovic, 2002a). The growth of international outsourcing also created opportunities for small and medium sized enterprises.

Domestic entrepreneurs that established production facilities to fill the demand for low cost original equipment manufacture (OEM) essentially acted as manufacturing order fulfillment specialists. With an ample supply of local

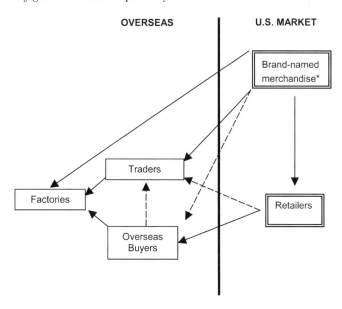

Figure 6. Buyer-driven global commodity chains. (Source: Gereffi, 1994.)

labour and a seemingly insatiable demand from foreign purchasing agents, sub-contractors were not encouraged to develop their organizational configurations. Later, subcontractors began to face increasing labor costs in their domestic factories and they responded by relocating production in neighbouring states with untapped labour that were also establishing an industrial base. For example, Singaporean electronics firms relocated to neighbouring Johor province in Malaysia and Battam Island in Indonesia (Hobday, 1994a) and Taiwanese and Hong Kong based firms relocated to south China (Hsing, 1996). These developments produced some of the necessary constituent parts of what have become highly structured vertically disaggregated production and marketing systems (Storper and Walker, 1989), which Gereffi (1994) has labeled 'global commodity chains'.

Economic geographers (Storper and Walker, 1989; Saxenian, 1990) and political scientists (Sabel, 1988) argue that the emergence of localized regional economies that house productive elements of a system populated by networks of indigenous small firms and transplanted branches of multinationals represent an alternative form of industrial organization. Vertically disaggregated and spatially concentrated production networks (Figure 6) are seen as a viable, and often desirable, alternative to the vertically integrated hierarchically coordinated corporation. Based on the advantages of agglomeration, proximity, social cohesion, and market contracting, networks are seen as presenting an ascendant post-industrial structure and model for economic development (Best, 1990).

Configuration

Gerrefi (1994) distinguishes between two forms of production network: producer-driven and buyer-driven global commodity chains. The former are production systems dominated by large MNEs in industries such as autos computers, electrical machinery and aircraft. What distinguishes producer-driven networks is that production control is exercised by the MNEs. In contrast, buyer-driven commodity chains are characterized by more downstream value added activities. In buyer-driven chains, US and European brand name merchandisers such as Nike and Reebok, which do not operate production facilities, and large retailers such as The Gap and Walmart, specify designs, quantities, and price points to local trading companies. Many former subcontractors from first mover states have become intermediary trading organizations that play an integrating role, linking manufacturers to markets. Their role is to provide a variety of commercial functions relating to the provision of credit, insurance, and logistics. However, the core function of the traders appears to be that of enforcement agents responsible for contractual compliance (Figure 6). Historically, this trading role was filled by Japanese sogo shosha (Yoshihara, 1982) and colonial trading and investment companies or 'Hongs' (Drabble and Drake, 1982). More recently, new indigenous firms such as Li and Fung have filled this role.

In their initial phase, Asian networks were composed of a vertically disaggregated system of single-phase producers, small in size but linked together through a system of market contracts. These networks emerged spontaneously in response to market demands and were minimally coordinated. For example, the Hong Kong watch and clock industry in 1993 was composed of some 1,455 establishments with an average of 12 employees (Hong Kong Census and Statistics Department, 1993). These firms produced to high quality standards and are capable of meeting the quality demands of Swiss industry, which now subcontracts to Hong Kong suppliers (Glasmeir, 1994). Production flows through several establishments in elaborate subcontractor networks; for example, work is further subcontracted into sub-phases such as die-casting, electroplating and polishing.

Constituent firms in these informal networks possess simple organizational structures (Mintzberg, 1989). The prevalent approach to labour management relations consists of authoritarian paternalism by owner-mangers engaged in close supervision of work processes (Wilkinson, 1996; Shieh, 1992). Minimal delegation is linked with informal task structuring. There is a minimal reliance upon formal written job descriptions or procedures (Whitley, 1992).

The emergence of consciously planned or coordinated buyer-driven production networks has resulted from changing global organizing forces. One discernable impact is upon the organization of production. The relocation of labour intensive production from land-constrained Hong Kong and Singapore to Malaysia and China permitted the concentration of formerly disaggregated production into larger green-field factories. These larger facilities retain their relatively simple operating structures. However, the cost of access to labour and other factors of production comes at the price of more complex local governance structures. Labour seeking foreign investment is often required to form joint ventures or contract with local partners. Consequently, factory management structures have become more complex, reflecting shared ownership and responsibilities. For example, local production in China by collectives, private firms and township and village enterprises (TVEs) has flourished (Jefferson and Rawski, 1996). The effect of diverse and often opaque local ownership requirements has reinforced the role of traders, whose stock in trade is knowledge of these constraints and an ability to procure contracts to keep the factories busy.

Secondly, since many Western companies are facing mounting public criticism of their procurement practices, they have engaged in strict monitoring of their subcontractor's factories. These companies often deploy on-site expatriate compliance officers that monitor and enforce a comprehensive set of labour standards (Frenkel, 2001). The external structuring of employment relations in local subcontract firms by Western firms tends to moderate prevailing organization patterns and promotes a more human resource oriented approach to labor management. In contrast with the more authoritarian systems (Shieh, 1992), Frenkel describes relations between senior managers and production workers as moving from an 'authoritarian to a constitutional style' (2001:556). Many contractor factories now establish personnel and labour relations departments and formalize their employment and recruitment practices and terms of work.

CONFIGURATION AND CAPABILITY

Structural configurations vary widely in their technical efficacy and in the scope of environmental conditions under which they are effective (Carney and Gedajlovic, 2002a). Performance attributes of organization designs stem from the structure of incentives and property rights among different organizational stakeholders (Gedajlovic and Shapiro, 1998; Williamson, 1991). Policy makers and entrepreneurs are capable of detecting the differential performance attributes of organizations and seek to utilize organizations in an instrumental manner. Such agents may not be fully successful in their aims because outcomes are also the product of unintended or emergent processes (Mintzberg and Waters, 1985). Agents differ in their relative power and their ability to influence organizational and institutional outcomes (Pfeffer and Salancik, 1978). Powerful organizations can obstruct institutional initiatives that threaten their resource base (Oliver, 1991). This survey of Asian organization designs reflects these realities and is premised on the notion that organizations are instruments for accomplishing tasks, and human agents (entrepreneurs and policy makers) seek to utilize them to promote their interests.

A strategic choice perspective on organization design draws attention to a firms' competitive capabilities. The resource-based theory of the firm views organizations as bundles of resources, competencies, or routines (Nelson and Winter, 1982). Higher order capabilities are viewed as intangible, unimitatable and proprietary since they are embedded in an organization's activity system (Nikerson, Hamilton and Wada, 2001). Core competencies are organizational attributes that can be neither contracted out nor in because those attributes constitute the very essence of what the organization does. With its emphasis upon the coordination and integration of a value chain consisting of diverse assets and activities, there is in contemporary resource theories a tight link between organization design and firm capability.

Several theoretical perspectives are beginning to view an organization's ability to organize resources as a key determinant of its performance. For example, institutional theorists have recently recognized the pressing need to incorporate a resource perspective into their models (Oliver, 1996). Both agency theory (Alchian and Demsetz, 1972) and transactions cost economics (Williamson, 1999) take it as axiomatic that the way a firm is managed and enabled to compete is affected by the way it is structured. Such a perspective draws attention to the kind of generic or dedicated asset regime a firm may establish. However, it is the strategic choice perspective that goes furthest in recognizing the close identity of organization structure and firm capability. In a reassertion of the contingency principle, Chandler (1990, 1992) contends that the choice of organizational form determines a firm's efficiency and long-term survival in different industrial and technological contexts. In this section, we highlight how such structural configurations delimit the range and type of capabilities a firm may effectively and efficiently create.

GLE Capabilities

GLEs are generally successful in their primary mission of establishing national capacity. Moreover, they have been profitable and, typically, financially stable. However, these accomplishments have often been achieved at the cost of inefficiency and entrepreneurial weakness. McVey (1992:28) suggests Singaporean SOEs "show signs of sinking into bureaucratic routine." Wade (1990:304) reports a widely held 'culture of pessimism' about government enterprise within Taiwanese business circles. He notes that calls for restructuring and privatization are based upon the perception that GLEs have not been entrepreneurially dynamic. Ownership changes through privatization do not appear to have ameliorated these perceived deficiencies. Lim notes that privatized entities have maintained strong links with the state and that assets were often distributed to "privileged, politically well-connected members of indigenous communities" (1996:97). Thus, GLEs have a mixed performance record.

Close government ties profoundly influence the size and composition of GLE asset bases. A soft budget constraint and a close government relationship promote asset growth (Averch and Johnson, 1962). Over-investment is also indicated by public choice literature, which suggests that government-related agencies have a propensity to empire-build and accrete activities beyond their original mission. In Asia these organizational phenomena manifested themselves in states that adopted a variant of the Japanese industrial policy model and of directed investments toward selected sectors. Resources were often allocated without regard to market demand or a firm's cash flows. For example, industrial programs designed to establish automobile and aerospace sectors were promoted as policy makers sought to repeat earlier successes in labor intensive sectors (World Bank, 1993). The initiatives often created over-capacity rather than competitive industries. The Asian Finacial crisis of 1997 curtailed the worst excesses of these programs, but did not end them entirely.

On the one hand, some analysts such as Wade (1990) view Asian industrial policy favorably and see GLEs as essential tools in the process of industrialization. GLEs were particularly successful absorbers of technology and manufacturing processes that were pioneered elsewhere (Hobday, 1995). In this regard, GLEs pioneered the process of technology catch-up in state favoured sectors, but GLEs did not face strong incentives to carefully allocate resources to the most profitable ventures. While successful at assimilating mature technologies, GLEs did not move down the product life cycle toward the product initiation stage. Rather GLEs proved more adept at implementing projects favoured by governments than in developing organizational structures and processes (Noble, 1998).

FBG Capabilities

FBGs enjoy advantages and disadvantages with respect to asset accumulation and capability creation. On the one hand, coupling ownership and control creates a powerful incentive for owner-managers to manage their operations efficiently and profitably. On the other hand, such tight control also allows majority owners to adopt inefficient practices that reflect their own particularistic values and interests. The coupling of ownership and control also has significant negative implications regarding a firm's ability to raise capital and manage risk (Carney and Gedajlovic, 2002b).

Since they have long operated in hostile business environments, FBGs have developed substantial personalized social capital. Such capital may be the FBGs most valuable asset. Lasserre and Schutte (1995) attribute FBG success to their carefully cultivated personal connections or 'guanxi' (Fukuyama,

1995) and the ability to exploit market imperfections based upon temporary scarcity or arising from access to privileged contacts and other non-publicly available information. Park and Luo (2001) suggest that Chinese firms develop and utilize guanxi as a strategic mechanism to overcome competitive and resource disadvantages by cooperating and reciprocating favours with resource gatekeepers. Guillen (2000) suggests that the business group's guanxi is especially important in asymmetric trading environments; that is, where states pursue nationalistic development policies aimed at protecting their domestic firms. Guanxi facilitates business groups acquiring the bureaucratic permissions needed to secure cooperation with foreign business partners. From this perspective, FBGs serve as resource conduits for inward and outward trading relations. Khanna and Palepu (1997) claim that business groups create value in underdeveloped institutional settings by imitating the functions of several institutions that are present in advanced economies. For example, a business group that has a reputation for enforcing contracts may use its reputation for reliability to enter new businesses even if those businesses are completely unrelated. As Khanna and Palepu put it: "because the misdeeds of one company in a group will damage the prospects of the other, all the group companies have credibility when they promise to honor their agreements with any single partner. They (business groups) provide a haven where property rights are respected" (1997:17). Both guanxi and institutional void filling are a function of trust in an individual's reputation and the personalized nature of the FBG configuration supports this strategic orientation.

However, the FBG propensity for capital dispersion weighs against success in capital intensive industries. There is growing consensus that FBGs are at a disadvantage in developing proprietary strategic assets and multiple functional capabilities needed to compete in oligopolistic product markets and technologically dynamic industries (Redding, 2000; Carney and Gedajlovic, 2002a). Chandler (1990) contends that lack of managerial capacity limits the ability of personally managed firms to compete internationally due to the lack of coordination and monitoring capabilities needed to manage geographically distant and dispersed business activities. In short, the organizational form utilized by FBGs limits both the entrepreneurial incentive and the managerial capacity to develop and coordinate proprietary and complex assets.

Chaebol Capabilities

At the outset of industrialization, chaebol possessed few strategic assets. In an environment of resource scarcity, the South Korean state charted an investment-driven (Porter, 1990) development trajectory aimed at accumulating a technologically advanced industrial base. To this end, chaebol structured a range of foreign alliances, joint ventures partnerships and licensing in an active strategy of technical learning and absorption to catch-up with more advanced nations (Hobday, 1995). There can be little doubt that chaebol were successful in this goal. Chaebol were organized as generalists established to leverage scarce managerial skills in mid-range technology and especially heavy industries such as construction, civil engineering, shipbuilding and automobile manufacture. Later, chaebols' generalist orientation and absorptive capacity facilitated a gradual and continuous upgrading in the technological scope of their operations to incorporate consumer electronics, and semi-conductors and other electronic components. In each case, chaebol were positioned as low-cost, high-quality producers based upon the establishment of minimum efficient scale plants. Many chaebol also created global distribution and marketing networks. Many concentrated in emerging markets such as Eastern Europe.

However, chaebol have been slow to exit declining businesses, and their corporate scope has become very broad. Initially, their growth and technology acquisition strategy spread scarce Korean managerial talent to new industries. However, the logic of linking increasingly unrelated businesses becomes more and more questionable. With close government ties and operating under a soft budget constraint, chaebol managers were not confronted with a profit-growth trade off and had little incentive to restructure their operations. Many chaebol are now financially indebted and in possession of a surfeit of largely generic and tangible assets concentrated in mature, overcapacity markets.

Consequently, their absorptive capacity strategies, as well new technology initiation strategies, are stalled. While chaebol appear to posses sufficient organizational capabilities, new and promising businesses are starved of both internal and external capital needed for growth. Like other states in the region, South Korea has recognized the importance of technological innovation, as distinct from technological imitation, but chaebol continue to experience difficulties in crafting incentives that would propel them into the initiating phase of the product life cycle.

A residual paternalism creates a poor fit between the demands of large-scale industry and the centralized and personalized nature of chaebol hierarchies, which produces a continuing 'net drag on efficiency' (Fukuyama, 1995:144). A conservative managerial emphasis upon control and discipline has mitigated productivity improvements (Young, 1995). Consequently, Chaebol's international production and marketing assets are weighted in unfavorable industrial positions. For example, chaebol production capability remains heavily dependent upon OEM manufacturing. Their own brand positions are focused in mature and price sensitive segments. Bloom (1994:149) concludes that chaebols have become international "in a way that denies them many of the major benefits" of being international.

Keiretsu & Kaisha Capabilities

With respect to capabilities, a great strength of the keiretsu and kaisha alliance system is its capacity to forge long-term relations with business partners. In such a context, the investors of financial capital are not very sensitive to minor firm performance variations, which affords a firm the opportunity to adopt a longer-term orientation toward the creation and development of resources and competencies (Kester, 1992). Firms and their business partners also have the opportunity to develop trust and forbearance with respect to inter-firm transfers. Most importantly, firms are provided with the ability to create and invest in highly productive dedicated assets (Hill, 1993) that are advantageous in industries that are characterised by technical complexity (Dyer, 1996).

The reciprocal nature of the incentives under the keiretsu configuration may be expected to produce firm advantages in capital intensive, technologically complex industries characterised by predictable or continuous environmental changes that do not disrupt the elaborate lattice of inter-firm arrangements. Keiretsu are especially successful at incremental change, as indicated by their commitment to continuous operational improvement, but are less inclined to initiate frame-braking innovations (Boeyer and Hollingsworth, 1997).

On the other hand, reciprocal relations create difficulties for firms in industries facing discontinuous change and uncertainty. Uncertainty and discontinuous change create risks that suppliers of capital to alliance firms are not well-equipped to bear and pose demands for restructuring that stakeholders are often loathe to confront (Dore, 1998). Generally, the culture of reciprocity and the norms of stakeholder consultation attenuate innovation and restructuring processes. With few exceptions, keiretsu have not been very successful in creating firms that can harness the full potential of the new economy and effectively motivate knowledge workers who tend towards individualism (Fukuyama, 1995). Similarly, such firms have not been overly successful in engendering innovation based upon entrepreneurship (Yoshimura and Anderson, 1999). In this regard, incentives stemming from multi-stakeholder relations and the need for parties to consider the impact of their actions on others may reinforce the cultural dispositions of a society which engendered alliance capitalism.

CBG Capabilities

While business groups are becoming a dominant enterprise form (Child, 2000; Keister, 1998), there is little published work on how they develop capabilities. Despite enormous social and economic problems, China at the end of the 20th century is arguably better positioned to compete in world markets than were Japanese firms in 1945 or FBGs in the 1950s and 1960s. CBGs are presently in their nascent stage of development, and current environmental conditions provide clues to their propensity for capability development. It is quite evident that China is in possession of substantial natural resources. Like the economies of Southeast Asia, the agricultural and mineral extraction industries are likely to produce a range large energy and mining enterprises that are closely linked to the State. Perhaps more decisive are the massive but latent power of China's human resources.

The persistence of institutional weaknesses such as ambiguous property rights suggests that, like the FBGs, social capital and guanxi cultivation will be a necessary capability (Park and Luo, 2001). However, a continuing state bureaux and party monitoring role suggests that the State will pursue objectives related to technology transfer and other distinct strategic goals, depending on the organization. In one scenario CBGs may operate like chaebol as mechanisms for absorptive capacity. However, many CBGs possess greater financial autonomy than chaebol did in their formative phases. The role of the Chinese Communist Party adds a political and moral dimension (Granovetter, 1994) and can impose certain strategic goals because of the ability to influence senior appointments. In this regard CBGs may develop along the lines of GLEs. In sum, CBGs have the potential to develop in different directions, and it is unclear which developmental path will be taken.

Global Commodity Chain Capabilities

The trading organizations that are so vital to the efficient functioning of global commodity chains represent an interesting case of capability development. From a governance perspective they possess many of the ownership characteristics of FBGs. They are largely owner-operated, entrepreneurial enterprises. However, rather than developing diversified business holdings they have focused upon diversifying the geographical scope of their trading activities. Like the FBGs, a core asset for traders is the development of 'personalised' social capital, or reputation.

One element of this capital is the traders' longstanding links with downstream foreign buyers, which is based upon years of successful export transactions (Gereffi, 1994). The second element is relationships with upstream agents that control access to production resources such as labour, land, and bureaucratic permissions, such as export quotas. The ability to cultivate favourable relationships with the bureaucracies in newly industrializing, state-dominated economies has long been recognized as a core competence for enterprises operating in weak institutional environments (Khanna and Palepu, 1997). However, the capacity for reputably entering and enforcing contracts goes beyond implicit contracts with the bureaucracy, but extends to relationships with producer elements in the commodity chain.

The capacity for effective contracting provides a range of qualities valued by downstream clients, including strict variable cost containment, low overhead, product diversity, capacity utilization, low information costs, and swift adjustment to changing volume requirements (Carney, 1998b). The production system consists of a generic asset base with the utilization of few dedicated assets.

A key advantage of low asset specificity is that firms and subcontractors are kept at full capacity. Firms with generalized assets can switch production rapidly to serve quite different product markets. Variation in demand volumes can be met by subcontracting or by adding additional labor. The system has numerical flexibility; when absolute volumes become too great, firms quickly drop less profitable lines. Generic assets permit firms to enter and exit niches in response to small price movements. There is little incentive for a firm to grow in these circumstances, so the optimal size of a firm remains small and firms carry little unproductive slack (Carney, 1998b).

However, this contractual division of labour has the effect of segmenting the value chain into tightly sealed compartments. The transfer of knowledge between production and downstream stages is largely unidirectional. Specifically, traders and downstream buyers facilitate the diffusion of best practice production techniques to the production system as a whole, which improves the market for downstream buyers. However, producers presently lack the organizational capability to internalize the resources needed to move downstream. Gereffi (1994) suggests that the traders have begun to move down the value chain into retail and design, and points to the development of local (within Asia) retail chains.

Porter (1990) suggests that competitive advantage dependent solely upon the exploitation of low factor costs is vulnerable to competition from other lower cost regions and nations. Arguably, continued access to low cost labor removes the incentive for networked firms to develop other, deeper, organizational capabilities. In the absence of mechanisms for making discontinuous adjustments the risk that down stream production networks remain technologically dependent. The latter threat reflects a weakness of networks with respect to coordinated adaptability (Williamson, 1990). One solution to the problem is vertical integration or the emergence of coordinating firms (Harrison, 1994). The region's business groups could undertake this task, but outside of Japan and Korea few have shown an interests in developing capabilities in this area.

CONCLUSION

The stock of Asian organizational configurations profoundly reflects the region's history. At the close end of WWII, Asian economies were damaged by war and faced the challenge of reconstruction in the context of cold war politics. Entrepreneurial and organizational responses to this environment were remarkably adept. Today, the absolute efficiency of Asian organizational configurations have significantly depleted Western economies of much manufacturing activity and has contributed to the development of modern, affluent societies where per capita incomes, in Japan and some NIES, surpass those of many OECD countries, such as Canada and the UK.

In the post-WWII period characterized by underdeveloped national systems of innovation, lacking stimulation from sophisticated local demand and located far from the main sources of innovation, firms were dependent on others for the core capabilities needed to break into international markets. Consequently, firms who succeeded were those willing to develop substantial absorptive capacity through relational mechanisms such as alliances, joint ventures, licensing, OEM/subcontracting and imitation (Hobday, 1995). To rapidly learn and catch-up with more advanced firms and to manage the wide range of transactions and commercial constraints that are associated with relational strategies, firms developed correspondingly complex corporate structures.

Housed within these complex structures are arrayed relatively simple organizational subunits that responded to the structural imperatives associated with latecomer industrialization. Characterized by low task complexity and routine technology, managers had little need for large support staffs or elaborate technostructures (Mintzberg, 1979). With product market strategies focused upon prices and costs, managers could rely upon centralized organizational structures with low horizontal complexity and vertical coordination based upon rules or personalized authority. In commodity markets governed by rapid price movements and lacking the reach to influence distant markets, managers did not develop extensive planning, control and marketing infrastructures. Because many functions such as R&D, logistics, distribution, and marketing were performed by business partners, information processing requirements were relatively low and managers did not perceive the need for complex lateral coordination mechanisms or an extensive middle management to implement such systems (Galbraith, 1977).

Simple organizational configurations were both efficient and flexible tools for the purposes of technological catch-up. Moreover, the fit between the structural imperatives of latecomer industrialization and organizational configurations that facilitated catch-up also permitted firms to cultivate a range of globally competitive capabilities. In several industries, most notably electronics, firms incrementally internalised high-quality, high-reliability manufacturing and design capabilities (Hobday, 1995; Hobday, Cawson and Kim, 2001). However, the signature capability developed by the regions firms is skill in relational contracting and the management of interorganizational relations. These skills stem from coping with institutional voids (Khanna and Palepu, 1997), but also reflect intangible skills in acquiring technological, financial and commercial resources (Gulati, 1998). Relatedly, as many anecdotal studies attest, the region produced a plethora of risk-taking entrepreneurs that have prevailed in often hostile operating environments. Finally, as firms from the first-tier NIEs organize several industries in the second tier NIEs and other emerging markets, we see that firms in the region have developed international capabilities with the capacity to transfer their technological and managerial capabilities to new and difficult environments (Hu, 1995).

However, as of these firms approach and reach the technological frontier, they confront competition from emerging economies that have joined the latecomer queue. In this context, sustained competitive advantage must increasingly come from the creation and commercialisation of locally created proprietary assets. In this new innovation-driven stage of economic development, a more diverse set of organizational vehicles is likely to be required to support the needs of firms which must now develop their own technologies rather than exploit technologies developed elsewhere.

Organization theory suggests firms adopt business practices and develop organizing routines (Nelson and Winter, 1982) that strongly reflect institutional environment and technical contingencies prevailing at their founding (Starbuck, 1965). These founding or 'nascent' contextual conditions imprint on firms a structural configuration that creates an administrative heritage (Bartlett and Ghoshal, 1989). Such structural configurations provide firms with initial competitive advantage but may leave firms ill equipped to meet the environmental challenges of a subsequent era (Carney and Gedajlovic, 2002a). Our understanding of organization theory suggests that the administrative heritage of latecomer firms presents serious challenges to managers.

Numerous writers have iterated the range of deficiencies exhibited by many of Asia's dominant configurations. For example, most lack the range of capabilities needed to discover, develop and commercialise complex technical systems, capital goods and innovative products. Few firms in the region have developed or acquired the downstream distribution assets or brand capital to compete in international markets. With the conspicuous exception of Japan, most firms remain centred in the lower value-added stages of the value chain. Because of the depths to which the administrative heritage been institutionalised, it may be that something akin to a paradigm shift that is needed to develop the business and organizational models necessary to participate and prosper at the technological frontier. This is not to suggest that Asian firms need to emulate Western organizational models used in knowledge-intensive sectors, such as strategic business units, matrix organizations, and professional bureaucracies. Rather, Asian firms will probably need to create Made-in-Asia organizational solutions for this task.

One legacy of latecomer industrialization particularly reinforces existing relational capabilities and perhaps blurs the magnitude of the challenge facing managers. The region's bank-dominated corporate financial systems that initially rationed and directed scarce capital to valuable 'catch-up' opportunities also put a premium upon relational contracting capabilities (Rajan and Zingales, 1998). Firms that prospered in the early phase of government-led industrialization were those focusing on investment-intensive physical infrastructure and export-led development opportunities (Carney and Geadjlovic, 2001). As their economies matured, the returns from these ventures diminished but continued reliance upon relational contracting produced a misallocation of resources, culminating in the Asian financial crisis and the long-lived Japanese economic stasis. Whether incumbent firms can adapt to new environmental imperatives by revitalizing their capability sets, or whether a nascent population of new firms can emerge and grow, are open questions.

Existing theory is equivocal on these questions. A number of recent accounts of Asian organization have focused upon their unchanging and inertial qualities (Lincoln, Gerlach and Ahmadjian, 1996). Several writers argue that despite the forces of globalization and changes in their local business systems, Asian firms exhibit a remarkable structural continuity (Fligstein and Freeland, 1995; Boyer and Hollingsworth, 1997; Whitley, 1999). Path-dependence perspectives suggest that incumbent firms have both the power and incentive to impede changes that threaten their dominant economic positions (Bebchuk and Roe, 1999).

On the other hand, recent developments in institutional theory suggest that institutions and organizations co-evolve (Carney and Gedajlovic, 2002). Peng (2002) argues that the incumbent firm's relational strategies in emergent markets become self-limiting as the institutional environment becomes more codified. Subsequently, the resource-based strategic choices of foreign and new entrant firms gradually grow in legitimacy. If the managers of these firms possess less cognitive commitment to relational strategies, then it is to these firms that we should look for the paradigm shift in organizational models in the region. Ultimately, these are empirical questions.

REFERENCES

Abegglen, J. and Stalk, G. 1985. *Kaisha: the Japanese Corporation*. New York: Basic Books.

Alchian, A.A. and Demsetz, H. 1972. Production, information costs and economic organization. *American Economic Review*, 62: 777-795.

Ampalaver-Brown, R. 1995. Introduction: Chinese business in an institutional and historical perspective. In R.A. Brown, (ed.), *Chinese Business Enterprise in Asia* (pp. 1-26). London: Routledge.

Amsden, A.H. 1997. South Korea: Enterprising groups and enterpreneurial government. In A.D. Chandler, F. Amatori and T. Hikino (eds.), *Big Business and the Wealth of Nations*. Cambridge: Cambridge University Press.

Amsden, A.H. 1989. *Asia's Next Giant: South Korea and Late Industrialization*. New York: Oxford University Press.

Aoki, M. 1988. *Information, Incentives, and Bargaining in the Japanese Economy*. New York: Cambridge University Press.

Averch, H. and Johnson, L.L. 1962. The behaviour of the firm under regulatory restraint. *American Economic Review*, 1053-11069.

Azuni, K. and Macmillan, C.J. 1975. Culture and organization structure: A comparison of Japanese and British Organization Structure. *International Studies of Management and Organization*, 35-4.

Bartlett, C. and Ghoshal, S. 1988. *Managing Across Borders: The Transnational Solution*. Cambridge, MA: Harvard Business School Press.

Best, M. 1990. *The New Industrial Competition: Institutions of Industrial Restructuring*. Cambridge, MA: Harvard University Press.

Biggart, N.W. and Hamilton, G. 1992. On the limits of a firm-based theory to explain business networks: The Western bias of neoclassical economics. In N. Nohria and R. Eccles (eds.), *Networks and Organizations: Structure, Form and Action*. Cambridge, MA: Harvard Business School Press.

Bloom, M.D.H. 1994. Globalization and the Korean electronics industry; A chandlerian perspective. In H. Schutte (ed.), *The Global Competitiveness of the Asian Firm*. New York: St. Martin's Press.

Boyer, R. and Hollingsworth, J.R. 1997. From national embeddedness to spatial and institutional nestednes. In J.R. Hollingsworth and R. Boyer (eds.), *Contemporary Capitalism: The Embeddeness of Institutions*. Cambridge: Cambridge University Press.

Brickley, J.A. and Dark, F.H. 1987. The choice of organizational form: The case of franchising. *Journal of Financial Economics*, 18: 401-420.

Carney, M. 1998a. A management capacity constraint? Barriers to the development of the China family business. *Asia-Pacific Journal of Management*, 15(2): 137-162.

Carney, M. 1998b. The competitiveness of networked production: The role of asset specificity and trust. *Journal of Management Studies*, 35(4): 457-480.

Carney, M. and Gedajlovic, E. 1991. Vertical integration in franchising systems: Agency theory and resource explanations. *Strategic Management Journal*, 12: 607-629.

Carney, M. and Gedajlovic, E. 2000. East Asian financial systems and the transition from investment driven to innovation driven economic development. *International Journal of Innovation Management*, 4(3): 253-276.

Carney, M. and Gedajlovic, E. 2001. Corporate governance and firm capabilities: A comparison of managerial, alliance, and personal capitalisms. *Asia Pacific Journal of Management*, 18: 337-356.

Carney, M. and Gedajlovic, E. 2002a. The co-evolution of institutional environments and organizational strategies: The rise of family business groups in the ASEAN region. *Organization Studies*, 23(1): 1-29.

Carney, M. and Gedajlovic, E. 2002b. The coupling of ownership and control and the allocation of financial resources: Evidence from Hong Kong. *Journal of Management Studies*, 39(1): 123-146.

Chalmers, J. 1982. *MITI and the Japanese Miracle*, Stanford University Press.

Chandler, A.D. 1962. *Strategy and Structure*. Cambridge, MA: MIT Press.

Chandler, A.D. 1977. *The Visible Hand: The Managerial Revolution in American Business*. Cambridge, MA: Belknap Press.

Chandler, A.D. 1990. *Scale and Scope: The Dynamics of Industrial Capitalism*. Cambridge, MA: Harvard University Press.

Chandler, A.D. 1992. Managerial enterprise and competitive capabilities. *Business History Review*, 34: 11-41.

Chandler, A.D. 1997. The functions of the HQ in a multibusiness firm. In R. Rumelt, D. Schendel and R.J. Teece (eds.), *Fundamental Issues in Strategy: A Research Agenda* (pp. 323-360). Boston Harvard Business School Press.

Chen, M. 1995. *Asian Management Systems: Chinese, Japanese and Korean Styles of Business*. London: Routledge.

Child, J. 1994. *Management in China during the Age of Reform*. Cambridge, England: Cambridge University Press.

Child, J. 2000. Management and organization in China: Key trends and issues. In J.T. Li, A.S. Tsui and E. Weldon (eds.), *Management and Organizations in the Chinese Context* (pp. 33-62). Basingstoke: Macmillan.

Child, J. and Mansfield, R. 1972. Technology, size and organization structure. *Sociology* (pp. 369-393).

Chirot, D. and Reid, A. (eds.) 1997. *Essential Outsiders: Chinese and Jews in the Modern Transformation of Southeast Asia and Central Europe*. Seattle: University of Washington Press.

Claessens, S., Djankov, S. and Lang, L.H.P. 2000. The separation of ownership and control in East Ownership Corporations. *Journal of Financial Economics*, 81-112.

Demsetz, H. and Lehn, K. 1985. The structure of corporate ownership. *Journal of Political Economy*, 93: 1155-1177.

Deyo, F.C. (ed.) 1987. *The Political Economy of the New Asian Industrialism*. Ithaca: Cornell University Press.

Drabble, J.H. and Drake, P.J. 1982. The British agency houses in Malaysia: Survival in a changing world. *Journal of South East Asian Studies*, 12(2): 297-328.

Dore, R. 1998. Asian crisis and the future of the Japanese model. *Cambridge Journal of Economics*, 22(6): 773-787.

Dyck, A. 2001. Privatization and Corporate governance: Principles, evidence and future challenges. *World Bank Research Observer*, 16(1): 59-84.

Dyer, J.H. 1996. Does governance matter? Keiretsu alliances and asset specificity as sources of Japanese competitive advantage. *Organization Science*, 7(6): 649-666.

Fama, E.F. and Jensen, M.C. 1983. The separation of ownership and control. *Journal of Law and Economics*, 26: 301-328.

Fligstein, N. and Freeland, R. 1995. Theoretical and comparative perspectives on corporate organization. *Annual Review of Sociology*, 21: 21-40.

Frenkel, S.J. 2001. Globalization, athletic footwear commodity chains and employment relations in China. *Organization Studies*, 22(4): 531-562.

Fukuyama, F. 1995. *Trust: The Social Virtues and the Creation of Prosperity*. New York: Free Press.

Galbraith, J.R. 1977. *Organizational Design*. Reading, MA: Addison Wesley.

Gedajlovic, E.R. and Shapiro, D.M. 2001. National systems of corporate governance. *Global Focus*, 13(1): 143-157.

Gedajlovic, E.R. and Shapiro, D.M. 1998. Management and ownership effects: Evidence from five countries. *Strategic Management Journal*, 19: 533-553.

Gedajlovic, E.R. and Shapiro, D.M. (In Press). Ownership and firm profitability in Japan. *The Academy of Management Journal*.

Gerlach, M.L. 1992. *Alliance Capitalism: The Social Organization of Japanese Business*. Berkeley: University of California Press.

Gereffi, G. 1994. The organization of buyer-driven global commodity chains: How US retailers shape overseas production networks. In G. Gereffi and M. Korzeniewicz (eds.), *Commodity Chains and Global Capitalism*. Westport, CT: Greenwod Press.

Glasmeir, A. 1994. Flexibility and adjustment: The Hong Kong watch industry and global change. *Growth & Change*, 25: 223-246.

Granovetter, M. 1994. Business groups. In N.J. Smelser and R. Swedberg (eds.), *Handbook of Economic Sociology*. Princeton, NJ: Princeton University Press.

Goold, M. and Campbell, A. 1987. *Strategies and Styles: The Role of the Centre in Diversified Corporations*. Oxford: Basil Blackwell.

Guillen, M.F. 2000. Business groups in emerging economies: A resource based view. *Academy of Management Journal*, 43(3): 362-380.

Gulati, R. 1998. Alliances and networks. *Strategic Management Review*, 19: 293-317.

Hall, R.H. and Xu, W. 1990. Run silent, run deep: A note on the ever pervasive influence of cultural differences on organizations in the Far East. *Organization Studies*, 11: 596-616.

Hamilton, G.G. 2000. Reciprocity and control: The organization of Chinese family-owned conglomerates. In H.W.-C. Yeung and K. Olds (eds.), *Globalization of Chinese Business Firms* (pp. 55-74). New York: St Martin's Press.

Hamilton, G.G. and Biggart, N.W. 1988. Market, culture and authority: A comparative analysis of management in the Far East. *American Journal of Sociology*, 94: S52-S94.

Harrison. 1994. *Lean and Mean: The Changing Landscape of Corporate Power in the Age of Flexibility*. New York: Basic Books.

Hobday, M. 2000. East vs south east Asian innovation systems: Comparing OEM and TNC-led growth in electronics. In *Technological Learning and Economic Development: The Experience of the Asian NIEs*. Cambridge: Cambridge University Press.

Hobday, M.L. 1995. East Asian latecomer firms: Learning the technology of electronics. *World Development*, 23: 1171-1193.

Hobday, M. 1994. Technological learning in Singapore: A test case of leapfrogging. *Journal of Developmental Studies*, 30: 851-858.

Hobday, M., Cawson, A. and Kim, S.R. 2001. Governance of technology in the electronics industries of East and Southeast Asia. *Technovation*, 21: 209-226.

Hodder, R. 1996. *Merchant Princes of the East: Cultural Delusions, Economic Success and the Overseas Chinese in Southeast Asia*. New York: Wiley.

Hsing, Y. 1996. Blood thicker than water: Interpersonal relations and Taiwanese investment in southern China. *Environment and Planning A*, 28: 2241-2261.

Hu, Y.S. 1995. The international transferability of the firms' advantages. *California Management Review*, 37(4): 73-88.

Jefferson, G.H. and Rawski, T.G. 1996. The paradox of China's industrial reform. In A.E. Safarian and W. Dobson (eds.), *East Asian Capitalism: Diversity and Dynamism*. Toronto: University of Toronto Press.

Kao, J. 1993. The worldwide web of Chinese business. *Harvard Business Review*, 71(2): 24-36.

Khanna, T. and Palepu, K. 1997. Why focused strategies may be wrong for emerging markets. *Harvard Business Review*, 75(5): 41-51.

Krugman, P. 1994. The myth of Asia's miracle. *Foreign Affairs*, 73(6): 62-78.

Koike, K. 1993. Introduction: Business groups in developing economies. *Journal of Developing Economies*, 31(4): 363-378.

Kester, C.W. 1992. Industrial groups as systems of contractual governance. *Oxford Review of Economic Policy*, 8: 24-44.

Keister, L.A. 1998. Engineering growth: Business groups structure and firm performance in China's transition economy. *American Journal of Sociology*, 104: 404-40.

Lall, S. 1990. *Building Industrial Competitiveness in Developing Countries: Organisation for Economic Co-operation and Development*. Paris.

Lawrence, P.R. and Lorsch, J.W. 1969. *Organization and Environment*. Homewood, IL: Irwin.

Lasserre, P. and Schutte, H. 1995. *Strategies for Asia-Pacific*. London: Macmillan.

Lim, L. 1996. Southeast Asian business systems: The dynamics of diversity. In A.E. Safarian and W. Dobson (eds.), *East Asian Capitalism: Diversity and Dynamism*. Toronto: University of Toronto Press.

Lincoln, J.R., Gerlach, M.L. and Ahmadjian, C.L. 1996. Keiretsu networks and corporate performance in Japan. *American Sociological Review*, 61: 67-88.

McVey, R. 1992. The materialisation of the Southeast Asian entrepreneur. In R. McVey (ed.), *Southeast Asian Capitalism*. New York: Cornell University Southeast Asia program.

McNaughton, B. 1997. *The China Circle: Economics and Electronics in the PRC, Taiwan, and Hong Kong*. Washington, D.C.: Brookings Institution.

Mintzberg, H. 1979. *The Structuring of Organizations*. Englewood Cliffs, NJ: Prentice Hall.

Mintzberg, H. and Waters, J.A. 1985. Of strategies, deliberate and emergent. *Strategic Management Journal*, 6: 257-272.

Morikawa, Hidemas. 1997. Japan: Increasing organizational capabilities of large industrial enterprises, 1880–1980s. In A.D. Chandler, F. Amatori and T. Hikinio (eds.), *Big Business and the Wealth of Nations*. New York University Press.

Morikawa, Hidemas. 1992. *Zaibatsu: The Rise and Fall of Family Enterprise Groups in Japan*. University of Tokyo Press.

Nee, V. 1992. Organizational dynamics of market transition: Hybrid forms property rights and mixed economy in China. *Administrative Science Quarterly*, 37(1): 1-27.

Nelson, R.R. and Winter, S.G. 1987. *Evolutionary Theory of Economic Change*. Cambridge, MA: Harvard University Press.

Nickerson, J.A., Hamilton, B.H. and Wada, T. 2001. Market position, resource profile, and governance: Linking Porter and Williamson in the context of international courier and small package services in Japan. *Strategic Management Review*, 22: 251-273.

Noble, G.W. 1998. *Collective Action in East Asia: How Ruling Parties Shape Industrial Policy*. Ithaca: Cornell University Press.

Numazaki, I. 1993. Tainanbang: The rise and growth of a banana-bunch-shaped business group in Taiwan. *The Journal of Developing Economies*, 31(4): 485-511.

Ohsono, T. 1995. *Charting Japanese Industry: A Graphical Guide to Corporate and Market Structures*. London: Cassels.

Oliver, C. 1991. Strategic responses to institutional processes. *Academy of Management Review*, 16: 145-179.

Oliver, C. 1996. Sustainable competitive advantage: Combining institutional and resource based views. *Strategic Management Journal*, 18(9): 697-713.

Orru, M., Biggart, N.W. and Hamilton, G.G. 1991. Organizational isomorphism in East Asia. In W.W. Powell and P. De Maggio (eds.), *The New Institutionalism in Organizational Analysis*. Chicago: University of Chicago Press.

Organization Charts, 1996. *The Structures of 200 Businesses and Nonprofit Organizations*. Maurer, J.G., Nixon, J.M. and Peck, T.W. Detroit: Gale Research.

Ouchi, W.G. 1981. *Theory Z: How American Business Can Meet the Japanese Challenge*. Addison Wesley.

Park, S.H. and Luo, Y. 2001. Guanxi and organizational dynamics organizational networking in Chinese firms. *Strategic Management Journal*, 22: 455-477.

Peng, M. 2002. Institutional changes and strategic choices. *Academy of Management Review* (In press).

Pfeffer, J. and Salancik, G.R. 1978. *The External Control of Organizations: A Resource Dependence Perspective*. New York: Harper & Row.

Porter, M.E. 1990. *The Competitive Advantage of Nations*. New York: Free Press.

Rajan, R.G. and Zingales, L. 1998. Which capitalism? Lessons from the East Asian crisis. *Journal of Applied Corporate Finance*, 11(3): 40-48.

Redding, S.G. 2000. What is Chinese about Chinese Family Business? How Much is Family and How Much is Business. In H.W.-C. Yeung and K. Olds (eds.), Basingstoke: Macmillan Press.

Redding, S.G. 1990. *The Spirit of Chinese Capitalism.* New York: De Gruyter.

Redding, S.G. and Whitley, R.D. 1990. Beyond bureaucracy; A comparative analysis of forms of economic resource co-ordination and control. In S.R. Clegg and S.G. Redding (eds.), *Capitalism in Contrasting Cultures.* New York: de Gruyter.

Robison, R. 1992. Industrialization and the economic and political development of capital. In R. McVey (ed.), *Southeast Asian Capitalism* (pp. 65-89). New York: Cornell University Southeast Asia program.

Sabel, C. 1988. The resurgence of regional economies. In P. Hirst and J. Zeitlin (eds.), *Reversing Regional Decline.* Oxford: Oxford University Press.

Saxenian, A. 1990. Regional networks and the resurgence of Silicon Valley. *California Management Review*, Fall 1990: 89-112.

Schein, E. 1996. *Strategic Pragmatism: The Culture of Singapore's Economic Development Board.* Cambridge, MA: The MIT Press.

Schulze, W., Lubatkin, M., Dino, R. and Buchholtz, A. 2001. Agency relationships in family firms: Theory and evidence. *Organization Science*, 12(2).

Shieh, G.Y. 1992. *"Boss" Island: The Subcontracting Network and Micro-entrepreneurship in Taiwan's Development.* New York: P. Lang.

Shenkar, O. 1991. (ed.), *Organization and Management in China, 1979–1990.* NY: M.E. Sharpe.

Sikorski, D. 1996. 'Public enterprise in the marine industry: A case study of the Keppel Shipyard' Conference on The Asian Multinational Enterprise. National University of Singapore.

Singh, A. 1998. Savings, investment and the corporation in the East Asian miracle. *The Journal of Development Studies*, 34(6): 112-138.

Storry, R. 1982. *A History of Modern Japan.* London: Penguin Books.

Starbuck, W.H. 1965. Organizational growth and development. In J.G. March (ed.), *Handbook of Organizations* (pp. 451-533). Chicago: Rand McNally.

Storper, M. and Walker, R. 1989. *The Capitalist Imperative: Territory, Technology and Growth.* Oxford: Basil Blackwell.

Stubbs, R. 1999. War and economic development: Export oriented industrialization in East and Southeast Asia. *Comparative Politics*, 31(3): 337-355.

Suehiro, A. 1993. Family business reassessed: Corporate structure and late starting industrialization in Thailand. *Journal of Developing Economies*, 31(4): 378-408.

Tam, S. 1990. Centrifugal versus centripetal growth processes; Contrasting ideal types for conceptualizing the development patterns of Chinese and Japanese firms. In S.R. Clegg and S.G. Redding (eds.), *Capitalism in Contrasting Cultures.* New York: de Gruyter.

Thompson, J.D. 1967. *Organizations in Action.* New York: McGraw Hill.

Tseo, G.K.Y. 1996. Chinese economic restructuring: Enterprise development through employee ownership. *Economic and Industrial Democracy*, 17: 243-279.

Twang, Peck Yang. 1998. *The Chinese Business Elite in Indonesia and the Transition to Independence 1940–1950.* Kuala Lumpar: Oxford University Press.

Ungson, G., Steers, R.M. and Park, S.H. 1997. *Korean Enterprise: The Quest for Globalization.* Boston: Harvard Business School Press.

Vogel, E. 1988. *One Step Ahead in China.* Cambridge, MA: Harvard University Press.

Vogel, E. 1991. *The Four Little Dragons: The Spread of Industrialization in East Asia.* Cambridge, MA: Harvard University Press.

Wade, R. 1990. *Governing the Market: Economic Theory and the Role of Government in East Asian Industrialisation.* Princeton, NJ: Princeton University Press.

Weidenbaum, M. and Hughes, S. 1996. *The Bamboo Network: How Expatriate Chinese Entrepreneurs are Creating a New Economic Superpower in Asia.* New York: Free Press.

Westwood, R. 1997. Harmony and patriarchy: The cultural basis for 'paternalistic headship' among the overseas Chinese. *Organization Studies*, 18(3): 445-480.

Whitley, R. 1999. *Divergent Capitalisms: The Social Structuring and Change of Business Systems*. Oxford: Oxford University Press.

Whitley, R. 1992. *Business Systems in East Asia: Firms, Markets and Societies*. London: Sage.

Wilkinson, B. 1996. Culture, institutions and business in East Asia. *Organization Studies*, 17(3): 421-447.

Williamson, O.E. 1975. *Markets and Hierarchies: Analysis and Antitrust Implications*. New York, NY: Free Press.

Williamson, O.E. 1985. *The Economic Institutions of Capitalism*. New York, NY: Free Press.

Williamson, O.E. 1991. Comparative economic organization: The analysis of discrete structural alternatives. *Administrative Science Quarterly*, 36: 269-296.

Williamson, O.E. 1999. Strategy research: Governance and competence perspectives. *Strategic Management Journal*, 20: 1087-1188.

Williamson, P.J. 1997. Asia's new competitive game. *Harvard Business Review*, Sept.-Oct.: 55-67.

Wong, S.L. 1985. The Chinese family firm: A model. *British Journal of Sociology*, 36(1): 58-72.

World Bank, 1993. *The East Asian Miracle: Economic Growth and Public Policy*. Oxford: Oxford University Press.

Wu, Yuan Li and Wu, Chun. 1980. *Economic development in Southeast Asia: The Chinese dimension*. Stanford, CA: Hoover Institution Press.

Yoshikawa, T. and Gedajlovic, E. 2002. The impact of global capital market exposure and stable ownership on investor relations practices and performance of Japanese firms. *Asia Pacific Journal of Management*, 19: 1.

Yoshihara, K. 1988. *The Rise of Ersatz Capitalism in South-East Asia*. Oxford: Oxford University Press.

Yoshihara, K. 1982. *Sogo Shosha: The Vanguard of the Japanese Economy*. New York: Oxford University Press.

Yoshimura, N. and Anderson, P. 1999. *Inside the Kaisha: Demystifying Japanese Business Behaviour*. Boston, MA: Harvard Business School Press.

Young, A. 1995. The tyranny of numbers: confronting the statistical realities of the East Asian growth experience. *Quarterly Journal of Economics*, August: 641-680.

Zutshi, R.K. and Gibbons, P.T. 1998. The internationalization process of Singapore government-linked companies: A contextual view. *Asia Pacific Journal of Management*, 15(2): 219-247.

Chapter 5

FIRM DIVERSIFICATION IN ASIA

Lu Yuan
Chinese University of Hong Kong

Garry Bruton
Texas Christian University

Hailin Lan
Southern China University of Technology

INTRODUCTION

Diversification has long constituted an important position in both firm strategic management practices and academic research (Ansoff, 1965; Argyres, 1996; Chandler, 1962; Hill, Hitt and Hoskisson, 1992; Palich, Cardinal, and Miller, 2000; Rumelt, 1974; Ramanujam and Varadarajan, 1989; Williamson, 1975). Students of economics and strategic management have developed various theories and perspectives to examine corporate activities relevant to firm diversification (Brush, 1996; Ramanujam and Varadarajan, 1989; Reed and Luffman, 1986; Rumelt, 1974). However, despite diversification being well-researched in Western countries, the topic as an academic inquiry is relatively new in Asia, where environments and business systems have characteristics considerably different from Western society. For example, in contrast to advanced market economies in the West where governments were usually kept away from market, most Asian countries adopted an 'other directed' development strategy in which governments consciously controlled and promoted economic development through policy, regulations, and/or even direct administrative intervention, such as state plans (Berlinger, 1966).

In addition to the distinctiveness of Asian societies vis-à-vis those of the West, there is also great variation among Asian countries themselves. Take an example of GDP per capita. In 2000 Japan, Hong Kong and Singapore entered into the top twenty GNI per capita in the world, varying between $34,210 and $24,740. At the same time, two Asian countries with the largest population in the world, the People's Republic of China (the PRC) and India, had GNI per capita of $840 and $460. A gap exists not only between different countries but also across regions which share similar cultural inheritances. For instance, mainland China, Hong Kong and Taiwan were assumed to operate within Greater China Economic Zone where Chinese traditional culture dominated in social norms and values system. In 2000 GNP per capita in Taiwan and Hong Kong exceeded $14,000 and $24,000, more than 60 and 180 percent over that in mainland China. There is also variation in the economic environments within the Greater China Economic Zone. Taiwan and Hong Kong have had a relatively developed market economy and their governments were largely kept away from business operations. By contrast, in mainland China the overall economic institution is in a transition from a centrally planned economy to a market one. A major characteristic of a transition economy is that the government exerts a strong influence over both macro and micro economic activities by allocation of resources allocation and control of or even direct administrative intervention in business organizations (Chen, 1995; Redding, 1990).

These differences between Western and Asian societies, and among Asian societies, have suggested many questions to scholars studying diversification. For example, does diversification in Asia exhibit the same or similar characteristics as that in Western countries if there are distinctive differences between the two societies? Are Western theories appropriate to the study of firm diversification in Asia? Does the research of Asia's diversification require new context-specific design for the purpose of testing the limits of Western theories and conclusions? Furthermore, given the great discrepancy across Asian countries, will such inter-societal variance within Asia cause organizational differences in terms of firm behavior?

In this chapter we review previous studies of corporate diversification in seven major Asian countries and areas, including mainland China, Taiwan, Hong Kong, Japan, South Korea, Singapore and India. It begins with a brief review of Western theories of firm diversification. The second section will introduce findings from a literature survey of existing empirical studies in the seven Asian countries and areas. Building on literature survey findings, we will in the third section attempt to identify distinctive characteristics of firm diversification in Asia. The final section suggests directions for future research in this subject.

WESTERN BASED AND DOMINANT PARADIGMS OF DIVERSIFICATION RESEARCH

Reed and Luffman (1986) pointed out that the term 'diversification' has had different meanings when research interest varied. Earlier definitions of diversification, such as Gort (1962) and Berry (1975), approached the subject from products or services across industry or market boundaries. Later definitions extended to the means, particularly investment or partnership, which enables a focal organization to achieve growth or reduce overall risk (Hoskisson and Hitt, 1990; Ramanujam and Varadarajan, 1989). Closely related to the definition of diversification is the term 'diversity' that 'describes the extent to which firms are simultaneously active in many distinctive businesses' (Ramanujam and Varadarajan, 1989). Two types of diversity are mostly frequently examined in the literature: product diversification that refers to a firm's entry into a new sector market; and geographical (or international) diversification to a firm's exploration of markets in a new geographical area.

Why do firms diversify? Reed and Luffman (1986) assumed that firms implement diversification to achieve two fundamental objectives: to pursue diversification as an important strategy for growth (Ansoff, 1965) when attractive external opportunities emerged or the speed of expansion was overwhelmingly emphasized (Key, 1997; Williamson, 1966); or to pursue diversification for survival due to the maturity of an existing industry or decline of corporate performance (Hoskisson and Hitt, 1990).

The study of diversification in Western society has long been dominated by economic theories that viewed firm diversification as a more efficient way to maximize economic benefits or to reduce costs. Diversification is attractive to firms because it enables them to create value from taking the cost advantages of the economies of scope; or to avoid risks by concentrating upon a single industry; or to obtain incentives from government favorable taxation policies relevant to specific industries (Hoskisson and Hitt, 1990; Ramanujam and Varadarajan, 1989; Shleifer and Wishny, 1986). A recent development is to draw attention to managerial motives as a force driving firm diversification (Besanko, Dranove, and Shanley, 2000). For instance, agency theory suggests that instead of pursuing economic efficiency or enhancing shareholder wealth, executives are motivated to diversify because they tend to maintain or enhance their positions (Hoskisson and Hitt, 1990). This can help explain why many firms pursued unrelated diversification despite poor conglomerate performance.

As a powerful apparatus to analyze firm diversification, economic theory focused on the relationship between diversification and firm performance. Much attention has been drawn to the configuration of diversification; i.e., structure-performance. For instance, an institutional economic perspective suggests that a multi-divisional form structure (M-form) is more appropriate for firms with diversified businesses than other forms of organizational structure because such an organizational arrangement enables multi-product firms to achieve lower transaction costs. As a result, the M-form is assumed to lead to better performance (Williamson, 1975).

However, an economic model of firm diversification is largely based upon a precondition of free market competition that conceives of ideal conditions for competition. This paradigm assumes that the market is open and free so that economic units, individual or collective (such as firms), act as independent and dispersed players who have complete knowledge of all offers to buy and sell. Under this assumption, price is the only leverage to determine a transaction, while any other factors, such as social relations, are commonly regarded as 'external'. Although features of social and institutional influences on firm decision making were indeed taken into account in Western theories, they are usually treated as external to a focal organization, which is assumed to be able to take strategic responses in order to achieve its purposes. For instance, government antitrust policy usually motivates firms to enter into a new business. However, to an economist, government influences are categorized as 'regulatory'. As a result, diversification is supposed to be a choice for firms to fit to this external factor.

The above economic model that assumed the market as ideal and universal has been questioned by sociologists who argue that the economy is embedded in social relations and is not the aggregate activity of isolated individuals (Granovetter, 1985). Studies of management practices in Asia suggest that markets in Asian countries differ considerably from that in the US (Orrù, Biggart and Hamilton, 1997; Whitley, 1992). As Biggart argued, 'Organizations and markets and other forms of social organization in Asia are built on groups and networks – of people and firms – not on the individual actors hypothesized by Western market theorists' (Biggart, 1997: 17). Firms in these countries were not isolated and independent from others, but formed complex networks with interest groups, such as governments, buyers, and sellers. Moreover, internal organizational arrangements within Asian firms were also characterized by intra-firm networks, considerably different from M-form structure. These studies suggested that in Asia diversification, as a firm-level strategy, might follow a different path from a Western model due to Asia's unique societal and traditional environments.

REVIEW OF EMPIRICAL STUDIES ON DIVERSIFICATION IN ASIA

Research on firm diversification in Asia is relatively new. In this section, we will review empirical studies of firm diversification in seven countries and regions, including the People's Republic of China (the PRC), Taiwan, Hong Kong, Japan, South Korea, Singapore, and India. Through several rounds of searches on ProQuest using the keywords of 'diversification' or 'diversified' together with 'Asia' and a country/region's name, we obtained a list of publications relevant to the topic. We then limited our focus on academic papers with empirical findings and eventually identified 19 entries of publication, including four comparative studies. Table 1 summarizes the key points of the empirical studies reviewed.

The People's Republic of China (the PRC)

The People's Republic of China committed to state socialism after the Communist Party took over the power in 1949. Till the late 1970s, China imitated the former Soviet Union's model to establish a centrally planned economy. Government agencies not only decided what a factory produced, but also issued planning quota on output quantities. Under this system, diversification was not determined by managers but by government ministries or bureaus.

In 1978 China embarked on an economic reform program that attempted to transfer her economic system from a centrally planned economy to a market oriented one. China's reform program was characterized with an evolutionary change, starting with a decentralization of decision making from government to enterprise management. With the progress of decentralization, enterprises began to enjoy autonomy in arrangement of production and selection of products and gradually sought opportunities to enter in new businesses. As a result, diversification became a popular strategy to achieve growth, particularly in the earlier 1990s (Yin, 1999). Associated with this development, many enterprises transformed from single product factories to multi-product business corporations and business groups, which played a strategic role in the national or local economies.

Although diversification has been fashionable in mainland China in the last few years, little research on it has been published. Guthrie (1997) conducted a quantitative method to analyze 81 industrial firms and found that diversified firms had poorer economic performance. This finding was consistent with that in the US (Hoskisson and Hitt, 1990). Guthrie (1997) also noted governmental influence on diversification. Firms controlled by a higher level of governments were more likely to diversify than those at a lower level. This finding suggests that old institutional influences remained in place during China's transformation period.

Li and his colleagues conducted an exploratory study of eight cases and found there were two motivations to drive managers to choose diversification. The first was to build resource and skill necessary for firm growth. The second was an attempt to manage external environment by entering into a new business. Similar to what Guthrie (1997) found, Li and his colleagues also noted that governments, both central and local, played an important role in a firm's decision on diversification. For instance, state-owned enterprises were more

Table 1. Diversification in Asia: Empirical studies and their findings

Author(s)	Location	Sample size	Research theme	Research findings
Guthrie (1997)	Mainland, the People's Republic of China (PRC)	81 industrial firms	• Influences of contextual factors (performance and location of administrative level) on diversification	• Poor economic health organizations more likely adopted diversification • Firms at upper levels of administrative hierarchies more likely adopted diversification
Li, Li and Tan (1998)	Mainland, the PRC	Case study of eight firms	• Purposes and motivation of diversification	• State owned and non-state owned diversify with different motives • Diversification is used as a growth strategy, to capture opportunities and deploy skill and resources
Lu et al. (2000)	Mainland, the PRC	Case study of 15 firms	• Contextual factors and diversification	• Foundation conditions and ownership structures had an impact on a firm's degree of diversification
Wan (1998)	Hong Kong	81, including 47 multinational corporations	• Impact of international and industrial diversification on performance	• Positive impact on profitability stability and sales growth but not on profitability • Industrial diversification enhanced profitability stability but reduces profitability
Hamilton (1997)	Taiwan	96 large business groups	• Ownership, organizational structure, and diversification	• Family ownership has an influence on firm diversification • Network-like organizational structure
Aw and Batra (1998)	Taiwan	Data drawn from Taiwanese Census of Manufacturers	• Product and geographical market diversification	• Large firms are more diversified while small and medium sized firms diversified into the export market rather than different product markets
Geringer, Tallman and Olsen (2000)	Japan	108 largest Japanese manufacturing multinationals	• The relationship of performance with product and international diversification	• Product diversity strategies varied between keiretsu and non-keiretsu firms but performance is not much different • Performance also varied over time considerably but strategies less variable

Table 1. (Continued.)

Author(s)	Location	Sample size	Research theme	Research findings
Ito and Rose (1994)	Japan	342 spinoffs	• Spinoffs and organizational arrangement between parent and subsidiaries	• Product diversity has weak effects on firm performance only in one time period while international diversification has negative profitability and positive growth consequences in some periods • A profitable parents tend to control and nurture its subsidiary, providing more protection • Profitable subsidiaries become more self-sustainable
Chang and Hong (2000)	South Korea	317 groups with a total of 12019 affiliated companies	• Corporate effects on performance of individual business units in a different institutional setting	• At the group level, both related and unrelated diversification achieved higher performance although these effects over time periods • Group corporate headquarters played a critical to coordinate resource allocation and sharing activities among affiliated units
Chang, See Jin, and Choi, Unghwan (1988)	South Korea	182	• Diversification-structure-performance configuration	• Group-affiliated firms show superior economic performance
Khanna and Palepu (2000)	India	1309	• Diversification-structure-performance relationship	• A quadratic relationship between performance and group diversification • Group structure added value
Lim and Teck (1995)	Singapore	41	• Diversification-performance relationship	• Negative moderating effect of size on the diversification-performance relationship
Chen and Ho (2000)	Singapore	145	• Ownership, diversification and performance	• No correlation between insider ownership and the level of diversification

Table 1. (Continued.)

Author(s)	Location	Sample size	Research theme	Research findings
				• A weak negative correlation between outside block ownership and the level of diversification • Diversified firms are valued less than single segment firms
Comparative studies				
Feenstra, Yang and Hamilton (1999)	South Korea, Taiwan and Japan	50 largest chaebol in Korea, 96 largest groups in Taiwan, and 16 largest keiretsu in Japan	• Trade pattern of product diversity, business group structure	• Japanese firms exceed either of Taiwan and Korea in product variety, and Korean firms market particular products with high volume production but more limited product variety. Taiwan exports more high-priced intermediate inputs, whereas Korea exports relatively more high-priced final goods
Lee and Belvins (1990)	Japan, South Korea and Taiwan, comparing to the US	400 (100 in each country)	• Determinant of performance	• Diversification was not important to performance determinants at least in Japan and Korea samples
Lins and Servaes (1999)	Germany, Japan and UK firms in 1992 and 1994	174 and 227 German, 808 and 778 Japanese, 391 and 341 British	• Diversification and shareholders wealth	• The effect of diversification on firm value is different. The value of diversification is related to the institutional structure of a country • In Japan, firms a strong association to an industrial group would be less diversified than independent firms
Khanna and Rivkin (2001)	14 emerging markets	Various data sources	• A comparison of performance among firms affiliated with group and outside of groups	• Differences in profitability vary across institutional contexts • In some countries, business group affiliates earn higher accounting profits than do otherwise comparable unaffiliated firms

likely to be diversified than non-state owned firms because the former enjoyed preferential conditions offered by the government (Li, Li and Tan, 1998). This finding was consistent with a study done by a local scholar (Yin, 1999) who studied 292 local firms and 36 public companies and noted that state-owned enterprises were more diversified because they received more resources from governments.

Our investigation of firm diversification in mainland China had similar findings; namely, that firms enjoying more government support were likely to have a higher level of diversification. Part of the explanation was that governmental resources were usually general, such as capital, land property, information, business licenses, or administrative personnel. As a result, firms supported by government resources were more diversified if they had no core competency that was built upon technology. Second, when an entry barrier to a specific market, such as real estate property, is subject to government approval, a firm receiving better governmental support was likely to enter into the respective market.

In addition to the interaction of firms with governments, foundation conditions played another crucial role to influence a firm's diversification level. Firms established based upon mergers and acquisitions or transformation from former industrial bureaus usually turned into highly diversified corporations, while those based upon a single product or technology became related diversifiers (Lu, Yeh, Lan, and Chow, 2000).

Our case study of firm diversification in Guangdong Province did not identify a causal relation between the level of diversification and a firm's economic performance, but found that firms diversifying during an earlier period of the 1990s had better performance. We also noted that firms experienced a similar cycle to that in the US during the 1990s; namely, those with a high degree of diversification began to restructure and focus upon building core competencies. Associated with the change in strategies was the adaptation of organizational structure towards centralization within the corporation. This change was largely caused by an increase in market competition. Governmental firms with general resources and unrelated diversification began to lose their prestigious positions (Lu, Lan, and Bruton, 2002).

To sum up, firm diversification in mainland China was contingent on multiple contextual factors, including foundation conditions, institutional authorities, and market competition. In this case, diversification was not simply an economic matter, but involved complex issues stemming from history, resource specificity, and pressures from the external environment, particularly institutional authorities. Since in a transition economy, like China, environments change rapidly, the relationship between diversification and performance became uncertain. However, as there is a lack of systematic empirical studies, further research, particularly quantitative surveys, on firm diversification and related topics is necessary.

Taiwan

In contrast to mainland China where a centrally planned economy used to dominate the overall economy, Taiwan chose a market economy in which family enterprises contributed significantly to the overall national economy (Hamilton, 1997). Many Taiwanese firms were owned either by a single family or jointly by several individuals in limited partnership. Large family enterprises usually chose a form of business groups that owned wholly or partly numerous member firms. Diversification was popularly adopted as a major growth strategy. As Hamilton (1997) observed: 'By tracing the growth of groups through their surviving firms, one can get a fairly clear impression of their emerging patterns of diversification. Groups that have been included in the top 100 business groups for more than 15 years are, unsurprisingly, the most diversified. ... The following pattern is typical. Once a group has established an area of economic importance as an upstream supplier or a provider of services and has enlarged its core firms to keep pace with increasing domestic demand, it subsequently diversifies its assets by creating new firms in unrelated business areas. Large business groups can be very large indeed, with network structures and assets that rival any other business groups located elsewhere' (Hamilton, 1997: 251).

It is noted, by a closer look at organizational arrangement of Taiwanese family enterprises, that they had unique ownership structure that is assumed to be an important factor to drive firm diversification. A family-owned firm is a business organization owned by persons of the same family. Instead of equally sharing management authority, all sons receive equal shares of their father's estate. The brothers may jointly cooperate in mutual business activities and a focal enterprise is therefore divided into a number of horizontally connected firms that operate either in different sectors or in geographical areas. Diversification is the way through which family members share household assets (Hamilton, 1997).

Aw and Batra examined larger Taiwanese firms and noted that they were diversified in both export market and products (Aw and Batra, 1998). A motive behind their diversification was to take advantage of the economies of scale and scope (Aw and Batra, 1998). This conclusion was supportive of Western economic theory.

However, if large business groups preferred unrelated diversification in different businesses, do small and medium enterprises (SMEs), which play an important role in Taiwan's economy, also adopt a similar pattern of diversification? Aw and Batra (1998) further analyzed the data collected as part of the Taiwanese Census of Manufacturing in 1986 and suggested that Taiwanese SMEs diversified more into export markets (geographical diversification) rather than different products. An explanation of this phenomenon was the limited size of

Taiwan's domestic market. In other words, SMEs diversified geographically into overseas markets for growth.

In a recent study of diversified conglomerates in Taiwan, Chiu (2002) examined the data collected from 42 listed companies for the years 1997 and 1998. He found no definitive relationship between the level of diversification and companies' profits. The main factor affecting companies' operational performance was an inappropriate capital and labor mix, resulting in inefficiency.

In short, these studies, although not adequate for our understanding of firm diversification in Taiwan, seem to suggest that the rationale behind firm diversification involves more complex factors than economic motivations. Social relations, such as family ownership, played an equally important role in firm strategy formulation. Diversification in this circumstance is therefore an outcome of social settings, in addition to economic incentives. However, since existing studies could not identify a definitive relationship between diversification and firm performance, we need further investigation into internal organizational arrangements within diversified firms, particularly family enterprises, before any conclusions can be drawn.

Hong Kong

As a former British colony, Hong Kong established an open and liberal market. Foreign direct investment on the one hand and local entrepreneurship on the other hand may account for major business organizational forms in Hong Kong. Actually, there has been no systematic study of firm diversification. The only one we identified was Wan's (1998) examination of the relationship between diversification and performance of Hong Kong multinational corporations (MNCs).

Wan concluded that 'Hong Kong MNCs were more internationalized but industrially as diversified as domestic firms' (Wan, 1998: 214). However, international diversification did not seem to contribute to superior economic performance, although it has a positive impact on profitability stability and sales growth. Wan explained that this might be because international diversification distracted management capability. Or, perhaps, in a high growth region like Hong Kong, firms focusing upon the local market might obtain ample opportunities to have good performance without exploring international markets.

On the other hand, Wan examined the relationship between industrial diversification and firm performance of Hong Kong MNCs. His finding was consistent with that in Western society: a negative impact on profitability, but positive impact on profitability stability.

To understand the level of firm diversification in industries, we have done our own study of publicly traded firms in Hong Kong. Our data came from the Hong Kong Economic Daily, a local newspaper that publishes data on public companies. According to the newspaper's categorization, there were 807 firms on Hong Kong's stock market. Since our focus was placed upon Hong Kong local firms, we then excluded 50 H-share and 28 Chinese capital companies whose capital came from mainland China. Of the remaining companies, 301 had businesses related to industries including electronics, logistics, textile and food. According to the newspaper's categorization, 65 had 'integrated business', i.e. unrelated diversification. This accounted for 21.6% of local public firms in industrial sectors. This seems to suggest that diversification is popular in Hong Kong.

In fact, the actual percentage of Hong Kong firms with product and geographic diversity is likely much higher than our estimation. In particular, many Hong Kong firms, including small and medium firms, entered into the mainland Chinese market. Since China adopted an open door policy in 1978, Hong Kong has remained the largest investor in mainland China (*Almanac of China's Foreign Economic Relations and Trade 2001*, p. 765).

However, since there has been little study of firm diversification in Hong Kong, it is difficult to draw any definite conclusions. Hong Kong's economy consists of family enterprises, small and medium enterprises and multinational corporations. Therefore, firms of different size and ownership might have different strategic choices concerning diversification in products and geographical markets. Moreover, since Hong Kong's domestic market is limited, even smaller than that in Taiwan, it would suggest that Hong Kong firms should be more diversified in geographical areas. Therefore, it is urgent to conduct further research on related topics, including the measurement of firm diversification, organizational arrangements within firms, and the geographic locations of Hong Kong firms.

Japan

Japanese firms have been well-examined by scholars who identified a few well-defined clusters of firms at the top of the Japanese economy (Orrù, Biggart and Hamilton, 1991). These clusters consist of complex corporate groups and subcontractors, which are generally referred to as '*keiretsu*' (Shimotani, 1997). Keiretsu are fundamentally social structural relations, not legal entities, which were embedded in a long history of Japanese political, social and economic development paths. Keiretsu organizations are unique organizational arrangement in which member firms are linked through multidimensional networks of direct or indirect ties, such as equity stakes, interlocking directorates, capital and buying and selling of goods and services. Such keiretsu structural arrangement made member firms enjoy protection advantages. If a subsidiary is under attack by a rival, the parent may initiate a rescue operation (Ito and

Rose, 1994). As a result, keiretsu firms were ascribed as having a different strategic profile than non-keiretsu firms (Geringer, Tallman, and Olsen, 2000).

In fact, Japanese keiretsu involve complex economic activities in diversified markets, both geographical and industrial. They commonly use stable subcontracting relations with small firms as one major method of diversification. Accordingly, there are two types of configuration occurring within Japanese enterprise groups: inter-market groups that consist of stable horizontal linkages across non-competing industrial sectors; and independent groups that represent a network of vertically integrated firms in one industrial sector (Orrù, Biggart, and Hamilton, 1991). As a result, control in Japanese business groups is not centralized but horizontally dispersed throughout the network of firms.

Geringer and his associates examined diversification in Japanese multinational enterprises (MNEs) during a period between the late 1970s to the early 1990s and found that the relationship between product diversification strategies and results varied over time due to changing environmental impact on corporate strategy (Geringer et al., 2000). For instance, exports of Japanese firms steadily increased before 1986. Afterwards, exports started declining but direct investment in the US increased. During the earlier 1990s, exports increased but direct investment declined. As Geringer et al. noted, 'As environmental conditions fluctuate, strategies also seem both to vary and to have varying effects on performance' (Geringer et al., 2000: 76). Moreover, they found that multinational diversification is less valuable to firm performance, at least over a short to medium period, perhaps because it is more difficult for Japanese firms to manage effectively globally. Finally, there was no dramatic difference in the diversification-performance relationship between keiretsu and non-keiretsu firms, although they seemed to adopt different strategic profiles.

As previous studies noted, inter- and intra-firm networks exhibited distinctive structures from either market or hierarchies. Firm diversification is therefore conceived as a historical heritage from Japan's traditional complex relations among organizations, through which economic transactions were conducted.

South Korea

Korea's chaebol have become recognized globally. Chaebol refer to business groups that are a gathering of formally independent firms under common administrative and financial control and owned and controlled by certain families. The size of chaebol can be very large, consisting of up to 80 affiliates (Chang and Hong, 2002).

Korean chaebol have several distinctive characteristics (Orrù et al., 1991). First, chaebol typically started their businesses in only a few related industrial sectors, such as automobile, shipbuilding or electronics. Second, chaebol diversified by creating new affiliated firms instead of new divisions within an existing organization (Chang and Hong, 2002). Korean chaebol are usually owned and controlled by a single person or family and are organized through a central holding company that integrates economic activities conducted by affiliated firms. Third, differing particularly from Japanese keiretsu, chaebol do not own banks but have minority shares in banks controlled by the government. In the 1960s the Korean government provided preferential treatment to large chaebol in specific sectors in order to accelerate a pace of national economic development. Through its control of respective banks, the government could retain the right to influence chaebol's decision-making and other activities. The State, bank and chaebol family are therefore closely linked to each other.

Previous studies of large chaebol noted that diversification was used as a major strategy to achieve rapid growth (Kang, 1997; Kim, 1993). A chaebol's diversification process was closely associated with the government's industrial policy. For instance, Samsung, one of the largest chaebol in South Korea, followed three stages of diversification: horizontal into the trade, textile and banking industries during the period from 1938 to the 1960s; into heavy and chemical industries throughout the 1970s; and then the formation of corporate groups as core subsidiaries in several sectors. During each of Samsung's development stages, the firm benefited from government subsidies and favoritism (Kang, 1997). As the firm expanded rapidly, it introduced a double ownership structure. The core firms were dominated directly by the owner and the subsidiaries were dominated not by the owner but by the core firms indirectly. This structure helped the owner solve the problem of a shortage of financial assets, but at the same time, maintain managerial authority. Since the capital market in Korea was immature and therefore participation of public shareholders in a chaebol's decision making was limited, such an ownership structure enables the owner to maintain managerial authority and coordinate resources to diversify by investing in new firms in non-core subsidiaries (Kang, 1997). However, it was observed that diversification made large chaebol shift their structure to the multidivisional one to effectively control affiliated firms by introducing corporate planning (Chang and Choi, 1988).

Chang and Choi (1988) present one of the earliest empirical studies concerning the relationships among diversification, structure and performance of Korean business groups. Deploying a transaction cost perspective, Chang and Choi (1988) argued that business groups diversified, vertically and horizontally, because of market imperfections in Korea. Accordingly, transaction costs within a group were assumed to be lower than those in the market. Chang and Choi (1988) examined 182 list companies, including 63 affiliated firm and 119 independent firms, and the research findings supported their hypothesis.

In a recent study of diversification, Choi and Cowing (2002) examined the 25 largest chaebols for the years 1985–1995 and found group diversification into additional industries may not contribute to an increase in group profitability, whereas expansion into existing industries through an increase in the number of member firms does. Their findings indicate that the existence of financial firms within the chaebol did not affect group profit, which could be explained by the development of more efficient external financial markets. Moreover, they noted that firm concentration within the chaebol might result in lower profit. This implied a decline in the dominance of the founding firm within the chaebol.

The above studies all suggest that the relationship between corporate and affiliated firms is key to understanding the performance of diversified business groups. Other studies of South Korean chaebols point to the complex structural arrangements within business groups and changes in relationships between the parent and affiliated firms (Chang and Hong, 2000, 2002). Chang and Hong (2000) noted member firms share resources, and thereby chaebols took advantage of economies of scale and scope. In their later study, Chang and Hong (2002) report consistent findings; namely, the importance of corporate effects in business groups for resource sharing among affiliated firms. More interestingly, they noted the corporate effect decreased over time among the largest groups.

To summarize, Korean business groups (chaebol) developed distinctive and unique organizational forms that were shaped jointly by the impact of government support and family ownership. The finding that firms with government support were likely diversified was similar to that in mainland China, but the structure of Korean chaebol is considerably different from that in Taiwan, although both had family ownership structure. History, the nation's path of development, and social relations all contributed to the existing formation of business groups. However, the above studies also suggested a change in the extent of diversification and the relationship between corporate and affiliated firms. If, as Choi and Cowing (2002) noted, external markets become more efficient, will the chaebol continue diversifying?

Singapore

Singapore has a small but open economy, although the government imposes strong regulation over economic activities (Toh and Tan, 1998). It coud be assumed that Singaporean firms were likely more diversified because of the small size of the market. There were other factors that also encourage Singapore firms to diversify. For example, it has been suggested that Singapore's capital markets are not developed as those in well-developed market economies, so firms would have established an efficient internal capital market through which they coordinate financial resources to invest in new markets.

Lim and Teck (1995) studied the relationship between diversification and performance in Singaporean firms. They noted that larger firms became more diversified, but their performance suffered. Moreover, related diversification strategies were not found to achieve superior performance over unrelated diversification. These findings were not supporting a curvilinear relation model of diversification-performance (Palich, Cardinal, and Miller, 2000).

Chen and Ho (2000) tested the relationship between ownership structure and corporate diversification in Singaporean firms. According to agency theory, Singaporean firms were assumed to have high ownership concentration and there was the lack of an efficient external market for corporate control. As a result, managers would be motivated to adopt a diversification strategy in order to seek private benefits, rather than value-creation, from diversification (Hoskisson and Hitt, 1990). Chen and Ho's findings were consistent with Lim and Teck (1995), as well as research findings in the US, that larger firms were more diversified than smaller ones, while diversified firms were less valued than non-diversified firms. However, they only found a negative relationship between the level of diversification to outside blockholder ownership, but no relationship to insider ownership (Chen and Ho, 2000). One explanation for these phenomena was that Singaporean firms diversified due to the limited domestic market while managers with lower ownership stakes in their firms have more incentives to pursue diversification, supporting the agency cost assumption.

Up to now, the study of Singaporean firm diversification is limited and inadequate to draw definitive conclusions. Similar to Hong Kong, the size of the Singaporean market is small, but the country's government played a more active role in the control of economic activities and business organizations. Both seem to suggest, as indicated in other Asian countries, that firms seek diversification in product and geographical markets. However, whether such diversification leads to better firm performance remains a question. Moreover, there is a need for further study of organizational arrangements within Singaporean diversified firms.

India

The Indian government had used a state planning system to regulate economic activities before the mid-1980s. The country then embarked on new economic liberalization policies in 1991 through deregulation and reduction of state control (Mammen, 1999). Traditionally, state-owned firms and large family business groups accounted for a major portion of the national economy. With the progress of economic liberalization and reform, entrepreneurs and foreign investors emerged as important players, particularly in hi-tech industries (*The Economist*, April 9, 1994; January 21, 1995).

A unique characteristic of Indian business groups are their conglomerate structure that embraces legally separate affiliated firms but, unlike Japanese keiretsu, there was no internal bank within a group, while internal capital markets contributed little to profitability in diversified firms.

Ghemawat and Khanna (1998) conducted case studies of the two largest Indian business groups and their changes in corporate scope during the post-1991 period. They noted two general rationales for diversification. One concerned information impactedness and entrepreneurial scarcity, both pointing to a business group's internal mechanism for allocation of resources, such as capital, information and entrepreneurship. The other came from specific policies, such as taxation, that distorted the market processes and forced firms to increase diversification by taking advantages of economies of scope. The two sampled organizations studied by Ghemawat and Khanna (1998) were reported to reduce their level of diversification as policy distortions were wholly or partially removed and market mechanisms were introduced.

Khanna and Palepu (2000) studied Indian business groups and found that most diversified business groups added value. This was different from prior studies of the relationship between diversification and performance in US conglomerates that showed lower performance. Moreover, Indian business groups were found to have a distinctive organizational form in which affiliated firms enjoyed substantial autonomy in gaining superior access to critical resources, such as foreign capital and technology. For instance, group affiliates were able to obtain access to international capital market. As a result, business groups had better performance than firms without affiliates. Khanna and Palepu explained this result by pointing to a group's organizational arrangements which were assumed to replicate 'the functions of institutions that are missing in this emerging market' (Khanna and Palepu, 2000: 887).

Ramaswamy and Li (2001) approached the topic of diversification from a perspective of ownership structure and corporate governance. They studied the relationship between foreign investors, foreign directors and corporate diversification and found that the level of foreign shareholding did not have any bearing on the scope of unrelated diversification. The proportion of foreign directors on the board was negatively related to the level of unrelated diversification.

These two studies to some extent noted Indian business groups were organized by a loosely coupled system. The most distinctive characteristic of this structure was the decentralized control of resource allocation within a group. Such a coordination mechanism resembles a holding company in a market economy, such as the US, but contributed to better performance. Khanna and Palepu attributed this to institutional voids because of India's less developed market economy. As a result, transactions were more effectively internalized within organizational hierarchies than arranged in the market (Khanna and Palepu, 2000). However, such an explanation, derived from a transaction cost perspective, is unsatisfactory. Previous studies in the US assumed that if there exist institutional voids, an organization had to rely upon an internal capital market for the allocation of financial resources instead of external financial markets. Accordingly, a group's internal banking or internal capital market should play a more significant role in the control of affiliates. This is inconsistent with the research findings of Khannna and Palepu (2000b). Moreover, if unrelated diversification could lead to a better performance when a firm adopted a group's structure embracing affiliates, why was there a negative relationship between the proportion of foreign directors and the level of unrelated diversification? Needless to say, there is a need of further systematic study of Indian business groups and the performance of diversified firms.

Comparative studies

The above studies of corporate diversification focused upon a single country or region. The generality of their findings is thus limited due to the specificity of research contexts. This requires a comparative study for the better understanding of diversification in different countries.

Feenstra, Yang, and Hamilton (1999) compared diversified business groups in three Asian countries – South Korea, Taiwan and Japan. They found that Taiwan exported a greater variety of high-priced intermediate inputs, while Korea tended to aggressively market final products of high volume production but of more limited product variety. Japan exceeded either of the above two countries in product variety, consistent with previous studies, such as Orrù et al. (1991).

Khanna and Rivkin (2001) compared the performances of business groups in 14 emerging markets, including six Asian countries and regions (India, Indonesia, Philippines, South Korea, Taiwan and Thailand). They found that Indian, Indonesian and Taiwanese business group affiliates earned higher accounting profits than do otherwise comparable unaffiliated firms. This group effect on profitability had weaker support in another Asian country – the Philippines. However, in Korea and Thailand there was roughly a balance between the costs and benefits of group affiliation. Interestingly, they also found that in Asian countries members of a business group shared costs and benefits.

The above comparative studies concerned diversified firms in Asia or emerging economies. There were two comparative studies identifying similarities and differences between Asian firms and those in developed countries. Lins and Servaes (1999) compared Japanese firms to those in Germany and the UK. Based upon an agency cost perspective, they found significant differences in the valuation of diversified firms in the three countries. Diversification seemed less likely to lead to a discount value in Japan than that in the UK, but this relationship was not clearly defined in Germany. Their findings suggest that diversification is less of a problem for shareholders in Japan (and possibly in Germany) than in the UK.

Lee and Belevins (1990) compared the performance of diversified firms in Taiwan, South Korea and Japan to those in the US. They noted that South Korean and Taiwanese firms were more diversified than the US firms, but Japan was the least diversified. In terms of performance, the US firms achieved better performance than the others in terms of profitability measures, ROE, ROA, ROS, and ROI. However, when comparing growth rates of sales, they found that South Korean and Taiwanese firms performed better than the US and Japanese firms.

Results from these comparative studies suggest that firm diversification in Asia as well as in other emerging markets differs substantially from that in Western societies. Although it is dangerous to draw any general conclusions, it seems that unrelated diversification in Asia may not be necessarily leading to poor performance, as is the case in the US. The key to explaining this difference is perhaps in the configuration of diversification-structure-performance. A distinctive difference among multi-product firms in Asia and Western societies is that the former was organized in business groups or affiliations that present considerable differences from the Western M-form. Business groups are not equivalent to conglomerates in Western societies because they embrace complex relations between the parent firm/headquarters/core firms and affiliates, as well as among the affiliates themselves.

DISCUSSION

Our review of the empirical evidence in Asia and comparative studies seem to suggest that despite the importance of economic motivation and external incentives such as government policies, social relations are and remain a significant factor explaining firm diversification. For instance, Japanese firms diversified in both geographical and industrial markets by using subcontracting relations with small firms. By contrast, Taiwanese firms diversified through a network of family members or personal connections, while South Korean groups diversified by control of a holding company that coordinates core firms but lets the latter integrate numerous affiliated firms at the operational level. Moreover, in Japan firms engaged in either horizontal or vertical integration within the organization, while in Taiwan diversification was noted in geographical markets rather than in product or industrial sectors. However, in Korea vertical integration was found to be a popular diversification choice. These research findings also suggest that the pattern of diversification varies across Asian societies.

How can we explain such variance? If diversification is a more efficient way for firms to deploy their resources or realize cost advantages, as economic theory suggests, we then should see a causal relationship between diversification and firm economic performance. The empirical findings so far do not confirm such a hypothesis.

There are two theoretical approaches to interpret Asian distinctiveness. The first, based upon the Western neoclassic economic theory, is to attribute of these differences to Asia's imperfect markets. In an imperfect market, information is either missing or inadequate and resource allocation or transaction is thus not fully directed by prices but influenced by non-market intervention forces, such as government or monopolistic control. In such a circumstance, diversification enables a firm to obtain necessary information in a respective market.

Another characteristic of an imperfect market are institutional voids: institutional functions governing economic exchange relations are dominated by government regulatory measures instead of law and legal systems. The involvement of governments in economic transactions, to an economist, is perceived to jeopardize market operation. Government support or intervention lead to two results. First, firms taking advantage of governmental support will enjoy excessive resources that encourage them to take an over-diversified growth strategy. Second, to avoid government intervention, firms deploy diversification in order to gain control over transaction activities across markets (Khanna and Palepu, 1997).

However, if diversification is driven by market imperfection, firms ought to engage in activities relevant to a product's adjacent activities where affiliated units conduct internal coordination and, therefore, vertical integration should be specifically preferred. According to our review, vertical integration was not popular in diversified firms in Asia, with only the cases of Korea and Japan generally following this path. Moreover, such an explanation based upon market imperfections is difficult to give reasons for unrelated diversification where specific activities and assets could not be transferred between affiliated units. It is also hard to explain firm diversity in geographical markets. In particular, following this logic, we would assume that internal banking or internal capital markets should contribute greatly to firm performance. Since there was no definitive conclusions from empirical research, there is a need for further investigation into the role of internal capital markets within the firm and on diversification.

Moreover, if firm diversification is attributed to market imperfections, it implies that the pattern of firm diversification will resemble a Western model as market conditions in Asia more closer to perfect. Our observation of an evolution of business groups in Guangdong, the People's Republic of China, seems to support this prediction. When markets were open, diversified firms were forced to restructure their business portfolios for the purpose of building core competency (Lu, Lan, and Bruton, 2002). However, empirical evidence in relatively developed market economies, such as Taiwan, Japan and South Korean, does not seem to support this argument. Therefore, further research, particularly longitudinal studies, are needed.

The second conceptual framework to explain the characteristics of Asian firms comes from sociology and organization theories. Students of sociology argue that market imperfection theory does not provide an adequate explanation for Asian distinctiveness because Asian "markets" are fundamentally different from Western ones. Asian markets are founded on institutional logics 'rooted in connectedness and relationships' (Biggart and Hamilton, 1977: 37). These logics differ dramatically from Western beliefs that conceive of economic actors as independent, isolated and autonomous. In Asia, economic exchange is molded by traditions and historical practices that emphasize relations between individuals, families and organizations (Biggart, 1997; Whitley, 1992).

Following this relational logic, firm diversification is assumed to be the outcome of social relations. Since the foundation of social relations varies across Asian societies, the pattern of diversification and organizational arrangement carrying on the diversification also vary. For instance, in Chinese families, the inheritance system grant all sons equal shares of the father's property. This tradition remains in Taiwanese family enterprises and has given rise to a preference for horizontal diversification, since family members divided the businesses into equal shares. By contrast, in South Korea, the kinship system supported 'a clearly demarcated, hierarchically ranked class structure in which core segments of lineages acquire elite rankings and privileges' (Hamilton and Feenstra, 1997: 83). The eldest son usually inherited a dominant share of the father's private estate, with the younger sons dividing up the rest. This insight into Korean tradition helps us understand why South Korean business groups conducted vertical integration with dominant family ownership in control of core firms. History, tradition, and social norms are constituent to organizational behavior instead of external factors to which firms have to fit.

To us, the two frameworks – the one based upon neoclassical economic theories to highlight market imperfection, and the perspectives of sociology to emphasize the importance of tradition, history, social practices and relations – are complementary rather than in conflict. Indeed, market conditions in Asia were institutionalized with distinctive logics and therefore firms are encouraged to diversify based upon social relations. However, the question is when a market becomes more open, such as the case in mainland China after the country was admitted to WTO, will social relations continue to dominate strategic choices? As we observed in our case study, local firms in mainland China were forced to restructure their business portfolios when market competition was intensified (Lu, Lan, and Bruton, 2002). Our finding was consistent with that of Ghemawat and Khanna (1998), who noted change from diversification to restructuring when policy distortions were removed, associated with the progress in market development. Similarly, South Korean chaebol served the Korean economy well in the 1960s and 1970s. However, when the Asian financial crisis occurred during 1997 and 1998, these large conglomerates became vulnerable. Their complex structure of corporate governance, oblique decision processes, and privileged positions relying upon government preferential support led to inefficiency in competition. *Business Korea* in even proclaimed, '*"Chaebol"* is part of the past, not the future' (*Business Korea*, September, 2000: 8).

We may incorporate these two perspectives simultaneously by identifying market and social surroundings as two related contexts which influence firm diversification by different ways. With the progress of marketization, the external constraints caused by institutional voids, such as government control and policy distortion, will be reduced and the market as a resource allocation mechanism will become more efficient. In other words, markets in Asia will eventually become open, free, and liberal. As a result, the pressure from market competition will force managers to enhance competitiveness and, for example, pay attention to cost advantage of the economies of scale and scope. This will have a negative impact on firm diversification, particularly unrelated diversification. Therefore, we expect a decrease in the level of firm diversification in Asia. At the same time, social surroundings remain in place as the institutional foundation to influence management practices. For instance, firms may choose a network strategy, such as the formation of partnership with others, to diversify. Most likely, social relations will continue to be reflected seen in organizational arrangements. For instance, firms may increase the number of member firms as an expansion strategy in existing industries instead of diversification in unrelated industries.

CONCLUSION

We have reviewed Western theories on firm diversification and empirical findings in Asia. The fundamental assumptions in Western society were derived from economic theories that view firms as independent, isolated and autonomous actors in an open and free market. Our survey of previous studies in seven Asian countries and regions has showed mixed results vis-a-vis Western theory and respective hypotheses. For example, Western economic theories cannot provide a powerful explanation for the reasons behind the variation across Asian societies in terms of patterns of diversification: vertical, horizontal, and unrelated; and of different organizational arrangements of Asian firms for implementing a diversification strategies.

An economist may attribute Asian distinctiveness in diversification and the network-like structure of Asian firms to imperfect market conditions, but sociologists offer an insight into Asia's histories, traditions, and social relations that incorporate the institutional logics of Asian markets. Firm diversification, according to a relational logic, is the presentation of constituent social relations instead of the best choice to fit to the external environments.

We view the two perspectives – Western economic and sociologic – as complementary and see it necessary to integrate them into one model. Based upon our observation in mainland China – a transition economy moving from a centrally planned economy to a market one, we believe that markets in Asia will become more open, free, and liberal, and to some extent firm diversification in Asia will come to resemble that in the USA, in which strategic choice is primarily based on a cost-benefit rationale. This assertion does not, however, deny the importance of social surroundings. Rather, we believe that social relations will remain in place as a fundamental institutional infrastructure to direct managerial practices. For instance, partnership and strategic alliances may be considered more appropriate by Asian managers as a means of pursuing a diversification strategy. Network-like organizational arrangements may remain effective as a basic building block of organization design in diversified firms.

Needless to say, to answer these and other questions, we suggest further study of diversification in Asia. Comparative studies of Asian diversification with that in advanced market economies is particularly recommended. Moreover, more longitudinal studies of evolutionary changes in diversified firms in Asia are also necessary in order to enrich our understanding of how diversification is managed, implemented and amended over a period when a market becomes more competitive, open and free.

REFERENCES

Agryres, N. 1996. Capabilities, technological diversification, and divisionalization. *Strategic Management Journal*, 17: 395-410.

Almanac of China's Foreign Economic Relations and Trade 2001. China Foreign Economic Relations & Trade Publishing House.

Ansoff, H.I. 1965. *Corporate Strategy; an Analytic Approach to Business Policy for Growth and Expansion*. New York: McGraw-Hill.

Aw, B.Y., and Geeta, B. 1998. Firm size and the pattern of diversification. *International Journal of Industrial Organization*, 16(3): 313-331.

Berlinger, J. 1966. The economics of overtaking and surprising. In H. Rosvosky (ed.), *Industrialization in Two Systems: Essay in Honor of Alexander Gerschekron* (pp. 159-185). New York: John Wiley.

Berry, C. 1975. *Corporate Growth and Diversification*. Princeton, NJ: Princeton University Press.

Besanko, D., Dranove, D. and Shanley, M. 2000. *Economics of Strategy* (2nd edn). New York: John Wiley.

Biggart, N.W. 1997. Explaining Asian economic organization. In M. Orrù, N.W. Biggart and G.G. Hamilton (eds.), *The Economic Organization of East Asian Capitalism* (pp. 3-32). London: Sage.

Biggart, N.W. and Hamilton, G.G. 1997. On the limits of a firm-based theory to explain business networks. In M. Orrù, N.W. Biggart and G.G. Hamilton (eds.), *The Economic Organization of East Asian Capitalism* (pp. 33-54). London: Sage.

Brush, T.H. 1996. Predicted change in operational synergy and post-acquisition performance of acquired businesses. *Strategic Management Journal*, 17: 1-24.

Buono, A.F. and Bowditch, J.L. 1989. *The Human Side of Mergers and Acquisitions.* San Francisco: Jossey-Bass.

Business Korea, September, 2000. "*Chaebol*" is part of the past, not the future, 17(9): 8-10.

Chandler, A.D., Jr. 1962. Strategy and structure: Chapters in the history of industrial enterprises. Cambridge, MA: MIT Press.

Chang, Sea Jin and Choi, Unghawan 1988. Strategy structure and performance of Korean business groups. *Journal of Industrial Economics,* 37(2): 141-158.

Chang, Sea Jin and Hong, Jaebum 2000. Economic performance of group-affiliated companies in Korea: Intragroup resource sharing and internal business transactions. *Academy of Management Journal,* 43(3): 429-448.

Chang, Sea Jin and Hong, Jaebum 2002. How much does the business group matter in Korea? *Strategic Management Journal,* 23(3): 265-274.

Chen, Min. 1995. *Asian Management Systems.* London: Routledge.

Chen, Sheng-Syan and Ho, Kim Wai 2000. Corporate diversification, ownership structure, and firm value: The Singapore evidence. *International Review of Financial Analysis,* 9(3): 315-326.

Chiu, Yung-ho 2002. The impact of conglomerate firm diversification on corporate performance: An empirical study in Taiwan. *International Journal of Management,* 19(2): 231-237.

Choi, Jeong-pyo and Cowing, T. 2002. Diversification, concentration and economic performance: Korean business groups. *Review of Industrial Organization,* 21(3): 271-282.

The Economist. April 9, 1994. India's businesses: blinking in the sunlight, pp. 72-74.

The Economist. January 21, 1995. Indian business shapes up, pp. SS8-9.

Far Eastern Economic Review. 1991. Let 100 firms boom. 5 September, 56-57.

Feenstra, R., Yang, Tzu-Han and Hamilton, G. 1999. Business groups and product variety in trade: evidence from Souther Korea, Taiwan and Japan. *Journal of International Economics,* 48: 71-100.

Geringer, J.M., Tallman, S. and Olsen, D.M. 2000. Product and international diversification among Japanese multinational firms. *Strategic Management Journal,* 21(1): 51-80.

Ghemawat, P. and Khanna, T. 1998. The nature of diversified business groups: a research design and two case studies. *Journal of Industrial Economics,* XLVI(1): 35-61.

Gort, M. 1962. Diversification and integration in American industry; A study by the National Bureau of Economic Research. Princeton, NJ: Princeton University Press.

Granovetter, M. 1985. Economic action and social structure: the problem of embddedness. *American Journal of Sociology,* 91: 481-510.

Gulunic, D.C. and Eisenhardt, K.M. (1994). Renewing the strategy-structure-performance paradigm. *Research in Organizational Behaviour,* 16: 215-225.

Guthrie, D. 1997. Between markets and politics: organizational responses to reform in China. *American Journal of Sociology,* 102: 1258-1304.

Hamilton, G.G. 1997. Organizationa and Market processes in Taiwan's capitalist economy. In M. Orrù, N.W. Biggart and G.G. Hamilton (eds.), *The Economic Organization of East Asian Capitalism* (pp. 237-293). London: Sage.

Hamilton, G.G. and Feenstra, R.C. 1997. Varieties of hierarchies and markets: an introduction. In M. Orrù, N.W. Biggart and G.G. Hamilton (eds.), *The Economic Organization of East Asian Capitalism* (pp. 55-94). London: Sage.

Hill, C.W.L., Hitt, M.A. and Hoskisson, R.E. 1992. Cooperative versus competitive structures in related and unrelated diversified firms. *Organization Science,* 3: 501-21.

Hoskisson, R.E., Eden, L., Lau, C.M. and Wright, M. 2000. Strategy in emerging economies. *Academy of Management Journal,* 43(3): 249-267.

Hoskisson, R. and Hitt, M.A. 1990. Antecedents and performance outcomes of diversification: a review and critique of theoretical perspectives. *Journal of Management,* 16: 461-509.

Hoskisson, R. and Hitt, M.A. 1994. *Downscoping: How to Tame the Diversified Firm*. Oxford: Oxford University Press.

Ito, K. and Rose, E. 1994. The genealogical structure of Japanese firms: parent-subsidiary relationships. *Strategic Management Journal*, 15(1): 35-51.

Kang, C.-K. 1997. Diversification process and the ownership structure of Samsung cheabol. In T. Shiba and M. Shimotani (eds.), *Beyond the Firm* (pp. 31-58). Oxford: Oxford University.

Keister, L. 1998. Engineering growth: business group structure and firm performance in China's transition economy. *American Journal of Sociology*, 104(2): 404-440.

Key, N.M. 1997. *Pattern in Corporate Evolution*. Oxford: Oxford University Press.

Khanna, T. and Palepu, K. 1997. Why focused strategies may be wrong for emerging markets. *Harvard Business Review*, 75(4): 41-51.

Khanna, T. and Palepu, K. 2000. Is group affiliation profitable in emerging markets? An analysis of diversified Indian business groups. *Journal of Finance*, 55(2): 867-892.

Khanna, T. and Rivkin, J.W. 2001. Estimating the performance effects of business groups in emerging markets. *Strategic Management Journal*, 22(1): 45-74.

Kim, Jin-Moon 1993. Driving for diversification. *Business Korea*, March: 28-31.

Kitching, J. 1967. Why do mergers miscarry? *Harvard Business Review*, 45(6): 84-101.

Lee, J. and Belvins, D.E. 1990. Profitability and sales growth in industrialized versus newly industrialized countries. *Management International Review*, 30: 87-100.

Li, Shaomin, Li, Mingfang and Tan, J.J. 1998. Understanding diversification in a transition economy: a theoretical exploration. *Journal of Applied Management Studies*, 7(1): 77-94.

Lim, G.E. and Teck, T.Y. 1995. Diversification strategies, firm characteristics and performance among Singapore firms. *International Journal of Management*, 12(2): 223-233.

Lins, K. and Servaes, H. 1999. International evidence on the value of corporate diversification. *Journal of Finance*, 54: 2215-2239.

Liu, Hong, Campbell, N., Lu, Zheng and Wang, Yanzhong 1996. An international perspective on China's township enterprises. In D. Brown and R. Porter (eds.), *Management Issues in China: Volum I: Domestic enterprises* (pp. 129-142). London: Routledge.

Lu, Yuan, Lan, Hailin and Bruton, G. 2002. Enterprise groups in a transition economy: diversification in government owned firms in the People's Republic of China. Paper presented at Asian Academy of Management Conference, Bangkok, Thailand, December 12 to 14.

Lu, Yuan, Yeh, Ryh-song, Lan, Hailin and Chow, Hau-siu 2000. Strategic choice of organizational structure under diversification strategies. In Lau Chun-Ming, K.K.S. Law, D.K. Tse and Chi-Sum Wong (eds.), *Asia Management Matters* (pp. 169-203). London: Imperial College Press.

Mammen, T. 1999. *India's Economic Prospects: A Macroeconomic and Econometric Analysis*. Singapore; River Edge, NJ: World Scientific.

Orrù, M., Biggart, N.W. and Hamilton, G.G. 1991. Organizational isomorphism in East Asia. In W.W. Powell and P.J. DiMaggio (eds.), *The New Institutionalism in Organizational Analysis* (pp. 361-389). London: The University of Chicago Press.

Orrù, M., Biggart, N.W. and Hamilton, G.G. 1997. *The Economic Organization of East Asian Capitalism*. London: Sage.

Palich, L.E., Cardinal, L.B. and Miller, C.C. 2000. Curvilinearity in the diversification performance linkage: an examination of over three decades of research. *Strategic Management Journal*, 21: 155-174.

Ramanujam, V. and Varadarajan, P. 1989. Research on corporate diversification: a synthesis. *Strategic Management Journal*, 10: 523-551.

Ramaswamy, K. and Li, M. 2001. Foreign investors, foreign directors and corporate diversification: an empirical examination of large manufacturing companies in India. *Asia Pacific Journal of Management*, 18(2): 207-222.

Redding, S.G. 1990. *The Spirit of Chinese Capitalism*. Berlin; New York: W. de Gruyter.

Reed, R., and Luffman, G.A. 1986. Diversification: The Growing Confusion. *Strategic Management Journal*, 7(1): 29-35.

Rumelt, R.P. 1974. *Strategy, Structure and Economic Performance*. Boston: Division of Research, Harvard Business School.

Shimotani, M. 1997. The history of structure of business groups in Japan. In T. Shiba and M. Shimotani (eds.), *Beyond the Firm: Business Groups in International and Historical Perspective*. Oxford: Oxford University Press.

Shleifer, A. and Vishny, R.W. 1986. Large shareholders and corporate control. *Journal of Political Economy*, 461-468.

Toh, Mun Heng and Tan, Kong Yam (eds.) 1998. *Competitiveness of the Singapore Economy: A Strategic Perspective*. Singapore: Singapore University Press.

Wan, Chun Cheong 1998. International diversification, industrial diversification and firm performance of Hong Kong MNCs. *Asia Pacific Journal of Management*; Singapore; Oct. 1998. 15(2): 205-217.

Whitley, R. 1992. *Business Systems in East Asia: Firms, Markets and Societies*. London: Sage.

Williamson, J. 1966. Profit, growth and sales mazimisation. *Economica*, 33: 1-6.

Williamson, O. 1975. *Markets and Hierarchies: Analysis and Antitrust Implications*. New York: Free Press.

Yin, Y. 1999. Appropriate diversification: firm growth and business restructuring (shidu duojiaohua: qiye chengzhang yu yewu chongzu). Beijing: Life, Reading and New Knowledge Tri-alliances Press.

Chapter 6

THE ASIAN MULTINATIONAL CORPORATION
Evolution, Strategy, Typology and Challenges

Nitin Pangarkar
National University of Singapore

BACKGROUND

While there are anecdotal examples of Asian companies expanding into international markets even a hundred years ago, many Asian companies started venturing into international markets during the 1960s. Much of the growth in the number as well as the size and scope of Asian multinationals (MNCs), however, occurred after the 1970s. The growth in Asian outward Foreign Direct Investment (FDI) has been even more remarkable in the mid-1990s. Between 1989 and 1994, FDI outflow from east, south and southeast Asia averaged $20 billion a year. In 2000, the outward FDI amounted to $85.3 billion. Over the 1995–2000 period, despite the negative impact of the Asian crisis in 1997 and 1998, the average outflow of FDI from this region was $48.7 billion (World Investment Report, 2001, Promoting Linkages).

Over the last 30 years, the achievements of several individual Asian MNCs have been striking (Aggarwal and Agmon, 1990). According to Business Week, 6 Japanese companies figure in the world's 50 most valuable brands (Business Week, August 6, 2001) and as many as 14 Japanese companies are included in the world's 100 leading MNCs. A few Japanese MNCs, such as Toyota, are comparable to global leaders in terms of the foreign assets (see Tables 1 and 2). In addition, there are several firms from Newly Industrializing Economies (e.g., South Korea, Taiwan) which have attained global leadership positions. By the year 2002, Hyundai Motor was ranked the 133rd (in terms of revenues) in Fortune's Global 500 listing (The 2002 Global 500, www.fortune.com). Hyundai Motor's sales exceeded those of well-known and long-established corporations such as Volvo, Mazda, Mitsubishi, Suzuki and Isuzu. Samsung Electronics had become a leading producer of memory chips and was widely considered as a technological leader. Within the electronics

Table 1. Leading Japanese Multinationals (2000)

Global rank	Company	Industry	Assets Foreign	Assets Total	Sales Foreign	Sales Total	Employees Foreign	Employees Total	Transnationality index
6	Toyota	Motor vehicles	44.9	131.5	55.2	101.0	113216	183879	50.1
18	Honda Motor Co Ltd	Motor vehicles	26.3	41.8	29.7	51.7		112200	60.2
20	Sony Corporation	Electronics	...	52.5	40.7	56.6	102468	173000	59.3
24	Mitsubishi Corporation	Diversified	21.7	74.9	43.5	116.1	3668	11650	32.7
25	Nissan Motor Co Ltd	Motor vehicles	21.6	57.2	25.8	54.4	...	131260	42.6
37	Mitsui & Co Ltd.	Diversified	17.3	56.5	46.5	118.5	...	7288	34.9
45	Itochu Corporation	Trading	15.1	55.9	18.4	115.3		5775	21.5
46	Sumitomo Corporation	Trading/machinery	15.0	45.0	17.6	95.0		5591	26.3
55	Matsushita Electric	Electronics	12.2	66.2	32.4	63.7	133629	282153	38.9
56	Fujitsu Ltd	Electronics	12.2	42.3	15.9	43.3	74000	188000	34.9
68	Marubeni Corporation	Trading	10.6	53.8	31.4	98.8		8617	25.8
92	Canon Electronics	Electronics/office equipment	7.4	23.4	17.8	24.4	41834	79799	52.3
93	Bridgestone	Rubber/tires	7.4	14.7	11.3	17.1		97767	58.2
100	Toshiba Corporation	Electronics	6.8	48.8	14.5	44.6		198000	23.3

Source: World Investment Report, UNCTAD (www.unctad.org).

Table 2. World's Leading Multinationals

	Company	Country	Industry	Assets		Sales		Employment		TNI
				Foreign	Total	Foreign	Total	Foreign	Total	
1	General Electric	US	Electronics	128.6	355.9	28.7	100.5	130000	293000	36.3
2	General Motors	US	Motor vehicles	73.1	246.7	49.9	155.5	...	396000	30.9
3	Royal Dutch/ Shell Group	Netherlands/ UK	Petroleum expl./ref./distr.	67.0	110.0	50.0	94.0	61000	102000	58.0
4	Ford Motor Company	US	Motor vehicles	...	237.5	43.8	144.4	171276	345175	35.4
5	Exxon Corporation	US	Petroleum expl./ref./distr.	50.1	70.0	92.7	115.4	...	79000	75.9
6	Toyota	Japan	Motor vehicles	44.9	131.5	55.2	101.0	113216	183879	50.1
7	IBM	US	Computers	43.6	86.1	46.4	81.7	149934	291067	53.0
8	BP AMOCO	UK	Petroleum expl./ref./distr.	40.5	54.9	48.6	68.3	78950	98900	74.9
9	Daimler Chrysler	Germany	Motor vehicles	36.7	159.7	125.4	154.6	208502	441502	50.4
10	Nestle SA	Switzerland	Food/beverages	35.6	41.1	51.2	52.0	225665	231881	94.2

Source: World Investment Report, UNCTAD (www.unctad.org).

and electrical equipment sector, Samsung Electronics was also ranked ahead of well-known global corporations such as Sharp, Ericsson and Emerson Electric (The 2002 Global 500, www.fortune.com).

The research attention devoted to the Asian multinationals exhibits a similar trend. Prior to 1973, the literature on Asian MNCs was sparse. Many Japanese firms were just beginning to get noticed and were in the early stages of internationalization. Between 1973 and 2001, scores of articles were published regarding the Asian multinational corporation (see Table 3, Yeung, 1999). While several articles were exclusively focused on analyzing Asian MNCs, some others devoted at least some attention to discussing the Asian MNCs, while dealing with the broader topic of multinationals from developing countries.

Though the volume of literature regarding the Asian multinationals has grown, there are several issues with this literature (see Table 3 for a summary of this literature). First, many papers are focused on studying firms from one or two countries (see second column in Table 3) and hence have missed out on significant insights that could be obtained by doing comparative studies across MNCs from several Asian countries (Yeung, 1999). Secondly, the theoretical underpinning of many earlier studies is either derived from developed country contexts or is sparse. Many studies have tried to adapt the imperfect competition framework proposed by Hymer (1960) Dunning (1979) and others (which assumes that firms must have some monopolistic advantage to become MNCs) for the Asian MNCs by arguing that these firms adapted technology to suit the unique requirements of host markets or employed more labor intensive technology (Jo, 1982; Lall, 1982). Many of today's Asian MNCs do not fit this stereotype. Several such as Samsung, Creative Technology, Hyundai and Acer compete quite successfully in high technology sectors and also in advanced economies. Clearly their basis of competitive advantage goes well beyond adaptation of an imported technology to a particular geographic context. Thirdly, methodologically, many studies (especially earlier studies) are of a descriptive nature and do not attempt rigorous hypothesis testing based on sound statistical methodologies. Recent literature on the strategies of Asian MNCs has improved the theoretical and methodological rigor but at the expense of breadth of issues (see the more recent studies in Table 3). In contrast to the early literature—which was addressing issues such as the theoretical justification of Asian MNCs, their basis of competitive advantage and MNC parent-level strategy—recent literature has focused on narrow parent-level issues (e.g., plant location) or subsidiary-level issues such as entry mode in particular markets and subsidiary-level performance. Issues such as the degree of global integration within the Asian MNCs' networks of affiliates have received sparse research attention. Fourthly, despite the growing volume of literature, there have been few attempts to synthesize what we have learned and what is different about the Asian multinationals. Finally, the existing literature has also not addressed one of the most interesting and complex conceptual issues

Table 3. Literature regarding the Asian Multinational Corporation

Authors and year	Geographic focus/MNCs from countries	Phenomenon/ Dependent variable	Independent variable	Data sources (primary/ secondary)	Methodology
Lecraw (1977)	Thailand	Impact (costs and benefits) of MNCs from LDCs on the local economy versus MNCs from developed economies	Motivations, ownership patterns, various aspects of strategy (R&D, advertising, exports & imports)	Primary (survey), $N = 200$	Econometric estimation of production function
Wells (1978)	Chinese firms from Hong Kong	Investment strategies— Pricing, basis of competitive advantage, sourcing strategies	N/A	N/A	Anecdotal evidence and some aggregate (country) level analysis
Ghymn (1980)	Korean Construction MNCs	Destination of FDI, key success factors	Home government policy	Secondary data, $N = 124$	Descriptive
Lall (1982)	Indian MNCs	Extent of investment, sectoral distribution, strategies (joint ventures)	NA	Secondary	Case studies + analysis of secondary data
Encarnation (1982)	Indian MNCs	Involvement in overseas joint ventures	Indian government policies regarding foreign trade and investment, membership in a business group	Secondary data from government agencies, chambers of commerce etc.	Descriptive analysis
Lall (1983)	Conceptual/ descriptive article	N/A	Nature of MNCs, competitive edge	N/A	N/A
Kumar and Kim (1984)	Korean manufacturing multinationals	Strategies—ownership advantages, technology, sourcing of machinery, parent-subsidiary linkages	N/A	Primary, $N = 18$	Tabulation

Table 3. (Continued.)

Authors and year	Geographic focus/MNCs from countries	Phenomenon/ Dependent variable	Independent variable	Data sources (primary/ secondary)	Methodology
Pang and Komaran (1985)	Singapore MNCs and Hong Kong manufacturing MNCs in Singapore	Mode of entry, finance, control and risk	Type of company	Secondary, $N = 117$	Cross tabulation, comparative analysis between Singapore and Hong Kong firms
Lall (1986)	Indian MNCs	Likelihood of foreign investment	Strategic variables— technological sophistication and adaptation, capital intensity, export performance, dependence on imported raw materials	Secondary, $N = 162$	Regression analysis—Probit and Tobit
Lim and Teoh (1986)	Singapore MNCs	Geographical and industrial distribution of FDI, motivations, basis of competitive advantage, technology strategy	N/A	Detailed case studies (Primary), $N = 18$	Descriptive case studies
Chen (1986)	Taiwanese MNCs	Magnitude of FDI by destination and time	N/A	Survey + secondary data	Descriptive
Jun (1987)	S. Korean consumer electronics MNCs in the US	Explain reverse investment by S Korean firms	N/A	Csae studies of Goldstar and Samsung	Descriptive analysis of production costs and capacity
Han and Brewer (1987)	Korean MNCs	Ownership advantages, strategic dimensions including exports	Year, size of FDI, Industry membership, host country's regulation, customer profile	Secondary data	Cross tabulations

Table 3. (Continued.)

Authors and year	Geographic focus/MNCs from countries	Phenomenon/ Dependent variable	Independent variable	Data sources (primary/ secondary)	Methodology
Buckley and Mirza (1988)	Pacific Asian MNCs	Typology	Home country characteristics, strategic variables	Secondary data—various sources	Cross tabulation
Tallman and Shenkar (1990)	Small and medium sized firms from Korea	Joint venture strategies— Choice between JV & contractual	Technology (high/low) and Destination (development) characteristics	Primary (survey), N = 340	Cross-tabulations
Aggarwal and Agmon (1990)	MNCs from India, Singapore and S. Korea	Growth of FDI from countries	Geographical distribution of destination, Business-government relations	Aggregate data on investment levels by countries	Descriptive analysis
McDermott (1991)	Taiwanese MNCs in the electronics sector	Location strategies	N/A	Secondary data regarding country market shares in selected sectors, plant location patterns	Simple quantitative analysis
Smart and Smart (1991)	Hong Kong MNCs in South China	Role of guanxi in Hong Kong investment	N/A	N/A	Descriptive
Chen (1992)	Taiwanese MNCs	Propensity to invest abroad	Size, growth performance, dependence on imported raw materials, labor intensity, export ratio	Survey data, N = 468	Regression analysis (Probit)

Table 3. (Continued.)

Authors and year	Geographic focus/MNCs from countries	Phenomenon/ Dependent variable	Independent variable	Data sources (primary/ secondary)	Methodology
Ferrantino (1992)	MNCs from Argentina and India	Destination of FDI	Sales, technology expenditures, exports, imports of capital equipment & raw materials, industry technology frontier	Not clear	Probit analysis
Gang (1992)	Chinese MNCs	Motives and benefits of investing abroad	N/A	Survey data, $N = 18$	Tabulation
Jeon (1992)	South Korean MNCs	Determinants of foreign investment in developed versus developing countries	Size, advertising/ sales, growth rate of Korean economy, cultural distance, concentration ratio of industry, non-tariff barriers, wage rates	Secondary data, $N = 67$	Regression analysis
Chang and Grub (1992)	Taiwanese MNCs in the PC sector	Stages of internationalization	24 strategic variables such as pricing, branding, innovation, capital structure etc.	Interviews + surveys, $N = 54$	Cluster analysis
Lee and Plummer (1992)	Korean FDI	Sectoral propensity for FDI (no. Of cases/ no. of firms)	Revealed comparative advantage, number of inward JVs in the sector, capital/ labor ratio, sectoral profitability	Secondary data, All firms in 90 sectors	Regression analysis
Lecraw (1993)	Indonesian MNCs	Motivation of FDI and improvement in performance dimensions such as size, exports, quality, costs	Pre- versus post-FDI performance	Primary qualitative, $N = 24$	Comparing means across Indoensian MNCs, domestic firms and developed country MNCs, while holding industry membership constant

Table 3. (Continued.)

Authors and year	Geographic focus/MNCs from countries	Phenomenon/ Dependent variable	Independent variable	Data sources (primary/ secondary)	Methodology
Luo and Howe (1993)	Taiwanese firms in Xiamen	Strategies including the level of integration and performance attained by Taiwanese MNCs	N/A	Secondary data sources including government statistics	Descriptive analysis and cross-tabulations
Ulgado, Yu and Negandhi (1994)	Asian MNCs from Hong Kong, Singapore, India, S. Korea, Thailand and Taiwan	Management and organizational characteristics including autonomy to subsidiaries, localization of management	Asian (developing countries) MNCs versus other MNCs	Primary survey, $N = 85$	Cross tabulation
Yeung (1994)	MNCs from Asian developing countries	Strategic dimensions including size of investments, forms of market entry & ownership, capital and sources of funding, choice of technology, foreign trade orientation, patterns of competition & collaboration, locational choice	NA	NA	Descriptive analysis
Li (1994)	MNCs from S. Korea and Taiwan	Realized performance	Eight composite variables: strategy profile, resource pool, value norm, game rule, internal profile, strategic process, intended goal	Survey of 6 South Korean & 8 Taiwanese firms	Tabulation, simple statistical analysis

Table 3. (Continued.)

Authors and year	Geographic focus/MNCs from countries	Phenomenon/Dependent variable	Independent variable	Data sources (primary/secondary)	Methodology
Wesson (1994)	Hyundai's investment in the US PC industry	Motivation for FDI, Performance	Porter's diamond in home & host countries	Descriptive/Case study	Case study
Lee and Beamish (1995)	Korean firms in LDCs	Characteristics, motivation and performance	Ownership level, control by MNC, partner need and commitment	Primary (survey). $N = 108$	Chi-squared and correlation analysis
Chen (1996)	Taiwanese MNCs	Patterns and analysis of Taiwanese investment in China versus Southeast Asia	N/A	Secondary data	Comparative analysis of aggregate-level data
Dent and Randerson (1996)	S. Korean MNCs in Europe	Determining forces behind outward FDI	Non tariff barriers to Korean exports	Secondary data	Aggregate analysis of investment patterns
Fung (1996)	Chinese investment in Hong Kong	Extent and characteristics of investment	N/A	Secondary data	Cross tabulation based on sectors, entry mode
Young, Hunag and McDermott (1996)	Chinese state-owned MNCs	Motivations, stage achieved in the internationalization process	N/A	Interviews of 5 companies	Case studies/descriptive analysis
Yeung (1997)	Hong Kong firms in the ASEAN region	Business networks; mechanisms of ASEAN operations	Mechanisms of control, channels of marketing and sourcing	Interview/surveys ($N = 111$)	Frequency analysis

Table 3. (Continued.)

Authors and year	Geographic focus/MNCs from countries	Phenomenon/ Dependent variable	Independent variable	Data sources (primary/ secondary)	Methodology
Erramilli, Aggarwal and Kim (1997)	Korean MNCs	Level of ownership by Korean MNCs in developing versus other countries	Technology intensity, product differentiation, capital intensity	Bank of Korea data on 177 subsidiaries of 132 MNC parents established between 1988 and 1990	Multinomial Logistic Regression analysis
Yeung (1998)	Singapore MNCs	Overseas investments	State policies, support (assistance programs) and leadership—investment by State-owned firms	Secondary data	Descriptive analysis & case studies
Makino and Beamish (1998)	Japanese MNCs in Asia	Financial performance and termination rate of subsidiaries	Entry mode, host government restrictions	Secondary data, N = 1732	Correlation analysis, Chi-squared tests, T tests
Carney (1998)	Overseas Chinese Family Businesses	Development of proprietary competencies	Formality of the organization and top management membership (kinship, ethnic origin)	Secondary data, N = 50	Descriptive analysis
Pananond and Zeithaml (1998)	Charoen Pokphand group (Thailand)	International expansions process (geographic and sectoral participation)	Time period	Case study, N = 1	Descriptive analysis
Oh, Choi and Choi (1998)	Daewoo Motor Company	Globalization strategy	N/A	Case study, N = 1	Descriptive analysis

Table 3. (Continued.)

Authors and year	Geographic focus/MNCs from countries	Phenomenon/ Dependent variable	Independent variable	Data sources (primary/ secondary)	Methodology
Wan (1998)	Hong Kong MNCs	Performance (ROE, Sales growth, Variance in ROE)	MNC versus local firms, Industrial diversification, Geographic diversification, size, sector	Secondary data, $N = 81$	Regression analysis
Zutshi and Gibbons (1998)	Government-linked MNCs from Singapore	Internationalization process	Development policy (Singapore govt.) and firm strategy	Case studies, $N = 2$	Descriptive analysis
Ernst (1998)	Korean MNCs in the electronics sector	Industrial upgrading, technological learning	N/A	Sectoral case study	Descriptive analysis
Delios and Beamish (1999)	Japanese MNCs	Performance of MNCs	Geographic scope, product diversification	399 Japanese MNCs, Secondary data	Partial least squares analyses
Padmanabhan and Cho (1999)	Japanese MNCs	Ownership strategy	Decision specific experience, relative size, cultural distance	Secondary data, 1519 FDI cases undertaken by 402 Japanese firms	Logit regression model
Basu and Miroshmik (1999)	Japanese MNCs	Human Resource Management in overseas affiliates versus in Japan	N/A	Case studies. $N = 2$ (Toyota and Nissan)	Descriptive analysis
Mansumitrchai, Minor and Prasad (1999)	US and Japanese MNCs	Entry strategies	Country of origin, diversification strategy	Secondary data, $N = 972$	Regression analysis

Table 3. (Continued.)

Authors and year	Geographic focus/MNCs from countries	Phenomenon/ Dependent variable	Independent variable	Data sources (primary/ secondary)	Methodology
Delios and Henisz (2000)	Japanese MNCs	Equity ownership in affiliates	Public and private expropriation hazard (R&D) intensity, parent size, Capabilities (parent experience), and advertising, Keiretsu/ Sogo shosha membership	2827 subsidiaries of 660 Japanese MNCs	Tobit estimation
Shah, Zeis, Ahamdian and Ragassa (2000)	American, Japanese and German companies operating in the US	Generic and business level strategies	Country of origin	Surveys, $N = 160$	Means, medians, ANOVA and Kruskal Wallis tests
Geringer, Tallman and Olson (2000)	Japanese multinationals	Performance	Product diversity, international diversification, time, Export sales Keiretsu membership	Secondary data, 108 Japanese MNCs	Comparison of means, Regression analysis
Taylor, Zou and Osland (2000)	Japanese MNCs	Foreign market entry strategies	Stake of the host country, need for local contribution, riskiness of the host country, resource commitment, and host government restrictions	Survey. 178 Japanese manufacturing MNCs	Discriminant analysis
Delios and Beamish (2001)	Japanese MNCs	Subsidiary survival and performance	MNC's experience in the host country, experience with the entry mode, Intangible assets of the MNC	3080 subsidiaries of 641 Japanese MNCs	Regression analysis

Table 3. (Continued.)

Authors and year	Geographic focus/MNCs from countries	Phenomenon/ Dependent variable	Independent variable	Data sources (primary/ secondary)	Methodology
Belderbos, Capannelli and Fukao (2001)	Japanese MNCs (Electronics sector)	Backward vertical linkages (subsidiary to parent)	Quality of infrastructure, size of the local components supply industry, host country restrictions, entry mode, R&D intensity of parent	272 affiliates in 24 countries	Regression analysis
Asakawa (2001)	Japanese MNCs	Evolution of HQ-subsidiary relations	N/A	Case studies of 5 Japanese MNCs	Descriptive analysis
Henisz and Delios (2001)	Japanese MNCs	Plant location	Prior plant locations by other firms in the country, sales, R&D and advertising expenditures, exports, host country characteristics	Secondary data – 2705 International plant location decisions	Discerete time logit specification

regarding the Asian multinationals—the rapid ascent of many Asian firms from relative obscurity to global prominence within a space of 30 years.

This paper aims to address the above issues through a review and synthesis of the existing literature on Asian multinationals. Our focus, however, is on the newly emerging' multinationals from Asian countries outside of Japan; the strategies of Japanese multinationals are discussed only briefly. One reason for doing so is to reduce complexity of the topic being addressed. Though geographically Japan is in Asia, it is far more developed, economically as well as technologically, than other Asian countries, and its MNCs are in these regards closer to those of Western countries. Furthermore, for those interested, there is already a significant amount of literature addressing Japanese firms and their strategies. Instead, we focus on firms from East, Southeast and South Asia, but do not include those from the Middle East (e.g., Saudi Arabia and Iran). Furthermore, while we do not propose a new comprehensive theory of the Asian multinational, we propose a conceptual framework to help explain the emergence of the most complex Asian multinationals. We also propose a new typology for structuring our thinking regarding the diverse nature of these firms.

The chapter begins with a brief discussion of the historical evolution of the Asian multinational corporation. Next, we consider the theoretical explanations for the existence of the Asian multinational corporation. We then go on to discuss the motivations of Asian multinationals and their profiles, followed by the strategies they have adopted. The conceptual core of the paper proposes a typology for parsimoniously describing the complex and diverse entities included under the broad category of Asian multinationals. We conclude the paper by identifying a few directions for further research in this area.

Before going further, however, it is necessary to define what a multinational firm is. We adopt the following definition proposed by UNCTC in 1984 (Bartlett and Ghoshal, 2000, p. 3): A MNC is an enterprise (a) comprising entities in two or more countries, regardless of the legal form and the fields of activity of those entities, (b) which operates under a system of decision making permitting coherent policies and a common strategy through one or more decision making centres, (c) in which the entities are so linked, by ownership or otherwise, that one or more of them may be able to exercise a significant influence over the activities of others, and, in particular, to share knowledge, resources and responsibilities with others.

ASIAN MULTINATIONALS: A HISTORICAL PERSPECTIVE

Multinationals from Asian countries have had a long history (Yeung, 1999). The Wing-On company an, ethnic Chinese company headquartered in Hong

Kong, was among the first instances of an Asian multinational firm. By the 1920s, the Guo brothers (founders of the Wing On Company) had established a complex organization including several foreign affiliates. Companies such as the Wing On Company, however, were the exceptions rather than the norm. Before WWI, most Asian countries were economically under-developed and several were under the influence of colonial powers. Japan, though not colonized, was inward-looking. Thus, several Asian businesses found it difficult to thrive in their home countries, let alone expand into other countries. The period between the two world wars proved to be a highly unfavorable environment for international expansion due to the poor economic performance of the world economy (e.g., the Great Depression) and the high barriers to international trade and investment. In the period following the end of WWII, many Asian countries gained independence from colonial powers. In 1960, the stock of FDI originating from Asian countries (other than Japan) was estimated at less than 0.8 percent of total worldwide stock—a minuscule figure (Tolentino, 1993).[1] Though Asian companies started venturing into international markets during the 1960s, much of the growth in the number as well as the size and scope of Asian MNCs, however, occurred after the 1970s. Out of the 33 largest multinational firms from developing economies in 1977, only 12 were (East or South) Asian (Yeung, 1999). The largest (East, Southeast or South) Asian company in the list was the Hyundai Group from S. Korea. All the Indian multinationals listed were either in natural resource based sectors, and also government-created monopolies, suggesting a lack of sophisticated strategies or significant achievements.

Being the most economically well-developed country in Asia, Japanese firms were the early Asian investors in foreign countries. During the 1970s, a wave of Asian FDI originated from Japan, Hong Kong, South Korea, and, to a lesser extent Singapore (Ghymn, 1980; Lall, 1982, 1983). By 1978, the stock of Japanese foreign direct investment stood at a level of US\$ 26.8 billion (Han, 1994). Hong Kong's investments were also significant and had reached a level of \$2 billion by the early 1980s (Lall, 1983). Though the outward FDI from these countries might have been contemporaneous, there were significant differences in the nature of this investment (Yeung, 1999). For instance, while much of South Korean investment was government supported and encouraged (Li, 1994; Dent and Randerson, 1996), most of the Hong Kong and Japanese investment was private capital. Compared to the other Asian countries, a larger proportion of Japanese investment was concentrated in high tech sectors such as electronics and some of it was also destined for developed countries in the US and Western Europe (Han, 1994; Aoyama, 1996). The growth of Asian FDI and consequently the Asian multinational corporations was, no doubt, facilitated by the rapid post war economic development throughout most of the world, the reduction in trade and investment barriers and the developments in communication technology which made it cheaper as well as more powerful (Young, Huang and McDermott, 1996; Govindarajan and Gupta, 2001). In 1979, with the opening up of their economy, Chinese multinationals also started investing abroad (Gang, 1992).

By mid-1980s, the Asian MNCs (with the exception of Chinese firms) were starting to attain significant positions in the world economy. The investment from China, was still at a low level. At the end of 1985, the number of non-trade overseas affiliates of Chinese enterprises was 187 and the total value of investment was equal to $290 million (Gang, 1992). On the other hand, Japanese multinational firms such as Sony, Matsushita Electric, Sanyo and Sharp had established global leadership positions in the consumer electronics sector. These leadership positions were often supported by offshore production (outside Japan)—mostly in other Asian countries. Several multinational firms from other Asian countries had also started to attain prominent positions by this time. The year 1986 marked the beginning of an aggressive international expansion by Korean as well as Chinese firms. Lee and Plummer (1992) observed that out of a total 329 Korean FDI cases by the end of 1989, 252 had been established since 1986 and 136 cases in 1989 alone. Between 1985 and 1990, the number of foreign affiliates as well as China's investment abroad increased more than threefold (Tseng, 1994).

In a (1995) ranking of the top 50 multinationals from developing economies, Yeung (1999) identified 35 Asian companies. The domination of Asian companies was as striking at the top of the list with 7 out of the top 10 and 14 out of the top 20 companies coming from Asia. In contrast to 1977 when natural resource based companies were the leading multinationals, the 1995 list had only 4 (just under 12%) natural resource based companies. Thus the prominent Asian MNCs were becoming successful at providing high value added goods and services rather than depending on exploitation of natural resources and government-granted monopolistic positions. Analysis by the World Investment Report also reveals some interesting trends about the Asian multinationals (see Table 4). The 59 firms in list belong to 8 different countries including Taiwan, Malaysia, Singapore, Philippines, China & Hong Kong, Thailand, S. Korea and India. Some of the firms in the list, such as Asia Pacific Breweries, Acer, Jardine Matheson, Fraser and Neave, and Hyundai Motor also exhibit high values of the Transnationality index.[2] These firms have indeed internationalized to a great extent and are comparable to global firms from developed countries in this respect (compare Tables 2 and 4).

IS THE ASIAN MULTINATIONAL A THEORETICALLY ANOMALOUS PHENOMENON?

Theoretical explanations of foreign direct investment and multinationals have often assumed that the home country (and its enterprises) enjoy tech-

Table 4. Leading non-Japanese Leading Multinationals

S. no.	Company	Country	Industry	Year	Assets		Sales		Employment		TNI
					Foreign	Total	Foreign	Total	Foreign	Total	
1	Acer	Taiwan	Electronics	2000	1449	3304	4192	5267	9373	16326	60.3
2	Amsteel Corporation Berhad	Malaysia	Metals	1996	209	1459	80	1066	7800	28200	16.5
3	Asia Cement Corp.	Taiwan	Cement	1995		1365	55	614	200	1376	11.0
4	Asia Pacific Breweries Limited	Singapore	Food and beverages	1995	544	857	618	839	3449	3955	74.8
5	Ayala Corporation	Philippines	Food	1995		1134	22	538		14809	2.2
6	Cathay Pacific Airways Limited	Hong Kong	Transportation	1998	2555.0	7968.0	2023.0	4151.0	4038	15757	35.5
7	CDL Hotels Intenational Ltd.	Hong Kong	Hotel	1995		1044	200	202		9000	35.8
8	Charoen Pokphand	Thailand	Food	1996	82	642	109	857	1077	8440	12.8
9	China Cereals, Oil, Food-stuff Import Export	China	Trading	1997	467.3		6230.0				
10	China Harbor Engineering Company	China	Construction	2000	860	2420	150	1540	1963	62652	16.1
11	China Iron and Steel Industrial and Trading Group	China	Metals	1996	188		257				25.1 (1995)
12	China National Chemicals Import and Export Corporation	China	Diversified	2000	3000	4950	7920	13800	510	8415	41.4
13	China National Foreign Trade Transportation Corp.	China	Transportation	1999	740	2160	440	750	488	57368	31.3

Table 4. (Continued.)

S. no.	Company	Country	Industry	Year	Assets		Sales		Employment		TNI
					Foreign	Total	Foreign	Total	Foreign	Total	
14	China National Metals & Minerals Import & Export Corp.	China	Diversified/Trading	2000	850	2260	880	3180	142	1409	25.1
15	China State Construction Engineering Corp.	China	Construction	2000	3290	7300	1950	5890	5535	239102	26.8
16	China Steel Corporation	Taiwan	Metals	1997	170	5737	467	2492	6	9561	7.3
17	Chinese Petroleum	Taiwan	Petroleum refining	1997		15406.0	248	11765.5		3651	2.1
18	Citic Pacific Ltd.	Hong Kong	Diversified	2000	1842	8771	908	1755	7639	11871	45.7
19	CLP Holdings Limited	Hong Kong	Electric utilities or services	2000	630	7115	180	3101	...	4420	4.9
20	Creative Technology	Singapore	Electronics	1997	405.0	661.2	1175.0	1202.0	2048	4185	69.3
21	Daewoo Group	S. Korea	Electronics	2000	...	22135	...	30547		15000	49.4
22	Dairy Farm International Holdings Ltd.	Hong Kong	Retailing	1998	...[d]	3124.0	...[e]	6967.0	...[F]	49900	46.5
23	Doi Construction Ind.,	S. Korea	Construction	1998	...[d]	5120.0	...[e]	3086.0	...[F]	6583	34.8
24	Dong Ah Construction Industrial Co.	S. Korea	Construction	2000	...	3926	...	1785	...	6403	34.8
25	Evergreen Marine	Taiwan	Transport	1996	117	1678	80	1152	91	1298	7.0
26	First Pacific Company Ltd.	Hong Kong	Electronics Parts	2000	4086	7646	2527	2894	15063	30673	63.3
27	Formosa Plastic	Taiwan	Chemicals	1997		2325.6	241	1650.0		3449	10.4
28	Fraser & Neave Ltd.	Singapore	Diversified	2000	1473	3993	1069	1507	13037	15082	64.8
29	Genting Berhad	Malaysia	Diversified	1997	691.5	2282.9	61.5	982.3			18.3

Table 4. (Continued.)

S. no.	Company	Country	Industry	Year	Assets Foreign	Assets Total	Sales Foreign	Sales Total	Employment Foreign	Employment Total	TNI
30	Guangdong Investment Limited	Hong Kong	Miscellaneous	2000	1695	2577	614	812	16015	17330	77.9
31	Hong Kong and Shanghai Hotels Ltd.	Hong Kong	Hotel	2000	642	2346	58	274	3606	6249	35.4
32	Hutchison Whampoa Limited	Hong Kong	Diversified	2000		13389	2191	6639	20845	39860	39.4
33	Hyosung Corporation	S. Korea	Trading	1996	117	553	2206	2812	470	1460	430
34	Hyundai Motor Co.	S. Korea	Motor vehicles & parts	2000	...	7094	...	3815	...	22787	37.6
35	??, and Shanghai Hotels Ltd.	Hong Kong	Hotel/transportation	1997	319.0	2712.0	55.1	297	3014	5772	27.5
36	Jardine Matheson Holdings Ltd.	Hong Kong	Diversified	2000	5954	9565	7921	11230		160000	67.6
37	Keppel Corporation Ltd.	Singapore	Diversified	2000	2598	17321	376	2127	1700	11900	15.7
38	Korea Electric Power	S. Korea	Utilities	1996	8	26439		9376		29892	2.0
39	LG Electronics Inc.	S. Korea	Electronics	2000	3127	12824	4841	12213	27819	60753	36.6
40	Malaysian Airline Berhad	Malaysia	Transportation	1998	559.0	5294.3	1045.9	1386.5	...F	13788	51.2
41	Malaysian International Shipping Co., Ltd.	Malaysia	Transport	1996	72	172	406	885	321	3004	32.8
42	Natsteel Group	Singapore	Steel and iron	2000	685	1296	208	885	8598	11695	50.0
43	New World Development Co. Ltd.	Hong Kong	Diversified	2000	3414	13465	376	2628	30	16512	13.3
44	Orient Overseas (International) Limited	Hong Kong, China	Transportation	2000	1247	1801	1820	1833	3314	3935	84.3

Table 4. (Continued.)

S. no.	Company	Country	Industry	Year	Assets		Sales		Employment		TNI
					Foreign	Total	Foreign	Total	Foreign	Total	
45	Petroliam Nasional Berhad	Malaysia	Petroleum expl./refin./distribution	2000	5564	26184	3757	11133	2700	18578	23.2
46	Reliance Industries	India	Chemicals	2000	...	5741	...	3160		15985	7.7
47	Sam Yang Co., Ltd.	S. Korea	Diversified	1996	170	1964	115	1487	864	5795	10.4
48	Sampo Corporatoin	Taiwan	Electronics	1996	38	71	107	500	20	3500	25.2
49	Samsung Group	S. Korea	Electronics	2000	...	17213		16640	...	42154	16.3
50	San Miguel Corporation	Philippines	Food	2000	1676	3552	287	1811	4338	15923	30.1
51	Shougang Corporation	China	Diversified	2000	1610	6990	830	4270	1548	212027	14.4
52	Sime Darby Berhad	Malaysia	Food	2000	1270	3198	1959	3178		32490	41.3
53	Singapore Airlines	Singapore	Transportation	2000	1517	9944	3284	4508	3115	27386	33.2
54	Singapore Telecommunications Ltd.	Singapore	Telecommunications	1997	1546.2	5661.7	66.2	2840.2	1625.0	10966.0	14.8
55	Ssangyong Cement Industrial Co. Ltd	S. Korea	Construction	1997	307.3	4001.0	207.6	4170.0	658	4488	9.1
56	Sunkyong Group	S. Korea	Energy/trading/chemicals	2000	3851	36944	12029	38274	2400	29000	16.7
57	Tata Iron and Steel Co.	India	Metals	1995	11	1904	226	1212		76400	6.4
58	Tatung Co. Ltd.	Taiwan	Electronics	2000	...	4483	...	2921	...	19719	28.1
59	Tong Yang Cement Mfg Co., Ltd.	S. Korea	Cement	1996	91	1733	39	736	116	2208	5.3

Year refers to the latest year for which data was available from the World Investment Report (WIR) for that particular company. WIR identifies the Top 50 multinationals from Developing economies. The list above was derived by identifying the Asian firms in the WIR listing that were mentioned at least once in the WIR listing over the 1995–2000 period.
Source: Various issues of the World Investment Report (www.unctad.org).

nological or other monopolistic advantages over (enterprises based in) other countries (Dunning 1981). FDI is undertaken to exploit these advantages in new geographic locations. Starting with this premise, FDI by several Asian firms almost appears to be an anomalous phenomenon.[3] The lower levels of economic development of many Asian countries imply that neither the countries nor the enterprises based in these countries are likely to possess significant monopolistic advantages versus other countries or enterprises based in those countries.[4] MNCs from Asian countries, however, have been an empirical fact for the last several decades.

Let us first consider country level explanations of FDI from Asian countries. The three perspectives considered below including Dunning's investment development cycle model, Agarwal and Ghauri's Extended Product Cycle model and the Pecking order approach, were all proposed with the intention of explaining FDI from developing countries. As noted earlier, however, since many Asian countries are (or were at the time of FDI by firms) developing countries, these explanations may be considered appropriate for the Asian context.

Dunning's (1986) investment development cycle model may be considered as one of the key explanations of FDI from Asian countries. The cycle consists of five stages. The first stage of the model is characterized by little inward or outward investment from the Asian (developing) country. In the second stage, the country experiences a sharp rise in inward FDI. This inward FDI is seeking to exploit the domestic market or neighboring markets, and often involves adaptation of the ownership advantages of the MNC parent. In the third stage of the investment development cycle, Dunning argues that there could be some outward investment from the Asian countries though, on a net basis, there could be an inflow of investment into these countries. Despite a negative balance of investments at the aggregate country level, there is a possibility of some outward FDI from private- or market-oriented public enterprises (Diaz-Alejandro, 1977). The outflow of investment may be helped by the policies of an outward-looking home government. In stage four, the net outward investment may become positive. In the fifth and final stage, there is growing intra-industry rationalized investment which is based on the competitive advantages offered by different locations.

Building on Vernon's (1966) Product Life Cycle model, Agarwal and Ghauri (1991) advocated the Extended Product Life cycle, consisting of seven stages. During the first three stages the following events take place in a sequential fashion: a product is invented in a technologically advanced country, domestic sales increase in the home market and typically export sales also witness an increase. In the fourth stage, production moves to other (than the innovating country) developed countries. In the subsequent stage, this production, in addition to satisfying local demand, also supplies (exports) products to Asian (developing) countries. During the sixth stage of Aggarwal and Ghauri's (1991) proposed cycle, products from the Asian country are increasingly able to out-compete imports, including those produced in countries other than the innovating country. During the seventh and the last stage of the extended product life cycle, firms from Asian countries are likely to export to, as well as produce in, the innovating country. Thus the Asian countries repeat the foreign direct investment pattern of developed countries, but with a significant time lag.

The 'pecking order' approach, which, in fact, predates the product life cycle theory, also aims to explain the phenomenon of FDI from developing countries. There are two crucial assumptions of this approach. First, there is assumed to be a hierarchy of developing countries in terms of their degree of technological sophistication. Secondly, it is assumed that factor costs vary significantly across different developing countries. Thus firms from the more advanced (or industrialized) Asian countries (e.g., Singapore, South Korea, Taiwan, Hong Kong) might undertake FDI in less advanced developing countries. This behavior is not anomalous since these firms might enjoy ownership advantages versus the local firms. Additionally, FDI may also be motivated by the Asian MNCs' desire to exploit the lower factor costs in the other developing countries (Euh and Min, 1986; Wells, 1977).

There are several issues with the country-level explanations of FDI from Asian countries. First, they assume that firms within a country are homogeneous, which may be quite inaccurate. There may be pockets of excellence even in developing Asian countries with some firms excelling in their chosen sectors and thus enjoying ownership advantages. Singapore Airlines, for instance, was known as one of the best-managed airlines even during the late-1970s when Singapore was still a developing country (Pangarkar, 1998a). Creative Technologies from Singapore, which excels in its chosen niche of sound cards, is another example in this regard. Secondly, the explanations offered by the theories are, also, not entirely satisfactory. While it is conceivable that firms from Asian countries will account for an increasing percentage of manufacturing of technologically mature products and possibly export from their home countries, the extended product life cycle theory is not clear regarding why these firms might undertake FDI in other countries unless one assumes that this FDI takes place in even less developed countries. Even then, it is not clear why MNCs from developed countries don't simply establish plants in these new locations—that is why firms from a developing Asian country enjoy an advantage for investing in another developing country. While a significant percentage of FDI by Asian countries is bound for less developed countries, some of it is also bound for countries that exhibit a similar (or sometime even greater) level of development. Investments by Acer and Creative Technologies in the US market are excellent examples in this regard. Similarly, the pecking order approach is silent regarding why firms from developed countries do not undertake FDI in the less advanced developing countries. If this were to happen, the firms from the Asian countries, will "lose" their ownership advantage unless further assumptions are made regarding specialization across the different countries in terms of the ability to produce specific goods.

Let us now briefly review the firm-level explanations of FDI and the multinational firm. In his pioneering work, Hymer (1960) argued that four factors lead to the emergence of the multinational firm, namely market imperfections in the goods market, market imperfections in factor markets, internal and external economies of scale and government's interference with production or trade. The crux of Hymer's argument was that, due to the above imperfections, firms engage in foreign direct investment despite the various costs of operating a subsidiary in a foreign country. The theory, however, does not offer a comprehensive explanation regarding when firms will choose each of the different modes of servicing foreign markets—exports versus licensing versus FDI. Buckely and Casson (1976) based their theory of multinational corporations on Coase's (1937) insight regarding the fundamental difference between market-mediated versus within-firm transactions. They argued that due to the existence of market imperfections (e.g., government intervention in the form of tariffs, non-existence of future markets for long projects, bilateral concentration of market power), firms have incentives to bypass the market and internalize transactions across national borders. Dunning (1979, 1981) proposed the Eclectic theory as a synthesis of the cumulative theoretical insights. The Eclectic theory offers a single integrated explanation regarding MNCs' choice of different foreign market servicing modes. According to the Eclectic theory, three types of advantages (factors) are essential for the existence of a multinational firm: ownership advantages, location advantages and internalization advantages. Ownership advantages refer to one or more of the following: advantageous cost position due to superior access to resources; the ability of a firm to use resources more efficiently than its competitors (economies of scale); or monopolistic position (brand name, technological patents, etc.). Location advantages, on the other hand, are related to the host country and include factors such as low wage rates or other factor endowments in the country, tariffs to imports (that can be avoided by undertaking FDI) and incentives offered by the host government. The existence of internalization advantages means that the MNC finds it advantageous to establish its own sister subsidiary (and thus create an internal market for knowledge or other intermediate goods) rather than deal with outside agencies through licensing or other means.

Many studies regarding the Asian multinationals have recognized that several of these firms do not possess strong ownership advantages to begin with. Without these advantages, the Asian MNCs could be potentially trapped in a negative feedback loop (vicious cycle)—polar opposite of the positive feedback cycle depicted in Figure 1. Early studies argued that the ownership advantages of Asian MNCs lay in their ability to adapt product and/or process technology to make them more appropriate to the host country context (Lall, 1983).

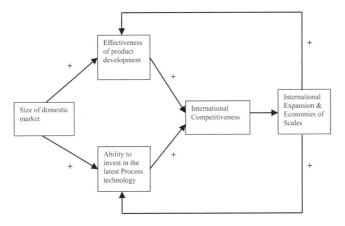

Figure 1. The internationalization process.

For instance the process technology may be changed to make it more labor intensive (Monkiewicz, 1986). They also used a variety of other strategic improvisations to enter foreign markets. Many firms from developing Asian countries that ventured abroad before 1980, undertook some firm-specific adaptation of foreign technology or standardized processes to a relatively small scale of operations and some adaptations of product designs to LDC conditions (Jo, 1981; Lall, 1982). Some scholars have argued that the state has played a significant role in the evolution of the Asian MNCs. In the Japanese context, while some observers believe that the bureaucrats had a significant role to play in Japan's economic development, including the spread of Japanese capital, Porter (1990: 420) asserts that market forces and astute firm strategies were responsible for the achievements of Japanese firms in the international markets. Yeung (1999) argues that strong economic role of domestic governments can compensate the lack of ownership or internalization advantages for these firms. Direct support and promotion of specific sectors, as done by the S. Korean government, is only one form of government support. Philippines, Korean and Indian governments, at various points in time, have helped construction companies to procure contracts in foreign markets (Tolentino, 1993). Yeung (1999) argues that sometimes FDI is governed by international cooperation agreements and may take place independently of the three advantages proposed by Dunning. Many Asian governments have also encouraged local firms to expand their overseas presence. Taiwan, for instance, had the Go-South policy. To facilitate the expansion of Taiwanese firms, former President Lee Teng Hui visited countries such as Indonesia, Philippines and Thailand. Since 1993, the Singapore government has encouraged local companies to develop an external wing (Yeung, 1999). FDI by some Asian firms was motivated by a desire to gain a window on technological developments in another part of the world (Young, Huang and McDermott, 1996; Hwang, 1994). Wesson (1994) terms this asset seeking FDI versus the asset exploiting FDI under the Eclectic theory. Thus even when the ownership advantages of these firms were not salient, they undertook FDI, sometimes in the technologically advanced countries (Ernst, 1998). Creative Technologies' and IPC's (Singapore) investments in the US are an excellent example in this regard.

While these explanations might have been adequate when the number of Asian multinationals was small and when their (MNCs') principal destinations were other developing countries, they are no longer adequate given the pervasiveness of Asian multinationals, the diversity of their destinations and sectors of participation, and the complexity of their strategies. As discussed below, several Asian multinationals have been able to create an ownership advantage while simultaneously becoming multinationals. The traditional theories also assume independence between ownership and location advantages. In the case of many Asian multinationals, the ownership and location advantages are, however, intertwined. For instance, the ownership advantage of firms such as the Thailand-based Charoen Pokphand Group—guanxi with various levels of the governments in China—is location specific, too (Pananond and Zeithaml, 1998).

Next, we turn our attention to how some Asian MNCs were able to attain global leadership positions within a relatively short period of time. We believe that these firms adopted strategies that were consistent with the strategy pyramid (see Figure 2). There are four key elements to the strategy pyramid. Firstly, direct or indirect state support played a vital role at several stages. The Korean government, for instance, provided the most successful exporters with a range of benefits including preferential access to loans at subsidized interest rates, exemptions from certain taxes, discounts on power and freight costs and access to import licenses for their machinery and components (Bloom, 1994). Secondly, many of these firms were consummate learners. Though they initially borrowed technology, they were able to improve upon it and, in some cases, come out with their own state-of the-art technology (Ernst, 1998; Ye-

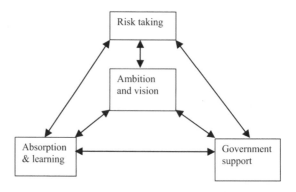

Figure 2. The strategy pyramid for attaining global leadership positions.

ung, 1999). In this sense, there are strong parallels between Japanese multinationals, on the one hand, and South Korean and Taiwanese multinationals, on the other hand. Another key factor behind their success was their ambition or organizational purpose. This ambition, which was often stated in the form of achieving global leadership positions (seemingly unattainable at that point in time) would have provided the constancy of purpose, so critical to global competitive success (Hamel and Prahald, 1985). An interesting contrast can be drawn between the development of Tata Engineering and Locomotive Company (TELCO) from India and Hyundai Motor Company. Even in the late 1970s, TELCO had several years of experience in making trucks. In fact, TELCO had been quite successful in adapting a Daimler Benz truck design to the unique operating conditions in India. By 1980, TELCO had five licensees in countries such as Indonesia, UAE and Guyana. It was also exporting trucks to parts of Africa and Southeast Asia. At that point in time, the Hyundai Motor Company was a fledgling producer of cars based on technology imported from Mitsubishi. By the year 2000, due to an aggressive technology push as well as a global orientation, Hyundai had become the eleventh largest automobile producer in the world whereas TELCO's competitive position had witnessed very little improvement over the previous twenty years. Thus a critical factor in the development of successful (at least in terms of size) Asian multinationals appears to be their ability to improvise and learn. This dynamic element of creation of ownership advantage, however, has not been accorded enough importance in the existing theoretical perspectives such as the extended product cycle model or the Eclectic theory.

MOTIVATIONS AND PROFILE OF ASIAN MULTINATIONALS

The Asian multinationals' internationalization efforts were motivated by several factors. The key factors included the following: limited size, cyclical nature, and vulnerability of domestic markets; quotas on imports set by developed countries; risk diversification; access to raw materials; and "learning" from new markets.

Limited size of domestic markets due to low per capita incomes was one of the key reasons for overseas expansion by several Asian MNCs. Large Indian business houses, for instance might have felt constrained due to the lack of opportunities in the home market. O'Brien (1980) notes that the capacity utilization in several major sectors of the Indian economy (1976) was only 53.7%. Many Singapore and Hong Kong firms might also be motivated by similar considerations.

During the 1970s and 1980s, the rapid penetration of some key sectors of the global economy by Asian firms also prompted several developed countries to impose quotas on products imported from these countries. Hong Kong firms set up textile plants in Singapore (1963, 1964), Taiwan, Macau and Thailand to get around these protectionist measures and the country of origin issue (O'Brien, 1980). Several Japanese and South Korean firms' investments in developed markets such as the USA and Europe were motivated by this consideration (Jeon, 1992). Goldstar set up a color television plant in the US (despite a relative cost disadvantage for manufacture in the US vis-à-vis South Korea) to overcome the quota on imports (Jun, 1987). Circumventing trade barriers and opening export markets was mentioned as an important motivation a decade later by Chinese MNCs (Gang, 1992).

Turning to the other motivations, many Asian countries including Korea and Japan have always faced shortage of key raw materials such as minerals, metals and oil. Some of Japanese and South Korean firms' investments in resource-rich Asian countries (e.g., Indonesia and Malaysia) were motivated by a desire to access these natural resources (Dicken, 1992; O'Brien, 1980). By entering foreign markets, these firms were also reducing their risk from political and economic instability at home (Ghymn, 1980; O'Brien, 1980).

Abundant and cheap labor force in host countries was another key motivation for the Asian MNCs (Dicken, 1992; Aggarwal and Agmon, 1990; Ghymn, 1980). This motivation was particularly salient for MNCs from countries such as Japan, Singapore and Hong Kong where land as well as labor was scare and rapid industrialization had raised the costs of these factors of production significantly (Han, 1994). Outward investment to address rapid appreciation of home currency was a phenomenon that was applicable only to Japanese (rather than other Asian) multinationals (Han, 1994). Recently many Asian firms have been motivated by developing a window on the developments in technologically advanced markets (e.g., the US) and learning from these markets (Gang, 1992).

The diversity of home market structural characteristics and economic conditions is reflected in the diverse profile of Asian multinationals. There are relatively few commonalties across the different countries. Firms involved in natural resource based sectors or essential services such as banking and airlines figure as prominent MNCs regardless of the country of origin. Another commonality is that the big business groups (keiretsu or chaebol) or houses account for a large percentage of investments originating in countries such as Japan, Philippines, South Korea and India.

Multinationals from several different Asian countries wield considerable market power in their home markets. Several studies have identified the influence wielded by large diversified Japanese firms, such as Hitachi, Toshiba and Matsushita Electric, in their home market. Lee and Plummer (1992) observe that the forty eight largest Chaebols accounted for as much as 2/3rds of the total Korean investment in the ASEAN4 (Singapore, Malaysia, Indonesia and Thailand) countries and the US. As much as 2/3rds of Indian equity investments overseas were made by large business houses, with the house of Birlas, alone, contributing about forty five percent (Lall, 1982). This is consistent with the domination of the Indian economy by the big business houses due to the excessive regulation by the government.

There are key differences, however, in the profiles across different countries. For instance, MNCs originating from market-oriented economies such as Hong Kong and Taiwan are likely to be small and medium-sized enterprises (Li, 1994). Lall (1982) observed that majority of Hong Kong multinationals seemed to be medium-sized firms. In the case of Japanese multinationals, there is an interesting dichotomy. Many Japanese SMEs have invested in neighboring Asian countries which exhibit a lower level of economic and technological development than their home country. As much as 70% of the Japanese capital in Korea and 82.3% in Asia has been invested by Japanese SMEs (Ozawa, 1979). These SMEs may be following their customers who have made similar investments.[5] Large Japanese companies, on the other hand, have invested in far-located developed countries which may be technologically and economically comparable (or even more advanced) than their home country (Han, 1994). Many Singapore MNCs are government-linked corporations reflecting the pervasive influence of the Singapore government, especially in capital intensive sectors such as telecommunications and airlines among others. Korean companies, on the other hand, are privately-owned but have received government support in the form of cheap capital, and protection from foreign competition, among other kinds (Li, 1994; Bloom, 1994).

In summary, Asian MNCs foreign investments have been motivated by a diverse set of reasons. The profile of Asian MNCs also differs across the country of origin and is at least partially influenced by the home market conditions. This profile could also change over time as in the case of India where MNCs based in high tech sectors might increasingly become more important than the traditional big business houses.

STRATEGY OF THE ASIAN MULTINATIONALS

The literature on the strategy followed by the Asian MNCs is voluminous with scores of studies addressing the issue. Prior to discussing the literature, a prefatory note is in order. First, there is considerable variation in the strategies followed by MNCs from different parts of Asia. For instance, the strategies followed by MNCs (especially large Chaebols) from South Korea are distinctly different from the strategies followed by Indian MNCs, which, in turn, are different from the strategies followed by Singaporean MNCs. There is another dimension to consider here. There is considerable variation in the strategies followed by multinationals from the same country over time. For instance, over the last 30 years, Korean firms such as Hyundai and Samsung have increased their focus on technologically intensive products, started offering own-branded products and also upgraded their technological capabilities by devoting significant resources to the R&D function. With the above caveats in mind, the following discussion will identify some of the common strategies adopted by multinational firms from the different countries.

It is generally well recognized that multinational firms in most Asian countries started out in a humble fashion by participating in low-technology industries. Lall (1982) pointed out that many Indian MNCs invested in less technologically advanced yet mature sectors such as textiles and garments, light engineering products (such as simple metallic objects), and palm oil. He argued that though some Korean investments were in technologically advanced sectors, many others were also in sectors such as textiles, plastics, cement and simple metal goods. Ghymn (1980) noted that several Korean construction companies had become MNCs and attained a fair degree of success.

In terms of destinations, the Japanese MNCs exhibit an interesting trend. During the second half of 1970s, a majority of Japanese multinational investment (55–57%) was bound for developing countries, mostly in Asia (Kojima, 1978). Mirroring the initial pattern of investment by the Japanese multinationals, other Asian multinationals also invested in developing countries that were either culturally or geographically close to their home countries. Lall (1982) identified 16 investments by India's then-preeminent business group, the Tatas, in countries such as Nigeria, Kenya, Malaysia, Indonesia and the Dominican Republic. O'Brien (1980) observed that forty six percent of Indian joint ventures were in countries with significant Indian migrants. Lall (1982) also observed that most of the Indian FDI was destined for South and Southeast Asia. Many other studies have observed that Taiwanese, Hong Kong and Singapore firms frequently invest in China (Yeung, 1994). Malaysia and the other Southeast Asian countries also form popular destinations for Singaporean MNCs. More than 80% of investments from Singapore and more than half of Malaysian investments are in South and Southeast Asia (UNCTC, 1983). At the end of 1985, though the Chinese MNCs had affiliates in 45 different countries, 40% of their affiliates were concentrated in Hong Kong and Macau, Thailand and Japan (Gang, 1992). In summary, geographic and cultural proximity is an important determinant of the location of investment (O'Brien, 1980). There are several reasons for this geographic pattern of investment. Firstly, when the trade and investment regime in many developing countries was not sufficiently liberalized, many of these (host) countries gave preference to investments from other developing countries (including Asian MNCs) over investment from developed countries. For instance, a former Sri Lankan minister was quoted as saying "We favor investors from small places like Hong Kong because nobody can talk about a sell-out to imperialism in the case of a country that is as small as or smaller than we are" (O'Brien, 1980).

In other words these multinationals may be perceived as less threatening by the host governments (Kumar and Kim, 1984). In addition, ethnic and cultural similarity may often be correlated with similarity of demand structures between home and host countries (Agarwal, 1985). MNCs may also find it easier to hire appropriate personnel in a culturally similar (or geographically proximate) environment, facilitating smoother handover from expatriates to the local personnel in the long run (Agarwal, 1985). Finally, the Asian MNCs might enjoy the advantage of superior market information in countries that are culturally or geographically proximate (Lee and Beamish, 1995; Ulgado et al., 1994).

Over time, however, the Asian MNCs increasingly invested in new locations. By the mid-1980s, the proportion of Japanese investment in Asia had declined to 45%. In late 1980s, as trade-barriers for Japanese goods went up in many developed markets, the proportion of Japanese FDI bound for developing countries further declined to 30% (Kojima, 1978, 1986). By 1991, the US accounted for 42.2% of the Japanese FDI and Europe accounted for another 19.5% (Han, 1994; JEI Report, 19th June 1992). Gang (1992) observed that between 1985 and 1988, the Chinese FDI became more diversified in terms of destinations. By 1988, the affiliates of Chinese MNCs had spread to 79 countries. Though a majority of these affiliates were in Asia, the rest of the world accounted for 44% of the total number (Gang, 1992).

Historically, the affiliates of several non-Japanese Asian MNCs have tended to be small in size (O'Brien, 1980). In 1978, 60% of Indian affiliates (sample size = 60) had sales below $2 million and thirteen had achieved sales above $6.3 million (Monkiewicz, 1986). At the same point in time, 64% of Korean overseas affiliates were characterized by an investment of less than $200,000; another 17% between 100,000 and 500,000 and only 10% had investments of more than $1 million (Monkiewicz, 1986). There could be significant variation for firms within the same country, however. Lee and Plummer (1992) note that the average investment by a Chaebol (1989) was three times as large as the average investment by other firms. However, over time, as they gained more experience, the Asian MNCs have moved towards establishing larger affiliates (Wei, 1993).

Japanese MNCs (especially the larger firms), on the other hand, have often invested in larger-sized affiliates. The mean employment size of all Japanese companies operating in Britain was 383 employees—roughly the same as US companies (Han, 1994).

In terms of ownership strategies for foreign affiliates, the Asian multinationals chose to form joint ventures, especially during the early stages of their internationalization. The average ownership of the Asian MNCs in these joint ventures was typically much less than other multinational firms. O'Brien (1980) noted the strong preference of Indian firms for minority joint ventures. This strategy was consistent with the MNC's resources (relatively weak ownership advantages) (Lall, 1983), host country policies (less liberalized investment regimes, especially in the 1970s and 1980s) and, in some cases, even, home country policies. Indian government, for instance, encouraged Indian MNCs to give their contribution in the form of export of capital equipment rather than cash (O'Brien, 1980). In this respect, the Asian MNCs were quite similar to broader category of Third World or Developing Country MNCs (Wells, 1978; Monkiewicz, 1986). Their willingness to accept minority stages in new ventures might have also made these multinationals more attractive to the host countries. It is noteworthy that many of the above studies were undertaken more than 15 years ago. In a more recent study of MNCs from Asian developing countries, Ulgado et al. (1994) found that sixty two percent of Asian MNCs' foreign affiliates were wholly-owned subsidiaries. Aoyama (1996) observed that Japanese MNCs tend to wholly own a roughly similar percentage of their affiliates. She also observed that a larger proportion (70%) of Japanese affiliates in Western Europe and USA tend to be wholly-owned versus developing countries (53%). Wei (1993) observed that, over time, Taiwanese firms have tended to establish a larger proportion of wholly owned subsidiaries. In another recent study, Yeung (1995) observed that Hong Kong TNCs prefer to set up wholly-owned subsidiaries. On the other hand, Lee and Beamish (1995) find that Korean firms form joint ventures while entering developing countries.

An important question relates to the degree of multinationality of the Asian multinationals—that is the progress they have made since their humble beginnings. Table 5 shows the Transnationality index for the major Japanese multinationals versus leading multinationals from other countries. It is apparent that Japanese firms lag behind comparable firms in all respects—percentage of foreign assets, sales and employees as well as the overall Transnationality index. One reason for this could be the perceived uniqueness of the Japanese management system which was believed to be strongly related to the national culture. Potential MNCs from Japan might have been concerned about the applicability of their management systems in other countries and hence were either reluctant or slow to establish plants in foreign countries. Figure 3 charts the movement of non-Japanese Asian multinationals in respect of the Transnationality index. As would be expected, the gap in the index was rather large in the beginning due to the nature (developing economies) of many Asian countries. The gap, however, has narrowed considerably over time. In summary, the Asian multinationals are still not as internationalized as MNCs from the rest of the world. With a few exceptions (e.g., the large Japanese and S. Korean firms), these MNCs also do not have a diversified presence though they are moving in that direction.

Table 5. Transnationality index for Japanese versus other leading multinationals

Criterion	1995			2000		
	Japanese	Non-Japanese (Top 100)	Top 100 (incl. Japan)	Japanese	Non-Japanese (Top 100)	Top 100 (incl. Japan)
Foreign assets	11.67 6	13.19 47	13.10 53	15.82 16	14.96 71	15.12 87
Total assets	49.94 21	34.69 78	37.92 99	53.23 17	40.72 82	42.87 99
Proportion of foreign assets	0.2345 6	0.4493 47	0.4250 53	0.3145 16	0.4342 71	0.4122 87
Foreign sales	24.38 21	13.39 78	15.72 99	26.26 17	19.29 82	20.49 99
Total sales	70.95 21	27.24 78	36.52 99	68.53 17	34.55 82	40.38 99
Proportion of foreign sales	0.3856 21	0.5587 78	0.5220 99	0.4324 17	0.6149 82	0.5836 99
Foreign employment	26681 18	63103 71	55737 89	68133 8	69737 63	69557 71
Total employment	98535 21	133538 78	126113 99	108850 17	129240 82	125739 99
Proportion of foreign employment	0.3158 18	0.4914 71	0.4559 89	0.4623 8	0.5762 63	0.5634 71
TNI	32.99 21	50.39 78	47.05 99	38.70 17	57.21 82	54.03 99

Source: Various issues of the World Investment Report (www.unctad.org).

THE ASIAN MULTINATIONALS' BASIS OF COMPETITIVE ADVANTAGE

Historically, the Asian MNCs did not possess the advantages that are typically attributable to a large multinational firm. By borrowing technology and subsequent improvisation and adaptation, they, however, achieved competitive advantages. It is noteworthy that even the Japanese MNCs used licensed technology from their European or American rivals. From this initial base of borrowed technology, further technological development took two paths: some

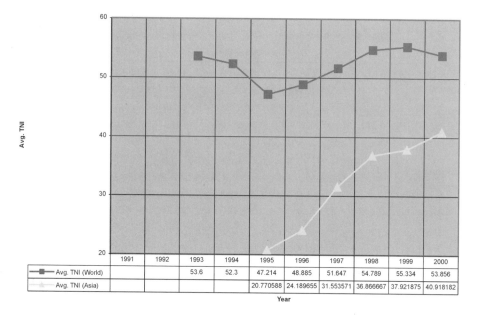

Figure 3. Transnationality index for Asian versus other MNCs 1995–2000.

firms undertook context-specific adaptation whereas others went on to develop their own unique technology. We will discuss each of these briefly.

Many Asian MNCs, especially those outside Taiwan, South Korea and Japan, modified the technology for use in their home markets (Monkiewicz, 1986). Such modifications might have been in the form of increasing the labor intensity of the manufacturing process, or altering the materials or components to suit local availability or, in some cases, minor innovations (Lall, 1983). Given the similarity in economic conditions across the home and host markets, these modified technologies were, often, more suitable for host countries than the technologies of MNCs from developed countries (Monkiewicz, 1986). In Ulgado et al.'s (1994) study also, Asian MNCs identified greater labor intensity of technology and manufacturing process as a key distinguishing feature of their strategy. In some cases (e.g., Hong Kong MNCs) the technology was further modified for use in host countries (Monkiewicz, 1986).

Under an alternative path of development, the Japanese MNCs imbibed the licensed technology and went on to develop their own unique technology which would be a basis of differentiation. For instance, Ampex (USA) served as the initial source of VCR technology for Japanese manufacturers. Firms such as Sony, JVC and Matsushita (Panasonic) were, however, able to improvise the technology and bring about a dramatic improvement, especially in the price/performance ratio of VCRs. Similarly, though Canon was a licensee of

Xerox in the 1960s, it was able to develop its own technological base by the late 1970s. Some of the South Korean and Taiwanese firms were also able to progress along similar paths, though the proportion of companies doing this successfully was lower than Japan. The most notable example of this would be Samsung which went on to become a technological leader in memory chips, liquid crystal displays, and Television sets, among other things.

In some cases, Asian MNCs tried to be early entrants in small markets (Lall, 1983), possibly to avoid confrontation with larger players. Hyundai Motor Company was among the first major investors in India (with investments totaling US$ 800 million) since the opening up of the Indian market to foreign investments in 1991. Taiwanese IT firms focused on Southeast Asia and also on international marketing activities in smaller European country markets such as Sweden and Spain (Chang and Grub, 1992). Daewoo Motors had invested in Poland and Kazakhstan—markets that might be low on the priority lists of most developed country MNCs. In a similar vein, Jollibee, a Philippines based fast food chain had invested in markets in the Middle East, in Brunei and Papua New Guinea (Bartlett and O'Connell, 1998).

In summary, the Asian MNCs have employed a variety of approaches to gain competitive approaches. While some approaches resulted in a localized advantage, others have led to a global competitive advantage. Absorptive capacity and learning appear to be the key drivers of competitive advantage of several Asian MNCs.

ROLE OF GOVERNMENTS

There is considerable variation in the role played by different countries in the development of the multinationals. Multinationals from Hong Kong and Taiwan have tended to be private firms. Many large multinationals from Singapore, including Singapore Airlines and Singapore Telecom, are government-linked. Many large Korean Chaebols, though private in terms of ownership, have received considerable support from their governments in the form of cheap capital as well as encouragement to develop an outward orientation. Typically, the governments in many Asian countries have created domestic conditions such as good quality infrastructure and maintaining high standards in education, that have encouraged or facilitated FDI by the local firms (Aggarwal and Agmon, 1990). With the exception of the semiconductor industry, where the government brought together industry participants in a consortium to bridge the technological gap versus the US industry, the Japanese government played a more indirect role through a competition policy that encouraged vigorous competition among firms (Porter, 1990).

Some Asian multinationals came into existence thru intergovernmental agreements though these are small in number and were formed in the early years—the 1960s and the 1970s. Monkiewicz (1986) notes that these MNCs were formed due to the strong desire of founding states and as either defensive measures against OECD states or offensive measures to integrate some segments of the national economies. In 1979, the governments of Indonesia (60% equity stake), Malaysia (13%), Philippines (13%), Thailand (13%) and Singapore (1%) formed PT Asian Aceh Fertilizers.

To summarize, governments have played a major role in the growth of several Asian MNCs. While some Asian governments have been directly involved, others have facilitated the strategies and growth of homegrown multinationals. It is amply clear, however, that, over time, the role of governments has been diminishing and is becoming more indirect (e.g., provision of appropriate regulatory or physical infrastructure).

TYPOLOGY OF ASIAN MULTINATIONALS

Since the strategies followed by Asian multinationals are diverse—reflecting the social, institutional as technological contexts of their home countries, it is a difficult task to devise a parsimonious typology of their strategies. Based on a survey of the literature, we identified the following key variables for devising the typology:

(1) Whether the company is government linked;
     Whether the company's main business is in natural resources or in highly regulated sectors such as banking;
(2) The degree to which the firm is internationalized or globalized;
(3) The degree of product diversification undertaken by the firm;
(4) Range of value creation activities performed by the firm within a given industry (narrow versus broad);
(5) Ethnic origin and ties.

Based on the above dimensions, we identified the following types of Asian multinationals (see Table 6 for the various dimensions as well as categories).

Expatriate multinationals

As pointed out by Buckely and Mirza (1988), these firms' roots can be traced back to the expansion of colonial powers (especially the British) into Asia. Prominent examples include Swire Pacific, and Jardines Matheson based in Hong Kong and Sime Darby based in Malaysia. The original intent of these firms was quite similar to the agenda of the colonial powers, which included the following: developing and exporting regional resources (e.g., plantations,

Table 6. Criteria and typology of Asian multinationals

Criteria	Category							
	Expatriate MNCs	Ethnic multinationals	Government linked multinationals	Intermediators	Advanced intermediators	Regional MNCs	Undiversified global MNCs	Diversified global MNCs
Origin from colonial companies	■							
Ownership by expatriates	■							
Focus on trading & real estate	■	■						
Family owned	■	■						
Business dealings based on kinship		■						
Conglomerate diversification	■	■						
Government linked or owned–Past or present			■					
Government granted monopoly–Past or present			■					
Narrow focus in value creation activities					■			
Intertwining between competitive advantage of Firm and comparative advantage of the country					■			
Participation in technologically progressive sectors					■		■ (selectively)	■ (selectively)
Local (host country) or regional (rather than global) basis of competitive advantage						■		
Global basis of competitive advantage							■	■ (selectively)
Focused (undiversified) product line	■	■				■	■	
Global presence							■	■
High product diversity								■

mining), facilitating regional trade and investment and acting as a conduit between the Asia Pacific and the Western economies. These firms are quite often focused in trading commodities and real estate sectors, but some have recently diversified into sectors where superior access to capital will yield a competitive advantage.

Ethnic Multinationals

Ethnic multinationals have played a prominent role in the development of their home economies and sometimes even in a larger (e.g., regional) context. The Hinduja group based in UK (but whose founders were of ethnic Indian origin) operated in 50 countries and employed 25,000 people. Overseas Chinese firms have been known to play a vital role in the regional circulation of capital, especially in East Asia (Buckley and Mirza, 1986). Hutchison Whampoa was ranked as one of the largest MNCs by the World Investment Report (2001). The most prominent examples of ethnic multinationals (in addition to the above) include Cheung Kong Holdings Group (Hong Kong), the First Pacific Group (Indoensia/Hong Kong), the Charoen Pokphand Group (Thailand), the Jack Chia Group (Singapore), and the Hinduja group (UK).

The ethnic multinationals adopt a unique combination of strategies. First, many of them are focused on trading and real estate sectors. Second, they often invest in locations where they can exploit their kinship network or host government connections. If opportunities for a network-based expansion, whether product or geographic, arise early in the life-cycle of an enterprise, these firms are quick to seize the opportunity. For instance despite having a relatively modest turnover of $33 million, the Jack Chia group had operations in Singapore to Malaysia, Thailand, Hong Kong, Indonesia, Philippines, Taiwan, United Kingdom and Australia (Lim and Teoh, 1986). Another characteristic of these firms is their opportunistic diversification strategy. The Hinduja group (2002) was involved in a wide range of sectors: film industry, oil, banking, media, pharmaceuticals, trucks, textiles, dried fruits, saffron, tea and other spices. Hutchison Whampoa, has used its superior access to capital to enter diverse sectors such as port development, telecommunications and energy infrastructure development (e.g., Husky Energy, one of Canada's largest integrated energy and energy related companies), and low technology manufacturing (e.g., water and beverage brands). Interestingly, their product diversity outside home markets might exceed their diversity in the home market. In its home country, the Charoen Pokphand (CP) group is focused on its core business of animal feed and integrated livestock. However, in China, the group is involved in a number of different sectors including the following: motorcycle manufacturing, acquaculture, downstream petrochemical projects and real estate development. The Hinduja group provides another example in this regard. Though the group is not involved in truck manufacturing in the UK, it has bought into an Indian truck manufacturing company which was strapped for capital and hence available at a bargain price (www.hindujagroup.com). These firms are also, typically, absent from high technology sectors and are often managed by family members rather than professional managers.

Government Linked Firms

These firms typically operate in highly regulated sectors and have been granted monopolistic rights in their home markets. From their substantial base of resources in the home markets, it's an easy progression for these firms to invest in other countries—often those that are less developed than their home markets. For instance, Singapore Telecom capitalized on the government granted monopoly to acquire two sets of skills and assets: experience in implementing the latest technologies and financial strength. Both skills were useful for entering developing country markets where the incumbents lacked experience with the latest technology as well as the financial resources (e.g., Bharati Telecom in India). The latter skill was useful for entering developed country markets (e.g., Belgium) where the incumbents were financially constrained (Singh and Heracleous, 2001).

In some cases, these firms are also able to effectively service multinational clients since they can offer similar services at home as well as host countries. The State Bank of India is a good example in this regard. Through its investments abroad, the bank services Indian government agencies, Indian companies as well as Indian citizens in the host countries. Due to its extensive network of branches at home, the bank can also offer some kinds of services (e.g., remittances to India) more effectively than even a global bank as Citibank, which has a far more limited reach in the Indian market.

Intermediators

This category was derived from Buckley and Mirza's (1988) paper. One of the key characteristics of these companies is that they are dependent on foreign corporations (especially Western and Japanese multinationals) who might provide critical skills such as the technological know-how and support or marketing skills, among other factors. The South Korean subcontractors who made footwear to the specifications of giant global firms, such as Nike and Reebok, exemplify one category of intermediators. In these arrangements, Nike and Reebok provided the footwear designs as well as the downstream marketing activities such as advertising, promotion and distribution. The subcontractors focused on the relatively simple and less risky tasks of employing the labor and operating the factories. A key source of competitive advantage for these firms lay with the comparative advantage of the home country itself—low wage rates and less stringent standards regarding minimum wage, occupational health and safety. Interestingly, if there was a dilution of the comparative advantage of home countries, the intermediators might move to foreign countries. For instance the South Korean subcontractors established factories in Indonesia to overcome the problem of rising wages in Pusan, South Korea (Rosenweig, 1994). Pao Cheng Shoe Co. (Taiwan) set up 17 production lines for making athletic shoes in China, 11 in indoensia (1994) and, in mid-1990s, committed to build a $30 million factory with 8 production lines in Vietnam (Chen, 1996). In another instance, a small rural town in Southern Fujian, home to 19 Taiwanese (owned) shoe factories, had been dubbed as the "Taiwan Shoe Town" (Luo and Howe, 1993).

Advanced Intermediators

Another class of intermediators includes semiconductor foundries such as UMC and Taiwan Semiconductor as well as other firms that are strategically focused on being OEM suppliers to their customers. Examples of the latter category include Flextronics based in Singapore. There are several critical distinctions as well as similarities between these firms and the intermediators operating in technologically less demanding industries. The key similarity is that both these classes of firms do not perform the full range of value creation activities. There are also two key distinctions. First, the advanced intermediators operate in technologically progressive industries. For instance, Wipro, Infosys and Tata Consultancy Services from India offer advanced software solutions to their customers. These firms do not, however, market their products to the end-users. Secondly, they might have developed a set of skills that are independent of the comparative advantage of their home countries. In a narrow sense, the skills of these firms might exceed those of their clients. For instance, Flextronics is widely reputed to be the most efficient contract manufacturer in the world. Its skills in managing the supply chain far exceed those of its customers.

Regional MNCs

These Asian MNCs do not excel in any particular dimension on a global basis. They, however, derive their competitive advantage from one of the following two sources. First, they might have superior skills versus local competitors. This may be coupled with the fact that the host market is not as attractive (or as open) to other multinational firms from developed countries that might have a stronger competitive position. For instance, during the 1970s, the Birla group from India operated the largest paper mill in Africa and the first export-oriented palm oil refinery in Malaysia (Lall, 1982). During the same time period, Tata Precision Industries, another Indian company operated a facility that was considered the most sophisticated of its kind in the Southeast Asian region (Lall, 1982).

In some cases, the Regional MNCs also have a unique set of competencies such as guanxi. Yeung (1997) argues that personal relationships in social and business networks is a critical factor in the FDI by Hong Kong firms into the ASEAN region. Charoen Pokphand (CP) group, an overseas Chinese group based in Thailand has often acted as a partner for foreign firms wishing to enter the China market. Interestingly the CPs group's diversity of products in China far exceeded the diversity in its home market (Pananond and Zeithaml, 1998).

The Undiversified Global Players

This category includes firms that have made the transition from some other categories such as the intermediators or the government supported multinationals. Through ambition and persistence, among other things, many of these firms have successfully made the transition to global players. A key feature of these firms is that they undertake a broader range of value creation activities versus the intermediators. Unlike the Government-linked multinationals, their dependence on government support for continued success is minimal (or even none). Unlike the Regional MNCs, this category of firms' enjoy competitive advantage on a global basis. Examples of undiversified global players abound but the most prominent ones include Acer (among intermediators) (McDermott, 1991) and Singapore Airlines (among the government-linked firms) and Creative Technologies from Singapore and Asian Paints from India which was ranked among the top 10 decorative coating companies in the world and had market leading positions in 6 countries (www.asianpaints.com).

The Diversified Global Players

If we use complexity as a measure of evolution, these firms have evolved the most. They typically operate in several industries (have high product diversity) and also have a truly global presence. They are distinguished from the previous category by their high degree of product diversity. They also share some similarities with the undiversified global players in the sense that they undertake the whole range of value creation activities including their own product development and marketing products under their own brand names. Examples of these include the Korean Chaebols such as Samsung and Hyundai. While these firms might have strong competitive position in some sectors (e.g., Samsung in semiconductor memory chips), they also might have weaker competitive position in other sectors (e.g., Hyundai in semiconductor memory chips or Kia in cars). There are several key characteristics of their strategies (see Figure 3 for a schematic regarding the key foundations of their strategy). First, they have benefited significantly from the government in the past, or sometimes even on a continuing basis. For instance, protected domestic markets would allow these firms to reduce the risks inherent in building capital intensive world-scale plants. Secondly, in their quest to achieve a globally prominent position in several sectors, they have often undertaken inordinate amount of risks—in the form of high debt loads. On the positive side, however, these firms are consummate learners. They have often started with borrowed technology but imbibed it fully. By improving upon the borrowed product technology, investing in world scale plants and process technology and an aggressive global push, these firms have been able to exploit the positive feedback cycle depicted in Figure 1 and rapidly match the size, scale and complexity of global leaders with a complex portfolio of products and strategies.

In the above typology, we were seeking a balance between parsimony, on the one hand, and comprehensiveness, on the other hand. Our list of key variables is, by no means, exhaustive, and nor is our categorization. We believe that each of the categories is distinct.[6] It is also noteworthy that, over time, firms can make the transition from one category to another. Hutchison Whampoa, for instance, has moved from being a Expatriate multinational to an Ethnic multinational; Singapore Airlines from a Government-linked MNC to an undiversified Global MNC and Acer from an advanced intermediator to an Undiversified Global MNC.

FUTURE RESEARCH ON ASIAN MULTINATIONALS

The large amount of literature on the topic of Asian multinationals suggests that the topic provides a fertile ground for research. There are several attractive aspects of the topic including the diversity of the Asian MNCs, the salient differences between the origins as well as the strategies of the Asian versus Western MNCs, several Asian MNCs' anomalous nature when viewed from a purely theoretical perspective and finally their dynamism which has enabled some of them to achieve global leadership positions.

One issue with the current literature on Asian MNCs is that a substantial proportion of research (especial research addressing the broad strategy of Asian MNCs) was undertaken more than 15 years ago. Even a casual observer of the Asian economic landscape will conclude that a typical Asian MNC today is quite different from its counterpart 15 years ago. For instance, a study on Indian MNCs today is more likely to focus on technology based firms, such as

Reliance Industries, Infosys and Wipro and Asian Paints, rather than large business houses such as Tatas and Birlas. Also if one were to study an Asian MNC making computer hardware today, Legend Computers from China (rather than Acer from Taiwan) would be one of the top candidates. Thus more research is needed to identify the profile, motivations, and strategies of the current crop of Asian MNCs (Ulgado, Yu and Negandhi, 1994).

Rapid technological change is a key characteristic of the today's global environment. It will be interesting to see how Asian MNCs are coping with this change. In the past Asian MNCs often borrowed technology but leveraged other forms of advantage such as lower labor costs. This strategy will, at best, result in limited success in today's environment. It will be indeed instructive to examine the technological strategies of Asian MNCs today to see if those strategies have changed from yesteryears. Though some Asian MNCs such as Samsung have been quite successful at becoming technological innovators, much less is known about the technological capabilities acquired by the average (or typical) Asian MNC. It can be seen from Table 3 there are very few recent studies regarding the technological strategies and capabilities of the Asian MNCs.

The research on Asian MNCs has also tended to focus on a few select countries such as S. Korea, Taiwan, Hong Kong, Singapore and India. Table 3 lists only 2 studies on multinationals from China.[7] As noted earlier, a distinguishing feature of the Asian MNCs is the diversity of the subject. A narrow focus, by definition, sacrifices the rich learning opportunities offered by this diversity. More specifically, future research might find it fruitful to study MNCs from China and the 'new' MNCs from India (such as Infosys, Wipro and Reliance), among others. Aspiring Chinese MNCs had historically been constrained due to government policy but some scholars predict that, by 2020, several MNCs from China and India will attain globally prominent positions (Govindarajan and Gupta, 2001). It is also noteworthy that the Chinese and the Indian MNCs would be blessed with a large domestic market and plentiful supply of highly skilled manpower—luxuries that most other Asian MNCs could only wish for.

Previous research on Asian MNCs has also tended to focus on large business groups in home countries. Today, it is amply clear that several small and medium-sized enterprises are also becoming multinationals. In a study dating back 12 years, Tallman and Shenkar (1990) observed that many small- and medium-sized Korean firms had become multinationals. Dicken (1992) found that small and medium sized Japanese companies account for a large share of the Japanese outward investment. Studying the profiles, motivations and strategies of these small- and medium-sized MNCs would prove to be another fruitful area of research since few recent studies have addressed this issue (see Table 3).

The information revolution that is sweeping across the world has strong implications for the multinationals. Today it may be easier to manage a geographically dispersed network of subsidiaries and affiliates since the costs of data processing and communication technologies have declined rapidly and yet these technologies have become more powerful. It will be interesting to see the extent to which Asian MNCs have harnessed the power of information technologies to better manage their organizations and/or to improve their strategies. It may also be worthwhile to undertake a longitudinal analysis of the impact of the change (increase?) in usage of information technology with the change in performance attained. Comparative studies of Asian MNCs versus developed country MNCs might reveal the gap (if any) between these two types of organizations in this respect. Table 3 shows that there are few studies comparing the strategies of Asian MNCs versus their Western counterparts.

When the Asian MNCs were in the early stages of evolution many studies observed that their management ranks were not professionalized, and their strategies were influenced by considerations such as extending their empires or keeping up with their rivals. Samsung's entry into the mature and competitive automobile industry would be an excellent example in this regard. It will be interesting to see if these organizational and behavioral patterns persist today. The younger generations of many Asian business houses have been educated in the prestigious western universities (e.g., Mukesh and Anil Ambani of the Reliance Group in India and Richard Li of Pacific Century Cyberworks/ Hutchison Whampoa, among others). The younger generation of leaders may also be less entrenched in the kinship- or ethnic-origin-based networks and hence conduct business in a different fashion. The previous generation of leaders also included a number of hard driving CEOs, many of whom founded their companies. It would be indeed interesting to witness the how the strategies of Asian MNCs change under the new generation of leaders and the impact of these changes on performance.

Direct or indirect government support has been a cornerstone of the achievements of several Asian MNCs. As the world moves towards an increasingly barrier-free trading and investment regime, the government support for Asian MNCs is expected to wither. Future research could examine if reduced government protection has brought about a change in the strategies of Asian multinationals. It will also be interesting to compare Asian MNCs that successfully made the transition to the new environment with others that struggled with the changes.

Over the last 5 years, the world economy has witnessed several crises. The Asian economic crisis of 1997 and the bursting of the internet and telecom bubbles (in 2001) hold particularly great relevance for Asian multinationals. During the Asian crisis, several prominent Asian MNCs faced financial difficulties—Kia entered bankruptcy, Samsung was forced to divest its newly-established automobile operations and the CP group was forced to abandon its octopus-like diversification strategy (Asian Wall Street Journal, July 28th, 1998). These instances raise doubts regarding the appropriateness of the some strategies adopted by several Asian multinationals. It would indeed be instructive to examine whether these strategies (e.g., octopus-like diversification) persist over time, especially with the occurrence of a number of crises over the last few years. If these strategies are changing, it would be useful to examine the rate of change as well as the profile of companies that are changing (versus others). Research based on Western data has concluded that conglomerate diversification adds little value and might even destroy value. Conglomerates are increasingly being broken up or de-merged in several countries (e.g., ICI and Hanson PLC in the UK; ITT in the US). It is also interesting that while the Asian MNCs have been quite open to borrowing technology from developed country firms, they have been slower to embrace the organizational and management strategies of Western firms.

Another issue pertains to the adaptability of several Asian multinational firms, especially firms falling under the categories of Intermediators and Advanced Intermediators. Historically these firms have accepted lower margins for lower risks. The lower risks may be attributed to the fact that these firms don't develop their own technology or brand names. This strategy, however, poses relatively weak barriers for would-be imitators. Over the long run, however, these firms face a significant threat of being supplanted by other firms, who might have even lower costs (or more efficient operations). Making a transition to designing and branding (in addition to manufacture) would require these firms to cultivate new skills—a strategic shift which would bring them in direct confrontation with some of their customers as well as other incumbent leaders—possibly provoking strong reactions. Future research might be able to generate significant insights by comparing and contrasting the firms that have made the above transition successfully versus others that did not (e.g., Acer which struggles as a standalone brand but is a major OEM supplier versus Hyundai which has enjoyed a fair amount of success with its own brand).

Though the amount of research of Asian MNCs is substantial, little is known regarding the sophistication of strategies adopted by the Asian MNCs—specifically the extent of global integration among the various affiliates. It would be interesting to identify the factors that explain the variation in the degree of integration across different firms. In Bartlett and Ghoshal's (2000) terminology, how many Asian MNCs are following the four different types of strategies: International, Multinational, Global and (the most evolved) Transnational strategy. In the past Japanese as well as Korean firms were believed to follow the global rather than the Transnational strategy. It would be instructive to examine if these firms, especially those competing in the high-technology sectors, have made the transition to the more integrated Transnational strategy.

The research of Asian MNCs also exhibits an interesting dichotomy. There are several studies addressing broad issues (e.g., typologies, theoretical basis) but employing less rigorous methodologies and analyses. On the other hand, several other studies studying narrower issues (e.g., mode of entry, strategic choices in a particular market). Future research might do well to bridge the gap between the above two categories. The literature will benefit from method- ologically and analytically rigorous studies addressing broader strategic issues regarding the Asian MNCs.

Future research also might find it worthwhile to develop a stronger theoreti- cal foundation specifically for Asian MNCs. The theoretical frameworks (e.g., the Eclectic theory) used in previous research have been adaptations of frame- works developed in the Western contexts. The substantial literature regarding Asian MNCs suggests that their strategies exhibit several distinguishing char- acteristics, namely, their ability to learn and improvise; the role of factors such as gaunxi- and kinship-based networks; the role of government-directed com- parative advantage; and their global ambitions. This uniqueness would further suggest that we need to radically re-think the theoretical frameworks for the Asian multinationals. In fact the traditional theories regarding MNCs and FDI might benefit by incorporating some of the insights from the literature regard- ing Asian MNCs.

In summary, previous research regarding Asian MNCs has generated signif- icant insights regarding the operations and the strategies of these firms. Oppor- tunities abound, however, for further exciting research in this area.

NOTES

1. Tolentino estimated the stock of FDI by all developing country firms at 0.8%. During that time period, most of the Asian countries would form a subset of the broader category of developing countries.

2. The Transnationality index is a simple unweighted average of the following three percent- ages: foreign assets to total assets, foreign sales to total sales and foreign employment to total employment. The higher the value of the index, the more internationalized the particular firm.

3. It is noteworthy that when many Japanese companies started to undertake FDI, Japan was far less developed than it is today. Canon, for instance, established its first overseas production in Taiwan in 1970 even when it did not possess an ownership advantage (www.canon.com).

4. It is noteworthy that firms from S. Korea, Taiwan and Hong Kong started becoming multina- tionals even when these economies were classified as developing economies.

5. There may be a multiplier effect at work here. For instance, the investment by automobile suppliers might easily exceed those by an automobile assemble such as Toyota.

6. It is more difficult to claim that the categories are mutually exclusive. A few firms may be following multiple strategies that would put them in multiple categories (e.g., Acer which exhibits some characteristics of an intermediator as well as an undiversified global firm).

7. This small number may be contrasted with the large number of studies addressing the strategy and operations of multinational firms in China.

REFERENCES

Agarwal, J.P. 1985. Intra-LDCs foreign direct investment: A comparative analysis of third world multinationals. *Developing Economies*, XXIII(3): 236-53.

Aggarwal, R. and Agmon, T. 1990. The international success of developing country firms: Role of government directed comparative advantage. *Management International Review*, 30(2): 163-80.

Aggarwal, R. and Ghauri, P.N. 1991. The evolution of multinationals from a small economy: A study of Swedish firms in Asia. In P.J. Buckley and J. Clegg (eds.), *Multinational Enterprises in Developing Economies* (pp. 248-69). London: Macmillan.

Aoyama, Y. 1996. From fortress Japan to global networks: Locational specificity of globalization for Japanese electronics industry in the 1990s. Ph D Dissertation, University of California, Berkeley.

Asakawa, K. 2001. Evolving headquarters-subsidiary dynamics in international R&D. *R&D Management*, 31(1): 1-14.

Asian Wall Street Journal 1998. Charoen Pokphand to sell its noncore businesses, July 28: 4.

Bartlett, C.A. and O'Connell, J.A. 1998. Jollibee Foods Corporation: international Expansion. Harvard Business School Case 399-007.

Bartlett, C.A. and Ghoshal, S. 2000. *Transnational Management: Text, Cases and Readings*. New York: Irwin, McGraw-Hill.

Basu, Dipak, R. and Miroshnik, V. 1999. Strategic human resource management of Japanese multinationals: A case study of Japanese multinational companies in the UK. *The Journal of Management Development*, 18(9): 714-32.

Belderbos, R., Capannelli, G. and Fukao, K. 2001. Backward vertical linkages of foreign manufacturing affiliates: Evidence from Japanese multinationals. *World Development*, 29(1): 189-208.

Bloom, M.D.H. 1994. Globalisation and the Korean electronics industry: A Chandlerian perspective. In H. Schutte (ed.), *The Global Competitiveness of the Asian Firm* (pp. 138-52) New York: St Martin's Press.

Buckley, P.J. and Mirza, H. 1988. The strategy of Pacific Asian multinationals. *Pacific Review*, 1(1): 50-62.

Buckely, P.J. and Casson, M.C. 1976. *The Future of the Multinational Enterprise*. London: MCMillan.

Business Week (August 6th 2001). The world's most valuable brands (pp. 60-63).

Carney, M. 1998. A Management Capacity constraint? Obstacles to the development of the overseas Chinese family business. *Asia Pacific Journal of Management*, 15(2): 137-162.

Chang, T.-l. and Grub, P.D. 1992. Competitive strategies of Taiwanese PC firms in their internationalization process. *Journal of Global Marketing*, 6(3): 5-27.

Chen, C.-h. 1986. Taiwan's foreign direct investment. *Journal of World Trade Law*, 20(6): 639-64.

Chen, T.-J. 1992. Determinants of Taiwan's direct foreign investment: The case of a newly industrializing country. *Journal of Development Economics*, 39: 397-407.

Chen, X. 1996. Taiwan's investments in China and southeast Asia: Go west but also go south. *Asian Survey*, XXXVI(5): 447-67.

Coase, R.H. (1937). The nature of the firm. *Economica*, 4: 384-405.

Delios, A. and Beamish, P.W. 1999. Geographic scope, product diversification and corporate performance of Japanese firms. *Strategic Management Journal*, 20(8): 711-27.

Delios, A. and Beamish, P.W. 2001. Survival profitability: The roles of experience and intangible assets in foreign subsidiary performance. *Academy of Management Journal*, 44(5): 1028-38.

Delios, A. and Henisz, W.J. 2000. Japanese firms' investment strategies in emerging economies. *Academy of Management Journal*, 43(3): 305-23.

Dent, C.M. and Randerson, C. 1996. Korean foreign direct investment in Europe: The determining forces. *Pacific Review*, 9(4): 531-52.

Diaz-Alejandro, C.F. 1977. Foreign direct investment by Latin Americans. In T. Agmon and C.P. Kindleberger (eds.), *Multinationals from Small Countries*, Cambridge, MA: MIT Press.

Dicken, P. 1992. *Global Shift: Industrial Change in a Turbulent World*. London: Paul Chapman.

Dunning, J.H. 1979. Explaining changing patterns of international production: In defense of the eclectic theory. *Oxford Bulletin of Economics and Statistics*, 41: 269-29.

Dunning, J.H. 1981. *International Production and the Multinational Enterprise*. London: Allen and Unwin.

Dunning, J.H. 1986. The investment development cycle revisited. *Weltwirtschaftliches Archiv*, 122(4): 667-75.

Encarnation, D.J. 1982. The political economy of Indian joint industrial ventures abroad. *International Organization*, 36(1): 31-59.

Ernst, D. 1998. Catching-up, crisis and industrial upgrading: Evolutionary aspects of technological learning in Korea's Electronics industry. *Asia Pacific Journal of Management*, 15(2): 247-284.

Erramilli, M.K., Agarwal, S. and Kim, S.-S. 1997. Are firm specific advantages location specific too? *Journal of International Business Studies*, 28(4): 735-57.

Euh, Y.-d. and Min, S.H. 1986. Foreign direct investment from developing countries: the case of Korean firms. *Developing Economies*, 24(2): 149-68.

Ferrantino, M.J. 1992. Transaction costs and the expansion of third world multinationals. *Economic Letters*, 38(4): 451-56.

Fung, K.C. 1996. Mainland Chinese investment in Hong Kong: how much, why and so what? *Journal of Asian Business*, 12(2): 21-39.

Gang, Y. 1992. Chinese Transantional Corporations. *Transnational Corporations*, 1(2): 125-33.

Geringer, J.M., Tallman, S. and Olsen, D.M. 2000. Product and international diversification among Japanese multinational firms. *Strategic Management Journal*, 21(1): 51-80.

Ghymn, K.-i. 1980. Multinational enterprises from the third world. *Journal of International Business Studies*, XI(2): 118-22.

Govindarajan, V. and Gupta, A.K. 2001. *The Quest for Global Dominance: Transforming Global Presence into Global Competitive Advantage*. San Francisco: Josey Bass.

Hamel and Prahalad. 1985. Do you really have a Global Strategy? *Harvard Business Review*, 63(4): 139-148.

Han, C.M. and Brewer, T.L. 1987. Foreign direct investment by Korean firms: An analysis with FDI theories. *Asia Pacific Journal of Management*, 4(2): 90-102.

Han, M.-H. 1994. *Japanese Multinational in the Changing Context of Regional Policy*. Hants, England: Ashgate Publishing Company.

Henisz, W.J. and Delios, A. 2001. Uncertainty, imitation and plant location: Japanese multinationals, 1990-96. *Administrative Science Quarterly*, 46(3): 443-75.

Hwang, J.S. 1994. Economic development and internationalization as viewed through the investment development path. Ph D Thesis, University of Reading.

Hymer, S. 1960. The international operations of international firms: A study of foreign direct investment. Ph D dissertation, Massachusetts Institute of Technology.

JEI Report (19th June 1992). Japan Economics Institute Weekly Publication.

Jeon, Y.-D. 1992. The determinants of Korean direct investment in manufacturing industries. *Weltwirtschaftliches Archiv*, 128(3): 527-41.

Jo, S.-H. 1982. Overseas direct investment by South Korean firms. In K. Kumar (ed.), *Multinationals from Third World Countries*. Lexington: DC Heath.

Jun, Y. 1987. The reverse direct investment: The case of the Korean consumer electronics industry. *International Economic Review*, 1(3): 91-104.

Kojima, K. 1978. *Direct Foreign Investment: A Japanese Model of Multinational Business Operations*, London: Croom Helm.

Kojima, K. 1986. Japanese style direct foreign investment. *Japanese Economic Studies*, XIV(3): 52-82.

Kumar, K. and Kim, K.Y. 1984. The Korean manufacturing multinationals. *Journal of International Business Studies*, 15(1): 45-61.

Lall, R. 1986. Third world multinationals: The characteristics of Indian firms investing abroad. *Journal of Development Economics*, 20: 381-97.

Lall, S. 1982. The emergence of third world multinationals: Indian joint ventures overseas. *World Development*, 10(2): 127-46.

Lall, S. 1983. The rise of MNCs from the third world. *Third World Quarterly*, 5(3): 618-26.

Lecraw, D.J. 1977. Direct investment by firms from less developed countries. *Oxford Economic Papers*, 29(3): 442-57.

Lecraw, D.J. 1993. Outward direct investment by Indonesian firms: Motivations and effects. *Journal of International Business Studies*, 24(3): 589-600.

Lee, C. and Beamish, P.W. 1995. The characteristics and performance of Korean joint ventures in LDCs. *Journal of International Business Studies*, 26(3): 637-54.

Lee, K. and Plummer, M.G. 1992. Competitive advantages, two way foreign investment and capital accumulation in Korea. *Asian Economic Journal*, VI(2): 147-70.

Li, P.P. 1994. Strategy profiles of indigenous MNEs from NIEs: The case of South Korea and Taiwan. *International Executive*, 36(2): 147-70.

Lim, M.H. and Teoh, K.F. 1986. Singapore corporations go transnational. *Journal of Southeast Asian Studies*, XVII(2): 336-65.

Luo, Q. and Howe, C. 1993. Direct investment and economic integration in the Asia Pacific: The case of Taiwanese investment in Xiamen. *China Quarterly*, 136: 746-69.

Lim, M.H. and Teoh, K.F. 1986. Singapore corporations go transnational. *Journal of Southeast Asian Studies*, 17(2), 336-65.

Makino, S. and Beamish, P.W. 1998. Local ownership restrictions, entry mode choice and FDI performance. *Asia Pacific Journal of Management*, 15(2): 119-36.

Mansumitrchai, S., Minor, M.S. and Prasad, S. 1999. Comparing the entry strategies of large US and Japanese firms. *International Journal of Commerce and Management*, 9(3): 1-18.

McDermott, M. 1991. Taiwan's electronic companies are targeting Europe. *European Management Journal*, 9(4): 466-74.

Monkiewicz, J. 1986. Multinational enterprises of developing countries: Some emerging characteristics. *Management International Review*, 26(3), 67-79.

O'Brien, P. 1980. The new multinationals: Developing country firms in international markets. *Futures*, 12(4): 303-16.

Oh, D., Choi, C.-J. and Choi, E. 1998. The globalization strategy of Daewoo Motor Company. *Asia Pacific Journal of Management*, 15(2): 185-204.

Ozawa, T. 1979. *Multinationalism, Japanese Style: The Political Economy of Outward Dependence*. Princeton: Pricneton University Press.

Padmanabhan, P. and Cho, K.R. 1999. Decision specific experience in foreign ownership and establishment strategies: Evidence from Japanese firms. *Journal of International Business Studies*, 30(1): 25-44.

Pananond, P. and Zeithaml, C. 1998. The international expansion process of MNEs from developing countries: A case study of Thailand's CP group. *Asia Pacific Journal of Management*, 15(2): 163-184.

Pang, E.F. and Komaran, R.V. 1985. Singapore multinationals. *Columbia Journal of World Business*, XX(2): 35-43.

Pangarkar, N. 1998a. The Singapore airlines group. *Asian Case Research Journal*, 2(2): 211-237.

Porter, M.E. 1990. *Competitive Advantage of Nations*. New York: The Free Press.

Rosenwrig, P.M. 1994. *International sourcing in athletic footwear: Nike and Reebok*. Harvard Business School case.

Shah, A., Zeis, C., Ahmadian, A. and Ragassa, H. 2000. Strategies of gaining competitive advantage at the generic and business unit level: A study comparing American, Japanese and German companies operating in the United States. *Multinational Business Review*, 8(1): 13-21. Shin, W.S. and Oh, E.J. 1990. Recent development in Korea's foreign investment. *Journal of World Trade*, 24(6): 31-56.

Singh, K. and Heracleous, L. 2001. Singapore Telecom: Strategic challenges in a turbulent environment. In K. Singh, N. Pangarkar and L.G. Eng, *Business Strategy in Asia: A Casebook* (pp. 1-22) Singapore: Thomson Learning.

Smart, J. and Smart, A. 1991. Personal relations and divergent economies: A case study of Hong Kong investments in south China. *International Journal of Urban and Regional Research*, 15(2): 216-33.

Tallman, S.B. and Shenkar, O. 1990. International cooperative venture strategies: Outward investment and small firms from NICs. *Management International Review*, 30(4): 299-315.

Taylor, C.R., Zou, S. and Osland, G.E. 2000. Foreign market entry strategies of Japanese MNCs. *International Marketing Review*, 17(2): 146-63.

Tolentino, P.E.E. 1993. *Technological innovation and the third world multinationals*. London: Routledge.

Tseng, C.-S. 1994. The process of internationalization of PRC firms. In H. Schutte (ed.), *The Global Competitiveness of the Asian Firm* (pp. 121-28). New York: St Martin's Press.

Ulgado, F.M., Yu, C.-M. and Negandhi, A.R. 1994. Multinational enterprises from Asian developing countries: Management and organizational characteristics. *International Business Review*, 3(2): 123-33.

UNCTC 1983. *Transnational Corporations in World Development: Third Survey*. New York: United Nations Centre on Transnational Corporations.

Vernon, R. 1966. International investment and the trade in the product cycle. *Quarterly Journal of Economics*, 80: 190-207.

Wan, C.-C. 1998. International diversification, industrial diversification and firm performance of Hong Kong MNCs. *Asia Pacific Journal of Management*, 15(2): 205-218.

Wei, Y.-s. 1993. The development and prospect of economic relations among mainland China, Hong Kong and Taiwan. In K.S. Lio and (ed.), *Politics of Economic Cooperation in the Asia Pacific Region* (pp. 161-189). Hong Kong: The Chinese University of Hong Kong.

Wells, Jr., L.T. 1977. The internationalization of firms from developing countries. In T. Agmon and C.P. Kindleberger (eds.), *Multinationals Firms from Small Countries* (pp. 133-56). Cambridge, MA: MIT Press.

Wells, L.T. Jr. 1978. Foreign investment from the third world: The experience of Chinese firms from Hong Kong. *Columbia Journal of World Business*, XIII(1): 39-49.

Wesson, T. 1994. Towards a fuller understanding of Foreign Direct Investment: The example of Hyundai's investment in the US personal computer industry. *Business and Contemporary World*, 3: 123-26.

Wan, C.-C. 1998. International diversification, industrial diversification and firm performance of Hong Kong MNCs. *Asia Pacific Journal of Management*, 15(2): 205-218.

World Investment Report (1995-2001). www.unctad.org.

Yeung, H.W.C. 1994. Transnational corporations from Asian developing countries: Their characteristics and competitive edge. *Journal of Asian Business*, 10(4): 17-58.

Yeung, H.W.C. 1994. Third world multinational revisited: A research critique and future agenda. *Third World Quarterly*, 15(2): 297-317.

Yeung, H.W.C. 1994. The political economy of transnational corporations: A study of the re-gionalization of Singapore firms. *Political Geography*, 17(4): 389-416.

Yeung, H.W.C. 1995. The geography of Hong Kong transnationals in the ASEAN region. *Area*, 27(4): 318-34.

Yeung, H.W.C. 1997. Cooperative strategies and Chinese business networks: A study of Hong Kong transnationals in the ASEAN region. In P.W. Beamish and J.P. Killing (eds.), *Cooperative strategies: Asia Pacific Perspectives* (pp. 22-56). San Francisco, CA: The New Lexington Press.

Yeung, H.W.C. 1997. Business networks and transnational corporations: A study of Hong Kong firms in the ASEAN region. *Economic Geography*, 73(1): 1-25.

Yeung, H.W.C. 1999. Introduction: Competing in the global economy: The globalization of business firms from emerging economies. In H.W.C. Yeung (ed.), *The globalization of Business Firms from Emerging Economies*. Cheltenham, Uk: Edward Elgar.

Young, S., Huang, C.-h. and McDermott, M. 1996. Internationalization and competitive catch up processes: Case study evidence on Chinese multinational enterprises. *Management International Review*, 36(4): 295-314.

Zutshi, R.K. and Gibbons, P. 1998. The internationalization process of Singapore government-linked companies: A contextual view. *Asia Pacific Journal of Management*, 15(2): 219-246.

Chapter 7

ASIAN ENTREPRENEURSHIP RESEARCH
A Profile and Assessment

John E. Butler
The Hong Kong Polytechnic University

Stephen Ko
The Hong Kong Polytechnic University

Wai Chamornmarn
Thammasat University

INTRODUCTION

Comprehensive treatments of entrepreneurship research are usually done in the context of an entire volume, rather than in a single chapter (e.g., Sexton & Smilor, 1986; Sexton & Landström, 2000). In the last twenty years a large quantity of managerially related entrepreneurship research has been published, but the majority of this has been conducted and published in Europe and North America. During this same period of time many Asian countries were experiencing rapid levels of economic growth, which was being driven by local entrepreneurs. Small and medium size businesses (SMEs) were accounting for much of the increase in employment and in many countries accounting for growth in exports. Research about Asian entrepreneurs gradually began to appear with the introduction of journals devoted to entrepreneurship. This trend was supported by the appearance of journals published in Asia about entrepreneurship.[1] More recently economic growth in China, Southeast Asian and South Asia has fueled research interest in entrepreneurship (Morris, 2001). Thus, there is now a considerable body of research literature, and the academic community can benefit from a comprehensive assessment of both what has been done, what has been learned, and what are the most meaningful directions for future research.

In this chapter some contextual background is provided, so that the continent's more than 50 political units can be seen as related entrepreneurship research groups, where the quantity of entrepreneurial behavior may or may not be related to the quantity of entrepreneurship research. Then, a framework is presented for discussing entrepreneurial research focused on this continent, and each of the distinct areas of research are discussed in terms of the entrepreneurial process. Finally, an assessment is made with respect to where the current state of research stands, what are the major gaps in this research, and what are the best ways to systematically fill these gaps.

THE CONTEXT OF ENTREPRENEURIAL BEHAVIOR IN ASIA

Some countries in Asia have been the source of larger numbers of entrepreneurship studies than other. The reasons for this relate to the variety in the counties, but there are some factors that are more obviously related to the discrepancy. The analysis here indicates that economic factors, including both per capita purchasing power parity and the absolute size of the economy are important drivers of research. In addition, the presence of a tradition of academic research, academic journals, and a willingness to support and/or collaborate with outsiders in such research appears to be important. Finally, the major journals of entrepreneurship tend to publish in English, which may be a limitation of this review, but which enhances the degree to which the research done can be diffused to academics in other countries. On balance, these factors help to explain why some countries are relatively more represented in this research area, either as active researchers or as research samples.

Per capital GDP based on purchasing power parity (PPP) is a useful way to measure of the rate of entrepreneurial activity that one might expect in a nation. Asia has 10 countries with PPP of over US $15,000.[2] However, four of these are small oil producing countries (Qatar, Brunei, Bahrain and Kuwait) that are unrepresented in the research literature. Hong Kong and Singapore have been the subject and source of much research, while Israel, South Korea and Japan have been the source of some research. There are a number of countries at the lower end of the PPP scale that are not represented in the research literature. However, lower PPP countries, which are also large economies such as China and India, are well represented. This suggests that both economic development, growth, and size act to attract academics involved in entrepreneurship research, in the same way that the availability of research grants and external funding attracts scholars to certain research topics. However, it also means that conclusions we draw from the existing bodies of research must be circumspect since mid-size and poorer economies are very under-represented in the published entrepreneurship research.

Our review indicates that a tradition of academic research and the presence of academic journals are important factors. Singapore and Hong Kong have been very aggressive with respect to encouraging academic research, while the presence of academic journals devoted to entrepreneurship in Singapore, Malaysia and India provide local researchers regional outlets for their manuscripts. This allows researchers to forge links and to identify themselves to others as potential contributors in joint research.

The presence of English as a first, or comfortable second language seems important. While this review has focused mostly on English language material, most entrepreneurship journals and major conferences on entrepreneurship use English.[3] In some cases, such as China, there is now a large number of overseas Chinese scholars fluent in English, and capable to using their Chinese language capabilities to form research links in China. This has resulted in China being well represented in the entrepreneurship research literature. In addition, researchers in the region are becoming more adept at collecting data, using native language surveys and interviews, and then reporting the results in English.

Entrepreneurship research also appears to benefit from both the interest in certain countries and the opportunities afforded to non-local researchers. For instance, some cases of entrepreneurship research in Israel, Indonesia and Thailand have been a function of a chance sabbatical or visit by a foreign academic researcher, which these countries have encouraged. In some cases these relationships have evolved into longer term relationships. In other cases, such as China, the level of interest in the country has increased dramatically. This has acted to draw researchers to the area, as well as encourage them to form research links with Chinese scholars.

Obviously, a lack of general interest or governmental encouragement works in the opposite direction, and helps account for the lack of research in most of the Arab countries as well as the newly independent Asian countries that used to form the Soviet Union. In addition, poorer countries such as Burma, Mongolia and Laos seldom appear in the existing literature. This presents a large geographical gap, and since these countries are sufficiently different from the areas where most research has been conducted, caution should be taken in generalizing bits of knowledge gained in one country or region to the entire continent. The return to political stability in some of these areas should bring some renew research interest in entrepreneurship research, as has already occurred in Cambodia (Dana, 1999; Webster & Boring, 2000).

The degree of diversity along almost any dimension is extremely high across Asia. In an entrepreneurial sense, and particularly from the perspective of researchers, this diversity provides a rich agenda for future research. All the dimensions of entrepreneurial behavior can be captured here, provided researchers have the links, language capability, energy and opportunity to engage in meaningful entrepreneurship research.

ENTREPRENEURIAL BEHAVIOR AND ASIAN ENTREPRENEURSHIP RESEARCH

The body of research relating to Asian entrepreneurship will be examined in terms of the entrepreneurship process. Figure 1 depicts the general direction of the entrepreneurial process and the topics that are reviewed, while the references for each topic are summarized in Figure 2. Obviously, there is some overlap, as some research covers more than one area, and papers may focus on the entire entrepreneurial process. In addition, some topics that are in the existing entrepreneurship literature are absent in the Asian literature, but highlighting their absence is one of the goals of this chapter.

ENTREPRENEURIAL CHARACTERISTICS

Traits and Characteristics

The debate about the usefulness of trait research continues in Europe and North America (Brockhaus & Horwitz, 1986; Gartner, 1988), but it is one of the most representative areas of entrepreneurship research in Asia. Research on the relationship between locus of control, risk taking, and tolerance for ambiguity and entrepreneurial behavior has been studied extensively, especially in Singapore. Singaporean entrepreneurs with high levels of these characteristics were found to be more adept at reducing stress and their firms had higher levels of performance (Teoh & Foo, 1997). Chew and Koh (1993) in an earlier study found a link between tolerance for ambiguity and performance, but no difference with respect to risk taking. The focus on business founding has also received some attention. Accounting students in Singapore, who had a high desire to open their own businesses had higher internal locus of control, greater propensity to take risks and higher levels of confidence than did their non-business founding inclined colleagues (Ho & Koh, 1992).

Trait research also raises the ongoing debate about the distinction between good entrepreneurs and good managers, since Ray (1994) found that managers did not differ from entrepreneurs on risk taking, with one exception: the risk of giving up their job to start a business. The risk of giving up a secure job is even more prominent in Japan (Ohe, Honjo & Oliva, 1991), which explains why well educated Japanese seldom leave secure positions to start a business, although this is now changing and may be an issue that needs to be re-examined.

If there is a substantive problem with the link between traits and entrepreneurial behavior and success, it may rest on the degree to which the items that compose these constructs have been taken from Western instruments. It may well be that the constructs are theoretically valid, but that more attention needs

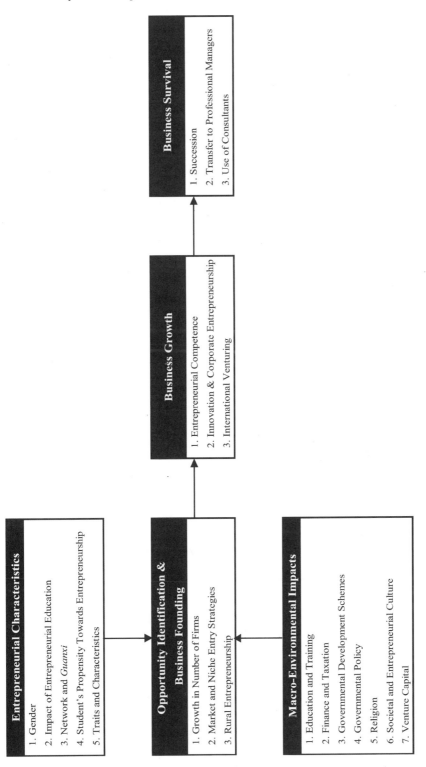

Figure 1. The entrepreneurial process as a research agenda.

Figure 2. Research topics and relevant studies. (To be continued.)

	RESEARCH TOPIC	RELEVANT STUDIES*
Entrepreneurial Characteristics	Gender (Women Entrepreneurs)	Singh IN (1993)•; Wimalatissa BN (1996); Lerher, Brush & Hisrich IL (1997)•; Das IN (1999)•; Kaur & Bawa IN (1999)•; Chu HK (2000); Milgram PH (2001); Ganesan, Kaur & Maheshwari IN (2002)•; Kantor SA (2002)
	Impact of Entrepreneurial Education	Ghazali, Chew, Ghosh & Tay SG (1994)•; Poonjary IN (1996)•; Saini & Bhatia IN (1996)•
	Networks and *Guanxi*	Ramachandran & Ramnarayan IN (1993); Brown & Butler VN (1994); Tsang CN (1994); Kanai JP (1995); Zhao & Aram CN (1995); Das IN (1996); Xin & Pearce CN (1996)•; Menning IN (1997); Bal IN (1998); Akizawa & Kijima JP (1999); Rutten MY & ID (2001)•
	Student's Propensity Towards Entrepreneurship	Ho & Koh SG (1992)•; Tan, Siew & Tan SG (1995)•; Doh, Tan & Chiong SG (1996)•; Kao & Chiang CN (2000)
	Traits and Characteristics	Ohe, Honjo & Oliva JP (1991)•; Ho & Koh SG (1992)•; Chew & Koh SG (1993)•; Ghazali, Chew, Ghosh & Tay SG (1994); Ng & Ng MY & SG (1994); Pareek IN (1994); Ray SG (1994)•; Sengupta & Debnath IN (1994)•; Sharpe SG (1994); Butler & Chamornmarn TH (1995)•; Chew & Koh SG (1995)•; Tan & Tay SG (1995)•; Arghiros TH (1997); Chan, Lau & Man HK (1997); Holt CN (1997)•; Teoh & Foo SG (1997)•; Abdullah MY (1998)•; Lee & Chan SG (1998); Mauysami & Goby SG (1998); Vijaya & Kamalanabhan IN (1998); Ray SG (1998); Misra & Kumar IN (2000); Choo & Mazzarol SG (2001)•; Lau & Busentiz CN (2001)•; Tan CN (2001)•
Macro-Environmental Impacts	Macro-Environmental Impacts	Reeder CN (1984); Tan CN (1987); Dandridge & Flynn CN (1988); Jia & Wang CN (1989); Ho HK (1992); Ghosh, Low, Tan & Chan MY & SG (1993); Wong, Wong, Kwan & Gansham SG (1994)•; Singh IN (1994); Lombardo CN (1995); Singh IN (1997)•; Honig IL (2001)•
	Education and Training	Aziz MY (1980)
	Finance and Taxation	Choy (1990); Hoshi, Kashyap & Scharfstein JP (1991)•; Murin & Sommariva CN (1993); Matsuda, VanderWerf & Scarbrough JP (1994)•; Teo & Cheong SG (1994)•; Cheung, Chan & Lam HK (1996); Boocock & Wahab MY (1997)•; Rao IN (1997); Chow & Fung CN (2000)•; Hall JP, SG, TW & ID (2000); Lerher & Haber IL (2001)•; Singh IN (2001)
	Governmental Development Schemes	Kashyap & Shah IN (1995)•; Ser EA & IN (1998); Singh IN (1999)

Figure 2. (Continued.)

	RESEARCH TOPIC	RELEVANT STUDIES*
Macro-Environmental Impacts	Governmental Policy	Hu CN (1993); Zhu CN (1993); Krishna & Awasthi IN (1994)•; Chau CN (1995); Lee CN (1995); Chow & Fung CN (1996); Tan CN (1996)•
	Religion	Akbar IA (1993)
	Societal Culture	Geertz ID (1963); McGrath & MacMillan CN & TW (1992)•; McGrath, MacMillan, Yang & Tsai TW & CN (1992)•; Swierczek PH, MY, SG & TH (1994)•; Kirby & Fan CN (1995); Siu & Kirby HK (1995)•; Selmer & de Leon SG (1996)•; Tsang CN (1996); Rutten ID (1997); Vachani TW, CN & TH (1998); Lo HK (1999)•
	Entrepreneurial Culture	Sharpe SG (1994); Tsang CN (1997); Ahlstrom & Burton CN (2002); Tan CN (2002)•
	Venture Capital	Keeley, Roure, Goto & Yoshimura JP (1990)•; Ray SG (1991); Ray & Turpin JP (1993); Rah, Jung & Lee KR (1994); Tashiro JP (1999); Wang & Sim SG (2001)•; Burton, Ahlstrom & Singh SG (2002); Cornelius & Naqui HK & SG (2002)•; Hindle & Lee SG (2002)•; Lockett & Wright AS (2002); Lockett, Wright, Sapienza & Pruthi IN, SG & HK (2002)•; White, Gao & Zhang CN (2002); Wright, Pruthi & Lockett IN (2002)•
Opportunity Identification & Business Founding	Business Founding	Liu CN (1992); Hawkins JP (1993); Siu, Liu & Tseng CN (1993); Sabbarwal IN (1994)•; Dobbins MM, CN, ID & PH (1996); Ray & Ramachandran IN (1996); Ray SG (1998); Kuemmerle CN & JP (2002)
	Growth in Number of Entrepreneurial Firms	Alexander TR (1960); Chew SG (1988); Bruun CN (1990); Lin CN (1990); Chang & MacMillan CN (1991); Awasthi IN (1992)•; Hu CN (1993); Cheung & Hoon SG (1994); Clark HK, TW, SG & KR (1994); Chau CN (1995); Trigo CN (1995); Wickramanayake, Chen & Wen CN (1995); Chattopadhyay & Ghosh IN (2002)•
	Market and Niche Entry Strategies	Tan CN (1996); Chan & Foster HK (2001)•; Tan SG (2001)
	Rural Entrepreneurship	Bruun CN (1990); Lin CN (1990); Bogaert, Das & Barik IN (1993); Kirve & Kanitkar IN (1993)•; Mall IN (1993)•; Singh & Krishna IN (1994)•; Zhang, Fu, Wong & Stewart CN (1996); Bal & Judge IN (2001); Singh IN (2002)

Figure 2. (Continued.)

	RESEARCH TOPIC	RELEVANT STUDIES*
Business Growth	Growth within the Entrepreneurial Firm	Chau HK (1993); Tambunan ID (1994); Cheah & Yu HK (1996); Mutahaly & Gunasekaran VN (1996)•; Sinha IN (1996)•; Wijewardena & Cooray JP (1996)•; Fam & Merrilees HK (1999)•; Yu HK (1999); Yu HK (2000); Cheung CN (2002)
	Entrepreneurial Competence	Man, Lau & ChariEA (2002)
	Innovation & Corporate Entrepreneurship	Jolly & Kayama JP (1990); Dana KR (1992); Ohe, Honjo & Merrifield JP (1992)•; Siu & Martin HK (1992); Morito, Chia & Oliga JP (1993); Williams & Li CH (1993); Dana VN (1994a, 1994b); Tang SG & TW (1994); Abetti JP (1997); Go & Chan HK (1997)•; Zutshi HK, SG & TW (1997); Chang MY (2001)•; Dana, Korot & Tovstiga SG (2001)•; Du CN (2001)
	International Venturing	Chang JP (1995)•; Grotenhuis, Neuijen & Dwiajmadja ID & JP (1999)•; Choo & Mazzarol SG (2001)•; Tsang SG (2002)
Business Survival	Firm Survival	Kantilal IN (1994)•
	Succession in Entrepreneurial Firms	Shi CN (1992); Cunningham & Ho SG (1994); Chin & Chan CN (1998); Butler, Phan, Saxberg & Lee HK & SG (2001)•
	Professional Managers/Consultants	Tan & Allampalli SN (1999)•; Awasthi & Pal IN (2000)•; Menkhoff, Kay & Loh SG (2002)

* Country of Asian sample for empirical and qualitative studies, or when specific country used for context in which issue is discussed, follows authors name (foreign country samples not indicated). Abbreviations as follow: AS (Asia), BN (Brunei), CN (China), EA (East Asia), HK (Hong Kong), IA (Islamic Asia), ID (Indonesia), IL (Israel), IN (India), JP (Japan), KR (South Korea), MM (Burma), MY (Malaysia), PH (Philippines), SA (South Asia), SG (Singapore), TH (Thailand), TR (Turkey), TW (Taiwan), VN (Vietnam).
•Indicates a large sample empirical study.

to be devoted to item development in the local context, which would make these constructs more valid and reliable in Asian research. For instance, one exception to the use of existing instruments is the critical incidents used by Chan, Lau and Man (1997) to identify personality attributes of Hong Kong entrepreneurs. They found that common attributes of Hong Kong entrepreneurs included a growth orientation, willingness to take calculated risks, innovativeness, opportunism, a learning mind, and flexibility.

Characteristics have also been the focus of some research on Asian entrepreneurs. For instance, important success characteristics that have been identified in the emerging population of Chinese entrepreneurs includes the ability to act quickly (Ng & Ng, 1994), a supportive social environment, rapid rates of firm growth and high levels of firm commitments (Lau & Busenitz, 2001). However, in Singapore the aging population (Mauysami & Goby, 1998) and the changing characteristics of the second generation of entrepreneurs (Lee & Chan, 1998) are seen as adversely affecting the rate of new entrepreneurial behavior.

While much of the trait and characteristic research has been empirical or based on the accumulated observations of the researchers, we identified one attempt to make a theoretical extension in the Asian context. Misra and Kumar (2000) developed a new concept "entrepreneurial resourcefulness", that sees this attribute as mediating the link between a favorable set of traits and characteristics and entrepreneurial behavior. They define entrepreneurial resourcefulness "as the ability to identify opportunities in the environment and regulate and direct behavior to successfully cope with the task of creating and managing organizational situations to pursue the opportunity" (Misra & Kumar, 2000: 144). While their model was developed in the context of entrepreneurial behavior in India and has not been tested empirically, it may mark another stage in Asian trait research. Efforts to link Asian entrepreneurial theory development to Asian items and instruments that uncover unique qualities of Asian entrepreneurship would be the next step in this line of entrepreneurship research.

Networks and Guanxi

While the impact of networks on entrepreneurial behavior came somewhat late in Western entrepreneurship research (Aldrich & Zimmer, 1986), networks and relationships have always been part of doing business in Asia, although reported network research is skewed towards East Asia. One of the earliest samples of entrepreneurs was an examination of 164 cremation books issued for Thai entrepreneurs born between 1837 and 1943 (Butler & Chamornmarn, 1995). Their study found that these early entrepreneurs had extensive foreign contacts, went to the same prestigious secondary schools, often attended universities in other countries, and had a wide network of family and social ties. This research, based on archival cremation books that served as mini-biographies, has been supported by subsequent survey based research on networks that found Thai manufacturing entrepreneurs still heavily depend on networks to help identify business opportunities as well to gain information on how to effectively operate their new businesses (Butler, Brown & Chamornmarn, 2003).

Entrepreneurs often indicate that networks are the source of their business ideas. Menning (1997), in a study of entrepreneurs in Gujarat province in India found that social networks are also quite important in gaining actual entry into an industry. His results suggest that they may have a more important role in some Asian countries, and serve as both a source of entrepreneurial ideas as well as provide the means to overcome barriers to entry in certain industries.

China's special form of networks, guanxi, has received considerable research attention in recent years (e.g., Xin & Pearce, 1996). In China entrepreneurs tend to use family and friends as a source of guanxi, and they use these links to others, including governmental officials to gain needed resources (Zhao & Aram, 1995). There has been some criticism of links between entrepreneurs and government officials because they have occasionally been based on bribes and led to tax evasion (Tsang, 1994). However, Tsang (1994) also found that normally competitive entrepreneurs actually network with each other to form a more effective bargaining unit when dealing with the government. Similar results were found in India, where Bal (1998) found that highly competitive entrepreneurs joined in social networks when dealing with government bureaucrats.

Asian network research has also uncovered some unique dimensions of how networks affect entrepreneurial behavior. For instance, Rutten (2001) found that social networks, especially those with family members, can enhance the prospects for initial entrepreneurial behavior and success, while later they can constrain their ability to make needed changes. He found that Muslim owners of small iron foundries in Java had business organizations that reflected their extended family and social networks, but that these acted to constrain change because some network members perceived change as a threat. In the same study, Chinese entrepreneurs in Malaysia, whose networks were much broader, were not so constrained and were able to make needed organizational changes and even entered new businesses.

Firm clustering also appears to be a special form of Asian networking. In developed countries maximizing one's distance from a competitor is often seen as optimal. However, Brown and Butler (1994) found that Vietnamese retailers selling similar products located on the same streets, often with as many as 60 of the same type shop. This facilitated the flow of information between retailers and allowed them to have a common posture vis-à-vis both consumers and suppliers. Bal's (1998) study, in India, found that lower middle class entrepreneurs benefited from situating their firms in clusters with other firms. Since the existing research relates to India and Vietnam, it may be that firms in developing economies, even in very basic businesses, benefit more from being clustered than they would from locating away from competitors.

Obviously, the internet is changing the forms of networks in Asia and elsewhere. While there is limited research on the topic, a study of internet networks in Japans showed that they were successful in terms of both growth and encouraging entrepreneurial behavior (Akizawa & Kijama, 1999). The role of the internet in building and maintaining networks may be one way to allow entrepreneurs, especially in Asian countries that have developing economies, to maintain networks that support their businesses without having to cluster with similar firms.

Gender

Research on women entrepreneurs in Asia is fairly rare, and much of the existing research reports samples that are predominantly male. The research reviewed here addresses three major themes: effort to encourage women to become entrepreneurs, characteristics of women entrepreneurs, and factors related to the success of women entrepreneurs' firms.

Micro finance, one way that governments tried to encourage poorer women to open firms, grew out of the success of the Grameen Bank in Bangladesh. Hashemi, Schuler and Riley (1996) found that micro finance programs were not effective in enhancing the status of women, while successful Asian male entrepreneurs tend to enjoy status gains if their business ventures are successful. Milgram (2001) examined a program in the Philippines to see if they were effective in stimulating entrepreneurial behavior. She found that these loans were useful in getting women to start very small scale businesses, but these programs failed to follow up with the expertise and support needed to make these businesses grow. One way for the process to be improved was proposed by Kantor (2002) who felt that there would have to be changes in cultural values in Asia, so that women could enter the types of professions and business occupations that would provide them with the experience and knowledge needed to open, and then grow a business.

The identification of traits and characteristics has also received some research attention. In a study of 200 members of the Indian Council on Women Entrepreneurs, Singh (1993) found 77% had university level education, most were married and had started their business after marriage, and had fathers with business experience. Women who started engineering, chemical or construction firms also attributed some of their success to the effective use of family networks. Their motivations for starting businesses included the desire to prove themselves and to gain some independence. Wimalatissa (1996) found similar results, in a less extensive study, in Brunei Darussalam. Women there indicated that the desire to put their education to practical use was a motivation to start a business. Most of the women in this sample were also married and started their business after marriage. Chu's (2000) study of Chinese women entrepreneurs in Hong Kong found that they also had founded businesses because they had a desire for higher status, personal achievement and independence. The subjects here were interviewed and often indicated that there was family pressure for them to start a business out of economic necessity. Research is needed on the barriers facing younger and unmarried women wishing to start businesses, in order to fill out this portion of the gender research agenda.

The final body of Asian women's entrepreneurship research relates to factors that affect firm's success. Lerher, Brush and Hisrich (1997), in a study of 220 Israeli women entrepreneurs, developed and tested a model of female business performance. They found that motivation and goals influenced firm performance, especially the desire for achievement, independence and economic necessity. Women who joined women's organizations also had firms with higher performance, which suggests such organizations are useful for women entrepreneurs as a source of expertise. Lack of education can act as a barrier to success in other ways. For instance, in China women involved in township and village enterprises seldom had the education needed to qualify for formal courses in business (Kao & Chiang, 2000), which blocked them from gaining the expertise needed for firm growth. Das' (1999) research in India found that economic necessity was also associated with poorer performance, but attributed this to the fact that women had less access to the investment funds needed for firm growth. This would be consistent with Kaur and Bana's (1999) study of 110 Indian women entrepreneurs where they found 54% provided their own funds while 23% got assistance from their parents. Poorer women would clearly lack these forms of assistance, and micro finance programs appear more interested in business founding than business growth.

Student's Propensity towards Entrepreneurship and Impact of Education

The existing research explores three questions: Do students want to be entrepreneurs? Do students have the attributes needed to be entrepreneurs? Does training and education have an impact on entrepreneurial success? Given the availability of students, and their willingness to participate in research, it is surprising there is not more research in this area. Most of what exists, in answer to the first two questions, has been done in Singapore which, given its size and prosperity, suggests more research in other parts of Asia is needed.

There is evidence that students in Singapore do want to start businesses. Doh, Tan and Chiong (1996), in a sample of 77 first year university students, found that 55.8% of students wanted to eventually start a business. Their results also indicated that students had realistic time frames with respect to when this might occur. 55.5% thought it would occur within the next 5 to 10 years, while 39.5% felt it would be more than 10 years before this occurred.

A large number of Asian students may want to be entrepreneurs, and research suggests many of them possess characteristics associated with successful entrepreneurial behavior (Ho & Koh, 1992). For instance, Tan, Siew and Tan's (1995) study of Singaporean university students found that 47% had what they call an "entrepreneurial spirit". This was defined as having a propensity towards risk taking, internal locus of control, innovative thinking, leadership qualities, strong determination and an achievement orientation. Since these characteristics are also associated with successful managers, the issue of why some choose to move up the corporate ladder while others take an entrepreneurial path remains unresolved.

The degree to which entrepreneurial education or training has an impact on entrepreneurial inclination or success has received limited research attention. Ghazali et al.'s (1994) study of 2486 university graduates in Singapore found that age and being Chinese were negatively correlated with starting a business. Given that the vast majority of Singaporeans are Chinese this is hardly encouraging. In addition, being a foreign university graduate was positively correlated with starting a business, which suggests education could, but is not currently having the desired impact. A study of SMEs in Malaysia found that entrepreneurs with university degrees only enjoyed a success advantage over entrepreneurs with a primary education, which confirmed an early study in this area (Aziz, 1980). Other studies in India found that business experience is much more useful than training courses (Poonjary, 1996), but that when training is very specific, such as how to access government funding, it can be useful (Saini & Bhatia, 1996).

MACRO-ENVIRONMENTAL IMPACTS

Governmental Policy

The link between governmental policies and entrepreneurship is both direct and indirect. For instance, Wong, Wong, Kwan and Gansham (1994: 459) concluded that the banking system and educational system, which are both affected by governmental polices and funding, were a negative environmental factor in Singapore. In fact, they describe the educational system, with its emphasis on exams as the "worst inhibiting factor affecting the entrepreneurial spirit" of students in Singapore. However, their empirical results, which linked environmental impacts to the personal attributes of the entrepreneur, showed that the presence of market opportunities had the biggest impact on entrepreneurial behavior. At a more specific level governmental policy can be quite effective, such as a freight equalization scheme that was introduced in India, and which made some regions very attractive and competitive locations, which had previously been considered undesirable (Singh, 1994).

In terms of environmental turbulence, the changes that begin in the 1980s in China have been the focus of much of the governmental policy research (e.g., Lombardo, 1995). Market orientated reforms changed the climate for independent business startups (Hu, 1993; Zhu, 1993). Industrial distribution (Lee, 1995) and collectively owned enterprises (Chow, 1996) led the way in exploiting these changes. The return of individual businesses (geti hu) has been rapid under new policies, and growth in dawu geti (large scale individual business) has been extremely rapid. While most of the research has been non-empirical, two empirical research efforts have focused on particular government efforts. Tan's (2001) study of 53 entrepreneurs in China found that the vagueness of, and propensity to change governmental policies did impact entrepreneurs, but that the entrepreneurs had high level of innovativeness, risk taking, and were highly proactive. These attributes were needed in this type of unstable regulatory environment.

More specific governmental policies may have some positive effects. Kashyap and Shah (1995) examined the impact of an Indian government policy on entrepreneurial success, which required firms in the same industry to cluster in the same industrial estate. Although it was not true in all cases, small firms that were similar and clustered in extremely large estates did appear to gain some of the scale benefits normally reserved for larger firms. However, it is not clear if the benefits came from their competitors or by learning from dissimilar larger firm in their industrial park.

Finance, Taxation, and Development Schemes

Although they had some criticisms, Wong, Wong, Kwan and Gansham (1994) gave favorable scores to governmental development and finance schemes, in terms of their impact on entrepreneurial behavior. Ser's (1998) study suggested that one of the reasons that development support programs are less successful is because they are often too narrowly focused. He suggested that SME expansion efforts have to include four elements, if they are to match SME diversity to governmental goals. His topology includes (1) welfare orientation, which would help absorb surplus labor, (2) efficiency orientation, which would be applied in cases where their were labor or trained labor shortages, (3) champion orientation, which would support firms with cutting edge technology, and (4) transaction cost reduction policies, which have a positive impact on most SMEs. The problem is that research examining links between development efforts and entrepreneurial behavior and success is sparse, and this and other models have not been tested empirically.

At a more specific level, we do have some information about how governmental policy has impacted entrepreneurs. Most of the existing research relates to the availability of funds. Smaller firms in Japan were found to lack network links to larger banks, which their larger counterparts had (Hoshi, Kashyap & Scharfstein, 1991). This prevented them from accessing funds during periods when they had liquidity problems. Research in other areas found a similar pattern in Singapore (Teo & Cheong, 1994), Malaysia (Boocock & Wahab, 1997) and India (Singh, 2001).

The existing research makes it difficult to determine the degree to which domestic banks or the government are responsible for SME funding problems. In Japan, strict IPO regulations make raising equity difficult (Matsuda, VanderWref & Scarbrough, 1994), but Cheung, Chan and Lam (1996) found many Hong Kong firms went to China to escape strict enforcement of tax laws. Since the tax rates are higher in China, the assumption is that enforcement is lax. The problem may just be one of coordination, as governments make efforts to stimulate entrepreneurial behavior in one area, but then ignore important issues such as banking reform that would be needed to make their original polices effective (Miurin & Sommariva, 1993). However, some research in India clearly lays the blame on the banking sector. Rao's (1997) analysis suggests firms were too tied to technical analysis and developed a model for bankers that included entrepreneurs' characteristics as an additional factor in the loan approval process, although there is not an indication that any banks in India have adopted this approach. Clearly, much more detailed and specific research, across the entire continent is needed in this area.

Venture Capital

Venture capital and financing have attracted research attention, as well as the attention of governments in the region. Most research is quite recent, and has focused more heavily on Singapore and Japan.[4] This region has always had a tradition of informal financing, but this obviously limited the scale of funds that were available (Butler, Brown & Chamornmarn, 2000; Choy, 1990).

Korea's first venture capital firm was founded in 1974 and the government began supporting venture capital firms in the early 1980s as a way to help develop its high technology industry (Rah, Jung & Lee, 1994). While these firms were not very profitable, Rah, Jung and Lee (1994) were able to develop a performance model that suggested they needed to focus more on firms with high potential, and value financing ability more than production ability in their evaluation. They also found that Korea's venture capital professional often lacked the technical training of their professional counterparts in other countries. Early research by Ray (1991; Ray & Turpin, 1993) looked at the venture capital industry in Singapore and Japan, in terms of how it differed from venture capital practices in the US. At this stage there were not many differences with respect to practices, although Japanese firms were more willing to examine any proposed deal and Singaporean venture capitalists were more comfortable with rational rather than intuitive decision making. We even have evidence that venture capital was establishing itself in Malaysia, which had 15 venture capital firms before the 1997 financial crisis (Boocock & Wahab, 1997).

Generally, IPOs are more difficult in Asian countries because of administrative and legal restrictions. As mentioned earlier, Japanese firms have a tough time getting permission for IPOs. In addition, SMEs were less likely to have the close relationships with banks that made securing funds for larger firms less problematical (Hoshi, Kashyap & Scharfstein, 1991). The economic problems that Japan has had in the past decade has resulted in a credit crunch for smaller firms, and despite the efforts of the Ministry of International Trade and Industry, substitutes for institutional financing have not increased. Thus, Japanese firms that had successful IPOs tended to be older and more likely to use the funds for research and development or investment in plant and equipment. US firms tend to use IPOs to exploit their current market value, and quite often the funds went into new ventures.

Singapore and Hong Kong have the largest population of venture capital firms, although Hong Kong's venture capital firms have received less research attention. Lockett, Wright, Sapienza and Pruthi (2002) provide a comprehensive contrast of the two regions along with India and the US. Cornelius and Naqui (2002) also used a common model based on resource exchange and value addition to describe the behavior of venture capitalists in both Hong Kong and Singapore. In addition, it appears that a community of investor "angels" may exist in Singapore, and although it just begins to uncover the subject, Hindle and Lee's (2002) research in this area in groundbreaking in an Asian setting. In most countries in the region, "angels" prefer to remain hidden in complex informal networks.

Hopefully, the recent research by Wright, Pruthi and Lockett (2002) on venture capital will start a trend of in depth examination of venture capital in countries that have and need this activity but are normally off the main research trail. They point out that venture capital funding in India now exceeds $1 billion and is increasing rapidly. Their research looked at the differences in monitoring behavior by domestic and foreign firms. Foreign firms had more expatriates and far more experience. However, in terms of their actual behavior they both tended to place high values on the same items, such as audited annual accounts and on restrictions on changes in ownership. However, domestic firms paid more attention to the requirements for certain accounting practices, which seems to suggest that they were more knowledgeable about the impact that various local accounting practices could have on reported income and profit. White, Gao and Zhang (2002) also examined monitoring behavior and found that Chinese venture capitalists were much less active monitors than were foreign VC firms, but related this to their lack of technical expertise.

Societal and Entrepreneurial Culture and Religion

The impact of culture on entrepreneurial behavior is often used as a justification for revisiting a topic in an Asian country, but there has not been a large amount of research that directly examines the issue. McGrath and MacMillan (1992), in a multi-country study that included China and Taiwan, found that culture had little impact on the core set of entrepreneurs' beliefs. They found that entrepreneurs tended to consider themselves and other entrepreneurs as part of an "in group", who were obtaining resources and building a business on their own. Swierczek (1994) had similar finding with respect to cultural differences producing attitude or behavior differences in a study of Filipino, Malaysian, Thai and Singaporean entrepreneurs. Neither study addressed the degree to which culture may have affected the way entrepreneurs went about achieving these common goals, which could relate to the quantity of entrepreneurs produced.

There is some research that suggests that culture does impact both the entrepreneurs and the ways they operate. For instance, in a study of Singaporeans working for Swedish firms, Selmer (1996) found that they took on the values of the Swedes with respect to uncertainty avoidance, power distance and individualism. These values are associated with entrepreneurial behavior, although evidence is not presented that the transfer of values led to such behavior. There is also research that shows culture can have a negative impact. Lo (1999) found that conformity was highly valued in Hong Kong, which would work against entrepreneurial behavior.

The religious diversity of the continent provides a "gold mine" for those looking to examine the impact of religion on entrepreneurial behavior. Max Weber (1935), in his examination of capitalism, suggested that Confucianism explained China's lack of economic development. To some, current economic growth in China suggests just the opposite but Kirby and Fan (1995) take a completely different track in pointing out that those who now attribute economic success to these same values may be equally skewing the argument. They point out that culture has an influence on entrepreneurial behavior but that it alone cannot induce such behavior, and we know very little about the precise role it plays when it interacts with other factors.

OPPORTUNITY IDENTIFICATION

Business Founding

Theoretical work, in Asia or using an Asian context, is rare. However, by examining some of the existing research relating to identifying opportunities, some inferences can be made about business founding. In the early 1980s the

Chinese government was still arresting entrepreneurs who started businesses or accumulated wealth, which suggests that opportunity identification and business founding are rather independent of government's efforts to limit them. In Japan, the SME as an institution is also under threat, although not from official governmental action. Hawkins' (1993) research suggested that the rate of business openings was slowing because of structural reasons related to a lack of skilled labor, high business starting costs including labor costs, and as mentioned earlier a lack of new venture funding. This would suggest that the viability of an opportunity is constrained by high costs in Japan. Ray's (1998) interview research of Singapore service entrepreneurs identified a group of 9 importers who were aware of and used Singapore constraints in deciding what to import. In this sense they appear to have the ability to see constraints as importing opportunities, which is central to the business founding process.

Business founding research in the immigrant communities has also been conducted in Asia. Much of this has been done by sociologists, historians, political scientists and anthropologists. However, Dobbin's (1996) research on entrepreneurial opportunities in the Philippines, India, China, Burma and Java examines immigrants in terms of their ability to identify opportunities in their new surroundings. For instance, after the British conquered Lower Burma in 1852, they attempted to settle large numbers of Indians there by giving them free land to farm. This was a complete failure because those attracted to the free land offer usually lacked any experience in farming. However, eventually large numbers of Nattukottai Chettiars, from Madras, did come and eventually outnumbered the Burmese in Rangoon. However, these Chettiars came as merchants and traders because these represented opportunities in areas where they had some expertise.

Growth in Number of Firms

Most countries in Asia are encouraging entrepreneurial behavior, with the underlying goal of achieving a larger absolute number of SMEs. Obviously, both business startup growth and high rates of new firm survival play a role in this process. Alexander's (1960) study of entrepreneurs in Turkey took a development economists approach and linked entrepreneurship to industrial growth, rather than making the entrepreneur the central focus. Later work, especially in China looked at the rise in entrepreneurial activity (Chang & MacMillan, 1991), the growth in entrepreneurial activity in rural regions (Chew, 1988; Bruun, 1990) and the supply of entrepreneurs (Wickramanayake, Chen & Wen, 1995). These studies tended to point out that entrepreneurial activity was increasing, and that the process seemed to be self-reinforcing because a larger supply of entrepreneurs acted to increase the rate of new entrepreneurial behavior. However, the focus of this research was not on the underlying factors driving this increase in entrepreneurial behavior, other than how they related to fewer governmental restrictions, which is an area where future research is needed.

The research suggests that assumptions about the stability of an entrepreneurial population need to be revised. For instance, Chew (1988) pointed out that Singapore was a hub of entrepreneurial activity in 1959, at the point of its independence. Now, the government has an active policy of trying to resurrect entrepreneurial behavior and claims that Singapore needs a larger force of entrepreneurs (Cheung, Hoon & Siew, 1994).

The aging population is also a concern in some countries with Japan, Singapore and Hong Kong all projected to have more that 26% of their populations over 60 years old by 2025 (Cheung, Hoon & Siew, 1994). Since research on entrepreneurs in industrial zones (Trigo, 1995) and in the dyestuffs industry in India found that younger people were more likely to engage in entrepreneurial behavior, this suggests that factors must be identified that will prompt older people to start more firms, or to increase the rate of entrepreneurial behavior in younger people. Awasthi (1992) research suggests that people born into entrepreneurial families acquire "entrepreneurial status" and higher levels of attributes associated with entrepreneurial behavior. More research on the transfer of attributes associates with entrepreneurial status needs to be carried out in other countries in the region.

Market and Niche Entry Strategies

In many cases the entrepreneur's success has been seen in terms of successfully formulating a strategy that exploits an open niche. However, this has received little research attention, at least where it is the direct focus of the research. This is true in general, as strategy formulation research has generally focused on larger firms, which means that niche strategies receive little attention in general. However, there is some evidence related to how niche strategies are formulated in Singapore, China and Hong Kong. Tan's (1996) discussion of business entry and adaptation of a Chinese entrepreneur on Hainan Island indicates that niche entry strategies may follow less organized and totally opportunistic approaches to earning money. In this case study he found that the entrepreneur first organized a business that opportunistically exploited supply chain faults by buying in one part of the country and selling in another. However, this entrepreneur eventually decided to move into the manufacture of computer disk drives because he saw this as a market niche opportunity. This gradual approach to moving towards a niche strategy has some support from a study of "gray market" entrepreneurs by Lim, Lee and Tan (1999). By working outside the manufacturer's controlled channels of distribution, these "gray market" local firms were able to sell well known cosmetics and luxury automobiles at lower prices than were authorized distributors. This research is important because it suggests that niches may exist even when distribution appears to be controlled, although the authors felt these "gray market" practices were a substitute for developing a niche strategy.

In Hong Kong, where entrepreneurs are viewed as being opportunistic and having a short-term perspective, Chan and Foster (2001) found they can be very proactive in the strategy formulation process. In a study of 42 entrepreneurs they found that entrepreneurs used their networks to help develop effective and proactive strategies, both with respect to identifying business opportunities and then getting the resources needed to exploit them. Moreover, they found that characteristics had no impact on the degree to which one's strategy was proactive or reactive. This may suggest that more firms will be proactive about formulating niche strategies as a way to be successful and grow.

Rural Entrepreneurship

Since many countries in Asia are either in the yet to develop or in the developing economy stage, rural development is extremely important. Although it has not received a lot of research attention, relative to the existing body of entrepreneurship research it is fairly well represented in Asian entrepreneurship research. The research covers three main areas: the emergence of rural entrepreneurs in China, rural entrepreneurship in India, and some factors that affect the rate of rural entrepreneurship.

In China, where rural enterprises began to appear in the late 1970s (Bruun, 1990; Lin, 1990; Hu; 1993), there have also been some efforts to link this growth to economic growth. For instance, Zhang, Fu, Wong and Stewart (1996) developed the notion that China's rural entrepreneurs were active in developing township village enterprises, which had a "catfish effect" on the economy, by essentially creating the turmoil needed to oxygenate the economy. Their study also found rapid growth in these rural enterprises and that over 50% of them had been founded by farmers.

While the emergence of rural enterprises surprised the government in China, they have emerged with governmental support in India. Gandhi's philosophy of self reliance encouraged production using local resources, which resulted in rural villagers starting businesses called panchayat udyog that produced goods in limited quantities, but which served local needs (Singh, 1999). However, some of these local businesses did attempt to generate growth. For instance, Bogaert, Das and Barik (1993) found that a group of rural people formed a craft cooperative in Orissa, and then opened a store in the nearest big city to increase demand for their products. The link between rural enterprise growth and economic growth has not been as dramatic in India as in China, but part of this is related to governmental restrictions on foreign investment and other restrictions on businesses.

On the research front, Singh and Krishna's (1994) study of agricultural entrepreneurs found that their success was related to their high scores on innovativeness, higher levels of knowledge and high levels of motivation. This suggests that rural entrepreneurs have many of the same characteristics as their urban counterparts. At the policy level, some training efforts have been successful in transferring skills, such as training tailors, but have resulted in few starting their own businesses (Kirve & Kanitkar, 1993). However, governmental and private finance assistance schemes have been very successful in generating rural startups (Mall, 1993). The links to success at the rural level and the relationship between rural entrepreneurial growth and national economic growth needs more research at both the theoretical and empirical level, and it needs to be addressed over a wider range of countries.

BUSINESS GROWTH

Growth within the Entrepreneurial Firm

Most new firms do not survive, and an even smaller number grow. However, those that do grow end up being extremely important to economic growth. There is a stream of research relating to Hong Kong that suggests that the ability to continue the opportunity identification process, after the founding of the business may be a key to firm growth. Chau (1993) coined the term "merchant entrepreneur" to categorize this behavior. Cheah and Yu (1996: 243) placed this behavior in the Austrian view of entrepreneurship and pointed out that Hong Kong's economic growth was "attributable largely to adaptive entrepreneurs who are alert to opportunities, maintain a high degree of flexibility in their production, and respond rapidly to change". They found that Hong Kong's entrepreneurs were able to quickly imitate foreign products, and then offer them at lower prices. Yu (2000) later used the term "creative imitation" to describe this behavior and found firms used a "guerrilla" business strategy to flood the market with their product and take their profits in the short term.

In a qualitative study of businesses in rural Indonesia, Tambunan (1994) found the opposite situation. The government actually encouraged smaller firm to enter the market because there were limited opportunities for growth, given the poverty of the region. This provided no growth opportunities for these new firms, which then became tied to the poverty of the region.

There is also some research that takes a more direct look at the factors that relate to firm growth. Modern promotional practices such as coupons, contests, and games were found to differentiate Hong Kong's retailers (Fam & Merrilees, 1999), suggesting that the ability to adapt may be important to growth. In another case the lack of exporting knowledge was found to hinder the growth of Vietnam's entrepreneurs, who wanted to grow but had no idea how to approach exporting (Mutahaly & Gunasekaran, 1996). In a study of 127 firms in

India, Saini and Bhatia (1996) found that training enhanced funding prospects, and that access to funding was related to growth. One of the most interesting studies involved investigating how entrepreneurs get squeezed out of a market. Cheung (2002) examined the growth and decline of entrepreneurial businesses by the People's Liberation Army in China and discovered that private businesses eventually pushed them out of some markets, accounting for the decline in the number of businesses operated by the military.

Entrepreneurial Competence

The issue of entrepreneurial competence is often addressed as a side issue. However, very little research has been done in Asia that focuses on the competence of entrepreneurs or the degree to which they acquire additional needed competences as their firms grow. We identified one study where competences were more directly addressed. Kantilal (1994) examined a sample of 32 private composite mills in the Ahmedabad textile industry in India, which seemed to be an industry that continually was facing some sort of crisis. Thus, competence was examined in terms of entrepreneurs' ability to adapt and effectively deal with these crisis situations.

Financial competence appeared to be extremely important to survival and performance. Firms that were able to add to their equity base by aggressively attempting to attract new investment and that tended to build adequate reserves during non-crisis periods were better performers. The degree of competence also appeared to be apparent in purchasing decisions. More successful firms tended to invest in semiautomatic looms, which were more suited to the Indian market, but they also had more plant space than others which suggests they were making decisions related to expanding capacity rather than in investing in modern but less suitable technology. Successful entrepreneurs also were more likely to engage in national advertising, which allowed them to get retailers to carry larger inventory stocks, which reduced their costs of distribution. All of the healthy mills had stayed in the same family and undergone one successful succession. This study, based on interviews and financial data, supports the notion that uniform levels of high competence across a wide range of business activities are important to Asian entrepreneurs.

Innovation and Corporate Entrepreneurship

While entrepreneurial activity in Japan at the SME level was slowing in the 1980s, there was considerable activity in larger firms. During this period the larger Japanese firms were engaged in the same types of internal venturing forms that were being used in the US (Burgelman, 1984; MacMillan &

George, 1985). Japanese firms encouraged employees to come up with new ideas and used four major structural adaptations to support these efforts (Jolly & Kayrma, 1990). Company wide task forces and project organizations were used by Honda. Kyocera used the same approach but also recycled successful innovators, which resulted in a high level of new venture activity at this firm. Jolly and Kayama (1990) also identified firms such as Meiji Milk that used more ad hoc approaches that encouraged managers to be more innovative by forming informal voluntary teams to work on new ideas.

At Asahi Glass, both managers and units were encouraged to come up with new ideas. The corporate support staff was then used to evaluate, but not discourage, new ideas. Obviously, top management provided tangible support only for those projects that were favorably evaluated. However, it is possible that unfavorable financial analysis could also be useful for those working on new innovations.

Separate new venture divisions, which were legally separate units in some cases, were also used by Japanese firms to encourage innovation. Toray had a new venture division with an independent pool of resources. These resources could be used to fund the development of any innovation or venture that was unrelated to the firm's existing lines of business.

Japanese firms were somewhat more conservative than many US firms during this period. However, the research of Ohe, Honjo and Merrifield (1992) showed that the criteria used to predict success in US projects, if plotted on what they called a "success curve", were equally accurate in a Japanese setting. They suggested that the use of these criteria by Japanese firms would result in much higher rates of funding for new ventures, and equally higher success rates.

Large Japanese firms may have developed structures to foster innovation, but Abetti's (1997) study of the birth and development of notebook computers at Toshiba found that keeping your idea "under the table" is a good initial strategy. He found that the developers of these products built up a network of supporters and champions before revealing their ideas to top managers. He also found that these corporate entrepreneurs had advanced engineering degrees, had been rotated though many jobs and had lots of contacts as a result, and had worked in other countries. Although it is hard to generalize from the case of Toshiba, it may be that credentials, contacts and an international perspective help in both the identification of ideas and in their implementation into new ventures.

International Venturing

An important area, where much more research needs to be done is on "born international entrepreneurial firms". However, there has been some research that examines the ability of Asian entrepreneurs to invest in new international operations. Tsang (2002), using a multiple case study, found that Chinese family firms from Singapore engaged in a number of practices that actually limited their learning from international ventures. He found that these firms were very reluctant to involve anyone but family members in the negotiations or operations of these firms. In addition, they took much longer periods to delegate responsibility and localize their management. In some ways, this constrained their ability to advance and resulted in very few people, other than a few close family members, being experienced in foreign operations. The non-Chinese family businesses in his study were much more adept at localization of management, in part because their expatriate managers wanted to return home. However, Choo and Mazzarol (2001) found that Singapore's entrepreneurs appear more likely to engage in all of the possible dimensions of forging market entry while Australians tended to focus only on direct exporting. Thus, non-Chinese family owned firms may have advantages in Singapore, but in general Singapore's entrepreneurs appear to be aggressive in entering foreign markets.

A similar situation occurred with respect to Japanese international ventures. Although Chang (1995) examined all size firms, it is likely entrepreneurial firms were following similar patterns of international expansion. Japanese firms tended to engage in sequential expansion, first investing in core businesses where they felt they had advantages and then expanding to other areas. This allowed them to pass the learning on from earlier ventures to later ones. While less likely to quickly localize management, they were more likely to expose a large number of managers to overseas operations.

BUSINESS SURVIVAL

Professional Managers and Consultants

Firm survival is the ultimate goal of all businesses, but it has an added dimension in the entrepreneurial firm. For instance, in the previously discussed study by Kantilal (1994), he found that a continued family presence in management was related to survival by textile mills in India. However, in many cases growth and survival can cause problems. It is for this reason that many countries offer assistance programs to entrepreneurs. However, Awasthi and Pal (2000) found that many entrepreneurs in Calcutta seldom accessed these services. In many cases they were unaware of their existence or exactly how they would help. In other cases they felt they would be unable to afford professional consulting and expertise. Even if firms do recognize their value and can afford their costs, Menkhoff, Kay and Loh (2002) found that Singapore's entrepreneurs were unwilling to use the services of accountants or consultants because they perceived them to be of little value. They also found that the consultants felt the entrepreneurs were too focused on revenue growth rather than on profit. The ability of entrepreneurs to cope with growth and the problems associated with it needs more research, especially with respect to the reasons why entrepreneurs appear so reluctant to use non-family professional managers and consultants.

Succession and Survival

Successful business succession means family member succession to many entrepreneurs, and the failure to achieve this is often characterized as a risk factor by entrepreneurs (Chin & Chan, 1998). In Asia, the topic's added importance is reflected in the response rates on surveys related to succession, where mailed surveys in Hong Kong and Singapore had extremely high response rates (Butler, Phan, Saxberg & Lee, 2001).

Many sons and daughters do not want to work for in a family firm, preferring the prestige that goes with working for the government or a larger firm in Singapore (Cunningham & Ho, 1994). However, Shi (1992) found that some entrepreneurs in China recognized their children's dilemma and did not want them to enter the family business because they also viewed it as less prestigious.

There is research that does outline some factors that are likely to lead to family member succession in an entrepreneurial firm, which indicates that the probability of having successful family member succession in Asia is higher if the family member works for the firm (Butler, Phan, Saxberg & Lee, 2001). They found in a large sample of firms in Hong Kong and Singapore that involvement at a high level, rapid firm growth, good financial performance, high levels of family involvement, and a differentiated image acted to attract children to want to succeed their parents. This suggests that founding entrepreneurs have to work to make the firm sufficiently attractive, in a financial sense, if they want their children to see succession as a desirable career route.

CONCLUSIONS AND IMPLICATIONS

Our review clearly suggests that the depth and extent of entrepreneurship research needs to be expanded across the continent. Regional coverage is lacking in both the Middle East, the central Asian republics, and in poorer countries. However, the focus of research should not be on revisiting areas that have been adequately researched. For instance, we may need more trait research, but in the context of entrepreneurial behavior and models of entrepreneurial behavior, rather than as an effort to differentiate entrepreneurs from others.

The body of research examined here also shows that theoretical research, and theory that is tested empirically, needs more development. Theories that are developed in the unique context of Asia are clearly missing from the entrepreneurship literature. This includes the impact of religion, cultural practices with respect to lending, rural development, issues related to gender in some countries and unique aspects of the Asian entrepreneurial process.

Policy issues also need more research. There are a number of policy issues that need to be addressed. For instance, the impact of various educational systems and in some cases the lack of education, the impact of taxation schemes on entrepreneurs and the degree to which the privatization or lack of thereof will impact on entrepreneurship needs to be addressed. Much more attention needs to be focused on examining the impact of proactive policies on entrepreneurship, not just the impact of more or less governmental restriction.

At a more specific level, research on born international firms and the role of networks is needed. Many firms in the region are founded on the basis of an exporting or importing opportunity. However, very little attention has been devoted to research that examines how these entrepreneurs become aware of these opportunities or the factors that affect the success and growth of these international entrepreneurship efforts.

Network research has made both theoretical and empirical contributions to our understanding of opportunity noticing and the effective operation of new firms. Given the importance of networking in most Asian countries, the amount of existing research is quite small. Network research at all levels needs to be expanded to determine if these networks have similar positive effects in an Asian context, how they transmit information, the degree to which they enhance competition, and the degree to which centrality, strength of ties, and network size impact entrepreneurial behavior.

Financing also needs considerably more attention. Unique topics, such as the role of Islamic banks in the entrepreneurial financing process, need to be examined. However, more research attention also needs to be focused on factors related to the development of venture capital and how financing "angels" get more connected to local entrepreneurs and begin to play a more significant role in the financing process. Micro financing schemes, especially those that represent new approaches, need to be examined to see if they are able to have an impact on the growth of firms rather than just assisting at the founding stage.

Relative to its population, not much entrepreneurship research has been done in Asia or using Asian samples. On the other hand, in terms of the absolute level of research, and taking into account the fact that most of it has been done recently, the research record is impressive. Most major areas of the entrepreneurial process are represented, as is indicated in Figure 2. Obviously, the next stage is to put a geographic dimension on that figure that would represent the geographic distribution of the existing published research. Without doing this, it is obvious that a very small number of counties account for most of the reported Asian research. Future research clearly needs to address this geographic dimension, in addition to the topics addressed above.

NOTES

1. For example, this would include journals such as *Journal of Enterprising Culture* (first published in 1993 in Singapore), *Entrepreneurship, Innovation and Change* (first published in 1992 in Singapore and later in Papua New Guinea, although it has since ceased publication), *The Journal of Entrepreneurship* (first published in 1992 in India), *China Venture Capital* (Chinese language, first published in 2002 in China), and *Journal of International Business and Entrepreneurship* (first published in 1992 in Malaysia).
2. Purchasing power parity data used here is taken from 2001 World Factbook by the US Central Intelligence. Washington, DC Superintendent of Documents.
3. It should be noted that entrepreneurship research is conducted in many of the countries not represented in this review, which draws the distinction between doing research and writing up the results. This research is often government sponsored, and technical reports are produced in the vernacular language, which are not widely disseminated.
4. The first research journal devoted to this area Venture Capital: An International Journal of Entrepreneurial Finance began publication in 1999, which account for an increase in published venture capital research.

REFERENCES

Abdullah, M.A. 1998. The impact of entrepreneurs' characteristics on financial performance and employment of SMEs in Malaysia. *Journal of International Business and Entrepreneurship*, 6(1,2): 1-28.

Abetti, P.A. 1997. The birth and growth of Toshiba's laptop and notebook computers: A case study of Japanese venturing. *Journal of Business Venturing*, 12(6): 507-529.

Adas, M. 1974. Immigrant Asians and the economic impact of European imperialism: the role of the South Indian Chettiars in British Burma. *Journal of Asian Studies*, 33(3): 385-401.

Ahlstrom, D. and Burton, G.D. 2002. An institutional perspective on the role of culture in shaping strategic action by technology-focused entrepreneurial firms in China. *Entrepreneurship Theory and Practice*, 26(4): 53-69.

Ainnrawut, P. 1985. *Drrchnipachon Na Don Pow Myndardi*. Bangkok: Siam Printing.

Akbar, M. 1993. Ideology, environment and entrepreneurship: Typologies from Islamic texts and history. *The Journal of Entrepreneurship*, 2(2): 135-154.

Akizawa, H. and Kijima, K. 1999. Comparative analysis of entrepreneurial networking and its implications for Japanese industry in the internet era. *Journal of Enterprising Culture*, 7(2): 155-177.

Aldrich, H. and Zimmer, C. 1986. Entrepreneurship through social networks. In D. Sexton and R. Smilor (eds.), *The Art and Science of Entrepreneurship* (pp. 3-24). Cambridge, MA: Ballinger Publishing Co.

Alexander, A.P. 1960. Industrial entrepreneurship in Turkey: Origins and growth. *Economic Development and Cultural Change*, 8: 449-365.

Arghiros, D. 1997. The rise of indigenous capitalists in rural Thailand: Profile of brickmakers on the central plains. In M. Rutten and C. Upadhya (eds.), *Small Business Entrepreneurs in Asia and Europe* (pp. 115-145). New Deli: Sage.

Awasthi, D.N. 1992. Entrepreneurship and the growth of firms: An exploratory study of the dyestuffs industry in Ahmedabad. *The Journal of Entrepreneurship*, 1(1): 37-74.

Awasthi, D.N. and Pal, S. 2000. Market for business development in India: A study of Calcutta. *The Journal of Entrepreneurship*, 9(2): 155-184.

Aziz, A. 1980. *Malay Entrepreneurship, Problems in Development: A Comparative Empirical Analysis.* Heng Press: Kuala Lumpur.

Bal, G. 1998. Communities and culture in entrepreneurship development in India. *The Journal of Entrepreneurship*, 7(2): 171-182.

Bal, G. and Judge, P. 2001. Terrorism and rural entrepreneurship in Punjab. *The Journal of Entrepreneurship*, 10(2): 191-208.

Birley, S. 1989. Female entrepreneurs: Are they really any different? *Journal of Small Business Management*, 27: 32-37.

Blunt, P. 1992. Do Moi: 'Renovating' enterprise management in Vietnam. *Journal of Southeast Asia Business*, 8 (2): 1-14.

Bogaert, M.V.D., Das, S.P. and Barik, S.S. 1993. Catching the tiger by the tail: Fostering entrepreneurship among craft groups in Orissa. *The Journal of Entrepreneurship*, 2(2): 155-176.

Boocock, G. and Wahab, I.A. 1997. The financing practices and problems of growth-orientated firms in Malaysia. *Journal of International Business and Entrepreneurship*, 5(2): 1-28.

Boyko, M. and Wakabayashi, M. 1995. Entrepreneurship in a developing country: Small and medium-size enterprises in the Roi Et province of Thailand. *Asian Review*, 8: 128-160.

Brockhaus, R.H. 1974. I-E locus of control scores as predictors of entrepreneurial intentions. In A.G. Bedeian, W.H. Holley, A.A. Armenakis and H.S. Field (eds.), *Proceedings of the Academy of Management* (pp. 433-435).

Brockhaus, R.H. and Horwitz, P.S. 1986. The Psychology of the Entrepreneur. In D.L. Sexton and R.W. Smilor (eds.), *The Art and Science of Entrepreneurship.* Cambridge, MA: Ballinger.

Brown, B. and Butler, J.E. 1994. Reaching the Vietnamese consumer. *The Vietnam Business Journal*, 2(5): 28-29.

Bruun, O. 1990. Small enterprise in the Chinese experience. *Small Enterprise Development*, 1(3): 27-37.

Burgelman, R.A. 1984. Designs for corporate entrepreneurship in established firms. *California Management Review*, 26(3): 154-166.

Burton, G.D., Ahlstrom, D. and Singh, K. 2002. The impact of institutional environment on the venture capital industry in Singapore. *Venture Capital*, 4(3): 197-218.

Butler, J.E. 1999. All the other kids were doing it: The Asian financial crisis from a managerial perspective. *Journal of Contemporary Business*, 11(2): 1-12.

Butler, J.E. and Chamornmarn, W. 1995. Entrepreneurial characteristics: Reflections of a changing economy. *Chulalongkorn Journal of Economics*, 7(1): 89-110.

Butler, J.E., Brown, B. and Chamornmarn, W. 2000. Guanxi and the dynamics of overseas Chinese entrepreneurial behavior in Southeast Asia. In J.T. Li, Anne Tsui and Elizabeth (eds.), *Management and Organizations in the Chinese Context* (pp. 245-268). London: Macmillan.

Butler, J.E., Keh, H.T. and Chamornmarn, W. 2000. Information acquisition, entrepreneurial performance and the evolution of modern Thai retailing. *Journal of Asian Business*, 16(2): 1-24.

Butler, J.E., Phan, P.H., Saxberg, B.O. and Lee, S.H. 2001. Entrepreneurial succession, firm growth and performance. *Journal of Enterprising Culture*, 9(4): 402-436.

Butler, J.E., Brown, B. and Chamornmarn, W. 2003. Informational networks, entrepreneurial action and performance. *Asia Pacific Journal of Management*, 20(2): 151-174.

Chakravarti, N.R. (1971). *The Indian Minority in Burma: The Rise and Decline of an Immigrant Community*. New York: Oxford UP for the Institute of Race Relations.

Chan, K.B. and Chiang, C. 1994. *Stepping Out: The Making of Chinese Entrepreneurs*. Singapore: Prentice Hall.

Chan, K.F., Lau, T. and Man, T.W.Y. 1997. The entrepreneurial personality of small business owner-managers in Hong Kong: A critical incident analysis. *Journal of Enterprising Culture*, 5(3): 249-271.

Chan, S.Y. and Foster, M.J. 2001. Strategy formulation in small businesses: The Hong Kong experience. *International Small Business Journal*, 19(3): 56-71.

Chang, J. 2001. Intrepreneurship and exopreneurship in manufacturing firms: An empirical study of performance implications. *Journal of Enterprising Culture*, 9(2): 153-171.

Chang, S.J. 1995. International expansion strategy of Japanese firms: Capability building through sequential entry. *Academy of Management Journal*, 38(2): 137-162.

Chang, W. and MacMillan, I.C. 1991. A review of entrepreneurial development in the People's Republic of China. *Journal of Business Venturing*, 6(6): 375-379.

Charoenloet, V. 2000. *Globalization, Economic Integration and Inequalities: Poverty, Unemployment and the Responsibility of Governments in Asia and Europe*. Unpublished manuscript presented at the ASEM 2000 People's Forum on People's Action and Solidarity Challenging Globalisation. Seoul, Korea, 17-21 October 2000.

Chattopadhyay, R. and Ghosh, A. 2002. Predicting entrepreneurial success: A sociopsychological study. *The Journal of Entrepreneurship*, 11(2): 21-31.

Chau, L.C. 1993. *Hong Kong: A Unique Case of Development*. Washington, DC: The World Bank.

Chau, S.S. 1995. The development of China's private entrepreneurship. *Journal of Enterprising Culture*, 3(3): 261-276.

Cheah, H.B. and Yu, T.F.L. 1996. Adaptive response: Entrepreneurship and competitiveness in the economic development of Hong Kong. *Journal of Enterprising Culture*, 4(3): 241-266.

Cheung, B.B.M. and Hoon, S.C.L.S. 1994. Moving Singapore entrepreneurship to new heights. *Journal of Enterprising Culture*, 2(4): 931-944.

Cheung, D.K.C., Chan, S.Y.S. and Lam, I.S.K. 1996. Taxation and its implications on crossborder profits of manufacturing businesses in Hong Kong. *Journal of Enterprising Culture*, 4(4): 410-415.

Cheung, T.M. 2002. *China's Entrepreneurial Army*. Oxford: Oxford University Press.

Chew, K.K. and Koh, H.C. 1993. Personality characteristics of entrepreneurs: A test of the locals at the Singapore International Monetary Exchange. *Journal of Small Business and Entrepreneurship*, 10(3): 59-68.

Chew, K.K. and Koh, H.C. 1995. The entrepreneurial decision and entrepreneurial success: A study of the locals at the Singapore International Monetary Exchange. *Entrepreneurship Innovation and Change*, 4(2): 105-131.

Chew, S.B. 1988. *Small Firms in Singapore*. London: Oxford University Press.

Chin, Y.W. and Chan, P.K. 1998. A risk management model for the preservation of a family business. *Journal of Enterprising Culture*, 6(4): 413-427.

Choo, S. and Mazzarol, T. 2001. An impact on performance of foreign market entry choices by small and medium-sized enterprises. *Journal of Enterprising Culture*, 9(3): 291-312.

Chow, C.K.W. and Fung, M.K.Y. 1996. Firm dynamics and industrialization in the Chinese economy in transition: Implications for small business policy. *Journal of Business Venturing*, 11(6): 489-505.

Chow, C.K.W. and Fung, M.K.Y. 2000. Small business and liquidity constraints in financing business investment: Evidence from Shanghai's manufacturing sector. *Journal of Business Venturing*, 15(4): 363-383.

Choy, C.L. 1990. Source of business financing practices: A comparison among U.S. and Asian countries. *Journal of Business Venturing*, 5(5): 271-275.

Chu, P. 2000. The characteristics of Chinese female entrepreneurs: Motivation and personality. *Journal of Enterprising Culture*, 8(1): 67-84.

Clark, G.L. 1994. The end of an era: Asian NIEs in the global economy. *Growth and Change*, 25(4): 487-508.

Cordes, Bernd 1991. Vietnam's economic "renovation". *Journal of Southeast Asia Business*, 7(1): 71-84.

Cornelius, B. and Naqui, S.A. 2002. Resource exchange and the Asian venture capital fund/portfolio company dyad. *Venture Capital*, 4(3): 253-265.

Cunningham, J.B. and Ho, J. 1994. The dynamics of growth and succession in entrepreneurial organizations. *Journal of Enterprising Culture*, 2(1): 571-600.

Dana, L.P. 1992. Changes in the South Korean model: Towards more entrepreneurship and innovation. *Entrepreneurship, Innovation and Change*, 1(3): 303-311.

Dana, L.P. 1994a. The doi-moi model: An ethnographic account of entrepreneurship, innovation and change in former French Indo-China. *Entrepreneurship, Innovation and Change*, 3(1): 61-83.

Dana, L.P. 1994b. A Marxist mini-dragon - entrepreneurship in today's Vietnam. *Journal of Small Business Management*, 32(2): 95-103.

Dana, L.P. 1999. *Entrepreneurship in Pacific Asia: Past Present and Future*. Singapore: World Scientific.

Dana, L.P., Korot, L. and Tovstiga, G. 2001. Convergence vs. divergence: A comparative analysis of Singapore versus Silicon Valley knowledge management practices. *Journal of Enterprising Culture*, 9(1): 7-20.

Dandridge, T.C. and Flynn, D.M. 1988. Entrepreneurship: Environmental forces which are creating opportunities in China. *International Small Business Journal*, 6(3): 34-41.

Das, K. 1996. Flexibility together: Surviving and growing in a garment cluster, Ahmedbad, India. *The Journal of Entrepreneurship*, 5(2): 153-177.

Das, M. 1999. Women entrepreneurs from Southern India. *The Journal of Entrepreneurship*, 8(2): 147-163.

Dobbins, C. 1996. *Asian Entrepreneurial Minorities: Conjoint Communities in the Making of the World Economy, 1570-1940*. Richmond, Surry: (Nordic Institute of Asian Studies Monograph Series No. 71) Curzon Press Ltd.

Doh, J.C., Tan, W.L. and Chiong, T.S.T. 1996. Entrepreneurship inclinations of Singapore business students. *Journal of Enterprising Culture*, 4(2): 209-223.

Du, Y. 2001. Research on technological innovation as seen through the Chinese looking glass. *Journal of Enterprising Culture*, 9(1): 53-89.

Dubini, P. 1988. The influence of motivations and environment on business start-ups: Some hints for public policies. *Journal of Business Venturing*, 4(1): 11-26.

Duckett, J. 2001. Bureaucrats in business, Chinese-style: The lessons of market reform and state entrepreneurialism in the People's Republic of China. *World Development*, 29(1): 23-37.

Ellis, V. 2002. *Liberating the Entrepreneurial Spirit*. New York Accenture.

England, V. 2001. Poverty of enterprise a new foe in East Timor struggle. *South China Morning Post*, September 2: 7.

Fam, K.S. and Merrilees, B. 1999. Small and medium sized retailers' promotion strategies in the Asia Pacific region – A comparative study. *Journal of Enterprising Culture*, 7(2): 179-196.

Ganesan, R., Kaur, D. and Maheshwari, R.C. 2002. Women entrepreneurs: Problems and prospects. *The Journal of Entrepreneurship*, 11(1): 95-93.

Gartner, W.B. 1988. "Who is an 'Entrepreneur?' is the Wrong Question. *American Journal of Small Business*, 12: 11-32.

Gartner, W.B. 2001. Is there an elephant in entrepreneurship? Blind assumptions in theory development. *Entrepreneurship Theory and Practice*, 25(4): 27-39.

Geertz, C. (1963). *Peddlers and Princes: Social Change and Economic Modernization in Two Indonesian Towns*. Chicago: University of Chicago Press.

Ghazali, A., Chew, S.B., Ghosh, B.G. and Tay, R.S.T. 1994. Tertiary education, gender and entrepreneurship: An empirical analysis. *Journal of Enterprising Culture*, 1(3-4): 473-495.

Ghosh, B.C., Low, A.M., Tan, T.M. and Chan, C. 1993. An exploratory study of strategic planning behavior in SMEs in Singapore/Malaysia Context. *Journal of Enterprising Culture*, 1(2): 255-278.

Go, F.M. and Chan, A. 1997. A normative framework for entrepreneurship and innovation in Hong Kong tourism. *Journal of Enterprising Culture*, 5(1): 75-88.

Goffee, R. and Scase, R. 1985. *Women in Charge: The Experiences of Female Entrepreneurs*. London: George Allen and Unwin.

Gomez, E.T. 1999. *Chinese Business in Malaysia: Accumulation, Ascendance, Accommodation*. Honolulu: University of Hawaii Press.

Grotenhuis, F.D.J., Neuijen, J.A. and Dwiajmadja, C. 1999. Culture, leadership styles and stress: A comparative study of Japanese and American joint ventures in Indonesia. *Journal of Enterprising Culture*, 7(2): 127-154.

Hall, C. 2000. Squeezing the Asian entrepreneurial engine: The impact of the credit squeeze on sustainable job creation in Asia. *Journal of Enterprising Culture*, 8(2): 141-167.

Hashemi, S.M., Schuler, S.R. and Riley, A.P. 1996. Rural credit program and women's empowerment in Bangladesh. *World Development*, 24: 635-653.

Hawkins, D.I. 1993. New business entrepreneurship in the Japanese economy. *Journal of Business Venturing*, 8(2): 137-150.

Henin, B. 2002. Agrarian change in Vietnam's northern upland regions. *Journal of Contemporary Asia*, 32(1): 3-19.

Hindle, K. and Lee, L. 2002. An exploratory investigation of informal venture capitalists in Singapore. *Venture Capital*, 4(2): 169-177.

Ho, P. (1962). *The Ladder of Success in Imperial China: Aspects of Social Mobility*. New York: Columbia University Press.

Ho, T.S. and Koh, H.C. 1992. Differences in psychological characteristics between entrepreneurially inclined and non-entrepreneurially inclined accounting graduates in Singapore. *Entrepreneurship, Innovation and Change*, 1(2): 243-254.

Ho, Y.P. 1992. *Trade, Industrial Restructuring and Development in Hong Kong*. London: MacMillan.

Hofstede, G. 1980. *Culture's Consequences: International Differences in Work-Related Values*. Newbury, CA: Sage.

Hofstede, G. and Bond, M.H. 1988. The Confucius connection: From cultural roots to economic growth. *Organizational Dynamics*, 16(4): 5-21.

Holt, D.H. 1997. A comparative study of values among Chinese and U.S. entrepreneurs: Pragmatic convergence between contrasting cultures. *Journal of Business Venturing*, 6(2): 483-505.

Honig, B. 2001. Human capital and structural upheaval: A study of manufacturing firms in the West Bank. *Journal of Business Venturing*, 16(6): 575-594.

Hoshi, T., Kashyap, A. and Scharfstein, D. 1991. Corporate structure, liquidity, and investment: Evidence from Japanese industrial groups. *Quarterly Journal of Economics*, 106(1): 33-60.

Hu, Y. 1993. Market orientated reforms in China. *Development Policy Review*, 11(2): 194-204.

Jia, T. and Wang, K. 1989. The emergence and development of private entrepreneurs in China. *Social Science in China*, 2: 89-100.

Jolly, V.K. and Kayama, H. 1990. Venture management in Japanese companies. *Journal of Business Venturing*, 5(4): 249-269.

Kanai, T. 1995. Seven entrepreneurial paradoxes and the taxonomy of networking: The cases of MIT Enterprise Forum, Smaller Business Association of New England, and the Yokohama Venturing Business Club. *The Annals of Kobe Business School*, 39: 33-102.

Kantilal, I. 1994. Entrepreneurship and survival strategies in a sick traditional industry: The case of the Ahmedabad textile industry. *The Journal of Entrepreneurship*, 3(1): 21-53.

Kantor, P. 2002. Gender, micro-enterprise success and cultural context. *Entrepreneurship Theory and Practice*, 26(4): 131-143.

Kao, R.W.Y. and Chiang, L.C. 2000. Training and development of women entrepreneurs in China: A conceptual model. *Journal of Enterprising Culture*, 8(1): 85-101.

Karkoviata, L. 2001. Getting down to business. *Asian Business*, 37(8): 46-47.

Kashyap, S.P. and Shah, A. 1995. Induced industrial clustering and efficiency: An exploratory study of Gujarat's industrial estates. *The Journal of Entrepreneurship*, 4(1): 71-87.

Kaur, R. and Bawa, S. 1999. Psychological correlates of entrepreneurial performance among women. *The Journal of Entrepreneurship*, 8(2): 195-205.

Kazmin, A. 2002. Burma's plight. *Financial Times*, April 4: 12.

Keeley, R.H., Roure, J.B., Goto, M. and Yoshimura, K. 1990. An international comparison of new ventures. In C.N. Churchill, W.D. Bygrave, J.A. Hornaday, D.F. Muzyka, K.Hl. Vesper and W.E. Wetzel Jr. (eds.), *Frontiers of Entrepreneurship Research 1990* (pp. 472-486). Wellesly, MA: Center for Entrepreneurial Studies, Babson College.

Kessler, R.J. 1989. *Rebellion and Repression in the Philippines*. New Haven: Yale University Press.

Kingston, J. 1991. Indonesia: Developing Agenda. *Journal of Southeast Asia Business*, 7 (3): 88-97.

Kirby, D.A. and Fan, Y. 1995. Chinese cultural values and entrepreneurship: A preliminary consideration. *Journal of Enterprising Culture*, 3(3): 245-260.

Kirve, H. and Kanitkar, A. 1993. Entrepreneurs at the grass-roots: Developing the income generating capabilities of rural women. *The Journal of Entrepreneurship*, 2(2): 177-197.

Krishna, K.V.S.M. and Awasthi, D.N. 1994. Responsiveness of small and tiny enterprises to policy reforms in India. *The Journal of Entrepreneurship*, 3(2): 163-189.

Kuemmerle, W. 2002. Home based knowledge management in international ventures. *Journal of Business Venturing*, 17(2): 99-122.

Landon, K. P. (1941), *The Chinese in Thailand*. London: Oxford University Press.

Lau, C.M. and Busentiz, L. 2001. Growth intentions of entrepreneurs in a transitional economy: The People's Republic of China. *Entrepreneurship Theory and Practice*, 26(1): 5-20.

Lee, D.Y. 1995. A projection of distribution system development trend in China. *Journal of Enterprising Culture*, 3(3): 367-387.

Lee, J. and Chan, J. 1998. Chinese entrepreneurship: A study of Singapore. *The Journal of Management Development*, 17(2&3): 131-141.

Lerher, M. and Haber, S. 2001. Performance factors of small tourism ventures: The interface of tourism, entrepreneurship and the environment. *Journal of Business Venturing*, 16(1): 77-100.

Lerher, M., Brush, C. and Hisrich, R. 1997. Israeli women entrepreneurs: An examination of factors affecting performance. *Journal of Business Venturing*, 12(4): 315-339.

Liao, D. and Sohmen, P. 2001. The development of modern entrepreneurship in China. *Stanford Journal of East Asian Affairs*, 1: 27-33.

Lim, G.H., Lee, K.S. and Tan, S.J. 2001. Gray marketing as an alternative market penetration strategy for entrepreneurs: Conceptual model and case evidence. *Journal of Business Venturing*, 16(4): 405-427.

Lin, Q. 1990. Private enterprises: Their emergence, rapid growth and problems. In W.A. Byrd and Q. Lim (eds.), *China's Rural Industry: Structure, Development and Reform* (pp. 172-188). Oxford: Oxford University Press.

Liu, Y. 1992. Reform from below: The private economy and local politics in the rural industrialization of Wenzhou. *China Quarterly*, 130: 293-316.

Lo, V.H.Y. 1999. The revealing of an inherent oriental perception on TQM implementation in Hong Kong. *Journal of Enterprising Culture*, 7(3): 299-308.

Lockett, A. and Wright, M. 2002. Venture capital in Asia and the Pacific Rim. *Venture Capital*, 4(3): 183-195.

Lockett, A.,Wright, M., Sapienza, H. and Pruthi, S. 2002. Venture capital investors, valuation and information: A comparative study of the U.S., Hong Kong, India and Singapore. *Venture Capital*, 4(3): 237-252.

Lombardo, G.A. 1995. Chinese entrepreneurs: Strategic adaptation in a transitional economy. *Journal of Enterprising Culture*, 3(3): 277-292.

Lufrano, R.J. 1997. *Honorable Merchants: Commerce and Self-Cultivation in Late Imperial China*. Honolulu: University of Hawaii Press.

MacMillan, I.C. and George, R. 1985. Corporate venturing: Challenges for senior managers. *Journal of Business Strategy*, 3(winter): 34-43.

Mall, C.P. 1993. Impact of financial incentives on entrepreneurial development in backwards regions – A case study of Deoria district of Uttar Pradesh. *The Journal of Entrepreneurship*, 2(2): 199-207.

Man, W.Y.T., Lau, T. and Chan, K.F. 2002. The competitiveness of small and medium enterprises: A conceptualization with focus on entrepreneurial competencies. *Journal of Business Venturing*, 17(2): 123-142.

Matsuda, S., VanderWerf, P. and Scarbrough, P. 1994. A comparison of Japanese and U.S. firms completing initial public offerings. *Journal of Business Venturing*, 9(3): 205-222.

Mauysami, R.C. and Goby, V.P. 1998. The impact of cultural trends on business practices. *Journal of Enterprising Culture*, 6(3): 333-346.

Maxwell, N. 1908. Imports, exports, and shipping. In A. Wright and O.T. Breakspear (eds.), *Twentieth Century Impressions of Siam: Its History, People, Commerce, Industries and Resources* (pp. 135-143). London: Lloyd's Greater Britain Publishing Company, Ltd.

McGrath, R.G. and MacMillan, I. 1992. More like each other than anyone else? A cross-cultural study of entrepreneurial perceptions. *Journal of Business Venturing*, 7(5): 419-429.

McGrath, R.G., MacMillan, I.C., Yang, E.A.Y. and Tsai, W. 1992. Does culture endure, or is it malleable? Issues for entrepreneurial economic development. *Journal of Business Venturing*, 7(6): 441-458.

Mellor, W. 2001. Enterprise: Cambodia: A hint of the future in a lawless land. *Asiaweek*. May 11: 1.

Menkhoff, T., Kay, L. and Loh, B. 2002. Worlds apart? Reflections on the relationship between small entrepreneurs and external change advocates in Singapore. *Journal of Asian Business*, 18(1): 37-65.

Menning, G. 1997. Ethnic enterprise in the decentralized textile industry of India. *The Journal of Entrepreneurship*, 6(2): 141-164.

Milgram, B.L. 2001. Operationalizing microfinance: Women and craftwork in Ifugao, upland Philippines. *Human Organizaton*, 60(3): 212-224.

Misra, S. and Kumar, E.S. 2000. Resourcefulness: A proximal conceptualization of entrepreneurial behavior. *The Journal of Entrepreneurship*, 9(2): 135-154.

Morito, K., Chia, J.K.H. and Oliga, J.C. 1993. An emerging intrepreneurship phenomenon in the Japanese labor process? *Entrepreneurship, Innovation and Change*, 2(3): 265-272.

Morris, M.H. 2001. Entrepreneurship is economic development is entrepreneurship. *Journal of Developmental Entrepreneurship*, 6(3): v-vi.

Murin, P. and Sommariva, A. 1993. The financial reforms in central and eastern European countries and in China. *Journal of Banking and Finance*, 17(5): 883-911.

Mutahaly, S.K.K. and Gunasekaran, A. 1996. The essentials of a successful export strategy for Vietnamese small and medium enterprises. *Entrepreneurship, Innovation and Change*, 5(4): 295-306.

Mydans, S. 2000. Religious warfare on Indonesia isles bodes wide chaos. *New York Times*, Feb. 9: A1.

Ng, B.K. and Ng, E.J. 1994. Dynamism of small Chinese business enterprises in Malaysia and Singapore. *Journal of Enterprising Culture*, 1(3-4): 497-508.

Norman, H. 1900. *The Peoples and Politics of the Far East, Travels and Studies in the British, French, Spanish and Portuguese Colonies, Siberia, China, Japan, Korea, Siam and Malaya.* London: T. F. Unwin.

Nyum, J. 2001. South Korea: Briefing on the economy and business environment. Minister's Speech East Asia Economic Summit [Internet]. Available from: http://www.mofe.go.kr/cgi-pub/content.cgi?code=e_sp&no=80 [Accessed on 16 April, 2002].

Ohe, T., Honjo, S. and Merrifield, D.B. 1992. Japanese corporate ventures: Success curve. *Journal of Business Venturing*, 7(3): 171-180.

Ohe, T., Honjo, S. and Oliva, M. 1991. Entrepreneurs in Japan and Silicon Valley: A study of perceived differences. *Journal of Business Venturing*, 6(2): 135-144.

Pareek, U. 1994. Entrepreneurial role stress. *The Journal of Entrepreneurship*, 3(1): 55-67.

Pearson, C.A.L. and Chatterjee, S.R. 2001. Differences and similarities of entrepreneurial characteristics in a diverse social setting: Evidence from Australian and Singapore managers. *Journal of Enterprising Culture*, 9(3): 273-289.

Petrick, J.A. and Quinn, J.R. 1994. Deforestation in Indonesia: Policy framework for sustainable development. *Journal of Asian Business*, 10(2): 41-56.

Poonjary, M.C. 1996. What creates an entrepreneur? Some observations from a micro study. *The Journal of Entrepreneurship*, 5(2): 253-260.

Putterman, L. 1997. On the past and future of China's township and village-owned enterprises. *World Development*, 25(10): 1639-1655.

Rah, J., Jung, K. and Lee, J. 1994. Validation of the venture evaluation model in Korea. *Journal of Business Venturing*, 9(6): 509-524.

Ramachandran, K. and Ramnarayan, S. 1993. Entrepreneurial orientation and networking some evidence. *Journal of Business Venturing*, 8(6): 513-524.

Rao, M.S.S. 1997. The entrepreneurial competency index: An assessment tool for financial institutions. *The Journal of Entrepreneurship*, 6(2): 197-208.

Ray, D.M. 1991. Venture capital in Singapore. *International Small Business Journal*, 10(1): 11-27.

Ray, D.M. 1994. The role of risk-taking in Singapore. *Journal of Business Venturing*, 9(2): 157-177.

Ray, D.M. 1998. Distinctive Singapore patterns of SME internationalization. *Journal of International Business and Entrepreneurship*, 6(2): 29-62.

Ray, D.M. and Turpin, D.V. 1993. Venture capital in Japan. *International Small Business Journal*, 11(4): 39-56.

Ray, S. and Ramachandran, K. 1996. Towards a framework for a comprehensive theory of entrepreneurship. *The Journal of Entrepreneurship*, 5(1): 1-22.

Reeder, J.A. 1984. Entrepreneurship in the People's Republic of China. *Columbia Journal of World Business*, 19(3): 43-51.

Reid, A. 1993. *Southeast Asia in the Age of Commerce 1450–1680.* New Haven: Yale University Press.

Reynolds, P.D., Hay, M., Bygrave, W.D., Camp, S.M. and Aurio, E. 2000. *Global Entrepreneurship Monitor: 2000 Executive Report.* Wellesley, MA: Babson College.

Rotter, J.B. 1966. Generalized expectation for internal versus external control of reinforcement. *Psychological Monographs*, 80: 609.

Rutten, M. 1997. Cooperation and differentiation: Social history of iron founders in central Java. In M. Rutten and C. Upandhya (eds.), *Small Business Entrepreneurs in Asia and Europe* (pp. 173-207). Chicago: University of Chicago Press.

Rutten, M. 2001. Family enterprises and business partnerships: Rural entrepreneurs in India, Malaysia and Indonesia. *The Journal of Entrepreneurship*, 10(2): 165-189.

Sabbarwal, S. 1994. Determinants of entrepreneurial start-ups. *The Journal of Entrepreneurship*, 3(1): 69-80.

Saini, J.S. and Bhatia, B.S. 1996. Impact of entrepreneurship development programmes. *The Journal of Entrepreneurship*, 5(1): 65-80.

Sanchez, Jr. C. 1983. How nontraditionals have spearheaded Philippine export growth. *International Trade Forum*, 19(2): 16-22.

Schermerhorn, Jr. J.R. 2000. Planning and investment minister Tran Xyan Gia on foreign investment and the Vietnamese business environment. *The Academy of Management Executive*, 14(4): 8-15.

Schumpeter, J.A. (1952). Capitalism, socialism and democracy. London: G. Allen & Unwin.

Selmer, J. and de Leon, C. 1996. Parent cultural controls through organizational acculturation. *Journal of Organizational Behaviour*, 17: 557-572.

Sengupta, S.K. and Debnath, S.K. 1994. Need for achievement and entrepreneurial success: A study of entrepreneurs in two rural industries in West Bengal. *The Journal of Entrepreneurship*, 3(2): 191-203.

Ser, T.T. 1998. A taxonomy of SME development schemes. *Journal of Enterprising Culture*, 6(3): 323-332.

Sexton, D.L. and Landström, H. 2000. *Handbook of Entrepreneurship*. Oxford: Blackwell.

Sexton, D.L. and Smilor, R.W. 1986. *The Art and Science of Entrepreneurship*. Cambridge, MA: Ballinger.

Sharpe, P. 1994. Building an entrepreneurial mindset in young children in Singapore. *Journal of Enterprising Culture*, 2(1): 617-628.

Shi, X. 1992. The development process of small businesses with a detailed breakdown: A case study of the Western district of Beijing. *Social Science in China*, 5: 19-38.

Sims, C. 2000a. Indonesia cracks down on terrorists in Irian Jaya. *New York Times*, Dec. 4: A6.

Sims, C. 2000b. Indonesia ponders the law, their hearts, Suharto's fate. *New York Times*, Sept. 30: A6.

Singh, K.A. and Krishna, K.V.S.M. 1994. Agriculture entrepreneurship: The concept and evidence. *The Journal of Entrepreneurship*, 3(1): 97-111.

Singh, K.P. 1993. Women entrepreneurs: Their profile and motivation. *The Journal of Entrepreneurship*, 2(1): 47-58.

Singh, N. 2002. Institutionalisation of rural entrepreneurship through NGOs: Introspection from case studies. *The Journal of Entrepreneurship*, 11(1): 55-73.

Singh, S.K. 1999. Panchayat udyogs in Uttar Pradesh: A democratic experiment in micro enterprise development. *The Journal of Entrepreneurship*, 8(2): 207-217.

Singh, S. 1994. Refugees as entrepreneurs: The case of the Indian bicycle industry. *The Journal of Entrepreneurship*, 3(1): 81-96.

Singh, S. 1997. Aspects of entrepreneurship in primary food processing industries in Asia. *The Journal of Entrepreneurship*, 6(2): 223-231.

Singh, S. 2001. Employment, efficiency and entrepreneurship in small industry: A study of baking industry in Punjab, India. *The Journal of Entrepreneurship*, 10(1): 71-88.

Sinha, T.N. 1996. Human factors in entrepreneurship effectiveness. *The Journal of Entrepreneurship*, 5(1): 23-39.

Siu, M. and Martin, R. 1992. Successful entrepreneurship in Hong Kong. *Long Range Planning*, 25(6): 87-93.

Siu, W.S. and Kirby, D.A. 1995. Marketing in Chinese small businesses: Tentative theory. *Journal of Enterprising Culture*, 3(3): 309-342.

Siu, W.S., Liu, Z.C. and Tseng, C.S. 1993. Private entrepreneurs in China: An exploratory study. *Journal of Enterprising Culture*, 1(2): 203-214.

Skinner, W.G. 1957. *Chinese Society in Thailand: An Analytical History*. Ithica, NY: Cornell University Press.

Swierczek, F.W. 1994. Exploring entrepreneurship cultures in Southeast Asia. *Journal of Enterprising Culture*, 21(2): 687-708.

Tambunan, T. 1994. Rural small-scale industries in developing regions: Sign of poverty or progress? A case study in Ciomas subdistrict, West Java province, Indonesia. *Entrepreneurship and Regional Development*, 6(1): 1-13.

Tan, C. 1987. Entrepreneurial development in the People's Republic of China. *International Small Business Journal*, 5(2): 37-42.

Tan, J. 1996. Regulatory environment and strategic orientation in a transitional economy: A study of Chinese private enterprise. *Entrepreneurship theory and Practice*, 21(1): 31-46.

Tan, J. 2001. Innovation and risk taking in a transitional economy: A comparative study of Chinese managers and entrepreneurs. *Journal of Business Venturing*, 16(4): 359-376.

Tan, J. 2002. Culture, nation, and entrepreneurial strategic orientations: Implications for an emerging economy. *Entrepreneurship Theory and Practice*, 26(4): 95-111.

Tan, W.L. and Allampalli, D.G. 1999. The professionalizaiton of Chinese family business in Singapore. *Journal of Enterprising Culture*, 7(2): 197-211.

Tan, W.L., Siew, L.K. and Tan, W.H. 1995. Entrepreneurial spirit among tertiary students in Singapore. *Journal of Enterprising Culture*, 3(2): 211-227.

Tan, W.C.M. and Tay, R.S.T. 1995. Factors contributing to the growth of SMEs: The Singapore case. *Journal of Enterprising Culture*, 3(2): 197-210.

Tang, H.K. 1994. The new audacious technopreneurs. *Journal of Enterprising Culture*, 2(3): 857-870.

Tashiro, Y. 1999. Business angels in Japan. *Venture Capital*, 1(3): 259-273.

Teo, S. and Cheong, S. 1994. Difficulties faced by SMEs in obtaining financing from financial institutions. *Journal of Enterprising Culture*, 2(4): 955-968.

Teoh, H.Y. and Foo, S.L. 1997. Moderating effects of tolerance for ambiguity and risk taking propensity on the role conflict-perceived performance relationship: Evidence from Singapore entrepreneurs. *Journal of Business Venturing*, 12(1): 67-81.

Thammapreechakorn, P. and Kritsada, P. 1990. *Ceramic Art in Thailand*. Bangkok: Acme Printing Co.

Trigo, V. 1995. Chinese entrepreneurs in action: The case of Tian He industrial development zone. *Journal of Enterprising Culture*, 3(3): 389-403.

Tsang, E.W.K. 1994. Threats and opportunities faced by private business in China. *Journal of Business Venturing*, 9(6): 451-468.

Tsang, E.W.K. 1996. In search of legitimacy: The private entrepreneurs in China. *Entrepreneurship Theory and Practice*, 21(1): 21-30.

Tsang, E.W.K. 1997. The intersector flow of entrepreneurial spirit in China. *Entrepreneurship, Innovation and Change*, 6(3): 229-236.

Tsang, E.W.K. 2002. Learning from overseas venturing experiences: The case of the Chinese family firm. *Journal of Business Venturing*, 17(1): 21-40.

Vachani, S. 1998. A preliminary framework for explaining the "success" of the international ventures of small- and medium sized companies. *Journal of Enterprising Culture*, 6(4): 429-455.

Vijaya, V. and Kamalanabhan, T.J. 1998. A scale to access entrepreneurial motivation. *The Journal of Entrepreneurship*, 7(2): 183-198.

Wang, C.K. and Sim, V.Y.L. 2001. Exit strategies of venture capital-backed companies in Singapore. *Venture Capital*, 3(4): 337-358.

Wang, T.E. 2000. *The "No haste, be patient" policy and Taiwan's security*. Division of Strategic and International Studies. Taiwan Research Institute.

Weber, M. 1935. *The Protestant Ethic and the Spirit of capitalism*. New York: Scribner.

Webster, L. and Boring, D. 2000. *The Private Manufacturing Sector in Cambodia: A Survey of 63 Firms*. Hanoi: Mekong Project Development Facility (Private Sector Discussion No. 11).

White, S., Gao, J. and Zhang, W. 2002. *China's Venture Capital Industry: Industry Trajectories and System Structure*. (Unpublished manuscript, presented at the International Conference on Financial Systems, Corporate Investment in Innovation and Venture Capital, Brussels).

Wickramanayake, E., Chen, Y. and Wen, M. 1995. Resurrection of the private micro-enterprises in China: Experience in urban and rural Areas. *Journal of Enterprising Culture*, 3(3): 293-307.

Wijewardena, H. and Cooray, S. 1996. Factors contributing to the growth of small manufacturing firms: Perceptions of Japanese owner managers. *Journal of Enterprising Culture*, 4(4): 351-361.

Williams, E.E. and Li, J. 1993. Rural entrepreneurship in the People's Republic of China. *Entrepreneurship, Innovation and Change*, 2(1): 41-54.

Wimalatissa, W.A. 1996. The emerging class of businesswomen and women-owned businesses in Brunei Darussalam. *Journal of Enterprising Culture*, 4(3): 287-300.

Wong, S.Y., Wong, C.L.Y., Kwan, R.Y.K. and Gansham, V.C. 1994. A conceptual model for depicting the relationship between entrepreneurs and the environmental factors in Singapore. *Journal of Enterprising Culture*, 1(3-4): 449-472.

Wright, M., Pruthi, S. and Lockett, A. 2002. Venture capital firm internationalization and monitoring high tech entrepreneurship: The case of India. In P. Phan (ed.), *Technology and Entrepreneurship* (pp. 149-181). Greenwich, CT: Information Age.

Xin, K.R. and Pearce, J.L. 1996. Guanxi connections as substitutes for formal institutional support. *Academy of Management Journal*, 39(6): 1641-1658.

Yoshihara, K. 1988. *The Rise of Ersartz Capitalism in South-East Asia*. Singapore: Oxford University Press.

Yu, T.F.L. 1999. Bringing entrepreneurship back in: Explaining the industrial dynamics of Hong Kong with special reference to the textile and garment industry. *International Journal of Entrepreneurial Behaviour and Research*, 5(5): 235-250.

Yu, T.F.L. 2000. Hong Kong's entrepreneurship: Behaviours and determinants. *Entrepreneurship and Regional Development*, 12(3): 179-194.

Yu, Y.S. 1986. *Rujia sixiang yu jingji faxhan: Zhongguo jinshi zongjiao lunli yu shangren jingshen* [Confucian thought and economic development: Early modern Chinese religious ethics and the spirit of the merchant class]. *Zhishi Fenzi* [The Chinese Intellectual], 2(2): 3-45.

Zapalska, A.M. and Edwards, W. 2001. Chinese entrepreneurship in a cultural and economic perspective. *Journal of Small Business Management*, 39(3): 286-292.

Zhang, Y., Fu, J., Wong, M.Y. and Stewart, S.E.A. 1996. The "catfish effect" of the private sector on the economy of the People's Republic of China. *Journal of Enterprising Culture*, 4(4): 331-349.

Zhao, L. and Aram, J.D. 1995. Networking and growth of young technology-intensive ventures in China. *Journal of Business Venturing*, 10(5): 349-370.

Zhu, M. 1993. Non-agricultural industrial development in Chinese rural area. *Development Policy Review*, 11(4): 382-392.

Zutshi, R.K. 1997. East Asian SMEs: Learning the technology. *Journal of Enterprising Culture*, 5(2): 165-191.

Chapter 8

THE DOUBLE-EDGED SWORD OF ORGANIZATIONAL CULTURE IN ASIA
Toward Transnational Reflexive Dialogues

Nobuyuki Chikudate
Hiroshima University

INTRODUCTION

The purpose of this chapter is to scrutinize published studies that, as a body, provide only a confused picture of issues related to organizational culture in the framework of comparative management between East and West. As such, it goes beyond the slew of reviews, books and handbooks of organizational culture that began to appear in the 1980s and continue to be published (e.g., Ashkanasy, Wilderom & Peterson, 2000; Eisenberg & Riley, 2001). It highlights the conceptual and epistemological limitations of the mass of research in this area, especially as applied to Asia, and shows how a reflexive methodology can advance the critical analysis of studies, often comparative, involving Asian contexts. Such reflexivity is valuable for those in search of a more comprehensive planisphere in which to locate the studies that propose to address the subjects of culture, management and organization.

A critical analysis of studies of organizational culture in Asian contexts must begin with studies related to Japan. First, the surge in interest in issues related to organizational culture coincided with the increased attention that management scholars began to focus on Japan and, more specifically, Japanese organizations. Second, as this review will discuss in more detail, there are extremely few academic studies of organizational culture (as opposed to "national" or ethnic culture) in Asian contexts besides Japan. Finally, the current malaise of Japanese companies—both in the financial and ethical senses—suggest new research questions related to organizational culture that can also construct a bridge between Western academic tradition and Asian contexts. It is important to note, however, that the "western" academic tradition referred to here does not mean that promoted and practiced in US-centric organizational science (e.g., Pfeffer, 1993), but that of German phenomenology and critical theory and French postmodern social theory. It is also necessary to clarify the terminology that I will use in this chapter. First, although many definitions of culture have been introduced (e.g., Louis, 1983; Pettigrew, 1979; Schein, 1985; Siehl & Martin, 1984; Van Maanen, 1988; Trice & Beyer, 1993), in this chapter I use Hatch's definition of organizational culture as "the way of life of an organization" (1997: 294). This definition precludes the alternative uses of "culture" to denote the general socio-conventional idiosyncrasies of the population of a particular nation-state, to which I refer as "national characteristics". Furthermore, "comparative" rather than "cross-cultural" is used to refer to differences among nation-states or organizations.

The chapter begins with a review the intellectual roots that have generated alternative paradigms for studying organizational culture in management studies. This is the basis for critically reviewing the studies of organizational culture in comparative and particular Asian contexts. The next section addresses the potential for bringing western intellectual approaches—in particular, critical theory and reflexive analyses—to bear on current management issues in Asia, such as organizational inertia and ethical lapses, for which an organizational culture perspective is particularly relevant. The chapter concludes with suggestions for comparative methodologies to advance the study of organizational culture in Asian contexts as well as across contexts.

ALTERNATIVE PARADIGMS OF ORGANIZATIONAL CULTURE

In spite of the views of organizational scholars such as Donaldson (1996, 1998) and Pfeffer (1993) who have criticized the profusion of terminologies and methodologies, alternative paradigms for the analysis and discourse regarding organizational culture have emerged and represent a positive, even necessary, aspect of academic inquiry. Three paradigms in particular—managerial, anthropological and critical—have emerged as the major schools of thought related to culture and organization in the Western literature. As discussed later in the chapter, however, the managerial perspective has dominated the few studies of organizational culture by researchers studying Asian contexts or making East–West comparisons. While the anthropological studies have a longer academic tradition, they are relatively scarce in management and especially comparative studies, for reasons discussed later. More recently, promoted by the clear weaknesses of "Japanese management" and fundamental corporate weaknesses across Asia that were exposed by the Asian financial crisis since 1997, the issues derived from the critical perspective are receiving increased attention.

MANAGERIAL APPROACH: CORPORATE CULTURALISM AND CULTURE AS A VARIABLE

From the early 1980s, management research saw an upsurge in the interest in both organizational culture and Japanese firms, and the result has been what Willmott (1993) describes as the rise of "corporate culturalism" and the successful marketing of corporate culture as a management mantra (Pettigrew & Whipp, 1991). Hatch (1997) even calls this a symbiotic relationship, with the search for sources of firm competitiveness during the 1980s leading to explanations based on organizational culture. This was reinforced by the perceived linkage between the organizational cultures and management practices of Japanese firms that differed considerably from US and Western firms, and the emerging dominance in particular industries of those Japanese firms during that period (e.g., Schein, 1981; Deutschmann, 1987). These cultural characteristics and practices became enshrined as "Japanese management" and were used to explain the high commitment, loyalty and morale of employees, docile unions and low turnover rates that prior work had noted in Japanese firms (e.g., Abegglen, 1958; Dore, 1973; Rohlen, 1974).

In parallel to the more practitioner-oriented analyses of "Japanese management", a number of scholars attempted to conceptualize what they saw in Japanese corporations (e.g., Ouchi, 1980; Wilkins & Ouchi, 1983; Wilkins, 1983). Wilkins (1983), for example, interpreted culture as an alternative form of organizational control, equating Perrow's (1979) third-order control (i.e., control over decision premises; [Simon, 1945]) to that of organizational control by culture. Ouchi (1980) labeled such control as "clan control", or control through shared traditions.

Of course, before the concept of culture was invoked, scholars and practitioners had recognized the role of bureaucratic rules and procedures as one means of integrating tasks and roles (a Taylorian approach), and goal congruence as another means of aligning individual activities to support company-level outcomes (e.g., Barnard, 1938). The fundamental point of departure of cultural control from these functionalist views, however, was that economic rationality among organizational members is not assumed. As Willmott (1993: 519) notes, programs of corporate culturalism and related management practices demand loyalty from employees. Cultural conformity on the part of employees—"do they behave and think as ideal Company X men or women"—is the key criterion. By behaving appropriately, individuals gain a sense of unity and fulfillment.

US-based scholars and consultants during this period found similarities between elements of "Japanese management" and successful firms in the US (e.g., Deal and Kennedy, 1982; Peters & Waterman, 1982). The underlying premise of this group of researchers, consultants and practitioners was that successful US companies, like those in Japan, used value-added leadership to unite individual and collective values, and these common values were the basis of the cohesiveness found in these firms. For example, Peters and Waterman concluded that top performing companies "... create a broad, uplifting, shared culture, a coherent framework within which charged-up people search for appropriate adaptations. Their ability to extract extraordinary contributions from very large numbers of people turns on the ability to create a highly valued sense of purpose. Such purpose inevitably emanates from love of product, providing top-quality services, and honoring innovation and contribution from all" (p. 516).

As a result, scholars and then practitioners began to describe an organization as "possessing" a good or bad, or strong or weak, culture. Shared values, corporate heroes, rites and rituals, and shared communication styles became indicators of the invisible power of a corporate culture. Furthermore, culture came to be conceived as one of many variables that should be managed, or "engineered", in order to achieve organizational goals. Positivist, hypothesis-testing studies then attempted to link different types of corporate culture to other managerial concepts and variables, such as strategy (e.g., Schwartz & Davis, 1981) and performance (Wilkins & Ouchi, 1983; Sorensen, 2002), as well as the compatibility between strategy and culture.

ANTHROPOLOGICAL APPROACH: ORGANIZATION AS CULTURE

The anthropological approach of the "cultural purists" (Willmott, 1993) provides a stark contrast to that of corporate culturalism and the conception of organizational culture as a managerial variable. Specifically, an organization is not described as "possessing" a culture, but the organization itself is a culture. Therefore, a culture is not described as "strong" or "weak" (or "good" or "bad" or ...), but each organization is itself a unique cultural manifestation. A further distinction between this approach and that of corporate culturalism is that researchers adopt a subjective/intersubjective epistemology (or "native's view"), whereas the functionalist "culture as managerial variable" researchers adopt an objective epistemology (or "received view") (e.g., Burrell & Morgan, 1979).

The conception of organization-as-culture is based on the assumption that a collectivity is held together by some sort of shared system of meaning amongst the individuals comprising it. These shared meanings are created and maintained through communication among organizational members, are the basis for understanding between members, and are in turn manifest as organizations. Accordingly, the unit of analysis is the organization, not individuals. In this tradition, one of the models and analytical frameworks that has gained the status of influential theory is that developed by Schein (1985), who defines organizational culture as "... the pattern of basic assumptions that a given group has invented, discovered, or developed in learning to cope with its problems of external adaptation and internal integration, and that has worked well enough to be considered valid and, therefore, to be taught to new members as the correct way to perceive, think, and feel in relation to these problems" (p. 6).

Researchers adopting this perspective seek clues to uncover the shared meaning systems, communication (i.e., patterns of social interaction within the meaning systems), and performance (e.g., Pacanowsky & O'Donnell-Trujilo, 1983). The clues vary according to the school and theories of cultural anthropology, such as cognitive anthropology and ethnoscience (e.g., Goodenough, 1971), symbolism (e.g., Geertz, 1973) and structuralism (Levi-Strauss, 1963). They usually include, however, an organization's rituals, symbols, language, stories and mythology. Researchers collect and interpret such cultural clues in order to induce the structure, elements and systems of shared meanings in an organization, relying primarily on qualitative methods such as ethnography and participant-observer techniques.

CRITICAL AND POSTMODERN APPROACHES: CULTURE AS TARGET OF CRITICISM

Beginning in the late 1980s, some management scholars pushed analyses of organizational culture further by returning to the thesis of corporate culturalism and culture as a control mechanism, questioning the validity of such means of managing people. These scholars draw on the works of Habermas and Foucault, and the substance of the Frankfurt critical theories and French poststructuralism/postmodernism (e.g., Alvesson, 1996; Alvesson & Willmott, 1992; Hassard & Parker, 1993; McKinlay & Starkey, 1998). The objective of critical analysis is to lay bare the hidden or concealed dimensions of power and domination disguised by cultural elements in organizational discourse and practices.

Thus, these scholars have drawn attention to the dark side of organizational culture, in contrast to the generally positive portrayal of culture by both the corporate culturalists and cultural purists. Kunda (1992), for example, discusses culture as a mechanism of social control that can be used to manipulate members into perceiving, thinking and feeling in certain ways. Willmott (1993) went so far to argue that culture was an instrument of slavery, equating its use by corporate culturalists to methods described in Orwell's (1989) Nineteen Eighty-Four. In his critique of corporate culturalism, he drew attention to the new problems that cultural control generated—suffocation from cultural indoctrination and a new type of domination—even as it was promoted as a remedy to authoritarianism and technical rationality.

EPISTEMOLOGICAL ISSUES IN THE COMPARATIVE STUDY OF ORGANIZATIONAL CULTURE

Although the three approaches to conceptualizing and studying organizational culture developed generally in the Western management literature, the situation is quite different when we consider studies in Asian contexts. This section reviews the work on organizational culture that has been done in Asian contexts, highlighting the narrow range of approaches that have been applied to analyses of related phenomena in the region.

QUANTITATIVE APPROACHES AND HOFSTEDE'S MIXED LEGACY

Much of the conceptual confusion surrounding the study of organizational culture in Asia (and perhaps elsewhere) can be traced to Hofstede's (1980) Culture's Consequences. His large-scale, multi-country, quantitative approach to deriving dimensions that were both "easy to interpret" (Hofstede & Bond, 1988) and comparable across nations represented a major innovation to the comparative study of culture. Until that time, qualitative description was the dominant approach to studying and characterizing national ("cultural") characteristics. The approach and results presented a major challenge to US-centric researchers and practitioners regarding the universality of American management methods. It has, for example, enabled researchers to study the correlation between the performance of local operations and the congruence (or not) of particular management practices in countries with different cultural characteristics (e.g., Newman & Nollen, 1996). For multinationals, it provided a basis for tackling the challenge of managing local operations across diverse national contexts. Furthermore, for Asians, it represented a welcome acknowledgment of local cultural norms and values, as well as a basis for increasing the cultural sensitivity of multinational managers coming to the region (Bedi, 1993a, 1993b).

Hofstede's triumph, however, has also been tragic for the comparative study of organizational culture. First, Hofstede and Bond (1988: 9) were careful to restrict their conclusions to the national level of analysis, but their research design in which individuals are the unit of analysis violates the theoretical assumption of organizational culture research that the unit of analysis should be organizations. In other words, perhaps a more accurate way of describing the study would be "the comparative and quantitative analysis of values and practices among workers across nation states". Other researchers, however, have linked or even failed to distinguish between national and organizational levels of analysis. Thus, we find studies in which variability in national characteristics is treated as an aspect of organizational culture (e.g., Aycan, Kanungo &

Sinha, 1999). In much of the literature, the distinction is lost completely. This is particularly obvious in the "Japanese management" version of corporate culturalism, discussed in the previous section, that was emerging in the 1980s just as Hofstede's results were gaining currency.

Perhaps even more tragic for the comparative study of organizational culture has been the emerging conviction that organizational culture can, and should, be studied through quantitative methodologies. The logic of this reductionist approach is that components of organizational culture (such as values, behaviors and practices) can be isolated, operationalized and measured on scales. Furthermore, in the case of comparisons of organizations across nations, it is assumed that variation within nations among organizations is less than variation between nations. This logic is represented by Hofstede et al.'s (1990) comparative quantitative study of twenty organizational cultures. This approach has also been advocated even for cross-cultural ethical studies (e.g., McDonald, 2000) that we would expect to involve highly subjective philosophical issues. Although such quantitative approaches may generate statistical significance, there is a fundamental question of whether organizational culture is actually being measured by aggregated scores marked by individual respondents. Because this topic goes beyond the scope of this chapter, we leave it as a question that should be asked of any study that claims to be one of "organizational" culture.

THE DILEMMA OF QUALITATIVE APPROACHES

A number of qualitative studies of organizational culture in Asian contexts have appeared in the literature, drawing on the anthropological and critical traditions. In addition to Brannen and Kleinberg's (2000) review of Japanese management studies from an organizational culture perspective, examples of empirical research has investigated partnerships and ethics in Japanese firms (Chikudate, 1999b, 2000a), cultures of a US subsidiary and local firm in Hong Kong (Kirkbride & Chaw, 1987), a Chinese organization undergoing change (Granrose et al., 2000), alternative decision-making styles in Japanese subsidiaries in Thailand (Kimura & Chikudate, 1996), and social structure and relations in a Japanese department store in Hong Kong (Wong, 1999).

Such qualitative and ethnographic studies of organizational culture, however, face a dilemma in the area of comparative research stemming from the nature of cultural analysis. On one hand, the advantage of qualitative studies is the ability to uncover and describe the idiosyncrasies of organizational life in each context. This can generate rich insights into local, context-specific sense-making organizational structures. On the other hand, such context-specificity becomes a liability when attempting to draw lessons for other contexts, or in pursuing comparative research questions. This is compounded when different national contexts are involved, since the insights may only be understood by those who share the same tacit knowledge in which the analysis is embedded.

To contribute to comparative management discourse, the challenge for qualitative researchers of organizational culture is to convert their context-specific "thick descriptions" into highly abstract concepts that can be decoded by others who may not share the same contextual tacit knowledge. Naming, nominalization and descriptions of findings are not enough to qualify for rigorous academism, even though such writings may appear "realistic" to natives familiar with the context. Otherwise, qualitative analyses of organizational culture run the risk of being no more than a "collection of pep talks and war stories" (Hofstede et al., 1990: 286) and chained to the context in which they were generated.

A further challenge for qualitative approaches to comparative organizational culture involves the relationship between external socio-cultural environments and institutions on the one hand, and organizational culture on the other. Typically, qualitative researchers have treated organizations as closed systems, in which shared values are imprinted by the founders and the way of life in the organization is unique to that organization. This may be appropriate if comparisons are being made between organizations in the same socio-cultural and institutional environment. However, for comparative studies between East and West, or among Asian contexts, it is necessary to incorporate such "external" influences into analyses of organizational culture because the clearly may have an important impact at the organizational level. For example, there may be commonly shared, taken-for-granted assumptions about approaches to management and doing business common to national or larger regional areas (Adler & Jelinek, 1986). Thus, comparative analyses across different external environments require that such elements be addressed. To this end, organizational culture could be usefully viewed as a subsystem of societal characteristics (Adler & Jelinek, 1986), object of societal effects (Mueller, 1994), and subject to "orders" represented by institutions and networks (Wilkinson, 1996; Zang, 1999).

CRITICAL PERSPECTIVES ON "ASIAN" MANAGEMENT

Many studies of organizational culture, and the interpretation of the apparent success of Asian firms and economies, have lacked critical analysis of the phenomena under study. This section shows how this weakness in prior analyses represents an opportunity for further research and improved management in Asian contexts.

PAROCHIAL UTOPIAN VIEWS AND THE FAILURE OF CORPORATE CULTURALISM

By the late 1990s, many of the same Japanese organizations that had been the icons of "Japanese management" and part of the legitimization of corporate culturalism among management researchers and practitioners during the 1980s, had lost their luster. These firms now populate the list of scandal-ridden and financially problematic organizations symbolic of Japan's ongoing domestic malaise. Top executives of these organizations now cite their cultures, conventions and traditions as a major reason behind the scandals in which they have been caught (Chikudate, 2002a, 2002b).

Similarly, the rest of Asia in the 1980s and early 1990s saw the emergence of supposedly unique national management systems (e.g., "K-type management" in Korea [Lee & Yoo, 1987]), ethnic management values and practices such as "Chinese values" (e.g., Miller et al., 1998; Xie, 1995). Perhaps one of the most pervasive buzz words at that time among both practitioners and supposed academics was the vaguely defined construct of "Asian values". This configuration of values, beliefs and behaviors, like the syndrome comprising "Japanese management", was used to explain the increasing competitiveness of both firms and national economies in the region at that time.

Even more dramatically than in the case of Japan, however, the 1997 Asian financial crisis revealed the specious link between those features and economic performance. Although the weaknesses of corporations and national business systems imbued with "Asian values" were present before the crisis, these were largely ignored in both the academic management literature and popular press. Backman (1999) draws the same conclusion, uncovering the fundamental weaknesses that accompanied the apparent strengths of companies and business systems across Asia and that have only drawn general acknowledgment in the aftermath of the Asian financial crisis of 1997.

Ironically, however, the current troubles of these firms actually verifies the thesis of organizational culture as a stabilizer of values and practices (Chikudate, 2000a). The critical weakness of the corporate culturalism approach to analyses of organizational culture and the sources of high performance was that scholars failed to recognize the potential disadvantages of "strong" cultures. The fundamental source of misunderstanding in this regard, particularly in the case of the "Japanese management" version of corporate culturalism, can be traced to Ouchi (1981) and Wilkins and Ouchi's (1983) misinterpretation of Perrow's (1979) third-order control to the case of Japanese organizations. Their analysis has two weaknesses. First, they mistakenly equated third-order control to that operating within Japanese firms, which Ouchi and Johnson (1978) described as clan-control. Second, they extrapolated positive effects of such control, even though Perrow himself did not discuss the desirability or not of outcomes of third-order control.

The problem of using Japanese organizations (and their competitive success, at least in the 1980s) as a basis for advocating clan control in organizations is Ouchi and Johnson's (1978) misunderstanding of the Japanese corporate cultural context. Into that context they read the positive connotations of Gemeinschaft in Tönnies (1940) dichotomous characterization of organizational forms, Gemeinschaft-Gesellschaft. According to Ouchi and Johnson, the clan-control of Gemeinschaft offers an escape from the stagnation by procedures and rules of bureaucratic control, and obtains flexibility, participation and loyalty.

This may be true to some extent in utopian German villages, but the Gemeinschaft ideal originating in Germany is not identical to that of Asian peasant villages. In Asian villages, both mobility and transportation were strictly controlled, and most villagers assumed that they were destined to be born, live and die in the same village. These villages were governed by the logic of rituals and ancestry worship, guided and controlled by village seniors. This evolved into multiple forms of control, including mechanisms of exploitation and punishment by authorities (Kaji, 1990), mutual surveillance to maintain the status quo (e.g., Foucault's (1977) panopticonism), and social ostracism for violators, deviants and strangers. Under such conditions, villagers developed a fundamental fear of deviating from the parameters of "normal" peasants, and conformed for the sake of surviving in their villages (Chikudate, 1999a). This is also fundamentally different from third-order, or "premise control", in which individuals make decisions after rational deliberation.

In Japanese and other Asian societies, the "village" can take other forms of association, including modern corporations, universities, media and political parties. However, individual behavior is still governed by the same type of normative control—and a preoccupation with being "normal", "traditional" and "natural"—as that which operated in Asian peasant villages. Whether wearing blue-collar uniforms in factories or white-collars in offices, employees in these modern villages have been subject to the same pressures for conformity, and excluded, silenced or punished if they question its "creed" (Willmott, 1993: 519). This has been reinforced in Japan through the conscious, and sometimes unconscious, efforts of the Japanese government, media, businessmen and academics (Chikudate, 2002b).

Although the same mechanisms were lauded in the 1980s as the basis of social and corporate cohesiveness, employee commitment and competitive performance, the 1990s have seen the negative implications of such extremely effective normative control. Ironically, there has been little research reported in the management literature that can shed light on such shortcomings of "Japanese management" or even "Asian values", even after more than a decade of scandals, corruption and poor economic performance (White, 2002).

THE YING AND YANG OF CONFUCIAN TRADITION

Although its impact on social norms and behavior varies across Asian societies (Lee and Jablin, 1992), Confucianism is perhaps the single most dominant intellectual tradition linked to Asian societies. Although the writings and interpretations of Confucius are extensive, the fundamental principles regarding social order are: 1) the stability of society is based on unequal relationships between people, 2) the family is the prototype of all social organizations, 3) virtuous behavior toward others consists of treating others as one would like to be treated oneself and 4) virtue with regard to one's skills in life consists of trying to acquire skills and education, working hard, not spending more than necessary, being patient, and persevering (Hofstede & Bond, 1988). Both Korean and Chinese scholars have focused on the only positive influence of Confucianism for economic development in the Pacific Rim (Chen, 1995; Chung, Lee & Jung, 1997; Horng, 1993; Leung et al., 2002; Yeung & Tung, 1996), and its basis for defining what Hofstede and Bond (1988) call the "Confucian connection".

A more critical analysis of Confucian principles, at least those described as the "secular Confucianism" used by the elites to maintain their dominance over the majority of society (Leung et al., 2002), reveals a system of normative control. Obedience in the face of hierarchical power, being "normal" and maintaining harmony are promoted as ideals. In a firm and, more generally, developing economy, such ideals help create a hardworking, obedient workforce that can support corporate and national economic development. With its emphasis on practical knowledge—basic reading and writing and mathematics, rather than abstraction (Kaji, 1990)—and repetition, Confucianism creates an intellectual ideal appropriate for blue-collar workers and production-oriented organizations. It is also possible to interpret many of the features and practices associated with Japanese management—on-the-job training, quality circles, incremental improvement ("kaizen"; Imai, 1986) and even Nonaka and Takeuchi's (1995) conceptualization of "knowledge-creation"—as manifestations of the Confucian values stressing practical knowledge and skills acquired through repetition.

Indeed, critical scholars have identified a number of serious implications when Confucianism is a strong influence on organizational values and practices. For example, the unequal relationships between people are based on recognized mutual obligations. A subordinate owes a senior respect and obedience, and the senior owes the subordinate production and consideration. The pathological result in such an organization is that a superior's authority is effectively insulated from challenge by subordinates, while the subordinate is always subject to censor and elimination by the superior (Kent, 1992). As a result, even if a subordinate sees unwise, questionable, unethical or even illegal behavior by a senior, he is unlikely to draw attention to it or challenge the senior. In a Confucian system, such a response by a subordinate is construed as "loyalty". Such behavior is further exacerbated in systems in which maintaining harmony is given precedent over introducing positive change.

A preoccupation with maintaining stability within the organization and harmonious relationships among members thus diminishes an organization's capacity for reflexivity and, thereby, acts as a source of inertia and resistance to change in these organizations. The "knowledgeable" members in Giddens' (1984) framework of structuration and cultural dynamics are either not produced or they are marginalized or expelled by authorities. The only exception is when someone in authority also has the ability and interest in introducing change, or allows a subordinate to do so.

The implication is that truly open and ideal communication (Habermas, 1984) is unlikely to be found in most Asian organizations, and empirical work seems to support this assumption. Lee (1989), for example, reported that most communication in Korean organizations is downward, although most directives do not contain detailed instructions. Being able to understand a superior's intentions out of the general context is a key skill for subordinates in such a system. This calls into question the true nature of participative management and decision-making practices, such as reported by Wai-Kwok and Wai-Kwok (1995) in their study of introducing TQM into Hong Kong organizations, or other "suggestion systems" (e.g., Imai, 1986) often associated with Japanese management practices. Chikudate (1999a) has found that such practices are corrupted in organizations in which members can make only positive comments, must avoid critical or sensitive issues, or the agenda for discussion is controlled by superiors. In other words, in organizations in which a subordinate's role is merely to interpret a superior's wishes, participative management practices do not have the same role or benefits as one in which Habermasian open/ideal communication is operating.

In such social contexts, even if they are noticed, raising discussion of negative, questionable or unethical issues in public is rejected (Chikudate, 2002a). In addition to submission to authority, many Asian organizations are characterized by norms of conflict avoidance (Swierczek, 1994; Leung et al., 2002), and raising such issues threatens conflict. This is reinforced by respect for the "face" of others and a developed sensitivity towards others' feelings (Blunt, 1988) that are also part of the social norms and values of these organizations.

The combination of normative control—especially when unrecognized and even reinforced by organizational members themselves—and the effects of Confucian-based values and practices have been shown to have other extremely negative consequences in Asian organizations. For example, Chikudate (1999a, 2002a) has used the term collective myopia to describe the process by which company—and institutional—level norms may diverge significantly from those of society at large, even to the point where illegal activities become "commonsense" within the organization and institution. Members objectivate facts (Berger & Luckmann, 1966) according to intra-organizational norms or those operating in wider communities, such as industries and business groups, insulated from society at large. This is one mechanism to explain how graduates of the most prestigious universities in their respective countries managing the most "respected" firms in their societies can undertake what, to their fellow citizens, is clearly unethical or illegal behavior.

SURPRISING EAST–WEST CONNECTIONS

A fundamental argument of this chapter is that more intellectually rigorous and methodologically diverse approaches can benefit the comparative study of organizational culture and reveal unexpected linkages between Asian and Western contexts. It also calls into question the pervasiveness of the East–West dichotomy in management research and practice. In his study of the cultural impediments to organizational change in Brunei and Malaysia, for example, Blunt (1988) found striking parallels between cultural orientations in those national contexts and in the UK. Across studies and time, Chikudate (1999a) found similar cultural features characterizing problematic organizational predispositions, as did Bate et al. (1984) in their study of UK organizations. Organizations in these national contexts seemed to have more in common, at least within the range of inquiry of the respective studies, than any of them (including the UK) with US organizations. Adler and Jelinek (1986) provide one basis for such an unexpected grouping, noting the strong American belief in individual free will and control. The British and other Europeans may have a greater sense of determinism or passivity when faced with the same circumstances, and this links them more closely with most Asians.

Other phenomena may be common across the artificial East–West dichotomy. Recent events in major US corporations suggest that collective myopia and organizational cultures that perpetuate unethical or even illegal behavior are phenomena not specific to any particular national context. Like their indicted Japanese counterparts, many of the American executives who have resigned or been indicted for illegal acts were leaders of some of the most respected firms in the US and were models of "successful professionals" (Ibarra, 1999). It is possible to infer that the dark side of normative control either made such behavior "acceptable" according to the values and practices comprising these organizational cultures, or certain issues were off-limits or impervious to critical reflection internally.

Indeed, similar questions and doubts can be leveled at most East–West dichotomies, which are at best simplistic and often inaccurate. For example, Triandis (1995, 1998) and many behavioral scientists have attempted to legitimize the dichotomy of Eastern cultures as collectivist and Western cultures as individualist. A broader intellectual analysis drawing on traditions within

sociology, cultural anthropology and philosophy—for example, symbolic in-
teractionism (Mead, 1934), ritual studies (Goffman, 1967), social construc-
tivism (Berger & Luckmann, 1966), critical theory and postmodernism (e.g.,
Foucault, 1977)—would show that such an attempt is both meaningless and
indefensible. In these and related approaches, individuals in any context are all
captured in normative webs by which conformity and social control continues.
The topics for research, therefore, are the particular mechanisms, processes and
power at play in the tug-of-war between individuality and collectivity. Similarities and differences between specific contexts are related to such constructs,
not an arbitrary geopolitical or ethnic boundary.

TOWARD REFLEXIVE ORGANIZATIONS AND
TRANSNATIONAL DIALOGUES

The analysis presented in this chapter has shown the weakness of corporate
culturalism as the dominant approach to the study of organizational culture in
Asian contexts. Not only did it draw specious correlations between features
of organizational cultures and performance, but in practice it also drew attention away from the dysfunctional elements of particular cultures. Furthermore,
the quantitative methodologies that were introduced as part of the reductionist
stream within that approach are at best questionable in terms of epistemology.
Qualitative methodologies, combined with a critical perspective on organizational culture, are better able to provide necessary balance to the positively
biased conclusions of corporate culturalist approaches. In particular, while values and practices associated with Confucianism had been promoted as the basis for organizational and national economic growth and competitiveness in
the region, a critical analysis reveals that the same values and practices act as
a mechanism for normative control which, when unchecked, can lead to organizational pathologies such as unethical or illegal behavior or resistance to
change.

Men of powers in Asia have programmed such a control through educational systems as well as equivocal and complex language systems, especially
Chinese, by giving Kŭn zi or Confucius, the inventor of Confucianism around
the time of 500. B.C. the similar status of a Greek philosopher Socrates (Hofstede & Bond, 1998) who taught the opposite principle of "asking questions
is the ultimate virtue". Even though Chinese and others fantasize that the natural acceptance of Confucianism by the majority of peasants finally ended the
continuous civil wars, it ripens at the time where Asians should ask such a
Foucaultian question into Asian contexts; "How are Asians shaped in the historical process of distorted intellectuality legitimacy, power and domination?"
(Chikudate, 2002b).

The chapter also reveals the tremendous potential that exists for comparative research of organizational culture, especially work that takes advantage of the diverse contexts found in Asia. First, more and more rigorous qualitative studies of Asian contexts could generate new abstract concepts that can then be used to compare organizations in diverse contexts. This would provide much more insightful, and perhaps unexpected, comparisons between organizations and contexts that prior approaches, such as East–West dichotomies, mask. Second, critical studies can draw attention to the negative implications of particular organizational types and features, providing balance to the generally positive bias of most studies of organizational culture. Such advances in research and understanding would then provide the basis for accurately diagnosing organizational problems and prescribing solutions. In conclusion, in the territories of organizational culture where the dark-sides of cultural control have been identified regardless East–West distinctions, I believe that we should bring various kinds of studies, which might have been screened in the legitimacy of US organization science, into the tables of transnational dialogues to learn and seek the solutions for mutual benefits. In this sense, future studies in organizational culture in comparison with Asia would be fruitful in comparative collaborative research toward reflexivity (Easterby-Smith & Malina, 1999; Chikudate, 2001, 2002b), going beyond simple inquiries of differences and similarities.

ACKNOWLEDGEMENTS

This study has been funded from the Grant-in-Aid C for Scientific Research from the Ministry of Education, Culture, Sports, Science and Technology of Japan.

REFERENCES

Abegglen, J. 1958. *The Japanese Factory*. Glencoe, IL: Free Press.
Adler, N.J. and Jelinek, M. 1986. Is "organization culture" culture bound? *Human Resource Management*, 25(1): 73-90.
Alvesson, M. 1996. *Communication, Power, and Organization*. Berlin: de Gruyter.
Alvesson, M. and Willmott, H. 1992. On the idea of emancipation in management and organization studies. *Academy of Management Review*, 17(3): 432-464.
Ashkanasy, N.M., Wilderom, C.P.M. and Peterson, M.F. (eds.). 2000. *Handbook of Organizational Culture & Climate*. Thousand Oaks: Sage.
Aycan, Z., Kanungo, R.N. and Sinha, J.B.P. 1999. Organizational culture and human resource management practices: The model of Culture fit. *Journal of Cross-Cultural Psychology*, 30(4): 501-526.
Backman, M. 1999. *Asian Eclipse: Exposing the Dark Side of Business in Asia*. Singapore: John Wiley & Sons (Asia) Pte.
Barnard, C. 1938. *The Function of the Executive*. Cambridge, MA: Harvard University Press.

Bate, P. 1984. The impact of organizational culture on approaches to organizational problem-solving. *Organization Studies*, 5(1): 43-66.

Bedi, H. 1993a. Sensitivity and success. *Asian Business*, March, 29(3): 4.

Bedi, H. 1993b. Stepping on cultural toes. *Asian Business*, April, 29(4): 4.

Berger, P. and Luckmann, T. 1966. *The Social Construction of Reality: A Treatise in the Sociology of Knowledge*. Garden City: Doubleday.

Blunt, P. 1988. Cultural consequences for organization change in a Southeast Asian state: Brunei. *Academy of Management Executives*, 11(3): 235-240.

Brannen, M.Y. and Kleinberg, J. 2000. Images of Japanese management and the development of organizational culture theory. In N.M. Ashkanasy, C.P.M. Wilderom and M.F. Peterson (eds.), *Handbook of Organizational Culture & Climate* (pp. 387-400). Thousand Oaks: Sage.

Burrell, G. and Morgan, G. 1979. *Sociological Paradigms and Organizational Analysis*. London: Heinemann.

Chen, M. 1995. *Asian Management Systems: Chinese, Japanese and Korean Styles of Business*. London: Routledge.

Chikudate, N. 1999a. The state of collective myopia in Japanese business communities: A phenomenological study for exploring blocking mechanisms for change. *Journal of Management Studies*, 36: 69-86.

Chikudate, 1999b. Generating reflexivity from partnership formation: A phenomenological reasoning on the partnership between a Japanese pharmaceutical corporation and Western laboratories. *Journal of Applied Behavioral Science*, 35: 287-305.

Chikudate, N. 2000a. A phenomenological approach to inquiring into an ethically bankrupted organization: A case study of a Japanese company. *Journal of Business Ethics*, 28, November (1): 59-71.

Chikudate, N. 2000b. Toward reflexive organizations: From the grounded theoretical study of non-manufacturers in Japan. In L. Songini (ed.), *Political and Economic Relations between Asia and Europe: New Challenges in Economics and Management* (pp. 195-205). Milan: Edizioni Giuridiche Economiche Aziendali.

Chikudate, N. 2001. Limitations and potentials of intercultural communication in unethical business conventions: A theoretical scrutiny in intercultural communication, business ethics, Habermasian discourse ethics, and Foucaultian aesthetics. In *Proceeding of 2001 EAMSA Annual Conference: Asia and Europe in the New Global System-Intercultural Cooperation and Competition Scenarios* (pp. 59-82). Berlin: Frei Universität Berlin.

Chikudate, N. 2002a. Collective myopia and disciplinary power behind the scenes of unethical practices: A diagnostic theory on Japanese organization. *Journal of Management Studies*, 39: 289-307.

Chikudate, N. 2002b. Collective myopia and defective higher educations behind the scenes of ethically bankrupted economic systems: A reflexive note from a Japanese university and taking a step toward transcultural dialogues. *Journal of Business Ethics*, 38, July (1): 205-225.

Chung, K.H., Lee, H.C. and Jung, K.H. 1997. *Korean Management: Global Strategy and Cultural Transformation*. Berlin: Walter de Gruyter.

Deal, T. and Kennedy, A. 1982. *Corporate Culture: The Rites and Rituals of Corporate Life*. Reading: Addison-Wesley.

Deutschmann, C. 1987. The Japanese type of organization as a challenge to the sociological theory of modernization. *Thesis Eleven*, 17: 40-58.

Donaldson, L. 1996. *For Positivist Organization Theory*. London: Sage.

Donaldson, L. 1998. The myth of paradigm incommensurability in management studies: Comments by an integrationist. *Organization*, 5: 267-272.

Dore, R. 1973. *British Factory, Japanese Factory: The Origins of National Diversity in Industrial Relations*. Berkeley: University of California Press.

Easterby-Smith, M. and Malina, D. 1999. Cross-cultural collaborative research: Toward reflexivity. *Academy of Management Journal*, 42(1): 76-86.

Eisenberg, E.M. and Riley, P. 2001. Organizational culture. In F.M. Jablin and L.L. Putnam (eds.), *The New Handbook of Organizational Communication* (pp. 291-322). Thousand Oaks: Sage.

Foucault, M. 1977. *Discipline and Punish: The Birth of the Prison*. New York: Vintage Books.

Geertz, C. 1973. *Interpretation of Cultures*. New York: Basic Books.

Giddens, A. 1984. *The Constitution of Society*. Cambridge: Polity Press.

Goffman, E. 1967. *Interaction Ritual: Essays on Face-to-Face Behavior*. New York: Pantheon Books.

Goodenough, W.H. 1971. *Culture, Language and Society*. Reading: Addison-Wesley.

Granrose, C.S., Huang, Q. and Reigadas. E. 2000. Changing organizational culture in Chinese firms. In N.M. Ashkanasy, C.P.M. Wilderom and M.F. Peterson (eds.), *Handbook of Organizational Culture & Climate* (pp. 483-496). Thousand Oaks: Sage.

Habermas, J. 1984. *Communication and the Evolution of Society*. Cambridge: Polity Press.

Hassard, J. and Parker, M. (eds.) 1993. *Postmodernism and Organizations*. London: Sage.

Hatch, M.J. 1997. *Organization Theory: Modern, Symbolic, and Postmodern Perspectives*. Oxford: Oxford University Press.

Hofstede, G. 1980. *Culture's Consequences: International Differences in Work-Related values*. Beverly Hills, CA: Sage.

Hofstede, G. and Bond, M.H. 1988. The Confucius connection: From cultural roots to economic growth. *Organizational Dynamics*, 16 (Spring): 4-21.

Hofstede, G., Neuijen, B., Ohayv, D.D. and Sanders, G. 1990. Measuring organizational cultures: A qualitative and quantitative study across twenty cases. *Administrative Science Quarterly*, 35: 286-316.

Horng, C. 1993. Cultural differences, trust, and their relationships to business strategy and control. In S.B. Prasad and R.B. Peterson (eds.), *Advances in International Comparative Management* (Vol. 8, pp. 175-197). Greenwich: JAI Press.

Ibarra, H. 1999. Provisional selves: Experimenting with image and identity in professional adaptation. *Administrative Science Quarterly*, 44: 764-791.

Imai, M. 1986. *Kaizen: The Key to Japan's Competitive Success*. New York: Random House.

Kaji, N. 1990. *Jyukyou Towa Nanika* [What is Confucianism?] Tokyo: Chuo Koron Shinsha.

Kent, D.H. 1992. Power, authority, and economic reform: The changing role of supervision in the Chinese state-owned enterprises. In S.B. Prasad (ed.), *Advances in International Comparative Management* (Vol. 7, pp. 169-184). Greenwich: JAI Press.

Kimura, Y. and Chikudate, N. 1996. The cross-cultural analysis of the life-world aspect of decision-making between Japanese and Thai Workers: An approach from the linguistic phenomenology to comparative studies in management. In *13th Annual Conference of Euro-Asia Management Studies Association Proceedings* (pp. 419-439). Tokyo: Chuo University.

Kirkbride, P.S. and Chaw, S.W. 1987. The cross-cultural transfer of organizational cultures: Two case studies of corporate mission statements. *Asia Pacific Journal of Management*, 5(1): 55-66.

Kunda, G. 1992. *Engineering Culture: Control and Commitment in a High-tech Corporation*. Philadelphia: Temple University Press.

Lee. H.C. 1989. Managerial characteristics of Korean firms. In K.H. Chung and H.C. Lee (eds.), *Korean Managerial Dynamics* (pp. 147-162). New York: Praeger.

Lee, J. and Jablin, F.M. 1992. A cross-cultural investigation of exit, voice, loyalty and neglect as responses to dissatisfying job conditions. *Journal of Business Communication*, 29(3): 203-228.

Lee, S.M. and Yoo, S. 1987. The K-type management: A driving forces of Korean prosperity. *Management International Review*, 27: 68-77.

Leung, K., Koch, P.T. and Lu, L. 2002. A dualistic model of harmony and its implications for conflict management in Asia. *Asia Pacific Journal of Management*, 19(2,3): 201-220.

Levi-Strauss, C. 1963. *Structural Anthropology*. New York: Basic Books.

Louis, M.R. 1983. Organizations as culture-bearing milieux. In L. Pondy, P. Frost, G. Morgan and T. Dandridge (eds.), *Organizational Culture* (pp. 39-54). Greenwich: JAI Press.

McDonald, G. 2000. Cross-cultural methodological issues in ethical research. *Journal of Business Ethics*, 27: 89-104.

McKinlay, A. and Starkey, K. (eds.) 1998. *Foucault, Management and Organization Theory*. London: Sage.

Mead, H. 1934. *Mind, Self, & Society: From the Standpoint of Social Behaviorist*. Chicago: University of Chicago Press.

Miller, D.J., Giacobbe-Miller, J.K., Zhang, W. 1998. A comparative study of Chinese and U.S. distributive justice values, goals, and allocative behaviors. In J.R. Cheng and R.B. Peterson (eds.), *Advances in International Comparative Management* (Vol. 12, pp. 185-206). Greenwich: JAI Press.

Mueller, F. 1994. Societal effect, organizational effect and globalization. *Organization Studies*, 15(3): 407-428.

Newman, K.L. and Nollen, S.D. 1996. Culture and congruence: The fit between management practices and national culture. *Journal of International Business Studies*, fourth quarter: 753-779.

Nonaka, I., Takeuchi, H. 1995. *The Knowledge-creating Company: How Japanese Companies Foster Creativity and Innovation for Competitive Advantage*. New York: Oxford University Press.

Orwell, G. 1989. *Nineteen Eighty-Four*. Hamondsworth: Penguin.

Ouchi, W.G. 1980. Markets, bureaucracies, and clans. *Administrative Science Quarterly*, 25: 129-141.

Ouchi, W.G. 1981. *Theory Z: How American Business Can Meet the Japanese Challenge*. New York: Addison-Wesley.

Ouchi, W.G. and Johnson, J.B. 1978. Types of organizational control and their relationship to emotional well-being. *Administrative Science Quarterly*, 23: 293-317.

Pacanowsky, M.E. and O'Donnell-Trujillo. 1983. Organizational communication as cultural performance. *Communication Monographs*, 50: 126-147.

Perrow, C. 1979. *Complex Organizations: A Critical Essay* (2nd edn). Glenview: Scott, Foresman Co.

Peters, T.J. and Waterman, R.H. 1982. *In Search of Excellence: Lessons from America's Best-Run Companies*. New York: Haper & Row.

Pettigrew, A. 1979. On studying organizational culture. *Administrative Science Quarterly*, 24: 570-581.

Pettigrew, A. and Whipp, R. 1991. *Managing Change for Competitive Success*. Oxford: Blackwell.

Pfeffer, J. 1993. Barriers to the advance of organizational science: Paradigm development as dependent variable. *Academy of Management Review*, 18: 599-620.

Rohlen, T. 1974. *For Harmony and Strength: Japanese White Collar Organization in Anthropological Perspective*. Berkeley: University of California Press.

Schein, E.H. 1981. Does Japanese management style have a message for American mangers? *Sloan Management Review*, 23: 55-68.

Schein, E.H. 1985. *Organizational Culture and Leadership*. San Francisco: Jossey-Bass.

Schwartz, H. and Davis, S.M. 1981. Matching corporate culture and business strategy. *Organizational Dynamics*, summer: 30-48.

Siehl, C. and Martin, J. 1984. The role of symbolic management: How can managers effectively transmit organizational culture? In J.D. Hunt, D. Hosking, C. Schriesheim and R. Steward (eds.), *Leaders and Managers: International Perspectives on Managerial Behavior and Leadership* (pp. 227-239). New York: Pergamon.

Simon, H.A. 1945. *Administrative Behavior*. New York: Free Press.

Sorensen, J.B. 2002. The strength of corporate culture and the reliability of firm performance. *Administrative Science Quarterly*, 47(1): 70-91.

Swierczek, F.W. 1994. Culture and conflict in joint ventures in Asia. *International Journal of Project Management*, 12(1): 39-47.

Tönnies, F. 1940. *Community and Society*. New York: American Book.

Triandis, H.C. 1995. *Individualism & Collectivism*. Boulder: Westview Press.

Triandis, H.C. 1998. Vertical and horizontal individualism and collectivism: Theory and research implications for international comparative management. In J.R. Cheng and R.B. Peterson (eds.), *Advances in International Comparative Management* (Vol. 12, pp. 7-36). Greenwich: JAI Press.

Trice, H. and Beyer, J. 1993. *The Cultures of Work Organizations*. Englewood Cliffs: Prentice-Hall.

Van Maanen, J. 1988. *Tales of the Field: On Writing Ethnography*. Chicago: University of Chicago Press.

Wai-Kwok, L. and Wai-Kwok, T. 1995. Company culture and total quality management: A case study. *Asia Pacific Journal of Quality Management*, 4(4): 41-45.

White, S. 2002. Rigor and relevance in Asian management research: Where are we and where can we go? *Asia Pacific Journal of Management*, 19(2,3): 287-352.

Wilkins, A. 1983. Organizational stories as symbols which control the organization. In L.R. Pondy, P.J. Frost, G. Morgan and T.C. Dandridge (eds.), *Organizational Symbolism* (pp. 81-92). Greenwich: JAI Press.

Wilkins, A. and Ouchi, W. 1983. Efficient culture: Exploring the relationship between culture and organizational performance. *Administrative Science Quarterly*, 28: 468-481.

Wilkinson, B. 1996. Culture, institutions and business in East Asia. *Organization Studies*, 17(3): 421-447.

Willmott, H. 1993. Strength is ignorance; Slavery is freedom: Managing culture in modern organizations. *Journal of Management Studies*, 30: 515-552.

Wong, H.W. 1999. *Japanese Bosses, Chinese Workers: Power and Control in a Hong Kong Megastore*. Honolulu: University of Hawaii Press.

Xie, J.L. 1995. Research on Chinese organizational behavior and human resource management: Conceptual and methodological considerations. In S.B. Prasad (ed.), *Advances in International Comparative Management* (Vol. 10, pp. 15-42). Greenwich: JAI Press.

Yeung, I.Y.M. and Tung, R.L. 1996. Achieving business success in Confucian societies: The importance of guanxi (connections). *Organizational Dynamics*, autumn: 54-65.

Zang, X. 1999. Research Note: Personalism and corporate networks in Singapore. *Organization Studies*, 20(5): 861-877.

Chapter 9

WESTERN AND ASIAN BUSINESS ETHICS
Possibilities and Problems

Daryl Koehn
University of St. Thomas

Alicia S.M. Leung
Hong Kong Baptist University

INTRODUCTION

Business ethics is a relatively new and increasingly important discipline, incorporating many approaches. This chapter examines these approaches and explores their possibilities and problems and identifies areas for future research.

It is useful to begin by broadly distinguishing the approaches. The approaches are either *macro* or *micro* in nature. *Macro-approaches* posit one or more values that are said to prevail in particular countries or throughout the world. Macro-approaches may be either *normative* or *empirical* in nature. *Macro-normative* approaches argue for the legitimacy of certain general norms, key values, or modes of reasoning. *Macro-empirical* approaches hypothesize the existence of general norms or values and then gather and analyze data with a view to determining the extent to which these norms or values prevail in the group surveyed. Macro-empirical approaches, in turn, are of two types: *analytical* and *documentary*. *Analytical* work considers the effect of values on practice; *documentary* work aims at establishing the presence of the hypothesized values in certain populations.

Like macro-approaches, micro-approaches can be normative or empirical. Unlike macro-approaches, micro-approaches do not argue or hypothesize that a set of values is shared by every member of a certain region or culture. Nor do micro-approaches suppose that a set of values applies to all practices within the country or countries being studied. Normative micro-approaches explicate and extend the arguments and justifications offered by particular thinkers in various traditions. Empirical micro-approaches document attitudes of individuals toward particular practices (e.g., whistleblowing; bribery). These empirical approaches typically do not evaluate whether one attitude is better than another.

Part One describes and evaluates the major macro-approaches; Part Two considers micro-approaches. We review arguments and findings of both approaches, discuss problems with the methodology employed and the assumptions made by those adopting the approach, and suggest areas for additional research.

PART ONE: MACRO-APPROACHES TO COMPARATIVE BUSINESS ETHICS

Section One: Normative Macro-Approaches

Most of the literature on international business ethics uses a macro-approach. Western philosophers and researchers, especially Anglo-Americans, generally adopt an approach based upon the ethics of Immanuel Kant or the norms of the Judeo-Christian tradition. The key idea in both ethics is that of human dignity. Human dignity is equated with personal worth. This worth stems from man's being as a creature of God or as a rational being. In both derivations, the worth is understood to be innate, a consequence of man's nature. According to the Judeo-Christian religion, human beings are created in the image and likeness of a good God. Man, the image and likeness of God, is thus good as well. In creating human beings, God has bestowed an intrinsic worth upon each individual. This dignity cannot be destroyed by any human authority. Such dignity is sacred; and so dignity may also be equated with the sanctity of life (Sevensky, 1983). By acquiring virtue, we reveal, as St. Thomas Aquinas has argued, an authentic human dignity (Cessario, 1989), but this dignity is always immanently present. Virtue reveals—it does not create—dignity.

Equally, Western ethical systems that take rationality (rather than our partly divine nature) to be the defining or characteristic mark of humans understand men and women to possess an intrinsic, innate worth. Kant, for example, argues that reason sets mankind apart from the animals. Animals exist quite well, living by instinct alone. The fact that we have reason means that reason serves another purpose—namely, to impose its own demands upon us (e.g., a demand to be logically consistent) (Kant, 1998). Experiencing and honoring these demands sets each of us apart from the animals and gives us worth in our own eyes and in the eyes of other rational beings. This worth belongs to us as members of a species. This dignity is fundamental and absolute (Llamzon, 1983; Wood, 1998).

It is fair to say that dignity-based ethics dominate Western thinking about theoretical and applied ethics. Some philosophers have gone so far as to argue that ethical reality is coextensive with human dignity and that being ethically good is identical with discerning the imperatives of human dignity (Glaser, 1989). Human rights organizations justify rights by appealing to human dignity. They argue that rights are necessary to protect dignity and that human beings possess rights by virtue of the inherent worth of persons (United Nations, 1948). Some governments explicitly base their legitimacy on human dignity. For example, Article One of the German Grundgesetz guarantees human dignity (Hofman, 1996). Prominent politicians have cited the need to protect human dignity and urged the founding of international institutions. Nelson Mandela has pressed for the establishment of an international criminal court in order to hold states accountable for human rights violations and to enable human dignity to "shine brightly" (Chothia, 1998).

Given the predominance of dignity-based ethics in the West, it should come as no surprise that normative macro-business ethics appeal to the need to respect human dignity. Stakeholder theory (Freeman, 2002) contends that every person who is significantly and relatively directly affected by a corporation's actions has a right to be respected by that corporation and its executives. Corporations are ethically good only to the extent that they heed and seek to accommodate the demands and concerns of all stakeholders—vendors, employees, communities, stockholders and managers. The social contract approach (Donaldson and Dunfee, 1999) argues for the existence of certain universal and controlling hypernorms (ultimately rooted in respect for human dignity) applicable to all business practice. Catholic social teaching has been used to analyze the ethical purpose of business firms and to evaluate work ethics (Abela, 2001; McCann, 1997). The norms implicit in Catholic social teaching embody the duty to respect each person's God-given dignity. Like Christian business ethics, Jewish business ethics treat God as the ultimate source of value, but stress that dignity inheres within human beings as members of a community. The community, therefore, holds a central place in Jewish business ethics (Pava, 1998b). Although a few Western theorists will speak of dignity as an acquired trait (Steur, 1989), all of these approaches treat human dignity or worth as an innate characteristic or property of individuals. While some Jewish norms are both legalistic and aspirational in character (Pava, 1998a), dignity itself is never aspirational: it is always a given in Kantian and Judeo-Christian business ethics.

Normative macro-approaches are equally popular among those evaluating business ethics practices in Asia. Instead of stressing universal norms, pure and applied ethical research often insists upon differences between Asians and Westerners. Asians are alleged to have a communitarian outlook, deriving from their Confucian tradition. This outlook

(1) gives primacy of place to the duties that persons have to the common good of the community and the virtues needed for the fulfillment of these duties; and

(2) casts reciprocal social relationships and roles as fundamental to communal flourishing and its shared vision of the good (Twiss, 1998:40).

Such communitarianism has numerous consequences. Organizations ask to trust and believe in superiors who have a moral duty to discern and to pursue the common good. The senior employee has prerogatives and authority not granted to more junior employees. Yang (1994) argues that relationships are asymmetric with more stringent requirements and restrictions being imposed on the less powerful role. As a consequence, juniors become relatively powerless. The emphasis on each person's duty to acquire social virtues is arguably tied to class distinctions, since each class is thought to make a distinctive contribution to the overall general welfare. Finally, some evidence suggests that Asian Confucian collectivists are more concerned with the consequences of their behaviors and more likely to sacrifice personal interests for the attainment of collective interest (Moorman and Blakely, 1995). In very general terms, the Western liberal arts education is designed to liberate students so that they can be more individually self-fulfilled. Countries with a strong Confucian ethical tradition, by contrast, historically have taught students to honor and fulfill the expectations of other people.

Like most Western ethics, the Asian Value approach focuses on dignity, but dignity is understood quite differently in Confucian and in Buddhist ethical systems than in Western theories. Dignity is not innate but is a worth that a person acquires by behaving properly within relationships. Liang contends that relationship is the most prominent and pervasive feature of Chinese culture (1949:86): "Relationships of ethics are also relationships of mutual favors, that is to say, there is a relationship of mutual obligation. The logic of ethical-relational principles is found in the components of feeling and obligation."

Guanxi is a well-known exemplification of relational ethics (Leung et al., 1996), but *guanxi*, like all of these ethical relations, is quite subtle and complicated (Dunfee and Warren, 2001). Favor-seeking *guanxi* is based in culture, while rent-seeking *guanxi* seems to be institutionally defined (Su and Littlefield, 2001). Women and men appear to differ in their understanding and use of *guanxi*. Men were found more likely to manipulate and construct *guanxi* through instrumental-personal ties (*renqing*) while women were more likely to develop social interaction through affective-personal ties (*ganqing*) (Leung, 2000). Dignity is achieved in highly specific ways, depending upon the rules and expectations implicit in each relation and the gender and class of the parties involved.

Confucian ethical systems are rooted in dyadic relations of family and kin that then extend outward to all types of interpersonal relationships. Filial piety and brotherly respect are specifically described as the roots of ethical virtue or *jen* (Dawson, 1981). Notice that this relationship-based ethic does not stress the intrinsic rights of individuals within the relationship as Western universalistic ethics do (Yang, 1994). Instead, Confucian business ethic mandates that individuals act as the relationships demand. The Confucian Mencius provides the classical expression of ethically correct human relationships:

Between parent and child there is to be affection;
Between ruler and minister, rightness;
Between husband and wife, [gender] distinctions;
Between older and younger [siblings] an order of precedence;
Between friends, trustworthiness (Mencius 3A:4).

Specific relationships are evaluated in light of the Confucian interdependent virtues of *jen* and *li*. *Jen* refers to human-relatedness (Hall and Ames, 1987). An individual qualifies as fully human only when he or she takes proper account of others and acts in accordance with relationship-specific norms and expectations. *Li* are the rules of propriety or proper behavior. At home and in social and commercial life, "*li* is the principle that channels respect for each other and for the world and regulates human nature" (Blackburn, 1994:75). While Western ethical systems emphasize rights deriving from intrinsic, inalienable dignity, Confucian ethical systems, which locate dignity in the relation, revolve around the obligation to observe these basic human proprieties (Pappu, 1982). Throughout Asia, business meetings begin with more general discussion, often on surprisingly philosophical topics. The visitor is always offered refreshment, and executives' offices often have pictures of family members and friends, a reminder of the larger human network in which we have our existence (Goodell, 1995).

Becoming fully human and having human dignity are thus equivalent notions in Confucian societies. Since humanity is an achievement—we must acquire the virtue of *jen* and learn the civilizing rules of *li*—it follows that neither our humanity nor our dignity are innate. While it might be argued that relational ethics assume that each person has the innate ability to become civilized, acquiring dignity requires effort on the part of the individual. Therefore, in Asian cultures structured around Confucian social relations, dignity is conditional. Everyone does not possess equal value, for the essence of rules of relational propriety is to distinguish among human beings. *Li* divide human society into superiors and inferiors (Dunkang, 1991). Acquiring human dignity entails not only realizing one's role-, gender- and class-based virtue but also taking note of others' family background, occupations, and social positions. Status differences must be respected and have strong behavioral implications. Those in lower ranks should honor those of higher rank (Westwood, 1992). Social status is always linked with wealth, authority and power—it is, in short, a matter of reputation and appearance. The son of a tycoon will be afforded a place of dignity in society because of his family's influence. Riches and honor command respect within the social system because they are signs that the individual has fulfilled his or her social duties successfully and therefore has dignity.

Confucian ethical systems link dignity to the person's level of education. Professions requiring a high level of education and self-discipline confer dignity. Becoming a doctor, lawyer, accountant or scholar bestows dignity upon the person occupying these roles. Dignity is role-specific in the Chinese and Japanese context. As Ho (1976:883) argues, "the respectability a person can claim for himself ... [varies according to the] relative position he occupies in his social network and the degree to which he is judged to have functioned adequately in that position as well as acceptably in his general conduct." A prestigious job is a social honor given to a person and grants that party a measure of secure dignity and ethical worth. Conversely, individuals can defer to others who are exercising role-specific authority without losing their dignity. In Japan, where the doctor has a great deal of authority to act in what he thinks to be in the best interest of the patient and family, individuals are comfortable with the paternalistic role of the doctor (Hayashi et al., 2000; Asai et al., 1997). The same logic seems to apply to corporate employees who are quite comfortable working for employers whom many Westerners would condemn as paternalistic (Umezu, n.d.).

Some feminists have argued that Confucian ethical systems devalue and oppress women. The sexual division of labor in China is captured by the Confucian principle that "men are primarily outside the home, and women are primarily inside the home". This principle can be read as meaning that women are to remain "inside" as "a spatial statement of virtuous femininity" (Rofel, 1994:235). Others, however, contend that Confucianism has allowed women to fulfill important and positive roles (Li, 2000). Although the level of dignity achievable by women within Confucian ethical systems can be debated, it is incontrovertible that some women face difficulty because their work is perceived as intrinsically shameful and thus lacking in merit. Prostitutes, for example, are in no position to command respect or to refuse to engage in certain shameful practices. As Whitehead (1997) observes, the paying customer may demand any sexual favor he desires because the "customer is always right". The prostitute–client relation is understood as one of domination. The client has all of the power because he owes the prostitute nothing unless she does what he wants. When she complies, she reinforces the relation by augmenting the client's sense of power. This case suggests that there are social relations at the margin in which it is not possible for a person to achieve dignity.

Although most discussions of business ethics in Asia have centered on Confucian values, scholars have begun to look for ethical norms within the logic of particular activities. Zhongzhi (2001) contends that the nature of consumption dictates that it be studied dialectically, as an activity regulated by both ethical and economic concerns. Lu (2001) sees globalization and the development of the knowledge economy as forces generating new ethical issues, including but not limited to problems of intellectual property protection, exploitation of native know-how by foreign companies, and cultural colonization. Since these are new issues, we need to develop ethical guidelines to grapple with emergent issues. Such guidelines must acknowledge the historical realities shaping particular people. Gier (2001) finds that moral virtue in China has been historically intertwined with arts such as archery, poetry, music and dance and suggests that this fusion of aesthetic and moral meaning could serve as a model for global ethics.

In addition, scholars have begun to articulate specific Hindu and Buddhist norms and to explore their compatibility with Western ethics. While Hindu religious and philosophical studies are well developed, Hindu ethical studies (normative and descriptive) are relatively undeveloped (Miller, 1981). Perrett (1998) has sought to demonstrate that traditional Hindu ethics are, at a minimum, consonant with Western ethics. He sees *karma yoga* as stressing the need to avoid developing reactive dispositions or habits. He also argues that Hindu ethics conceives of the relation between morality and fulfillment in many ways. As a result, the Indian Hindu ethical system is intrinsically pluralistic and able to incorporate and accommodate insights from many Western ethical traditions, including, one presumes, business ethics.

Works on Islamic business ethics in English are scarce. Rice (1999) tries to provide an overview of Islamic perspectives on business ethics, while documenting how actual practice diverges from that philosophy. Abeng (1997), a Muslim business leader, offers a general, but not very rigorous, account of fundamental Islamic principles for business conduct and sound business leadership. There are more works on Buddhist business ethics. Wolfe et al. (1999) have developed a case study contrasting the interests of the company with that of the family. The researchers evaluate the case from Buddhist as well as Jewish perspectives. Gould (1995) sketches what he takes to be the basic Buddhist view on business ethics, a view that focuses on the psychological state of the individual business decision-maker. Contrasting Western economics with the ethical economic outlook of Buddhism, Alexandrin (1993) maintains that Buddhism would have managers operate with patience, generosity, perseverance, compassion, impartiality and mindfulness. Instead of stressing competition in the here and now, Buddhist ethics will point to the impermanence of all economic transactions and conditions and urge the individual to treat his or her interests and skills as capacities to be developed rather than as givens.

Macy (1979) offers a more rigorous macro-normative ethical analysis of Buddhism. She observes that: "The Buddha Dharma (as Buddhists call Buddhism) is not alone among the world's religions in upholding certain ideals of moral behavior. Self-restraint, compassion, non-violence, social and economic justice—all these virtues have been preached by other faiths...What is distinctive about Buddhist ethics is the view of the world and self which they express, and with which they are imbued. Their uniqueness resides not in the values they present so much as in their logical and provenance—their rootedness in a vision of relativity and the degree to which they are empowered by this relativity . . ." (Macy: 38).

When one looks more closely at Buddhism, one wonders whether a Buddhist business ethic truly is compatible with the Kantian, Judeo-Christian, or Confucian dignity-based ethical systems. According to Macy, Buddhism does not speak of the self that *has* experience. The self *is* the shifting and changing process of experience. The self has no essence or nature. Given that there is no self in which dignity can inhere or acquire dignity, Buddhism requires that we rethink all business ethical norms in light of the impermanence of the self.

Empirical Macro-Approaches

Empirical macro-approaches have sought to test to what extent members of a culture act on a value (or set of values) and exhibit certain types of moral reasoning. Western researchers frequently have used Kohlberg's scale of ethical development (based on Kantian ethics) to measure the extent to which individuals in a sample set are capable of truly respecting each other's dignity. The more the individual is controlled by reason and has internalized moral standards of universal justice, the more developed Kohlberg found the person to be (Kohlberg, 1976, 1981a, 1981b, 1984). Employees who are controlled by fear or by peer pressure operate at an ethically less developed, conventional level, while employees who use rule-based logical norms of justice are said to operate at an ethically superior, autonomous, postconventional level. Baumhart (1961) found that Western employees rank their conscience or their internal moral standards as the primary force guiding their behavior and company policy is secondary. Sheng et al. (1994) found that businesspeople and government officials in Taiwan reason at both the conventional and post-conventional level.

Comparative business ethics research and work in Asia is dominated by efforts to measure the prevalence of Confucian values. This Confucian notion of role-based dignity has been found to be prevalent not only in China but also in Taiwan (Ma and Smith, 1992), Japan, Hong Kong and South Korea. Relationships, not individual conscience, provide guidance as to what qualifies as right behavior (Brenner and Molander, 1977; Jackall, 1989). In China, peer and social pressure have been found to be very controlling (Triandis et al., 1988). In Japan, company policy, social pressure, ethics codes and industry practices play the largest role in regulating people's behavior. Studies in Japan have shown that the example set by business leaders who function as father figures is crucial as well as when it comes to establishing the controlling ethical norms (Nakano, 1999). East Asian countries emphasize Confucian values of hierarchy and obedience to superiors. As a result, senior management establishes the dominant organizational norms constitutive of the senior–junior relation. It becomes crucially important for juniors to be seen by their superiors as loyal, which may account for why workers in Hong Kong, Korea and Japan are loath to take holiday and leave time that they have accrued (Lincoln and Kallerberg, 1990). The reason does not seem to be organizational commitment, for American workers appear to have a stronger organizational commitment than Japanese and Korean workers (Luthans et al., 1985). Asian junior employees seem rather to forego vacation because they want to be seen by their superiors in whose eyes they achieve dignity. In Pacific Rim countries, concern over being disciplined by the employer or by a professional organization and thereby losing face are major deterrents to unethical behavior (Baker and Veit, 1998).

Kinship relations, which lie at the heart of Confucian ethics, pervade business dealings throughout Asia. Employment positions are typically filled through personal networks. Forty-five percent of business loans made in Taiwan in 1993 were made in the private sector, primarily among family members (Goodell, 1995). When businesses in Thailand wanted to raise capital, they invited in businesspeople on the basis of the latter's clan affiliations (Goodell, 1995). In Confucian thought, "family" serves as the paradigm for harmony, and an individual's primary moral obligations are to social institutions, such as corporations and the state. Given that so much business is transacted through family networks, it is not surprising that empirical macro-studies have found that the familial emphasis on harmony is replicated in the corporate setting in China, Japan and Korea. According to Korean Confucianism, the universe consists of li, which are the forms of life unique to each type of relationship, and ch'i, which is the matter. Since li are group archetypes, Korean culture stresses that individuals should adapt to preserve harmony and should be loyal to the group (Bae and Chung, 1997). Vogel (1963) has argued that the diligence of Japanese employees similarly derives from the Japanese cultural and ethical norms of respecting the collective.

Loyalty to the company becomes a primary value within collectivist ethical systems. In the past, Japanese managers have viewed themselves as chiefly loyal to their company, not to the shareholders, a perspective that may be reinforced by the fact that the Japanese release earnings less often than US companies do and, therefore, are not as sensitive to short-term fluctuations in profit (Hazera, 1995). Since employees so strongly align their dignity with the company, it is not surprising that Japanese and Korean managers do not seem to distinguish between what is doing right and doing what conduces to long-term profit for their company (Lee and Yoshihara, 1997). While Western business ethics is filled with cases in which executives must choose between profits and principles, a striking 42% of Japanese managers and nearly 20% of Korean managers claim never to have experienced ethical conflicts at all (Lee and Yoshihara, 1997).

Another popular form of empirical micro-research uses Hofstede's four cultural dimensions to compare and contrast ethical values prevalent in various cultures. (Geletkanycz, 1997; Hickson, 1996; Vitell et al., 1993). Hofstede hypothesizes and tests for four ethical dimensions:

(1) Individualism understood as the degree to which an individual or group orientation prevails;
(2) Power Distance understood as the level of preference for equality versus inequality within groups;
(3) Certainty understood as the individual's preference for risk as opposed to structure;
(4) Achievement understood as the relative degree of a relation vs. task-oriented mentality. Hofstede associates the task mentality with masculinity and the relation-orientation with femininity.

The Hofstedian approach overlaps with macro-empirical research using an Asian Values/Confucian approach. Indeed, Hofstede and Bond (1988) suggest that citizens of neo-Confucian countries will score high on power distance, low on individualism and in the mid-range of masculinity measures. Research articles applying Hofstedian measures to Asian countries number in the scores, if not hundreds.

Recent research has branched out beyond Hofstedian and Confucian approaches. A few management theorists have begun to explore the relations among ethics, success and job satisfaction. Viswesvaran and Deshpande (1996) found that employee job satisfaction was reduced when the employees perceived that successful managers were behaving unethically. Khan and Atkinson (1987) have provided an empirical analysis of attitudes of British and Indian senior executives toward the issue of corporate social responsibility and involvement in social action programs, and compared these findings with studies of American companies. Gilligan's work on justice vs. care ethics has had a significant impact on macro-empirical business ethics. Miller, Bersoff and Harwood (1990) compared the moral reasoning of Indian Hindus (the sample contained some managers and professionals) with that of Americans with a view to determining to what extent each group resorted to rule-based moral reasoning instead of interpersonal obligations of care. They found that culture is more determinative of attitudes than is gender and that Indians tended to invoke obligations of care more than their American counterparts. They attribute their findings to the Hindu emphasis on social duties and responsibilities; American culture, by contrast, stresses individual rights and rules of justice. The contrast, though, between Asians and Westerners is often not so clear. Vasquez et al. (2001) found that both Americans and Filipinos invoked rules involving autonomy issues and cited cases of physical harm as a primary ethical violation. Filipinos, however, appear to be more "morally multi-lingual" insofar as they mentioned themes of community and divinity (e.g., pure body, pure spirit, pure thought), while Americans did not.

Section Three: Problems with Normative and Empirical Macro-Approaches & Recommendations for Future Research

Normative macro-analysis in business ethics, especially those proposed by Western theorists, articulates a supposedly universal business ethic. Almost all of these universalistic ethics are grounded in the notion of human dignity. But as the above section has made clear, various ethical systems understand this term "dignity" quite differently. While we would not deny that many, and maybe even all, cultures and nations value something that may be translated as "dignity", the same cultures impute vastly different meanings to the term. These local or regional differences often will result in disagreement over which actions or choices are ethically good.

Given this possibility of disagreement, it is not surprising that universal rules or hyper norms have proven to be incapable of actually addressing or resolving ethical issue. Ethical issues inevitably get defined and addressed using virtues and values implicit in the local culture or in the specific profession or practice in question (Lee and McCann, 2000). If so, it becomes crucially important to attend to differences in the ways in which groups of people or cultures conceptualize ideas such as "human dignity", "worker rights", "stakeholders", etc. Business ethicists must do a better job of sensitively modeling the terms they use when promulgating a business ethic supposedly valid in all countries at all times.

The Asian Values approach is similarly riddled with problems. Asian and Western practices embody a wide array of ethical norms from a variety of religious traditions—Confucian, Buddhist, Shintoist, Taoist, Jewish, Christian, Islamic, to name but a few. Other theorists have observed that, in Asia, there are legalistic as well as Confucian philosophies (Ma, 2000). Talk of Asian Values grossly oversimplifies the values that are in play in a single country, much less a huge region such as Asia. Moreover, practices have their own intrinsic norms as well, norms learned through doing the particular practice (MacIntyre, 1997). Therefore, it would be more accurate and far less misleading if we were to refer to American or Korean "ethical systems" rather than to American or Korean ethics. Both Western and Asian ethical systems contain individualistic and communitarian or collectivist strands (Nie, 2000). As Kim and Nam (1998) have argued, collectivism is an incomplete concept of culture, inadequate to the complication reality of interpersonal behavior of Asians. Macronormative and macro-empirical cross-cultural business ethics needs to become more interpretive and pluralistic than it has been to date.

The normative and empirical business ethics macro-approaches used by philosophers and management scholars have been too superficial. If it is true that Asian ethics are relationship-based, then it would seem to follow that even abusive relations would qualify as ethically good. Abusive relations embody social expectations as to how each party should behave. Yet we question whether an individual can have relationship-based respect within an abusive relationship. A deeper reading of Confucius reveals that only certain types of relations will bestow dignity. Even in relationships of unequal power, the dominant party, who expects obedience and loyalty, must reciprocate by protecting and caring for the weaker party. Only if we refrain from treating others inhumanely will they reciprocate by treating us well. If "... you yourself desire rank and standing; then help others to get rank and standing. [If] you want to turn your own merits to account, then help others to turn theirs to account" (Confucius, 1979).

A proper inner state, then, is reflected in proper social behavior. Taken collectively, such inner states produce a properly ordered social system. In China, dignity is acquired by cultivating an inner disposition toward reciprocity and by adhering to jen and li (Westwood, 1992). In Japan, dignity comes from cultivating a true and sincere heart (Watsuji, 1996). If so, then some thought needs to be given as to what it means to acquire the appropriate inner disposition. Research needs to be done on how and whether business companies in Asia are helping individuals to cultivate the appropriate inner dispositions. Such research might well show that Asian values are not so different from Western individualized ethics that stress having the appropriate inner disposition.

Most of the empirical macro-research tends to be documentary, not analytic. Researchers survey employees to establish their values or mode of moral reasoning and then summarize their findings. With few exceptions (e.g., Whitcomb et al., 1998; Dolecheck and Bethke, 1990), little thought is given to the implications of these findings. Empirical researchers should consider questions such as: what do these findings suggest about the best way to organize a corporation in a given country? Do these findings mean that it will be more or less difficult to organize teams or to empower people in the United States as opposed to, say, Korea? One might hypothesize that the ethical norms within Asian countries are more homogeneous than in the West, since the latter's understanding of dignity elevates autonomous and self-determining choices, while the Confucian understanding encourages society-wide, uniform norms and expectations. Shared norms may favor a centralization of power and may make teamwork more attractive. Japan is famous for its well-functioning teams and its centralization of power. This centralization has resulted in a system of local government characterized by standardization and an emphasis on equity (Cupaiuolo, 1994). Have the same results obtained in the private corporate sector in Japan and elsewhere in Asia? Or has the practice of business engendered its own intrinsic norms and values in both the West and East?

To take another example: since a Confucian ethical system structures relationships, some scholars have claimed that the Chinese look to these implicit moral relationships to maintain order, instead of imposing order through jurisdiction (Redding, 1990). The same may be true in other parts of Asia. Although Americans tend to equate legality with ethics (Lee and Yoshihara, 1997), only

8% of Koreans and 5% of the Japanese think that adhering to the letter of the law would suffice to make one ethical (Lee and Yoshihara, 1997). If so, what are the prospects for establishing a truly viable rule of law within China or in business communities with a large ethnic Chinese population? If the prospects are not good, or if it will take years to get such a system in place, what sort of ethical practices are people likely to rely upon to fill the void? Ma (1971) has explored what legal philosophers can do to reconcile traditional Chinese norms with the Taiwanese legal system. More scholars need to follow his lead in making practical recommendations.

Sorting out the analytical connections among values and between values and practice is especially important because differences in values or modes of reasoning do not necessarily result in differences in action. Husted (1996) found that, although the form of moral reasoning by Mexican, Spanish, and US MBAs varied considerably, there was substantial agreement on the twelve most morally objectionable practices. Steidlmeier (1999) has shown that both Chinese and Western ethical systems will offer ethical guidance as to how to compete while avoiding corruption. While some research suggests that managers are effective only if their values are congruent with those of the national culture (Newman and Nollen, 1996), congruence in values or modes of moral reasoning may be less important than congruence in behavior. In addition, we should remember that economic forces transform people's values. Kantian, Judeo-Christian, and Japanese and Confucian ethical systems would condemn the harvesting and marketing of bodily organs, yet the US, Japan, and China have all been moving in the direction of allowing such practices, largely for economic reasons (Becker, 1999).

The empirical macro-approaches of both Western and Asian researchers treat cultures as if they are homogeneous. As a result, many findings are highly suspect. Hofstede, for example, makes sweeping generalizations about culture, claiming that a given culture is either masculine or feminine and individualistic or collectivistic. Hofstedian analyses assume that a term such as "feminine" is univocal. Yet how the feminine is understood may vary dramatically within a single culture. The wife of a fundamentalist American preacher will not understand that term in the same way as an academic feminist. Various cultures and subgroups within a given culture will understand such a characterization very differently, so such terminology is potentially very misleading. Furthermore, America and increasingly European countries consist of many linguistic and religious cultures. A single culture may consist of many subgroups with very different norms. The Hakka consider themselves to be part of Hong Kong, yet they worship different gods and do not subscribe to the democratic liberalism of Hongkongese from Guangdong. While some research acknowledges differences in values within countries (Albert and Triandis, 1985; Dorfman and Howell, 1988), much work remains to be done on this topic.

Indeed, it could be argued that foreign nationals studying in a country constitute a subgroup and possibly even a subculture. Many comparative ethical studies contrast US citizens studying at US universities with foreign nationals at these same universities (Hegarty and Sims, 1979; McCabe et al., 1993; Wafa, 1990). Foreign nationals are a self-selected group and may not be representative of the values of their homeland. When Asian nationals are used instead of Asian students studying in America, fewer consistent differences emerge (Nyaw and Ng, 1994; White and Rhodeback, 1992). Foreign students at American universities may misunderstand the scenarios, which are presented in English (Priem and Shaffer, 2001). Or foreign nationals may feel alienated and thus inclined to set themselves in opposition to what they perceive as American values. In either case, it is misleading to assume that the attitudes of foreign nationals studying in the US will correspond with those of native employees. Empirical macro-approaches frequently fail to distinguish sufficiently among cultural subgroups and industries. Future research using an empirical macro-approach should more finely discriminate among subcultures within countries being studied and compared.

A subculture may be collectivist within a dominant individualistic culture. Furthermore, within supposedly collectivist culture, individuals are always interpreting what they are being told. Reed (1995) found that individual citizens within China constructed their own interpretations of socialist role models. Moreover, there is some evidence that collectivists are collectivistic only with respect to in-group members; toward out-group members, they become individualistic and apply different principles of justice (Leung and Bond, 1984; Jones and Bock, 1960). Asian workers have been found to be more motivated to achieve goals assigned by in-group members (i.e., superiors) than those they set for themselves (Kim and Nam, 1998). In-group members in Japan tend to discount the interests of those who are more distant, perhaps because some dimensions of the ethical system stress only face-to-face relations (Koehn, 2001b). Employees and employers are not especially concerned with the consequences of their actions for anonymous members of the larger community. This indifference to the larger community was apparent in Mitsubishi's disregard of consumer complaints and the Japanese parent company Bridgestone's initial lack of concern over the exploding Firestone tires. Researchers should remember as well that differences in ethical perceptions vary not only with respect to culture but also with respect to industry (Schlegelmilch and Robertson, 1995).

Business managers within a country may evolve a distinctive ethical outlook reflecting the constraints and opportunities they face. As the old joke goes, the conservatives see the glass of water as half-empty; the liberals see a glass that is half-full; and the business manager sees a glass that is twice as big as it needs to be. Recent research suggests that the values of Indonesian and US managers are converging (Heuer et al., 1999), despite substantial divergence in the values embedded in national cultures (Barkema and Vermeulen, 1997). The research of Barach and Elstrott (1988) suggests that Hong Kong managers view private life as governed by a non-competitive ethic, while business ethics requires a "mutually beneficial transaction (whose legitimacy) can be found in the Golden Rule" (Barach and Elstrott: 547). Organizations have distinctive cultures as well. Although Hofstede contends that organizational culture derives from workplace practices, symbols, heroes and rituals instead of from deeply rooted values (Hofstede, 1980a, 1980b; Hodgetts, 1993), this claim is suspect. Peters and Waterman (1982) have argued that an organization's values constitute the core of its culture. The values of an organization's founders may be especially influential when it comes to a firm's behavior (Van Muijen and Koopman, 1994). Future research should examine the possible links between organizational and national culture. Such research should reflect the fact that many large corporations and organizations are now multinational.

Since most business ethics studies look at the mores and values within particular countries, they provide no guidance as to how we should proceed when two or more ethical systems collide. If each side argues that its system should "trump" that of the other, then this attempt at a solution will simply perpetuate the ethical conflict. An appeal to hypernorms is not useful or attractive in those cases in which one of the quarreling parties does not recognize the existence or legitimacy of such norms. The parties could try to find common ground by considering the extent to which their notions of human dignity overlap. Or perhaps the parties could agree to certain dialogical norms (Habermas, 1985; Koehn, 1998), adopt helpful negotiating practices (Fisher and Ury, 1983), try to articulate and realize as many situational goods as possible so that both sides will be relatively satisfied (Koehn, 2001b), or institute small steps to build trust (Lewicki and Bunker, 1995; Lewicki et al., 1994). More normative and empirical research needs to be done to illuminate the sources of intercultural conflict and to document the efficacy of various ways of dealing with such conflict.

Normative and empirical macro-analyses are quite static. They assume that a culture's values do not change through time. However, no culture is an island unto itself. Cultures are permeable and evolve through interaction and through migration. As business becomes more international, cultures will have even more contact than they have had in the past. It is reasonable to hypothesize that people's values will evolve for three reasons. First, as individuals from different cultures meet, they may decide that the practices in the other's country are superior to their own and change their behavior accordingly. As Lu (1997a) argues, business ethics in China have been influenced by business ethics from abroad. There is no reason not to think that a similar dynamism obtains in other parts of Asia. Second, the members of a culture have many latent values (Lu, 1997b). As they interact with citizens of other countries, some of these latent values likely will come to the fore. Third, as political systems change, some values are favored, while others are repressed (Kristof and

Wudunn, 1995). Maoism consciously repressed the Confucian value of familial loyalty and piety when it claimed that "Father and mother are close, Chairman Mao is closer still." Repressed values may simply go "underground" for a
period, or they may be supplanted by the values favored by the new regime.

Longitudinal studies of values are urgently needed, and researchers must develop a methodology recognizing the existence of latent values and acknowledging the dynamic quality of individual and collective values. Few studies
of business ethics examine intergenerational changes. Although the Koreans
score close to the Japanese in believing in the importance of harmonious teamwork and in having lower worker autonomy, Korean workers' self-reported
ties with their co-workers appear less strong than in Japan or the United States
(Hong, 2001). Perhaps these weaker ties are due to the fact that the average
Korean worker is now younger than in Japan or in the US. Younger workers
may have new values. For example, young Koreans are embracing the internet as a way to rebel against what they see as conservative Confucian values
(MacIntyre, 2000). Or perhaps young Korean workers have simply had less
time to cement ties with fellow employees. Some research suggests that Koreans a show a higher work commitment and place greater importance on getting
a job promotion than do the Japanese (Bae and Chung, 1997). This claim must
be carefully interpreted. In the past, the number of top slots in Japanese companies was quite limited. We would hypothesize that, since employees rarely
changed jobs, opportunities for promotion were not necessarily that plentiful.
Consequently, the Japanese wisely refused to make their dignity depend upon
job advancement. Now that the system of lifetime employment is breaking
down within Japan, research should be done to see whether younger Japanese
are increasingly valuing job promotions.

PART TWO: MICRO-APPROACHES TO BUSINESS ETHICS

Section One: Normative Micro-Approaches

There are two types of normative micro-approaches. The first approach is
thinker-based. Philosophers consider the arguments of a particular thinker and
then try to extrapolate what this thinker would say about a host of applied
ethics issues. Most of the normative Western micro-analyses rely upon Kantian
or quasi-Kantian arguments (Bowie, 2002; Donaldson and Dunfee, 1999), although there have been some attempts to offer Aristotelian analyses of the
nature of the business corporation (Solomon, 1993). Aristotelian analyses focus less on intrinsic human dignity and more on human excellences or virtues
and on character development. One might say that Aristotelian ethics resemble Confucian ethics insofar as Aristotle makes dignity more of an achievement

and less of a given than does Kant. Recent Aristotelian analyses have described virtues specific to the practice of business and have analyzed features of the excellent or virtuous firm (Hartman, 1996).

Gilligan (1982) has argued that women have a distinctive way of conceiving of ethical issues. Gilligan claims that women are more caring, dialogical, and relational in their thinking, while men appeal to hierarchical and absolute norms of justice. Gilligan's work has formed the basis for describing the caring firm, feminist firm (Derry, 1996) and for reinterpreting Kantian stakeholder theory (Wicks et al., 1994). While Dobson (1996) has provided theoretical reasons for why a feminist theory of the firm is not logically sound and for why such a firm would rapidly perish in the real world, little empirical work has been done to establish the existence or viability of caring feminist firms.

These *thinker-based* normative micro-analyses elaborate the thinking of a single philosopher with a view to providing a theoretical foundation of the corporation and of business activity in general. A second type of normative micro-approach—*practice-based analysis*—evaluates particular business practices using the ethical principles practices of a single ethical thinker or single ethical tradition. The focus of the second approach is less on interpreting the thinker and providing theoretical ethical underpinnings for business and more on teasing out the ethically problematic character of the practices under consideration. Practice-based analyses often rely (implicitly or explicitly) upon the Kantian notion of respect for the person. Business ethicists have argued that labor-management collective bargaining negotiations should be less adversarial and more cooperative in order to better respect human dignity (Bowie, 1985). Critics of excessive managerial incentives, power, and discretion contend that these excesses disrespect individual dignity (Vredenburgh and Brender, 1998). Corporate downsizing has been criticized as an affront to both employee and employer dignity (Grosman, 1989). Business practices such as polygraph and drug testing, extensive employer surveillance of employees, and the use of integrity exams are problematic to the extent that they undermine respect for employees (Ottensmeyer, 1991).

Kantian micro-analyses often elaborate conditions that must be met in order for certain types of practices to qualify as ethically sound. Velasquez (2002) argues that marketing is morally acceptable if and only if the firm complies with the claims it makes about its product; discloses exactly what the customer is buying; marketing is morally unacceptable if the firm misleads the consumer as to the nature of the product; manipulates the consumer emotionally to make a sale, etc. Paine (1993) contends that competitive intelligence gathering is ethically good only if the techniques avoid misrepresentation, respect privacy rights, and sustain relationships of trust and confidence. Radin and Werhane (1997) offer Kantian reasons for why employment at will is ethically suspect and propose that hiring and firing, to be ethically good, must protect employees' fundamental rights to due process, free speech and privacy and must provide adequate information to employees about their future and the company's prospects.

Aristotelian analyses of particular business practices are rare. A few ethicists have used Gilligan to evaluate particular practices. White (1998) has argued that the ethic of care helps explain why sexual harassment has a larger and more direct emotional impact on women than on men. Catholic social teachings, as enunciated by particular popes, have been applied to some particular practices. Barrera (2000) uses Catholic social principles to determine whether currency markets should be taxed to deter speculation; McMahon (1991) draws on these papal principles to critique moneylending. Drawing upon Jewish ethics, Tamari (1997) argues that charity is an obligation, creditors must show debtors both justice and mercy, and businesspeople must take care to protect the vulnerable against fraud and theft. Jewish ethics mandate that debtors repay their loans (Tamari, 1990). Green (1997) adds that Jewish business ethics require sellers to truthfully represent transactions and businesses to protect human life. Invoking Jewish norms, Pava (1996) stresses that businesspeople must go beyond the mere letter of the law.

Very little has been written discussing specific international business practices from the perspective of particular Asian thinkers. Normative and empirical macro-approaches in business ethics invoke Confucian values but do not examine Confucius' writings in any detail. The human rights literature, by contrast, provides several excellent and sustained in-depth analyses of how a Confucian, Taoist and Buddhist ethical systems might view the nature of rights (Woo, 1980; Davis, 1995) and the nature of the self (Tao, 1990). Goodman (1980) attempts to apply the Taoist idea of "wu wei" (actionless activity) to issues in environmental ethics and the business of farming. Hansen (1991) has gone beyond Confucian traditionalism to examine Mozi's utilitarianism, Mencius' innate intuitionism, Zhuangzi's relativism, and Xunzi's highly pragmatic Confucianism, but it is unclear how these ethical systems would handle various business ethics issues. Wawrytko (1982) offers a sustained comparison of the ethics of respect advanced by Confucius and Kant, but she, too, says little about how such differences "cash out" in practice. Danto (1972) critically surveys key ethical doctrines in religio-philosophical Indian and Chinese texts, but says little about concrete practical applications.

The business ethics literature to date has avoided grappling in any detail with the subtleties of the ethical systems offered by Asian thinkers. Some recent research tries to apply some of the teachings of Buddha to evaluating various approaches to management (Wick, 1996) and administration (Brahmawong, 1994), and to critiquing economic exploitation (Norberg-Hodge, 2000). Koehn (2001b) uses the ethical analysis of the famous Japanese philosopher Watsuji Tetsuro to evaluate specific Japanese business practices. Gruzalski (1993) documents efforts by some grass root activists in India to exemplify central tenets of Mohatma Gandhi; this work might be extended to business ethics. Harvey (1999) argues that Confucian *jen* requires that sellers respect the interests of buyers. Ethicists need to articulate Confucian, Taoist, Buddhist, Hindu, Islamic, and Gandhian standards that must be met in order for a particular practice to qualify as ethical. Such standards would allow researchers to compare Kantian and Judeo-Christian ethical criteria with those that emerge from other well-established ethical traditions in Asia.

Section Two: Empirical Micro-Approaches

Empirical micro-analyses seek to establish cultural attitudes toward particular practices such as gift-giving, bribery or whistleblowing or to measure the efficacy of teaching business ethics within some specific culture(s). Some studies examine whether norms of conduct support or undermine people's willingness to engage in certain behaviors. Chua and Gould (1995) found that Confucian norms encourage whistleblowing. Vinten (1999) looked at Confucian norms and the effects of a Weberian culture on individuals and concluded that Confucian norms would not necessarily require that one become a whistleblower.

Chen and Liu (1998) surveyed advertising practitioners in Taiwan. They found that almost 32.5% of the respondents denied that there were any ethical problems in their profession. Those who admitted the existence of problems thought that the main ethical issues centered on unethical products, under-the-table rebates, the credibility of advertising research and the quality of service.

This finding is consistent with McDonald and Zepps' (1988) discovery that Hong Kong managers did not view deceptive advertising as especially unethical. Wafa (1990) compared the attitudes of US students with those of foreign students from Indonesia, Malaysia, and Thailand toward bribery. He found that US students have higher ethical standards in general and that students from Thailand were less likely to reject bribery than those from the US and Malaysia. The mean for women rejecting bribery was higher than that of male students in the sample. In general, ethical standard scores increased positively as the age, work experience and income of students increased, although Thai students exhibited a reverse relation.

Whether to teach business ethics to management students is an important question meriting cultural and cross-cultural investigation. There have been a few attempts to measure the effectiveness of teaching business ethics. Lee (1997) established that teaching business ethics had a positive impact in Korea, especially on young male students with no work experience. McDonald (1997) contends that there is no evidence that the Western model of pedagogy has been effective. The Western approach fails to ask students to examine their own behavior. He recommends that the Indian approach stressing self-examination and personal transformation is more effective.

Section Three: Problems with Normative and Empirical Micro-Approaches & Recommendations for Future Research

The tendency to equate Asian ethics with superficially understood Confucian ideals (e.g., filial piety) is unfortunate. Unless we delve deeply into the ethical thinking of specific philosophers and theorists, we will be tempted to settle for easy generalizations that more frequently reflect our prejudices than the truth. For example, there is no distinction between the normative and descriptive in Japanese ethics as understood by Watsuji (1996). Moreover, Watsuji categorically rejects the Western tendency to use organic metaphors (e.g., Mente, 1989) to describe collective harmony or *wa*. We could find no work in English that extrapolates the thinking of major philosophers from Thailand, Indonesia, Vietnam, Cambodia, or Korea and then applies such thinking to business ethics in Asia or the West.

We would also argue that cultures consist of *individuals*, and individuals are never merely cultural exemplars. Hofstede himself warns: "If you are going to meet a person from a particular country, the validity of cultural information is limited because in interpersonal contact, any statement about a person's culture should only be used as a working hypothesis. If you are going to spend time with a Japanese colleague, you shouldn't assume that overall cultural statements about Japanese society automatically apply to this person. In our own country, we are aware of the existence of a wide range of different personalities. We should try to develop this same open-mindedness to other cultures." (Quoted in Hodgetts, 1993:61.)

We would caution against the marked propensity of both normative and empirical business ethics researchers to reify what are merely theoretical dimensions. The Hofstedian dimensions are theoretical constructs, not facts of the universe. As Hofstede notes, "We should retain a healthy does of realism about the entire concept of 'dimensions'. ... Some of the younger students and researchers, in my view, tend to look at the dimensions as concrete entities. However, the sole purpose of the dimensions is to add some structure to a mass of cultural information that otherwise is too complex to grasp." (Quoted in Hodgetts, 1993:63.)

Theoretical sociological constructs are not the same thing as individual character traits. Focusing on the ethical arguments of particular thinkers has the merit of keeping the individual character and personality before us. Business ethicists and management theorists need to devote more attention to the nuances of ethical theorists' work while keeping a sharp lookout for bad research that hypostatizes ethical constructs and then imputes these constructs to individuals.

The majority of business ethics studies evaluate personal and cultural factors affecting individual behavior. Much more attention needs to be paid to environmental dimensions associated with people's willingness to perform certain concrete behaviors. The Confucian requirement that the agent make sure he or she is trustworthy before accusing other people (Koehn, 2001a) might militate against whistleblowing in countries such as Korea and Taiwan where Confucianism appears still to be strong. Whistleblowing could be viewed as a threat to hierarchical authority and to organizational harmony. On the other hand, Korea passed an anti-corruption law effective in 2002 protecting and compensating whistleblowers. This law may lead people to overcome their Confucian hesitation. If Koreans do become whistleblowers and are treated as heroes, then the next generation of businesspeople may be more accepting of whistleblowing. Care must be taken to specify what counts as whistleblowing. Gorta and Forell (1995) point out that employees may talk with other employees, report internally, or report externally. Employees with strong Confucian values might be willing to report problems to an internal ethics officer while refusing to subvert hierarchical authority by speaking to the press or to regulators. The extent of protection might be an important variable as well. If protections are weak, or if the government does not enforce anti-corruption laws, employees may fear retaliation.

Employee values do not exist in a vacuum, so empirical micro-approaches should include many variables. Empirical work on factors affecting people's willingness to blow the whistle should include not only an environmental dimensions but also measures of employee's level of education and length of employment, given that some research suggests that these factors are important (Miceli and Near, 1992; Dworkin and Near, 1987).

Empirical micro-approaches, like their macro counterparts, are primarily documentary. While recent research purports to unearth the values of business managers in China, Taiwan, Thailand (Singhapakdi and Salyachivin, 2000), etc., such research tells us little about why people have these attitudes or how their attitudes toward one behavior (e.g., employee theft) is related to their stance toward other activities (e.g., whistleblowing). Future empirical micro-research should probe the normative reasons for these stances. Findings that Buddhist students have lower ethical standards than do Catholics and Protestants (Wafa, 1990) should be taken with a large grain of skepticism. This finding may be an artifact of the way in which the researcher understands ethics. As we observed in Part One, Buddhist ethics do not fit comfortably within the standard dignity-based approach of Kantian and Judeo-Christian ethics. Researchers should try to elicit Buddhist norms and then test how well Asian and Western Buddhists measure up to their own norms.

Like empirical macro-analysis, empirical micro-research centered on particular practices has focused almost exclusively on quasi-criminal behavior. Future studies might compare the types of incentives prevalent in different countries and industries and examine practical, non-criminal consequences of such behavior. There are relatively few articles in major marketing journals on advertising journals (Hyman et al., 1994) and almost no cross-cultural business studies documenting and comparing marketing or advertising ethics in Asia, Europe, Africa and North and South America. Multi-level marketing (MLM) schemes are popular in the Americas, while China recently took steps to curtail the operations of Amway and Avon. It would be helpful to know whether this difference in tolerance of MLMs reflects a fundamental difference in a Confucian, as opposed to Kantian or Judeo-Christian, ethical schemes or whether political factors unique to China were at work.

We would conclude by uttering a plea for more empirical work to be done of the values and practices of business managers and employees in Thailand, Korea, Malaysia, Vietnam, Sri Lanka, Indonesia, Burma, Cambodia, and the Philippines. Little or no micro- or macro-empirical work on business ethics in these countries has appeared in English.

REFERENCES

Abela, A. 2001. Profit and more: Catholic social teaching and the purpose of the firm. *Journal of Business Ethics*, 31(2): 107-116.

Abeng, T. 1997. Business ethics in Islamic context: Perspectives of a Muslim business leader. *Business Ethics Quarterly*, 7(3): 47-54.

Albert, R.D. and Triandis, H.C. 1985. Intercultural education for multicultural societies: Critical issues. *International Journal of Intercultural Relations*, 9: 391-397.

Alexandrin, G. 1993. Elements of Buddhist economics. *International Journal of Social Economics*, 20(2): 3-11.

Asai, A., Fukuhara, S., Inoshita, O. and Miura, Y. 1997. Medical decisions concerning the end of life: A discussion with Japanese physicians. *Journal of Medical Ethics*, 23(5): 323-327.

Bae, K. and Chung, C. 1997. Cultural values and work attitudes of Korean industrial workers in comparison with those of the United States and Japan. *Work and Occupations*, 24(1): 80-96.

Baker, H.K. and Veit, E.T. 1998. A comparison of ethics of investment professionals: North America versus Pacific-rim nations. *Journal of Business Ethics*, 17(8): 917-937.

Barach, J. and Elstrott, J. 1988. The transactional ethic: The ethical foundations of free enterprise reconsidered. *Journal of Business Ethics*, 7: 545-551.

Barkema, H.G. and Vermeulen, F. 1997. What cultural differences are detrimental for international joint ventures? *Journal of International Business Studies*, 28: 846-864.

Barrera, A. 2000. Social principles as a framework for ethical analysis (with an application to the Tobin tax). *Journal of Business Ethics*, 23(4): 377-388.

Baumhart, R. 1961. How ethical are businessmen? *Harvard Business Review*, July-August: 6-17.

Becker, C. 1999. Money talks, money kills: The economics of transplantation in Japan and China. *Bioethics*, 13(3-4): 236-243.

Blackburn, S. 1994. *The Oxford Dictionary of Philosophy*. Oxford: Oxford University Press.

Bowie, N.E. 1985. Should collective bargaining and labor relations be less adversarial? *Journal of Business Ethics*, 4: 283-291.

Bowie, N.E. 2002. A Kantian approach to business ethics. In T. Donaldson, P. Werhane, and M. Cording (eds.), *Ethical Issues in Business*. Upper Saddle, NJ: Prentice Hall.

Brahmawong, C. 1994. The application of Buddhist principles to administrative arts. *Buddhist Behavioral Codes and the Modern World*. Connecticut: Greenwood Press.

Brenner, S.N. and Molander, E.A. (1977). Is the ethics of business changing? *Harvard Business Review*, Jan.- Feb.: 57-71.

Cessario, R. 1989. The meaning of virtue in Catholic moral life: Its significance for human life issues. *The Thomist*, 53: 173-196.

Chen, A. and Liu, J. 1998. Agency practitioners' perceptions of professional ethics in Taiwan. *Journal of Business Ethics*, 17(1): 15-23.

Chothia, F. 1998. Mandela supports an international criminal court. *Business Day*, July 2: 9.

Chua, A.C.H. and Gould, D.B. 1995. Whistleblowing: Public interest or personal interest? The experience of a Hong Kong Government Pharmacist. *Hong Kong Public Administration*, 4(2): 251-264.

Confucius (trans. 1979). *The Analects*. London: Penguin Books.

Cupaiuolo, A. 1994. Comparing localities in Japan and America. *PM. Public Management*, 76(11): 14-18.

Danto, A. 1972. *Mysticism and Morality: Oriental Thought and Moral Philosophy*. New York: Basic Books.

Davis, M. 1995. *Human Rights and Chinese Values: Legal, Philosophical, and Political Perspectives*. Hong Kong: Oxford University Press.

Dawson, R. 1981. *Confucius*. Oxford: Oxford University Press.

Derry, R. 1996. Toward a feminist firm: Comments on John Dobson and Judith White. *Business Ethics Quarterly*, 6(1): 101-109.

Dobson, J. 1996. The feminine firm: A comment. *Business Ethics Quarterly*, 6(2): 227-232.

Dolecheck, M. and Bethke, A. 1990. Business ethics in Hong Kong: Is there a problem? *The Hong Kong Manager*, 26(5): 13-23.

Dorfman, P. and Howell, J.P. 1988. Dimensions of national culture: Hofstede revisited. In E.G. McGoun (ed.), *Advances in International Comparative Management* (Vol. 3). Greenwich, CT: JAI Press.

Donaldson, T. and Dunfee, W. 1999. *Ties That Bind: A Social Contracts Approach to Business Ethics*. Cambridge: Harvard Business School Press.

Dunfee, T. and Warren, D. 2001. Is *Guanxi* ethical? A normative analysis of doing business in China. *Journal of Business Ethics*, 32(3): 191-204.

Dunkang, Y. 1991. The Concept of 'Great Harmony' in the Book of Changes (Zhou Yi). In S. Krieger and R. Trauzettel (eds.), *Confucianism and the Modernization of China*. Germany: V. Hase and Koehler Verlang Mainz.

Dworkin, T.M. and Near, J.P. 1987. Whistleblowing statutes: Are they working? *American Business Law Journal*, 25: 241-263.

Fisher, R. and Ury, W. 1983. *Getting to Yes: Negotiating Agreement Without Giving In*. New York: Penguin Books.

Freeman, R.E. 2002. Stakeholder theory of the modern corporation. In T. Donaldson, P. Werhane, and M. Cording (eds.), *Ethical Issues in Business*. Upper Saddle River, NJ: Prentice-Hall.

Geletkanycz, M.A. 1997. The salience of 'culture's consequences': The effects of cultural values on top executive commitment to the status quo. *Strategic Management Journal*, 18(8): 615-634.

Gier, N. 2001. The dancing ru: a Confucian aesthetics of virtue. *Philosophy East and West*, 51(2): 280-305.

Gilligan, C. 1982. *In a Different Voice*. Cambridge, MA: Harvard University Press.

Glaser, J.W. 1989. Hospital ethics committees: One of the many centers of responsibility. *Theoretical Medicine*, 10(4): 275-288.

Goodell, G. 1995. Another way to skin a cat: The spirit of capitalism and the Confucian ethic. *The National Interest*, Winter, 1995/96: 66-71.

Goodman, R. 1980. Taoism and ecology. *Environmental Ethics*, 2: 73-80.

Gorta, A. and Forell, S. 1995. Layers of decision: Linking social definitions of corruption and willingness to take action. *Crime, Law & Social Change*, 23: 315-343.

Gould, S. 1995. The Buddhist perspective on business ethics: Experiential exercises for exploration and practice. *Journal of Business Ethics*, 14(1): 63-70.

Green, R. 1997. Guiding principles of Jewish business ethics. *Business Ethics Quarterly*, 7(2): 21-30.

Grosman, B.A. 1989. Corporate loyalty, does it have a future? *Journal of Business Ethics*, 8: 565-568.

Gruzalski, B. 1993. *The Chipko Movement: A Gandhian Approach to Ecological Sustainability in Ethical and Political Dilemmas of Modern India*. New York: St. Martin's Press.

Habermas, J. 1985. *The Theory of Communicative Action: Reason and the Rationalization of Society (The Theory of Communicative Action, Vol. 1)*. Boston: Beacon Press.

Hall, D. and Ames, R. 1987. *Thinking Through Confucius*. Albany, NY: State University of New York Press.

Hansen, C. 1991. Classical Chinese Ethics. In P. Singer (ed.), *A Companion to Ethics*. Cambridge: Blackwell.

Hartman, E. 1996. *Organizational Ethics and the Good Life (The Ruffin Series in Business Ethics)*. Oxford: Oxford University Press.

Harvey, B. 1999. 'Graceful merchants': A contemporary view of Chinese business ethics. *Journal of Business Ethics*, 20(1): 85-92.

Hayashi, M., Hasui, C. and Kitamura, F. 2000. Respecting autonomy in difficult medical settings: A questionnaire study in Japan. *Ethics and Behavior*, 10(1): 51-63.

Hazera, A. 1995. A comparison of Japanese and U.S. corporate financial accountability and its impact on the responsibilities of corporate managers. *Business Ethics Quarterly*, 5: 479-97.

Hegarty, W.H. and Sims, H.P. 1979. Organizational philosophy, policies, and objectives related to unethical decision behavior: A laboratory experiment. *Journal of Applied Psychology*, 64: 331-338.

Heuer, M., Cummings, J. and Hutabarat, W. 1999. Cultural stability or change among managers in Indonesia? *Journal of International Business Studies*, 30(3): 599-610.

Hickson, D. 1996. The ASQ years then and now through the eyes of a Euro-Brit. *Administrative Science Quarterly*, 41(2): 217-228.

Ho, D.Y.F. 1976. On the concept of face. *American Journal of Sociology*, 81: 867-884.

Hodgetts, R. 1993. A conversation with Geert Hofstede. *Organizational Dynamics*, 21(4): 53-61.

Hofman, H. 1996. The promised human dignity. *Humboldt Forum Recht*, 8 at http://www.rewi.hu-berlin.de/HFR/8-1996/English.html.

Hofstede, G. 1980a. *Culture's Consequences: International Differences in Work-Related Values*. Newbury Park, CA: Sage.

Hofstede, G. 1980b. Motivation, leadership, and organization: Do American theories apply abroad? *Organizational Dynamics*, 9(1): 42-63.

Hofstede, G. and Bond, M.H. 1988. Confucius and economic growth: New trends in culture's consequences. *Organizational Dynamics*, 16(4): 4-21.

Hong, Y. 2001. The practice of business ethics in China: We need a parent. *Business Ethics*, 10(2): 87-91.

Husted, B. 1996. The impact of cross-national carriers of business ethics on attitudes about questionable practices and form of moral reasoning. *Journal of International Business Studies*, 27(2): 391-411.

Hyman, M., Tansey, R. and Clark, J. 1994. Research on advertising ethics: Past, present, and future. *Journal of Advertising*, 23(3): 5-11.

Jackall, R. 1989. *Moral Mazes: The World of Corporate Managers*. Oxford: Oxford University Press.

Jones, L.V. and Bock, R.D. 1960. Multiple discriminant analysis applied to 'ways to live' ratings from six cultural groups. *Sociometry*, 23: 162-176.

Kant, I. 1998. *Groundwork of the Metaphysic of Morals*. In M.J. Gregor (ed.), Cambridge: Cambridge University Press.

Khan, A.F. and Atkinson, A. 1987. Managerial attitudes to social responsibility: a comparative study in India and Britain. *Journal of Business Ethics*, 6: 419-432.

Kim, J.Y. and Nam, S.H. 1998. The concept and dynamics of face: Implications for organizational behavior in Asia. *Organization Science*, 9(4): 522-534.

Koehn, D. 1998. *Rethinking Feminist Ethics: Care, Trust, and Empathy*. London: Routledge.

Koehn, D. 2001a. Confucian trustworthiness and the practice of business in China. *Business Ethics Quarterly*, 11(3): 415-429.

Koehn, D. 2001b. *Local Insights, Global Ethics for Business*. Amsterdam: Rodopi.

Kohlberg, L. 1976. Moral stages and moralization: the cognitive-developmental approach. In T. Lickona (ed.), *Moral Development and Behavior*. New York: Holt, Rinehart & Winston.

Kohlberg, L. 1981a. *The Meaning and Measurement of Moral Development*. Worcester, MA: Clark University Heinz Werner Institute.

Kohlberg, L. 1981b. *Philosophy of Moral Development*. New York: Harper & Row Publishers.

Kohlberg, L. 1984. *The Philosophy of Moral Development: Moral Stages and the Idea of Justice*. New York: HarperCollins.

Kristof, N. and Wudunn, S. 1995. *China Wakes: The Struggle for the Soul of a Rising Power*. New York: Vintage.

Lee, C.Y. 1997. Impacts of teaching business ethics in Korea. *Teaching Business Ethics*, 1(2): 131-149.

Lee, C.Y. and Yoshihara, H. 1997. Business ethics of Korean and Japanese managers. *Journal of Business Ethics*, 1(16): 7-21.

Lee, K.H. and McCann, D. 2000. Marketing ethics, social contracts and sources of moral wisdom. *Unpublished manuscript*.

Leung, A. 2000. Gender differences in *guanxi* behaviors: An examination of PRC state-owned enterprises. *International Review of Women and Leadership*, 6(1): 48-59.

Leung, K. and Bond, M.H. 1984. The impact of cultural collectivism on reward allocation. *Journal of Personality and Social Psychology*, 47:793-804.

Leung, T.K.P., Wong, Y.H. and Wong, S. 1996. A study of Hong Kong businessmen's perceptions of the role *guanxi* in the People's Republic of China. *Journal of Business Ethics*, 15(7): 749-758.

Lewicki, R.J. and Bunker, B.B. 1995. Trust in relationships: A model of trust development and decline. In B.B. Bunker and J.Z. Rubin (eds.), *Conflict, Cooperation and Justice*. San. Francisco: Jossey-Bass.

Lewicki, R.J., Litterer, J., Minton, J. and Saunders, D. 1994. Negotiation. *Social Forces*, 63(4), 967-985.

Li, C. 2000. *The Sage and the Second Sex*. Chicago: Open-Court.

Liang, S.M. 1949. *The Essential Meanings of Chinese Culture*. Chengdu: Lu Ming Shudian.

Lincoln, J.R. and Kallerberg, A. 1990. *Culture, Control, and Commitment: A Study of Work Organization and Work Attitudes in the United States and Japan*. Cambridge, UK: Cambridge University Press.

Llamzon, B. 1983. Toward a holistic approach in moral decisions. *Listening*, 18: 23-29.

Lu, X. 1997a. Business ethics in China. *Journal of Business Ethics*, 16(14): 1509-1518. 28(3): 9-17.

Lu, X. 1997b. On economic and ethical value. *Online Journal of Ethics*, 2(1): 1-8.

Lu, X. 2001. Ethical issues in the globalization of the knowledge economy. *Business Ethics*, 10(2): 113-119.

Luthans, F., McCaul, H.S. and Dodd, N.G. 1985. Organizational commitment: A comparison of American, Japanese and Korean employees. *Academy of Management Journal*, 28: 213-219.

Ma, H. 1971. Law and morality: Some reflections on the Chinese experience past and present. *Philosophy East and West*, 21: 443-460.

Ma, L. 2000. A comparison of the legitimacy of power between Confucianist and legalist philosophies. *Asian Philosophy*, 10(1): 49-59.

Ma, L.C. and Smith, K. 1992. Social correlates of Confucian ethics in Taiwan. *The Journal of Social Psychology*, 132(5): 655-659.

MacIntyre, A. 1997. *After Virtue: A Study in Moral Theory*. Indiana: University of Notre Dame Press.

MacIntyre, D. 2000. Wired for life. *Time Asia Online*, 156(23).

Macy, J. 1979. Dependent co-arising: The distinctiveness of Buddhist ethics. *Journal of Buddhist Ethics*, 7(1): 38-52.

McCabe, D.L., Dukerich, J.M. and Dutton, J.E. 1993. Values and moral dilemmas: a cross-cultural comparison. *Business Ethics Quarterly*, 3: 117-130.

McCann, D. 1997. Catholic social teaching in an era of economic globalization: a resource for business ethics. *Business Ethics Quarterly*, 7(2): 57-70.

McDonald, G. and Zepp, R. 1988. Ethical perceptions of Hong Kong Chinese business managers. *Journal of Business Ethics*, 7: 836.

McDonald, R. 1997. Information and transformation in teaching businesses ethics. *Teaching Business Ethics*, 1(2): 151-162.

McMahon, T. 1991. A reaction to Vogel's 'The ethical roots of business'. *Business Ethics Quarterly*, 211-222.

Mencius (trans. 1970). D.C. Lau. London: Penguin Books.

Mente, B. 1989. *Chinese Etiquette & Ethics in Business*. Lincolnwood, Ill.: NTC Business Books.

Miceli, M.P. and Near, J.P. 1992. *Blowing the Whistle – The Organizational and Legal Implications for Companies and Employees*. New York: Lexington Books.

Miller, D. 1981. Sources of Hindu ethical studies: A critical review. *Journal of Religious Ethics*, 9(2): 186-199.

Miller, J.G., Bersoff, D.M. and Harwood, R.L. 1990. Perceptions of social responsibilities in India and in the United States: Moral imperatives or personal decisions? *Journal of Personality and Social Psychology*, 58: 33-47.

Moorman, R.H. and Blakely, G.L. 1995. Individualism as an individual difference predictor of organizational citizenship behavior. *Journal of Organizational Behavior*, 16: 127-142.

Nakano, C. 1999. Attempting to institutionalize ethics: Case studies from Japan. *Journal of Business Ethics*, 18(4): 335-343.

Newman, K. and Nollen, S. 1996. Culture and congruence: The fit between management practices and national culture. *Journal of International Business Studies*, 27(4): 753-780.

Nie, J. 2000. The plurality of Chinese and American medical moralities: Toward an interpretive cross-cultural bioethics. *Kennedy Institute of Ethics Journal*, 10(3): 239-260.

Norberg-Hodge, H. 2000. Economics, engagement, and exploitation in Ladakh. *Tricycle: The Buddhist Review*, 10(2): 77-79, 114-117.

Nyaw, M.K. and Ng, I. 1994. A comparative analysis of ethical beliefs: a four country study. *Journal of Business Ethics*, 13: 543-555.

Ottensmeyer, E.J. 1991. Ethics, public policy, and managing advanced technologies: The case of Electronic surveillance. *Journal of Business Ethics*: 519-526.

Paine, L. 1993. Corporate policy and the ethics of competitor intelligence gathering. In T. Beauchamp and N. Bowie (eds.), *Ethical Theory and Business*. Englewood Cliffs, NJ: Prentice Hall.

Pappu, S.S.R.R. 1982. Human rights and human obligations: An East-West perspective. *Philosophy and Social Action*, 8: 15-28.

Pava, M. 1996. The Talmudic concept of 'beyond the letter of the law': relevance to business social responsibilities. *Journal of Business Ethics*, 15(9): 941-950.

Pava, M. 1998a. Developing a religiously grounded business ethics: a Jewish perspective. *Business Ethics Quarterly*, 8(1): 65-83.

Pava, M. 1998b. The substance of Jewish business ethics. *Journal of Business Ethics*, 17(6): 603-617.

Perrett, R. 1998. *Hindu Ethics: A Philosophical Study*. Honolulu: University of Hawaii Press.

Peters, T. and Waterman, R. 1982. *In Search of Excellence*. New York: HarperCollins.

Priem, R. and Shaffer, M. 2001. Resolving moral dilemmas in business: A multi-country study. *Business & Society*, 40(2).

Radin, T. and Werhane, P. 1997. Employment at will, employee rights, and future directions for employment. In T. Donaldson, P.H. Werhane, and M. Cording (eds.), *Ethical Issues in Business: A Philosophical Approach*. Upper Saddle River, NJ: Prentice-Hall.

Redding, S.G. 1990. *The Spirit of Chinese Capitalism*. New York: de Gruyter.

Reed, G. 1995. Moral/Political education in the People's Republic of China: Learning through role models. *Journal of Moral Education*, 24(2): 99-111.

Rice, G. 1999. Islamic ethics and the implications for business. *Journal of Business Ethics*, 18(4): 345-358.

Rofel, L. 1994. Liberation nostalgia and a yearning for modernity. In C.K. Gilmartin, G. Hershatter, L. Rofel, and T. White (eds.), *Engendering China*. Cambridge, MA: Harvard University Press.

Schlegelmilch, B. and Robertson, D. 1995. The influence of country and industry on ethical perceptions of senior executives in the U.S. and Europe. *Journal of International Business Studies*, 26(4): 859-881.

Sevensky, R. 1983. The religious foundations of health care: A conceptual approach. *Journal of Medical Ethics*, 9: 165-168.

Sheng, P. Chang, L. and French, W. 1994. Business's environmental responsibility in Taiwan – moral, legal or negotiated. *Journal of Business Ethics*, 13(11): 887-897.

Singhapakdi, A. and Salyachivin, S. 2000. Some important factors underlying ethical decision making of managers in Thailand. *Journal of Business Ethics*, 27(3): 271-284.

Solomon, R. 1993. *Ethics and Excellence: Cooperation and Integrity in Business (The Ruffin Series in Business Ethics)*. Oxford: Oxford University Press.

Steidlmeier, P. 1999. Gift giving, bribery and corruption: Management of business relationships in China. *Journal of Business Ethics*, 20: 121-132.

Steur, A.D. 1989. Freedom and dignity as acquired traits. In P. Creighton (ed.), *Freedom, Equality, and Social Change*. Lewiston: Mellon Press.

Su, C. and Littlefield, J. 2001. Entering *guanxi*: a business ethical dilemma in mainland China. *Journal of Business Ethics*, 33(3): 199-210.

Tamari, M. 1990. Ethical issues in bankruptcy: A Jewish perspective. *Journal of Business Ethics*, 785-789.

Tamari, M. 1997. The challenge of wealth: Jewish business ethics. *Business Ethics Quarterly*, 7(2): 45-56.

Tao, J. 1990. The Chinese moral ethos and the concept of individual rights. *Journal of Applied Philosophy*, 119-127.

Triandis, H.C., Bontempo, M., Villareal, M. and Lucca, N. 1988. Individualism and collectivism: Cross-cultural perspectives on self-ingroup relationships. *Journal of Personality and Social Psychology*, 54: 323-338.

Twiss, S. 1998. Discussing Confucianism and human rights. In W. De Bary and T. Wiming (eds.), *Confucianism and Human Rights*. New York: Columbia University Press.

Umezu, M. (ed.). Ethics and the Japanese miracle: Characteristics and practice of Japanese business practice. Unpublished paper. 1-25.

United Nations 1948. *Universal Declaration of Human Rights.*

Van Muijen, J. and Koopman, P. 1994. The influence of national culture on organizational culture: A comparative study between ten countries. *European Work & Organizational Psychologist*, 4(4): 367-380.

Vasquez, K., Keltner, D., Ebenbach, D. and Banaszynski, T. 2001. Cultural variation and similarity in moral rhetorics: Voices from the Philippines and the United States. *Journal of Cross-Cultural Psychology*, 32(1): 93-120.

Velasquez, M. 2002. *Business Ethics: Concepts and Cases.* Upper Saddle River, NJ: Prentice Hall.

Vitell, S., Nwachukwu, S. and Barnes, J. 1993. The effects of culture on ethical decision-making: An application of Hofstede's typology. *Journal of Business Ethics*, 753.

Vinten, G. 1999. Whistleblowing – Hong Kong style. *Public Administration and Policy*, 8(1): 1-19.

Viswesvaran, C. and Deshpande, S. 1996. Ethics, success, and job satisfaction: a test of dissonance theory in India. *Journal of Business Ethics*, 15(10): 1065-1069.

Vogel, E. 1963. *Japan's New Middle Class.* Berkeley, CA: University of California Press.

Vredenburgh, D. and Brender, Y. 1998. The hierarchical abuse of power in work organizations. *Journal of Business Ethics*, 17(12): 1337-1347.

Wafa, S. 1990. A cross-cultural study of business ethical standards among graduate business students from Indonesia, Malaysia, Thailand, and the U.S. *Journal of International Business Studies*, 21(2): 347.

Watsuji, T. 1996. *Watsuji Tetsuro's* Rinrigaku *Ethics in Japan*, trans. Y. Seisaku and R.E. Carter. Albany: New York Press.

Wawrytko, S. 1982. Confucius and Kant: The ethics of respect. *Philosophy East and West*, 32: 237-257.

Westwood, R.I. 1992. Culture, cultural differences, and organizational behavior. In R.I. Westwood (ed.), *Organizational Behavior*: 27-62. Hong Kong: Longman.

Whitcomb, L., Erdener, C. and Li, C. 1998. Business ethical values in China and the U.S. *Journal of Business Ethics*, 17(8): 839-852.

White, L.P. and Rhodeback, M. 1992. Ethical dilemmas in organization development: a cross-cultural analysis. *Journal of Business Ethics*, 11: 663-670.

White, T. 1998. Sexual harassment: trust and the ethic of care. *Business & Society Review*, 100(101): 9-21.

Whitehead, K. 1997. *After Suzie: Sex in the South China.* Hong Kong: Chameleon.

Wick, G. 1996. Zen in the workplace: approaches to mindful management. *Tricycle: The Buddhist Journal*, 5: 14-19.

Wicks, A., Gilbert, D. and Freeman, E. 1994. A feminist reinterpretation of the stakeholder concept. *Business Ethics Quarterly*, 4(4): 475-497.

Wolfe, R., Payne, R. Benor, E. and Green, R. 1999. The successful sarariim. *Ethics and World Religions*, 280-297. New York: Orbis.

Woo, P. 1980. A metaphysical approach to human rights from a Chinese point of view. *The Philosophy of Human Rights.* Westport: Greenwood.

Wood, A.W. 1998. Kant on duties regarding nonrational nature I. *Aristotelian Society*, Supp (72): 189-210.

Yang, M. 1994. *Gifts, Favors, and Banquets: The Art of Social Relationships in China.* New York: Cornell University.

Zhongzhi, Z. 2001. Ethical and economic evaluations of consumption in contemporary China. *Business Ethics*, 10(2): 92-96.

PART III

ORGANIZATIONAL BEHAVIOR AND HUMAN RESOURCE MANAGEMENT

Chapter 10

ORGANIZATION BEHAVIOR
East and West

Oded Shenkar
The Ohio State University

INTRODUCTION

The epic of "East versus West" has been at the center of scholarly attention centuries before organization behavior (OB) were to become a formal field of study. To the West, the "East" has been carrying the allure of the exotic, and, most saliently, an antithesis to things Western. "Oh, East is East and West is West, and never the twain shall meet" wrote Rudyard Kipling towards the end of the 19th century. At least as far as OB is concerned, East and West are yet to meet. While trade and foreign investment have been generating East–West flows of people, ideas and resources in both directions, the East–West flow of ideas within the OB community has been limited and asymmetrical.

Today, the OB field remains firmly rooted in Western civilization and in the US industrial landscape of the twentieth century in which it was born, deeply embedded in the institutions and social context associated with its emergence. It has failed, in fact not even tried, to break away in other directions. The East has become a topic of interest to OB scholars but it remains more a testing ground and a sounding board for Western ideas rather than a genuine source of inspiration and innovation in either theory or method. To understand why, and to appreciate the scholarly ramifications, we need to first go back in time and reflect on some of the fundamental roots of the Western attitude towards the East.

Spanning from Egypt to China or variably delineated somewhere in between, "the East" has been not only an enigma to the West, but also, and perhaps more importantly, a symbol of "distance" from Western civilization. In historical times, this distance was measured from the European heart of Western civilization, producing the *Near* East (e.g., Greece), the *Middle* East (e.g., Israel), and the *Far* East (e.g., China). If the geographic distance may have been narrowed over time via transportation and communication advances, the mental or "psychic" distance remains very much in place. That we continue to use those same terms today, in fact classifying regions and civilizations according to how far they have strayed from the Western "core", is a testimony to the endurance of language as well as of the frame of reference and meaning in which it is anchored. The staying power of the terminology is also a reflection, however, of a perception that the West has triumphed, which, in a culture who appreciates success and the bottom line above all, is the ultimate yardstick of relevance.

The resulting ethnocentrism, I suggest, has been especially pronounced in the relatively new social science disciplines which emerged in the West in the 20th century, ironically the only century during the last millennium in which an Eastern economy (China) was not the largest in the world. These new social science disciplines, OB included, are especially susceptible to a narrow Western approach since they do not possess the institutional memory and diversity that would encourage the development of an alternative frame of reference. Failing to expand the current frame of reference may prove fatal, however, particularly in a global age when fields of knowledge are expected to intersect and develop predictive capability that exceeds national boundaries. In other (blunt and strictly non-Asian) words, the stubborn adherence to past frames may accelerate the march of OB towards irrelevance, signs of which already abound (e.g., membership numbers in the Academy of Management, number of positions offered).

Ethnocentrism is of course not a Western monopoly. China, "The Middle Kingdom", saw itself as the center of a civilization surrounded by half-civilized "semi-barbarians" and full fledged "barbarians" at its outer perimeters. Here too the other side was generalized, stereotyped, and labeled fundamentally different; alternately despised, rejected, admired, and feared. Chinese modern history is dotted with debates, not to mention violent struggles, surrounding the alternate threat and promise of Western ideas, leading to discussions of how, for instance, to adopt Western technology without adopting Western values. This debate perhaps diminished the stereotyping of the other side but has by no means done away with it. At the least, the debate introduced some measure of Western thought and institutions as an alternative, desirable or not, to the local frame of thought.

The mutual stereotyping of East and West could have resulted in a balance that would have kept ethnocentric tendencies in check. It did not. The ascent of the West towards the end of the millennium has made Eastern ethnocentrism less visible and also less relevant. With the exception of a brief, fledgling interest in "Japanese Management" in the 1980s (see later discussion), the East did not become a serious alternative to things Western. A prolonged recession in Japan and the Asian Financial crisis shattered even this brief, fragile interest by convincing Westerners, especially in the US, that theirs was the only viable model of economy, society, business and management. Very much a product of a Western perspective, it was what worked that counted. Japan became interesting to the West when it seemed that it has found a winning formula and that its firms would soon "take over" the West, but fell from grace as soon as it appeared not to be the case.

Globalization notwithstanding, "East" and "West" continue to represent fundamentally different frames of meaning and reference. It often seems that the two sides do not really converse but rather talk to each other each in its own language, incomprehensible as it may be to the other. When Taiwan, Hong Kong, Singapore and South Korea surprised the world with their rapid industrialization, Western observers sought a metaphor that will articulate not only the might but also the menace posed by the newcomers. They came up with "little dragons" a perfectly fitting term to the readers of Greek mythology who grew up admiring brave dragon slayers. Luckily, perhaps, this was hardly read as an insult by East Asians for whom the dragon was a rather benevolent creature entrusted with so many virtues that parents would try to plan the birth of their offspring to occur in the year of the dragon. The ramifications of such misunderstandings are rarely humorous however, neither for the corporations engaged in international trade and investment nor for the scholarly community who struggles to produce a truly global science. At the risk of sounding too pessimistic, I will argue that the downside risk of retreating into an exclusively Western paradigm of scholarly discourse is equal to if not greater than the prospect of Western dominated OB thought being expanded to include an East–West frame of reference.

To those who find my judgment too harsh, I should concede that much more management and OB research is being conducted in "the East" and in other non-US locations today than at any time in recent memory, and that more such research finds home in US outlets who in the past questioned its relevance for their readers. This author, for instance, has long ago discarded a standard pitch sent with his journal submission, explaining why editors should consider a China related material for their journals. My pessimism comes rather from the observation that there seems to be a precipitous decline in the willingness of OB scholars to question fundamental assumptions as the result of such research and to integrate this knowledge within the research mainstream. In other words, the price of acceptance and legitimacy has been the tacit acknowledgement that existing paradigms are the lightning rod for all to follow. While most textbooks nowadays have "windows" calling attention to the peculiarities of foreign countries, many of the classical management and OB models do not even boast adequate theory testing outside the US. For instance, Mintzberg's model of the managerial role has been seldom tested or validated in Asian countries, yet is continued to be taught as universal reality across the globe. And those who have tested existing models in foreign waters have seldom ventured beyond testing.

In this brief preface, I take the reader on a somewhat eclectic journey into the twilight zone where East and West meet, or, more often, miss each other's trajectory in the OB field. I will not be looking as much into *East versus West*, the contrasting exercise which has been the dominant but I believe erroneous emphasis in OB. Rather, I will be looking into *West on East*, that is, on how the West has looked on the East and especially on the ramifications of this perspective for the development (or rather lack of) in the field. In this journey, I will follow the underlying causes of the current state of the field, both scholarly and institutional, e.g., the ascent of strategy as the macro equivalent of OB, both being context-devoid disciplines, and the business school staffing models. In this discourse, I will be using what I consider to be "critical incidents" in the Western, OB view of the East, among them, the rise and fall of Japanese management, the brief Western interest in Confucianism, and the ascent of China. I will also touch on the few Eastern concepts that have drawn the interest of OB scholars, e.g., *guanxi*, and will attempt to explain why they have gained favor with Western researchers and in what light they appeared. Finally, in a concession to a "no nonsense" American approach that insists on producing some tangible, "bottom line" results, I will make some suggestions on "where do we go from here".

ORGANIZATION BEHAVIOR EAST AND WEST

If the boundaries of "East" and "West" were often poorly defined in the scholarly and practitioner community, this was not the case in OB, which was from the outset a largely American product. While significant scholarly work on organizational issues was initiated in another Anglo-Saxon culture, the UK, in the 1950s and 1960s, it rapidly lost ground. Furthermore, the UK work had a strong macro, organization theory flavor, which did not endear it to OB scholars in the US. In the absence of fresh inputs, and with a staunchly micro perspective, OB remained firmly rooted in the US context, probably more than any other field of management. When McGregor wrote "The Human Side of Enterprise", he made the argument that man has already fulfilled his basic needs and was now ready for higher order needs and a "Theory Y" type of organization. It did not occur to him to qualify his statement based on realities in other nations. Nor did the question occur to most OB scholars, from those writing on core leadership and motivation issues to those dwelling on esoteric Pygmalion type topics. Yes, there were exceptions, such as McClelland's (1963) comparison of children stories in various nations, but these forays received very little attention and following compared to supposedly universal models. Further, McClelland's style of investigation set the stage for what was to continue decades later, namely the testing of a Western derived paradigm, in this case, his motivational framework.

Many decades and a healthy dose of "globalization" later, it still does not occur to most OB authors to question the universality of the basic frames of reference used in their research. Interestingly, even those who hail from "Eastern" nations quickly adopt the traditional Western view. Rather than injecting a measure of diversity, they seem more interested in dissecting Eastern concepts for Western consumption by alternately showing equivalence or contrast, than in introducing East and West to the intricacies of their respective frames of thought and to developing the interface between the two.

A casual reader of the OB literature is unlikely to guess that the US accounts for merely 20 percent of the world's economic output or that it has been running a huge trade deficit for almost a quarter of a century. Admittedly, the skewed representation is true for most fields of business, including, ironically, international business. A survey published by the *Journal of International Business Studies* (JIBS) shows the US, by a huge margin, as the most frequently studied country (Thomas, Shenkar & Clarke, 1994). Other countries are only interesting to the extent they can be benchmarked against the US anchor. More ominously, perhaps, from a perspective of scholarly pursuit, the study shows that the probability of inclusion in *JIBS* is best predicted by a country's trade importance for the US, i.e. by "practical" relevance. The reality has generated its own self-fulfilling prophecy, where reviewers would often reject, say, a French-Chinese study because it lacks the US as a comparative anchor.

If OB's "West" is represented by the US, then what is "East"? In disciplines which have been around much longer, such as history and literature, as well as in social science disciplines such as political science which adopted the comparative perspective with considerably more zeal, "East" represents a broad territory, including the Near and Middle East. The case is different in OB, however. By and large, "OB East" consists of East Asia, primarily Japan (in its turn), Korea and (in particular today) Greater China. Articles on other Eastern countries, e.g., Turkey or Egypt, are few and far between. There are some exceptions, e.g., work on Greece initiated by the personal interest of Harry Triandis, or on Israel, skewed by the very high per capita publication level in that country. However, East Asia is by far the most represented part of the East in the eyes of a largely Western OB scholarly community. There are a number of reasons for that designation as well as for the concomitant failure of this focus to elicit a truly global discourse within the OB community.

The first reason for the emergence of East Asia and in particular certain nations within this geographic sphere is practical relevance. As earlier noted, the East Asian "dragons" (or "tigers") rose to relevance in the OB scholarly community on the back of their economic success and strategic importance to the US rather than as a result of scholarly search and thirst for new paradigms. Further, this relevance was born engulfed in what was perceived to be a crisis atmosphere ("Japan is taking over" and "the decline of American civilization") and seems to have gone the same way (the Asian crisis and "the triumph of American capitalism"). In between these two events that generated more hysteria than serious scholarly pursuit, relevance defined and drove the scholarly interest in East Asia in the OB community. If OB and management as a whole are sometimes criticized for lacking relevance, this was rather a case of relevance without sufficient rigor, where academics rushed to cash in on the sudden but huge demand in the practitioner community.

The crisis to the West represented by the advance of Japan and later the "little dragons" (it was never clear if Japan or China were the "big dragon") generated soul searching focused on the competitive position of the US. Was there another means to that same end of economic efficacy? At the same time, foreign direct investment by US firms in Asia was beginning to grow, requiring practical responses. It became a matter of practical exigency to inquire, for instance, whether Western models of motivation would work in a US affiliate in Singapore or Taiwan. As we will later discuss in some detail, the OB scholarly community by and large saw the East in the same vein of practicality, except that exigency meant the use of the emergent interest to resuscitate old ideas with Japan mobilized to counter skeptics in other business disciplines. The Human Relations movement, for one, saw Japan a vindication of its call for empowerment, paying scant attention to considerable evidence to the contrary, e.g., one showing "orchestrated empowerment". Later, Japan has been replaced with China, but this new focus of attention was not to become even an illusory alternative. At best, China has become a testing ground for Western concepts and theories, in itself not a bad idea but one that hardly takes us forward in terms of theory development.

The second reason why East Asia has become "OB East" is the "exotic" allure of the "Far East". The distance from the West, mental as much as geographic, made East Asia appears as the most intriguing portion of the East. As an "antithesis" to the West, East Asia came to be used as a form of a "contrast effect", allowing the West to examine itself from the outside while maintaining a Western frame of reference. Surprisingly, while doctoral programs in the West started to churn out an increasingly large number of East Asian graduates, this seems to have done little to support the advance of an "eastern" approach – one where ideas and concepts originating in the East are the driver rather than one representing mere application of Western models. In the absence of legitimacy or incentives to do otherwise, these Asian scholars quickly embraced the US anchored approach. Survival in US academia and even in their local institution meant publication in US outlets, and those were, and are still very much embedded in the same Western research tradition.

The timing and circumstances surrounding the emergence of East Asia as a focus of interest had ominous repercussion for the OB field. It defined the scholarly debate in terms of national competitiveness, often confusing OB issues with those of industrial policy and institutional environments with which the OB community was ill prepared to deal. This could have led to theoretical advance in the sense of challenging the traditional boundaries of a field that remained largely closed to other disciplines, including other areas in business and even in management such as organization theory. The opportunity was missed because the OB field undertook East Asia as a chance to revisit old paradigms and settle old accounts rather than as a platform from which to reassess fundamental frames of reference and develop new paradigms. From hereon, the debate on "universality", to the extent that it developed at all, would take the form of exportation of Western ideas and models rather than a truly global exchange that could have enriched the field immensely.

EAST MEETS WEST

In this section, I present two "critical incidents" covering the introduction of East Asia to a Western OB community. The two, Japan and China, played a quite different role in the process. They are also anchored in different time periods. The era of "Japanese management" dawned around 1979, reached its peak in the mid-1980s, and started its gradual descent in the 1990s until its demise towards the end of the century. While an association for the study of Japanese management is still around, it looks more like the textbook case of the polio society hanging on once the disease has been eradicated, than a fountain of new ideas and concepts. The Chinese era in OB starts in the mid 1980s as a purely "exotic" play, though sporadic interest in the Maoist managerial systems existed earlier among Sinologists. The OB interest in China evolves much more slowly than in the Japanese case, however it too has left vital imprints on the field that are likely to govern the future development of academic discourse for years to come.

The Rise and Fall of "Japanese Management"

No case is more important to the understanding of the East–West saga in organization behavior than that of Japanese management. The story begins in the 1970s, when Americans find themselves faced with an unprecedented onslaught of Japanese products, including the most visible symbol of the American economic might and way of life – the automobile. Japanese success was first attributed to the oil crisis of October 1973, a myth that by now has been institutionalized. It is indeed a myth: a big jump in Japanese car imports took place in 1972–1973 just prior to the oil crisis and the oil embargo itself merely accelerated a trend that was already in full swing. The attribution was important however in that it enabled many in media and industry to argue the Japanese were merely lucky, that they happened to have economy cars for sale just when the market suddenly needed them.

The argument of luck was followed by another explanation for Japanese success, namely that the Japanese were not playing fair. This argument was not without merit, but taken together with the first further delayed a serious look at the Japanese managerial system. Only when these arguments (and their economic counterparts in the realms of exchange rates and such) were largely discredited, came the conclusion that the Japanese were doing something right and that the US would better figure out what that was if it wanted to halt its decline. With one discipline after another raising its hands in frustration over its inability to explain the "Japanese phenomenon", management, and especially OB, made their move via a quick string of best sellers that introduced not only Japan but also management and OB to the mass market, a rare opportunity that would not be soon repeated. The honeymoon with "Japanese management" was about to begin.

By the later 1970s, US business schools, that until then did not want anything to do with Japan or any other Asian country, began a period of enchantment with everything Japanese. Centers for Japanese business were established complete with abundant resources and tea houses, and scholarly attention shifted to a country that until then was almost nowhere to be found on either curriculum or research agenda. Frustration built up quickly, for instance, economics scholars discovered that Japan refutes the assumptions of economic theory on such key issues as the relationship between exchange rates and trade. To resolve the dissonance, they ended up with the now famous statement that "Japan does not fit the model". Building a model that will accommodate Japan or other Asian nations was not on anyone's agenda, however, an ominous sign of things to come in strategy (the management discipline most closely aligned with economic thought) that would soon cast a shadow over business school education. However it was in management that Japan received the widest attention, generating a halo effect onto other Asian nations. The undersigned, having written his thesis on the evolution of Chinese management against the opinion of many of his advisors, must therefore thank Japan for having obtained an academic job at that time.

The managerial chapter in this fascination with Japan begins with a project undertaken by California professors that included a very brief stay in Japan. The resulting best sellers had little to do with the realities of Japanese business and everything to do with the perceptions and misperceptions of Americans about it. Their descriptions of an ideal environment were much in line with the image emanating of the popular media, such as Time's magazine description of Japan as "industrial nirvana". Respectable academic outlets such as AMR quickly fell into the same trap with rosy accounts written by people with little understanding of the Japanese environment but a keen eye for the emerging publishing opportunity associated with this new product life cycle (e.g., Hatvani & Pucik, 1981).

All of the above sources portrayed an idyllic system in which empowered, life-long employees and their managers worked for the greater benefit of the firm and in which union and management acted as one. There was very little mention, if any, of the life of Japanese workers in supplier, satellite firms, in small and home businesses; of the violence that accompanied the introduction of such celebrated techniques as Just-in-Time management, or of the dissatisfaction expressed by many in the Japanese workforce. The fact that "Japanese management" was never practiced by a majority of the Japanese workforce was also rarely reported. Books such as Kamata's (1983) *In the Passing Lane*, which provided a first hand and infinitely more negative view of the Japanese workplace, had never attracted large audience, failing to counterbalance the emerging myth. Nor was there much interest in books such as Morishima's (1982), which attributed Japanese success to a much more complex web of history, culture and institutional legacy.

While Japanese management fascinated almost everyone, it was adopted more eagerly by a number of constituencies whose agenda predetermined their interest in the "human element". In the "real world", the natural constituencies were labor unions, who naturally attributed Japanese success to the job security accorded to employees. The unions' information came from the misinformed best sellers, who forgot to mention that the life-time employment enjoyed by core employees in large corporations could not be exercised without the convenient buffer of temporary employees in the same firms and especially among their secondary and tertiary suppliers. By now, however, life-time employment, seniority and rotation were taken for granted, as were quality circles and other features of so-called "Japanese management".

In the scholarly community, the quickest to jump on the opportunity was the then dormant Human Relations movement in OB. The movement and its adherents were desperate to show that empowered employees in decentralized organizations produced higher performance, something that empirical data did not bear and which practitioners were then questioning openly. Japan was a godsend: it supposedly provided consensus decision-making, quality circles and other means for "empowerment". Almost no one in management questioned (at that time) the superior performance of Japanese firms (some economists did but for the wrong reasons). The missing piece was to show that Japanese organizations fitted the bill for empowerment. This was provided by the aforementioned best sellers and by a string of articles and "educational" videos that reinforced the utopian view of Japanese management. The empowerment myth was now taken for granted not only by scholars but also by unsuspecting US employees who joined Japanese transplants often believing in the pipe dream of industrial nirvana.

The embrace of the "Japanese model" by the Human Relations movement proved suffocating, however, when Japan faltered. Since what supported the story was the belief in the infallibility of Japanese firms, their troubles and the eventual decline of the Japanese economy as a whole dealt a deathblow to the nascent attempts to leverage the interest in Japan and reach towards universal theories of management or at least a broadening of scholarly horizons. Presumably, Japan was the alternative, it failed, and that was it. We could all go back to the safety and comfort of US models. The US continued to run huge trade deficits, first with Japan and then with China, but this time no one was paying much attention.

China: The Big Dragon as a Silent Sounding Board

With Japan gone as an alternative model of management in the 1990s, China gradually emerged from the "exotic" category. To an extent, the country has already become less exotic when it incrementally abandoned its command economy, since it was supposedly becoming less different and hence less interesting. China was becoming however more relevant, drawing more foreign investment than any other developing economy, and gradually competing with Japan for the number one place on the US list of trade deficit culprits. However it was a far cry from the position Japan enjoyed in its heydays. While both Japan and China were considered somewhat of a menace to things Western, China did not become in any way an alternative model for Westerners to consider, not even one cast in Western eyes. China's trade powers was easy to explain in terms of low cost advantage and a host of negative practices such as nepotism, corruption and counterfeiting, so there was little to suggest the emergence of a new competitive model. Further, with Chinese outward foreign investment a tiny fraction of the money pouring into China, there was no immediate sense as yet of a Chinese economic menace. My index of China bashing which is the sum of anti-China best sellers published in a given year is still at a very low level. This is likely to change in the future though my guess is that even then China will not gain the cult following Japan enjoyed at the time. China will come to be perceived, however, as a threat, and, as the Japanese experience shows, this is likely to further dim prospects for open and rigorous East–West research flow.

Early on, China enjoyed a short lived spill-over from the success of Japan and the little dragons, when Confucianism became the subject of many best sellers trying to explain the "Japanese miracle" and emerging contenders, such as "the new Japan" (South Korea). Those books lauded the Confucian emphasis on frugality, hard work and loyalty and used them to explain the rise of East Asian economies. Other attributes of Confucianism, including, ominously, the explicit ranking of economic activity at the bottom of human action (only the military fared worse), were obviously not reported. And Mainland China, mired in the economic problems of a Communist system just starting to reform, was not an example to follow anyway.

The roots of the Western interest in Chinese management go much deeper however. More than Japan, China always represented the exotic, whether in its legendary bureaucracy or in its organizations and management during the Communist era that triggered an interest akin to that of circus goers – fascination with the different and the "bizarre" but not something you would want to try at home. It was always easy to make the point that one could not disregard the largest workforce in the world when formulating assumptions about people's behavior in organizations though that too was not an easy sell (the undersigned repeatedly used this argument when pleading with editors not to dismiss a China based study offhand because "it was irrelevant to our readers").

If China was considered "too different" under its command economy, its reforms produced a new interest. The interest was mainly formulated as an opportunity to test managerial assumptions in a "giant lab" undergoing a dramatic, albeit incremental change. However this test lab was a place to test theories, not to develop new ones. And once the reforms have gathered steam, there was even a rationale to avoiding such new development. Indeed, one of the strongest arguments against paying much attention to China was that as the country changed, it was becoming more "like us". Wait a few more years, and there will be no need to worry about that at all. Nothing could be further from the truth. What worries me most however is not the story itself but the fact that it repeats an argument that has been discredited more than half a century ago, when the idea that modernization was to be equated with Westernization was summarily rejected. What scholars discovered instead was that each country found its own path of change and reform with both means and ends varying dramatically. That we have to revisit the same fallacy time and time again suggests that beyond East and West, we may have a basic problem of failing to learn about past scholarship especially when it comes from other disciplines. In this atmosphere, reinventing the wheel is to be expected and indeed often found.

IN SEARCH OF AN EASTERN CONSTRUCT

The Chinese challenge to OB begins at the most fundamental level, that of terminology. For instance, autonomy, undoubtedly one of the core constructs in OB, cannot be adequately translated into Chinese. Not surprisingly, such problems are more likely to come from Sinologist circles than from traditional OB sources even when the topic is OB (e.g., Falkenheim, 1981). Unfortunately, while the Sinologists looked into OB as a potential source of ideas and explanations, the same was not true for OB scholars, who by and large neglected

Sinology and other disciplines. Yet, one can make the point that the reason a construct cannot be translated is that it is based on a fundamentally different perspective, in this case, one that is based on interdependence of the self.

Such examples abound. And the basic ramifications they raise, e.g., the use of the group instead of the individual as a frame of reference, are not considered. They are not, I would argue, for a number of reasons. The first reason is simply lack of knowledge, however, this would not explain why many Chinese born authors follow the same path. The second reason has to do, ironically, with the likely emergence of an alternative paradigm, one that cannot be merely understood using a Western perspective, as a similar or contrasting effect, but one that would necessitate a radically new approach and the possible discard of existing theories that together make the current "body of knowledge" in OB.

Over the years, there have been only a few *Eastern* constructs that seem to have drawn the attention of OB scholars at large, providing an opportunity to go beyond the testing of Western constructs and into the realm of Eastern theory development. One of those constructs was face, a concept treated as much simpler than it really is and whose impact, if any, was confined to methodological debate (e.g., that Eastern respondents will not utter negative feedback). Even this methodological advice was not often heeded, however. Nor were other indications that Chinese method of discourse was basically different from Western parlance, e.g., delaying key points to the end of a conversation and hence frustrating even emic, qualitative data collection.

More recently, *"guanxi"* emerged as a Chinese construct to raise broad interest. It is important to understand why and how this came to be. The word "guanxi" can be roughly translated as "connections" or "relationships". The concept was easy to grasp (after all, even Westerners knew about networking), appealing in its mistaken simplicity (quite akin to the Western over-simplistic interpretation of "face"), and, most of all, within easy grasp as a supposed contrast to things Western and hence, ironically, explainable within the same framework.

Typical of the genre, Lovett, Simmons & Kali (1999) present a formula from which to calculate the cost and benefit of guanxi, in effect "translating" this complex construct into a paradigm understandable to economic rationalists. Guanxi is presented as an alternative, alright, but the alternative can only be appreciated using the same yardsticks as those of the Western model. Much in the same way Chinese hierarchy had to be marketed as a "substitute" to Western leadership behavior (e.g., Schemerhorn, 1987), the theoretical contributions emanating from the analysis of guanxi appear in the form of "substitutes" to existing western constructs (e.g., Xin & Pearce, 1996), making them sellable in Western outlets. Defining a phenomenon as a "substitute" is clearly a way to acknowledge variation while safely maintaining the existing paradigm, for it merely shows a variation on an existing variable rather than questioning the variable itself or its relationship with other constructs in a system. Hence, the fundamental challenges raised by guanxi to an individual level of analysis and to western concepts of a "network" are not pursued and probably would have little chance of getting accepted without the Western "anchor" – but it is precisely this anchor that severely limits the theory development potential of the imported construct.

Interestingly, while the bulk of the management and OB articles on guanxi appeared in the last four or five years, the area study literature was already discussing its declining importance (Guthrie, 1999). It would be a serious (though often committed) mistake however to equate this decline with "convergence", that is the historically false illusion of things foreign becoming more similar with time.

IN SEARCH OF AN EASTERN INSTRUMENT

It is a sad commentary that almost no Eastern-derived instruments exist in organization behavior. Few authors have had the openness of Adler, Campbell & Laurent (1989) who acknowledged the inappropriateness of Western instruments in the context of China. While work by Michael Bond and others has made remarkable strides in weighing equivalencies, the Chinese Cultural Connection (1987) remains a noble but isolated attempt to establish a genuinely Chinese instrument that unfortunately yielded very little continuity. While the cross-cultural literature has lamented the bias of Western derived instruments for years, we continue to use the same instruments without having developed an alternative. "Validation" techniques in organization behavior as well as in its parent disciplines of psychology and sociology continue to "test" the applicability of Western instruments in a different context, an effort that means little in a context that is fundamentally different. Twenty-five years ago, Donald Trieman (1977) made the classical mistake of arguing for the universality of prestige scales without realizing the fundamental difference in the institutional context of different societies (e.g., Japanese do not see the occupation as their anchor of social identity – it is the organization that fulfills this purpose). Lacking indigenous instrumentation and area study understanding, we are liable to continue and make the same mistake over and over again.

If Eastern instrumentation is virtually non-existent, it is not at all surprising that no genuine theory development anchored in an Eastern approach has ever emerged. Virtually all models of motivation, from Maslow to Vroom, have been developed in the US. It is hardly surprising that all of these theories are strongly focused on the individual – after all the US is the most individualistic country in the world. What is more disconcerting is that the latest theories, e.g. expectancy, show much less inclination to even test their basic assumptions than earlier theorists, e.g., McClelland, which at least tested their models across societies early on (see McClelland, 1963). It is difficult, from this perspective, to argue that the scholarly community is indeed set on a course that will eventually take us to a truly universal science.

THE INSTITUTIONAL CONTEXT

The failure of OB to utilize Japan and China opportunities as genuine platforms for theory developments rather than as sounding boards for Western perspectives is a fundamental problem that needs to be understood within an institutional context. The shift of much of the OB literature into schools of business, a largely American invention, supported an environment in which even Asian scholars embraced the Western paradigm as the only one available. The trend was further assisted by a staffing model that brought in PhD graduates of business schools rather than those with degrees in underlying disciplines, especially sociology, political science, modernization and, most importantly, area studies. The typical graduate doing international research today, East or West, comes with economics background and a "disciplinary" knowledge in strategy. This graduate is likely to see culture and institutions – if at all – as something that can be conveniently packaged in a quantified measure of cultural and institutional distance. He/she is satisfied to reduce any social, political and economic complexity to residual "externalities", a fantasy term set to support a presumably universal model. Such a scholarly environment is unlikely to support theory development based on comparative and international research. Worse, as earlier argued, it is likely to take us back in time, forfeiting years of progress.

In OB, the shift in the make-up of business schools has marginalized the field and pushed scholars away from the mainstream of what was once called "cross-cultural" and comparative research into the increasingly confining boundaries of their own discipline. This is a problem in all business areas, but especially in strategy which is in the process of claiming its own legitimacy against more entrenched players such as finance and marketing. However, with OB losing ground in both management (as the declining numbers of students, positions and membership will attest) and international business, it quickly retreated into ever-narrower confines. It did not help that organization theory was losing ground even faster, devastated by the loss of its sociological base that delivered much of the managerial thinking of the time, such as structural contingency theory.

The fatal blow to prospects for the internationalization of organization behavior is what Child (2000) has pinpointed as the growing disconnection between comparative and international management. Comparative management refers to such questions, as how and why the management styles of Japanese and US executives are similar in some respects but different in others. International management refers to the actual *crossing* of national boundaries, e.g., the conflict produced by US and Japanese management style within the context of a joint venture. Unfortunately, comparative and international management and organization behavior remain separate, with little or no communication, minimal crossover, and no systematic mechanisms for cooperation. To comparative organization behavior, the exclusion of an international management perspective has meant a steady decline in relevance. At the same time, the neglect of a comparative perspective has robbed international management and organization behavior of what could have been its most important theoretical and methodological base.

It is the meeting of comparative and international management that makes the juxtaposition of theoretical perspectives possible. What is a better way to examine the role of culture than to subject it to the test of international encounter between firms and individuals? Likewise, how is it possible to examine claims for behavioural universals in the absence of an in-depth comparison of national systems? If we fail to answer those questions, we run the risk of what I would call "the fallacy of economics": when frustrated economists discovered that Japan was not behaving quite as expected in its reaction to exchange rate alignment, i.e. it was not increasing its import goods consumption to the tune of the Yen appreciation, they proclaimed that "Japan did not fit the model". If we fail to grant more than a testing ground status to foreign environments, we too will embrace false universality just because we have never given serious consideration to the alternative.

ORGANIZATION BEHAVIOR EAST AND THE FUTURE OF ORGANIZATION BEHAVIOR

The focus of our story, the East, is only a parable, for the issues raised in this chapter are not confined to East Asia or to the "East" as a whole. It is admittedly easier to focus on East-Asian societies due to their visibility ("challenge to the West") and their particular position on the cultural and social landscape. For instance, it is pedagogically easier to expose the vulnerabilities of a "low context discipline" (Adler & Boyacigiller, 1996) using cultures that are "high context" (Hall, 1959). To say that East Asia does not fit the model is to fall back on the economic fallacy described earlier in this chapter. The fundamental problem is obviously not with the empirical case that does not fit the model but rather with the model itself, whose parameters and perimeters fail to capture the empirical phenomenon.

The fundamental problem of OB exposed by the Eastern journey is, to this author, the failure to converse with other disciplines with overlapping interests, primarily, organization theory, and the removal of all but one of the elements of an environmental and institutional setting. Leaving the "macro" domain to organization theory and later to strategy creates a closed-system scholarly environment that is unlikely to make much progress in a highly interdependent world. The artificial extension into the single environmental sector of culture to the neglect of other sectors such as the legal, the political, and the social as well as of structure, institutions and other "macro" variables, undermines the ability of OB to provide a coherent, rigorous and, especially, relevant picture of organizational phenomena. On an institutional level, OB remains in all probability the one business administration discipline that retains formal and close affiliation with a parent discipline, psychology, via its SIOP (Society for Industrial-Organizational Psychology) branch. This affiliation has its advantages in terms of continuous theoretical and methodological feed, but it is also quite detrimental in the sense of buffering OB from other business disciplines that could have been extremely helpful in terms of broadening its scope as well as enhancing its relevance. Is it a coincidence, for instance, that while virtually all business disciplines have by now produced a coherent body of knowledge on alliances, a phenomenon which has been exploding in the real world, OB has not?

Another disconnect occurred in the potentially promising link between OB and non-business disciplines, e.g., anthropology and sociology, and, in particular, with area studies. If you examine carefully the Sinologist outlets, you will find substantial inputs from sociology, anthropology and organization theory, but very little from OB. While it would be easy to blame Sinologists for lack of appreciation of OB ideas, there is a strong possibility that the approach taken by OB has at least something to do with it. Apparently, like their business school counterparts on the other side of the spectrum, area study people found little in the OB literature that was useful and relevant to them. Perhaps a narrow approach that does not recognize or establish links beyond its narrow confines is to blame.

Paradoxically, the narrow, over-specialized approach adopted by many OB scholars is also detrimental to the field's treatment of culture, the only environmental sector that OB seems to acknowledge. For instance, one of the classical problems in cross-cultural research is the treatment of culture as a residual variable. This problem is much more likely to occur when alternative explanations are absent, and as long as no other facets of the environment are considered, neither will alternative explanations. I once attended a presentation by an OB scholar who attributed a certain phenomenon in a Chinese enterprise to cultural disposition. When I drew his attention to the fact that the phenomenon was much more in line with the firm's practices and governance than with culture, he countered, to my amazement, that this was "outside his domain".

Given this context, is not at all surprising that OB remains virtually the only discipline to employ the term cross-cultural research rather than the broader and more diversified "international", "comparative" or "global" research. It is equally not surprising that there continues to be a fundamental divide between "Cross-cultural OB" and mainstream OB. Take a look, for instance, at the must have chapter on motivational theories in an OB textbook, and you will be hard pressed to find anything that is comparative or international *embedded in the theory, model and instrument*. When this changes, we will know that East and West shall meet. Unfortunately, the preceding analysis suggests that this is unlikely to happen any time soon. More alarmingly, I do not believe we are any closer today than two decades ago.

WHERE DO WE GO FROM HERE?

As I have forewarned the reader of this chapter, the analysis of OB in the Asian context is admittedly gloomy and far from promising. Can anything be done? Probably, and at the urging of the editors of this Handbook I am pleased to offer some constructive ideas to that effect in the following pages. I should note however that my own reading of the institutional landscape and disciplinary inertia suggests that the likelihood of those steps being actually taken is not particularly high. While as I am writing these final comments, the Enron mess and subsequent accounting scandals unfold, casting a long shadow over the aforementioned argument that the American model of efficiency and transparency is the model of choice for everyone around the globe, it remains to be seen whether this will trigger the necessary soul searching not only in accounting, finance and strategy but also in the OB area.

What OB needs is nothing less than a paradigm-shift, a radical realignment in underlying assumptions, constructs, analytical tools and research instruments, all the way down to scholarly discourse where we must refrain from using generic statements of the sort "what motivates people is" until and unless they have been validated in multiple countries. Asian management can play a vital role in such a paradigm shift, but only if it is willing to undertake a more entrepreneurial, risk-taking approach, embodying the charting of an independent theory development course rather than a limited theory testing effort. What I envision is the emergence of an "Asian school" whose influence will go well beyond East Asia but which will trigger soul searching and revival of creative and relevant OB throughout the globe.

At the institutional level, the change noted above is unlikely to happen unless there is a will to challenge existing outlets such as AMR and AMJ as quality benchmarks and encourage submission to and publication in Asian and international business journals. It is especially vital for scholars of Asia who have shown their ability to publish in the prestigious Western outlets to lead the change, as they are less likely to be accused of making the shift because of inability to publish in those journals. Growing criticism of these outlets in the West as being repetitive, narrow, irrelevant, and out of touch make this an opportune moment to make the shift and begin offering the contours of an alternative.

Another constructive step where the "Asian school" could contribute to OB at large is in forcing a long overdue opening of the field beyond assessing the role of culture on individual and group processes to include other sectors of the environment or, at the least, the interplay of culture with social and economic forces. Opening to "emic" research will resurrect both anthropological and business forces that seem to have been lost in the march of OB towards irrelevance. Specifically, this could be triggered by the submission and publication of articles that consider non-culture variables as well as those adopting a qualitative approach. Publication of OB pieces in non-OB outlets may be an innovative way to circumvent some of the obstacles within the disciplines. Another "radical" idea is to encourage the publication of OB-focused case studies which would challenge the customary emphasis on strategy in existing cases and will show that enhanced relevance goes hand in hand with growing internationalization, towards which an Asian school can lead the way.

Until the developments suggested above take hold, mid range theory development is probably the most realistic course. Such mid-range theory development involves targeting a specific construct or instrument and going beyond testing into adaptation. For instance, the findings reported by Farh, Dobbins & Cheng (1991) comparing the self-rating of Chinese and US workers should be taken to the next step, which would be charting the context for Chinese supervisory behaviour, with all its open system implications, and then devising a model for leader-subordinate dyads that may or may not be parallel to the Western construct. It is this model which then needs to be juxtaposed with the Western model. In other words, we need to go, in reverse, from instruments to constructs to underlying assumptions.

The mid-range theory development effort must not be confined however to single constructs or instruments. To borrow a page from the strategic repertoire, the real value of such contributions by and large depends on the ability to build synergies, that is to utilize dispersed contributions towards the building of a value added whole, e.g., producing an Asian model of motivation. My pessimism stems from the observation that it is unlikely that such synergies will be allowed to emerge within the existing institutional framework any time soon. I remain open, and hopeful, to be proven wrong and trust that this book is an important step in this direction.

REFERENCES

Adler, Cambell and Laurent 1989. The globalization of our mental map: evaluating the geographic scope of jibs coverage. Reprinted, *Journal of International Business Studies*, Fourth Quarter, 1994.

Adler, N. and Boyacigiller, N. 1996. Global management and the 21st century. In B.J. Punnett and O. Shenkar (eds.), *Handbook for International Management Research*. Oxford: Blackwell.

Child, J. 2000. Theorizing about organization cross-nationally. In J. Cheng and R.B. Peterson (eds.), *Advances in International Comparative Management*. Stamford, CT: JAI Press.

Chinese Culture Connection (1987). Chinese value and the search for culture-free dimensions of culture. *Journal of Cross-Cultural Psychology*, 18: 143-164.

Donald, T. 1997. *Occupational Prestige in Comparative Perspective*. Academic Press, Inc.

Falkenheim, V.C. 1981. Autonomy and control in Chinese organizations: Dilemmas of rural administrative reform. In S.L. Greenblatt, R.W. Wilson and A.A. Wilson (eds.), *Organizational Behavior in Chinese Society*. NY: Praeger.

Farh, J.L., Dobbins, G.H. and Cheng, B.S. 1991. Cultural relativity in action: A comparison of self-ratings made by Chinese and US workers. *Personnel Psychology*, 44: 129-147.

Guthrie, D. 1999. The declining significance of guanxi in China's economic transition. *The China Quarterly*, 254-282.

Hall, E.T. 1959. *The Silent Language*. Greenwich, CT: Fawcett.

Hatvany and Pucik, V. 1981. An integrated management system: Lessons from the Japanese experience. *Academy of Management Review*.

Kamata, S. 1983. *Japan in the Passing Lane: An Insider's Shocking Account of Life in a Japanese Auto Factory*. New York, NY: Knopf Publishing Group.

Lovett, S., Simmons, L.C. and Kali, R. 1999. Guanxi versus the market: Ethics and efficiency. *Journal of International Business Studies*, 30(2): 231-248.

McClelland, D. 1963. Motivational patterns in Southeast Asia with special reference to the Chinese case. *Social Issues*, 19: 6-19.

Morishima, M. 1982. *Why Has Japan 'Succeeded'? Western Technology and the Japanese Ethos*. Cambridge, UK: Cambridge University Press.

Schermerhorn, J.R. 1987. Organizational features of Chinese industrial enterprise: Paradoxes of stability in times of change. *Academy of Management Executive*, 1: 345-349.

Xin, C. and Pearce, J.L. 1996. Guanxi: Connections as substitutes for formal institutional support. *Academy of Management Journal*, 39(6): 1641-1658.

Chapter 11

KEEPING OTHERS IN MIND
The Very Social Cognition of Asian Managers

Zhixing Xiao
INSEAD

Steven K. Su
INSEAD

INTRODUCTION

Does culture impact the way in which managers process information and make decisions? Will Asian and Western managers evaluating the same business decision take fundamentally different paths and as a result reach different conclusions? This chapter reviews current scholarship on this intriguing question. One possible answer is that just as the rules of mathematics are identical in the East and West, the rules of analysis in business will be very similar, and hence no special differentiation is necessary to describe the Asian context. However, while managers in the East and West often behave similarly, we will argue that profound cultural differences in social beliefs and values affect how information is processed. As this area is relatively unexplored, we present research and conjecture to map out directions for future research.

To illustrate how cross-cultural differences can affect cognition in a particular context, consider an analogy to the restaurant context. In both Asia and the West, the principal activity is that patrons go to a business establishment to receive a meal in exchange for payment. There are obvious differences between the two, most noticeably in the taste of the food. Of greater interest to us are the differences that might seem trivial at first glance, but actually signify important divergences in social practices. Restaurants in the West are typically equipped with rectangular tables well suited for two to four people, at which patrons randomly choose their seats. In Eastern countries such as China, it is more common to have large round tables that allow each patron to directly face a larger number of compatriots. Here seating arrangements are not random, but have hierarchical significance. Seats facing the door are usually taken by those who are more senior in status, in the same way that seats on the left tend to be taken by the more senior. Differences in food selection procedures also exist. In the West, each patron is presented a menu from which personal selections are made. In China, only one menu is presented to the host, who orders all the dishes to be shared by the group.

Such differences of practice testify to differences of orientation regarding group and individual roles. As compared to the West, Asian restaurant scripts place more exacting emphasis on one's precise relationship to the group, specifying one's commonality with others and one's rank within the group. This emphasis is also reflected in social cognition, as participants gather and process information about things that happen at the table. At a very manifest level, participants make sense of social events by matching observed behaviors to culturally recognized patterns and role expectations. For instance, a person who orders the dishes is quickly recognized by observers to be the host and would be expected to pay for the group. At a more subtle level, perceivers make sense of observed behaviors within the context of unarticulated theories about cause and effect. For instance, Chinese participants implicitly expect people to perform acts in order to accommodate others, rather than to satisfy personal desires. Thus, in China, when the host orders an expensive or unusual dish, observers may view him less as personally liking the dish, and more as dutifully trying to cater to others. Furthermore, it is also likely that the very type of information to which observers are attuned will be distinctive. At a Chinese table, observers are more likely to notice any detail that might confer relationship status: for instance, who is seated closer to the honored guest, who is served first or takes the first bite of food, who serves food to whom, and who directs the conversation.

Our central theme is that cultural differences in social values will be reflected in social cognition. We begin by reviewing broad cultural patterns that lead Asians to orient their thoughts more exclusively around personal relationships and social context. From there, we begin our analysis of the workplace by exploring how individuals perceive the behaviors of co-workers and of the self. We also examine how one's coworkers influence one's views and decisions. In the final section, we explore how people work interactively to jointly process information. In all three areas of workplace cognition, we will suggest that cultural differences leave a distinctive imprint.

MODES OF THINKING: RELATIONSHIPS AND CONTEXT VS. INDIVIDUAL COMPONENTS

The greater tendency for Asians to orient reasoning and logic around interrelationships and context is a central distinction emphasized in comparisons to Western modes of thinking. This contrast is evident even in the historical roots of Western analytic thinking and Eastern holistic thinking. Analysts have noted that the Western analytic style is grounded in traditions such as Aristotelian physics, which account for the behavior of each object by reference to its own particular attributes (Shweder & Bourne, 1984). It has been only in relatively recent history, the time of Galileo, that Western theorists acknowledged the interactions between objects and their environment (Choi, Nisbett, & Norenzayan, 1999). In contrast, Eastern thought has long been rooted in a more holistic approach that models phenomena according to interrelationships between the various elements that constitute a whole. In ancient China, the principles of action and distance were studied and applied to the movement of tides and magnetism 1,500 years before Galileo (Needham, 1962; Choi, Nisbett, & Norenzayan, 1999). Beliefs about the very basis of matter focused on the interrelationships between various elements. The ancient philosophy of *Wuxing* (a holistic view of the world that states that all things are comprised by the five elements of metal, wood, water, fire and soil) has long been the dominant paradigm in Chinese thinking. Similarly, Chinese medicine is characteristic for a holistic diagnosis of health that focuses on the overall balance between various conflicting forces. This holistic approach even extended to the interrelationships between events within the body and forces external to it. As opposed to a dualism in the Western tradition, which made a major distinction between the rules that apply to the inner being and to the physical environment, Asians applied a monolistic model (Bond, 1986; Markus & Kitayama, 1991a). Traditional Chinese medicine proposed that people are made of the same substances as the nature around them: the same five elements of matter are internalized to represent the five main organs in the human body.

Psychologists have argued that such differences in epistemology are reflected in how Asians and Westerners perceive the relationship between individuals and their social environment. A much-noted cultural difference in cognition is that of field independence, or the ability to separate a perceived item from its context (Witkin, Dyk, Fattuson, Goodenough, & Karp, 1962; Witkin & Berry, 1975; Berry, 1991). A field dependent person (who by definition lacks field independence) tends to orient the self with reference to the environment. Berry finds differences in degree of field dependence in different cultures and correlates these differences in "cognitive style" to ecological conditions. In comparisons of the West to Asia, Chiu (1972) observes that the Chinese are more situation-centered, and Americans are more individual centered. Similarly, Kuhnen, Hannover and Schubert (2001) have distinguished the context-dependent mode of thinking that prevails in the East to the context-independent mode of the West.

A related formalization of cultural differences in social cognition concerns how people draw boundaries between the self and others (Markus & Kitayama, 1991a). Westerners tend to have a self-construal that is "independent" as it stresses the "self as an individual whose behavior is organized and made meaningful primarily by reference to one's own internal repertoire of thoughts, feelings, and actions, rather than by reference to thoughts, feeling, and actions of others" (p. 226). In contrast, the Asian model of the self is "interdependent" in that it emphasizes the self "as part of an encompassing social relationship" and recognizes that "one's behavior is determined, contingent on, and, to a large extent organized by what the actor perceived to be the thoughts, feelings, and actions of others in the relationship" (p. 227). Many other models have proposed similar ways to distinguish the Eastern from the Western self, postulating for instance that the Asian self is more socially embedded (Reykowski, 1994), more contextualized with less of a boundary between the self and others (Kim, 1994), and more likely to assume compatibilities between individual and group goals (Triandis, 1995).

Markus and Kitayama propose that differences in self-concept are reflected in the manner in which people mentally collect, organize, and retrieve information. People attuned externally to their relationships with others will likely organize information differently than those attuned internally to themselves. Thus for people with interdependent selves, knowledge about the self is more likely to be embedded in specific contexts, and less likely to be generalized and abstract across contexts. Some of the first systematic evidence of this came from studies in which participants were asked to finish 20 statements about themselves that begin with the words "I am." Results from these Twenty Statement Tests reveal that in describing themselves the Chinese and Japanese use fewer abstract stable traits, such as "I am an honest person," than do Americans (Bond & Cheung, 1983; Cousins, 1989). Asian self-descriptions were more concrete and role specific, for example in statements such as "I play cards on Sunday with my sisters." Importantly, these same patterns also appear to govern how people organize and retrieve information about others. In a comparison of how people in India and America describe close acquaintances, Shweder and Bourne (1984) found that Indian descriptions focus more on behaviors, and are more context and relationship specific.

Parallel differences have been noted in the very style of logic that is applied in the East and West. Peng (1997) notes that Western logic focuses on decomposing issues down to their unique constitutive elements. Western reasoning is influenced by philosophical beliefs such as the three laws of Aristotelian logic: the *law of identity*, the *law of non-contradiction*, and the *law of the excluded middle*. Rules of logic such as these suggest that there is one consistent truth that is deduced by introducing and discarding individual propositions until contradictions are eliminated. Chinese epistemology, on the other hand, places emphasis on appreciating the totality and complexity of an entire situation, rather than on the purity of its constitutive elements. In sharp contrast to the Western tradition, Chinese epistemology presupposes that because truths are in constant opposition, contradictions are inherent and to be accepted.

Scholars have distinguished the thinking style of the East as being less linearly logical than that of the West (Reischauer, 1977; Torrance, 1980). For example, research on multi-attribute product choices has shown that selections made by the Japanese were less closely determined by the weighted-average model than those of Americans (Chu, Spires, & Sueyoshi, 1999). In other words, when a Japanese person chooses from a group of options, the decision criteria are less likely to be a simple linear function of preference weights multiplied by attribute levels. Americans are more willing to decompose options into individual attributes that can be weighed and summed to produce an overall value. Similar patterns are suggested in the numerical probabilities estimation of students and managers in Britain and Asia (Philipe & Wright, 1977). Asian estimates of numerical probabilities were more extreme and less accurate, leading to the speculation that Asians take a more fatalistic point of view with less emphasis on a Laplacean probabilistic-causal view of world. This seeming difficulty in separating out and focusing on singular distinct elements has led to yet other charges. One controversial claim has been that Asians are less adept in forming and considering counter-factuals, or in other words, constructing a simulation of what would have happened had an event in the past transpired differently (Bloom, 1984; Au, 1983).

MAKING SENSE OF WORKPLACE BEHAVIORS

In the current section, we begin our analysis of how differences in thinking style affect management. The workplace is a context in which managers and subordinates engage and interact in joint activities. In order to adapt one's own activities to those of others, each worker must continuously gather and process information about the self and about others. We suggest that the tendency to attend to relationship and context – as opposed to individual components in isolation – has a distinctive imprint on how workers compare themselves to others, interpret the behaviors of others, and view their own skills and motivations.

Comparing Employees

Perhaps the most ubiquitous requirement in management theory is that managers identify the people or practices that most aid or obstruct the performance of the enterprise (Ilgen, Fisher, & Tylor, 1979; Cleveland, Murphy, & Williams, 1989). This determination forms a basis for allocating rewards or making staffing decisions to promote the most competent, and to correct the least competent. Managers are not the only ones to make such comparisons across individuals. Employees who are subject to their decisions also engage in the same process of comparison, and use the conclusions to gauge the level of effort they should apply and to assess the fairness of their superiors. Interpersonal comparisons of performance are not only commonplace, but of great interest to many.

Researchers have sought evidence of cognitive factors that influence the way people assess the performance of others (DeNisi & Williams, 1988), and have pointed to the role of culture (McEvoy & Cascio, 1990; Vallance, 1999). One hypothesis focuses specifically on how people in Asia and the West make interpersonal comparisons. It notes that Asians are more likely to focus on the commonalities that bond individuals into a group, and less likely to engage in analysis that decomposes the group into distinct individuals. Thus, in comparison to Westerners, Asians should be less likely to perceive differences across individuals belonging to the same group.

Indeed, research does indicate that Asians perceive a higher degree of self-other similarity (Markus & Kitayama, 1991a). When asked to evaluate the degree to which they are personally similar to others in their class, American students tend to see themselves as more dissimilar to others than do Asians. Interestingly, much research indicates that people in the West are more likely to view themselves not only as different from others, but also as better (Turner & Mo, 1984; Watkins & Dong, 1994). In one example, Markus and Kitayama (1991b) asked college students to assess the percentage of the population that was better than themselves on many different types of capabilities. On average, students in the United States rated themselves as better than two thirds of the population on socially desirable attributes. In contrast Japanese students provided responses that were significantly lower, approaching the mathematically correct average response of one half. Other studies have found that Chinese students in Taiwan provide lower self-ratings (Stigler, Smith, & Mao, 1985) on the Perceived Competence Scale (PCSC) than those in the US. The Chinese students provided lower self-ratings in academic competence, physical competence, and general self-esteem, though interestingly not in social competence.

This tendency on the part of Asians to self-deprecate is reinforced by the manner in which they provide accounts for their performance. Researchers have observed systematic differences in explanations for one's own successful and unsuccessful outcomes. In explaining failure, Chinese students are more likely to attribute the outcome internally to themselves – for instance, to a lack of effort. In explaining success, the pattern reverses as explanations focus on external factors such as luck and ease of task (Crittenden, 1996). These explanatory styles appear to have implications for self-esteem (Kashima & Triandis, 1986). For instance, Kitayama (1993) presented descriptions of various situations in which there is success or failure to Japanese and American participants and asked them to evaluate the impact on their self-esteem. Americans were more likely to react to successes, with their self-esteem boosted, whereas Japanese were more likely to be affected by failures, with their self-esteem diminished.

Research does suggest that these cognitive behaviors also manifest in work contexts. As compared to the West, in Asia employers make less dramatic distinctions across employees based upon individual performance. For instance, industry analyses indicate that, compared to Western enterprises, there is less wage dispersion in Japanese enterprises. For workers of the same rank, it is unusual to have large differences in pay based upon individual performance (Lincoln & McBride, 1987). Instead of focusing on themselves as distinct and better than others, employees in Asia have a tendency to self deprecate. Focusing on how people cognitively evaluate performance, Farh, Dobbins and Cheng (1991) find that Taiwanese workers exhibited a modesty bias. In their sample, worker self-ratings were lower than those provided by their superiors. Researchers have also investigated the types of feedback workers find more informative. Bailey, Chen and Dou (1997) find that when receiving performance feedback, Japanese persons were more likely to seek failure feedback, or information about the mistakes they had made. In contrast, Americans were more likely to seek success feedback, or information about things that they had done correctly.

Assessing the Causes of Actions

The workplace is a context in which participants constantly assess the causes of other people's behaviors. From a managerial perspective, knowledge about the causes of an employee's good or bad performance is essential to crafting a productive response. Take the case of a manager who discovers that one employee has just committed a costly mistake. Should the employee be punished or fired? A beneficial response requires knowing why the employee made the mistake. If for instance the mistake occurred because the employee was not given adequate information or direction from co-workers, acts to punish the worker will seem unfair and are unlikely to correct the underlying problem. If on the other hand, the mistake occurred because of a more permanent character trait, such as persistent laziness or carelessness, failure to discipline or remove the employee might make recurrence inevitable. Thus, determinations of whether actions are caused by factors internal or external to the employee are essential in management.

Much research in social cognition focuses specifically on how observers attribute cause to behavior. Researchers have amply documented a tendency for people to explain the behaviors of others in terms of internal attributes or personality traits (Gilbert & Malone, 1995; Ross & Nisbett, 1991), a process that appears to spontaneously occur with minimal intention and effort on the part of the observer (Winter & Uleman, 1984). In characterizing this phenomenon, Ross refers to it as no less than "the fundamental attribution error" (Ross, 1977). Such behavior, if applied to the workplace, would suggest that managers and employees have a tendency to err by over-attributing outcomes such as success or failure internally to the actor, even when they have access to information about external causal factors.

Initial research on the fundamental attribution error was drawn on data collected from Western samples. However, as we have discussed, Asians are more likely to orient their thinking externally, towards the actor's relationships to others and the external environment. Asians are also less likely than Westerners to organize information around the stable qualities that distinguish oneself as different from others. These perspectives suggest that perceptual processes in Asian work contexts might differ in that more credit is given to external causes of behavior.

Indeed, ethnographers have noted that everyday explanations in China are more likely to refer to an actor's social context than to personality characteristics (Hsu, 1953). In more scientifically controlled examinations of the matter, researchers have found less evidence of the fundamental attribution error in Asian samples (Miller, 1984; Morris & Peng, 1994). Morris and Peng (1994) argue that implicit theories of social behavior that prevail in different cultures engender different patterns in explaining cause. The Western implicit theory, which is centered on the autonomous person, channels attributions to the actor's internal, stable traits. In contrast, the Asian implicit theory, focused on situations and groups, directs attributions to the actor's embeddedness in groups and relationships. To test this hypothesis, school children in the US and China were presented with animated displays of social objects, such as fish in motion. Results showed that US school children interpreted displays of an individual moving near a group in terms of the individual's personal characteristics, whereas Chinese school children focused on the individual's accommodation to the group. Similar patterns were evident in analyses of explanations provided by adults for several real world crimes.

An interesting question that has surfaced is whether these differences are due to an Asian aversion to dispositional inference, or a preference for situational explanations. Some evidence indicates that through engagement in their culture, individuals come to acquire aversions or preferences for dispositional reasoning (Miller, 1984). An analysis was performed on how people of various ages in India and the US explain an acquaintance's behavior in daily life. Explanations of Children in two cultures were similar, but with age, Americans became more dispositional, and Indians became less dispositional, especially in explanations of deviant behaviors. However, Choi, Nisbett, and Norenzayan (1999) also find that Asians do engage in dispositional inference. Participants in the US and China were asked to predict a person's future behavior given information on their past behaviors or a trait label. Results indicated that, in making predictions, both samples were similarly influenced by personality labels. Moreover, both relied on personality traits for predicting behaviors in similar situations and also across different types of situations. These investigators suggest that the central cross-cultural difference in attribution is the greater willingness on the part of Asians to integrate information about the situation. To test this, they asked Korean and American students to predict the future behavior of an actor, given information about facilitating or inhibiting factors in the context. Their results showed that Koreans were more likely to rely on situational information to make predictions.

Menon and colleagues provide yet another explanation based on cultural differences in the construal of agency (Menon, Morris, Chiu, & Hong, 1999). They argue that Americans conceive of individual persons as free agents, whereas Asians conceptualize individuals as more constrained and less agentic than social collectives. Support of this hypothesis can be found in Morris and Peng's (1994) survey of graduate students. Participants were presented with details regarding two murders that had been committed by young men living alone and far from home. Respondents were presented with a list of hypothetical changes to the murderer's situation and asked to judge whether the tragedy might have been averted if the world had been different in this one particular way. The responses showed that Chinese respondents gave more weight to the actor's social situation than to the actor's dispositions. While Chinese respondents felt the presence of close others might have appropriately constrained the individual's actions, Americans imagined that the person would have engaged in the same action regardless of group context.

In both Asia and the West, research confirms that attribution patterns are important in shaping how people make sense of workplaces events. An analysis of reactions to critical supervisory feedback in Hong Kong and the US indicates that in both cultures, people often make dispositional attributions for the actions of the supervisor. For instance, the reason for the negative feedback can be attributed to unpleasant personality dispositions of the supervisor, rather than to one's own faulty performance (Leung, Su, & Morris, 2001). In both cultures, the attributional path taken has important implications. People who attribute the cause internally to the supervisor are less willing to accept the content of the feedback and have more negative workplace intentions than those who believe external factors were responsible.

Research has also illustrated East–West differences in explanatory style regarding workplace events. Menon and her colleagues performed an analysis of newspaper articles about the "rogue trader" scandal, in which a currency trader at Barings singlehandedly bankrupted the venerable British banking institution though illegal trades. They found that US newspapers made more mention of the individual traders involved, whereas Japanese newspapers were more likely to refer to the organization (Menon, Morris, Chiu, & Hong, 1999). Compared to Americans, Asians are less likely to attribute causality for workplace behavior to the stable trait characteristics of individuals. Instead, Asians are more likely to explain behaviors with respect to more external factors such as the constraints of the situation, or the influence of the social group.

While cultural differences in attributional style have been linked to workplace cognitions, less research has been conducted to investigate any impact on business practices. However, the Asian tendency to find external explanations for actions, if applied to evaluations of success or failure, could provide another reason why credit and reward are apportioned more equally in the Asian workplace. If the unique traits of the employee are not the cause of success or failure, there is less of a basis to apportion rewards according to accomplishment. In this case, other entities that are considered to be independently agentic with respect to performance might be given more consideration in apportioning reward. Indeed, Asian enterprises are often scrutinized for their willingness to emphasize group level rewards (Schuler and Rogovsky, 1998). This tradition extends as far back as to before the birth of Christ, when collective responsibility became a distinguishing feature of Chinese law. The widely enforced system of *Lianzuo* held that superiors, kinsmen, and neighbors shared the responsibility for the criminal behavior of an individual offender (Chiu and Hong, 1992; Nishisda, 1985; Zhang, 1984).

The stronger tendency for Asians to confer agency to groups may also play a role in the system of "guanxi." Under this system of social exchange, a businessperson's behaviors are expected to be consistent with and responsive to the influence of the various groups to which he or she belongs. Thus, businesspeople often rely on other people's group memberships and relationships to gauge their trustworthiness and social value (Farh, Tsui, & Xin, 1997; Ting-Toomey, 1988).

Assessing the Reasons for Work Performance

A central organizational imperative is to motivate employees to engage in behaviors that will benefit the business entity. Clearly, this is often a challenge. In workplaces in the East and West alike, employers expend significant resources to offer their employees material compensation in exchange for task performance. While research has demonstrated that behavior can be a straightforward result of the mathematical correspondence between rewards or punishments and beneficial or harmful behavior (Skinner, 1963), psychologists have also established an undeniable role for people's cognitions about their work activities.

One important stream of research concerns a person's beliefs regarding the reason why they perform a task. Researchers have noted that people find certain activities to be rewarding in and of themselves. For instance, a graphic artist may enjoy drawing for its own sake, just as a novelist may enjoy writing. For such activities, controlled experiments have shown that the payment of material rewards can actually cause individuals to view the task as less intrinsically attractive and interesting (Lepper & Greene, 1978). Without deliberate effort, people process information about their situation to determine the reasons for their own behavior. When an extrinsic reward is provided for task performance, there is a tendency to conclude that one performed the task for the sake of the reward, and to ignore the intrinsically pleasing aspects of the task. As a result, if extrinsic rewards are discontinued, people often reduce or discontinue the activity.

In the West, a rich tradition of research in motivation has given central attention to the individual's ability to control and manage situations that are confronted. The sense of self-efficacy in a domain produces a wide range of positive and reinforcing outcomes (Bandura, 1986). Individuals are more likely to engage in tasks for which they have a strong sense of personal competence, and are more likely to view them as challenges that can be mastered. They are also more likely to expend greater effort and find them to be intrinsically interesting. When they encounter difficulties, they are more likely to persist, and even heighten their effort. Finally, when failures occur, they are more likely to attribute the outcome to temporary or external factors and recover their confidence. Conversely, the loss of the belief that one can influence and control one's situation has been linked to depression, difficulty in learning, and ill-health (Seligman, 1975).

Research specifically in work contexts has provided further evidence that the sense of personal competence has important positive benefits (Deci, 1975). Because of the strength of such findings, Bandura (1986, 1997) asserts that beliefs of personal efficacy constitute the key factor of human agency. The importance placed on the process whereby an individual gains control of a situation appears also to be deeply imprinted on business practice and thought (Wilkinson, 1998; Shipper & Manz, 1992). Many schools of leadership exhort managers to avoid "micro-managing" by granting employees autonomy. It is suggested that "empowered" employees, who are given latitude to act and even to fail independently, learn to build self-confidence and ability.

However, cultural psychologists have wondered whether the sense of personal competence plays an equally dominant role in all cultures. Markus, Kitayama, and Heiman (1997) note that while "in some cultural contexts the most powerful impetus for behaviors appears to be self-determination and free choice … in other cultural groups, where people are required to be continually receptive and responsive to particular others, the energy and direction for individual behaviors seems to reside in the expectation of others" (p. 857).

In Asia, where less emphasis is placed on the distinctive qualities of the self, more attention is likely to focus on external factors – such as one's relations to others or to the group. In studies conducted in actual work contexts, Earley

(1994, 1999) differentiated between the competencies and abilities of the group and those of the individual. With participants from different samples in the Asia and in the West, he found that for individualists, efficacy training that focused on individual abilities had a more dramatic impact on performance. The pattern was reversed for collectivists, for whom efficacy training exercises focused on groups were more productive.

In cultures where attention is focused on one's relationships to others, it seems likely that task motivation will be connected to things that signal the ability to maintain strong relationships. While in the West individuals derive motivation from behaviors that make actors feel competent and skillful, it is likely that in Asia people will be motivated by behaviors that make them feel responsive and receptive to others. Su and his colleagues (Su, Chiu, Hong, Leung, & Morris, 1999) have argued that Chinese social actors are constrained by social structure to meet obligations to others. In Chinese culture, glory is bestowed to the dutiful person who suppresses personal desires to accommodate others. Kanungo and Wright (1983) argue that in Japan the very sense that one is engaging in self-sacrifice for the good of the organization is a source of intrinsic motivation and self-fulfillment.

As compared to the West, the Asian workplace is likely to place less emphasis on empowering the employee to develop personally distinctive competencies. Studies of Japanese workplaces suggest that close supervision and control of corporate culture are more effective tools to manage salespersons than more Western approaches, which focus on individual financial incentives given to more autonomous individuals (Money & Graham, 1999). Similarly, Agarwal (1993) finds that while in the US, salespersons reacted negatively to job codification and rule observation, in India, rule observation had a favorable influence on the organizational commitment of the salesperson. In Asia, it is not unusual to see practices that seem to publicly suppress an individual's sense of self competence. In one very successful Chinese firm, Haier, workers witness a daily ritual in which the poorest performer of the previous day stands inside big footprints painted beside the manufacturing line, performs self-criticism, and accepts the criticism of others.

Aside from making inferences about personal competence, people also make inferences about the source and nature of their competence. One influential research program has focused on implicit theories about human characteristics or skills. Dweck, Hong, and Chiu (1993) propose that people differ with respect to whether they view skills as fixed or malleable. At one extreme are individuals who believe that personal characteristic are fixed and not easily changed (entity theorists), and at the other extreme are those who believe that they are flexible and malleable (incremental theorists). Implicit theories about the nature of intellectual ability or skill have been shown to dramatically influence how people respond to information about performance. When presented with fictional feedback indicating that they are performing poorly on a task, entity theorists are more likely to abandon the activity or react with a sense of helplessness. Incremental theorists, on the other hand, are more likely to increase their effort in an attempt to improve their skill.

Not surprisingly, cultural psychologists have suspected cross-cultural differences in implicit theories of skill. The Western inward emphasis on identifying the unique stable attributes of individuals seems to correspond to an implicit theory that holds that skills are fixed. The Asian outward emphasis on relationships to others seems likely to correspond to an implicit theory that allows for responsiveness to the demands of the situation. Indeed empirical results indicate that compared to Westerners, Asians are significantly more likely to hold an incremental theory of skill (Norenzayan, Choi, & Nisbett, 1998). This finding is consistent with a strong cultural notion, embodied in philosophies such as Confucianism, that the individual can through effort and sacrifice make changes in the self to accommodate situational requirements. Individuals are exhorted not only to learn from, but also to closely imitate the actions of acknowledged masters.

Summary

Current research indicates that there are profound cultural differences in how individual workers make sense of the behaviors of others in their workplace. Westerners are more likely to interpret behaviors within a framework emphasizing individuals as unique self-contained units that are distinct from others. Asians, on the other hand, focus on the individual's relationship to others. Their framework portrays individuals as similar and more tightly integrated with others in their group. These differences are reflected in the workplace. As compared to the West, workers in Asia are less likely to perceive large individual differences in performance and are more likely to believe that an individual's behavior is derivative from group affiliation. Workers are less focused on the sense of individual competency, and more responsive to the sense of group efficacy. Whereas in the West, individuals are encouraged to discover and exploit their unique talents, in Asia individuals are encourage to apply effort to master the skills necessary to accommodate the situation.

SOCIALLY RESPONSIVE DECISION-MAKING

In the current section, we take an even more social approach to cognition by exploring ways in which individuals are influenced by others at the workplace. We will suggest that compared to people in the West, Asians process information in a manner that is more responsive to the reactions or imagined reactions of closely related others. When making decisions, people can search internally within their personal thoughts or externally to others for rationales to guide action. We propose that Westerners are more likely to favor approaches that focus on analysis of personal preference. In contrast, Asians are more likely to search externally to others for socially sanctioned decision rules.

Socially Sanctioned Decision Rules

In the workplace, managers and subordinates alike are continually confronted with the need to make choices from different options. Managers may have to do so in decisions involving capital purchases, hiring employees, or forming alliances. Employees also may have to decide which jobs or assignments to take, which compensation or investment plans to enroll in, or with whom to associate. To explain how people choose between options, scholars have also suggested a role for culture.

One hypothesized cross-cultural difference concerns the decision rules favored by people in the East and West. When making such choices, people may search internally or externally for rationales to guide or affirm their decisions. An internal rationale might require the decisionmaker to focus on his own past experiences to ascertain his personal preferences, and then evaluate the desirability of each option. A more external rationale might instead focus on knowledge about the experiences or beliefs of others. In this case, the desirability of each option could be evaluated based upon what we know about other people's experiences, either by direct observation or word of mouth.

To illustrate an internal rationale, consider the case of a manager who is contemplating the purchase of a computer. It may be said that in making this choice, the manager is assessing the utility corresponding to the various computers she examines. A straightforward approach might be to consider how much she would benefit from having each particular computer. This might be calculated by considering issues such as the functional specifications of each computer, the nature of the tasks she is likely to perform, and the extent to which she values the impact on her work. For many people, this would be a functional approach that rational managers would take. Theorists however have noted that people often depart from rational decision making behavior (Kahneman & Tversky, 2000; Thaler, 1985, 2000), leading other scholars to attempt to identify other more external approaches that are commonly utilized.

Consider again the manager who is seeking a computer. While at the sale of the assets of a small company that went bankrupt, she finds a three year old computer at a very low price. She is excited when she discovers that the computer is selling for half of its fair market value and decides to purchase it, perhaps without extensive consideration of its capabilities relative to more current machines. In this case, the decision is based on a factor other than the usefulness of the computer – the fact that the computer was available at a steep discount. Building on research demonstrating that justifications (Tetlock & Kim, 1987) and reasons (Shafir, Simonson, & Tversky, 1993; Wilson, Dunn, Kraft, & Lisle, 1989) profoundly influence how people make choices, Hsee (1999) characterizes this decision as one motivated by rationale utility. This particular decision is taken because a commonly appreciated rationale, purchasing at a steep discount, can be produced to make it seem well founded. This rationale, to the extent that it is not specific to the particular circumstances or preferences of any individual, provides a more external basis for choice behavior. Moreover, one can provide a public account of the decision choice to demonstrate skill in adhering to socially approved decision rules.

Building on this distinction, Weber and Hsee make a connection to culture by proposing that different decision modes prevail in Asia and the West (Weber & Hsee, 2000). External rationales are likely to play a larger role in explaining the decision-making of people in Asia, while internal rationales are more emphasized in the West. Certainly it is true that in both the East and West, rationales such as purchasing at a steep discount exist. However, as Western culture gives greater recognition to individually distinct preferences, more weight is likely to be given to an inward analysis that focuses more on the specific needs of the buyer. Moreover, Westerners are more likely to engage in linear analytic thinking in which the various attributes of a product are dissected and evaluated for desirability, as suggested by the finding that the Japanese are less systematic in making multiple-attribute product choices (Chu, Spires, & Sueyoshi, 1999). Such analyses are of course more conducive to a functional analysis of the use value of the proposed purchase. Thus, in the West, we expect greater sensitivity to internal considerations such as the personal use value of a decision outcome. In the East, we expect greater sensitivity to the external guidance provided by other people and deeper consideration of how one's choices might affect relationships to others.

Much basic research needs to be completed in order to validate such hypotheses. Such research promises to be influential, as scholars have identified important workplace behaviors in which external rationales play a role. In proposing the retrospective rational model of behavior, Pfeffer (1997) suggests that businesspeople are often motivated to "maintain their self-identity, to appear to others and themselves to be acting consistently, to make their past decisions appear sensible or turn out well, to avoid the political cost of being discovered as having made a mistake" (p. 67). This motive leads to behaviors to maintain a positive public account, for instance by altering one's expressions regarding preferences. As a result, individuals who endured a very complicated recruitment process are more likely to commit to the organization (Pfeffer, 1997). People who turned down jobs that offered higher salaries are more likely to report high satisfaction and commitment to the job their chose (O'Reilly and Caldwell, 1981). Similarly, in their analysis of situations in which people escalate commitment to failing courses of action, Staw and

Ross (1987) have noted that one causal factor relates to concerns about public image. Managers who have publicly endorsed a project are less likely to terminate it upon receiving unfavorable information about it. Indeed, studies of how Japanese managers react to product failures have found a tendency to persist in investing in weak products. Tse, Lee, Vertinsky, and Wehrung (1988) find that executives in China are more likely to persist with an unprofitable production line than Canadian executives. Chow, Harrison, Linquist, and Wu (1996) use student sample in Taiwan and the US and find the same pattern.

Estimates about the Uncertain

Virtually all management decisions are based on predictions about the future or estimates of details about which one is uncertain. Accuracy in estimation of real-world parameters has been studied in both Asia and the West. One of the most widely utilized experimental paradigms involves asking participants to make estimates of real-world parameters, and at the same time, assess the probability that each estimate is correct. For example, participants may be asked to estimate the ideal temperature for growing potatoes and the probability that their estimate is accurate. Overconfidence within a sample of participants is measured by taking the average probability estimate and comparing it against the percentage of actual answers that are correct. This methodology, when utilized in different cultures, allows for comparisons of the degree of overconfidence (Yates, Zhu, Ronis, Wang, Shinotsuka, & Toda, 1989; Yates, Lee, & Bush, 1997). Such studies have documented a tendency for samples in the East and West to overestimate the likelihood of correct estimation. Such studies have also shown that this overconfidence is more pronounced in Asian samples. This pattern has been found to generalize to even probabilistic predictions of economic indices by professional forecasters in China (Zhang, 1992).

These cultural patterns can be understood within our approach of attending to the use of internal or external rationales in information processing. As compared to Westerners, Asians appear less eager to decompose probability estimates into the individual pieces of knowledge or considerations that comprise them. For instance, in making a probability estimate about an economic indicator, the person might attempt to collect arguments on conflicting sides of an issue (i.e., reasons why the inflation rate will increase, reasons why it will decrease). Yates and colleagues have suggested Asians are less vigilant in mentally recruiting extensive evidence supporting both sides of an issue, and in playing off competing ideas to personally reach a conclusion (Yates, Lee, & Shinotsuka, 1996). Instead, they suggest that Asians are more likely to seek information on matters that are already known or accepted as correct by others.

Emulation is a heavily stressed method of learning in traditional Asian culture. For instance, the Chinese word signifying "to learn" has been traced entomologically to "to imitate" (Nakamura, 1964). Zhang (1992) has proposed that Asians often utilize the decision mode of "precedence matching." It is proposed that when facing a decision, instead of detailed analysis of available information Chinese persons search folk history for a precedent that appears relevant. When a precedent is founded, the decision maker follows it to the exclusion of further processing of decision-specific details. In a culture thick in idioms and references to folk history, past history is relied on by actors and observers to confer validity and legitimacy. As Martin (1992) has documented that work organizations also have folklike stories that are collectively recognized, it seems likely that precedence matching would be robust and specific to each organization.

Despite the stronger tendency for Asians to be overconfident, empirical research has not established that this translates into more risk-seeking behavior (Clifford, Lan, Chou, & Qi, 1989; Wright, Philips, & Wisudha, 1983). Risk preference can be assessed through experiments in which participants are asked to choose between a safe-low payoff choice and risky-high payoff choice. Participants are asked, for example, to give advice to a person deciding between two options. These might include a safe option of a job with a secure but undistinguished future and a risky option of a job with an insecure but potentially prosperous future. Cultural comparisons utilizing such techniques have revealed that Taiwanese participants are actually more risk-averse than American participants (Hong, 1978; Yates & Lee, 1996). This Asian preference for risk aversion in action appears to generalize to academic, medical, and social risks. Weber and Hsee (1998, 1999) do find some evidence that Chinese students are more risk-seeking in financial decisions. They propose a "cushion" hypothesis to explain the results in this particular domain: Chinese persons have a larger and more helpful social network to help and offer security, should a risky financial gamble fail.

The lack of close congruence between overconfidence in estimation and actual risk behavior might also be understood by reference to the strong Asian sensitivity to self-presentation issues. Overconfident assessments serve the social expectations placed on a social actor, but do not lead to misbehavior by intruding into actual behavior. Confucian philosophy extols the virtues of industriousness and hard work as the path to success. Risk seeking behavior, as an alternative path that requires less sacrifice, may be viewed negatively. However, the greater risk seeking behavior in the financial domain may reflect the strong entrepreneurial tradition in Asia. Clearly, more research is needed to further clarify the connection between estimation behavior and risk taking behavior.

The Social Route to Persuasion

Managers often wish to convince others to adjust if not alter their behavior to serve personal goals or business strategy. Consider the case of a group manager in a large conglomerate who would like to persuade a division director in another part of the company to utilize his software programming group. How might the manager convince the division director that she would benefit from his services? One approach might be for the manager to present the director with a report detailing the best features of his software and the expected benefits. The director then has access to extensive information that will hopefully help her accept its desirability. An alternative approach might be for the manager to ask a mutually trusted and respected person to speak to the director on his behalf.

A sizeable literature on the role of guanxi seems instructive on Asian managerial persuasion (see Ting-Toomey, 1994 for an overview). Scholars and practitioners alike have noted the important role played by intermediaries in bridging business relationships. One reason provided for this phenomenon is that the requirement to "give face" to the other party requires an indirect method, in which the latter is not placed in an uncomfortable position. Other reasons focus on the greater credibility perceivers extend to people that are close to themselves. In the West, business people also value the benefits of intermediaries in making introductions when "networking." However, there is a stronger sense that the intermediary is needed only in facilitating the early stages of contact. Afterwards one is expected to approach the other party directly to make a strong case for one's position. In light of this difference in practice, it is natural to wonder about cultural differences in responsiveness to different types of persuasive appeals.

Research in persuasion has focused on how, and to what extent, people process the arguments and details offered to support a position. Several models have been proposed to differentiate influence based upon strength of argument, and that based on other less logic oriented factors. One dual process theory proposes that people engage in systematic, or diligent and thoughtful, processing of evidence when they have the motivation and capacity to do so (Chaiken, 1980). In the absence of motivation and cognitive capacity, people rely on heuristics, or mental shortcuts, in responding to a persuasive appeal. An equally prominent dual process theory is the Elaboration Likelihood Model (Petty & Cacioppo, 1981). This theory proposes two similar routes to persuasion. The central route involves persuading a person through evidence and argument, while the peripheral route entails persuasion through other factors such as source credibility or attractiveness.

These theories are both very well supported empirically, and have much in common. Consider the proposition that the same arguments will have more persuasive effect if delivered by a college professor rather than a prison inmate, or by a lifelong friend rather than an unfamiliar person. In this case, the heuristic processing is based on source credibility. It is also at this same juncture that we expect cross-cultural difference. We propose that Asians will be more likely than Westerners to be influenced by source characteristics.

Source credibility is often premised on factors such as the social rank or affiliation of the person attempting to persuade others. Scholars of culture have long noted that, compared to people in the West, Asians are more highly attuned to hierarchical status and group affiliation of others (see Su, Chiu, Hong, Leung, & Morris, 1998 for a review). The imperative to defer to those of greater hierarchical status is deeply engrained in Asian religions, philosophies, and upbringing. Children are exhorted to imitate role models and not to defy or contradict others of higher rank, a predisposition that carries over to adulthood. Also, we have already proposed that, consistent with their implicit beliefs regarding the agentic influence of groups, Asians will have a stronger expectation that the behaviors of individuals will serve the interests of the groups to which they belong. Thus, the group affiliations of the source are likely to be given much weight in Asia. Statements associated with a competing or untrustworthy group are likely to be interpreted as biased or untrustworthy. In summary, our hypothesis is that compared to people in the West, Asians will be more sensitive to source characteristics such as rank and group affiliation.

Our second hypothesis is that these cultural effects interact with public evaluation. Tetlock (1985; Tetlock & Kim, 1987) has persuasively argued that the sense that others will evaluate our behaviors has a profound impact. He marshals an impressive amount of evidence showing that many types of cognitive biases disappear when individuals believe that they will be accountable for their behaviors. In a sense, it may be said that when individuals feel accountable for their actions, they are more vigilant in applying the rules of behavior that are socially held to be rational and correct. We borrow from this perspective to argue that the presence of observers will have different effects in Asian and Western cultures, as they will lead Asians to adhere more strongly to culturally expected rules of behavior. As the West places stronger emphasis on rational analysis, decision makers will give more weight to argument quality when publicly evaluated. And as respect for status and affiliation is socially expected and enforced in Asia, the felt presence of observers will magnify this motive.

Summary

When processing information and making decisions in the Asian workplace, we have argued that workers will be more sensitive to views or imagined views of others who are closely associated. While much basic research remains to be done, existing scholarship on Asian culture and on cognition suggests the hypothesis that Asians are more likely to incorporate the views of close others in choice behaviors, estimation of probability, and in reacting to persuasion. These hypotheses may be somewhat pessimistic from the Western perspective, suggesting that Asian employees may be less willing to engage in rigorous individualized analysis. However, the willingness to be influenced by close others may serve to improve group coordination in the Asian workplace, a possibility we will examine in the next section.

PROCESSING AS A GROUP

In our final section, we consider the workplace as an arena in which individuals interact and mutually influence each other simultaneously. We focus specifically on the impact of organizing as a group on how people process information. As a central difference between Asian and Western cognition concerns one's relationship to the group, we expect cross-cultural differences to be robust. Our exposition will show that group processing in Asia promises important benefits, as well as shortcomings.

Decision-Making as a Group

Consistent with the assumption held by Asians that groups are agentic entities, groups in Asia actually do make decisions that are often left to individuals in Western countries. For instance, in Japanese firms, the *ringi* system specifically confers decision powers to groups rather than individuals. Research on the psychology of work indicates that when Asians are asked to make decisions as individuals, they experience greater decision stress, have a greater tendency to avoid decisional conflict, and have lower confidence and esteem. When asked to individually make a decision for their group, Asians are more likely to engage in behaviors such as avoidance, procrastination, and even panic (Lee, 2000; Mann, Radford, Burnett, Ford, Bond, Leung, Nakamura, Vaughan, & Yang, 1998; Radford, Mann, Ohta, & Nakane, 1993).

In Asia, the organization of work activities around groups appears to have produced many beneficial consequences. The much-hailed concept of Total Quality Management (TQM), a manufacturing approach that emphasizes the involvement of all employees and all departments in decision making, has its origins in the Japanese tradition of inclusive group decision making. Operating through organizational structures such as quality circles in which employees attempt to solve problems of strategic importance, TQM has been credited for important improvements in product quality (Powell, 1995). In contrast to the US, where strategic decision-making is concentrated among top executives, in

Japan, lower level managers contribute actively to corporate level decisions. Thus while employees in typical leading US companies produce on average 2 suggestions for improvement per year, employees at leading Japanese companies produce between 38 and 833 suggestions. It has been argued that the group approach taken by Japanese industry helps to explain their success in formulation and implementation of incremental strategies.

Research has specifically addressed the issue of whether controlled experiments can demonstrate performance improvements as a result of organization by group. Earley (1993) examined performance in in-basket tasks as a function of culture and group structure. His results indicate that for Asians, performance is indeed better when working with one's close associates. For Asians, performance when working in ingroups is higher than that in outgroup and individual contexts. For Westerners, performance is highest in when working alone than in either of the two group contexts. A similar set of findings is provided by Harris and Nibler (1998), who asked groups of Chinese and American students to perform the "Lost at Sea" exercise, a group-consensus decision-making task. The results show that Chinese ingroups were more effective than outgroups, while American outgroups were more effective than ingroups.

These results indicate that for Asians, performance depends not only on being placed jointly with others to fulfill a function. To gain functional benefits, the quality of the social relationship between group members is critical. Earley suggests that such cognitive benefits are tied to motivation of the individuals in the group. When collectivists identify with the group they are in, they are more likely to place group goals ahead of individual interests and plans. "They view their individual actions as an important contribution to their group's well-being and they gain satisfaction and a feeling of accomplishment from their group outcomes" (p. 341). Not surprisingly, much deliberate care is taken in Asian organizations to emphasize common membership and to reinforce group cohesion. For instance, large numbers of Asian firms create company anthems and flags. In rituals designed to foster strong firm identity, many even conduct a daily ritual in which employees collect in a company square and sing the company anthem as the company flag is raised.

Integration and Different Perspectives

In some endeavors, the amount of information processing that is required is too voluminous or complex to be handled by one person alone. Organizations exist so that several people can work jointly to solve problems. Certain models of innovation give a central role to conflict and competition. For instance, many models suggest that several theories or ideas should be compared against each other so that the best idea can be distinguished from the rest. Kuhn's (1970) theory of paradigm shift focuses centrally on the accumulation of contradictions that set the background for a new revolutionary thought system. Other theories of innovation suggest that new ideas are found through conflicts in which decision makers reject stale old ways of doing things (Gray & Starke, 1984; Baron, 1991). Theorists have also suggested that for innovation to occur, groups should seek to encourage cross-fertilization of ideas. A novel reformulation of the perspectives held by different individuals can bring new insights to the problem at hand (Galbraith, 1982; Sutton & Hargadon, 1996). These models jointly suggest that innovation and progress require conflict and clear communication of differences of perspective.

In the Western tradition, philosophical beliefs such as the three laws of Aristotelian logic suggest that one consistent truth can be found, principally by forcing to surface the contradictions posed by untrue beliefs. In the East, a different imperative to strive for harmony is embedded in epistemology that for instance calls for unity between heaven and man and harmony of the five basic elements. According to Asian philosophies such as Taoism, ultimate wisdom is attained not through conflict, but through simultaneous coexistence of opposing perspectives. The icon of yin and yang is an expression of the belief that opposites depend on each other. A similar cross-cultural division exists with respect to how individuals should interact with others. In the Western tradition, a righteous person must uphold the truth without compromise in the face of the false opinions held by others. In contrast, Chinese epistemology presupposes that truths are inherently in constant contradiction. A righteous person attempts to understand the multiple truths that pervade circumstances and searches for compromise.

Peng (1997) illustrates this difference by asking US and Mainland-Chinese participants to analyze two social contradictions (a mother–daughter value conflict and a conflict between having fun and going to school). The responses of most of the American participants was uncompromising, blaming one side for causing the problem and demanding acquiescence from it. In contrast, Chinese participants were more likely to assign blame to both sides and to recommend mutual concessions. This epistemological difference seems to translate into in a preference for compromise in choice situations. Briley, Morris, and Simonson (2000) presented participants with a choice of three product options which vary on two attribute dimensions: the first option was strong on attribute A and weak on attribute B; the second option was strong on attribute B and weak on attribute A; and the third option was moderate on both attributes. The results in a large number of decisions reveal that Asians have a greater tendency to choose the compromise option.

In the work context, Asian manager have a stronger tendency to seek perspectives that favor compromise, for instance preferring equality-oriented outcomes when resolving conflicts (Leung, 1997; Tinsley & Pillutla, 1998).

Asians also seem less eager to directly engage others in conflicts. In an analysis of conflict resolution preferences, Leung and Lind (Leung & Lind, 1986; Leung, 1987) found that compared to the Americans, Chinese were less likely to seek adversarial arrangements. Chinese managers have a greater preference for avoidant conflict styles (Morris, Williams, Leung, Larrick, Mendoza, Bhatnagar, Li, Kondo, Luo, & Hu, 1998), whereas US managers are more likely to choose a competing style.

Whereas Western organizations may have a propensity to seek well-defined resolutions to troubling issues, Asian organizations seem more willing to formally tolerate ambiguity. Western organizations are often known for having written rules on hiring practices, division of responsibilities, and even value statements; even if it is unclear that such rules are followed. Asian organizations are marked for their relative absence of formal rules.

Asian workplaces also appear to be unlikely places for clear or sharp communication of differences. To begin, subordinates often find it difficult to express ideas that might contradict those of more senior co-workers, as it would violate hierarchical standing and embarrass the latter. Similarly, coworkers of the same level may avoid disagreement for fear of embarrassing each other in the presence of a superior. Thus, to avoid confrontation and conflict, it is not surprising that Asians often appear to be less willing to express their true beliefs (Ohbuchi and Takahashi, 1994).

Indeed, it appears that Asians may have few expectations that others are communicating their true opinions or intentions. Inexperienced observers of Chinese business often express amazement at how some managers routinely engage in behavior that contradict previously expressed attitudes and behaviors. Asians, on the other hand, express little surprise when an official, who is renowned as utterly ruthless and corrupted, makes a string of passionate speeches condemning corruption. There is even a common slang to describe such behavior ("He speaks on the stage, everyone else talks about him offstage"). Foreign managers in China often perceive their employees to "say one thing, believe a second, and do a third." Consistent with these observations, psychologists have found less evidence in Asia of the Western need to maintain consistency between behavior and beliefs.[1] In a workgroup, this tendency to alter one's statements to maintain harmony across situations may be less likely to yield a diverse and direct exchange of opinions.

This discussion suggests that social processing of information in Asia could potentially be inhibited by a lack of willingness to engage in critical conflict and to clearly express differences. Without effective conflict resolution measures, it may be the case that conflict in Asia has a more deleterious impact on the ability of a group to work together (Xie, Song, & Stringfellow, 1998). However, these conclusions are in large part based on Western theories of innovation and progress. Little if any research has directly studied the psychology of innovation from a cross-cultural perspective.

Decision-Making Syndromes

In the West, investigators of decision-making have noted the tendency for groups to reach more extreme decisions than individuals acting alone (Myers & Lamm, 1976). Many mechanisms have been proposed to explain this polarization, including diffusion of responsibility, and the emergence of "thought" guardians. One particularly important mechanism focuses on the pressure to maintain group conformity, which causes individuals to avoid statements that might contradict the group. However, each person's hesitation in expressing dissent can be taken as a sign by others of agreement with the decision, further increasing the pressure on others not to object. In summarizing this body of research, Gilbert, Fiske, and Gardner (1998) note that groups tend to make decisions that are either more cautious or risky than those of individuals. The direction of this shift is a function of the group members' initial position. While the group polarization effect is not necessarily a bias, it is a significant shift in outcome with potentially important repercussions.

In light of the importance of group conformity and self-presentation as mechanisms for this phenomenon, a natural hypothesis is that group polarization will be more extreme in Asia, where people place more emphasis on group harmony and on social approval. Saha and Ghosh (1999) asked subjects from India and Bangladesh to make group decisions on risk-taking items. They find that more group-oriented subjects showed more group polarization and took riskier consensual decisions as compared to self-oriented subjects. Hong (1978) finds that when Chinese participants are required to produce consensus risk-taking advice in groups, they display a "cautious shift" and are more risk-aversive than when they arrive at their advice alone.

Summary

The precise relationship between group setting and task performance is of course complicated, as it is likely to depend on the types of task being performed and the distribution of skills in the group. The current literature indicates that Asians process information most effectively in groups, and there are many instances particularly of Japanese firms that have operated effectively by emphasizing the group approach. However, there are also potential weaknesses in the Asian workgroup. Further research is necessary to explore the tradeoff between the negative consequences of suppression of differences and the positive consequences of inclusion and harmonizing with close others. One possibility is that Asian ingroups follow certain behavioral patterns that create a safe context for subtle expression and incorporation of information about differences.

DISCUSSION

Managerial social cognition is rooted in the values emphasized by culture. The Asian thinking style attends diligently to interrelationships within a situation, rather than to entities in isolation. In the social context of work, a defining feature of Asian cognition is the implicit imperative to keep others in mind. Asians are more likely to view each person as connected to and similar to others in his or her group. At work, this translates into performance evaluations that make less detailed distinctions across individuals and a tendency to attribute the causes of people's behavior to their group memberships. In making decisions, Asians favor external rationales that provide a favorable public account of their choices and are more open to the influence of others closely associated to them. Finally, Asians not only prefer groups, they tend to perform better in them. However, their willingness to accommodate others in order to preserve harmony may impede the honest exchange of differences of opinion, an important ingredient in innovation and change. Altogether, these propositions suggest that social cognition in the Asian workplace both reflects and supports cultural values.

While many managers and cross-culture researchers will consider cultural practices to be the outcome of different value orientations, a cognitive approach provides a different perspective that adds in yielding a richer understanding. For instance, the tendency for Asians to self deprecate when evaluating their own performance can be interpreted by outsiders as behaviors that satisfy the desire to be modest or polite. Social cognition research, by examining the way in which people gather, encode, and process information, provides a different understanding. This approach suggests that the collectivist concept of the self – which views the self as intimately interdependent on close others and closely connected to the group – leads Asians to actually perceive less difference between their own performance and those of others in the group. The cognitive approach provides a different set of mechanisms to explain behavior. Social cognition research has helped us to understand that the mechanism responsible for self deprecating appraisals also leads Asians to confer credit or fault for individual behaviors to the group.

The need for further research is evident. Much work remains to be done in exploring the manner in which Asians rely on external rationales when making decisions. Foremost, basic research is necessary to better identify the types of internal and external rationales that might be accessed by a decision maker, and to demonstrate cultural differences. The current scholarship paints a pessimistic view of external rationales, as factors that cause individuals to neglect rational analysis of functional value. However, external rationales can also be beneficial since they may convey the collective wisdom that has resulted from the trials and errors of many people. Another promising area of research relates to the way in which Asian firms deliberately control and communicate external

rationales. Weick (1979, 1995) has argued that organizations function as entities that coordinate the cognitive processes of their members. An interesting
question is whether greater reliance on external rationales provides a positive
benefit to Asian businesses by coordinating the activities of their employees.
For instance, it may be that certain explicit external rationales help Japanese
quality circles to elicit contributions from employees to further the common
goal of increasing productivity. One interesting question is whether the skill
and manner in which Asian firms control external rationales can be linked to
their ability to collectively learn or innovate.

Another intriguing issue is the precise nature of estimation and risk taking in
business. The existing literature indicates that Asians are more likely to make
overconfident probability estimates and to take risks in financial matters, suggesting the possibility that Asian businesses would be run in a more aggressive
manner. Yet, no clear evidence has surfaced to prove definitively that Asian
business concerns are more reckless or innovative than those of the West. Indeed, many examples provided by large successful business concerns in Korea,
Japan, and China seem to portray a story about success through government
intervention or control. Thus, a clearer explanation of the exact relationship
between estimation and actual risk taking behavior is needed. The identification of factors that translate confidence into risk taking would certainly help in
understanding and predicting the behaviors of Asian firms. One factor that will
likely receive examination in research on business risk taking is the influence
of group decision making, and its consequences for risky shift or cautious shift
behavior.

An exciting direction for future research is intracultural social cognition. As
the business world becomes more international, more and more business units
have simultaneously individuals from different cultures. Often times, these individuals are themselves multi-cultural in that they have extensive experience
with different cultures. Scholars have found that differences in the environmental context can lead individuals to exhibit cognitive patterns that correspond to
different nationalities. By priming bicultural Hong Kong Chinese subjects with
culturally laden symbols of the East and West, Hong and her colleagues have
successfully elicited culturally corresponding cognitive patterns (Hong, Chiu,
& Kung, 1997; Hong, Morris, Chiu, & Benet-Matinez, 2000). Hence, they
have called for shift from the examination of cross-cultural differences to that
of cross situation differences (Hong & Chiu, 2001). The possibility exists that
in the multinational firm of the future, different cultural symbols might be invoked in order to elicit cognitive patterns that are functionally desired. Perhaps,
an organizational division that requires revolutionary discontinuous changes
might invoke Western symbols, while in the same firm, another division that
requires collaboration from all employees might invoke Asian symbols.

Finally, we explicitly acknowledge the need for caution in presenting results
from different countries as representative of "Asia." Asia comprises a wide ge-

ographical span with many different countries and cultures. In this chapter, we aggregated many countries into the rubric of Asia because the empirical research is not sufficiently expansive to allow a more fine-grained analysis. The likelihood is that this aggregation has led to overgeneralization of certain conclusions. Scholars such as Lie (1990) have noted that the management style is very different even in cultures that are geographically proximate, such as Japan and South Korea. Similarly, the basic texture of collectivism differs in China and Japan, two countries with many historical and cultural ties (White, 2002). We look to future research to helps us arrive at a more nuanced understanding of managerial cognition.

NOTE

1. For instance, researchers have had difficulty inducing cognitive dissonance when replicating forced compliance experiments (Festinger & Carlsmith, 1959) to Chinese (Hiniker, 1969) and Korean (Choi, Choi, & Cha, 1992) participants.

REFERENCES

Agarwal, S. 1993. Influence of formalization on role stress, organizational commitment, and work alienation of salespersons: a cross-national comparative study. *Journal of International Business Studies*, 24: 715-739.

Au, T.K. 1983. Chinese and English counterfactuals: The Sapir-Whorf hypothesis revisited. *Cognition*, 15: 162-163.

Bailey, J.R., Chen, C.C. and Dou, S.G. 1997. Conceptions of self and performance-related feedback in the U.S., Japan and China. *Journal of International Business Studies*, 28: 605-625.

Bandura, A. 1986. *Social Foundations of Thought and Action: A Social Cognitive Theory*. Englewood Cliffs, NJ: Prentice Hall.

Bandura, A. 1997. *Self-efficacy: The Exercise of Control*. New York: WH Freeman.

Baron, R.A. 1991. Positive effects of conflicts. *Employee Responsibility and Rights Journal*, 4: 281-296.

Berry, J.W. 1991. Cultural variations in field dependence–independence. In S. Wapner and J. Demick (eds.), *Field Dependence–independence: Cognitive Style Across the Life Span* (pp. 289-308). Hillsdale, NJ: Lawrence Erlbaum.

Bloom, A. 1984. Caution – the words you use may affect what you say: A response to Au. *Cognition*, 17: 281.

Bond, M.H. 1986. *The Psychology of Chinese People*. New York: Oxford University Press.

Bond, M.H. and Cheung, T.-S. 1983. College students' spontaneous self-concept: The effect of culture among respondents in Hong Kong, Japan, and the United States. *Journal of Cross-Cultural Psychology*, 14: 153-171.

Briley, D.A., Morris, M.W. and Simonson, I. 2000. Reasons as carriers of culture: Dynamic versus dispositional models of cultural influence on decision making, *Journal of Consumer Research*, 27: 157-178.

Chaiken, S. 1980. Heuristic versus systematic information processing and the use of source versus message cues in persuasion. *Journal of Personality and Social Psychology*, 37: 1387-1397.

Chiu, L.-H. 1972. A cross-cultural comparison of cognitive styles in Chinese and American children. *International Journal of Psychology*, 8: 235-242.

Chiu, C. and Hong, Y. 1992. The effects of intentionality and validation on individual and collective responsibility attribution among Hong Kong Chinese. *Journal of Psychology*, 126: 291-300.

Choi, I., Choi, K.W. and Cha, J.-H. 1992. A cross-cultural replication of Festinger and Calsmith, 1959. Unpublished Manuscript, Seoul National University, Seoul, Korea.

Choi, I., Nisbett, R.E. and Norenzayan, A. 1999. Causal attribution across cultures: variation and universality. *Psychological Bulletin*, 125: 47-63.

Chow, C.W., Harrison, P. Linquist, T. and Wu, A. 1996. Escalation commitment to unprofitable projects: Replication and cross-cultural extension. In *Proceedings: American Accounting Association Annual Meeting*. Chicago.

Chu, P.C., Spires, E.E. and Sueyoshi, T. 1999. Cross-cultural differences in choice behavior and use of decision aids: A comparison of Japan and the United States. *Organizational Behavior and Human Decision Process*, 77: 147-170.

Cleveland, J.N., Murphy, K.R. and Williams, K.J. 1989. Multiple uses of performance appraisal: Prevalence and correlate. *Journal of Applied Psychology*, 74: 130-135.

Clifford, M.M., Lan, W.Y., Chou, F.C. and Qi, Y. 1989. Academic risk-taking: Developmental and cross-cultural observations. *Journal of Experimental Education*, 7: 321-38.

Cousins, S.D. 1989. Culture and self-perception in Japan and the U.S. *Journal of Personality and Social Psychology*, 56: 124-131.

Crittenden, K.S. 1996. Causal attribution process among the Chinese. In M.H. Bond (ed.), *The Handbook of Chinese Psychology* (pp. 112-148). Hong Kong: Oxford University Press.

Deci, E.L. 1975. *Intrinsic Motivation*. New York: Plenum Press.

DeNisi, A.S. and Williams, K.J. 1988. Cognitive approaches to performance appraisal. In G. Ferris and K. Rowland (eds.), *Research in Personnel and Human Resources Management*, 6: 109-155.

Dweck, C.S., Hong, Y.-Y. and Chiu, C.-Y. 1993. Implicit theories: Individual differences in the likelihood and meaning of dispositional inference. *Personality and Social Psychology Bulletin*, 19: 644-656.

Earley, P.C. 1993. East meets West meets Mideast: Further explorations of collectivistic and individualistic work groups. *Academy of Management Journal*, 36: 319-348.

Earley, P.C. 1994. Self or group? Cultural effects of training on self-efficacy and performance. *Administrative Science Quarterly*, 39: 89-117.

Earley, P.C. 1999. Playing follow the leader: Status-determining traits in relation to collective efficacy across cultures. *Organizational Behavior & Human Decision Processes*, 80: 192-212.

Farh, J.L., Dobbins, G.H. and Cheng, B.S. 1991. Cultural relativity in action: A comparison of self-rating made by Chinese and U.S. workers. *Personnel Psychology*, 44: 129-147.

Farh, J.L., Tsui, A.S. and Xin, K. The influence of relational demography and Guanxi: The Chinese case. *Organizational Science*, 9: 471-488.

Festinger, L. and Carlsmith, J.M. 1959. Cognitive consequences of forced compliance. *Journal of Abnormal and Social Psychology*, 58: 203-211.

Galbraith, J.R. 1982. Designing the innovative organization. *Organizational Dynamics*, Winter: 3-24.

Gilbert, D.T., Fiske, S.T. and Gardner, L. *The Handbook of Social Psychology*. New York: McGraw-Hill.

Gilbert, D.T. and Malone, P.S. 1995. The correspondence bias. *Psychological Bulletin*, 117: 21-38.

Gray, J.L. and Starke, F.A. 1984. *Organizational Behavior*. Columbus, OH: Charles E. Merrill.

Harris, K.L. and Nibler, R. 1998. Decision making by Chinese and U.S. students. *Journal of Social Psychology*, 138: 102-114.

Hiniker, P.J. 1969. Chinese reaction to forced compliance: Dissonance reduction or national character? *Journal of Social Psychology*, 77: 157-176.

Hong, Y. and Chiu, C. 2001. Toward a paradigm shift: From cross-cultural differences in social cognition to social-cognitive mediation of cultural differences. *Social Cognition*, 19: 181-196.

Hong, Y., Chiu, C. and Kung, M. 1997. Bring culture out in front: Effects of cultural meaning system activation on social cognition. In K. Leung, U. Kim, S. Yamaguchi and Y. Kashima (eds.), *Progress in Asian Social Psychology* (Vol. 1, pp. 139-150). Singapore: Wiley.

Hong, Y., Morris, M.W., Chiu, C. and Benet-Matinez, V. 2000. Multicultural minds: A dynamic constructivistic approach to culture and cognition. *American Psychologist*, 55: 709-720.

Hong, L.K. 1978. Risky shift and cautious shift: Some direct evidence on the culture-value theory. *Social Psychology*, 41: 342-346.

Hsee, C.K. 1999. Value-seeking and prediction-decision inconsistency. *Psychonomic Bulletin and Review*, 6: 555-561.

Hsu, F.L.K. 1953. *American and Chinese: Two ways of life*. New York: Schuman.

Ilgen, D.R., Fisher, C.D. and Tylor, M.S. 1979. Consequences of individual feedback on behavior in organization. *Journal of Applied Psychology*, 64: 349-371.

Kahneman, D. and Tversky, A. (eds.) 2000. *Choices, Values and Frames*. Cambridge, England: Cambridge University Press.

Kanungo, R. and Wright, R.W. 1983. A cross-culture comparative study of managerial job attitudes. *Journal of International Business Studies*, 14: 115-129.

Kashima Y. and Triandis, H.C. 1986. The self-serving bias in attribution as coping strategy: A cross-cultural study. *Journal of Cross-Cultural Psychology*, 17: 83-98.

Kim, U. 1994. Introduction. In U. Kim, H.C. Triandis, C. Kagitcibasi, S.-C. Choi and G. Yoon (eds.), *Individualism and Collectivism: Theory, Method and Applications*. Newbury Park, CA: Sage.

Kiyatama, S. 1993. Culture, self and emotion: The nature and functions of "good needs/feelings" in Japan and the United States. Lecture at East-West Center, Honolulu, Hawaii, Oct. 21.

Kuhn, T. 1970. *The Structure of Scientific Revolutions*. Chicago, IL: University of Chicago.

Kuhnen, U., Hannover, B. and Schubert, B. 2001. The semantic-procedural interface model of the self: the role of sex-knowledge for context-dependent versus context independent modes of thinking. *Journal of Personality and Social Psychology*, 80: 397-409.

Lee, J.-Y. 2000. A cross-cultural investigation of college students' environmental decision-making behavior: Interactions among culture, environmental, decisional, and personal factors. Doctoral Dissertation, Ohio State University.

Lepper, M.R. and Greene, D. (eds.) 1978. *The Hidden Cost of Reward*. Hillsdale, NJ: Erlbaum.

Leung, K. 1987. Some determinants of reactions to procedural models for conflict resolution: A cross-national study. *Journal of Personality and Social Psychology*, 53: 898-908.

Leung, K. 1997. Negotiation and reward allocation across cultures. In P.C. Earley and M. Erez (eds.), *New Perspectives on I/O Psychology* (pp. 640-675). San Francisco, CA: Jossey-Bass.

Leung, K. and Lind, E.A. 1986. Procedural justice and culture: Effects of culture, gender and investigator status on procedural preferences. *Journal of Personality and Social Psychology*, 50: 1134-1140.

Leung, K., Su, S.K. and Morris, M. 2001. When is criticism not constructive? The roles of fairness perception and attribution in employee perceptions of critical supervisory feedback. *Human Relations*, 54: 1155-1188.

Lie, J. 1990. Is Korean management just like Japanese management? *Management International Review*, 30: 113-119.

Lincoln, J.R. and McBride, K. 1987. Japanese industrial organization in comparative perspective. *Annual Review of Sociology*, 13: 289-312.

Mann, L., Radford, M., Burnett, P., Ford, S., Bond, M., Leung, K., Nakamura, H., Vaughan, G. and Yang, K.-S. 1998. Cross-cultural differences in self-reported decision-making style and confidence. *International Journal of Psychology*, 33: 325-335.

Markus, H.R. and Kitayama, S. 1991a. Culture and the self: Implications for cognition, emotion, and motivation. *Psychological Review*, 98: 224-253.

Markus, H.R. and Kitayama, S. 1991b. Culture variation in the self-concept. In J. Strauss and G.R. Goethal (eds.), *The Self: Interdisciplinary Approaches* (pp. 18-48). New York: Springer-Verlag.

Markus, H.R., Kitayama, S. and Heiman, R.J. 1997. Culture and 'basic' psychological principles. In E.T. Higgins and A.W. Krulanski (eds.), *Social Psychology: Handbook of Basic Principles* (Vol. 4, pp. 857-913). New York: Guiford.

Martin, J. 1992. *Cultures in organizations: Three perspectives*. London: Oxford University Press.

McEvoy, G. and Cascio, W. 1990. The United States and Taiwan: Two different cultures look at performance appraisal. In B. Shaw and J. Beck (eds.), *International Human Resources Management*, Research in Personnel and Human Resource Management Series, Supplement Two, Greenwich, Co: JAI Press.

Menon, T., Morris, M.W., Chiu, C.-Y. and Hong, Y.-Y. 1999. Culture and construal of agency: attribution to individual versus group dispositions. *Journal of Personality and Social Psychology*, 76: 701-717.

Miller, J.G. 1984. Culture and the development of everyday social explanation. *Journal of Personality and Social Psychology*, 46: 961-978.

Money, R.B. and Graham, J.L. 1999. Salesperson performance, pay, and job satisfaction: Tests of model using data collected in the United Stated and Japan. *Journal of International Business Studies*, Winter: 149-172.

Morris, M.W. and Peng, K. 1994. Culture and cause: American and Chinese attributions for social and physical events. *Journal of Personality and Social Psychology*, 67: 949-971.

Morris, M.W., Williams, K.Y., Leung, K., Larrick, R., Mendoza, M.T., Bhatnagar, D., Li, J., Kondo, M., Luo, J. and Hu, J. 1998. Conflict management style: Accounting cross-national differences. *Journal of International Business Studies*, Winter: 729-748.

Myers, D.G. and Lamm, H. 1976. The group polarization phenomenon. *Psychological Bulletin*, 83: 602-627.

Nakamura, H. 1964. *Ways of thinking of Eastern people: India, China, Tibet and Japan*. Honolulu, HI: East-West Center Press.

Needham, J. 1962. *Science and Civilization in China* (Vol. 4) Physics and physical technology. Cambridge, England: Cambridge University Press.

Nishisda, T. 1985. *A Study of The History of Chinese Criminal Laws*. Beijing: Peking University Press.

Norenzayan, A., Choi, I. and Nisbett, R.E. 1998. *Eastern and Western Folk Psychology and the Prediction of Behaviors*. Manuscript submitted for publication.

Ohbuchi, K. and Takahashi, Y. 1994. Cultural styles of conflict management in Japanese and Americans: Passivity, covertness and effectiveness of strategies. *Journal of Applied Social Psychology*, 24: 1345-1366.

O'Reilly, C.A. and Caldwell, D.F. 1981. The commitment and job tenure of new employees: Some evidence of post decisional justification. *Administrative Science Quarterly*, 39: 603-627.

Peng, K. 1997. Naïve dialecticism and its effects on reasoning and judgement about contradiction. Doctoral Dissertation, University of Michigan.

Petty, R.E. and Cacioppo, J.T. 1981. *Attitudes and Persuasion: Classic and Contemporary Approaches.* Dubuque, IA: Wm. C. Brown.

Pfeffer, J. 1997. *New Directions for Organization Theory: Problem and Prospects.* New York: Oxford University Press.

Philipe, L.D. and Wright, G.N. 1977. Culture differences in viewing uncertainty and assessing probabilities. In H. Jungermann and G. de Zeeuw (eds.), *Decision Making and Change in Human Affairs* (pp. 507-519). Dordrecht, Netherlands: Reidel.

Powell, T.C. 1995. Total quality management as competitive advantage: A review and empirical study. *Strategic Management Journal,* 16: 15-37.

Radford, M.H., Mann, L., Ohta, Y. and Nakane, Y. 1993. Difference between Australian and Japanese students in decisional self-esteem, decisional stress, and coping styles. *Journal of Cross-Cultural Psychology,* 24: 284-297.

Reischauer, E.O. 1977. *The Japanese.* Tokyo: Tuttle.

Reykowski, J. 1994. Collectivism and individualism as dimensions of social change. In U. Kim, H.C. Triandis, C. Kagitcibasi, S.-C. Choi and G. Yoon (eds.), *Individualism and Collectivism: Theory, Method and Applications.* Newbury Park, CA: Sage.

Ross, L. 1977. The intuitive scientist and his shortcomings. In L. Berkowitz (ed.), *Advances in Experimental Social Psychology* (Vol. 10, pp. 174-220). New York: Academic Press.

Ross, L. and Nisbett, R.E. 1991. *The Person and the Situation: Perspectives of Social Psychology.* New York: McGraw-Hill.

Saha, A. and Ghosh, E.S.K. 1999. *Individualism-collectivism Revisited: Some Consequences for Group Decision-making.* Paper presented on the Fourteenth International Congress of the International Association for Cross-cultural psychology.

Schuler, R.S. and Rogovsky 1998. Understanding compensation practice variations across firms: the impact of national culture. *Journal of International Business,* Spring: 159-177.

Seligman, M.E. 1975. *Helplessness: On Depression, Development, and Death.* Oxford, England: W.H. Freeman.

Shafir, E., Simonson, I. and Tversky, A. 1993. Reason-based choice. *Cognition,* 49: 11-36.

Shipper, F. and Manz, C.C. 1992. Employee self-management without formally designated teams: An alternative road to empowerment. *Organizational Dynamics,* 20: 48-61.

Shweder, R.A. and Bourne, E.J. 1984. Does the concept of person vary cross-culturally? In R.A. Shweder and R.A. LeVine (eds.), *Cultural Theory: Essay on Mind, Self, and Emotion* (pp. 158-199). Cambridge, England: Cambridge University Press.

Skinner, B.F. 1963. Operant behaviour. *American Psychologist,* 18: 503-515.

Staw, B.M. and Ross J. 1987. Behavior in escalation situations: Antecedents, prototypes, and solutions. *Research in Organizational Behavior,* 9: 39-78.

Stigler, J.W., Smith, S. and Mao, L. 1985. The self-perception of competence by Chinese children. *Child Development,* 56: 1259-1270.

Su, S.K., Chiu, C., Hong, Y., Leung, K., Peng, K. and Morris, M.W. 1999. Self-organization and social organization: American and Chinese construction. In T.R. Tyler and R.M. Kramer (eds.), *The Psychology of the Social Self* (pp. 193-222). Mahwah, NJ: Erlbaum.

Sutton, R.I. and Hargadon, A. 1996. Brainstorming groups in context: Effectiveness in a product design firm. *Administrative Science Quarterly,* 41: 685-718.

Tetlock, P.E. 1985. Accountability: A social check on the fundamental attribution error. *Social Psychology Quarterly,* 48: 227-236.

Tetlock, P.E. and Kim, J.J. 1987. Accountability and judgment process in the personality prediction task. *Journal of Personality and Social Psychology,* 52: 700-709.

Thaler, R.H. 1985. Mental accounting and consumer choice. *Marketing Science,* 4: 19-214.

Thaler, R.H. 2000. Mental accounting matters. In D. Kahneman and A. Tversky (eds.), *Choices, Values and Frames*. Cambridge, England: Cambridge University Press.

Ting-Toomey, S. 1988. Intercultural conflict styles: A face-negotiation theory. In Y.Y. Kim and W.B. Gudykunst (eds.), *Theories in Intercultural Communication* (pp. 213-233). Newbury Park, CA: Sage.

Ting-Toomey, S. 1994. *The Challenge of Facework: Cross-cultural and Interpersonal Issues*. New York: SUNY Press.

Tinsley, C.H. and Pillutla, M.M. 1998. Negotiation in the U.S. and Hong Kong. *Journal of International Business Studies*, 29: 711-725.

Torrance, E.P. 1980. Lessons about giftedness and creativity from a nation of 115 million achievers. *Gifted Child Quarterly*, 24: 145-151.

Triandis, H.C. 1995. *Individualism and Collectivism*. Boulder, CO: Westview Press.

Tse, D.K., Lee, K., Vertinsky, I. and Wehrung, D. 1988. Does culture matters? A cross-cultural study of executives' choice, decisiveness and risk adjustment in international marketing. *Journal of Marketing*, 52: 81-95.

Turner, S.M. and Mo, L. 1984. Chinese adolescents' self-concepts as measured by the offer self-image questionnaire. *Journal of Youth and Adolescence*, 13: 131-43.

Vallance, S. 1999. Performance appraisal in Singapore, Thailand and the Philippines: A cultural perspective. *Australian Journal of Public Administration*, 58: 78-85.

Watkins, D. and Dong, Q. 1994. Accessing the self-esteem of Chinese school children. *Educational Psychology*, 14: 129-37.

Weber, E.U. and Hsee, C.K. 1998. Cross-cultural differences in risk perception but cross-cultural similarities in attitudes towards risk. *Management Science*, 44: 1205-1217.

Weber, E.U. and Hsee, C.K. 1999. Models and mosaics: Investigation of cultural differences in risk perception and risk preference. *Psychonomic Bulletin and Review*, 6: 611-617.

Weber, E.U. and Hsee, C.K. 2000. Culture and individual judgment and decision-making. *Applied Psychology: An International Review*, 49: 32-61.

Weick, K.E. 1979. *The Social Psychology of Organization*. Reading, MA: Addison-Wesley.

Weick, K.E. 1995. *Sense Making in Organizations*. Thousands Oaks, CA: Sage.

White, S. 2002. *Organizational and Network Collectivism*, unpublished manuscript, INSEAD.

Wilkinson, A. 1998. Empowerment: Theory and practice. *Personnel Review*, 27(1): 40-56.

Wilson, T., Dunn, D., Kraft, D. and Lisle, D. 1989. Introspection, attitude change, and attitude-behavior consistency: The disruptive effects of explaining why we feel the way we do. In L. Berkowitz (ed.), *Advances in Experimental Social Psychology* (Vol. 19, pp. 123-205). Orlando, FL: Academic Press.

Winter, L. and Uleman, J.S. 1984. When are social judgement made? Evidence for spontaneousness of trait inferences. *Journal of Personality and Social Psychology*, 47: 237-252.

Witkin, H.A., Dyk, R.B., Fattuson, H.F., Goodenough, D.R. and Karp, S.A. 1962. *Psychological Differentiation: Studies of Development*. New York: Wiley.

Witkin, H.A. and Berry, J. 1975. Psychological differentiation in cross-cultural perspective. *Journal of Cross-Cultural Psychology*, 6: 4-87.

Wright, G.N., Philips, L.D. and Wisudha, A. 1983. Cultural variation in probabilistic thinking: Alternative ways of dealing with uncertainty. *International Journal of Psychology*, 15: 239-57.

Xie, J., Song, X.M. and Stringfellow, A. 1998. Interfunctional conflict, conflict resolution style, and new product success: A four-culture comparison. *Management Science*, 44: 192-206.

Yates, J.F., Lee, J.W. and Bush, J.G. 1997. General knowledge overconfidence: Cross-national variation. *Organizational Behavior and Human Decision Processes*, 70: 87-94.

Yates, J.F. and Lee, J.W. 1996. Chinese decision making. In M.H. Bond (ed.), *Handbook of Chinese Psychology* (pp. 338-351). Hong Kong: Oxford University Press.

Yates, J.F., Lee, J.W. and Shinotsuka, H. 1996. Beliefs about overconfidence, including its cross-national variation. *Organizational Behavior and Human Decision Process*, 70: 138-147.

Yates, J.F., Zhu, Y., Ronis, D.L., Wang, D.F., Shinotsuka, H. and Toda, W. 1989. Probability judgement accuracy: China, Japan, and the United States. *Organizational Behavior and Human Decision Processes*, 43: 147-171.

Zhang, B. 1992. Culture conditioning in decision making: A prospect of probabilistic thinking. Unpublished Ph.D. dissertation, Department of Information Systems, London School of Economics.

Zhang, J. 1984. Exploratory investigations on the characteristics of the judicial system in feudal China. *Theses of Law of China*, I: 245-266.

Chapter 12

WORK MOTIVATION IN ASIA
Review and Future Directions

Chun Hui
The Chinese University of Hong Kong

Jessica Y. Y. Kwong
The Chinese University of Hong Kong

Cynthia Lee
Northeastern University

INTRODUCTION

We have witnessed rapid changes in Asia in the last decade including changes in their economy, culture, and political climate. These changes affect individuals' motivation to work, their values, behavior, and organization's motivation practices. However, theories and empirical studies of motivation seldom incorporate such changes in their theoretical framework. Universal or etic frameworks were used instead of incorporating the necessary differences in the studies of work motivation. Recent studies have made great progress in incorporating emic aspects in their theorizing (Chen, Chen, & Meindl, 1998; Farh, Earley, & Lin, 1997; Lee, Allen, Meyer, & Rhee, 2001; Lee, Pillutla, & Law, 2000; Lee, Tinsley, & Bobko, 2003; Lee, Tinsley, & Chen, 2000; Turban, Lau, Ngo, Chow, & Si, 2001). These studies, in addition to examining boundary conditions of the theories, also studied the relationships of and interplay between the individual and the organizations in cultural contexts. This chapter thus reviews empirical studies of work motivation in Asia by examining: (1) national versus cultural differences; (2) testing of mean differences versus patterns; and (3) studies of etic versus emic approaches. We conclude this chapter by providing suggestions for future research that are culture and change-based.

THE PRESENT REVIEW

Our present review is based on two decisions. The first dealt with the literature base to be reviewed. We primarily consider empirical studies conducted in Asia since 1990. We do not, however, provide a comprehensive listing of all research published over this time period. This is because doing so would require citing hundreds of references without considering the impact of individual contributions. Secondly, we decided against organizing our review based on traditional motivation theories. Instead, we focus on publications particularly related to the three themes we identified above.

REVIEW THEMES

National versus Cultural Differences

Our first theme deals with studies examining national versus cultural differences. Research in this category has typically focused on motivational differences between nations. For example, Alpander and Carter (1991) examined the importance of five basic human needs of employees from eight countries (e.g., Belgium, Japan, and Spain). Based on the works of Herzberg (1966), Maslow (1954), and McClelland (1961), the categories of need that may motivate employees examined by Alpander and Carter are: need for economic security, control, recognition, personal self-worth, and belongingness. Twenty-two professionals and first-line supervisors from eight subsidiaries (Belgium, Spain, Germany, Italy, Venezuela, Mexico, Colombia, Japan) of a multinational company completed questionnaires (total $N = 176$). They were asked to indicate the importance of each of the five human needs. Across the eight countries, the need for control was the most important need (e.g., having autonomy over one's own decisions and influence over a situation or another individual's thinking, attitudes, or behavior). The ranking of the other four needs varied across countries. The five European countries (Belgium, Spain, Germany, Italy, and Venezuela) ranked need for economic security as second most important, while the two Latin American countries (Mexico and Colombia) ranked belongingness as second. Only Japan ranked recognition as the second most important need. More specifically, the Japanese valued the need for control the most, recognition as second, belongingness as third, economic security as fourth, and self worth as least important.

Yamauchi, Beech, Hampson and Lynn (1991) compared the eight achievement related motives in the Achievement-Related Scale between Japanese, British, Irish students. These eight achievement motives included four motives related to hope of success, two related to fear of failure, and two related to fear of success. They also related these achievement motives to examination success for the Irish students, and found that Japanese students scored higher on work tension and confidence in success, and lower on work effort, ambition and fear of failure scales (i.e., facilitating anxiety and deliberating anxiety). They did not find country effect for fear of success (fear of loss of affiliation and of competitiveness).

Yamauchi, Lynn, and Rendell (1994) examined whether there is cross-cultural consistency on gender differences in work motivations between occidental and oriental cultures. They compared participants from Japan and Northern Ireland on motivations such as work ethic, mastery of work, competitiveness, attitude toward money (in terms of saving), achievement motivation, valuation for money, and achievement via conformity, a dimension from the California Personality Inventory (CPI; Gough, 1957). Yamauchi et al. hypothesized that Japanese women would have weaker work motivation when compared with Japanese men and that such differences would be greater than those observed in western cultures. Participants were middle class adults. Japanese males scored higher on mastery and Japanese females scored higher on achievement motivation than their counterparts. Surprisingly, no gender difference was found in competitiveness, achievement via conformity, or work ethic for the Japanese participants. They found that Northern Ireland male scored higher on competitiveness than female.

Furnham et al. (1993) compared the Protestant Work Ethic (PWE) across thirteen nations, including, Australia, Ciskei, Great Britain, Germany, Greece, Hong Kong, India, Israel, New Zealand, South Africa, United States, West Indies, and Zimbabwe. Furnham et al. suggested that PWE beliefs should be lower in more liberal, less conservative or authoritarian cultures. PWE beliefs should be lower in more "scientific" countries and those with better established and more efficient bureaucracies. Subjects in countries that stress power distance, uncertainty avoidance, and individualism ought to score higher on PWE beliefs than subjects in countries that do not. Strong PWE scores ought to be found in countries that had large inequalities. Participants were all students at prominent universities or institutions of higher education. They found that First World countries tended to have lower scores than those from Third World countries. Those with higher gross national product – Germany, the US, Britain, Australia, and New Zealand – tended to have lower PWE scores, whereas those with relatively low GNP – India, Zimbabwe, and the West Indies – tended to have higher PWE scores. Hong Kong had an intermediate score, and Israel, a low score. Poorer, Third World countries that have high power distance relationships and value collectivism over individualism seem to endorse PWE most. PWE beliefs were strongly correlated with power-distance $(r = 0.91)$ and individualism $(r = -0.57)$ (Hofstede, 1984). This indicated that PWE was associated with traditional ethics and countries that emphasize authoritarianism.

Dubinsky, Kotable, Lim, and Michaels (1994) examined motivational differences among sales personnel from US, Japan, and Korea using the framework of expectancy theory of motivation. Participants were sales personnel from the electronics industry in the US, Japan and Korea. They found that the American respondents had higher expectancy estimates than those from Japan and Korea, with no difference between the latter two. One reason for the national difference as suggested by the authors is that neither the Japanese nor the Korean firms generally provide as much detailed job-related information as firms in the US do. Asian employees may be unable to identify what levels of effort are necessary for good performance. Moreover, the Asian tendency to focus on group rather than individual performance may render it difficult to estimate how their individual efforts contribute to the group. Among the three respondent groups, American participants reported the highest scores on extrinsic instrumentality beliefs (i.e., instrumentality of pay increase, job security, promotion, and formal recognition), with the Japanese in second and Koreans last. For example, the American salespeople believed most strongly that effective performance would lead to a pay raise and promotion. Results also showed that American participants had a higher valence for pay increase, job security, promotion, formal recognition, personal growth and development, and feelings of worthwhile accomplishment than did the Japanese or Koreans. Apparently the American sales personnel found those rewards particularly desirable relative to the Japanese and Koreans.

Xiang, Lee and Solmon (1997) investigated the generality of goal orientations (task vs. ego) (Nicholls, 1984) across American and Chinese culture using elementary school students. Task orientation involves the goal of developing one's ability through learning or task mastery, while ego orientation involves demonstrating one's superiority over others. The nations studied included the USA and PRC. The dependent measures were students' perceived ability in physical education (PE) class, satisfaction in PE (enjoyment and boredom) and task choice (preferences for challenging tasks in PE and courage to try new skills). Xiang et al. attempted to examine the similarities and differences in the goal orientations between Anglo-American and Chinese students. They found that the factor structure of the Goal Orientation Scale was similar for the two samples. Anglo-American students differed from the Chinese students in task orientation but not on ego orientation. Anglo-American were more task oriented (had a higher mean) than their Chinese counterparts.

In another study comparing United States and Hong Kong university students, Lee, Tinsley, and Bobko (2003) found that while the students from the US embrace both learning (tendency to adopt goals related to developing ability) and performance goal orientations (tendency to adopt goals related to demonstrating ability) as separate and distinct ideas, the Hong Kong students do not readily distinguish between the two goal orientations. They also found that both goal orientations showed positive associations with classroom performance while only learning goal orientation was positively related to performance in the US sample. Further, female students in Hong Kong had higher performance goal orientations than male students while gender was unrelated to goal orientations in the US sample.

Niles (1998) also tested national, but not cultural differences. Niles questioned the prevailing belief that achievement is predominately an individualistic phenomenon. He argued that Westerners and non-Westerners are not necessarily more or less motivated as a group; rather, achievement-related behaviors and goals may be culture specific. For example, Singhal and Misra (1989) found that Indians emphasized group-related goals more than individual goals. Goal orientation may be considered an index of the individualist and collectivist orientations of diverse cultural groups. Nations examined in Niles' study were Australia and Sri Lanka. The dependent variables were the importance of 28 achievement goals (that are desired in life) and 31 means (important ways in which one gets what one wants in life). Niles hypothesized that salient achievement goals as well as achievement means may be either group oriented (collectivist) or person oriented (individualists). Results showed that Sri Lankans would choose more group-oriented goals and means than would Australians. A significant difference was found only on achievement goals concerning *family/social responsibility*, with Sri Lankans scoring higher than Australians. Although not statistically significant, the data reflected an individualist orientation in preferred achievement goals (material prosperity and personal fulfillment) among Australians. Sri Lankans, although predominantly more family and group oriented, also have important individual goals (scored higher than Australian on personal development). In respect of preferred means for achieving goals, both groups were remarkably similar. Both groups believe strongly in individual or internal means (e.g., the efficacy of hard work, determination, and dedication), and do not endorse external means such as powerful others and social support.

The studies reviewed above explored people's endorsement of a specific human need, work-related value, or achievement-related motive and goal in different nations. Results of the above studies are quite inconsistent, however. For example, Alpander and Carter (1991) found that one important human need that differentiates Japanese subjects from the European and Latin American subjects was the need for recognition. Dubinsky et al. (1994) reported that American salespeople valued extrinsic rewards (e.g., formal recognition, pay increase) more than Japanese and Koreans did. Yamauchi et al. (1991) found that Japanese, in general, endorsed motives related to work tension and confidence in success more than motives related to fear of failure. Gender difference in terms of competitiveness was found in Northern Ireland but did not uphold in Japan (Yamauchi et al., 1994). The Lee et al. (2003) study found gender differences in goal orientations among Hong Kong students but not among US students. By separating achievement goals into task- versus ego-orientation,

Xiang et al. (1997) showed that the Anglo-American students endorsed more task-oriented goals than did the Chinese. Using individual versus group orientation to characterized different achievement goals, Niles (1998) noted that Sri Lankans chose more group-oriented goals than did Australians.

The above studies used nation as the independent variable. Some of these studies even labeled their study as "cultural" studies but indeed what they tested were national differences. A nation is an aggregation of people organized under a single government. This government may be a federation. A nation is marked by specific representation of sovereignty and a geographical boundary. While the definitions of culture vary across time and scholar (cf. Kroeber & Kluckhohn, 1952), in general, a culture refers to the totality of socially transmitted behaviors, symbols and patterns that characterize a people. Even though culture may correspond with geographical boundary, cultures may influence each other. Thus, one may find some components of American culture in Japan (e.g., values, fashion) or vice versa. But one will not find another US in Japan.

The confusion of nation with culture is more than a semantic issue, however. Nation is not the same as culture. Because a nation is a collection of people marked by a sovereign government, what ties a particular nation together is normally explained via other cultural, social, psychological, economic or political mechanisms. In an attempt to understand motivation, hence, it requires explanatory mechanisms that are not normally afforded at the "nation" level. Culture, on the other hand, can be the property of a nation and culture is typically used to explain collective behavior within national boundaries. Hence, when attempting to understand human motivation within national contexts, we may build cultural theories of motivation but not quite national theories of motivation.

Summary

Research focusing on the differences in motivational characteristics across nations represents attempts to contribute to the general knowledge of what may differ across nations. The issue of whether nations differ in their motivational characteristics can be important, as well as interesting. For example, whether Americans are more motivated by the need for achievement than Chinese are can be an interesting question in itself and may even have practical implications. However, as discussed above, finding out these differences may represent only an incipient step in cross-cultural research because much would still have to be learnt about why there are such differences. To compound these problems, when comparing motivational characteristics across nations, many researchers relied on using statistical means as the basis for comparison. The following section discusses the problems with comparing nations on mean values.

Comparing Mean Differences versus Patterns

Our second theme deals with testing the mean differences versus patterns. Mean differences refer to the use of statistical mean to index what is different between nations. Patterns, on the other hand, refers to the use of the pattern of relationships between a number of related constructs to enhance the understanding of what distinguish one nation or culture from another. A number of studies use statistical means as the operationalization for the differences in specific types of motivation across different nations. For example, Yamauchi et al. (1994) compared a number of motivations, including, among others, work ethic and achievement motivation between nations and gender. Furnham et al. (1992) compared the level of work ethics across different nations. Alpander and Carter (1991) compared the importance ratings of five basic needs across eight nations. Yamauchi et al. (1991) compared eight achievement motives across three national groups. Dubinsky et al. (1994) compared the mean differences of expectancy, valence and instrumentality estimates across US, Japan and Korean salespeople. Xiang et al. (1997) compared the mean differences of goal orientation between Anglo-American and Chinese American. Niles (1998) compared the mean differences in achievement goals and means to attaining these goals across Australians and Sri Lankans.

The effective comparison of national differences in motivation necessitates an identification of what can be compared. Sartori (1994) suggests that to compare is to both assimilate and differentiate, meaning that we need to know what is in common and what is not in common between the objects that we are comparing. Different nations are pears and apples until we can conceptualize the properties that we can compare them on. This suggests that in comparing nations, one needs conceptualization before measurement (Kaplan, 1964). After assuring conceptual comparability, researchers need to establish measurement equivalence before they may make meaningful comparisons (van de Vijver & Leung, 1997). van de Vijver and Leung argued that the same mean across different cultures could convey very different meanings, whereas different means could convey the same meanings across cultures because of measurement inequivalence. Equivalence of the measurement means that researchers must ensure that the translation is accurate, the instrument is appropriate in the new context, and that the scores are equivalent and can be compared.

Using mean individual differences for comparing cultures may also suffer from aggregation bias (e.g., Lang, Dollinger, & Marino, 1987; Sego, Hui, & Law, 1997; Robinson, 1950) because there is variance within culture. The variance within a culture represents intra-cultural differences, and can refer more specifically to the population distribution of a particular characteristic within a culture (Au, 1999). Conceptually, it is important to consider intra-cultural variations because cultures are shared by their members. However, different members share a particular culture in various degrees. Au showed that intra-cultural variation has substantial influence on the statistical power of cross-cultural research, which in turn may result in an inability in detecting true differences. Further, it is possible to have similar cultural means but large differences in intra-cultural variation. To the extent that there is variance within a particular culture, the aggregation of individual values into a statistical mean and to use this as the basis for comparison may lead to erroneous conclusions unless we take variance and patterns of relationship into account. In the contrary, the consideration of intra-cultural variation would help researchers gain a better understanding of the degree of "sharedness" of a particular culture. Indeed, Au (1999) found that some countries appeared to have either large or small intra-cultural variations. For example, Au showed that the Netherlands tend to have smaller variations across work related (e.g., job satisfaction) and change-related (e.g., the belief that change is good) variables than India has.

Perhaps the most significant inadequacy of examining motivation differences as national mean differences relates to the lack of an explanation for why such differences occur, even if such differences do exist and can be compared. Przeworski (1987, p. 35) suggests that "comparative research consists not of comparing but of explaining. The general purpose of cross-national research is to understand." Similarly, Ragin (1987, p. 6) suggests that comparative knowledge "provides the key to understanding, explaining and interpreting." In other words, comparative research that makes a contribution is the ones that provide theories for specific observations that differ across nations. Examining national differences in motivation do not reveal what really takes places in the "black-box" of the nations. But it is precisely an account for what takes place in the "black-box" of nations that should be of the greater interest to researchers. For example, finding that there is a difference between the US and Japan on some dimensions of achievement orientation may be informative. But readers are still left with the question of what accounts for these differences and the substantive meaning of these differences, which is a more serious issue of comparing mean differences across nation or culture.

One way to get into the "black-box" of national differences is to examine differences in patterns as opposed to means. Pattern may be interpreted in terms of the inclusion of contextual variables in cross-cultural research (van de Vijver & Leung, 1997). Contextual variables are cultural factors that can account for observed cross-cultural differences. Inclusion of contextual variables enables researchers to rule out alternative interpretations, control for nuisance variables and may constitute a framework for interpreting cross-cultural differences. In essence, the inclusion of contextual variables moves the research away from the simple exploration of cross-cultural differences to the explanation of such differences.

Besides examining the similarities and differences in goal orientations between Anglo-American and Chinese students, Xiang et al. (1997) also addressed the issue of the relationships of goal orientations to perceived ability, satisfaction, and task choice for the two different cultural groups. Consistent with previous research on goal orientation, task orientation was positively linked to perceived ability (competence) and enjoyment in the American students. On the other hand, task and ego orientation was positively related to perceived ability and enjoyment. In addition, ego orientation correlated positively with physical challenge. This is one example of how the use of pattern of relationships may supplement the use of mean differences.

Summary

As culture is shared by its members, cross-cultural researchers frequently have to find ways to index this "sharedness" when conducting their studies. Statistical means can be a useful tool to index such "sharedness" because it represents an important central tendency of a group. As discussed above, however, comparing means across nations can be misleading, if not dangerous because they can lead to erroneous conclusions. To avoid the pitfalls in comparing statistical means, researchers should ensure that they are comparing only the comparable and to examine the constructs of interest in relation to other constructs. To accomplish this and to understand cross-cultural research accurately and substantively, researchers may further distinguish between etic and emic research, which is discussed in the next section.

Etic versus Emic

Our third theme deals with studies of etic versus emic approaches. Berry (1969, 1997) elaborated on Pike's (1966) formulation of the etic versus emic perspective of culture and identified three stages of cultural research. The etic perspective refers to the studying of behavior from a position outside the system and examining the same phenomenon across different cultures for comparison purposes. The emic perspective refers to the studying of behavior from within the system and examining the phenomenon within specific cultural systems, so specific that often times the examination involves only one culture. Berry (1997) suggested that both the etic and the emic approach were essential for cross-cultural understandings. Cross-cultural studies can benefit from an integration of these two approaches along three stages. The first stage was what Berry labeled "imposed etic," which could be the first step of cross-cultural research. Researchers carry with them their cultural understandings, as well as biases, into the study of cultures other than their own when conducting imposed etic research. The second stage was labeled emic exploration and refers to the development of an understanding of phenomena in local cultural terms. The third stage is derived etic which refers to the derivation of truly etic understandings across cultures. Supposedly, it is more probable for derived etic to emerge following extensive use of emic approaches across a number of cultures. These three stages correspond to the three goals of cross-cultural psychology: to transport and test, to explore and discover, and to integrate. In other words, in Berry's terms, to contribute to cultural understanding and to global knowledge, the goal of cross-cultural research should be derived etic and there should be a progression from an etic to an emic and then to a derived etic research.

Morris, Leung, Ames and Lickel (1999) suggested that emic and etic research may lead to important synergies other than derived etic research. Emic and etic research can stimulate each other's progress by identifying new research questions and cultivating richer understandings of culture. For example, emic research has the advantage of generating substantial amount of details whereas etic research has the advantage of offering a map or an overview of the interesting or important cross-cultural issues. The map provided by etic research may guide second generation emic research whereas the details and in-depth understanding of a culture garnered from emic research may provide a strong challenge to etic researchers.

Based on Berry's notion of derived etic research or Morris et al.'s notion of synergistic or integrative research, the objectives of cross-cultural researchers should be to raise new, important theoretical cross-cultural issues and to cultivate better understandings of cultural phenomena. Unfortunately, most studies on cross-cultural motivation that we examined used the etic approach, without sufficient emic or integrative considerations. For example, Chang, Wong, Teo and Fam (1997) study the existence of a transcultural construct of intrinsic motivation to achieve in Singapore. Despite the manifestations of the motive may be guided and shaped by the type of achievement goals and patterns of working behavior that are valued by the culture, motivation to achieve may be a basic human need. Participants were university and polytechnic students, as well as employed workers. Factor analysis of the Work and Family Orientation Scale (WOFO) responses revealed three oblique factors similar in content to those of reported US data. LISREL modeling indicated that this three-factor structure: mastery, competitiveness, and work ethics is appropriate for the Singaporean data. Comparison of the factor structure from subsamples in Singapore revealed good reliability. Confirmatory factor analysis between results from Singapore and those results of Helmreich and colleagues (Helmreich, Beane, Luker, & Spence, 1978; Helmreich & Spence, 1978) showed a higher degree of correspondence. This is an example of the use of a Western scale in an Asian country.

Clugston, Howell and Dorfman (2000) examined the effects of culture on organizational commitment. They operationalized cultural effects in terms of the four cultural values identified by Hofstede (1984): power distance, individualism–collectivism, uncertainty avoidance and masculinity–femininity. They examined both the basis of commitment that was suggested by Meyer and Allen (1991) and the foci of commitment suggested by Becker and colleagues (Becker, 1992; Becker, Billings, Eveleth, & Gilbert, 1996). Meyer and Allen (1991) distinguished between the affective, continuance and normative components of organizational commitment. Becker and his colleagues suggested that commitment could have different foci such as the organization, supervisor and work group. Clugston et al. did not include other cultural samples other than the US, however. Instead, they measured the cultural value orientation at an individual level and as a within culture variable. Because many Asian nations are suggested to have high power distance and be collectivistic, this study has implications for motivation in Asian contexts. Participants were employees from a public agency in a sparsely populated Western state in the US. Clugston et al. found that a nine-factor model of organization commitment (3 bases × 3 foci) had acceptable fit. They further found that cultural values predicted different components of organizational commitment, thus supporting the assertion that cultural socialization is antecedent to organizational commitment.

Chay and Aryee (1999) examine the generalizability of the concept of careerist orientation and its implications for work attitudes in a collectivist culture – Singapore. They found that careerist orientation (e.g., perceived an incompatibility between personal and organizational goals, is driven by a search for self-fulfillment) was negatively related to job involvement and organizational commitment but was positively related to turnover intention. Further, career growth opportunities (i.e., expected utility of present job) moderated the relationship between careerist orientation and turnover intentions. The effects of careerist orientation on turnover intentions were stronger when the expected utility of a present job was low than when it was high. Career growth opportunities were positively related to job involvement, organizational commitment and was negatively to turnover intentions (i.e., the effects were in the opposite direction of those of careerist orientation). They concluded that careerist orientation may not be culture-bound. Employees in Singapore, much like their individualist American counterparts, seem to have developed an individualist, self-oriented (careerist) orientation to their careers. The findings suggest that organizational dependence on employees as a competitive resource may be facilitated through a relational and not a transactional psychological contract (as the latter promote careerist orientation).

Silverthorne (1996) attempted to discover what motivates Taiwan employees and whether the same factors motivate civil servants and private sector employees. Silverthorne compared rank (managers and non-mangers) and sector (public and private) differences on the reasons for an individual taking their jobs (e.g., "The pay is good," "My work is challenging") and preference for Theory X, Y, and Z styles of management as measured by the XYZ Inventory (Reddin & Sullivan, 1977). A preference for Theory X management reflects that the respondent believes employees dislike responsibility and managers should actively intervene to motivate the employees. A preference for Theory Y management reflects that the respondents believes employees have a capacity for responsibility and management's job is to arrange conditions and operations so that people can achieve their own goals best by directing their efforts toward organizational goals. A preference for Theory Z management indicates that the respondent believes long-term employment is the basis of effective organizations and employees should be allowed to participate in helping their organizations be successful. Participants were 120 Taiwanese employees from public service sector (40 managers and 80 non-managers) and another 120 Taiwanese employees from private sector. Silverthorne found slight variability between managers and non-managers and between public and private sectors in their reasons for taking a job, indicating little differences in their motivational needs. Rank and sector had no effect on the preference for Theory XYZ management. In general, the Taiwanese respondents preferred Theory Z approach to management, followed by Theory X and finally Theory Y. The emphasis on the Theory Z approach replicated a finding by Swierczek (1991). He found that Asian managers preferred leaders who practiced participation over giving direction.

Using an imposed etic approach, the above studies substantiate the generalizability of a number of motivation constructs in Asian cultures. For example, there was a high consistency in the way Singaporeans and Americans conceptualize "motivation to achieve," as measured by WOFO (Chang et al., 1997). The usefulness of the concept, careerist orientation, and its impacts on job attitudes such as commitment and job involvement in Singapore have been demonstrated by Chay and Aryee (1999).

By adopting Theory XYZ inventory, Silverthorne (1996) revealed that Taiwanese employees preferred participatory management practices.

Summary

Progressing from imposed etic to emic research and ultimately to derived etic research and the generation of integrative cross-cultural research offers a model for researchers to understand how true cross-cultural and universal knowledge can be advanced. Motivational research in Asia will contribute to local, regional and universal knowledge only if researchers move beyond the imposed etic phase and begin to accumulate emic knowledge. Without true emic knowledge, one can hardly safeguard against comparing apples in one culture to pears in another. The question that remains is what constitutes good emic and derived etic research.

ASIAN PROGRESS AND RESEARCH STYLES

In reviewing the motivation literature in Asia since 1990, several observations present themselves. Studies on simple cross-national comparisons have given way to examining specific theoretical relationships in Earley and Singh's (2000) unitary, gestalt, reduced and hybrid forms. They call for more studies using the hybrid form. A hybrid form attempts to identify and isolate which of various alternative explanations accurately captures a given phenomenon by identifying specific aspects of the nation or culture that are related to a given explanation. The key to understanding complex relationships in this form is in understanding how and why differences exist in their context rather than simply identifying these differences.

Unitary form is one of the four research styles. Emphasis is being placed on understanding a given phenomenon in a particular circumstance on its own terms. One example of the unitary form is the studies of *guanxi*, a particular kind of interpersonal relationship or connection that serves as a form of social currency. Tsui, Farh, and Xin (2000) clarify the conceptual domain of *guanxi*, review the research findings about the effect of *guanxi* bases on employment relationships, and suggest future directions for *guanxi* research. *Guanxi* is the construct that has unique meaning and interpretation in China and is not shared in the United States. Another example is the work on paternalistic leadership by Farh and Cheng (1999). Paternalistic leadership, which combines strong discipline and authority with fatherly benevolence and moral integrity couched in a "personalistic" atmosphere, has been found to be prevalent in overseas Chinese family businesses. After critically reviewing the extant literature, Farh and Cheng identify three constituent elements of paternalistic leadership: authoritarianism, benevolence, and moral leadership. They trace the deep cultural roots of each element and explore their relevance to organizations in contemporary Chinese societies. They then identify key research issues and propose a preliminary paternalistic leadership model for future studies on leadership in Chinese organizations. These emic research themes or unitary form is very important for understanding a given group or cultural context. However, it does not provide the opportunity for establishing universal principles afforded by other research paradigms, assuming that such universals exist (Earley & Singh, 2000).

Studies in the gestalt form can be characterized as comparative studies. According to Earley and Singh (2000), this approach requires a researcher to examine a cultural or national system as an intact whole rather than breaking it part. Using this approach, researchers study relationships among variables as they occur across different cultural or national contexts. The constructs and hypothesized relationships are derived from general principles rather than from within the systems themselves. Lastly, interpretations of results are developed with reference to the specific cultural context. These interpretations informs researchers as to the generalizability of the given theory or principle. For example, Lee, Allen, Meyer, and Rhee (2001) studied the generalizability of Meyer and Allen's (1991) three-component model of organizational commitment. Using two studies, they concluded that the three commitment constructs are likely to generalize to non-Western cultures, but that there might be a need to refine the measures for cross-cultural research. Another example is the Lam, Hui and Law's (1999) study of organizational citizenship behavior. They used the Podsakoff et al. (1990) measure developed and validated in the USA to examine the definitions of job roles across the ranks of supervisors and subordinates across USA, Australia, Japan and Hong Kong. They found the measure to have more general applicability across these national samples. They reported that the participants from Hong Kong and Japan were also more likely to regard some categories of OCB as an expected part of the job than were participants of USA and Australia. Although the conceptual orientation was based on USA, they interpreted their findings in light of each cultural or national context. According to White (2002), comparative research studies are clearly the dominant concern of researchers focused on Asia. While identifying differences among populations of individuals, groups and organizations is certainly important, most of the studies are less than satisfying in terms of insights into the sources of those differences or their performance implications (White, 2002). The next research style takes White's criticism into account.

The third research style is the reduced form that emphasizes breaking down a system into component parts to understand process functioning within the system. This form assumes that a cultural system is divisible and that any given facet of the system can be examined independently of other facets. As in the gestalt form, constructs and hypothesized relationships are arrived at deductively based on general principles observed from other cultural or national contexts. Results are also interpreted based on specific aspects of the cultural contexts. One example of this is the Chay and Aryee (1999) study discussed earlier. Another example is the Lee, Pillutla, and Law (2000) study, using a sample of Hong Kong employees, examining the cultural role of power distance as the moderator of organizational justice and contract fulfillment and trust in supervisor. Further, Xie (1996) found support for the cross-cultural applicability of Karasek's job demands-decision latitude model from a study of 1,200 employees from five Chinese cities. She further found that what some individuals perceived as stimulating and challenging, others found it excessively demanding and stressful. Her findings extend Karasek's model theoretical assumption that high strain jobs lead to high stress and active jobs lead to high satisfaction for everyone.

The last research style is the hybrid form that uses aspects from both the gestalt and the reduced perspectives. Earley and Singh (2000) suggest that this approach has the advantage of building etic relationships from emic analyses. Theories that are developed from this approach can cross over national and cultural borders. The cultural values of power distance, individualism–collectivism, uncertainty avoidance and masculinity–femininity identified by Hofstede (1984) is an example of this hybrid form. We echo Earley and Singh's (2000) call for more research in this particular research approach. As the emic or indigenous constructs and issues in the unitary form are being examined and accepted in mainstream studies, research in Asia management is gaining ground into top tier journals (cf. Lau, 2002; Li & Tsui, 2002). As we are heading for higher impact research, stronger focus should be placed in theory development and contribution to conceptual issues beyond our audience in Asia. The search for new theories originating from unique Asian societal and cultural factors is a viable way to start (Lau, 2002). We suggest future research to focus on combining the research styles suggested by Earley and Singh (2000). Further, we suggest research effort should also focus on studying a mid-range hybrid form where we develop an Asian paradigm that has high potential for global impact. Lau (2002) suggests that it is fruitful to address some Asian phenomenon and generate theory for global-relevant issues. Although it is meaningful to use Asian-developed constructs to study local and global issues, it is also meaningful to examine the broader existence and applicability of the constructs and issues developed in Asia that cut across different cultural contexts.

Integrating 'Time' in our Research

Rousseau (1997), in her chapter on "organizational behavior in the new organizational era," stated that changes in contemporary firms and their competitive environment translate into a new focus in organizational research. There appears to be an adaptive quality in the field's work that shifts attention toward particular applied problems firms face within a given decade (Goodman & Whetten, 1998). For example, of the studies conducted in North America, organizational development was a theme in the 1950s and 1960s. However, organizational decline, mergers and acquisitions were themes in the 1980s and 1990s. As organizations restructured or downsized, we further witnessed studies on work and family, employment relationships issues in the 1990s and currently. This pattern is also observed in motivation studies in Asia. For example, as firms in China were trying to recruit and retain talented employees, Chen, Hui, and Sego (1998) studied organizational citizenship behavior as a behavioral predictor of employee turnover. Further, China has been restructuring its state-owned enterprises in the 1990s. Recently, Hui, Lee, and Rousseau (2002) examined the employee–employer's beliefs concerning their reciprocal obligations. Additionally, Lee, Bobko, and Chen (2002) studied issues related to job insecurity perceptions in China. Together, these collective writings have served to demonstrative the futility of examining the so-called real world issues in organizations during changing times.

Recently, Goodman, Lawrence, Ancona, and Tushman (2001) call attention on how to think about and integrate time in our research. According to White (2002), the majority of studies conducted in Asia are dominated by correlational analyses or cross-sectional designs. The majority of the literature in Asia management on cross-cultural measurement is focused exclusively on cross-section data, addressing cross-cultural differences in measurement and constructs without examining the temporal dimension of measurement and constructs (Chan, 2002). Again, the lack of longitudinal designs is ironic, given that a common justification for undertaking a study in an Asian context is that the organizational environments have undergone dramatic changes in recent decades (Chan, 2002; White, 2002). Consider the study of psychological contracts. Will employees' obligations to the employer change as newcomers are socialized into their organizations? Research in Asia should make time explicit in their research designs regardless of whether the focus of the study is on time. According to Mitchell and James (2001), in non-time based research, the independent and dependent variables are not about time. They could be about the relationship between perceptions of job insecurity and job satisfaction or between trust and organizational citizenship behaviors. Mitchell and James' argument is that time is a critical issue both in terms of lags between variables and the stability of the variables, and that time must be made explicit in all studies.

Most recently, Chan (1998, 2002) categorized different possible aspects of change over time into nine fundamental questions and proposed a unified data analytic framework to analyze each of the change patterns over time in cross-cultural organizational research. Although these nine questions are not an exhaustive list, they provide a framework for researchers to consider in designing research in cross-cultural context. Additionally, Ancona, Goodman, Lawrence, and Tushman (2001) advise researchers to think carefully about the duration of X and Y and when Y might occur. If we follow the above suggestions, the theoretical formulation and methodological approaches of our work will help provide new opportunities for explanations and prediction.

CONTEXTUAL RELEVANCE

In his review of the forty years of organizational studies, Porter (1996) commented that we have tended to the "B" in the micro-OB studies and have ignored the "O" as critical contexts affecting the behavior occurring within them. Porter calls for researchers to take the organization into account more explicitly as a context influencing behavioral phenomena relating to individuals and groups. Porter's view is shared by Heath and Sitkin (2001), Johns (2001), and Rousseau and Fried (2001). They call for researchers to contextualize their studies linking observations to a set of relevant facts, events, or points of view that make possible research and theory that form part of a larger whole. According to Rousseau and Fried (2001), contextualization occurs in many stages of a research process. It takes place from question formulation, site selection, and measurement to data analysis, interpretation, and reporting. Contextualization helps us theorize, understand, and interpret the pattern of relationships we identified and help us advance our emic and etic knowledge. Differences within a country, and among the employees of various firms located therein, can be as great as those observed between countries. For example, studying loyalty to the supervisor in Qingdao, Peoples' Republic of China may yield very different results as studying the same phenomenon in Hong Kong, China. The cultural context of these two cities can serve as a main effect and/or as a moderator of relationships at another unit or level of analysis.

Further, in a study of Chinese achievement orientation, Yu (1996) explains that the Chinese view of self is a social construction that exists between individuals or between an individual and his/her family, clan, society, or state. The true nature of the Chinese self is revealed when placed in the context of affective relationships between an individual, significant others, and the in-group to which the individual belongs (Yu, 1996). Therefore, according to Yu (1996), Chinese achievement motivation can only be understood when placed in the context of the developmental processes of an individual's life history and experience. This may also explain the inconsistent results reported by the Yamauchi et al. (1994) and the Lee et al. (2003) studies on gender differences. Gender difference in terms of competitiveness was found in Northern Ireland but did not uphold in Japan (Yamauchi et al., 1994). The Lee et al. (2003) study found gender differences in goal orientations in Hong Kong but not in the United States.

Future research in motivation in Asia should take the socio-cultural context and the changes that are occurring into account. Contextual differences can be a major source of conflicting findings, and teasing out underlying pattern requires us to pay more attention to research settings (Rousseau & Fried, 2001). We suggest that research in Asia should carefully contextualize their research. One of the reasons is that the Asia culture is constantly influx. Although cultural values change slowly most of the time, they seem to change much faster during periods of drastic social upheaval such as what is occurring in China and other parts of Asia. Simply exploring cultural dimensions of power distance, collectivism/individualism are inadequate to address the dynamic aspect of cultural change within Asia.

One way to contextualize Asian motivation research is to conceptualize the different contexts and examines how these various contexts affect employee motivation. For example, Borman and Motowidlo (1993) distinguished the technical core from the social-psychological core of an organization. The technical core deals with the technical aspects of the job and the technology that the organization relies on for survival. The social-psychological core deals with the software of the organization and refers the social and psychological dynamics in the workplace, including among others, organizational culture and human relations. A society, as well as an organization, may also have technical and social-psychological cores. There may be different antecedents and consequences of these two cores of a culture and an organization. For example, Borman and Motowidlo suggested that contextual performance, a form of extra-role performance, is related to the social-psychological but not the technical core of an organization. Technical characteristics of an Asian nation or an Asian organization may impact human motivation differently than the social-psychological characteristics. Thus, conceptualizing Asian contexts may guide researchers to go beyond the sole reliance on cultural values in explaining Asian motivation and organizational outcomes.

CONCLUSION

Looking to the Future

Where do we go from here? Unfortunately, there are no experts on the future, only on the past (Porter, 1996). However, we can talk about what we think *should* happen in the future, even if we don't know what *will* happen (Porter, 1996). Here are some of our concluding thoughts.

The studies of motivation in Asia have made great progress in moving from simple comparative studies across nations, studying mean differences to the studies involving the unitary, gestalt, reduced research forms identified by Earley and Singh (2000). Theoretical and methodological advances have been made and will continue. We have advanced from examining differences in goal orientation by comparing factor structures of scales (Xiang et al., 1997) to comparing differences or similarities in correlations of goal orientations and performance (Lee, Tinsley, & Bobko, 2003). As stated in the reduced form of research styles, we extend general principles or established theoretical assumptions by including contextual factors. Instead of simply testing etic theories, we have seen attempts at theory building and testing as in the case of Tsui et al.'s work on guanxi and Farh's work on paternalistic leadership. However, we must also remember to contextualize our studies by providing 'thick' description. Combining qualitative and quantitative methods are ways to highlight context (Johns, 2001) and help us understand why differences exist and how differences emerged.

Next, time is context and researchers should also foster context by being sensitive to time (Johns, 2001). According to Chan (2002), many phenomena of interest in cross-cultural organizational research are temporal in nature. These phenomena are about processes or changes that unfold over time. Time is a surrogate for a number of environmental stimuli in place when the research is conducted. The job insecurity perceptions followed by the reorganization of state-owned enterprises in China may give new meaning to organizational citizenship behaviors as compared to the 'iron rice bowl' period. Viewing time as context also suggests the possibility that the very meaning of constructs and work behaviors changes over time (Johns, 2001; Rousseau & Fried, 2001). In turn, the correlates of these behaviors change as well. Does 'trust' in management carry the same meaning as the state-owned enterprise is downsizing? Will the definition of my psychological contract change as I learned more about my employing organization and as my organization change externally (e.g., labor market) and internally (e.g., change in leadership)? Therefore, it is important that historical factors be taken into account in describing research settings, including the timing of data gathering and events that might impact their meaning (Rousseau & Fried, 2001). Additionally, since our constructs may change over time, it is important that we build 'time' in our theorizing and research design.

Lastly, we have been diligently trying to understand behavior of individuals in organizations. It is a challenge for us to examine the influence of the organization on individual and group behavior or the influence of individual and group behavior on the organization or context. Research in Asia has been keeping pace with research in the west by extending the work at the individual level to the group level, or have begun to study group level constructs. For example, Lee and Farh (in press) examined the sources of group efficacy and the joint roles of group efficacy and gender diversity on the relationship between group efficacy and outcomes among 45 groups of Hong Kong students. They found that past performance and self-efficacy were both positively related to group efficacy. Additionally, the interaction of gender diversity and group efficacy was positively related to group effectiveness.

Another study conducted by Lee, Tinsely, and Bobko (2002) examines the power of group confidence, group potency (generalized confidence) and group efficacy (task specific confidence). These constructs are embedded in a causal model including both antecedent and consequent variables. Results, obtained within a collective cultural context using 27 student groups from Hong Kong, suggest that group cohesion and group norms are antecedents to group confidence, and task performance and satisfaction are consequences. The empirical effects for group potency are robust, but those for group efficacy were surprisingly non-significant. This study shows that generalized confidence (group potency) is a stronger predictor of group outcomes than group efficacy when the group members are unfamiliar with the complex tasks at hand. Future studies might directly investigate the role of a group's culture in transmitting confidence across group members.

In a study of 288 senior managers from England, France, Thailand, and the United States, Earley (1999) tested the hypothesis that power distance would moderate the influence of member status on collective decisions made by a group. His results demonstrate that in high power distance cultures (France and Thailand), collective judgments of group capability, or collective efficacy, are more strongly tied to higher rather than to lower status group members' personal judgments. In low power distance cultures such as England and United States, members appear to contribute comparably to collective efficacy judgments. Collectively, the tasks used by these researchers were short-term nature using a group structure. No doubt that studying group level constructs or at the group level will emerge as key motivation topics in Asia, we, however, must take into consideration the role of context and time as the study of cross-cultural or Asian organization behavior moves forward.

The above studies have given attention to show individual actions can affect group actions. Future research would also benefit from forging a stronger link between the macro and micro part of the filed. In building multilevel theories, we can hopefully bridge the micro–macro divide, integrate the micro domain's focus on individuals and groups with the macro domain's focus on organizations, environment, and strategy (Klein, Tosi, & Cannella, 1999), and contribute to a more in-depth and systematic understanding of work motivations in Asian contexts. According to Klein et al., multi-level theorizing provides a deeper, richer portrait of organizational life that acknowledges the influence as organizational context on individual behavior and the influence of individual behavior on the organizational context. Their thinking has also been reflected in Rousseau's (1985) work addressing issues pertinent to the development of cross-level and multi-level theories, including the guidelines for conducting cross-level and multi-level research.

White (2002) draws on 840 articles from 30 journals from the last 20 years to assess the state of management research in Asian contexts. His basic conclusions, similar to our review themes, are that too much of the research effort has been limited to simplistic comparisons, correlational analyses providing no insight into underlying processes, and skewed, idiosyncratic sampling. The result has been a lack of theory development and contribution to conceptual discourse beyond an audience specifically interested in Asia, with little relevance for management practice. His analysis points to clear recommendations for increasing both the rigor and relevance of this collective research effort, while at the same time acknowledging the considerable institutional and cognitive barriers to moving forward.

Recently, we have seen the quality of our research methods, of our theory development, and of our attempts to integrate knowledge about behavior in organizations become better now than it ever has been. While established themes such as achievement motivation or self-efficacy endure, others shift focus or level of analysis. Still new or indigenous topics may emerge such as paternalistic leadership or moral justice (Law, Lee, Farh, & Pillutla, 2001). We should also go beyond emic studies and develop theories that are etic and hybrid in nature. As suggested by Lau (2002), work done with Asian-developed theories focusing on or applicable to issues of global interests accounts for a relatively small portion of management studies. The lower originality and lack of methodological rigor have now been replaced with high quality research as the reward system of the academic institutional environment in Asia changes. We are excited that the quality of contribution from Asia is making inroads to the globalizing academic community.

ACKNOWLEDGMENTS

This research was fully supported by a grant from the Research Grants Council of the Hong Kong Special Administrative Region, China (Project CUHK6197/98H) awarded to Chun Hui and Denise Rousseau.

REFERENCES

Alpander, G.G. and Carter, K.D. 1991. Strategic multinational intra-company differences in employee motivation. *Journal of Managerial Psychology*, 6: 25-32.

Ancona, D.G., Goodman, P.S., Lawrence, B.S. and Tushman, M.L. 2001. Time: A new research lens. *Academy of Management Review*, 26: 645-663.

Au, K.Y. 1999. Intra-cultural variation: Evidence and implications for international business. *Journal of International Business Studies*, 30(4): 799-812.

Becker, T.E. 1992. Foci and bases of commitment: Are they distinctions worth making? *Academy of Management Journal*, 35: 232-244.

Becker, T.E., Billings, R.S., Eveleth, D.M. and Gilbert, N.L. 1996. Foci and bases of employee commitment: Implications for job performance. *Academy of Management Journal*, 39: 464-482.

Berry, J.W. 1969. On cross-cultural comparability. *International Journal of Psychology*, 4: 119-128.

Berry, J.W. 1997. An ecocultural approach to the study of cross-cultural industrial/organizational psychology. In P.C. Earley and M. Erez (eds.), *New Perspectives on International Industrial-Organizational Psychology*. San Francisco: The New Lexington Press.

Borman, W.C. and Motowidlo, S.J. 1993. Expanding the criterion domain to include elements of contextual performance. In N. Schmitt and W.C. Borman (eds.), *Personality Selection* (pp. 71-98). San Francisco: Jossey-Bass.

Chan, D. 1998. The conceptualisation and analysis of change over time: An integrative approach incorporating longitudinal means and covariance structures analysis (LMACS) and multiple indicator latent growth modeling (MLGM). *Organizational Research Methods*, 1: 421-483.

Chan, D. 2002. Questions about change over time in cross-cultural organizational research. *Asia Pacific Journal of Management*, 19: 449-457.

Chang, W.C., Wong, W.K., Teo, G. and Fam, A. 1997. The motivation to achieve in Singapore: In search of a core construct. *Personality and Individual Differences*, 23: 885-895.

Chay, Y.W. and Aryee, S. 1999. Potential moderating influence of career growth opportunities on careerist orientation and work attitudes: Evidence of the protean career era in Singapore. *Journal of Organizational Behavior*, 20(5): 613-623.

Chen, C.C., Chen, X.P. and Meindl, J.R. 1998. How can cooperation be fostered? The cultural effects of individualism-collectivism. *Academy of Management Review*, 23: 285-304.

Chen, X.P., Hui, C. and Sego, D. (1998). The role of organizational citizenship behavior in turnover: Conceptualization and preliminary tests of key hypothesis. *Journal of Applied Psychology*, 83: 922-931.

Clugston, M., Howell, J.P. and Dorfman, P.W. 2000. Does culture socialization predict multiple bases and foci of commitment? *Academy of Management Journal*, 26: 5-30.

Dubinsky, A.J., Kotabe, M., Lim, C. and Michaels, R.E. 1994. Differences in motivational perceptions among U.S., Japanese, and Korean sales personnel. *Journal of Business Research*, 30: 175-185.

Earley, P.C. 1999. Playing follow the leader: Status-determining traits in relation to collective efficacy across cultures. *Organizational Behavior and Human Decision Processes*, 80: 192-212.

Earley, P.C. and Singh, H. 2000. *Innovations in International and Cross-cultural Management*. Thousand Oaks: Sage Publications, Inc.

Farh, J.L. and Cheng, B.S. 1999. A cultural analysis of paternalistic leadership in Chinese organizations. In J.T. Li, A.S. Tsui and E. Weldon (eds.), *Management and Organizations in the Chinese Context* (pp. 84-127). London: MacMillan Press Ltd.

Farh, J.L., Earley, P.C. and Lin, S.C. 1997. Impetus for action: A cultural analysis of justice and organizational citizenship behavior in Chinese society. *Administrative Science Quarterly*, 42: 421-444.

Furnham, A., Bond, M., Heaven, P., Hilton, D., Lobel, T., Masters, J., Payne, M., Rajamanickam, R., Stacey, B. and Van Daalen, H.A. 1993. Comparison of Protestant work ethic beliefs in thirteen nations. *Journal of Social Psychology*, 133: 185-197.

Goodman, P.S., Lawrence, B.S., Ancona, D.G. and Tushman, M.L. 2001. Introduction to special topic forum on time and organizational research. *Academy of Management Review*, 26: 507-511.

Goodman, P.S. and Whetten, D.A. 1998. Fifty years of organizational behavior from multiple perspectives. In M. Neufeld and J. McKelvey (eds.), *Industrial Relations: The Dawn of the New Millennium* (pp. 33-53). Ithaca, NY: Cornell School of Industrial and Labor Relations.

Gough, H. 1957. *Manual for the California Personality Inventory*. Palo Alto, CA: Consulting Psychologists Press.

Heath, C. and Sitkin, S.B. 2001. Big-B versus Big-O: What is organizational about organizational behavior? *Journal of Organizational Behavior*, 22: 43-58.

Helmreich, R.L., Beane, W., Luker, G.W. and Spence, J.T. 1978. Achievement motivation and scientific attainment. *Personality and Social Psychology Bulletin*, 4: 222-226.

Helmreich, R.L. and Spence, J.T. 1978. Work and Family Orientation Questionnaire: An objective instrument to assess components of achievement motivation and attitudes toward family and career. *Catalog of Selected Documents in Psychology*, 8: 1677-35.

Herzberg, F. 1966. *Work and the Nature of Man*. Cleveland, OH: World Publishing Co.

Hofstede, G.H. 1984. *Culture's Consequences: International Differences in Work-related Values*. Newbury Park: Sage Publications.

Hui, C., Lee, C. and Rousseau, D.M. 2002. Psychological contract and organizational citizenship behaviors in China: Exploring generalizability and instrumentality. Northeastern University working paper.

Johns, G. 2001. In praise of context. *Journal of Organizational Behavior*, 22: 31-42.

Kaplan, A. 1964. *The Conduct of Inquiry*. San Francisco, CA: Chandler.

Klein, K.J., Tosi, H. and Cannella, Jr., A.A. 1999. Multilevel theory building: benefits, barriers, and new developments. *Academy of Management Review*, 24: 243-248.

Kroeber, A.L. and Kluckhohn, C. 1952. *Culture: A Critical Review of Concepts and Definitions*. Cambridge, MA: Harvard University Peabody Museum of American Archeology and Ethnology.

Lam, S.S.K., Hui, C. and Law, K.s. 1999. Organizational citizenship behavior: Comparing perspectives of supervisors and subordinates across four international samples. *Journal of Applied Psychology*, 84: 595-601.

Lang, J.R., Dollinger, M.J. and Marino, K.E. 1987. Aggregation bias in strategic decision-making research. *Journal of Management*, 13: 689-702.

Lau, C.M. 2002. Asian management research: Frontiers and challenges. *Asia Pacific Journal of Management*, 19: 171-178.

Law, K.S., Lee, C., Farh, J.L. and Pillutla, M.M. 2001. Organizational justice perceptions of employees in the PRC: A grounded investigation. Paper presented at the Global Business and Technology Association 2001 International Conference, July 11–15, 2001, Istanbul, Turkey.

Lee, C., Bobko, P. and Chen, Z.X. 2002. Investigation of the multidimensional model of job insecurity: Are all components necessary. Northeastern University working paper.

Lee, C. and Farh, J.L. (in press). Group efficacy and outcomes: Moderating role of gender diversity. *Applied Psychology: An International Review*.

Lee, C., Pillutla, M. and Law, K.S. 2000. Power-distance, gender and organizational justice. *Journal of Management*, 26: 685-704.

Lee, C., Tinsley, C.H. and Bobko, P. 2002. An investigation of the antecedents and consequences of group-level confidence. *Journal of Applied Social Psychology*, 32: 1628-1652.

Lee, C., Tinsley, C.H. and Bobko, P. 2003. Cross-cultural variance in goal orientations and their effects. *Applied Psychology: An International Review*, 52: 271-296.

Lee, C., Tinsley, C.H. and Chen, Z.X. 2000. Psychological normative contracts of work group members in the U.S. and Hong Kong. In D.M. Rousseau and M.J.D. Schalk (eds.), *Psychological Contracts in Employment: Cross-Cultural Perspective* (pp. 87-103). Thousand Oaks: Sage.

Lee, K., Allen, N.J., Meyer, J.P. and Rhee, K.Y. 2001. The three-component model of organizational commitment: An application to South Korea. *Applied Psychology: An International Review*, 50: 596-614.

Li, J.T. and Tsui, A.S. 2002. A citation analysis of management and organizational research in the Chinese context: 1984–1999. *Asia Pacific Journal of Management*, 19: 87-107.

Maslow, A.H. 1954. *Motivation and Personality*. NY: Harper & Row.

McClelland, D.C. 1961. *The Achieving Society*. New Jersey: Van Nostrand.

Meyer, J.P. and Allen, N.J. 1991. A three-component conceptualization of organizational commitment. *Human Resource Management*, 1: 61-89.

Mitchell, T.R. and James, L.R. 2001. Building better theory: Time and the specification of when things happen. *Academy of Management Review*, 26: 530-547.

Morris, M.W., Leung, K., Ames, D. and Lickel, B. 1999. Views from inside and outside: Integrating emic and etic insights about culture and justice judgment. *Academy of Management Review*, 24: 781-796.

Niles, S. 1998. Achievement goals and means: A cultural comparison. *Journal of Cross Cultural Psychology*, 29(5): 656-667.

Nicholls, J.G. 1984. Achievement motivation: Conceptions of ability, subjective experience, task choice, and performance. *Psychological Review*, 91: 328-346.

Pike, K.L. 1966. *Language in Relation to a Unified Theory of the Structure of Human Behavior*. The Hague: Mouton.

Podsakoff, P.M., MacKenzie, S.B., Moorman, R.H. and Fetter, R. 1990. Transformational leader behaviors and their effects on followers' trust in leader satisfaction and organizational citizenship behaviors. *Leadership Quarterly*, 107-142.

Porter, L.W. 1996. Forty years of organization studies: Reflections from a micro perspective. *Administrative Science Quarterly*, 41: 262-269.

Przeworski, A. 1987. Methods of cross-national research, 1970-83: an overview. In M. Dierkes et al. (eds.), *Comparative Policy Research: Learning from Experience*. Aldershot: Gower.

Ragin, C. 1987. *The Comparative Method: Moving Beyond Qualitative and Quantitative Strategies.* Berkeley, CA: University of California Press.

Reddin, W.J. and Sullivan, B. (1977). *XYZ Test.* Fredericton, Canada: Organizational Tests.

Robinson, W.S. 1950. Ecological correlations and the behavior of individuals. *American Sociological Review*, 15: 351-357.

Rousseau, D.M. 1985. Issues of level in organizational research: Multi-level and cross-level perspectives. In B.M. Staw and L.L. Cummings (eds.), *Research in Organizational Behavior* (Vol. 7, pp. 1-37). Jai Press Inc.

Rousseau, D.M. 1997. Organizational behavior in the new organizational era. *Annual Review of Psychology*, 48: 515-548.

Rousseau, D.M. and Fried, Y. 2001. Location, location, location: Contextualizing organizational research. *Journal of Organizational Behavior*, 22: 1-13.

Sartori, G. 1994. Compare why and how. In M. Dogan and A. Kazancigil (eds.), *Comparing Nations: Concepts, Strategies, Substance.* Cambridge, MA: Blackwell Publishers.

Sego, D., Hui, C. and Law, K.S. 1997. Operationalizing cultural values as the mean of individual values: Problems and suggestions for research. In C. Earley and M. Erez (eds.), *New Perspectives on International Industrial/Organizational Psychology* (pp. 148-159). San Francisco: The New Lexington Press.

Silverthorne, C.P. 1996. Motivation and management styles in the public and private sectors in Taiwan and a comparison with United States. *Journal of Applied Social Psychology*, 26: 1827-1837.

Singhal, R. and Misra, G. 1989. Variations in achievement cognitions: The role of ecology, age and gender. *International Journal of Intercultural Relations*, 13(1): 93-107.

Swierczek, F.W. 1991. Leadership and culture: Comparing Asian managers. *Leadership and Organizational Development Journal*, 12(7): 3-10.

Tsui, A.S., Farh, J.L. and Xin, K.R. 2000. Guanxi in the Chinese context. In J.T. Li, A.S. Tsui and E. Weldon (eds.), *Management and Organizations in the Chinese Context* (pp. 225-244). New York: St. Martin's Press Inc.

Turban, D.B., Lau, C.M., Ngo, H.Y., Chow, I.H.S. and Si, S.X. 2001. Organizational attractiveness of firms in the People's Republic of China: A person-organization fit perspective. *Journal of Applied Psychology*, 86: 194-206.

Van de Vijver, F. and Leung, K. 1997. *Methods and Data Analysis for Cross-cultural Research.* Thousand Oaks: Sage Publications.

White, S. 2002. Rigor and relevance in Asian management research: Where are we and where can we go? *Asia Pacific Journal of Management*, 19: 287-352.

Xiang, P., Lee, A.M. and Solmon, M.A. 1997. Achievement goals and their correlates among American and Chinese students in physical education: A cross-cultural analysis. *Journal of Cross Cultural Psychology*, 28(6): 645-660.

Xie, J.L. 1996. Karasek's model in the People's Republic of China: Effects of job demands, control, and individual differences. *Academy of Management Journal*, 39: 1594-1618.

Yamauchi, H., Beech, J.R., Hampson, S.L. and Lynn, R. 1991. Japanese–British differences on achievement-related motives. *Psychologia: An International Journal of Psychology*, 34: 157-163.

Yamauchi, H., Lynn, R. and Rendell, I. 1994. Gender differences in work motivations and attitudes in Japan and Northern Ireland. *Psychologia: An International Journal of Psychology*, 37: 195-198.

Yu, A.B. 1996. Ultimate life concerns, self, and Chinese achievement motivation. In M.H. Bond (ed.), *The Handbook of Chinese Psychology* (pp. 227-246). Oxford University Press.

Chapter 13

LEADERSHIP RESEARCH IN ASIA
Developing Relationships

Dean Tjosvold
Lingnan University

Alfred Wong
Lingnan University

Chun Hui
Chinese University of Hong Kong

LEADING IN ASIA: APPLYING EASTERN VALUES AND WESTERN THEORY

Leadership has stimulated thousands of research studies and many models, but the resulting knowledge base has been disappointing with a modest impact on practice (Hunt & Dodge, 2000; Kouzes & Posner, 1995). Especially when compared to stories of managers re-invigorating and re-directing their organizations, leadership research seems placid and removed from the demands and opportunities of running today's organizations.

A major challenge to research progress is the very complexity of leadership. Leaders daily confront many issues in many settings in large and small, public and private, growing and shrinking organizations. Leadership is a performing art that requires actions and strategies as well as beliefs and ideas. Leadership occurs in conjunction with followers: A leader who leads alone is not a leader. How can leadership research respond to these realities yet develop elegant frameworks that deepen understanding and improve practice?

Asian researchers have highlighted the additional challenge of understanding the role of culture. Effective leadership in one culture may be counterproductive in another. Within multinational corporations and international alliances, leaders and employees often have distinct cultural values and expectations. Indeed, persistent workforce immigration flows mean that significant cultural differences increasingly occur within domestic organizations in Europe and East Asia as well as in such traditionally diverse countries as Australia and Canada. How can leadership knowledge be applied in cross-cultural settings?

White (2001) has recently criticized Asian management research as too focused on simplistic comparisons, often between Asia and the West. Studies rely on unrepresentative samples and on correlational analyses that show possible associations but do not document the dynamics by which variables are related. Consequently, Asian researchers have not developed their frameworks much nor contributed to theorizing and practice beyond an audience specifically interested in Asia.

Although we generally agree with White's critique of Asian research, we argue that research in Asia can very much contribute to theorizing about leadership more generally. Asian research questions long-held assumptions and proposes alternative concepts that potentially can create enduring, elegant approaches to understanding leadership. The need to develop frameworks that are relevant for cross-cultural management is stimulating efforts to develop more universal approaches.

This chapter argues that the Asian emphasis on relationships is key to developing a powerful, applicable framework. Recent cross-cultural studies suggest that this leader relationship has to be negotiated by managers and employees. Studies have begun to document that the theory of cooperation and competition can help managers and employees contend with their cultural differences and develop effective leader relationships.

DEFINING LEADERSHIP

Leadership has traditionally been considered in terms of influence and moving a group toward its goals. Roger Stogdill (1974), a pioneer in leadership research, defined leadership as influencing the activities of an organized group toward setting and achieving goals. Leadership involves actions that engage group members to direct and coordinate their work.

In his comprehensive review, Bernard Bass (1990) defined leadership as interaction between two or more group members that structures or restructures the situation and alters the perceptions and expectations of members. Leaders are agents of change. They modify the motivation and competence of group members so that the group is more able to reach future goals.

Leaders are especially potent and constructive. They use their power and persuasion to have a positive impact on group success. For leaders to have a constructive impact on followers, employees must be open and responsive to

their managers but that in turn requires that managers be open and responsive. Leadership involves interdependence and demands coordination between
managers and employees.

ASIAN VALUES: ORGANIZATION AS A FAMILY

An initial, fundamental issue has been to characterize the nature of leadership in Asia. In doing so, Asian research has clearly indicated that the culture
of leaders and employees very much affects how they behave and respond to
each other.

Researchers have emphasized that Asians consider organizations as "families" (Cheng, 1995; Farh & Cheng, 2000; Redding, 1999; Silin, 1976; Westwood, 1997). Organization as family is a metaphor that orients managers and
employees' expectations of each other. But family is also a description. In addition to the prevalence of small companies in Asia, prestigious family companies play a very substantial role in Asian society.

The organization as family should be tightly knitted and managed by the
"father." The in-group of actual family members and long-term employees accepted as "family" is considered entitled to power and special treatment. This
section discusses relationship values and the leader as head as components of
the ideal of the organization as family.

Relationships

Asian leaders and employees are thought to be especially concerned about
relationships. Indeed, researchers have emphasized that personal connections
are critical for doing business in Asia (Hui, Law, & Chen, 1999; Tung, 1991).
Guanxi and collectivism values are reinforcing ideas to understand relationships in Asia.

Guanxi is a close, personal relationship based upon particularistic ties
(Hwang, 1987; Leung, Koch, & Lu, 2002; Tsui & Farh, 1997). For example,
leaders and employees may develop *guanxi* based in part because their families
are from the same village. They are considered part of the in-group whereas
those from other villages are the out-group. But the relationship has to be personal between the two persons; just having the same background is typically
insufficient. *Guanxi* should help develop trust and contribute to leader effectiveness.

Cheng, Farh and Chang (1999) conducted a quantitative study by selecting
173 superior-subordinate dyads from six private Taiwanese companies. Their

findings indicated that close manager-employee relationship leads to more generous treatment. Managers tended to be more considerate and concerned about the welfare of their employees with whom they had close ties.

Consistent with the idea of *guanxi*, researchers have proposed that Asians are collectivists who value a socially defined self. They give priority to in-group goals and accept that social norms should determine behavior (Kashima, Siegel, Tanaka, & Kashima, 1992; Kim, Triandis, Kagitcibasi, Choi, & Yoon, 1994; Markus & Kitayama, 1991; Mills & Clark, 1982; Sampson, 2001; Triandis, 1995). In contrast, individualists value a personal self, give priority to personal goals, and believe that their individual attitudes should determine their behavior. Chinese people have been found to see themselves as part of a larger whole and place high priority on their in-groups (Triandis, 1990; Trompenaars, 1993; Tung, 1991).

Collectivist values have been hypothesized to affect behavior, including leadership (Morris, Williams, Leung, Larrick, Mendoza, Bhatnagar, Li, Kondo, Luo, & Hu, 1998; Leung, 1997). Studies have shown that employees with high quality relationships with leaders perform their own jobs well and are willing to contribute as good citizens to the organization (Hui, Law, & Chen, 1999; Law, Hui, & Tjosvold, 1998). Personal relationships in particular are thought to contribute to effective leadership (Hui, Law, & Chen, 1999). For example, strong relationships helped Hong Kong managers and employees believe they were powerful, productive, and democratic (Tjosvold et al., 1998).

Collectivist values were found to promote leader relationships and commitment in China. Employees who indicated that their relationship was collectivist with their managers rated their own commitment high and were effective organizational citizens as rated by their manager (Tjosvold, Yu, & Liu, 2001). The mediating variable between collectivism and constructive outcomes was openness, measured by direct discussion of opposing views and acceptance of the manager's influence. Similarly, Chinese employees with collectivist relationships with their Japanese managers were able to discuss their differences open-mindedly and productively (Tjosvold, Wong, & Liu, 2002). These results challenge typical thinking that collectivism promotes conflict avoidance. However, as argued in the next section, they are consistent with theorizing and recent evidence that the traditional value of leader as head promotes open, supportive interaction between managers and employees.

Leader as Head

Theorists have proposed that in Asia, just as the father should be a strong leader in a family business, managers are expected to act as the "head of household" in private companies (Westwood, 1997). Based on the collectivist, harmony, and social order values of Asia, paternalistic leadership is culturally endorsed. In contrast, the individualistic, freedom-oriented West endorses open, participative leadership. Paternalistic leaders explain and teach employees but maintain some social distance from them. They strengthen their authority, expect employee obedience, and minimize conflict among employees.

But Asian paternalistic leaders are not simply autocratic as often assumed in the West. The values of *guanxi* and collectivism support a strong element of benevolence in the Asian model. Asian leaders develop personal relationships with employees and show favoritism toward in-group members. More generally, they are expected to care for their employees. Their employees are to accept their direction but in return leaders are obligated to understand and to provide for employee needs. Asian leaders feel a moral obligation for their employees' well being. Chinese employees described those managers who ascribed to the traditional idea of leadership as head as very supportive and effective (Tjosvold, Wong, & Liu, 2002). Traditional Chinese leadership values involve encouragement and relationship building, not coercion.

Farh and Cheng (2000) argued that the three major dimensions of Asian leadership are authoritarian, benevolence, and morality. Leaders assert control, build up their authority, and instruct employees who are expected to comply respectfully. Benevolent leaders privately show their personal caring of individuals as well as avoid embarrassing employees in public. Asian moral leaders serve unselfishly and model appropriate good citizenship behavior. Employees reciprocate the benevolence and morality of their leader with gratitude, respect, and identification.

Asian paternalistic leadership also differs from the Western idea of autocratic leadership in its emphasis on discussion between leaders and employees. Whereas autocratic leaders are closed, Asian leaders are expected to share and discuss their ideas. Dialogue is the ideal. Personal relationships and taking care of employees require leaders to listen to employee ideas and concerns. Although public debate may be difficult, private discussions are needed to show concern and caring, deal with issues, and maintain relationships and harmony (Farh & Cheng, 2000).

Paternalistic leadership also differs from the West's concept of autocracy in its orientation toward power. Theorists have proposed that in Asia power and authority are associated with moral obligation to use that capacity to protect and further the interests of the less powerful (Pye, 1985; Spencer-Oatey, 1997). Power is not primarily a tool for suppression and domination.

Impact of Asian Research

Asian leadership research is already having an impact on leadership theorizing. Specifically, research in the West has made progress by investigating the interpersonal relationship between managers and employees as an important antecedent to successful leadership across a wide variety of situations. Understanding the differences between Asian paternalistic leadership and West's autocratic leadership can also contribute to our understanding of authority and power.

Recently, researchers have joined those in Asia in emphasizing the role of relationships in successful leadership as well as decision-making and teamwork (Gersick, Bartunek, & Dutton, 2000; Howell & Hall-Merenda, 1999; House & Aditya, 1997; Kramer & Messick, 1995). George Graen and his colleagues have developed an impressive empirical base that the individual relationship between managers and employees has a critical impact on leader effectiveness (Bauer & Green, 1996; Brower, Schoorman, & Tan, 2000; Delugua, 1998; Gerstner & Day, 1997; Graen & Uhl-Bien, 1995; Howell & Hall-Merenda, 1999; Schriesheim, Neider, & Scandura, 1998). Early studies had direct Asian influences (Wakabayashi & Graen, 1984; Wakabayashi, Graen, & Uhl-Bien, 1990).

Emerging Western research on transformational leadership also emphasizes the importance of leaders developing effective relationships with and among employees (Bass, 1997; Chen & Farh, 2001). High quality leader relationships appear to be so useful because they foster interaction that helps employees feel committed and motivated to contribute to the organization. Argyris and Schon (1978, 1996) have argued that open, mutually supportive interaction is the foundation for leader effectiveness.

Asian paternalistic leadership can also have an impact on theorizing on nature of productive leadership relationships. Researchers in the West have tended to assume that directive leadership has to be autocratic and that leaders are either open and participative or directive and controlling. But paternalistic leaders in Asia develop personal, caring, and open relationships where they discuss and dialogue with their employees.

Paternalistic leadership explores assumptions in Western theorizing about authority and power. Asian researchers emphasize that authority is not established just because a manager has a superior position. Leaders must earn authority, especially its moral aspects, by demonstrating a commitment and openness to employees.

Paternalistic leadership also challenges the common belief in the West that power is invariably corrupting as it involves suppression and domination (Kipnis, 1976). Indeed, power in the West is assumed to be competitive where the power of the leader is at the expense of the power of employees (Pfeffer, 1981; Weber, 1947). However, in Asia, power is associated with benevolence and moral standing (Pye, 1985).

A few voices in the West have also argued that power need not be dominating and corrupting (McClelland, 1975). Rosabeth Kanter (1977, 1979) proposed that power is often a highly productive force in organizational life. Power does not frustrate employee involvement but promotes participation. It is the more powerful managers who assist and support their subordinates, the less powerful who resist employee influence. Powerful managers have the confidence as well as ability to aid their employees and influence them collaboratively.

Coleman (2000) found that managers who viewed power as expandable so that both the leader and the follower can enhance their power involved employees in decision making and developed constructive relationships. Experiments in North America and in China suggest that when power is considered expandable and cooperative, rather than limited and competitive, power is used to provide support and resources, not to coerce and limit the less powerful (Tjosvold, Coleman, & Sun, 2003).

Asian research and values support recent research and theorizing on the centrality of relationships for leadership and on the positive role of power and authority. The next section examines the complexities of understanding cross-cultural leadership.

UNDERSTANDING CULTURAL DIFFERENCES

In addition to characterizing Asian leadership, researchers in Asia have contributed to research on cultural differences. Indeed, much of the writing on Asian leadership compares it with well-known Western leadership models. This section briefly reviews these approaches and discusses comparisons across Asia.

Leader Orientations and Approaches

Researchers have applied transformational and transactional and other approaches developed in the West to understand similarities and differences with leadership in Asia (Chen & Farh, 2001). Productivity and maintenance values have historically been considered valuable in understanding leadership (Bass, 1990; Kerr & Schrieshiem, 1974; Matsui, Ohtsuka, & Kikuchi, 1978; Misumi & Peterson, 1985; Stogdill & Coons, 1957). Productively getting the work done and maintaining people and their relationships so that they can continue to get the work done are considered the two central functions of leaders.

Misumi (1985) has proposed that these general functions cross cultural boundaries. However, the specific ways these people and productivity functions are effectively accomplished depend upon the specific situation and more generally on the cultural context. From questionnaires collected in Hong Kong, Japan, UK and USA, items measuring the general functions of productivity and people and the specific ways to implement them correlated with each other in different ways depending upon the country, but the general items predicted leader effectiveness across the cultures (Smith, Misumi, Peterson, Tayeb, & Bond, 1989; Smith, Peterson, Misumi, & Bond, 1992). These results suggest that effective leaders communicate both a productivity and people orientation but how they operationalize these values depends upon the cultural context.

The GLOBE Program

The Global Leadership and Organizational Behavior Effectiveness program (GLOBE) has also found that there are universally endorsed leader dimensions and that the operationalizations of these dimensions – the specific strategies and actions that communicate the dimension – vary from one culture to another. Although there are approaches that universally promote or impede organizations, the behaviors by which these are implemented differ across countries.

The overall aim of the GLOBE project is to develop an empirically based theory that relates the effects of cultural values on leader behavior and effectiveness. The GLOBE team has tried to identify the leadership behaviors that are universally endorsed across cultures and those that are culture-specific, that is, those that are valued within a national culture. These culturally endorsed leadership dimensions are in turn based on the nation's collectivism, individualism, and other underlying values.

A major finding of this research is that there are universal dimensions of leadership and these dimensions have similar effects (facilitative or obstructive) across many nations (Brodbeck, Frese, & Javidan, 2002; den Hartog, House, Hanges, Dorfman, Ruiz-Quintana, & GLOBE Associates, 1999). Universally valued dimensions include: *Charismatic/Value Based Leadership*. Here the leader espouses a vision congruent with the values and cultural norms of followers. *Self-Protective Leadership*. These leaders are bossy, self-interested, and evasive and rely on formalities and procedures. These leaders were found to be ineffective across national cultures.

National cultures also have their own understandings of what constitute effective leadership that result in behaviors that while facilitative in one cultural context may not be in another. Dimensions that were found to be more dependent upon the national culture include: *Team Orientated Leadership*. These leaders focus on the team and emphasize relationships among team members. *Humane Leadership*. Leaders are generous, compassionate, patient, and modest. *Participative Leadership*. A participative leader works well and directly with employees on the task. *Autonomous Leadership*. Leaders are independent and autonomous.

. Recent research has applied this framework to Asia. Results supported the hypotheses that in both Australia and New Zealand effective leaders, in addition to being Charismatic/Value Based and having low levels of Self-Protection, have high levels of Participative leadership and Team Orientation, and moderately high levels of Humane leadership (Ashkanasy, Roberts, & Lincoln, 2003).

Comparisons across Asia

The traditional assumption has been that the differences among Asian countries are not significant given the dominance of collectivist values in Asia. However, the GLOBE project departed from the usual practice of comparing Asian and Western approaches to management to examine national cultures. Recent analyses suggest specific differences in leadership across Asian countries.

Filipino and Thai leaders operate within clearly collectivist milieus where maintaining good relationships is considered critical (Bhanthumnavin & Bhanthumnavin, in press; Teehankee, in press). There is a traditional Thai saying that, "a crowded environment is livable, but an uneasy relationship is unbearable." Good leaders are expected to support employees and to foster a caring, even fun-oriented work environment. Although these values would seem to make cooperative relationships culturally appropriate, they do not automatically translate into effective work relationships. Indeed, Filipino and Thai employees may be particularly sensitive to losing social face and public criticism. When leaders fail to know their employees as individuals, treat each employee with enough personal regard and consideration, or in other ways not live up to high standards, Filipino and Thai employees may feel frustrated and become suspicious of their leader.

Filipino and Thai employees often want their relationships with in-group and family members to be recognized and at times given priority over work relationships. Developing cooperative relationships focused on productivity and efficiency may frustrate their expectations. Open controversy in the workplace may seem unusual, even culturally inappropriate for people are oriented toward "getting along." Leaders may have to focus to help their employees understand the value of open discussion of differences and develop strong relationships in which it can occur.

Leading in Thailand and the Philippines are not the same. The Philippines experienced centuries of Spanish rule and more recently strong American influence. In Thailand, learning the ceremony to serve tea may be an important way to communicate concern and interest in employees (Bhanthumnavin & Bhanthumnavin, in press).

Leading in Singapore poses some similar but also additional obstacles to effective leader relationships (Ko, in press). Although a Chinese society, Singaporeans have also adopted values of individualism as their economy has become closely linked with the West. Continually reminded that they have few natural resources, Singaporeans recognize that they must continually develop themselves and their organizations to remain competitive in the global marketplace. They have developed language and other skills of high standards.

However, many Singaporean leaders believe that they need to be heroic and dominating and they exert considerable pressure on employees to perform efficiently. Indeed, humor and good spirits are often lacking in Singaporean workplaces. Also troubling is that because of the pressure to succeed, Singaporeans have strong fears of failure and avoid experimenting. Western managers often complain that their Singaporean employees avoid risk, perhaps because they have become accustomed to highly directive leadership where making a mistake is seen as highly costly. Yet there is a wide spread belief that Singapore must change and become a more knowledge-based economy to flourish in the future. Developing norms and skills for open-minded discussion for mutual benefit and change in Singapore may require especially sensitive leadership.

Australia and New Zealand are the most Western societies in Asia. But the values of individualism do not mean that Australian and New Zealand employees are uninterested in cooperative relationships with their bosses. Indeed, recent evidence suggests that Australia has a strong "we are all mates" climate that emphasizes the equality among employees and their bosses (Ashkanasy, Roberts, & Kennedy, in press). No one person's interests are superior to those of another. Leaders are to be generous and compassionate, sincere and modest.

While New Zealand may not be so rapidly equalitarian, leaders are very much expected to focus on developing the team and fostering high levels of performance. They are to be consultative, loyal, and group-orientated but they are also should be diplomatic and credible. Much is expected of leaders in Australia and New Zealand yet they have to lead with little formal power and authority.

Methodological Issues

Questions of how leadership in one culture compares to leadership in another culture are easy to ask, very difficult to answer. Developing a generally acceptable theoretical framework to compare cultures is challenging. Despite hundreds of empirical studies, a recent review suggests that the ideas of collectivism and individualism suffer from conceptual weaknesses and their measurement instruments from low reliability (Oyserman, Coon, & Kemmelmeier, 2002). Evidence, when considered together, does not suggest that collectivism and individualism have large, consistent, replicated effects. People in a national culture were also found to be both collectivist and individualistic (Sampson, 2001; Sinha, Sinha, Verma, & Sinha, 2001). Oyserman et al. (2002) concluded that it is at best premature to conclude that collectivism and individualism represent distinct ways of psychological functioning.

There are numerous methodological issues that frustrate comparisons of leadership across national cultures. A fundamental obstacle is to develop representative samples of the national cultures. Even when, for example, both Japanese and American samples are all MBA students they are likely to differ on other characteristics, such as age, in addition to their national culture. Even when they have the same chronological average age, they may still differ in their psychological maturity, business experience, and many other dimensions. How can any differences be attributed to national culture?

The results of comparisons are limited in time. Values are theorized to be relatively enduring but they change over time (Heuer, Cummings, & Hutabarat, 1999; Ralston, Egri, Stewart, Terpstra, & Kaicheng, 1999). The time frame for significant change is unknown (Smith, 2002).

There are questions of identifying cultural groups. Typically, the nation state is used to demarcate different cultures. However, studies have documented significant regional differences within countries such as China in their endorsement of basic values (Schlevogt, 2001; Kozan & Ergin, 1999).

Even when these issues are dealt with reasonably, results remain correlational. Findings suggest possible relationships but do not provide direct evidence on the dynamics underlying cultural differences and the conditions under which these differences are particularly strong.

Conclusions about how leadership compares across cultures remain general with many possible exceptions. Our confidence in these conclusions should be tempered with the understanding of the weaknesses in the empirical foundation. The next section argues that research on cultural differences in leadership suggests the need for additional approaches to understanding leadership.

THE CROSS-CULTURAL CHALLENGE

Leadership is often cross-cultural in multi-national companies and increasingly within domestic organizations. Traditional cross-cultural management research highlights potential value differences between the leader and employee. It can help leaders and employees use reasonably accurate stereotypes to form their expectations of each other. Recent studies though underline the limitations of traditional cross-cultural knowledge and suggest more useful approaches.

Negotiating Leadership

Cross-cultural interaction and leadership are particularly complex (Adair, Okumura, & Brett, 2001). Cross-cultural interactions have the potential to communicate a disrespect for others identity and values (Ting-Toomey, 1999). Although there are often significant gains when people of diverse cultures work together, research is needed on how they are able to overcome barriers and collaborate effectively (Earley & Mosakowski, 2000).

In a recent study, Japanese managers indicated that they were more assertive, used appeals to reason, made threats and appealed to higher authority with Canadian employees; whereas with Japanese subordinates, they were indirect (Rao & Hashimoto, 1996). US employees of a Japanese firm evaluated a Japanese who had somewhat adapted his behavior to US styles as more effective than those who did not adapt (Thomas & Ravlin, 1995). However, they believed a Japanese managers who adopted a highly American way was not genuine. Japanese managers were found to adapt their behavior somewhat when negotiating with US Americans (Adair et al., 2001).

These studies suggest the limits of knowledge on cultural values for the understanding and practice of cross-cultural leadership (Smith, 2002). Managers do not simply act out of their national values nor just adopt the culturally endorsed approach of the employee. Managers must have the abilities and procedures to apply their knowledge of cultural values in sensitive, adaptive ways. They must develop methods so that employees understand them and feel motivated to get things done.

Event Management Approach

Evidence about cross-cultural differences, even if they are reasonably accurate and timely, provide only general guidance. It cannot be assumed that the manager and employee exactly represent their "cultures" in that they have the same values as national samples. What counts are the orientations of the specific individuals involved, not national averages.

More generally, the behavior of leaders and employees very much depends upon the specific situation. The tasks and demands, the organization's climate and its intergroup relations, the particular aspirations of the individuals, and many other variables all impact leadership. Cultural values, even if they can be specifically identified, are only one part of the situation in which leadership occurs (Salk & Brannen, 2000).

Smith and his colleagues have recently proposed that event management theory can help to understand leadership as it occurs within situations (Smith & Peterson, 1988; Smith, Peterson, & Schwartz, 2002). Leaders must deal with numerous work events daily. They first must understand the event and determine how to respond to it all under the time and other pressures of organizational life.

Interviews with Chinese middle-level managers with foreign managers from Asia and the West in joint venture hotels in the mid-nineties revealed a number of problematic events, including ways of making decisions, ways of allocating tasks, conduct of meetings, bonus payments, and poor work by subordinates (Smith, Wang, & Leung, 1997). The Chinese managers were found to rely upon traditional Chinese methods of using indirect influence and relying on widespread Chinese beliefs to deal with these events. However, they believed that Western ways of direct talk and following usual policies and procedures were more effective. These managers also indicated that they found different ways effective with different foreigners. Direct talk was seen as effective but not with Japanese supervisors.

These Chinese managers recognized that certain Western methods were more effective; however, they still relied upon their Chinese methods. Perhaps they were in the middle of the adaptation process. Later they might be able to reconcile their proclivity for Chinese approaches with their understanding that at least within their joint ventures, Western approaches were more effective. A companion study conducted in Belarus suggested that Western managers had adapted and had begun to rely upon culturally endorsed tough, autocratic methods though they would have preferred more Western methods (Smith, Yanchuk, & Sekun, 2001).

Managers and employees negotiate how they will behave toward each other. Cultural values do not dictate their behavior. Managers must deal with cultural differences as they act in specific settings with specific events. Research is needed to understand and help managers and employees with different cultural and national backgrounds find ways to work effectively together.

COOPERATION AND COMPETITION RESEARCH

Asian and current Western research has emphasized the vital role of relationships in leadership. Recent research on cross-cultural leadership further supports the centrality of relationships. Managers and employees, in addition to having reasonable expectations for their cultural differences, must be able to negotiate a way to work together across a variety of tasks and situations. This section proposes that Asian as well as Western managers can use the theory of cooperation and competition to develop their relationships so that they can work effectively across situations and over time. A few studies directly suggest that the theory is useful in cross-cultural settings.

Theory

Morton Deutsch (1949, 1973) argued that how people believed their goals are related has a pervasive impact on underlying expectations and interaction that then affect outcomes. Managers and employees can believe that their goals are cooperatively or competitively related or unrelated (Deutsch, 1949, 1973; Johnson & Johnson, 1989). In cooperation, they perceive that they can reach their goals if and only if the others also reach their goals. As they succeed to the extent that others succeed, they encourage and support each other's efforts. In competition, managers and employees work against each other to achieve a goal that only one or a few can attain. Goal achievements are negatively correlated; each person perceives that when one achieves his or her goal, others fail to achieve their goals. Thus, they are tempted to frustrate and obstruct others from performing well and reaching their goals.

With independent goals, there is no correlation among goal attainments. Each person perceives that he or she can reach his or her goal regardless of whether other individuals attain their goals. They seek an outcome that is personally beneficial without concern for the outcomes of others. Results of over 575 experimental and 100 correlational studies conducted mostly in North American when taken together in meta-analyses strongly support the theorizing on goal interdependence on interaction and outcomes (Johnson & Johnson, 1989).

The dynamics induced by cooperative goals and contributing to effective joint work has been characterized as constructive controversy (Tjosvold, 1998, 1985b). Controversy occurs when persons discuss their opposing views about how a problem should be solved. Research indicates that it is through open-minded, controversial discussion that people combine and integrate their ideas to resolve issues and strengthen their relationships (Tjosvold, 1998, 1985b). Through controversy, people develop and express their own perspectives on an issue. When confronted with another's opposing views, they feel uncertain about the most effective solution and search for additional information and a more adequate way of understanding the issue. Then they are prepared to integrate other ideas to create new, more elegant conceptualizations of the problem. This exploration of positions and the creation of new solutions during controversy result in high quality, high commitment decisions.

The theory of cooperation and competition, like any other, cannot be assumed to apply in another culture. A cooperative, bicultural network has tested the theory in Asian organizations. Trained both in the East and West and based in Hong Kong, Mainland China, Korea, Japan, Taiwan, and other East Asian countries, researchers have debated the theory and developed the methods. We now review our findings using experimental and field methods.

Field Studies on Leadership in Asian Organizations

Research first was to determine the extent that the theory of cooperation and competition was useful for understanding leadership in Asian organizations. In an initial study, 89 Hong Kong leaders and employees were interviewed on specific incidents (Tjosvold et al., 1998). An open-minded discussion of opposing views between leaders and employees was found to be highly crucial, resulting in productive work, strong work relationships, experiencing the leader as democratic, and believing that both the leader and employee are powerful.

In a survey study, managers and their employees in a watch case manufacturing factory in southern China participated on a study of the leader relationship and employee citizenship (Law, Hui, & Tjosvold, 1998). Structural equation analysis confirm the hypotheses that strong cooperative goals as measured by the employees, but not competitive or independent ones, promote a high quality relationship between leader and employee, which in turn leads to high levels of job performance and citizenship behavior as described by their manager.

106 pairs of supervisors and employees from 10 State Owned Enterprises in Nanjing and Shanghai participate in a leadership study on goal interdependence, justice, and citizenship behavior (Hui, Tjosvold, & Ding, 1998). The analysis supported the model that a strong sense of justice promotes cooperative goals that lead to open-minded, constructive controversy whereas competitive and independent goals result in closed-mindedness. Controversy in turn resulted in job performance and citizenship behavior.

Experiments on Power and Conflict

Experimental studies are needed in leadership to document directly causal relationships and the dynamics between variables. Building upon previous experiments in North America (Tjosvold, 1985a, 1985c, 1981), managers with cooperative, compared to competitive, goals with their employees used their valued resources to assist and support employees, especially employee who demonstrated high needs by being unable to complete the task themselves (Tjosvold & Sun, 2001; Tjosvold, Coleman, & Sun, 2003). Field studies have similarly found that managers with cooperative goals use their abilities to assist employees (Tjosvold & Poon, 2001).

Experiments have also shown that cooperative compared to competitive goals promote the open-minded consideration of opposing ideas (Tjosvold & Sun, 2001). Chinese participants in an experiment placed in the role of managers were committed to mutual benefit, were interested in learning more about the opposing views, considered these views useful, came to agree with them, and tended to integrate them into their own decisions in cooperative compared to competitive situations. They were more attracted to the other protagonist and had greater confidence in working together in the future than participants in the competitive condition.

Open discussion, compared to avoiding conflict, strengthened relationships, and induced epistemic curiosity where Chinese people asked questions, explored opposing views, demonstrated knowledge, and worked to integrate views (Tjosvold, Hui, & Sun, 2000; Tjosvold & Sun, 2001). They characterized people who disagreed directly and openly as strong persons and competent negotiators whereas "avoiding" protagonists were considered weak and ineffectual. In another experiment, open discussion compared to avoiding developed a cooperative relationship and open-minded understanding of the opposing view (Tjosvold & Sun, in press).

Although the Asian value of social face (Ho, 1976) is commonly hypothesized to lead to conflict avoidance (Ting-Toomey, 1988), social face has been found, under certain conditions, to promote openness. Chinese negotiators who confirmed social face were able to discuss their opposing views open-mindedly (Tjosvold et al., 2000; Tjosvold & Sun, 2001). Participants taking the role of managers who believed they were seen as effective emphasized their cooperative goals with the employee, learned, considered the opposing views useful, and came to agree with some of them. A field study also indicated that confirmation of face helped Chinese people to discuss their opposing views cooperatively and productively.

Cross-Cultural Studies

A few studies have directly suggested that the theory is useful in cross-cultural settings. Hong Kong senior accounting managers were found to be able to lead employees working in the mainland of China when they had cooperative goals, but not when their goals were competitive or independent (Tjosvold & Moy, 1998). They were then able to discuss their views open-mindedly that led to stronger relationships and productivity, consequences that in turn resulted in future internal motivation.

Chinese employees described specific examples of when they worked with their American or Japanese manager (Su, Chen & Tjosvold, 2003). Results indicated that cooperative goals contributed to an open-minded discussion of views that led to productive collaborative work and strengthened relationships. Similarly, managers in the Hong Kong parent company and new product specialists in Canada who developed cooperative links and engaged in constructive controversy were able to develop strong, trusting relationships despite their cultural differences and geographic separation (Tjosvold, 1999).

Applying the Theory in Asia

Our results provide good support for the theory of cooperation and competition in Asia and, in particular, that cooperative goals and open-minded discussion are a strong basis for successful leader relationships. However, unlike leadership research that identifies major strategies and actions that managers can take, the implications of the theory of cooperation and competition are social psychological. Managers and employees have to develop their own ways of interacting; there are no scripts that insure they are developing a cooperative relationship.

Managers and employees must come to their own conclusions that what is good for one is good for all; success for one is success for all. Already developed procedures suggests broad outlines of how managers and employees may proceed, but they must modify these to take into account their situation and cultures (Deutsch, 1994; Tjosvold, 1991, 1993). In particular, they should develop norms and procedures that jointly consider and incorporate their diverse cultures (Leung, in press).

For example, developing common tasks, recognizing the necessity for joint effort, and shared rewards for success can convince managers and employees that they have cooperative goals so that they feel that they are "on the same side" and are "in this together." They can also develop skills and procedures to voice and integrate their different views but these ways should be acceptable to both cultural groups. The theory of cooperation and competition does not provide a quick fix to leadership but it does suggest how managers and employees, even from culturally diverse backgrounds, can together develop it.

CONCLUDING COMMENTS

Asian research documenting the role of cultural context and identifying the demands of cross-cultural leadership underlines the complexity of leadership and the need to develop elegant, applicable frameworks. Asian research also proposes that relationships are the foundations of leadership and, contrary to common Western stereotypes, these relationships are mutual and two-way. Asian managers believe that as heads of the organization they must care for and be open with their employees; in turn employees are respectful and accepting of influence.

Cross-cultural research has also reminded us that managers and employees must negotiate and develop their relationships and ways of interacting that are effective and appropriate for their situation, tasks, and cultures. Recent research has documented that the theory of cooperation and competition can guide the development of these relationships. Common interests and open-minded discussion where leaders support and listen and with their employees engage in constructive controversy characterize effective leader relationships.

But the idea of relationship still may seem too far removed from images of leaders shaping their company's strategy and forging its competitive advantages. Isn't this the core of leadership, not developing relationships? Strategic management researchers have recently emphasized that top management teams, not just one person, are needed to continue to update strategies and their implementation (Kilduff, Angelmar, & Mehra, 2000; Knight, Pearce, Smith, Olain, Sims, Smith, & Flood, 1999). A recent study directly documents the value of the relationships among top management team members for strategic leadership in Asia. Results from 378 executives and 105 CEOs in China indicate that cooperative goals form the basis for an effective top management team (Tjosvold, Chen, & Liu, 2001). Within these teams, executives recognized and applied their ideas and other abilities so that they created strategic advantages. Successful CEOs work with and through their executives to develop the capacities that will help their companies succeed in the marketplace.

Leadership requires an intellectual understanding but is also a complex performing art. Every leader and every employee have their own styles, aspirations, and values. Leading one person is not the same as leading another. Each leadership setting is unique with its own requirements and opportunities. Cross-cultural leadership highlights the demands on managers and employees to adapt to each other. Studies have documented the importance of the Asian value of two-way relationships where leaders and employees are sensitive and open to each other. Managers lead with employees as together they set their direction, solve problems, and encourage each other. Although much more research is needed, recent studies in Asia have begun to develop frameworks with the potential to help managers and employees forge their own effective leader relationship.

ACKNOWLEDGMENTS

This work has been supported by the Research Grants Council of the Hong Kong Special Administrative Region, China, (Project No: LU3013/01H) to the first author and RGC grant project No: HKUST6197/98H to the third author.

REFERENCES

Adair, W.L., Okumura, T. and Brett, J.M. 2001. Negotiation behavior when cultures collide: The United States and Japan. *Journal of Applied Psychology*, 86: 371-385.

Arygris, C. and Schon, D.A. 1978. *Organizational Learning: A Theory of Action Perspective*. Reading, MA: Addison-Wesley.

Arygris, C. and Schon, D.A. 1996. *Organizational Learning II: Theory, Method, and Practice*. Reading, MA: Addison-Wesley.

Ashkanasy, N.M., Roberts, E.T. and Kennedy, J. (in press). The Egalitarian leader: Leadership in Australia and New Zealand. In D. Tjosvold and K. Leung (eds.), *Leadership in Asia Pacific: Managing Relationships for Teamwork and Change*. Singapore: World Scientific Publishing.

Bass, B.M. 1990. *Bass and Stogdill's Handbook of Leadership* (3rd edn). New York: The Free Press.

Bass, B.M. 1997. Does the transactional-transformational leadership paradigm transcend organizational and national boundaries? *American Psychologist*, 52: 130-139.

Bauer, T.N. and Green, S.G. 1996. Development of leader-member exchange: A longitudinal test. *Academy of Management Journal*, 39: 1538-1567.

Bhanthumnavin, Duangduen and Bhanthumnavin, Duchduen. (In press). Leadership effectiveness in Thailand. In D. Tjosvold and K. Leung (eds.), *Leadership in Asia Pacific: Managing Relationships for Teamwork and Change*. Singapore: World Scientific Publishing Co.

Brodbeck, F.C., Frese, M. and Javidan, M. 2002. Leadership made in Germany: Low on compassion, high on performance. *Academy of Management Executive*, 16: 16-29.

Brower, H.H., Schoorman, F.D. and Tan, H.H. 2000. A model of relational leadership: The integration of trust and leader-member exchange. *Leadership Quarterly*, 11: 227-250.

Chen, X.P. and Farh, J.L. 2001. Transformational and transaction leader behaviors in Chinese organizations: Differential effects in the People's Republic of China and Taiwan. In W.H. Mobley and M.W. McCall, Jr. (eds.), *Advances in Global Leadership* (Vol. II, pp. 101-126). Oxford: Elsevier Science.

Cheng, B.S. 1995. *Authoritarian Values and Executive Leadership: The Case of Taiwanese Family Enterprises*. Taiwan's National Science Council. Taiwan: National Taiwan University (In Chinese).

Cheng, B.S., Farh, J.L. and Chang, H. 1999. Employee categorization and managerial behavior in the Chinese context: A theoretical model and its validation. Unpublished Paper.

Coleman, P. 2000. In M. Deutsch and P.T. Coleman (eds.), *The Handbook of Conflict Resolution: Theory and Practice* (pp. 475-495). San Francisco: Jossey-Bass.

Delugua, R.J. 1998. Leader-member exchange quality and effectiveness ratings. *Group & Organization Management*, 23: 189-216.

den Hartog, D.N., House, R.J., Hanges, P.J., Dorfman, P.W., Ruiz-Quintana, A. and GLOBE Associates. 1999. Culture specific and cross-culturally generalizable implicit leadership theories: Are attributes of charismatic/transformational leadership universally endorsed? *Leadership Quarterly*, 10(2): 219-256.

Deutsch, M. 1994. Constructive conflict resolution: Principles, training, and research. *Journal of Social Issues*, 50: 13-32.

Deutsch, M. 1949. A theory of cooperation and competition. *Human Relations*, 2: 129-152.

Deutsch, M. 1973. *The Resolution of Conflict*. New Haven, CT: Yale University Press.

Earley, P.C. and Mosakowski, E. 2000. Creating hybrid team cultures: An empirical test of transnational team functioning. *Academy of Management Journal*, 43: 26-49.

Farh, J.L. and Cheng, B.S. 2000. A culture analysis of paternalistic leadership in Chinese organization. In A.S. Tsui and J.T. Li (eds.), *Management and Organizations in China*. London: Macmillan.

Gersick, C.J.G., Bartunek, J.M. and Dutton, J.E. 2000. Learning from academia: The importance of relationships in professional life. *Academy of Management Journal*, 43: 1026-1045.

Gerstner, C.R. and Day, D.V. 1997. Meta-analytic review of leader-member exchange theory: Correlates and construct issues. *Journal of Applied Psychology*, 82: 827-844.

Graen, G.B. and Uhl-Bien, M. 1995. Relationship-based approach to leadership: Development of leader-member exchange (LMX) theory of leadership over 25 years: Applying a multi-level multi-domain perspective. *Leadership Quarterly*, 6: 219-247.

Heuer, M., Cummings, J.L. and Hutabarat, W. 1999. Cultural stability or change among managers in Indonesia? *Journal of International Business Studies*, 30: 599-610.

Ho, D.Y. 1976. On the concept of face. *American Journal of Sociology*, 81: 867-84.

House, R.J. and Aditya, R. 1997. The social scientific study of leadership: Quo vadis? *Journal of Management*, 23: 409-473.

Howell, J.M. and Hall-Merenda, K.E. 1999. The ties that bind: The impact of leader-member exchange, transformational and transactional leadership, and distance on predicting follower performance. *Journal of Applied Psychology*, 84: 680-694.

Hui, C., Law, K.S. and Chen, Z.X. 1999. A structural equation model of the effects of negative affectivity, leader-member exchange, and perceived job mobility on in-role and extra-role performance: A Chinese case. *Organizational Behavior and Human Decision Processes*, 77: 3-21.

Hui, C., Tjosvold, D. and Ding, D. 1998. Organizational justice and citizenship behavior in China: Goal interdependence as mediator. Paper, submitted for publication. Chinese University of Hong Kong.

Hunt, J.G. and Dodge, G.E. 2000. Leadership de ja vu all over again. *Leadership Quarterly*, 11: 435-458.

Hwang, K.K. 1987. Face and favor: the Chinese power game. *American Journal of Sociology*, 92: 944-974.

Johnson, D.W. and Johnson, R.T. 1989. *Cooperation and Competition: Theory and Research*. Edina, MN: Interaction Book Company.

Kanter, R.M. 1977. *Men and Women of the Corporation*. New York: Basic Books.

Kanter, R.M. 1979. *Power Failure in Management Circuits* (pp. 65-75). Harvard Business Review.

Kashima, Y., Siegel, M., Tanaka, K. and Kashima, E.S. 1992. Do people believe behaviors are consistent with attitudes? Toward a cultural psychology of attribution processes. *British Journal of Social Psychology*, 331: 111-124.

Kerr, S. and Schrieshiem, C.A. 1974. Consideration, initiating structure, and organizational criteria: An update of Korman's 1966 review. *Personnel Psychology*, 27: 555-568.

Kilduff, Angelmar, R. and Mehra, A. 2000. Top management-team diversity and firm performance: Examining the role of cognitions. *Organization Science*, 11: 21-34.

Kim, U., Triandis, H.C., Kagitcibasi, C., Choi, S. and Yoon, G. 1994. *Individualism and Collectivism: Theory, Method and Applications*. Newbury Park, CA: Sage.

Kipnis, D. 1976. *The Powerholders*. Chicago: University of Chicago Press.

Knight, D., Pearce, C.L., Smith, K.G., Olain, J.D., Sims, Jr., H.P., Smith, K.A. and Flood, P. 1999. Top management team diversity, group process and strategic consensus. *Strategic Management Journal*, 20: 446-465.

Ko, W. (in press). Leadership challenges and excellence in Singapore. In D. Tjosvold and K. Leung (eds.), *Leadership in Asia Pacific: Managing Relationships for Teamwork and Change*. Singapore: World Scientific Publishing.

Kouzes, J.M. and Posner, B.Z. 1995. *The Leadership Challenge: How to Keep Getting Extraordinary Things Done in Organizations*. San Francisco: Jossey-Bass.

Kozan, M.K. and Ergin, C. 1999. The influence of intra-cultural value differences on conflict management practices. *International Journal of Conflict Management*, 10: 249-267.

Kramer, R.M. and Messick, D.M. 1995. *Negotiation as a Social Process*. Thousand Oaks, CA: Sage Publications.

Law, S.A., Hui, C. and Tjosvold, D. 1998. *Relational Approach to Understanding Conflict Management: Integrating the Theory of Cooperation and Competition, Leader-Member Relationship, and In-Role and Extra-Role Performance*. Paper submitted for publication, Hong Kong University of Science and Technology, Hong Kong.

Leung, K. 1997. Negotiation and reward allocations across cultures. In P.C. Earley and M. Erez (eds.), *New Perspectives on International Industrial/Organizational Psychology* (pp. 640-675). San Francisco: Jossey-Bass.

Leung, K. (In press). Effective conflict resolution for intercultural disputes. In T. Gärling, G. Backenroth-Ohsako, B. Ekehammar and L. Jonsson (eds.), *Diplomacy and Psychology: Prevention of Armed Conflicts After the Cold War*.

Leung, K., Koch, T.P. and Lu, L. (2002). A dualistic model of harmony and its implications for conflict management in Asia. *Asia Pacific Journal of Management*, 19: 201-220.

Markus, H.R. and Kitayama, S. 1991. Culture and self: Implications for cognition, emotion and motivation. *Psychological Review*, 98: 224-253.

Matsui, T., Ohtsuka, Y. and Kikuchi, A. 1978. Consideration and structure behaviour as reflections of supervisory interpersonal values. *Journal of Applied Psychology*, 63(2): 259-62.

McClelland, D.C. 1975. *Power: The Inner Experience*. New York: Irvington Publishers, Inc.

Mills, J. and Clark, M.S. 1982. Exchange and communal relationships. In L. Wheeler (ed.), *Review of Personality and Social Psychology* (Vol. 3). Beverly Hills, CA: Sage.

Misumi, J. 1985. *The Behavioral Science of Leadership*. Ann Arbor, MI: University of Michigan Press.

Misumi, J. and Peterson, M.F. 1985. The Performance-Maintenance (PM) theory of leadership: Review of a Japanese research program. *Administrative Science Quarterly*, 30: 198-223.

Morris, M.W., Williams, K.Y., Leung, K., Larrick, R., Mendoza, M.T., Bhatnagar, D., Li, J., Kondo, M., Luo, J.L. and Hu, J.C. 1998. Conflict management style: Accounting for cross-national differences. *Journal of International Business Studies*, 29: 729-748.

Oyserman, D., Coon, H.M., and Kemmelmeier, M. 2002. Rethinking individualism and collectivism: Evaluation of theoretical assumptions and meta-analyses. *Psychological Bulletin*, 128: 3-72.

Pfeffer, J. 1981. *Power in Organizations*. Boston: Pittman.

Pye, L.W. 1985. *Asian Power and Politics: The Cultural Dimensions of Authority*. Cambridge, MA: Harvard University Press.

Ralston, D.A., Egri, C.P., Stewart, S., Terpstra, R.H. and Kaicheng, Y. 1999. Doing business in the 21st century with the new generation of Chinese managers: A study of generational shifts in work values in China. *Journal of International Business Studies*, 30: 415-428.

Rao, A. and Hashimoto, K. 1996. Intercultural influence: A study of Japanese expatriate managers in Canada. *Journal of International Business Studies*, 27: 443-466.

Redding, S.G. 1990. *The Spirit of Chinese Capitalism*. Berlin: Walter de Gruyter.

Salk, J.E. and Brannen, M.Y. 2000. National culture, networks, and individual influence in a multinational management team. *Academy of Management Journal*, 43: 191-202.

Sampson, E.E. 2001. Reinterpreting individualism and collectivism: Their religious roots and monologic versus dialogic person-other relationship. *American Psychologist*, 55: 1425-1432.

Schlevogt, K.A. 2001. Institutional and organizational factors affecting effectiveness: Geoeconomic comparison between Shanghai and Beijing. *Asia Pacific Journal of Management*, 18: 519-551.

Schriesheim, C.A., Neider, L.L. and Scandura, T.A. 1998. Delegation and leader-member exchange: Main effects, moderators, and measurement issues. *Academy of Management Journal*, 41: 298-318.

Silin, R.F. 1976. *Leadership and Values*. Cambridge, MA: Harvard University Press.

Sinha, J.B.P., Sinha, T.N., Verma, J. and Sinha, R.B.N. 2001. Collectivism coexisting with individualism: An Indian scenario. *Asian Journal of Social Psychology*, 4: 133-145.

Smith, P.B. 2002. Culture's consequences: Something old and something new. *Human Relations*, 55: 119-135.

Smith, P.B., Misumi, J., Peterson, M.F., Tayeb, M.H. and Bond, M.H. 1989. On the generality of leadership styles across cultures. *Journal of Occupational Psychology*, 62: 97-110.

Smith, P.B. and Peterson, M.F. 1988. *Leadership, Organisations and Culture: An Event Management Model*. London: Sage.

Smith, P.B., Peterson, M.F., Misumi, J. and Bond, M.H. 1992. A cross-cultural test of the Japanese PM leadership theory. *Applied Psychology: An International Review*, 41: 5-19.

Smith, P.B., Peterson, M.F., Schwartz, S.H. and 36 co-authors. 2002. Cultural values, sources of guidance and their relevance to managerial behaviour: A 47 nation study. *Journal of Cross-Cultural Psychology*, 33: 188-208.

Smith, P.B., Wang, Z.M. and Leung, K. 1997. Leadership, decision-making and cultural context. *Leadership Quarterly*, 8: 413-431.

Smith, P.B., Yanchuk, V.A. and Sekun, V.I. 2001. Management behaviour in Belarus organizations. Report to International Association for the promotion of co-operation with scientists from the newly independent states of the former Soviet Union (INTAS): Brussels.

Spencer-Oatey, H. 1997. Unequal relationships in high and low power distance societies: A comparative study of tutor-student role relations in Britain and China. *Journal of Cross-Cultural Psychology*, 28: 284-302.

Stogdill, R.A. and Coons, A.E. 1957. *Leader Behavior: Its Description and Measurement.* Columbus, OH: Ohio State University, Bureau of Business Research.

Stogdill, R.M. 1974. *Handbook of Leadership: A Survey of Literature.* New York: Free Press.

Su, F., Chen, Y.F. and Tjosvold, D. 2003. *Goal Interdependence for Working Across Cultural Boundaries: Chinese Employees with Foreign Managers.* Paper, Academy of Management, Seattle, Washington.

Teehankee, B.L. (in press). Culturally sensitive leadership in the Philippine setting. In D. Tjosvold and K. Leung (eds.), *Leadership in Asia Pacific: Managing Relationships for Teamwork and Change.* Singapore: World Scientific Publishing.

Thomas, D.C. and Ravlin, E.C. 1995. Responses of employees to cultural adaptation by a foreign manager. *Journal of Applied Psychology*, 80: 133-146.

Ting-Toomey, S. 1988. A face negotiation theory. In Y.Y. Kim and W.B. Gudykunst (eds.), *Theory and Intercultural Communication* (pp. 47-92). Thousand Oaks, CA: Sage.

Ting-Toomey, S. 1999. *Communicating Across Cultures.* New York: Guilford Press.

Tjosvold, D. 1981. Unequal power relationships within a cooperative or competitive context. *Journal of Applied Social Psychology*, 11: 137-150.

Tjosvold, D. 1985a. Effects of attribution and social context on superiors' influence and interaction with low performing subordinates. *Personnel Psychology*, 38: 361-376.

Tjosvold, D. 1985b. Implications of controversy research for management. *Journal of Management*, 11: 21-37.

Tjosvold, D. 1985c. Power and social context in superior-subordinate interaction. *Organizational Behavior and Human Decision Processes*, 35: 281-293.

Tjosvold, D. 1991. *Conflict-Positive Organization: Stimulate Diversity and Create Unity.* Reading, MA: Addison-Wesley.

Tjosvold, D. 1993. *Learning to Manage Conflict: Getting People to Work Together Productively.* New York: Lexington Books.

Tjosvold, D. 1998. The cooperative and competitive goal approach to conflict: Accomplishments and challenges. *Applied Psychology: An International Review*, 47: 285-313.

Tjosvold, D. 1999. Bridging East and West to develop new products and trust: Interdependence and interaction between a Hong Kong parent and North American subsidiary. *International Journal of Innovation Management*, 3: 233-252.

Tjosvold, D., Chen, G. and Liu, C.H. 2001, July. Interdependence, Mutual Enhancement and Strategic Advantage: Top Management Teams in China. Paper, Social Interdependence Theory Conference, Minneapolis, MN.

Tjosvold, D., Coleman, P.T. and Sun, H. (2003). Effects of organizational values on leader's use of information power to affect performance in China. *Group Dynamics: Theory, Research, and Practice*, 7: 152-167.

Tjosvold, D., Hui, C. and Law, K. 1998. Empowerment in the leader relationship in Hong Kong: Interdependence and controversy. *Journal of Social Psychology*, 138: 624-637.

Tjosvold, D., Hui, C. and Sun, H. 2000. Building Social face and open-mindedness: Constructive conflict in Asia. In C.M. Lau, K.S. Law, D.K. Tse and C.S. Wong (eds.), *Asian Management Matters: Regional Relevance and Global Impact* (pp. 4-16). London: Imperial College Press.

Tjosvold, D. and Moy, J. 1998. Managing employees in China from Hong Kong: Interaction, relationships, and productivity as antecedents to motivation. *Leadership & Organization Development Journal.*

Tjosvold, D. and Poon, M. 2001. *Power, Conflict, and Scarce Resources: Using Conflict to Develop Quality Budgets.* Paper, submitted for publication. Hong Kong: Lingnan University.

Tjosvold, D. and Sun, H. 2001. *Faces of Power in China: Effects of Social Contexts on Use of Managerial Power.* Paper, submitted for publication. Hong Kong: Lingnan University.

Tjosvold, D. and Sun, H. (in press). Openness among Chinese in conflict: Effects of direct discussion and warmth on integrated decision making. *Journal of Applied Social Psychology.*

Tjosvold, D. and Sun, H. (2001). Social face in conflict among Chinese: Effects of affronts to person and position. *Group Dynamics: Theory, Research, and Practice*, 4: 259-271.

Tjosvold, D., Wong, M.L. and Liu, C.H. 2002, June. *Collectivist Values and Open-Mindedness for Chinese Employees Trust of their Japanese Leaders.* Paper, San Juan, Puerto Rico: Academy of International Business.

Tjosvold, D., Yu, Z.Y. and Liu, C.H. 2001. *Collectivist and Individualistic Values in the Leader Relationship: Openness and Employee Commitment and Performance.* Paper. Hong Kong: Lingnan University.

Triandis, H,C. 1995. *Individualism and Collectivism.* Boulder, CO: Westview Press.

Triandis, H.C. 1990. *Cross-cultural studies of individualism and collectivism.* In J. Berman (ed.), *Nebraska Symposium on Motivation, 1989* (pp. 41-133). Lincoln, Nebraska: University of Nebraska Press.

Trompenaars, F. 1993. *Riding the Waves of Culture.* London: Economist Books.

Tsui, A.S. and Farh, J.L. 1997. Where Guanxi matters: Relational demography and guanzi in the Chinese context. *Work and Occupation*, 24: 56-79.

Tung, R. 1991. Handshakes across the sea: Cross-cultural negotiating for business success. *Organizational Dynamics*, 14: 30-40.

Wakabayashi, M. and Graen, G. 1984. The Japanese career progress study: A 7-year follow-up. *Journal of Applied Psychology*, 69: 603-614.

Wakabayashi, M., Graen, G. and Uhl-Bien, M. 1990. Generalizability of the hidden investment hypothesis among Japanese line managers in five leading Japanese corporations. *Human Relations*, 43(11): 1099-1115.

Weber, M. 1947. *The Theory of Social and Economic Organization.* New York: Oxford University Press.

Westwood, R. 1997. Harmony and patriarchy: The cultural basis for "paternalistic headship" among the Overseas Chinese. *Organization Studies*, 18: 445-480.

White, S. 2001. Asian management matters: Regional relevance and global impact. *Asia Pacific Journal of Management*, 18: 121-124.

Chapter 14

INTERCULTURAL COMMUNICATION AND EFFECTIVE DECISION MAKING
Contributions to Successful International Business Ventures

Richard W. Brislin
University of Hawaii

Brent R. Mac Nab
University of Hawaii

INTRODUCTION

The analysis of intercultural communication for international business dealings must begin with a cultural universal. All people are socialized as children into a culture and one of the major purposes is to prepare them to be responsible and respected adults. Even when there are failures, as with criminals and adults who spend long periods of time on welfare, people are judged according to the standards set by successfully socialized individuals. People learn many skills that mark the well-socialized individual in their culture: how to meet and interact with strangers, appropriate topics for conversation, who should be given special attention (relatives, powerholders, etc.) and how to negotiate with others. A major aspect of intercultural communication in international business is that people who were socialized in different cultures come together for the purpose of identifying shared goals and working toward their accomplishment. Many times, they bring different culturally-influenced preferences for how best to interact, how best to communicate, and how best to follow through on business agreements.

The purpose of this chapter is to introduce theoretical concepts and analytical frameworks that will assist people in international business dealings that transcend cultural boundaries. Since there have been book-length treatments that deal with this and related topics (Brislin, 2000; Hofstede, 2001; Triandis, 1995), our goal will be to highlight what we feel are especially important issues. We will begin with a discussion of intercultural business success and how effective communication facilitates the goal of productive international business dealings. We will use the term "sojourner" to refer to people who accept overseas business assignments and who expect to return to their own culture after they complete these assignments. People on the receiving end of visits from sojourners are called "hosts" or "host nationals." We then review research on the traits and abilities of people who are likely to be successful. This is followed by a treatment of key intercultural communication issues that sojourners must face: stylistic differences, an understanding of attributional processes, and awareness of well-researched cultural dimensions that have effects on many specific interpersonal misunderstandings, and high- order management issues like ethical dilemmas.

There is an interesting, perhaps ironic, aspect of effective intercultural communication. As people become more skillful and more successful during their international assignments, they will be asked to become involved in more and more business dealings. Some of these dealings will challenge the ethical standards that have guided people's behavior in their own culture. For example, sojourners from the United States might be asked to serve on a hiring committee. Should the best candidate be sought, or should the less qualified nephew of the company's vice president be hired? To obtain government clearance for a new construction project, should the company provide key public officials with financial incentives? Given that there is absolutely no enforcement of applicable laws, shall the company ignore intellectual property rights and purchase low cost pirated software for its computers? To assist in decision making when faced with difficult questions such as these, we review treatments of ethical considerations that could prove helpful in complex international business dealings.

International Business Success

When sojourners are considered successful, they have satisfied requirements of a four part criteria. (1) They enjoy their intercultural assignments, feel that they have been productive, and feel that the assignments have been good for their careers. These feelings (2) must be reciprocated by host nationals who should report that the sojourners made contributions and that their presence was welcome. Overseas businesspeople (3) have tasks that are central to their overseas assignments, such as the establishment of joint ventures, and these should be accomplished in a timely manner. The final part of the criteria of success is that (4) people manage stress effectively. The term "culture shock" is used to refer to a special set of stresses that almost always cause emotional difficulties for sojourners (Bochner, 1994). These stresses include dealing with very different ways of accomplishing goals in different cultures, and the sheer number of small adjustments that must be made in a short period of time. These adjustments can be due to work demands (interacting effectively with coworkers and bosses), and to family issues (finding appropriate schooling for children and productive use of time for one's spouse). One of the goals of this chapter is to help people with culture shock reactions through an understanding of various concepts that will help them adjust effectively to their overseas assignments.

The Traits of Successful Sojourners: Linkages to Cultural Differences

With an understanding of success on overseas assignments, we can begin to discuss the traits of people likely to achieve success (Kealey, 1996). Before discussing these traits, we need to note our agreement with other theorists (Ross, 1977; Zimbardo & Leippe, 1991) who argue that traits are best understood as they contribute to goal accomplishment in various social situations. We need information about people's traits and the social situations, or social context, in which these traits might be used. A leader with entrepreneurial traits, for example, could be effective in the fast moving computer software industry where risk taking (Stewart & Roth, 2001) is valued. These same traits might be unhelpful in a profitable company that owns a quarry and produces sand for concrete in the same way as it has for the last fifty years.

Businesspeople on overseas assignments find themselves in social contexts that can be analyzed with the help of important cultural concepts that have been researched over the last twenty years. Two concepts, that will be briefly reviewed here, are individualism vs. collectivism (Hofstede, 2001; Markus & Kitayama, 1998) and power distance (Hofstede, 2001). In individualistic cultures such as the United States and Canada, there is great emphasis placed on individuals and their abilities, opinions, and work accomplishments. People enjoy feeling that they are unique and appreciate recognition for their individual accomplishments. When they succeed as individuals, they want to be rewarded in an equitable manner and are comfortable when surpassing age peers in the quest for career success. In collectivist cultures such as Japan and Korea, there is great emphasis placed on membership in and contributions to group. People enjoy feeling that they have cooperative and harmonious relations with others in their ingroup, and this group very much consists of coworkers in their organizations. They value succeeding as members of their group and are comfortable with equal recognition compared to peers (Hofstede, 2001; Triandis, 1995). They are noticeably more uncomfortable than people socialized in individualistic nations when asked to accept promotions that would place them above former peers.

The concept "power distance" is best understood if a universal aspect of culture is analyzed. All cultures have distinctions in the amount of power that people possess: bosses have more power than employees, politicians have more power than those who elected them to office, and men very often have more power than women (Glick & Fiske, 2001). The distinction between cultures high (Philippines, Japan, Korea) and low (United States, Israel) in power distance is the *amount* of the distinction and people's *acceptance* of how power is distributed. In high power distance cultures, relatively few people have large amounts of power and these people are given a great deal of deference and respect. They take their power seriously, are not pleased with public disagreements, and expect their directives to be followed. Subordinates are sensitive to the preferences of powerholders and will use phrases like, "The boss wants this project to be given special attention," to persuade peers to move in a certain direction. "High power distance" connotes a wide psychological gap between powerholders and their subordinates. This gap has implications such as use of titles rather than first names in interactions, few out-of-work interactions as social equals, and the sense that powerholders *deserve* their place in society as well as the deference that they receive.

In low power distance cultures, more people share control and influence, but in more delimited areas. There is not an automatic deference to those who have power. Subordinates recognize a psychological gap between themselves and bosses, but the gap is relatively small. Consequently, people can refer to each other by first names, socialize as equals (e.g., golf, attendance at cultural events), and treat each other with respect given that powerholders and their subordinates recognize each other's talents. There are more likely to be jokes about powerholders: in some low-power distance cultures, entertainers make handsome livings by making high status people the targets of their humor. Subordinates do not feel that powerholders are better people and, in fact, often look forward to the day that they become promoted to higher level positions in their companies such that today's boss will be tomorrow's assistant.

Traits: Personality in Culture

With this introduction to two important cultural dimensions, we can begin a discussion of the traits of successful sojourners. Other cultural dimensions will be introduced throughout this chapter. Treatments of people's traits need to be discussed along with cultural dimensions since, on overseas assignments, people must integrate their traits into the cultural context where they find themselves working. A good example is the trait, "open-mindedness."

Open-mindedness as a predictor of overseas success has been frequently discussed (Adler, 2002; Bhawuk & Brislin, 1992; Kealey, 1996). It refers to people's willingness to consider various viewpoints and various potential solutions to problems. People may have strong preferences on topics such as how best to motivate workers and how to run effective business meetings, but if they are open-minded they recognize that there are alternative methods for meeting these goals. Integrating the concept "goals" means that people have targets for traits such as open-mindedness and they can apply these traits given their knowledge of cultural differences. With knowledge of collectivism, for example, an open-minded manager would not automatically recommend a system for rewarding the initiative and productivity of specific people. Rather, the manager would also consider a system for recognizing the efforts of the group of which the highly productive people are members. Productive people in a collectivistic culture will often not object to such a system. They will make statement such as, "Members of my group will be together for a long time. Maybe next year someone else will be especially productive, and so it is important to recognize the long-term efforts of the group. I don't want to interfere with group harmony by being centered out for special attention today."

The trait "flexibility," another predictor of overseas success, takes open-mindedness into the realm of actual behaviors that are observable by others. One can be open-minded and *know about* high power distance. With flexibility, people are willing to modify their everyday behaviors so that they are more effective with managers and executives who take their power very seriously. For example, sojourners might have the strong behavioral tendency to address bosses by their first names. If they are flexible, they will put this tendency aside and refer to their bosses by their formal titles. They will modify other tendencies and use a more deferential tone of voice and more respectful gestures. In some cultures, these gestures will include standing when the boss enters a room and not disagreeing in a public forum.

A sense of humor is another desirable trait, and the target of this trait is the mistakes and cultural blunders that sojourners will surely make. A sense of humor about one's mistakes can increase the chances that people can objectively step back and assess the reasons for their mistakes. Humor usually is associated with a lack of rigidity. If people can see the humor in their mistakes, this implies that they can consider alternative behaviors that may have been more appropriate in certain social situations. Humor is also a stress reducer, and it can humanize people in the eyes of hosts. Everybody makes mistakes, and if people can admit this and joke about it, hosts will often laugh along with them and not at them. The advantages of a sense of humor are well-enough known that companies will specify it as a job requirement when advertising for international managers and executives in publications such as the New York Times.

Traits: Using and Sharing Skills

We are using the term "traits" broadly to refer to aspect of people that become part of their reputations. These include personality traits such as those already discussed, but they also refer to skills, abilities, and interests. The adjustment of sojourners is facilitated if they have skills that hosts value and want to learn. Further, sojourners develop good reputations among hosts if they are able to transfer their skills to hosts (Kealey, 1989). For example, if sojourners can introduce advanced computer technology to organizations and also transfer their skills to hosts, they will develop good reputations. Further, after the sojourners return to their own country hosts can continue the efforts if the sojourners have introduced skill such as updating software technology and troubleshooting glitches in the computer hardware.

Another useful trait related to skills is that the best-adjusted sojourners often have a wide variety of interests. This is undoubtedly related to open-mindedness, already discussed. If sojourners have many interests, they are more likely to find that they can pursue at least a few of those interests in other countries. People play chess and bridge all over the world, and there is often an outlet for guitar and piano players in most countries. Before their actual move overseas, sojourners are well advised to do some research on various clubs and volunteer organizations in their country of assignment. If these are interest based, it could be cost-effective to bring the materials necessary to pursue the interest. Sojourners need a certain amount of social interaction outside their workplaces, and for adults these interactions very often start with shared interests among sojourners and hosts. Without shared interests such as music, athletics, or book discussion groups, sojourners sometimes engage in lowest-common-denominator activities such as alcohol use. This can lead to health problems as well as to difficulties in the workplace.

Dealing With Cultural Differences: Preparation

Everyone goes through an adjustment process when they are assigned to another country. The adjustment is hastened if sojourners have access to various types of formal and informal assistance. These can include formal training programs (Brislin & Yoshida, 1994), mentoring programs where newly arrived sojourners are paired with experienced people, and integration into supportive groups of people. The latter is especially critical in collectivist cultures where people often get things done through their social networks composed of people whom they know. The ambitious, hardworking, but socially unconnected sojourner often has a difficult time being productive when assigned to a collectivist country.

Formal efforts to assist sojourners are aided if four aspects of effective intercultural interactions are kept in mind. We recommend that sojourners review the specific advice they receive and organize it according to these four points. The first is (1) awareness of cultural differences. People are sometimes chosen for challenging international business assignments because they have been successful in their own countries. It is easy to forget that they have been successful because they know how to accomplish difficult tasks in their own country. This record of success may not transfer to work in another country unless the sojourners are *aware* that they will be encountering major cultural differences. When sojourners know that they will be encountering cultural differences, they are said to be at "the awareness stage." This is not a trivial stage on the way to greater intercultural sophistication. Many adults, quite successful people, go through their lives impervious to the existence of culture and cultural differences.

The second aspect of successful intercultural interactions is based on the recognition that not all knowledge is universal. Rather, (2) different cultures socialize their members into accepting different "facts" and "knowledge." For example, in individualistic cultures, the "fact" is that employees will often receive yearly workplace evaluations based on their individual accomplishments. In collectivistic cultures, the evaluations will often be based on team performance and/or individual contributions to a team. Another and related piece of knowledge is that if a worker has a problem, it is proper to share it with team members when working in a collectivist culture. In turn, the worker should be ready to help other team members when they ask for help.

Intercultural interactions are (3) more anxiety laden and emotion arousing than interactions among similar people in one's own culture. The reasons are plentiful: in a dyadic interaction, one of the people is often using a second language. The two people were socialized in different cultures and so do not have similar socialization experiences that lead to interpersonal attraction based on various similarities in attitudes and interests. There is always a point that sojourners reach where activities are limited to hosts and the sojourners are not encouraged to participate. These can be visits to homes, religious ceremonies, certain types of parties late at night, and so forth. If sojourners feel rejected, this can lead to emotional upheavals. Taking the advice of hosts regarding applications of newly-acquired knowledge, discussed above, can also lead to anxiety since many sojourners will be unfamiliar with "facts" such as sharing work related problems with team members.

The fourth aspect of successful interpersonal interactions is that sojourners should consider modifying their behaviors when appropriate in other cultures. Sojourners should frequently ask themselves questions such as these: "What are my workplace goals? In my own country, what behaviors would I engage in to achieve these goals? Given similar goals (e.g., workplace productivity, good interpersonal relations), are there different behaviors that would be more likely to lead to goal accomplishment?" If they ask and answer such questions, different behaviors will be identified. In Korea and Japan, good interpersonal relations are aided by after-hours socializing with colleagues. This may involve more alcohol than the level to which sojourners are accustomed. Both the time spent with colleagues and alcohol use may involve behaviors that the sojourners engaged in less frequently in their own country. There are other advantages of "knowing the behaviors." If they know about alcohol consumption, sojourners may be able to quietly ask restaurant personnel to bring ginger ale in a manner similar to whiskey.

Culture and Interaction Styles

Discussions of culture and appropriate behaviors lead directly into a discussion of interaction styles. The term "style" refers to the manner in which a collection of behaviors is performed, guided by the norms of various cultures. Interaction styles can be a difficult topic to communicate since there is not a common, well-accepted set of terms that allows easy description of styles. There is a well-developed set of terms for the content of communication ("there were different demands: labor wanted an 8% pay raise, management insisted that the limit be 4%), but fewer clear terms to communicate interaction styles. We will review several styles, and terms to describe them, that have been based on recent research.

Direct and Indirect Styles

In the simplest interpersonal interaction, two people are trying to communicate. One person has a message and wants to make it clear to the other person. In a direct style, common in individualistic cultures, the major goal is to get the message across, and so the style include features such as a firm tone of voice, precise choice of vocabulary, simple declarative sentences, and so forth. "This company should improve its leadership development by hiring the Bates consulting firm," said in a firm voice tone with eye contact directed at major decision-makers, is an example. In an indirect style, common in collectivistic cultures (Gudykunst, 1998), the goal of communicating the message is integrated with other goals such as smooth interpersonal relations. The communicator has additional knowledge: perhaps the nephew of a decision-maker works for one of Bates' competitors. Others at the meeting may not be prepared to make a decision immediately and would rather ponder various alternative recommendations over the next several weeks. If the Bates firm is chosen and does a poor job, the person recommending it may "lose face" and be held responsible for a poor decision. These considerations lead to a preference for an indirect style of communication. "The Bates consulting firm may be one of several that we look into further," said with a tentative voice tone and without eye contact directed at anyone in particular, is an example.

Sender and Receiver Orientations

Direct and indirect styles of communication are assisted, respectively, by another aspect of interpersonal relations captured by the terms "sender and receiver orientation" (Brislin, 2000). Consider again the simplest case of a person desirous of communicating a message to a second person. Who has the responsibility for making sure that the message is received as clearly as possible? If the culture has a "sender orientation," it means that the speaker has the responsibility. Consequently, communication skills such as a clear and energetic voice tone, multiple examples of any recommendation in the communication, and careful use of redundancy are employed. If the culture has a "receiver orientation," the responsibility for making sure the message is communicated is shared between the speaker and the listener. The speaker presents a message, and the listener is expected to put time and effort into receiving the message. If the speaker is being indirect so as to be gentle to those who might disagree, then the listener is expected to know this and to interpret the meaning behind the indirectness. The phrase, "We are supposed to read the speaker's mind, especially if it is a high status speaker," is commonly heard.

An especially clear example of the distinction between speaker and receiver orientations takes place in the college classroom. In an individualistic culture such as the United States or Australia, the professor has the responsibility for presenting important information in a clear and interesting manner. In a collectivist culture such as Japan, Korea, or Thailand, the students share the responsibility for receiving the professor's information. If the professor was disorganized and dull, the students still have the responsibility for gathering nuggets of information from the lecture. If students learn nothing, it can be their fault for being unprepared or inattentive to the wisdom emanating from the professor. Similarly, sojourners are ill advised to complain after a bone-numbing and dreary presentation from the company president. It is the employee's responsibility to be attentive and to understand the president's message.

Open Discussions and Behind the Scenes Agreements

In individualistic and low power distant cultures, people often attend business meetings and argue the merits of their proposals. Given that there is a cultural appreciation of individual opinions and the development of expertise in specific areas, people are accustomed to hearing and reacting to proposals in open meetings. In other cultures, with Japan being the most well-researched on this point (Yoshida, 1994), the presentation of proposals takes place "behind the scenes" in collections of one-on-one meetings in people's offices.

After reactions are gathered from these multiple meetings, the proposal developer integrates various suggestions and presents a possible consensus position in another set of one-one-one meetings. If there is agreement, a meeting of many people is called, but the goal is to announce and perhaps celebrate the decision already made. If someone brings up a previously undiscussed issue, this would be a major cultural error and the speaker would likely be chastised through non-verbal glares and other negative body language reactions (Cushner & Brislin, 1996). There are naturally pros and cons to this "behind the scenes" approach. For example, although the process of consensus decision making (a.k.a. – *ringi* in Japan) might take longer compared to other approaches, a more cohesive and efficient implementation process can result; some of the potential downsides can include increased *groupthink* or the lack of exploring a more robust set of options.

Using Time

There are varying approaches to how time is used that affect intercultural communication (Levine, 1997; Brislin & Kim, 2003). The workday can be organized around clocks or events. "Clock time" means that people keep schedules according to the time of day, and will be attentive to starting a meeting at 11:30 a.m. if that is on their schedules. "Event time" means that people have a sense of how long events take, whether a certain event should continue, and when a new event should start. There may be a clock reference point, but it is much looser. An executive may be entertaining a client in a restaurant. Another businessperson may be waiting for the executive to return to his office. The executive feels that the client needs more time. This "event" takes precedence over any clock-time agreement. This can be maddening for businesspeople socialized in clock time cultures, and intercultural "war stories" based on time are some of the most commonly shared among sojourners. There is advice for people frustrated with working in event time cultures. They should be willing to start new events on their own while waiting for the executive. They could talk with the executive's assistants or secretaries, who often do a great deal of work to support their boss and so know a great deal about the company's business. The businesspeople should not interpret the missed start of the appointment as a snub but rather should demonstrate their knowledge of cultural differences by "flowing with the development of events."

Another aspect of time is that there are cultural difference regarding the acceptability of long periods of silence. In some countries (e.g., United States), people feel pressured to fill long periods of silence and view silence as a signal that communications with others are not going well. In other countries, people are far more comfortable with silence and do not feel the need to fill it with talk. The difference can be seen at receptions in the workplace. In the United

States, if people arrive at a reception no one talks to them, they are very uncomfortable. Good hosts and hostesses often keep a lookout for people who need someone to talk to and rush to make proper introductions among attendees. In many Asian countries, people might stand by themselves for long periods of time, and there is less likely to be the norm that people should be talking with others. Quiet participation at the reception is far more acceptable.

Knowing the American desire to fill periods of silence, businesspeople in Asia will sometimes use this information in decisions about negotiation tactics (Pye, 1992). Americans will make an offer at the negotiation table, and their Asian counterparts will remain silent. The Asians realize that the Americans will become uncomfortable, may interpret the silence as rejection of the offer, and will make a counterproposal with more favorable terms for the Asians. Americans should know about this tactic and learn to become more comfortable with silence.

Various Cultural Differences and Their Impacts on International Business Dealings

Given previous discussions of intercultural success, sojourner traits, and communication styles, we can now discuss other cultural differences that will have an impact on international business dealings. Space limitations demand conciseness, and so reference will be given for longer treatments.

Particularism and Universalism

In some cultures, various type of work get done through a complex set of interpersonal relationships, and so there is a great deal of emphasis on the particular set of people whom an individual knows well. In China, this has been institutionalized and the collection of relationships people have is known as their "guanxi" (Luo & Chen, 1996). Without good guanxi, people have a very difficult time getting important work done, such as contacting government officials for permits or meeting potential investors. If an individual wants to talk with a certain official, he or she has to either know that person or know someone who has a guanxi relationship with the official. Large amounts of time and energy are needed to maintain one's guanxi. In a culture marked by universalism, there is emphasis placed on equal treatment of others. The term comes from the goal of a universal manner of dealing with others rather than a collection of particular and specific manners depending upon relationships with others. This means that people can contact others for government and business dealings whether they know those others well or not. This can sound impersonal, but it can also be very efficient. Universalism can lead to effective bureaucracies. If bureaucrats are expected to meet certain people and to distribute information as part of their job descriptions, they should do this regardless of whether they know other people or not. We are not naïve. There will always be favoritism toward certain individuals because of their status, wealth, political connections, and so forth. Universalism refers to the goal to treat others equally, even though this goal is not always achieved given pressures to treat certain privileged people well.

High and Low Context

We introduced the importance of sensitivity to the social context of behavior early in this chapter. Another reason for its importance is that some people in some cultures are expected to be especially attuned to the context in which people communicate. In high context communications (Hammer, 1997), much of a person's message is contained in the social context that surrounds any choice of words. People are expected to know the social context and consequently extensive verbal communication is not necessary. In the example of proposing new ideas, for instance, consider this taking place in a high context culture such as Korea, Japan, or Hong Kong. People should know what to do given their knowledge of culture and the social context where behavior takes place. In high context cultures, people often do not have extensive experience explaining what might happen to people. There are well-internalized social norms that provide guidance for people's behavior. If people are well-socialized members of their culture, they are supposed to know what to do!

In low context cultures (in North America, Western Europe) the message is less contained in a context and must be found in the choice of words, voice tone, specific examples, etc., that the communicator chooses. Since there is no assumed accuracy of communication based on context alone, people are much more accustomed to explaining themselves and also explaining what might be going on in back-and-forth communications among people. This example may capture the difference between high and low context. In the United States, a couple becomes engaged in 1930. Where do they live? In 1930, the answer was high context and there had to be little discussion: they live where the male has a job with good career prospects. Where does a couple live in the year 2002? This is now a low context issue and must be discussed extensively. The modern answer may involve where the female has good prospects, the age of parents who might need care, plans concerning when to have children, and so forth. In 1930 clear, largely unspoken norms established the couple's location decision – little discussion was required. In 2003 these unspoken norms are not as well established and an explicit a low context process of communication (for our example) is the result. If people find it necessary to explain themselves and to present reasons for their actions, this is a sign of low context. For example, both of us find that we should explain what might happen in decision-making meetings when attendees include our Asian colleagues. We point out that people may disagree openly, may challenge each other's ideas, and may ask direct questions such as, "What do you think of this marketing plan for teenagers in Korea?" The meetings are low context: these behaviors may occur, but again they may not. There is no well-established set of norms to guide exactly what will happen in business meetings, and people should be prepared for this low context approach to decision making.

Cross-Cultural Communication and Technology

Language can be viewed as one of the more important gateways to culture that has challenged human interaction since our earliest history as exemplified through accounts like the Tower of Babel. As an integral and prominent artifact of culture, language, and the process of understanding known as semantics, plays a critical role in a world community that has been moving toward globalization (Sands, 2001; Nadesan, 2001). Trends like the globalization of business and trade, world-wide communication networks, new technology, improved transportation and geo-political economic unions will continue to increase the incidence of foreign language contact (as exemplified by the business context of the previous section) and thus the need for effective, efficient cross-cultural communication. These needs also drive both practitioners and academia toward new studies and aspects of communication, language, semantics and translation.

In developing a forward-looking view of cross-cultural communication the authors would be remiss by not discussing the use of technology. New technology including fuzzy logic, neural networks and parallel processing (aka – artificial intelligence) are developing in ways that stand to radically alter the reality of communication (specifically with translation issues) as we know it today (Lehman-Wilzig, 2001). The task of holistic, global communication, taken from an individual's perspective, is indeed daunting. There are between 3,000 to 6,000 languages globally (depending on the source quoted) with about 200 of those being spoken by a million people or more and around 100 serving as official, national languages. Given that even the best human translators are able to manage working effectively with only a hand full of these languages, a significant gap remains. Translation technology not only promises to functionally assist the facilitation of cross-cultural communication between individuals, groups and organizations, it also may help to eventually preserve more fringe languages – by acting as an intellectual crutch, translation technology could discourage the learning of a new language, entrenching the native tongue. Or from another perspective, it could stave off the parochialistic domination of a few language types. In general the potential disincentive for language studies could have some negative residual effects if not replaced with other cross-cultural contact activities/studies.

Currently, textual translation programs and software are integrated and being used on the web, in business and in other organizational contexts. For example, the European Union currently uses translation software to handle about ten percent of its translation duties. Large, global organizations are predicting a significant increase in the total amount of material which will need to be localized to fit regional language patterns by an amount as much as six fold by 2005 (Freivalds, 1999). These trends, coupled with a stagnating number of human translators, are driving forces within the translation industry that has been growing in gross revenue by 15 to 20 percent a year. Nevertheless, we are just beginning to use technology as an effective tool for translation and as an effective leverage for managing language and assisting in cross-cultural communication.

Although automated translation software has been used since the Cold War era, some of the more modern, advanced programs are able to translate in one hour, with 90 percent accuracy, what might take a human two or three days (Freivalds, 1999). For example, *Synchronous Automated Translation Systems (SATS)* represent highly advanced technology that will allow seamless translation without any perceptible time delay. SATS based systems are also expected to handle basic aspects of idioms and will be able to alert communicators of potentially vague language which would have a high probability of multiple meaning – thus prompting for more clarification. Advanced SATS systems are projected to be mainstream and in the market by 2015 (Lehman-Wilzig, 2001). One of the main trials for this type of advanced cross-cultural communication system will be how effectively it will be able to handle a variety of unique translation issues like interaction patterns between low and high context cultural societies and the relative importance of contextuality in the communication process (Ting-Toomey, 1985).

Multinational Organizations and High Order Communication

As the global economy moves forward, the phenomena of the International Joint Venture (IJV) and Foreign Direct Investment (FDI) have become more common than ever before and this trend is only increasing. Over the past 15 years FDI has risen from $47 bn to $827 bn in 1999 (Domke-Damonte, 2001). Also, the number of foreign countries listed on stock exchanges outside their country of origin is significantly increasing and the number of non-US companies trading on the NYSE has tripled in the last decade (Deloitte & Touche, 1999). As countries move to gain certain advantages and efficiencies that can be gleaned from multinational operations (e.g., market penetration, low cost labor, local expertise, better access to capital and materials) high order communication interactions become more common. *High order* communication interactions are characterized by the weight of importance placed on successfully navigating the process. For example, when Volkswagen AG negotiates an IJV relationship with a plant in China, the importance of successfully navigating the entire process of communication is significant. The organization has spent important resources, time and capital in investigating and entering into negotiations. Critical future plans ride on the success of the operation and negotiation. Clearly this is quite different from a *low order* cross-cultural communication interaction that is more common in other contexts like tourism. Although the IJV format of partnership would normally exemplify the most binding type of multinational business interaction between groups, other significant formats exist that will also require consistent *high order* communication interaction; these include: export/import partnerships, licensing agreements, turnkey projects, franchising and consulting.

Multinational corporations (MNCs) operate through foreign subsidiaries across national borders, across cultures and across languages. The amount of information flow within these operations can be staggering. MNCs can be managed in a number of distinct styles from a decentralized approach to regionalization to a more centralized standard. Hybrid approaches of management are also apparent as MNCs seek advantages of a variety of approaches in relation to different areas of the organization. Nevertheless, modern MNCs tend to foster flows of information, products, people and capital between the various subsidiaries that form the corporation (Mirjaliisa & Marschan-Piekkari, 2002). This connectedness between units emphasizes the need for staff at different levels to communicate *horizontally* with the help of a shared language (Bartlett & Goshal, 1990). Such interactions can benefit the organization by increasing the transfer of knowledge (Kogut & Zander, 1993; Gupta & Govindarajan, 2000), sharing of subsidiary core competencies, increasing collaboration (Goshäl et al., 1994), and increasing creativity while protecting against group think.

Language Specific v. Holistic Communication Styles

Although the effect of language as a facilitator to a variety of communication contexts within the MNC construct seems significant (Nickerson, 1998, 1999, 2000) – and to some intuitive – other research suggests that a less language-specific approach in managing and training for cross-cultural communication may be in order for other contexts – particularly horizontal communication (Mirjaliisa & Marschan-Piekkari, 2002). Domke-Damonte (2001) argues that MNCs need to develop a more holistic *communication competence* that considers special contextual nuances of these high order communication exchanges like regulatory and investment climates and cultural understanding.

The reliance on heavy language training and emphasis of a central language for the organization can create feelings of isolation for those out-group language employees and it is cautioned that an employee's communication evaluation in such contexts should embrace a broad perspective and not simply competency in any one language(s). Nevertheless, it has also been noted that the centralization of communication facilitation provides significant power to those members of the organization who take on the role of communication brokers or intermediaries (Marschan-Piekkari et al., 1999b) while knowledge of the parent company native language is also a significant source of power (Marschan-Piekkari et al., 1999a). Also, other researchers have clearly linked the importance of solid language skills to expatriate assignment success (Lane et al., 1997; Black et al., 1992).

Also, some researchers have missed a treasure chest full of valuable communication-oriented information that can be drawn from cross-cultural studies. For example, cultures of high uncertainty avoidance will be more comfortable with a precise type of communication style whereby details are clearly spelled out in writing. Also, cultures higher in masculine characteristics will be more persuaded by information/communication styles that emphasize facts more than emotion, intuition or instinct. To not recognize the important explicit and implicit links to cross-cultural communication that can be found in already well established cross-cultural studies is to miss valuable foundation work. However, solely relying on past studies and the informed stereotypical treatments of specific styles may not be very longitudinally effective (Yoneyama, 1999). There is evidence from recent research that cultural artifacts, as manifest in organizational behavior, communication and practice, is more of a moving target than a static reality (Worthley, Brislin & Mac Nab, 2004; Kelley et al., 2002; Ralston et al., 1997). This may have an important and profound impact on how multinational organizations approach organizational communication in a variety of contexts and provides sound warning for organizations that are resistant to longitudinally altering their approach to communication and employee interaction.

REFERENCES

Adler, N. 2002. *International Dimensions of Organizational Behavior* (4th edn). Boston: PWS-Kent.

Bartlett, C. and Goshal, S. 1990. Matrix management: Not a structure, a frame of mind. *Harvard Business Review*, July-August: 138-147.

Bhawuk, D.P.S. and Brislin, R. 1992. The measurement of intercultural sensitivity using the concepts of individualism and collectivism. *International Journal of Intercultural Relations*, 16: 413-436.

Black, J. Gregsen, H. and Mendenhall, M. 1992. *Global Assignments*. San Francisco: Jossey-Bass.

Bochner, S. 1994. Culture shock. In W. Lonner and R. Malpass (eds.), *Psychology and Culture* (pp. 245-251). Needham Heights, MA: Allyn and Bacon.

Brislin, R. 2000. *Understanding Culture's Influence on Behavior* (2nd edn). Fort Worth, TX: Harcourt.

Brislin, R. and Yoshida, T. 1994. *Intercultural Communication Training: An Introduction.* Thousand Oaks, CA: Sage.

Brislin, R. and Kim, E. 2003. Cultural diversity in people's understanding and uses of time. *Applied Psychology: An International Review*, 52: 363-382.

Cushner, K. and Brislin, R. 1996. *Intercultural Interactions: A Practical Guide* (2nd edn). Thousand Oaks, CA: Sage.

Deloitte and Touche. 1999. Getting real about going global. *Fortune*, 139(3): 170-171.

Domke-Damonte, D. 2001. Language learning and international business. *SAM Advanced Management Journal*, 66(1): 35-40.

Freivalds, J. 1999. The technology of translation. *Management Review*, 88(2): 48-52.

Glick, P. and Fiske, S. 2001. Ambivalent sexism. In M. Zanna (ed.), *Advances in Experimental Social Psychology* (Vol. 33, pp. 115-188). San Diego, CA: Academic Press.

Goshal, S., Korine, H. and Szulanski, G. 1994. Interunit communication in MNCs. *Management Science*, 40: 96-110.

Gudykunst, W. 1998. Individualistic and collectivistic perspectives on communication: An introduction. *International Journal of Intercultural Relations*, 22: 107-134.

Gupta, A. and Govindarajan, V. 2000. Knowledge flows within MNCs. *Strategic Management Journal*, 21: 473-496.

Hammer, M. 1997. Negotiating across the cultural divide: Intercultural dynamics in crisis incidents. In R. Rogan, M. Hammer and C. Van Zandt (eds.), *Dynamic Processes of Crisis Negotiation* (pp. 9-24). Westport, CT: Praeger.

Hofstede, G. 2001. *Culture's Consequences: Comparing Values, Behaviors, Institutions, and Organizations Across Nations* (2nd edn). Thousand Oaks, CA: Sage.

Kealey, D. 1989. A study of cross-cultural effectiveness: Theoretical issues, practical applications. *International Journal of Intercultural Relations*, 13: 387-428.

Kealey, D. 1996. The challenge of international personnel selection. In D. Landis and R. Bhagat (eds.), *Handbook of Intercultural Training* (2nd edn, pp. 106-123). Thousand Oaks, CA: Sage.

Kelley, L., Huff, L., Worthley, R. Mac, Nab, B. and Pagano, I. 2002. Adaptability and change in Japanese management practice: A longitudinal inquiry into the banking industry – through the bubble economy and beyond. Paper presented at *AJBS Conference* (June) St. Louis.

Kogut, B. and Zander, U. 1993. Knowledge of the firm and the evolutionary theory of the MNC. *Journal of International Business Studies*, 24(4): 625-645.

Lane, H., DiStephano, J. and Maznevski, M. 1997. *International Management Behavior.* Cambridge, MA: Blackwell.

Lehman-Wilzig, S. 2001. Babbling our way to a new Babel: Erasing the language barriers. *The Futurist*, 35(3): 16-23.

Levine, R. 1997. *A Geography of Time.* New York: Basic Books.

Luo, Y. and Chen, M. 1996. Managerial implications of guanxi-based business strategies. *Journal of International Management*, 2: 293-316.

Markus, H. and Kitayama, S. 1998. The cultural psychology of personality. *Journal of Cross-Cultural Psychology*, 29: 63-87.

Marschan-Piekkari, R., Welch, D. and Welch, L. 1999a. Adopting a common corporate language: IHRM implications. *The Journal of International Human Resources Management*, 10(3): 337-390.

Marschan-Piekkari, R., Welch, D. and Welch, L. 1999b. In the shadow: The impact of language on structure, power and communication in the multinational. *International Business Review*, 8(4): 421-440.

Mirjaliisa, C. and Marschan-Piekkari, R. 2002. Language training for enhanced horizontal communication: A challenge for MNCs. *Business Communication Quarterly*, 65(2): 9-29.

Nadesan, M. 2001. Fortune on globalization and the new economy. *Management Communication Quarterly*, 14: 498-506.

Nickerson, C. 1998. Corporate culture and the use of written English within British subsidiaries in the Netherlands. *English for Specific Purpose*, 17(3): 281-294.

Nickerson, C. 1999. The use of English in electronic mail in multinational corporations. In F. Bargiela-Chiappini and C. Nickerson (eds.), *Writing Business: Genres, Media and Discourses*. London: Longman.

Nickerson, C. 2000. *Playing the Corporate Language Game. Studies in Language and Communication*. Amsterdam: Rodopi.

Pye, L. 1992. *Chinese Negotiation Style: Commercial Approaches and Cultural Principles*. New York: Quorum Books.

Ralston, D., Holt, D., Terpstra, R. and Cheng, Y. 1997. The impact of national culture and economic ideology on managerial work values: A study of the U.S., Russia, Japan and China. *Journal of International Business Studies*, First Quarter: 177-207.

Ross, L. 1977. The intuitive psychologist and his shortcomings. In L. Berkowitz (ed.), *Advances in Experimental Social Psychology* (Vol. 10, pp. 173-220). New York: Academic Press.

Sands, D. 2001. Getting global. *Insight on the News*, 17(8): 33.

Stewart, W. and Roth, P. 2001. Risk propensity differences between entrepreneurs and managers: A meta-analytic review. *Journal of Applied Psychology*, 86: 145-153.

Ting-Toomey, S. 1985. Toward a theory of conflict and culture. In W. Gudykunst, L. Stewart and S. Ting-Toomey (eds.), *Communication, Culture and Organizational Processes*. Beverly Hills: Sage.

Triandis, H. 1995. *Individualism & Collectivism*. Boulder, CO: Westview.

Worthley, R., Brislin, R. and Mac Nab, B. 2004. Evolving perceptions of Japanese workplace motivation – An employee v. manager comparison. *International Journal of Cross-Cultural Management*. In review.

Yoneyama, L. 1999. Habits of knowing cultural differences: Chrysanthemum and the Sword in the US liberal multiculturalism. *Topoi*, 71-80.

Yoshida, T. 1994. Interpersonal versus non-interpersonal realities: An effective tool individualists can use to better understand collectivists. In R. Brislin and T. Yoshida (eds.), *Improving Intercultural Interactions: Modules for Cross-cultural Training Programs* (pp. 243). Thousand Oaks, CA: Sage.

Zimbardo, P. and Leippe, M. 1991. *The Psychology of Attitude Change and Social Influence*. New York: McGraw-Hill.

Chapter 15

IN THE EYE OF THE BEHOLDER
Culture and the Perception of Organizational Justice

Mara Olekalns
University of Melbourne

INTRODUCTION

In any social exchange, individuals look for fairness. However, what 'fairness' means has become progressively more complex over time. According to Bies and Moag (1986), there are three points in the exchange process that can influence justice judgements. In assessing fairness, individuals can consider the procedure by which resources are allocated, individual treatment during this process, and the final allocation itself. These three forms of justice – procedural, interactional, distributive – all contribute to justice judgements. Although different aspects of the social exchange process influence each type of justice, the consequences of violating justice are uniform. Unfair treatment leads to a range of adverse organizational consequences and motivates individuals to redress the injustice. When individuals believe their outcomes or treatment are unfair, they report lower job satisfaction, lower organizational commitment and a greater willingness to leave the organization. Moreover, research shows that it can result in such as actions as increased organizational theft (Greenberg, 1990). Understanding and remedying the antecedents of injustice is therefore an important part of effective management.

Initial analyses of fairness focused on individuals' outcomes. Adams' equity theory (1965) proposed that fairness is a relative construct based on a comparison of an individual's outcomes with the outcomes of similar others. This theory of *distributive justice* stated that we perceive our outcomes to be fair when others, who exert the same level of effort, also receive the same outcomes. It also focused attention on how individuals redress unfair outcomes and restore fairness, that is, *retributive justice* (McLean Parks, 1997). Although perceptions of distributive justice were able to explain some of the variations in individuals' satisfaction with organizational outcomes such as pay, they could not account for all of it.

As a result, attention turned to the processes by which decisions were made. Not only did research show that *procedural justice* is an important predictor of individual and organizational outcomes, but some analyses suggest that it may shape perceptions of distributive justice: Individuals appear more willing to accept unfair outcomes if the procedures by which those outcomes are determined are fair. Yet other research has linked distributive justice to outcome fairness and procedural justice to system fairness (e.g., McFarlin & Sweeney, 1992; Sweeney & McFarlin, 1993).

More recent analyses have separated early conceptions of procedural justice into two components. The first more closely mirrors the initial definition of procedural justice and focuses on the decision making process. Assessments of this form of procedural justice take into consideration whether the decision-maker is free of bias, the extent to which information used in the decision is accurate and the degree to which grievance processes allow redress of unfair decisions. A second form of procedural justice, known as interactional justice, captures aspects of interpersonal treatment. Interactional justice judgements are made along four criteria: truthfulness, respect for the individual, absence of bias and appropriate explanations for decisions (Bies & Moag, 1986; Cohen, 1991).

In this chapter, I focus on the relationship between culture and two forms of justice, distributive and procedural. This focus reflects the considerably larger body of research examining distributive and procedural justice and draws attention to the need for research on the remaining two forms of justice, interactional and retributive.

Frameworks for Understanding Culture

Research examining the effects of culture can take one of two paths. The first is to follow the well-trodden *cultural dimensions* path and to use constructs such as individualism–collectivism, power distance and uncertainty avoidance (Hofstede, 1980; Schwartz, 1990) to test for and explain country differences in behaviour. The second is to follow the *country context* path, that is, to compare countries and identify differences without making assumptions about the dimensions that underlie those differences.

The two approaches have complementary strengths and weaknesses. The major benefit of a cultural dimension approach is that it provides a more general, theoretical framework for unifying observations made in individual countries. However, because it focuses on similarities rather than differences, this approach carries the risk of overlooking the more subtle differences between countries. In particular, research within this paradigm rarely considers more than one dimension – usually individualism–collectivism – and so provides no insight into how the various cultural dimensions combine. Given Fiske's (1992) work on relational forms, this is problematic for researchers working from a cultural dimension perspective: Fiske argues that how two dimensions (collectivism and status recognition) combine determines individual preferences for allocating resources. It is precisely this problem that is overcome by adopting a country context perspective. By focusing on countries, we highlight their differences rather than their similarities and recognize the multiple dimensions that influence behaviour within each country. Of course, it creates a greater challenge in attempting to develop a unifying framework for understanding how culture affects behaviour.

Organizational justice research is evenly split between the two approaches. Of the studies reviewed in this chapter, approximately half follow the country context path while the other half follow the cultural dimensions path. Research following both approaches has limitations other than those described above. The *country context* path is limited in the comparisons that it makes and the countries that are included in research. The first limitation of this approach is that considerably more of the cross-cultural comparisons are along an East–West divide than within Eastern cultures. Second, the samples contributing to this research are limited in two ways. All of the research focusing on East–West comparisons uses the United States as the Western benchmark against which to compare Eastern countries. Research providing comparisons between Asian countries is also limited in the comparisons that it makes, largely focusing on a small subset of East Asian countries. Finally, this approach is atheoretical – although it successfully identifies differences between countries, it is yet to provide a theoretical account of why such differences emerge.

The *cultural dimensions* approach also has its limitations. The most evident is that researchers adopting this approach almost always select countries based on differences along the individualism–collectivism dimension. Moreover, this dimension is used as the explanatory variable for any observed differences. Only recently has research focused on dimensions other than individual-collectivism (for example, power distance) or adopted a country context approach to understanding organisational justice. It has, however, provide a stronger framework for building theories of culture and justice. As a result, in this review, I will develop arguments drawing on the cultural dimensions approach. However, the review includes research findings from both perspectives.

DISTRIBUTIVE JUSTICE AND CULTURE

Distributive justice focuses on the perceived fairness of reward allocations. According to Adams (1965), fairness is determined through a comparison of individuals' inputs, such as effort, to their outcomes, such as pay, relative to the inputs and outcomes of similar others. This original formulation of the principles of distributive justice, known as *equity theory*, contains a strong element of social comparison. According to equity theory, individuals perceive their outcomes as fair when they receive the same level of rewards as similar others who have similar inputs. Individuals may experience two forms of inequity, *over-reward*, in which they receive more than their inputs demand and *under-reward*, in which they receive less than their inputs demand. In theory, both forms of inequity motivate individuals to restore balance, either by changing their inputs or outcomes. There is a substantial body of research showing that when individuals experience under-reward inequity, they engage in a range of organizationally destructive behaviours including higher levels of organizational theft (see Greenberg, 1990, for a review).

Building on Adams' seminal work, researchers have argued that any one of three distribution rules can be used to evaluate the fairness of reward allocations. Although equity is one such rule, fairness may also be evaluated on the basis of equality or need (Deutsch, 1973, 1975). In comparison to equity, *equality* emphasizes an equal distribution to all and *need* essentially reverses the equity principle, allocating the most resources to the most needy individual. In trying to understand which of these rules dominates reward allocations and perceptions of fairness, researchers have argued that equity and equality meet different goals. Whereas equity focuses on individual performance and highlights the need for productivity, equality focuses on group goals and serves to maintain positive relationships. Not surprisingly, cross-cultural researchers have been quick to highlight the parallels between individualism and equity, and between collectivism and equality.

Incorporating Culture into Models of Distributive Justice

Early analyses of the culture–justice relationship focused on how culture shapes preferences for allocation rules. Drawing on the work of Deutsch (1985), researchers noted that the dominant values of individualistic cultures – productivity, competition, self-gain – align strongly with the principles of equity. The distribution of resources according to individual inputs focuses individuals not only on their task, but also on individual performance. Conversely, the dominant values of collectivist cultures – solidarity, harmony, cohesion – align with the principles of equality. The equal distribution of resources to all members of a group fosters cohesion and builds group relationships, and promotes team rather than individual performance (cf. Leung, 1997). Notwithstanding this strong theoretical link, researchers have failed to find a consistent relationship between individualism–collectivism and preferred distribution rules. Theory and research identify four factors that modify this relationship: shifts in preference strength, social context, the interpretation of inputs and outcomes, and the role of other cultural dimensions.

Shifts in Preference Strength

The typical assumption is that individuals select either one or other allocation rule. In individualistic cultures, the dominant choice should be equity, whereas in collectivist cultures the dominant choice should be equality. Although this may be the case, it presents a model that allows for little situational variation in preferences. It implies that individualists never choose equality and that collectivists never choose equity. Chen, Chen and Meindl (1998) argue that culture does not influence behavior in an absolute way, but that it acts to shift preferences. This has two implications. The first is that the extent to which individuals in a given culture endorse cultural norms may vary, but the mean level of endorsement differs across cultures. The second is that there will be some overlap in the distribution of values within two different cultures. One conclusion that we can draw from this analysis is that, rather than seeing absolute preferences for different allocation rules, we may see more subtle shifts. Taking up this point, James (1993) argues that individualism–collectivism does not result in the consistent endorsement, respectively, of equity and equality; rather it leads to a preference shift. Collectivists prefer equality to equity, whereas individualists prefer equity to equality. This argument leaves open the possibility that, under certain circumstances, the reverse pattern may be observed. It leads to the question of how situations interact with cultural values to shape the selection of allocation rules.

Social Context

Leung (1997) takes up this question. The dominant theme in his analysis is the role of group membership. Leung argues that collectivist cultures are more sensitive to in-group, out-group distinctions than are individualists. According to this argument, equality applies only when resources are being allocated to an individual's in-group. When resources are being allocated to an out-group, collectivists adopt an equity rule even more strongly than do individualists (James, 1993). Within in-groups, the choice of allocation rules is further complicated by an individual's assessment of his or her inputs to the group. It appears that collectivists adopt a 'generosity' rule: When they perceive their inputs to be greater than those of other group members, they endorse an equality rule, whereas when they perceive their inputs to be lower than those of other group members, they endorse an equity rule. In short, they select a rule that does not unduly advantage them or give them a greater share of the resources than other group members.

Interpreting Inputs

The third way in which culture might impact on reward allocation relates to how individuals interpret inputs and outcomes. Morris and Leung (2000) argue that cultures may differ in how they interpret inputs, or in what performance dimensions are weighted most heavily in assessing effort. For example, in assessing inputs, individualists might look for personal attributes such as skills, qualifications and contribution to the task whereas collectivists might look for social attributes such as ability to maintain group harmony, relationship building and promotion of group outcomes. In assessing equity, each may be indifferent to aspects of behavior that are culturally incongruent 'inputs'. Similarly, whereas individualists may focus on personal outcomes, collectivists may focus on group or social outcomes when assessing the input-outcome relationship.

This argument has at least two important implications. First, it suggests that the nature of meaningful rewards will differ across cultures. Second, as I go on to discuss, it provides us with a unifying construct to explain variations in cultural preferences that are not accounted for by individualism–collectivism, that of *interaction goals* (Leung, 1997). Interaction goals capture both the tangible (resource allocation) and intangible (relationship) goals that individuals hope to achieve (e.g., Dillard, Palmer & Kinney, 1995; Waldron & Cegala, 1992). Broadly, such goals focus on the independence or interdependence of individuals' outcomes, and on whether the underlying relationship is viewed as a transactional (exchange) or communal one. How these goals combine has the potential to shape individuals' perceptions of what is fair.

Other Dimensions of Culture

The last factor that needs to be considered when assessing the culture–reward relationship is how values other than those derived from individualism–collectivism might impact on preferences. Relatively less attention has been paid to these dimensions. However, there is some tentative evidence that Hofstede's masculinity–femininity dimension also influences preferences for reward allocation in a way that parallels the effects for individualism–collectivism. Researchers have argued that femininity (communal orientation) will promote a preference for equality, whereas masculinity (agentic orientation) will promote a preference for equity (James, 1993). Similarly, power distance may influence the extent to which departures from equality are tolerated. In cultures that incorporate status and hierarchy in their value systems (high power distance), allocation according to individuals' roles or positions may be perceived as more fair than in cultures that are low in power distance (James, 1993; Morris & Leung, 2000). Interaction goals provide a way of integrating these dimensions. Whether we are considering individualism–collectivism, femininity–masculinity, or power distance, we can identify two broad interaction goals. One focuses more on the individual or task and accentuates differences whereas the other focuses on the group or social relationships and attenuates differences.

Summary

The various models described in this section suggest two principles. The first is that when cultural values emphasize difference, an equity norm will be preferred and when they emphasize similarity an equality norm will be preferred. The second is that when an equity rule is applied, the nature of the inputs and the outputs that underpin justice judgements will differ depending on the dominant interaction goal (see James (1993) for a similar argument).

Distributive Justice Research: How Culture Shapes the Allocation of Rewards

The preceding discussion suggests that, while culture might direct individuals to prefer either an equity or an equality rule, context plays a large part in determining which rule is chosen. Many of the theoretical ideas described earlier are yet to be investigated. To date, researchers in this field have tested two propositions: (a) that culture determines preferences for allocation rules and (b) that the factors contributing to perceived equity are culturally-determined.

Shifts in Preferences

Although the theoretical links from individualism to equity and from collectivism to equality are strong, there is little empirical support for this relationship. Instead, several studies suggest that, independent of culture, individuals endorse an equity principle more strongly than either equality or a needs-based principle of reward allocation. A comparison of Australian and Japanese students shows that both groups rate equity as being more fair than equality when judging reward allocations (Kashima, Siegal, Tanaka & Isaka, 1988). Similarly, comparisons of students from the United States, Japan and South Korea (Kim, Park & Suzuki, 1990) show that all cultures allocate the highest rewards to those individuals making the greatest contributions. These findings suggest that equity is a dominant principle and that violations of equity will be detrimental in a wide range of cultures. One research study, however, shows that despite the dominant preference for equity, culture modifies the application of equity principles: Collectivism more strongly influences reward allocations in Hong Kong than in the United States (Chen, Meindl & Hui, 1998). This research suggests that, if culture does impact on perceptions of distributive justice, it has its effects at a more fine-grained level than the selection of allocation rules.

Social Context

Several findings highlight the role of social context in determining resource allocations. Consistent with the ingroup–outgroup effects proposed by Leung (1997), a collectivist (Hong Kong Chinese) sample displayed more generosity when allocating rewards to friends than did an individualist (US) sample (Hui, Triandis & Yee, 1991). There is also evidence suggesting that task structure shapes reward allocations. For example, in comparing the US and China, Hui et al. (1991) find that culture does not affect allocation rules when rewards are zero sum; however, when they are nonzero sum, collectivists favor equality whereas individualists favor equity. Third, Chiu (1990) highlights the role of person perception in a survey of Hong Kong Chinese students. Chiu (1990) found that when allocating grades to group members, equality was perceived as fair when individuals weighted social factors and took into consideration that other group members' were likeable and committed to the group, and when group cohesiveness was high. However, equity was preferred when individuals weighted performance and took account of their own contribution the group. Finally, there is also some evidence that interaction goals shape allocation preferences. Across cultures when tasks are high in interdependence or when individuals have productivity goals, they adopt an equity-based rule. Conversely, when tasks are low in interdependence, or when individuals have a solidarity goal, they endorse equality (Chen et al., 1998). Overall, these findings suggest that, in applying an equity principle, cultures vary in their sensitivity and responsiveness to contextual cues. Chen et al.'s (1998) findings further suggest that interaction goals may provide a unifying construct for understanding these patterns.

Interpreting Inputs and Outcomes

Culture can shape perceptions of distributive justice because it influences perceptions of inputs and outcomes. Earlier, I highlighted the possibility that different kinds of inputs will be relevant in different cultures. Three studies bear on this argument. Kim et al. (1990) distinguish between two types of rewards, instrumental (grades) and social (friendship). In a comparison of three countries, the United States, Japan and Korea, they demonstrate that United States students are more generous than either Korean or Japanese students in giving grades. Conversely, South Korean students are more generous than the other cultural groups in giving social rewards. Extending these findings, research shows that workplace justice is assessed on different criteria in the

United States and South Korea. Mueller, Iverson and Jo (1999) demonstrate that culture influences the kinds of rewards that shape expectations in the workplace: Whereas in the United States, autonomy shapes justice perceptions, in South Korea these perceptions are influenced by advancement opportunities. Finally, culture affects responses to over-reward inequity. In a large-scale organizational survey, Levine (1993) showed that US workers are not responsive to either over- or under-reward inequity. However, Japanese workers report lower job satisfaction and commitment, and higher turnover intentions when they are *over-rewarded.*

Other Dimensions of Culture

The above findings clearly demonstrate that, even if culture does not influence preferred allocation rules, it shapes the kinds of rewards that contribute to distributive justice as well as reactions to those rewards. Interestingly, they raise the possibility that the individualism–collectivism dimension is not the sole determinant of justice perceptions. For example, Mueller et al.'s (1999) finding that opportunities for advancement are important to perceived justice in the South Korean sample highlights the importance of status and seniority, a characteristic associated with Hofstede's power distance dimension. Other findings also suggest that power distance plays a role in determining perceived fairness. For example, whereas individual performance is a strong predictor of perceived pay fairness in the United States, seniority and education levels are stronger predictors in pay fairness in South Korea (Hundley & Kim, 1997). Similarly, whereas age affects preferred allocation rules in Japan, need affects the choice of equity or equality in Australia (Kashima et al., 1988). And, research by Lam, Schaubroeck and Aryee (2002) provides preliminary evidence that power distance and distributive justice interact to influence the organizational outcomes of job performance, absenteeism and job satisfaction: Individuals with low power distance are more sensitive to variations in justice than those with high power distance.

PROCEDURAL JUSTICE AND CULTURE

One of the problems facing equity theory and analyses of distributive justice is that they cannot account for all aspects of perceived fairness. As a result, researchers turned their attention to the way in which rewards are allocated, that is *procedural justice.* Research in this field shows that individuals judge outcomes to be more fair when they have control over the processes by which those outcomes are determined. Several factors contribute to whether the procedures themselves are judged to be fair: neutrality, consistency, use of accurate information and the ability to change outcomes all contribute to higher perceived procedural fairness (Bies & Moag, 1986; Cohen, 1996). Importantly, research suggests that the impact of unfair outcomes is mitigated when the procedures by which the outcomes were determined are judged to be fair. If culture impacts on procedural justice in the same way that it impacts on distributive justice, we would expect to see that the perceived fairness of procedures influences justice judgements across cultures, but that what contributes to fair procedures is culture-specific.

Incorporating Culture into Theories of Procedural Justice

There are several theoretical reasons for expecting that culture will influence perceptions of procedural justice. Many of the same arguments that applied to considerations of distributive justice can be found in discussions of procedural justice. As was the case for distributive justice, early analyses of procedural justice focused on individualism–collectivism. Initial analyses of the culture-procedural justice relationship centered around the idea that process control sits with notions of autonomy and independence. These concepts, in turn, align more with individualistic than with collectivist values (Leung & Lind, 1986). Researchers argued that individualists and collectivists would prefer different kinds of conflict resolution processes because they had different preferences for direct confrontation. This resulted in the prediction that individualists would prefer processes in which they had a high degree of control, such as adjudication, whereas collectivists would prefer processes that promoted harmony, such as mediation (Morris & Leung, 2000). Again, the failure to find consistent effects highlights the impact of other situational factors. To enable a comparison with models of distributive justice, I will consider four broad variables: shifts in preference strength, social context, interpretation of procedural justice criteria and other cultural values.

Shifts in Preference Strength

Paralleling the analyses of distributive justice, one way in which culture might influence procedural justice is by shifting individual preferences for specific procedures. In the context of procedural justice, this implies that both collectivist and individualist cultures will endorse a number of procedures, but that the endorsement of mediation will be enhanced in collectivist cultures and weakened in individualistic cultures. Conversely, the endorsement of adjudication will be stronger in individualistic cultures than in collectivist cultures. The argument that culture affects preference shifts is also made by Brockner et al. (2000), although in a slightly different form. These authors propose that procedural justice is based on the principle of social exchange. They go on to argue that culture, because it affects the degree to which individuals view themselves as interdependent, may also affect the relative importance that they place on maintaining the social exchange (Brockner et al., 2000). Again, this raises the possibility that social context and interaction goals shape justice judgements.

Social Context

Two authors have addressed the issue of social context. Both present the argument that group membership will be influential in shaping those procedures that are perceived as fair. Lind and Earley (1992) identify three dimensions of procedural justice: voice, dignitary processes and fair processes. They argue that whereas voice and dignitary process will be culture-general, assessments of fair process will be culture specific. These authors draw on their group value model of justice, to discuss the relationship between culture, voice and justice judgements. Lind and Earley (1992) propose that two factors determine the perceived fairness of any procedure. The first is the extent to which procedures are consistent with the core values of the group; the second is the extent to which those procedures accord full membership to individuals. According to Lind and Earley (1992), whereas the first of these factors will be culture specific, the second will be culture-general. That is, independent of culture, individuals will perceive those procedures that treat them as full status group members to be fair; however, the nature of those procedures, because they reflect group values, will differ from culture to culture.

Leung (1997) also takes up the issue of group membership. He argues that, within collectivist cultures, two goals shape the assessment of procedural justice. The first is harmony enhancement, which has the goal of strengthening relationships and results in yielding to others in a conflict. The second is disintegration avoidance, which aims to prevent the weakening of relationships, and results in avoiding behaviors. According to Leung (1997), collectivists will select harmony-enhancing behaviors when interacting with their core in-group and disintegration avoidance behaviors when interacting with their peripheral in-group. More generally, we can conclude that whereas the preference for harmony-enhancing procedures is culture-general, beliefs about the procedures that achieve this goal are culture-specific (Morris & Leung, 2000).

Interpretations of Process

Third, Morris and Leung (2000) argue that, as was the case for distributive justice, culture might affect the interpretation of procedural justice criteria. They identify three criteria on which justice judgements are made, benevolence, neutrality and status recognition. In each case, culture can impact in the interpretation of a decision-maker's behavior. What is viewed as benevolent can differ across cultures, as can the perception that third party involvement is appropriate and desirable. Similarly, they propose that in high power distance countries the expression of negative emotions may be perceived as disrespectful. Furthermore, three components that contribute to procedural justice, trust in an authority's benevolence, the extent to which an individual is treated with dignity and the extent to which decisions are based on accurate information, might be weighted differently in justice judgements (Lind & Earley, 1992). All of these arguments point to the importance of considering how interpretations of behavior are shaped. They also highlight the possibility that whether cultures are high- or low-context may be an important determinant of such interpretations.

Other Dimensions of Culture

Finally, James (1993) raises the possibility that power shapes justice judgements. For example, Lind, Tyler and Huo (1997) argue that countries that emphasize hierarchy (high power distance) will weight trust in the benevolence of authorities more highly whereas cultures that emphasize egalitarianism (low power distance) will weight status recognition (dignity) more highly in their justice judgements. This implies that individual roles may be influential in shaping justice judgements. Consistent with this, Brett et al. (1998) report that, in some cultures, negotiators identify their role as a source of power (see, also, Graham, Minton & Rodgers, 1994). Extending this line of argument, Morris and Leung (2000; Leung, 1997) argue that high power distance may result in greater tolerance of harsh treatment.

Procedural Justice Research: How Culture Shapes the Interpretation of Fair Process

There is relatively little research examining how culture influences perceptions of procedural justice. However, like the distributive justice literature, there are two distinct patterns of findings. The first identifies a set of common themes across cultures. Broadly, these findings show that the same processes underlie justice judgements. The second again identifies the role of interaction goals and other dimensions of culture shaping the relationship between specific procedures and justice judgements.

Preference Shifts and Interaction Goals

As was the case for distributive justice, there is little evidence that culture influences the assessment of fair procedures. Research shows that trust in an authority's motives, status recognition, neutrality and voice all contribute to higher procedural justice in United States, German and Hong Kong Chinese samples (Lind et al., 1997). There is also agreement, in United States and Hong

Kong Chinese samples, that adversarial procedure give greater process control (Leung & Lind, 1986). There is, however, evidence that interaction goals may underpin this effect: Independent of the procedures that are assessed, the belief that they increase process control and harmony increases perceived procedural justice in both Japanese and Spanish respondents (Leung et al., 1992).

Interpretations of Process

Comparisons within collectivist cultures extend the theme of interaction goals, and suggest that there are distinct cultural differences in the processes that contribute to perceived fairness and favourableness. Comparing two collectivist cultures, Leung et al. (1992) report two related differences. The first is that Japanese respondents express a stronger preference for mediation and arbitration than Spanish respondents. The second is that the relationship between perceptions of fairness and favorableness differ in the two cultures. Whereas they form a single dimension for Japanese, their relationship is influenced by the procedure that is used for Spanish. In this latter sample, four procedures – threatening, accusing, mediating and complying, are evaluated separately on the two dimensions whereas another four – ignoring, complying, mediating and arbitrating, are not. Moreover, whereas perceived favorableness and fairness predict procedural preferences in the Japanese sample, they only predict preferences for four procedures – ignoring, complying, accusing and threatening – in the Spanish sample. These findings return to my earlier argument that only culturally congruent 'inputs' are recognized. They suggest that four of the procedures included in Leung et al.'s study may be irrelevant to justice judgements in Spain.

Other Dimensions of Culture

Two studies look not at individualism–collectivism, but at the degree to which cultures endorse hierarchy, that is their power distance. In a series of experiments, Lind et al. (1997) show that Hong Kong Chinese, who place the greatest emphasis on hierarchy, are also more likely to use mediation and arbitration that individuals from either the United States or Germany. Interestingly, the Hong Kong Chinese group also reports higher levels of procedural justice than either of the other groups does. This suggests that procedural choices map on to perceived justice, and further suggests that the Hong Kong Chinese group is most likely to select procedures that result in procedural fairness. In a second study, these authors also report that, consistent with their lower power distance, the procedural justice judgements of United States respondents are more sensitive to status recognition than are those of Japanese respondents. Finally, Lam et al. (2002) provide preliminary evidence that power distance and procedural justice interact to influence the organizational outcomes of job performance, absenteeism and job satisfaction. As was the case for distributive justice, these authors show that individuals with low power distance are more sensitive to variations in justice than those with high power distance.

AT THE CROSSROADS: DISTRIBUTIVE AND PROCEDURAL JUSTICE TOGETHER

Distributive justice is typically linked to outcome satisfaction, for example salary levels, whereas procedural justice is thought to be associated with system satisfaction and linked to organizational outcomes such as turnover, absenteeism and commitment. In addition to exploring how each type of justice affects individual and organizational outcomes, researchers have examined how the two kinds of justice interact. Early research in the United States has demonstrated an interaction between these two variables. This research shows not only that perceived procedural justice moderates the relationship between distributive justice and a range of organizational outcomes, but also that outcomes are especially poor when both forms of justice are low. For example, McFarlin and Sweeney (1992), reported that dissatisfaction with pay, jobs and supervisors, as well as organizational commitment were lowest when individuals perceived *both* distributive *and* procedural justice to be low. Satisfaction increased markedly if either of these factors was high. Recent research examines whether and how culture influences this interaction between the two forms of justice.

Within Culture Studies of Justice

Several studies have examined the relationship between procedural and distributive justice and organizational outcomes within Asian countries. Paralleling findings from the United States, research in Asian countries shows relationships between procedural justice, distributive justice and a range of organizational outcomes including organizational citizenship behavior, job satisfaction and turnover intentions. For example, in Singapore, procedural justice moderates the relationship between perceived union support and organizational citizenship behaviors, as well as between union instrumentality and organizational citizenship behaviors (Aryee & Chay, 2001). Similarly, in Hong Kong, procedural justice predicts higher job satisfaction, more positive evaluations of supervisors (Fields, Pang & Chiu, 2000) as well higher trust in supervisors and the perception that expectations have been met (Lee, Pillutla & Law, 2000). Distributive justice predicts turnover intentions (Fields et al., 2000) and also increases the perception that an organization has fulfilled its psychological contract (Lee et al., 2000). Finally, Leung, Chiu and Au (1993) show that Hong Kong residents are more positive about grievances that are based on violations of interactional or procedural justice than those that are based on violations of distributive justice. Action against such grievances is perceived as fairer and generates more support than action to remedy distributive injustice.

These findings suggest that procedural and distributive justice function in very similar ways across a broad range of cultures. It is only when we turn to the interactions between these two forms of justice that some subtle differences emerge. The first is that whereas, in the United States, procedural justice moderates the relationship between distributive justice and evaluations of supervisors, in Hong Kong it moderates the relationship between distributive justice, turnover intentions and job satisfaction. The second relates to gender effects. For example, whereas research in the United States suggests that gender moderates the relationship between distributive justice and two outcome variables, job satisfaction and turnover intentions, Fields et al. (2000) find no such relationship in their Hong Kong sample. In addition, whereas Sweeney and McFarlin, drawing a sample from the United States, find that women are more sensitive to procedural justice than men, Lee et al. (2000) report that in their Hong Kong sample, men are more sensitive to justice issues than women.

The two kinds of justice interact to shape organizational outcomes. Fields et al. (2000) observed that job satisfaction was highest and turnover intentions were lowest when both distributive and procedural justice were high. Similarly, Lee et al. (2000) report that the two forms of justice interact to predict perceived contract fulfillment. An interesting feature of this second study is the inclusion of a power distance measure. Although power distance is typically used to differentiate countries, in any country we might also expect some individual variation along this dimension. Following this line of argument, Lee et al. (2000) establish that individuals with low power distance are more sensitive to justice issues. Compared to high power distance individuals, those who score low on this dimension are more responsive to changes in the level of justice. When both procedural and distributive justice are low they report lower levels of trust in supervisor and a stronger perception that contracts have been not been fulfilled. However, when both forms of justice are high they report higher levels of justice and a stronger perception that contracts have been fulfilled than high power distance individuals. These findings suggest that individuals who place less emphasis on hierarchy are more attuned to the procedural aspects of the workplace. When status does not provide a sufficient or acceptable norm of resource allocation and other organizational procedures, the perceived fairness of outcomes plays a much stronger role in shaping organizational outcomes.

Comparative Studies of Justice

Two studies provide cross-cultural comparisons of how justice is perceived and used. As is the case in much of the research described in this chapter, there are some global as well as some culture-specific effects. In a comparison of Israeli and Hong Kong respondents, both groups reported similar expectancies about the role of different resource allocation rules. Individuals in both countries believed that an equity rule would enhance harmony, that a needs-based rule would enhance performance, and that using an equality rule would enhance both harmony and performance (Bond, Leung & Schwartz, 1992). They differed in their perceptions of procedural justice, with Israeli respondents indicating a stronger preference for the use of threats and arbitration than did Hong Kong Chinese. Interestingly, this effect could be attributed to the perception of Israeli respondents that threats increased process control whereas arbitration increased harmony (Bond et al., 1992). It suggests that procedural preferences are driven by the functions that they are perceived to serve, and further suggest that none of the procedures in this study (threatening, negotiation, meditation or arbitration) were seen, by Hong Kong respondents, to strongly serve a process control of harmony enhancing function.

In a series of two experiments, Brockner et al. (2000) shed light on the interaction between procedural justice and distributive justice. A comparison of Taiwanese and Canadian participants found that these two variables had quite different effects on individuals' willingness to protest a selection decision. Canadians were equally willing to protest if either the outcome or the process, or both were unfair and unwilling to protest if both were fair. However, Taiwanese were less willing to protest when either the outcome, the process or both were fair and willing to protest only when both the outcome and the process were unfair. Put differently, any aspect of unfairness *provoked* protest from Canadians, and any aspect of fairness *prevented* protest from the Taiwanese in the study. A similar pattern emerged in a second study, comparing a United States sample to one from the People's Republic of China (PRC). In this case, United States respondents were most willing to interact again with negotiators when both procedural and distributive justice was high, whereas a more complex pattern emerged for negotiators from the PRC. In this sample, when outcomes were fair, procedural justice did not influence willingness to interact in the future. However, when outcomes were unfair, negotiators were more willing to interact again in the future when procedural justice was high than when it was low. These findings suggest that, in Western cultures, both aspects of justice must be present for positive outcomes. However, in Eastern cultures, the relationship is more complex and requires further investigation.

Finally, three studies test the relationship between culture, justice and organizational outcomes. Like many of the preceding studies, they highlight both general and culture-specific effects. A comparison of India, China and the

United States shows that distributive justice consistently predicts higher levels of trust in all countries (Pillai, Williams & Tan, 2001). Similarly, procedural justice predicts increased organizational commitment in these three countries, as well as a decreased likelihood of retaliation in both the United States and Taiwan (Blader, Chang & Tyler, 2001).

There are, however, also several differences between countries. For example, distributive justice predicts job satisfaction only in China and India, not the US (Pillai et al., 2001) and turnover in the US but not in Bangladesh (Rahim, Magner, Antonioni & Rahman, 2001). Research also shows that distributive justice predicts organizational commitment in India, but not in the US, China or Bangladesh (Pillai et al., 2001; Rahim et al., 2001). Although country comparisons show that there are some differences in the impact of distributive justice, there are many more in the impact of procedural and interactional justice. Procedural justice predicts trust in the United States and India, but not China; and it predicts organizational commitment in the US, China and Bangladesh but not India. It does not predict job satisfaction in any of the countries studied so far but does predict turnover intention in the Bangladesh sample studied by Rahim et al. (2001). Moreover, the interaction of procedural justice and interactional justice plays a role in determining organizational commitment in US samples whereas it plays a role in determining turnover intentions in Bangladesh samples (Rahim et al., 2001).

JUSTICE, CULTURE AND FUTURE RESEARCH

Comparative studies of organizational justice are limited in two potentially serious ways. The first is that all of the research works from within existing frameworks developed in Western cultures, largely the United States. In the same way that using cultural dimensions can mask differences between countries, applying these frameworks may hide important differences in the antecedents and consequences of justice judgements. Perhaps differences fail to emerge because we are looking in the wrong places. Scholars must ask whether the constructs identified as critical to perceptions of justice and to the antecedent–justice–outcome relationship hold universally. This review suggests that, while there are some surface similarities, the interplay of different forms of justice show subtle variations across countries. These differences highlight the need for scholars to ask whether there are new constructs and new processes that better capture justice judgements in Asian countries. A second limitation of the research reviewed in this chapter is in the range of countries that are included. As I noted earlier, our ability to understand the culture–justice–outcome relationship is limited in two ways. First, research focusing on differences between Asian countries has limited sample selection to a very small number of East Asian countries. Second, East–West comparisons have all used the United States as the Western point of reference. Future research clearly needs to expand the range of Asian and Western countries that are included in comparative studies of organizational justice.

In terms of theoretical development, one of the themes that has emerged from this research is the possibility that interaction goals provide a unifying construct for understanding the relationship between culture and justice judgements. In both research on distributive and procedural justice, it appears that individuals seek to obtain the same interaction goals. Culture exerts its influence by shaping the procedures and other factors that are thought to contribute to goal attainment. The importance of interaction goals is further highlighted by research looking at organizational culture. This research shows that organizations that endorse economic goals also select equity, whereas those that endorse personal development or have a more humanistic orientation endorse equality (Chen, 1995; Mannix, Neale & Northcraft, 1995). These findings strengthen the case for using interaction goals as a broad framework for understanding how culture shapes justice judgements. At the moment, however, this remains a theoretical proposition that requires more systematic investigation in a cross-cultural context.

A second feature that stands out from this review is the dominance of individualism–collectivism as the key dimension for classifying cultures. In examinations of both distributive and procedural justice, almost all research has focused on these dimensions. Very few studies have considered or measured other dimensions. This raises two issues. The first is that, without examining other cultural dimensions, we do not have a complete picture of the relationship between culture and justice judgements. Although the links between individualism–collectivism and distributive justice judgements are theoretically strong other dimensions seem better able to explain procedural justice judgements. Moreover, the inability to find consistent effects for individualism–collectivism suggests that other dimensions play a role in shaping justice judgements. The second issue is that, if other dimensions have been considered it has been in isolation from other dimensions. However, several models of justice suggest that these dimensions combine in unique ways to shape both distributive and procedural aspects of justice (e.g., Fiske, 1992; Kabanoff, 1991). Future research should consider not only how dimensions such as power distance and masculinity–femininity shape justice judgements, but how these various dimensions combine to influence the way in which resources are allocated.

Finally, this review has also made clear that there is much work to be done in building our understanding of the relationship between culture and justice judgements. Although the area of distributive justice has been quite systematically explored, relatively less attention has been paid to how culture shapes procedural justice judgements. Although some procedural justice research has incorporated dimensions of interaction justice, this area also needs to be more systematically addressed. Morris and Leung's (2000) argument that high power distance cultures are more willing to accept harsh treatment has implications for our understanding of the culture–interactional justice relationship. Finally, even less work has addressed the issue of retributive justice. Although researchers have discussed how culture might impact on retributive justice (e.g., Leung & Morris, 2001), this relationship is yet to be systematically tested.

JUSTICE, CULTURE AND ORGANIZATIONAL PRACTICES

The findings reviewed in this chapter also have several implications for management practice. The overall conclusion from this research is that there are some global effects in the factors that shape justice judgements and their consequences for organizational outcomes such as trust and commitment. However, there are also several differences, not only along the East–West divide but also between Asian countries. This suggests that multinational and other companies in which there is significant cultural diversity face challenges in designing their organizational systems. Organizations need to be sensitive not only to the possibility that different systems will be required in different countries, but that in any one country different subgroups may react differently to the same organizational systems.

One clear implication is for the design of organizational reward systems. Analyses of distributive justice suggest that the nature of inputs and rewards used in the equity equation differs across cultures. It appears that whereas collectivist cultures weight social inputs and rewards, individualist cultures weight task inputs and more concrete rewards. Moreover, at least one collectivist culture found over-reward to be unfair. This suggests that the process of designing reward systems becomes significantly more complex when groups have different cultural backgrounds and so may be indifferent to culturally incongruent inputs and processes. Although the concept of 'cafeteria style' reward systems is not new, these findings suggest that organizations must focus not only on the outcomes of reward systems but on the appraisal processes that yield those rewards. Distributive justice research suggests that whereas appraisals based on task contributions will be transparent in individualistic cultures, they will be less readily understood in collectivist cultures; conversely, transparency will be increased in collectivist cultures and decreased in individualistic cultures when appraisals focus on social inputs. For example, research shows that individuals overestimate their input and underestimate the input of other groups when assessing distributive justice.

Culture also affects the kinds of organizational grievance and dispute resolution systems that will be effective. Procedural justice research shows that, although individuals in all cultures look for procedures that enhance harmony, the procedures that accomplish this goal show considerable cultural variation. Similarly, although cultures all use trust, neutrality and voice to assess procedural justice, they differ in what is viewed as achieving these goals. These findings suggest that the design of grievance mechanisms and other dispute resolution processes is not 'one size fits all', but needs a tailor made approach taking into consideration the culture specific nature of justice judgements.

Turning to issues of diversity management, analyses of both procedural and distributive justice suggest that there are subtle differences in responses to organizational injustice. Research shows considerable variation in the effects of justice on organizational outcomes such as trust, commitment, job satisfaction and organizational commitment. It also shows that how different forms of justice interact to affect organizational outcomes differs across countries. However, the culture–justice–outcome research is relatively limited and it is difficult to draw clear implications for organizational practice. What is clear is that organizations with well-designed and fair systems are not necessarily guaranteed positive outcomes. For example, even if resource allocations and reward systems are judged to be fair (high distributive justice), this perceived fairness will increase commitment and job satisfaction in only a handful of countries. These findings underscore the need for organizations not just to attend to cultural differences in designing organizational systems and management practices, but also in considering their likely consequences.

CONCLUSION

Notwithstanding the research reviewed in this chapter, there is considerable work to be done in developing our understanding of the culture–justice–outcome relationship. First and foremost, as I have already noted, current justice research works from a framework developed in a Western context. Researchers pursuing the cultural aspects of justice judgements must, as a first step, re-evaluate the utility of this approach and ask whether by adopting this approach they are masking important cultural differences. Second, the number of countries studied to date is limited – both in terms of the Asian countries that have been included in research and in the use of the United States as the benchmark Western culture. The inclusion of more Asian and Western countries in future research can only increase our understanding of how culture shapes the antecedents and consequences of organizational justice. Finally, current research has a strong focus on distributive justice. Relatively little research has focused on other forms of justice (procedural, interactional, retributive) or on how these forms of justice interact to shape perceived justice. Given the considerable cultural variability in the effects of procedural justice, it is especially important that cross-cultural justice research addresses this substantial gap in our knowledge.

With these comments in mind, this review has identified two culture-general patterns in justice judgements. The first is that, across cultures, individuals endorse equity as a fair principle for the allocation of resources. The second is that trust in an authority's motives, status recognition, neutrality and voice all contribute to the perception of fair process in several countries. The effects of culture are subtler than to alter the rules used for allocating rewards or the strategies that contribute to fair process. In this review, I identified three factors that shape the relationship between culture and justice judgements, preference shifts, social context, the interpretation of inputs and procedures, and highlighted the possibility the dimensions other than individualism–collectivism play a role in shaping these judgements. In analyzing existing research, I argued that interaction goals provide a means for capturing the essential differences between cultures and understanding the culture–justice judgment relationship. Interaction goals that minimize differences and emphasize relationships differ in their effects from those that accentuate difference and emphasize performance.

REFERENCES

Adams, J.S. 1965. Inequity of social exchange. In L. Berkowitz (ed.), *Advances in Experimental Social Psychology* (Vol. 2). New York: Academic Press.

Aryee, S. and Chay, Y.W. 2001. Workplace justice, citizenship behavior, and turnover intentions in a union context: Examining the mediating role of perceived union support and union instrumentality. *Journal of Applied Psychology*, 86: 154-160.

Bies, R.J. and Moag, J.S. 1986. Interactional justice: Communication criteria of fairness. *Research on Negotiation in Organizations*, 1: 43-55.

Blader, S.L., Chang, C.-C. and Tyler, T.R. 2001. Procedural justice and retaliation in organizations: Comparing cross-nationally the importance of fair group processes. *The International Journal of Conflict Management*, 12: 295-311.

Bond, M.H., Leung, K. and Schwartz, S. 1992. Explaining choices in distributive and procedural justice across cultures. *International Journal of Psychology*, 27: 211-225.

Brett, J.M., Adair, W., Lempereur, A., Okumura, T., Shikhirev, P., Tinsely, C. and Lytle, A. 1998. Culture and joint gains in negotiation. *Negotiation Journal*, 14: 61-86.

Brockner, J., Ackerman, G., Greenberg, J., Gelfand, M.J., Franscesco, A., Chen, Z., Leung, K., Bierbauer, G., Gomez, C., Kirkman, B., Shapiro, D. 2001. Culture and procedural justice: The influence of power distance on reactions to voice. *Journal of Experimental Social Psychology*, 37: 300-315.

Brockner, J., Chen, Y.-R., Mannix, E.A., Leung, K. and Skarlicki, D.P. 2000. Culture and procedural fairness: When the effects of what you depend on how you do it. *Administrative Science Quarterly*, 45: 138-159.

Chen, C.C. 1995. New trends in reward allocation preferences: A Sino-U.S. comparison. *Academy of Management Journal*, 38: 408-428.

Chen, C.C., Chen, X.-P. and Meindl, J.R. 1998. How can cooperation be fostered? The cultural effects of individualism–collectivism, *Academy of Management Review*, 23: 285-304.

Chen, C.C., Meindl, J.R. and Hui, H. 1998. Deciding on equity or parity: A test of situational, cultural and individual factors. *Journal of Organizational Behavior*, 19: 115-129.

Chiu, C.-Y. 1990. Distributive justice among Hong Kong Chinese college students. *The Journal of Social Psychology*, 130: 649-656.

Cohen, R.L. 1991. Justice and negotiation. *Research on Negotiation in Organizations*, 2: 259-282.

Deutsch, M. 1975. Equity, equality and need: What determines which value will be used as the basis for distributive justice? *Journal of Social Issues*, 31: 137-149.

Deutsch, M. 1973. *The Resolution of Conflict*. New Haven: Yale University Press.

Dillard, J.P., Palmer, M.T. and Kinney, T.A. (1995). Relational judgements in an influence context. *Human Communication Research*, 21: 331-353.

Fiske, A.P. 1992. The four elementary forms of sociality: Framework for a unified theory of social relations. *Psychological Review*, 99: 689-723.

Fields, D., Pang, M. and Chiu, C. 2000. Distributive and procedural justice as predictors of employee outcomes in Hong Kong. *Journal of Organizational Behavior*, 21: 547-562.

Graham, J.L., Mintu, A.T. and Rodgers, W. (1994). Explorations of negotiation behaviors in ten foreign cultures using a model developed in the United States. *Management Science*, 40: 72-95.

Greenberg, J. 1990. Organizational justice: Yesterday, today and tomorrow. *Journal of Management*, 16: 399-432.

Hiu, C.H., Triandis, H.C. and Yee, C. 1991. Cultural differences in reward allocation: Is collectivism the explanation? *British Journal of Social Psychology*, 30: 145-157.

Hofstede, G. 1980. *Culture's Consequences: International Differences in Work-related Walues*, Beverly Hills: Sage.

Hundley, G. and Kim, J. 1997. National culture and the factors affecting perceptions of pay fairness in Korea and the United States, *International Journal of Organizational Analysis*, 5: 325-341.

James, K. 1993. The social context of organizational justice: Cultural, intergroup and structural effects on justice behaviors and perceptions. In R. Cropanzo (ed.), *Justice in the Workplace*.

Kabanoff, B. 1991. Equity, equality, power and conflict. *Academy of Management Review*, 16: 416-441.

Kashima, Y., Siegal, M., Tanaka, K. and Isaka, H. 1988. Universalism in lay conceptions of distributive justice: A cross-cultural examination. *International Journal of Psychology*, 23: 51-64.

Kim, K.I., Park, H.-J. and Suzuki, N. 1990. Reward allocations in the United States, Japan and Korea: A comparison of individualistic and collectivist cultures. *Academy of Management Journal*, 33: 188-198.

Lam, S.S.K., Schaubroeck, J. and Aryee, S. 2002. Relationship between organizational justice and employee work outcomes: A cross-national study. *Journal of Organizational Behavior*, 23: 1-18.

Lee, C., Pillutla, M. and Law, K.S. 2000. Power-distance, gender and organizational justice. *Journal of Management*, 26: 685-704.

Leung, K. 1997. Negotiation and reward allocations across cultures. In P.C. Earley and M. Erez (eds.), *New Perspectives on International Industrial/Organizational Psychology*. San Francisco: Jossey-Bass.

Leung, K. and Lind, E.A. 1986. Procedural justice and culture: Effects of culture, gender and investigator status on procedural preferences, *Journal of Personality and Social Psychology*, 50: 1134-1140.

Leung, K. and Li, W.-K. 1990. Psychological mechanisms of process-control effects. *Journal of Applied Psychology*, 75: 613-620.

Leung, K. and Morris, M.W. 2001. Justice through the lens of culture and ethnicity. In J. Sanders and V.L. Hamilton (eds.), *Handbook of Justice Research in Law* (pp. 343-378). Dordrecht, Netherlands: Kluwer Academic Publishers.

Leung, K., Bond, M.H., Carment, D.W., Krishnan, L. and Liebrand, W.B.G. 1990. Effects of cultural femininity on preference for methods of conflict processing: A cross-cultural study. *Journal of Experimental Psychology*, 26: 373-388.

Leung, K., Au, Y.-F., Fernandez-Dols, J.M. and Iwawaki, S. 1992. Preference for methods of conflict processing in two collectivist cultures. *International Journal of Psychology*, 27: 185-209.

Leung, K. and Chiu, W.-H. and Au, Y.-F. 1993. Sympathy and support for industrial actions: A justice analysis. *Journal of Applied Psychology*, 78: 781-787.

Levine, D.I. 1993. What do wages buy? *Administrative Science Quarterly*, 38: 462-483.

Lind, E.A., Tyler, T.R. and Huo, Y.J. 1997. Procedural context and culture: Variation in the antecedents of procedural justice judgements. *Journal of Personality and Social Psychology*, 73: 767-780.

Lind, E.A. and Earley, P.C. 1992. Procedural justice and culture. *International Journal of Social Psychology*, 27: 227-242.

McFarlin, D.B. and Sweeney, P.D. 1992. Distributive and procedural justice as predictors of satisfaction with personal and organizational outcomes. *Academy of Management Journal*, 35: 626-637.

McLean Parks, J. 1997. The fourth arm of justice: The art and science of revenge. *Research on Negotiation in Organizations*, 6: 113-144.

Mannix, E.A., Neale, M.A. and Northcraft, G.B. 1995. Equity, equality, or need? The effects of organizational culture on the allocation of benefits and burdens. *Organizational Behavior and Human Decision Processes*, 63: 276-286.

Morris, M.W. and Leung, K. 2000. Justice for all? Progress in research on cultural variation in the psychology of distributive and procedural justice. *Applied Psychology: An International Review*, 49: 100-132.

Mueller, C.W., Iverson, R.D. and Jo, D.-G. 1999. Distributive justice evaluations in two cultural contexts: A comparison of U.S. and South Korean teachers. *Human Relations*, 52: 869-893.

Pillai, R., Williams, E.S. and Tan, J.J. 2001. Are the scales tipped in favour of procedural or distributive justice? An investigation of the U.S., India, Germany, and Hong Kong (China). *The International Journal of Conflict Management*, 12: 312-332.

Rahim, M.A., Magner, N.R., Antonioni, D. and Rahman, S. 2001. Do justice relationships with organization-directed reactions differ across U.S. and Bangladesh employees? *The International Journal of Conflict Management*, 12: 333-349.

Schwartz, S.H. 1994. Beyond individualism/collectivism: New cultural dimensions of values. In U. Kim, H.C. Triandis and G. Yoon (eds.), *Individualism and Collectivism* (pp. 85-117). London: Sage.

Sweeney, P.D. and McFarlin, D.B. 1997. Process and outcome: Gender differences in the assessment of justice. *Journal of Organizational Behavior*, 18: 83-98.

Sweeney, P.D. and McFarlin, D.B. 1993. Workers' evaluations of the 'ends' and 'means': An examination of four models of distributive and procedural justice. *Organizational Behavior and Human Decision Processes*, 55: 23-40.

Waldron, V.R. and Cegala, D.J. 1992. Assessing conversational cognition: Levels of theory and associated methodological requirements. *Human Communication Research*, 18: 599-622.

Chapter 16

CONFLICT MANAGEMENT IN ASIA
A Dynamic Framework and Future Directions

Catherine H. Tinsley
Georgetown University (USA)

Susan E. Brodt
Queen's University (Canada)

INTRODUCTION

Interpersonal conflict, the perception of differences or incompatibilities (Thomas, 1992), is pervasive in organizational life. Indeed, managers spend an abundant amount of time intervening in disputes and resolving work place conflict (Mintzberg, 1975). Although conflict may not always be detrimental to a company (Thomas, 1992), the proper management of conflict can contribute to the efficiency, effectiveness, and possibly longevity of an organization (McCann & Galbraith, 1981). Yet, understanding the "proper" process for managing conflict continues to be a challenging topic for researchers.

One of the most prominent proposals is Pruitt and Rubin's (1986) dual concern model. This model, building off Blake and Mouton (1964) and Thomas and Killman (1974), posits that a conflict management strategy hinges on how much one cares about him/her self and how much one cares about the other party. High concern for self and high concern for the other party should lead one to adopt a *problem solving* strategy, high concern for one's self and low concern for the other party should lead one to adopt a *forcing* strategy, low concern for one's self and high concern for the other party should lead one to adopt an *accommodating* strategy, moderate concern for both parties should lead one to adopt a *compromise* strategy, and low concern for both parties should lead one to adopt an *avoidance* strategy.

This paradigm, which continues to receive empirical support (see DeDreu, Weingart, & Kwon, 2000), provides researchers with a useful framework for both describing the various ways in which conflict could be managed and for prescribing how conflict should be managed. One implication is that when parties value both their own concerns and those of the other party, then problem solving should be used. This squares with similar prescriptions from the field of negotiation and labor relations, namely that parties should problem solve or "integrate" their specific interests, in order to reach higher quality outcomes that both parties are motivated to implement (Walton & McKersie, 1965; Raiffa, 1982). Other empirical studies confirm the usefulness of this approach with findings that show that when parties used interests-based problem solving to manage conflict they are more satisfied with the outcome, because they feel their unique needs and goals have been addressed (Shapiro, Drieghe, & Brett, 1985).

Although this dual concern model and the problem solving strategy in particular have proven extremely useful both descriptively and prescriptively, it is important to remember that this research was framed largely through a US perspective—generated by US scholars, conducted on US samples. More recent research has shown that interest-based problem solving, while a preferable method for resolving workplace conflict in the US, is not necessarily the most preferred method elsewhere (Tinsley, 1998, 2001; Tinsley & Brett, 2001). Tinsley and Brett (2001), for example, found US managers used comparatively more interest-based problem solving strategies while their Hong Kong Chinese counterparts were more likely to incorporate upper management.

Indeed a plethora of comparative work has found cross-cultural differences in how conflict is resolved (cf. Gulliver, 1979; Trubisky, Ting-Toomey, & Lin, 1991; Chua & Gudykunst, 1987; Leung, 1987, 1997; Dyer & Song, 1997; Tse, Francis, & Walls, 1994; Gire, 1997). The majority of these studies link differences in conflict resolution to cultural dimensions, or characterizations of differences in values and beliefs. As Tinsley (1998, 2001) explains, each strategy for resolving conflict has a number of underlying assumptions (about conflict goals, what information is important, how people should interact, etc.). If there is a poor fit between these assumptions and the dominant value patterns of the national culture, then this particular strategy is unlikely to be used or preferred in that culture.

In this chapter, we blend two approaches. First, we consider the dominant value patterns in Asia and the implications of these value patterns for conflict resolution. We review prior research on conflict resolution in an Asian context to discuss what new constructs have emerged and how consideration of these constructs helps inform the predominantly Western-based theories of conflict resolution. Second, adopting a social cognitive analysis of culture and conflict resolution (Hong & Chiu, 2001), we propose a framework in which psychological frames, schemas, and scripts help us understand the numerous ways in which conflict may be resolved and how these ways relate to each other, and to culture. That is, most prior cross-cultural conflict research looks at disputants' behavioral differences based on differences on individual-level or cultural-level values. We begin with these values and behavioral differences and then delve into the cognitive dynamics underlying them. Essentially, we believe that these value and behavioral differences have socio-cognitive roots and can be explained by disputants' conflict frames, schemas, and scripts. Thus we use basic social psychological tools (frames, schemas, and scripts) as well as cultural findings (on value and behavioral differences) to broaden and deepen our understanding of conflict resolution. We offer commentary as to which types of conflict resolution frames, schemas, and scripts might be most likely in an Asian context, but we caution that the particulars of our framework are still a work-in-progress. We conclude with questions we hope future research might answer.

CONSTRUCTS FROM ASIA

Asia has enjoyed a rich history of comparative cultural research. There are many studies that detail responses to conflict by Chinese, Japanese, Korean or Taiwanese managers typically in comparison to Western counterparts, as well as some studies that incorporate Thailand, India, or Indonesia (cf. Sriussadaporn-Charoenngam & Jablin, 1999; Leung & Tjosvold, 1998). Quite conveniently for the field of conflict research, interest in Asia coincided with the rapid rise of these economies in the 1980s (at a time when conflict scholars in the region were beginning research and those in the US were starting cross-cultural studies) as well as the marked differences between Asian cultures and the West.

Collectivism

One of the most striking characteristics of Eastern cultures is the collectivism or embeddedness of the parties. People are not isolated individuals but rather are embedded in a rich social fabric of others. People are viewed as social or relational beings; indeed Ho (1993) has suggested that the unit of analysis for Asian research should not be the individual, but rather the "individual-in-relations." Whereas Western individuals tend to characterize themselves as autonomous units with boundaries that stop at their own skin, Eastern people tend to characterize themselves as units that are intimately linked to various social groups (Markus & Kitayama, 1991). Triandis (1986) for example, reports that collectivists characterize themselves as actors in relation to others, such as "I am a sister of___; I am a friend of ___ ", whereas individualists characterize themselves by their own discrete characteristics, such as "I am smart; I am a basketball player." In fact, many scholars argue that while personality may explain a large part of behavior in a Western context, it is an individual's social context such as his or her place within a social hierarchy that predicts behavior in an Eastern context (Ho, 1993; Yang, 1993). People's lay theories about the causes of others' behaviors also correspond to these differences (Choi, Nisbett, & Norenzayan, 1999; Masuda & Nisbett, 2001).

Because of its impact on how people perceive themselves and others, embeddedness has several implications for how parties manage conflict. First, embeddedness or collectivism should affect parties' *conflict goals*. Tinsley (1997), for example, argues that the goals underlying the dual concern model should be modified for a collective context. She argues that while individualists might choose a conflict resolution strategy based on how much they care about their own concerns and those of the other party, collectivists might choose a conflict resolution strategy based on how much they care about their own concerns and those of the *collective*. Similarly, Leung (1987, 1997) has argued that "animosity reduction" is a major goal for collectivists in severe disputes, and "disintegration avoidance" is the goal in milder disputes, both of which address concerns for the collective. The notion of embeddedness highlights the specific conflict context and that in certain cultures there may be value placed on maintaining relationships over transactional goals. Hence, this introduces a concern for the broader collective.

Second, a party's embeddedness or collectivism has implications for *conflict resolution behavior*. Triandis and colleagues consider individualism–collectivism to be the most widely studied cultural dimension (Triandis, Brislin, & Hui, 1988), and a number of studies have examined how this dimension affects conflict behavior. Generally, collectivists use more avoidance and less problem solving than individualists (Trubisky, Ting-Toomey, & Lin 1991; Tang & Kirkbride; 1988; Chua & Gudykunst, 1987). And there is some evidence that collectivists are more prone to compromise than individualists (Cushman & King, 1985). Indian disputants, for example, are less competitive than their US counterparts (Morris et al., 1998). In the framework presented in this chapter, we incorporate both of these implications and propose that collectivism influences a party's goals or conflict frame (i.e., concern for the self, the other party, and the broader community) as well as their behavior of conflict scripts.

Indirect Communication

Another phenomenon prevalent in Asia is communication by indirect or more covert codes and signals. Individuals select more roundabout ways of expressing themselves as opposed to sharing thoughts and feelings overtly and directly. These methods may involve communicating through a third party or simply communicating in a certain scripted "code" so that in-group members understand the true meaning of what is being communicated. In Japan, for example, there exist a number of verbal formulas for expressing disagreement without explicitly voicing any differences and hence maintaining a surface harmony (Eastman, 2000). It has been said that while US President Nixon was on a trip to Japan urging then Prime Minister Tanaka to open up his country to further imports, Tanaka replied, "I will do my utmost." This remark pleased Nixon, whereas most Japanese understood that this verbal formula is used frequently to imply nothing will be done (Eastman, 2000). Similarly, in Thailand, "competent" communication is characterized as being tactful, modest, and polite (Sriussadaporn-Charoenngam & Jablin, 1999).

Hall (1976) calls this high context communication, where members share a highly developed context and therefore less information needs to be transmitted explicitly. Although there is less research on the implications of indirect or high context communication, it is the dominant explanation behind Ting-Toomey's (1988) conflict-face negotiation theory. She argues that concerns over a person's social face or reputation drive their conflict resolution behavior, and those with a higher need to save face, i.e., those living in high context cultures, will resolve conflict using more indirect techniques. In the related field of negotiation, Brett and her colleagues (Adair, Brett, Lempeurer, Okumura, Shikhirev, Tinsley, & Lytle, 2004; Brett & Okumura, 1998; Brett, Adair, Lempeurer, Shikhirev, Tinsley, & Lytle, 1998) have shown that Eastern cultures (here Japan, Hong Kong, and Russia) that value indirect communication tend to negotiate via a different script than those who value direct communication. Members of Eastern cultures tend to make fewer statements about their own preferences and priorities, make fewer remarks explicitly comparing and contrasting parties' statements and positions, offer fewer direct reactions, and make considerably more package solutions to the other side. This indirect process of coming to agreement through an exchange of packaged offers (rather than an explicit discussion of parties' positions and interests) is called a "heuristic trial and error" script. In the framework presented in this chapter, we discuss how indirect communication influences parties' conflict behavior or script as well as the different meanings (schemas) that might be associated with that behavior.

Hierarchy

Also prevalent in Asia is the importance of hierarchical social structure, often called a high power distance culture. Hierarchy or high power distance describes a value for social inequality rather than equality (Haire, Ghiselli, &

Porter, 1966), as well as value on autocratic leadership and centralized authority, rather than participative leadership and decentralized authority (Hofstede,
1980). Social hierarchy is beginning to enjoy some attention in conflict management research (cf. Adair et al., 2004; Leung & Lind, 1986; Tinsley, 1998,
2001; Tinsley & Brett, 2001; Tse, Francis, & Walls, 1994; Brett et al., 1998),
perhaps because status and decision power are intimately connected to conflict
resolution (Walton & McKersie, 1965). For example, using status imbalance
may be the best way to resolve a conflict, at least in the short term (Goldberg,
Green, & Sander, 1985), and when power is distributed unequally parties tend
to adopt a forcing conflict management strategy (over problem solving, compromise, and legalistic strategies) (Lin & Germain, 1998).

There are two general findings regarding hierarchy. The first is that in
high power distance cultures, parties tend to accept an imbalanced resolution that was fashioned based on the social power of the varying parties.
For example, parties from high power distance cultures are more likely to
accept insults from a high status party (Bond, Wan, Leung, & Giacalone,
1985) and unequal allocations favoring the high status party (Triandis et al.,
1988), than are parties from low power distance cultures. As a corollary to
this finding, we also see that when power imbalances exist, parties find it
completely acceptable to use power to force an imbalanced resolution (Lin
& Germain, 1998). The second finding is that in high power distance cultures,
disputants tend to look to higher status members for guidance and input. For
example, Hong Kong Chinese and Japanese (high power distance) litigants
are more likely to look to a judge for discretionary guidance, whereas US
(low power distance) litigants prefer to argue their own case (Leung & Lind,
1986). Similarly, Chinese executives are more likely to consult their superior
about a conflict than are their Canadian counterparts (Tse, Francis, & Walls,
1994). And Hong Kong Chinese parties are more likely to defer conflict issues to upper management than are their US counterparts (Tinsley & Brett,
2001).

These findings suggest that hierarchy affects a party's conflict goals, or
frame, as well as that party's resolution behavior. Parties from a high power
distance culture are often concerned about soliciting the input of authority figures with the goal of ensuring resolution that satisfies these authority figures.
Thus, hierarchy, like collectivism, may focus parties towards collective or community concerns. In the framework presented in this chapter, we discuss how
hierarchy, like collectivism, might influence an individual's goals or perspective and reflect varying amounts of concern for the self, for others, and for
the community. As well, parties from high power distance cultures seem more
comfortable with forcing and other power-based resolution behaviors. Thus we
will also discuss how hierarchy influences parties' conflict resolution behavior
(scripts) and its meaning (schemas).

INCORPORATING CULTURAL FINDINGS INTO A FRAMEWORK OF CONFLICT RESOLUTION

Before detailing our particular framework of conflict resolution, it is important to understand how this framework was built from cultural findings. Our general argument is that cultural knowledge (for example, research exploring cultural differences in conflict management practices) can be used to both *deepen* and *broaden* our Western-based conflict resolution theories, or those that were built primarily from one cultural perspective. Comparative research, which has elucidated several constructs prevalent in Asia (collectivism, indirect communication, hierarchy), broadens Western-dominant theories by highlighting their assumptions of individualism, direct communication, and egalitarian social structures. These theories and frameworks become more inclusive and better at understanding (and predicting) conflict management across cultures. Cultural findings also allow us to probe the variability of conflict management strategies within a culture. Cultural groups are not monolithic; each culture has a distribution of various characteristics, meaning that even typically individualistic US parties can and will espouse collective values and display collective-based conflict behaviors in some situations (such as within family conflicts). These values and behaviors are present but just not typical. Therefore, looking at dominant approaches in other cultures helps us see what might be less typical—but present—values and behavior in our own cultures. Without such highlighting, these approaches might otherwise be overlooked. As well, because culture is continuously changing, these alternatives may prove to be valuable conflict management choices in the future. So cultural knowledge not only helps us better understand our present and dominant choices, deepening our conflict management knowledge, but also offers alternatives that may prove to be valuable options in the future, broadening our conflict management knowledge.

In the remainder of this chapter we use cultural findings from Asia to expound a rich framework of conflict frames schemas and scripts. We use cultural findings to suggest that there are three focal orientations or social goals: self-concern, mutual concern (concern for both parties),[1] and community concern. As we explain below these foci are conflict management frames, which focus attention and define the scope of the conflict. As well, we use cultural findings from Asia to catalogue several conflict management scripts or behavior. This variety of behavior, documented in prior cross-cultural research, certainly broadens our conflict management knowledge, however we caution that other conflict management scripts certainly exist. The ones we have chosen simply reflect the current empirical-based literature.

We deepen our knowledge by using cultural findings to explore the links between conflict frames and scripts, elucidating the meaning underlying behavior in light of a party's social goals. Here is where we introduce the notion of conflict resolution schemas, which comprise the meaning of the conflict behavior. All in all, we show that there may be a very complex interplay among frames, schemas, and scripts across cultures. Again, we propose to have only skeletal knowledge at this point of the variety of conflict management behaviors, what they mean, and what goals they are serving. We offer what we have developed as a work-in-progress upon which future research might build.

DEFINING FRAMES, SCHEMAS, AND SCRIPTS

Conflict management is an individual's attempt to reconcile a perceived incompatibility with another. During this activity, an individual sets goals for the interaction and then engages in behavior that is meant to forward those goals. Goals, behavior, and the meaning of that behavior are the key elements to conflict management and these elements are reflected (respectively) in conflict frames, scripts, and schemas.

Elsewhere (Brodt & Tinsley, 2001) we have explained that a *frame* is an active filtering mechanism that reflects a party's primary concern or goal orientation. Frames direct attention toward certain aspects of the social environment and away from others (Minsky, 1977), broadening or narrowing the scope of what one attends to or what is perceived as important. Hence, they embody a party's conflict goal. *Schemas* are dynamic knowledge structures that help make sense of, and give meaning to, one's social world (Ross & Nisbett, 1991; Fiske & Taylor, 1991). They comprise the vast reservoir or web of information about facts, persons, and things learned by members of a social group through both instruction and experience. In essence, schemas provide the underlying meaning of surface behavior. Finally, *scripts* are a special type of schema—i.e., an event schema—consisting of information about actions or events (Fiske & Taylor, 1991). They include knowledge about when and where people play different roles, and include the various behavioral options that are part of a role. In essence, scripts comprise the set of behavioral options available to an individual. They include concrete, visible behaviors and as such they are the enactment of a person's response to a situation.

Taken together, we have called these frames, schemas, and scripts the social-cognitive system—how an individual's cognitive processes interact with the social world (Brodt & Tinsley, 2001). Frames filter information reflecting a person's social goal orientation, schemas embody the meaning or interpretation of surface behavior, and scripts are the enacted responses to a situation as construed. Our use of these terms is somewhat unique due to our desire to delve deeply into the workings of the social cognitive system. Thus we include all three concepts and distinguish among them whereas others focus on either frames or schemas, for example, and use them interchangeably. We believe that this precision brings different aspects of the conflict resolution process to life. As well, we intentionally violate the purely cognitive nature of the original constructs most notably by linking frames with motivation.

DELINEATING THE FRAMES, SCHEMAS, AND SCRIPTS OF CONFLICT RESOLUTION

Table 1 lists the conflict frames, schemas, and scripts we have been able to delineate from the literature to date that examines conflict management in both Western and Asian contexts.

CONFLICT FRAMES

Conflict frames reflect a party's primary underlying social goal or orientation and serve to actively focus attention on some aspects of the dispute and not on others. The dual concern model distinguishes between two different orientations (or frames): self-concern and mutual concern (a combination of concern for self and concern for other). As Pruitt & Carnevale (1993) have explained, the movement between forcing, compromising, and accommodating conflict management strategies is really an adjustment along a "distributive" or "value-claiming" continuum, whereas the movement between avoidance, compromise, and problem solving is really adjustment along an "integrative" or "value creating" continuum. Hence, these five behaviors (scripts) reflect two underlying orientations or goals (frames) that one might have—a self-orientated, distributive frame or a mutual-oriented, integrative frame. This model is wonderful for capturing the types of goals (frames) most frequently

Table 1. Conflict resolution frames, scripts, and schemas

Frames	Scripts	Schema
Self-concern	Problem solving	Collaborating
Mutual-concern	Forcing	Claiming value
Community-concern	Yielding	Saving face
	Compromising	Satisfying collective
	Avoiding	Respecting rights
	Heuristic trial and error	Terminating involvement
	Consulting others	Co-opt high status 3rd party
	Objective standards	Satisfy high status 3rd party's concern
	Involving high status 3rd parties	Getting information or external perspective
	Tacit coordination	

seen in Western conflict management. Yet, collectiveness, indirect communication, and hierarchy, which are so prevalent in Asia, force us to consider whether these two frames are exhaustive.

Both social collectivity and hierarchy suggest that a third frame is needed— a collective or community orientation. Western conflict management tends to isolate conflict from its context, to treat conflict as a discrete event between the focal parties. The relevant scope is often the two (or more) focal parties who are directly involved in the conflict, rather than anyone who might be more tangentially related to either the parties or to the issues in conflict (Tinsley, forthcoming). Yet, when parties are intimately connected to others in their social world (collectivism) and when parties care about the wishes and interests of superiors (hierarchy), then parties are likely to consider the dispute embedded in its social context. This embeddedness would encourage parties to consider a broader community orientation frame. Hence, our conflict framework has 3 frames corresponding to 3 different answers to the question: what is the main goal of this conflict resolution behavior? Disputants may be interested in self, self and other disputants, or the greater community (family, organization) in which the disputants are embedded. These answers lead (respectively) to self-concern, mutual-concern, and community-concern frames.

As noted previously, cultures are not monolithic; hence, we do not mean to imply that a community-concern frame is only found in Asian cultures and not in the West. Indeed, in certain circumstances we argue just the opposite: when representatives from labor and management consider the collateral damage of a strike and how that impacts customers, we would expect Western parties to adopt a community-concern frame. Our point is simply that community-concern is not a dominant frame for Western parties, and hence is less likely to be a focus of inquiry. On the other hand, this frame is naturally investigated in Asia, since it is used under more circumstances.

CONFLICT SCRIPTS

In the dual concern model there are five scripts: problem solving, forcing, yielding, compromising, and avoiding. Yet, cross-cultural comparative work has elucidated a number of differences between Asian and Western conflict management behaviors, leading us to delineate additional scripts. As noted above, Brett and colleagues (Adair et al., 2004; Brett & Okumura, 1998; Brett et al., 1998) found that instead of interest based problem solving, Asians negotiated using a heuristic trial and error method. As well, Tse et al. (1994) found that instead of problem solving, Chinese were more likely to turn the matter over to a third party. Tinsley (1998, 2001) found that instead of problem solving, Japanese tended to try to co-opt a third party authority figure whereas

Germans were more likely to use objective standards or standard operating procedures. Moreover, Ting-Toomey (1998) found that instead of interest-based problem solving, Asians were more likely try an indirect resolution by tacit coordination or consulting others.

Taken together, these studies broaden the original list of 5 conflict resolution scripts to 10, including: (1) problem solving (2) forcing, (3) yielding (4) compromising (5) avoiding (6) heuristic trial and error, (7) consulting others (8) relying on objective standards, rules and procedures, (9) involving high status third parties, and (10) tacit coordination. These scripts are listed in Table 1. Again, we clarify that we do not mean to imply that the latter five scripts are not found in the West. These are conflict management behaviors that any Westerner would recognize and potentially use; they simply may not be common choices.

CONFLICT SCHEMAS

To understand how conflict frames (social goals) relate to scripts (behavior), we invoke the psychological concept of a schema. Recall that schemas embody the meaning of the surface behavior, as they represent the vast web of declarative knowledge accumulated through instruction and experience. In order to delineate the schemas in our framework, we turn to culture. Schemas are directly related to culture because culture is the source of shared understanding and experiences (Malinowski, 1944; Kluckhohn & Strodtbeck, 1961), therefore culture influences an individual's interpretation or meaning of behavior (schemas). To delineate our specific schemas, we look at cross-cultural comparisons of conflict management and the implied meaning of various behaviors. Because culture is intimately related to schemas, we examine the comparative work that uses collectivism, indirect communication, and hierarchy, for as noted above the Asian context highlights the importance of these three concepts.

Collectivism

Compared to collectivists, individualists engage in more problem solving information exchange and forcing (Leung, 1987; Chan, 1992; Chua & Gudykunst, 1987), whereas collectivists tend towards compromise or yielding behavior. These findings may seem surprising in that individualists espouse behavioral extremes, whereas collectivists show less extreme behavior, such as compromise (Thomas, 1976). Yet, these results make sense by considering the meaning (schema) of each script in its cultural context and by considering the cultural characteristics and conflict situations that influence the person's goal orientation (frame). Specifically, in individualist societies, problem solving behavior means that a person is *collaborating* (they are using a collaborative schema). Problem solving, with its sharing information about preferences and priorities, thus emanates from a mutual-concern orientation or frame (Pruitt & Rubin, 1986). Forcing and compromise behaviors both mean that a person is trying to *claim as much value* as possible (schema), consistent with a self-concern orientation (Raiffa, 1982). In collectivist societies, however, the same compromise behavior tends to mean something quite different. Along with yielding and consulting others, compromise might indicate a *face saving* schema (Ting-Toomey, 1988). These behaviors (that mean saving face) are enacted because among in-groups, collectivists value harmony and thus adopt a mutual concern frame (Yang, 1993).

Collectivists also show a proclivity towards tacit coordination to resolve conflict (Ting-Toomey, 1988). What determines whether a collectivist will use this behavior versus compromise or yielding? Again the answer lies in understanding the meaning (schema) of the behavior and the parties' goal orientation (frame). Whereas compromise, yielding, and using social networks mean saving face for parties in conflict (Ho, 1993), tacit coordination might mean parties are *satisfying the collective* (schema) implying a focus on the broader social community (frame). To predict which meaning a collectivist will wish to convey, we consider his or her goal orientation—is it mutual concern or concern for the broader collective? We predict that if a collectivist broadly construes the in-group to include the community or social system, he or she would be driven to adopt a community orientation or frame and espouse a tacit coordination script. If a collectivist adopts a narrower construal of the in-group (i.e., the immediate parties to the conflict), he or she would adopt a mutual-orientation frame and espouse a compromise or yielding script.

Research shows that collectivists are more likely to consult others in negotiating conflict (Tinsley, 1997). Once again, this behavior can have two meanings. On the one hand, this script indicates that a party may be trying to exploit the coalition to personally claim value (schema); this would occur when a person adopts a self-orientation frame. On the other hand, this same behavior may mean that a party is trying to *satisfy the collective* (schema); this will occur when a party adopts a community-orientation frame. Distinguishing between these two frames or orientations hinges on the interaction of culture and social context, such as in-group/out-group definitions. When a collectivist is resolving a conflict with out-group members, he or she will likely adopt a self-orientation frame whereby coalition building is done to exploit the out-group for the benefit of the in-group. On the other hand, when resolving a conflict among in-group members, he or she is likely to adopt a community-orientation frame, thus here coalition building behavior means satisfying the in-group collective.

Indirect Communication

Research shows that people in high context cultures use more indirect methods of conflict resolution such as a heuristic trial and error script, than do those in low context cultures (Adair et al., 2004; Brett & Okumura, 1998; Brett et al., 1998). This heuristic trial and error script means that parties are collaborating by exploring agreements, but without openly discussing the conflict or their interests. Brett & Okumura (1998) found that negotiators from the same culture might adopt a mutual concern frame and attempt to convey collaboration through their behavior (scripts). However, during intercultural negotiations, low context US negotiators used information sharing (script) to mean collaboration (schema) and reflect mutual concern (frame), whereas high context Japanese used heuristic trial and error (script) to mean collaboration (schema) and reflect their mutual concern (frame). Intercultural dyads had lower joint gains than intra-cultural dyads, a difference that likely arose from each side misunderstanding the meaning (schema) of the other side's behavior (script).

Members of low context cultures have also been shown to use objective standards, rules, and procedures when resolving conflict (Tinsley, 1998, 2001). This behavior can mean two things. On the one hand, it can mean parties selectively use rules that promote their own issues (claiming value), which would be the case when parties are adopting a self-orientation. On the other hand, it can mean parties are trying to *respect what is right* for everyone (because following rules can be argued to create the most good for the most people, Glenn & Glenn, 1981), which would be implied by parties adopting a mutual orientation.

Ding (1996) has argued that there are many times when Chinese will simply avoid an issue. This avoidance may mean the Chinese are trying to *terminate involvement* (schema), which is similar to what avoidance often means in the West. However, as Ding (1996) and others explain, this avoidance may signal a trying to satisfy the collective by keeping peace or harmony. Hence, avoidance of discussion may not always be terminating involvement, but may stem from a community concern frame and be meant to satisfy the collective.

Hierarchy

Egalitarian cultures tend to have more face-to-face discussions, whereas hierarchical cultures tend to incorporate authority figures (Tse et al., 1994; Tinsley & Brett, 2001). The tendency to involve authorities may have several different meanings. On the one hand, it can mean a person is *co-opting the third party's status* and authority to forward one's own agenda (Leung, 1997; Tinsley, 1997). This is likely to occur when adopting a self-orientation frame. On the other hand, this behavior can mean that a *party is satisfying the third party's concern* (Tinsley, 1997), which is likely to occur when adopting a mutual-orientation frame (because here what is best for both parties is that high status figures are satisfied). Yet again, this behavior can be enacted to simply *get information or an external perspective* (schema) when parties are adopting either a self, mutual, or community-orientation frame.

Thus looking at the impact of collectivism elucidates several schemas: collaboration, claiming value, saving face, and satisfying the collective. Indirect communication highlights the additional schema of respecting rights and terminating involvement. Hierarchy research underscores still more schemas—co-opting high status parties, satisfying high status parties, and getting information or an external perspective. These schemas are listed in the last column of Table 1.

RELATIONSHIPS AMONG THE FRAMEWORK ELEMENTS

By delineating conflict schemas, we begin to piece together how the elements (frames, schema, and scripts) relate to each other. Table 2 shows the relationships expressed in the above examples. Problem solving can mean collaboration (schema) to promote mutual-concern frame or can mean claiming value (schema) to promote a self-concern frame. We argue that forcing will tend to always be associated with a claiming value schema to promote a self-concern frame. Yielding can be done to claim value by minimizing personal losses (schema) if one is adopting a self-concern frame or it can be a face saving gesture (schema) if one is adopting a mutual-concern frame. Compromise can mean claiming value schema to promote a self-concern frame or it can mean a saving face schema to promote a mutual-concern frame. Avoiding can mean a terminating involvement schema if one has either a self or a community concern frame. Alternatively, avoiding can signal satisfying collective concerns (schema) if one has a community concern frame. Heuristic trial and error can mean someone is offering lopsided proposals for claiming value (schema) if one has a self-concern frame, or it can be used to try to explore agreements and collaborate if one has a mutual-concern frame. Consulting others can be done to build a coalition and claim value (schema) if one has a self-concern frame or it can signal satisfying collective concerns (schema) if one has a community-concern. Use of objective standards, rules and procedures can be done to claim value (schema) if one has a self-concern frame, or to respect rights (schema) if one adopts a community-concern frame. Involving authorities can reflect behavior designed to co-opt the authority figure (schema) if one has a self-concern frame, or it can reflect a satisfying of high status parties (schema) if one adopts a mutual- or community-concern frame, or it can be used to get an external perspective (schema), which might be used

Table 2. The relationships between conflict resolution scripts, schemas, and frames

Scripts (surface behavior)	Schemas (meaning or interpretation)	Frames (social goal or perspective)
Problem solving	Collaboration Claiming value	Mutual concern Self-concern
Forcing	Claiming value	Self-concern
Yielding	Claiming value (by minimizing personal losses) Saving face	Self-concern Mutual concern
Compromising	Claiming value Saving face	Self-concern Mutual concern
Avoiding	Terminating involvement Satisfying collective	Self- or Community concern Community concern
Heuristic trial and error	Claiming value Collaboration	Self-concern Mutual concern
Consulting others	Claiming value Satisfying collective	Self-concern Community concern
Objective standards, rules or procedures	Claiming value Respecting rights	Self-concern Community concern
Involving authorities	Co-opting high status Satisfying high status parties Getting information or External perspective	Self-concern Mutual or Community concern Self, Mutual, or Community concern
Tacit coordination	Satisfying collective	Community concern

if one has a self, mutual, or community-orientation frame. And finally, tacit coordination is almost always done with a collective concern schema and a community-concern frame.

As noted in the introduction, we offer Table 2 as a skeletal understanding of how this complex social cognitive system works. We have used existing research on culture and conflict management to delineate the possible relationships—how various surface behaviors (scripts) reflect a variety of underlying schemas and how these scripts and schemas are motivated by various frames. Obviously, this table will be further refined as cultural findings increase and as researchers directly test these relationships. We do offer a few concluding syntheses of the various relationships outlined in Table 2.

CONCLUSIONS AND FUTURE QUESTIONS

Cultural characteristics such as collectivism, indirect communication, and hierarchy, influence the possible meanings behind people's conflict management behavior. For example, parties from different cultures may have similar social goals (such as a mutual-concern frame) but show very different behavior (such as a problem solving versus heuristic trial and error scripts) when managing their conflict because these scripts have the same meaning (collaborate) in the different cultural contexts. Similarly, parties from different cultures might adopt the same script, but have it imply a very different meaning. Shapiro and Rognes (1996), for example, found that for US negotiators information sharing meant collaboration (schema), whereas for Norwegian negotiators information sharing was seen as an aggressive claiming value (schema). Hence, as we have argued elsewhere, culture has a main or direct effect on schema (Brodt & Tinsley, 2001). And because of this direct effect, there can be a mismatch between frames and scripts across cultures (the same frame can manifest in different scripts or the same scripts can emanate from a different frame).

Additionally, to understand whether a disputant intends one meaning over another requires looking at that disputant's social goals or frame. We posit that all three frames exist both in the West and in Asia, and that determining a party's frame requires looking at both the cultural context (degree of collectivism, indirect communication, and hierarchy) and the features of the situation or dispute context. In other words, culture interacts with features of the dispute context to encourage a particular conflict frame (Brodt & Tinsley, 2001). Although Table 2 shows that scripts, schemas and frames are associated with each other, we do not mean to imply a linear causal chain. That is, we are not arguing that frames cause schemas, which cause scripts. We are saying, however, that to understand conflict resolution behavior (scripts), we must examine both the underlying meaning (schemas) and social goals (frames) of the disputant.

Obviously, there are questions here of indeterminancy that future research might address. For example, how do people choose a certain conflict script from several that are able to attain the same goal? How do we infer the goals (frames) of people who adopt a certain conflict script, given that the script can signify multiple goals? Moreover, we propose that culture influences conflict resolution scripts directly via conflict resolution schemas and indirectly via frames. Yet it is still an open question as to how a particular frame, schema, or script is chosen and which is selected first. For example, does a person's frame influence his or her schema and script? Or is it more often the case that a person's script (as a reciprocal response to the other party's conflict behavior) induces a corresponding schema and frame? Perhaps even more intriguing is the question of how conscious these choices really are. Are these strategic decisions (conscious) or are they the natural manifestation of one's culture or of a social interaction and outside of one's conscious awareness? We believe the answer will fall somewhere in between these extremes and eagerly await research addressing this issue.

Although we suspect that our three frames are somewhat universal, we do wonder about the universality of our scripts and schema, as well as the possibility that other scripts and schema are still unaccounted for. We suspect that further research (particularly on under-represented parts of Asia such as India, Malaysia, and Vietnam) will elucidate additional scripts and schemas. Naturally, as well, we hope future research will continue to refine the linkages among the elements of the conflict management framework. For example, we propose that perhaps for high context cultures, where behavior tends to be more tightly scripted, there may be fewer scripts associated with any schema, compared to in low context cultures

Studying conflict management in Asia stands to significantly enhance existing theories and frameworks of conflict management by broadening our understanding of conflict goals and scripts, as well as deepening our understanding of the meaning of various conflict management behaviors. Although Asian and Western conflict management often differ, the combined set of goals and behaviors offers managers from both regions a richer spectrum of alternatives from which to choose. Together this rich set of alternatives combined with the deeper understanding of how conflict behaviors relate to a party's intentions, social goals, and culture should help managers consciously and intelligently choose among a variety of conflict strategies and more effectively manage conflict.

NOTE

1. We use the term "mutual concern" to avoid confusion with the dual concern model (Pruitt & Rubin, 1986), yet we highlight that we are at the individual level of analysis. Thus mutual concern means that a party cares about both his own outcome and his opponent's.

REFERENCES

Adair, W.A., Brett, J.M., Lempereur, A., Okumura, T., Shikhirev, P., Tinsley, C.H., Lytle, A. 2004. Culture and negotiation strategy. *Negotiation Journal*, 20(1): 87-111.

Blake, R.R. and Mouton, J.S. 1964. *The Managerial Grid*. Houston: Gulf publishing.

Bond, M., Wan, K., Leung, K. and Giacalone, R. 1985. How are responses to verbal insults related to cultural collectivism and power distance? *Journal of Cross-cultural Psychology*, 16: 111-127.

Brett, J.M. and Okumura, T. 1998. Inter- and intracultural negotiation: U.S. and Japanese negotiators, Academy *of Management Journal*, 41(5): 495-510.

Brett, J.M., Adair, W., Lempereur, A., Okumura, T., Shikhirev, P., Tinsley, C.H. and Lytle, A. 1998. Culture and joint gains in negotiation. *Negotiation Journal*, 14: 61-86.

Brodt, S.E. and Tinsley, C.H. 2001. Diving beneath the surface: Exploring the role of frames, schemas, and scripts in understanding conflict resolution behavior across cultures. Working paper.

Chan, D.K.S. 1992. Effects of concession pattern, relationship between negotiators, and culture on negotiation. Unpublished master's thesis, University of Illinois, Department of Psychology.

Choi, I., Nisbett, R. and Norenzayan, A. 1999. Causal attribution across cultures: Variation and universality. *Psychological Bulletin*, 125: 47-63.

Chua, E. and Gudykunst, W.B. 1987. Conflict resolution styles in low and high context cultures. *Communication Research Reports*, 4: 32-37.

Cushman, D.P. and King, S.S. 1985. National and organizational culture in conflict resolution: Japan, the United States, and Yugoslavia. In W.B. Gudykunst, L.P. Stewart and S. Ting-Toomey (eds.), *Communication, Culture, and Organizational Processes* (pp. 114-144). Thousand Oaks, CA: Sage.

DeDreu, K., Weingart, L. and Kwon, S. Influence of social motives on integrative negotiation: A meta-analytic review and test of two theories. *Journal of Personality and Social Psychology*, 78: 889-905.

Ding, D.Z. 1996. Exploring Chinese conflict management styles in joint venture in the People's Republic of China. *Management Research News*, 19: 45-55.

Dyer, B. and Song, X. 1997. The impact of strategy on conflict: A cross-national comparative study of U.S. and Japanese firms. *Journal of International Business Studies*, Third Quarter 1997: 467-493.

Eastman, R.A. 2000. The Cultural dimension in transactions with Japanese Companies. June 2000. *The Metropolitan Corporate Counsel*, Northeast Edition.

Fiske, S. and Taylor, S. 1991. *Social Cognition* (2nd edn). New York: McGraw Hill.

Gire, J.T. 1997. The varying effect of individualism-collectivism on preference for methods of conflict resolution. *Canadian Journal of Behavioural Science*, 29(1): 38-43.

Glenn, E.S. and Glenn, C.G. 1981. *Man and Mankind*. Norwood: Ablex publishing.

Goldberg, S.B., Green, E.D. and Sander, F.E.A. 1985. *Dispute Resolution*. Boston: Little, Brown and Co.

Gulliver, M.P. 1979. The effect of the spatial visualization factor on achievement in operations with fractions. *Dissertation Abstracts International*, 39(9-A): 5381-5382.

Haire, M., Ghiselli, E.E. and Porter, L.W. 1966. *Managerial Thinking: An International Study*. New York: John Wiley & Sons.

Hall, E.T. 1976. *Beyond Culture*. Garden City: Anchor/Doubleday.

Ho, D.Y.F. 1993. Relational orientation in Asian social psychology. In U. Kim and J.W. Berry (eds.), *Indigenous Psychologies: Research and Experiences in Cultural Context* (pp. 240-259). Newbury Park, CA: Sage.

Hong, Y.-y. and Chiu, C.-y. 2001. Toward a paradigm shift: From cross-cultural differences in social cognition to social-cognitive mediation of cultural differences. *Social Cognition*, 19: 181-196.

Hofstede, G. 1980. *Culture's Consequences: International Differences in Work-related Values*. Newbury Park, CA: Sage.

Kluckhohn, C. and Strodtbeck, F. 1961. *Variations in Value Orientations*. Westport: Greenwood.

Leung, K. and Lind, E.A. 1986. Procedure and culture: Effects of culture, gender, and investigator status on procedural preferences. *Journal of Personality and Social Psychology*, 50: 1134-1140.

Leung, K. 1987. Some determinants of reaction to procedural models for conflict resolution: A cross-national study. *Journal of Personality and Social Psychology*, 53: 898-908.

Leung, K. 1997. Negotiation and reward allocations across cultures. In P.C. Earley and M. Erez (eds.), *New Perspectives on I/O Psychology* (pp. 640-675.) San Francisco: Jossey-Bass.

Leung, K. and Tjosvold, D. 1988. *Conflict Management in the Asia Pacific*. Singapore: John Wiley & Sons.

Lin, X. and Germain, R. 1998. Sustaining satisfactory joint venture relationships: The role of conflict resolution strategy. *Journal of International Business Studies*, 29(1): 179-196.

Malinowski, B. 1944. *A Scientific Theory of Culture and Other Essays*. Chapel Hill: UNC Press.

Markus, H. and Kitayama, S. 1991. Culture and the self: Implications for cognition, emotion and motivation. *Psychological Review*, 98: 224-253.

Masuda, T. and Nisbett, R. 2001. Attending holistically versus analytically: Comparing the context sensitivity of Japanese and Americans. *Journal of Personality and Social Psychology*, 81: 922-034.

McCann, J. and Galbraith, J.R. 1981. Interdepartmental relations. In P.C. Nystrom and W.H. Starbuck (eds.), *Handbook of Organizational Design* (Vol. 2, pp. 60-84). New York: Oxford.

Minsky, M. 1977. A framework for representing knowledge. In P. Winston (ed.), *The Psychology of Computer Visions* (pp. 211-277). New York: McGraw-Hill.

Mintzberg, H.R. 1975. The manager's job: Folklore and fact. *Harvard Business Review*, (July/August): 49-61.

Morris, M.W., Williams, K.Y., Leung, K., Larrick, R., Mendoza, M.T., Bhatnagar, D., Li, J., Kondo, M., Luo, J. and Hu, J. 1998. Conflict management style: Accounting for cross-national differences. *Journal of International Business Studies*, 29(4): 729-748.

Pruitt, D.M. and Rubin, J.Z. 1986. *Social Conflict: Escalation, Stalemate, and Settlement*. New York: McGraw-Hill.

Pruitt, D.M. and Carnevale, P. 1993. *Negotiation in Social Conflict*. Pacific Grove, CA: Brooks/Cole.

Raiffa, H. 1982. *The Art and Science of Negotiation*. Cambridge: Harvard University Press.

Ross, L. and Nisbett, R. 1991. *The Person and the Situation*. New York: McGraw Hill.

Shapiro, D.L., Drieghe, R.M. and Brett, J.M. 1985. Mediator behavior and the outcome of mediation. *Journal of Social Issues*, 41(2): 101-114.

Shapiro, D.L. and Rognes, J. 1996. Can a dominating orientation enhance the integrativeness of negotiated agreements. *Negotiation Journal*, 12(1): 81-90.

Sriussadaporn-Charoenngam, N. and Jablin, F.M. 1999. An exploratory study of communication competence in Thai organizations. *Journal of Business Communication*, Oct: 382-418.

Tang, S.F. and Kirkbride, P.S. 1986. Developing conflict management skill in Hong Kong: An analysis of some cross cultural implications. *Management Education and Development*, 17: 287-301.

Thomas, K.W. and Killman, R.H. 1974. *Thomas-Killman Conflict Mode Instrument*. Tuxedo, NY: Xicom.

Thomas, K.W. 1976. Conflict and conflict management. In M. Dunnette (ed.), *Handbook of Industrial and Organizational Psychology* (pp. 889-935). Chicago: Rand McNally.

Thomas, K.W. 1992. Conflict and negotiation processes and organizations. In M.D. Dunnette and L.M. Hough (eds.), *Handbook of Industrial and Organizational Psychology* (Vol. 3, 2nd edn). Palo Alto, CA: Consulting Psychologists Press.

Ting-Toomey, S. 1988. A face-negotiation theory. In Y. Kim and W. Gudykunst (eds.), *Theory in Intercultural Communication*. Newbury Park, CA: Sage.

Tinsley, C.H. 1997. Understanding conflict in a Chinese cultural context. In R. Bies, R.J. Lewicki and B. Sheppard (eds.), *Research on Negotiations in Organizations* (pp. 209-225). Beverly Hills: Sage.

Tinsley, C.H. 1998. Models of conflict resolution in Japanese, German, and American cultures. *Journal of Applied Psychology*, 83: 316-323.

Tinsley, C.H. 2001. How we get to yes: Predicting the constellation of strategies used across cultures to negotiate conflict. *Journal of Applied Psychology*, 86: 583-593.

Tinsley, C.H. (in press). Culture and Conflict: Enlarging our Dispute Resolution Framework. In M.J. Gelfand and J.M. Brett (Eds.), *Culture and Negotiation: Integrative Approaches to Theory and Research*. Palo Alto, CA: Stanford University Press.

Tinsley, C.H. and Brett, J.M. 2001. Managing work place conflict in the United States and Hong Kong. *Organization Behavior and Human Decision Processes*, 85(2): 360-381.

Triandis, H. 1986. El individualismo y la teoria sociopsicologica / Individualism and sociopsychological theory. *Mexico: Asociacion Mexicana de Psicologia Social*, 2(2): 23-28.

Triandis, H.C., Brislin, R. and Hui, C.H. 1988. Cross-cultural training across the individualism-collectivism divide. *International Journal of Intercultural Relations*, 12: 269-289.

Trubisky, P., Ting-Toomey, S. and Lin, S.-L. 1991. The influence of individualism-collectivism and self-monitoring on conflict styles. *International Journal of Intercultural Relations*, 15: 65-84.

Tse, D.K., Francis, J. and Walls, J. 1994. Cultural differences in conducting intra- and inter-cultural negotiations: A Sino-Canadian comparison. *Journal of International Business Studies*, 25: 537-555.

Walton, R.E. and McKersie, R.B. 1965. *A Behavioral Theory of Labor Negotiations*. New York: McGraw-Hill.

Yang, K.S. 1993. Chinese social orientation: An integrative analysis. In L.Y. Cheng, F.M.C. Cheung and C.N. Chen (eds.), *Psychotherapy for the Chinese: Selected Papers from the First International Conference*. The Chinese University of Hong Kong.

Chapter 17

A NEW PERSPECTIVE ON DIVERSITY AND GROUP DYNAMICS IN ASIA

Hun-Joon Park
Yonsei School of Business, Seoul, Korea

Sang-Hyeon Sung
Samsung Economic Research Institute, Seoul, Korea

INTRODUCTION

Asia is growing dynamically. What is the source of this dynamism in Asia, exemplified by Japan's economic success, China's emergence in the world market, and Korea's rise? This chapter will trace its cause to diversity processes and group dynamics in Asian organizations. In doing so, we attempt to develop several propositions that highlight the differences in group dynamics in organization in the West and in Asia.

There are several ways to define the culture of a group or an organization (Deal and Kennedy, 1982; Harrison, 1986; Grave, 1986; Hampden-Turner, 1992). This chapter deals with socio-cultural group dynamics in Asia on a more macro level, and attempts to link cultural characteristics to group dynamics in the Asian context. One point to note is that taxonomizing culture into regional, racial, and national categories may fall into the trap of gross generalization that overlooks cultural subtleties. An Asia-based parochialism that overemphasizes Asian uniqueness is unlikely to generate universal theoretical frameworks that allow inter-regional applications and comparisons (White, 2002). It is therefore our goal to develop propositions based on the East Asian cultural traditions that are applicable to other cultural regions as well.

DIVERSITY AND GROUP DYNAMICS

Diversity in human resources has become an obvious trend for many reasons: the diversity of the labor market and employment patterns; labor migration; new technologies; the professionalization of various tasks; diversification; and borderless competition.[1] It is important to manage this diversity, thereby creating synergy and increasing productivity. In addition, cultural diversity and intercultural interaction is increasing. The disappearance of borders and interregional migration occur widely in both corporate and non-profit organizations. The proliferation of virtual organizations triggered by information technologies, the frequency of mergers and acquisitions, the extension of strategic alliances, and the development of network organizations are making the range of human interactions wider and more frequent (DeSanctis and Monge, 1999; Mowshowitz, 1994; Nohria and Berkley, 1994; Barner, 1996). The rapid increase of inter-firm alliances further accelerates the fusion of human and cultural resources. For instance, the fusion of technologies in the case of digital home appliances increases technological interactions, and the diversification of consumers' needs demands close interaction between production and marketing.

Corporate organizations either create new knowledge or follow current diversity trends, achieving corporate goals by deliberately promoting diversity. Countries that prohibit employment discrimination require firms to hire ethnic minorities, women, and the disabled. Although the Asian situation is different from that of the US or Europe, Asia has also been adopting the legislation of anti-discriminatory policies. Amid rapid changes, corporations want to sustain competitive advantages by nurturing and organizing diversity, which promote positive interactions and enhance organizational efficiency. To manage diversity effectively is a necessary agenda for enhancing competitiveness (Herriot and Pemberton, 1993). In particular, the management of human resources diversity is important to ensure optimal utilization of human resources by putting the right people in the right positions.

Diversity in a group tends to increase the uncertainty, complexity and disorder of group processes, and can eventually decrease productivity. On the other hand, cultural and temporal (generational) diversity can obviate groupthink and facilitate the creation of new ideas. However, firm conclusions about the effects of diversity on group performance have not yet been drawn. Early studies on diversity ran into difficulties in clarifying the relationship between types of diversity and performance changes, and failed to generate viable theoretical frameworks (Webber and Donahue, 2001). For instance, Milliken and Martins (1996) pointed out that studies on task experience are lacking in the extant literature on diversity. Most studies center on the functional experiences of top management teams (TMT) (e.g., Bantel and Jackson, 1989; Smith, Smith,

Olian, Sims, O'Bannon and Scully, 1994), and explore the relationship between the diversity of functional experiences and team dynamics. The diversity of TMT may yield positive influence on international communication, although that is not always the case (Smith et al., 1994). Bantel and Jackson (1989) argue that the diversity of TMT encourages innovation in financial industries, while Korn et al. (1992) found a positive relationship between diversity and innovation in furniture industries. Ancona and Caldwell (1992) reported some contradictory results in their sample of product development teams. They concluded that functional diversity had a positive influence on innovative performance through the increase of external communication, although functional diversity also had a negative influence directly on innovative performance. Glick et al. (1993) failed to corroborate the validity of a scheme for classifying the structural and demographic diversities of TMT, which measured TMT's market, geographic, and functional diversities, and task functions, age, and seniority, respectively. Jackson et al. (1995) operationalized personal attributes by means of individual attributes that are not relevant to tasks and task-relevant attributes such as skills and abilities. Milliken and Martins (1996) divided diversity into readily detectable and less observable diversities to include sex, race, nation, and age for the former category and value, skills, and knowledge for the latter.

Recent studies on this topic are more theoretical and systematic. Pelled (1996), for instance, provided a matrix of visibility (easily detectable attributes, such as age, gender, race, tenure, etc.) and job relatedness (attributes needed for task performance, such as experience, skill, education, functional background, etc.). A combination of high visibility and low job relatedness includes age, sex, and race, and another combination of low visibility and high job relatedness included seniority, education, and functions. Jehn et al. (1999) classified diversity into social categorical diversity, information diversity, and value diversity. Barsade (2000) added to the conventional demographic diversity a new category of affective diversity, which refers to the cumulative affective fit or misfit among group members. Harrison, Price and Bell (1998) introduced surface-level and deep-level diversities and showed that deep-level diversity increased with the duration of teamwork. Surface-level diversity can be defined as differences among group members in overt, biological characteristics that are typically reflected in physical features. Such characteristics include age, sex, and race/ethnicity. Deep-level diversity includes differences among members' attitudes, beliefs, and values. Information about deep-level diversity is communicated through verbal and nonverbal behavioral patterns and is only learned through extended, individualized interaction and information gathering. Baek et al. (2002) conducted an empirical study of the Korean TMT with two categories of knowledge-based diversity (seniority, task skills, and educational level) and social categorical diversity (age and birthplace). Webber and Donahue (2001) found that diversity patterns change according to different types of groups, as complex tasks require highly diverse knowledge bases, and simple tasks require a low level of knowledge diversity.

Diversity may affect performance outcomes through mediating or moderating variables. Many procedural variables are possible in the study of diversity: task structures such as task complexity, mutual dependency, and constancy (Jehn, 1997; Jehn et al., 1999; Pelled et al., 1999); the decision-making environment in groups, such as discussion (Simons, 1995; Simons et al., 1999), participatory decision-making, and the frequency of communication (Baek et al., 2002). Cho and Cho (2002) found that relational conflicts had a negative influence on performance, while task conflicts had a positive influence.

Studies on the diversity of human resources in the West have emphasized diversity factors that are demographic in nature, such as national, ethnic, gender, age, religion, and disability (Kluttz, 2002). Demographic diversity belongs to the inter-individual diversity category, and individual knowledge, skills, capacity, and personality are factors that constitute inter-individual diversity. Examples include professional area, work experience, seniority, educational background, and personal styles. These diversity factors differ from intra-individual diversity, in that the latter emphasizes the multiple selves of one individual.

Western corporations in particular have emphasized job based human resource management (HRM), which takes the route of training an individual to be a professional and placing him or her in a team of professionals. If they have to create a cross-functional team, these corporations recruit professionals from different teams. On the other hand, "multifunctionalized individuals" refer to those who have education and training in different areas. Japanese firms have traditionally adopted multifunctionalization (Nonaka and Takeuchi, 1995; Kusunoki and Numagami, 1996). The benefits of this system are multifold. First, individuals have a wide perspective on their tasks, which allows them to be more innovative and cooperative with others. This also allows for the efficient utilization of a workforce that can handle a variety of tasks with a small number of people, simultaneously reducing the boredom of the job by avoiding simple repetition. This system, however, cannot deepen the professionalism of an individual, making it necessary to introduce a T-model of training where individuals retain a professional area, but also enjoy diversified work experiences in other areas.

In most organizations, inter- and intra-individual diversity occurs at the same time. Multifunctional members can participate in a multifunctional as well as a monofunctional team. Western firms' learning about Japanese production methods, and Asian firms' adoption of Western style teams, have made the picture much more complicated than before. In order to understand the Asian style of diversity correctly, it is important to consider not only the Western framework of diversity that focuses on inter-individual diversity, but also intra-individual diversity, which is important for understanding the effects of a team leader's intra-individual diversity on team learning.

This chapter also emphasizes what can be learned about diversity from its various effects. Thomas (1996) proposed to treat diversity from the viewpoint of learning and suggested three ways of managing diversity. In the case of the discrimination-and-fairness paradigm, he suggests a managerial solution for the homogenization of diversity by disregarding individual differences. In the access-and-legitimacy paradigm, he suggests to reinforce diversities by respecting individual differences (e.g., establishing transactions with a minority group). Both paradigms create a problem in terms of exploiting minority groups and reducing them to peripheral members of an organization. His third paradigm underscores learning. In order to induce creativity and innovation, proper leadership recognizes and respects differences among groups and initiates inter-group learning about different experiences and cultures. The management of diversity eventually aims at ensuring the synergistic co-existence of individuals and organizations through learning. Thus, it is necessary to view diversity and group dynamics from the standpoint of learning for leveraging diversity as management resources for organizational performance. The research on diversity in the West may contribute to identifying the optimal approach in Asia, where the experience in diversity management and research is still insufficient. To transcend the limit of the first and second paradigms that focus on preventing discrimination and utilizing differences for achieving organization goals, the approach to diversity in Asia should adopt the third paradigm – focusing on the facilitation of learning. This learning viewpoint is desirable for managing diversity, and should be applicable across regions and cultures.

NEW PERSPECTIVES ON DIVERSITY AND GROUP DYNAMICS IN ASIA

Hierarchical Complementarity vs. Heterogeneous Age Diversity

Many studies found that differences among group members lead to conflict instead of mutual learning. The temporal diversity of a team, i.e., the diversity among group members, which varies along length of service, seniority, age or the starting point of service, may create difficulties in job transfers (Jackson et al., 1991; O'Reilly et al., 1989; Wagner, Pfeffer and O'Reilly, 1984) and reduce positive attitudes toward team members (Judge and Ferris, 1993). In a similar vein, seniority diversity leads to the reduction of communication (Zenger and Lawrence, 1989) and low levels of social cohesion among group members (O'Reilly, Caldwell and Barnett, 1989), which in turn lead to low performance (O'Reilly and Flatt, 1989). These negative behaviors and attitudes become barriers to the utilization of broad perspectives and diverse ideas in task performance (Watson, Kumar, and Michaelsen, 1993). Harrison, Price and Bell (1998) found that surface-level diversity is supplanted by deep-level diversity as cooperation within a team and significant interactions between team members increase. These studies are based on the similarity-attraction and social categorization paradigms, which assume that interpersonal differences create insecurity and crisis, leading to the argument that diversity of age and seniority will engender a negative relationship with learning and performance.

On the other hand, with respect to an organization whose culture values seniority, can one generate a competing hypothesis? Unlike the horizontal diversity emphasized in an individualistic culture, Asian cultures that put weight on seniority can produce positive effects from hierarchical complementarity through hierarchical diversity. In other words, due to the cultural norms of revering the elderly and the relatively large power distance, temporal diversity among group members can have a positive effect on the overall team process (Hofstede, 1991). "Power distance" refers to the degree of acceptance among group members of the fact that power is unequally distributed, a term measured from a subordinate's point of view (Hofstede, 1991). Hofstede (1991) found that large power distance exists in Latin American and European, Asian, and African countries, whereas power distance is lower in North America and non-Latin European countries. Korea was found to have a relatively large power distance.

The origin of this cultural tradition of respecting the elders can be traced back to the Greek and Roman Senate, making it impossible to argue that seniority reverence is only an Asian phenomenon. In the 8th century BC, the Roman Empire relied on senators to make decisions, and the Senate was composed of elders from noble families. This tradition can still be found in the elder system of Protestant churches. Elders tend to uphold principles that are based on experience, and reverence towards elders reflects an implicit procedure by which members can utilize the elders' experience. It is customary to determine seniority based on the year a person enters a company, the military, a government agency, or a university. The year of entrance functions just like one's birthday, imparting one with a stable status. Age or seniority is a symbol of hierarchy in an organization, and members accept the fact that scarce resources are distributed according to this attribute.

Cultures that have large power distance will expect juniors to accept the natural order of respecting the elders, which then leads to fewer conflicts between generations. The juniors are also eager to learn from the elders. Asian cultures assume that intergenerational interactions can be negative only when junior members defy the authority of the seniors and disrupt this implicit demographic hierarchy. Therefore, we can advance an assumption that the diversity of age and seniority would not lower the overall performance of a team, as is the case in Western corporations. Instead of causing negative or regressive attitudes toward other members, diverse in seniority contributes to a socially acceptable hierarchy within a team.

The following is an interview with the Dutch team manager of the Korean National soccer team who led the team to the semi-final of the World cup:

Interviewer: What was your first impression of the Korean players?

Guus Hiddink: At first I noticed an enormous difference from the European players. In Europe everybody gets along, but here [Korea] two senior members maintained a strict hierarchy. Frankly, I am still afraid of Hong Myong Bo [smiles]. I flinch whenever he says, "No, Hiddink!," although other players don't seem to fear him any longer. I thought Hwang Sun Hong was different [from Hong] because his smile was so innocent. I thought Hwang was under the control of Hong. But I cracked up to see Hwang was teaching Hong a lesson [because Hong was junior to Hwang]. Now, everything is fine. Here, everybody listens to me. No one defies my words. Everybody works as hard as I want. (Quoted from http://www.daum.net.)

Socially acceptable differences under this cultural background will not invite a crisis of identity. On the contrary, temporal diversity will result in positive effects in role identity and transparency. If roles are clear, job satisfaction and commitment increase, and job turnover decreases (Jackson and Schuler, 1985). Therefore, we propose seniority diversity in Asia is a requisite resource for positive group dynamics and team learning through hierarchical complementarity. When temporal diversity is high, intra-team learning is promoted through hierarchical complementarity in Asia. But in an individualistic culture, temporal diversity leads to increased conflict and a low level of learning and performance.

Leader's Diversity in Experience vs. Horizontal Functional Diversity among Members

Studies that support diversity argue that problem-solving skills, knowledge, and information increase with diversity (Tziner and Eden, 1985). For example, a team of high diversity will perform better than a low-diversity team, because the former has a larger variety of skills, knowledge, information, and other resources to utilize (Tziner and Eden, 1985). McEvily and Zaheer (1999) argue that diverse network resources made it easier for members to have access to information and ideas and hence enhanced corporate competitiveness. Kusunoki and Numagami (1996) argue that exchanges among engineers of different task groups increase overall corporate performance. It has been suggested from time to time that Japanese corporations tried to promote functional diversities of individuals in order to deliberately increase technological competitiveness (Kusunoki and Numagami, 1996). In reality, the reason a corporation selects a team of people of diverse experience is to utilize their diverse set of resources. However, although the diversity of task experiences elevates performance, it is difficult for a team of diverse perspectives to agree on a common goal and an effective task procedure (Dougherty, 1987; Souder, 1987). Team members of limited experience can be myopic in identifying solutions, and team members with different work experiences and functional backgrounds may have different task processes, terminologies, and understanding of products and the market (Dougherty, 1987; Lawrence and Lorsch, 1969).

The increased diversity of employees brings in their wake complexity and procrastination in the decision making process. Diverse teams typically take more time and effort than simple teams in hammering out consensus and actions. Depending on the diversity of employees and organizational practices, job evaluation and remuneration plans can change drastically across departments and groups even within one corporation. Consequently, members may complain about the inequality within a group, an important source of intragroup conflict. This is why teams of diversity sometimes fail to take advantage of its diversity, one of the main reasons for creating a diverse team in the first place.

If corporations want to maximize the benefit of diversity in the improvement of performance, there must be organizational means of accommodating diversity. Harmony between organizational goals and the functions of each group within an organization is a consequence of overcoming the confusion that diversity can cause. Many variables affect the achievement of a team's defined goal. Among others, the role team leaders play is especially significant in neutralizing the threats emanating from endogenous and exogenous factors. Team leaders resolve conflicts of interest, coordinate members to increase mutual understanding, and define and redefine team goals. Their primary job concerns include finding a proper organizational means of executing tasks, and simultaneously collecting and providing information and resources from external sources. According to Hofstede (1991), the reliance of the weak on the powerful is large in cultures where the power distance is large. Therefore, we can assume that the dependence of team members on team leaders is large in Asia. In particular, it can be said that in a Korean corporate culture that encourages members to revere authority, leadership style and orientation can create a significant impact on group members. This is because leaders *qua* initiators of a team provide initial guidelines for members' behavior and thinking patterns, which will have a prolonged lock-in effect.

Therefore, this chapter argues that team learning and its benefits are affected positively by the leaders' diversity of experiences. In other words, the richer the experiences of a leader, the higher the team performance, even when the diversity of team members is noticeable. If the degree of diversity in a group increases, negative behaviors such as conflict are likely to increase, and it becomes difficult to transform the diverse resources into positive performance. But if the group has a leader with a broad scope of experience, member diversity can be converged into creative synergy and high performance (Park and Sung, 2000). Because of the considerable power distance in Asian cultures, this tendency – that team leaders with diverse personal experiences have stronger effects on team learning and performance than leaders with homogeneous experiences – will be stronger in Asian cultures than in individualistic cultures.

Democratic Co-existence of Diversity vs. the Catalytic Transformation of Homogeneity

Individualistic societies maintain loose interpersonal relationships, as most people are expected to take care of themselves and their immediate family members. Collective societies take care of individuals as long as they maintain unconditionally loyalty to the group. Hofstede (1991) found that East-Asian countries such as Korea and Japan have strong collectivism. Furthermore, in an effort to reduce Eurocentric cultural biases, Hofstede (1991) turned to items that reflected the Chinese culture and value system, which led to a new dimension labeled as Confucian dynamism. The newly industrialized nations of Hong Kong, Taiwan, Japan, and Korea all retain a relationship with Confucian teachings and values, which are argued to be the motor of their economic growth. Asian collectivism has a particular dynamism, which is not based on social contracts, but on dynamic energy for economic development.

This argument explains how the four small dragons, unlike the Anglo-Saxon model of individualism, have accomplished economic miracles through government initiatives, Confucian hierarchy, and educational zeal, which can be called Confucian capitalism. Some Asian scholars even argue that Confucian capitalism should be a "universal value on a global level" not confined to East Asia. However, the late 1980s and early 1990s witnessed a new wave of economic growth in Malaysia, Indonesia, Thailand, and Vietnam, suggesting that Confucian capitalism is an outdated model of economic analysis. Dissatisfied with the utility of Confucian capitalism, American scholars tried to find a new model for explaining the economic success of these South East Asian countries. Other approaches include the "Asian value" model (Park, 1998).

Is the learning pattern of a collectivistic culture different from that of an individualistic culture? The clue to this question can be found in the World Cup game hosted by two East Asian nations, Korea and Japan. The Korean soccer team successfully completed the co-hosted games with a miraculous winning record. The swarming of people in the streets to cheer for the Korean team occurred voluntarily. The spread of national uniforms, slogans, gestures, and peaceful parades after the game was also done in a voluntary manner. Street support for the Korean team began without any organization or plans, and this support was echoed and spread nationwide, as well as to Koreans overseas. Soccer fans provided a catalyst for others to join their street demonstration of support through a snowball effect of self-reproduction and psychological resonance.

A recent, mass civil demonstration with candlelight, held to honor the memory of two middle school girls who were run over and killed by a US army armored car, can also be understood as a snowball effect of psychological resonance. Once the idea of a candlelight demonstration gathered enough active support from people, the movement spread very quickly. These phenomena can be interpreted as a reflection of strong collectivism through networking among people and psychological resonance.

Similar kinds of phenomena can be observed in corporate organizations. Korea's largest conglomerate, Samsung, has succeeded in management change triggered by CEO Kun Hee Lee and his self-disciplined New Management Movement (Jun and Han, 1994; Lee, 1999). The recent change of management of Yuhan-Kimberly, the health care company co-invested by Yuhan and Kimberly in Korea, also shows self-disciplined corporate transformation through shared values shaped by its founder, Yu, who has made many contributions to society. G. H. Moon, CEO of Yuhan-Kimberly, said that the company's effort to overcome the management crisis experienced during the IMF bailout was successful due to the employees' voluntary cooperation. This company did not lay off any employees and therefore received strong loyalty and commitment from employees. The psychological resonance to save the company proliferated and led to high performances from all employees. These cases show that a respectful leader or a sympathetic cause can generate great resonance and concentrate energy for goal attainment.

Collectivism provides a catalyst for the expansion of energy or passion. Although collectivism enables a rapid spread of passion, it does not need to suppress individuality and self-control. In this sense it is difficult to interpret this type of phenomena only through a traditional collectivism argument. Hofstede (1991) first treated Asian collectivism as detrimental to capitalist development. He subsequently shifted his position due to the rise of the four dragons in East Asia, and explained their economic success using the concept of Confucian dynamism as the fifth dimension. Confucian dynamism allowed him to retract from his earlier negative view of collectivism. We argue that there is no necessary connection between the ability of collectivism to mobilize people effectively and its drawbacks, which are often associated with the suppression of individuality. Other negative aspects of collectivism include collective selfishness, nepotism, and totalitarianism. Nazism and fascism are examples of extreme realization of collectivism in a negative way. However, the World Cup and civil candlelight demonstration exemplify how collectivism can promote creativity and sanguine group cohesiveness through learning. These achievements were possible because the Red Devils (the self-organized cheerleading group supporting the Korean soccer team) and the civil groups, both of which were founded purely on a voluntary basis, functioned as genuine leaders. Of course, examples similar to the World Cup and the civil demonstration can be seen in other countries, but these Korean cases were especially remarkable in both scale and speed.

In individualistic cultures, because the standard of judgment lies in oneself, the spread of learning can be slow. But because the standard of judgment lies in other persons in a collectivistic culture, the learning and imitation process may accelerate. Individuals committed to the goal of an organization or a society tend to demonstrate their membership by actively absorbing and learning organizational or social needs. Therefore, we can suggest a hypothesis that Asian collectivism can produce a more positive effect on intra-team learning than can individualistic cultures. That is, an individualistic culture allows the coexistence of diversity through interactions, and incremental learning occurs through consensus. On the other hand, a collectivistic culture encourages quick and innovative learning when diversity is allowed, and psychological resonance leads to an explosive expansion of homogeneity that allows continued learning and performance improvement. Respect for the senior and leadership based on experience in a collectivistic culture can facilitate hierarchical complementarity, which facilitates organizational learning and performance.

DISCUSSION

The question of how diversity affects group dynamics in Asia can now be made more specific: "How does diversity affect group dynamics in real-life circumstances?" When we can answer this question, we can also provide a rationale for the practical applications of our knowledge to managerial situations. In Asia, the demographic diversity of an organization develops differently from the pattern observable in the West, and the underlying processes are different. This chapter starts with the premise that group dynamics of diversity in Asia are different from the extant Western point of view. These new propositions, we think, can lead to more practical and specific studies of the issue.

We need a new interpretation of seniority. The extant Western point of view assumes that the diversity of members' ages and seniority have a negative effect on collective processes and organizational performance. A big gap in age and seniority among team members would freeze intra-organizational communication and collaboration, which in turn leads to organizational inefficiency. Furthermore, the negative aspects of seniority-based pay system have been emphasized in the corporate world, and a pay-for-performance system is spreading quickly. The myth of lifetime employment predominantly adopted by Japanese corporations began to be destroyed in the face of a long-lasting economic recession in Japan. The Korean seniority-based system was also destroyed after the 1997 foreign currency crisis. Instead, "performance-firstism" spreads widely and quickly. Seniority as a part of Asian culture and Confucian order was considered a bad thing. However, are we certain that a seniority-based order always cause negative outcomes?

In this chapter, we propose that diversity of age and other temporal attributes, such as seniority, can accelerate hierarchical complementarity and positively affect learning and performance in Asia. Unlike horizontal complementarity, hierarchical complementarity refers to offsetting each other's weaknesses in a hierarchical division of labor, and diversity of ages and seniority can promote hierarchical complementarity. Respect towards seniors is not a waste or inefficiency, but provides a framework for learning from their wisdom. Disregard for seniority highlights the possible failure of modern management in sustaining an effective organization on a long-term basis by putting organizational efficiency first and treating human resources as dispensable tools. We need to understand the loss of social balance through the mindless destruction of the seniority order. A candid reflection on this issue is possible only when we can discuss diversity in the context of maximizing creativity through learning, beyond the social needs of affirmative action and anti-discriminatory legislation (Thomas, 1996; Thomas and Woodruff, 1999).

The role of the leader's diverse experiences should be emphasized in channeling team members' diversity into a converging direction. The formation of a diverse team permits the initial attempt at increasing collaboration and accelerating organizational learning.[2] In this case, firms usually want to organize teams in terms of horizontal functions. In this chapter we emphasize the diversity of leaders, because through formal and informal influence, they determine the initial conditions of a team, and it is important to train leaders to have a diversity of experiences. If it is a Western tradition to form a team of professionals with diverse expertise, in Asia it is important to train leaders to have a diverse array of experiences.

Asian teams should pursue the synergy of mutual differences, going beyond the idea of the coexistence of differences that is rampant among Western teams. A democratic order based on logic and rationality does not usually go beyond the mutual tolerance and coexistence of differences, although it is highly likely in Asia that differences can develop into synergistic assimilation. The theory of complexity that views organizations as systems of complex adaptation can be a theoretical tool for explaining the explosive resonance of learning (Lewin and Regine, 2002). From an administrative point of view, Asian managers should encourage emotional acceptance of mutual differences, instead of rational acceptance. The emotional acceptance of a leader becomes an especially critical factor of success. Despite the excellent ability of a leader, its leadership will falter if no emotional acceptance occurs among his/her members. A leader's mistakes can be accepted, if the members accept the leader emotionally. In these teams, a high level of performance and an explosion of learning based on creativity is expected.

These propositions about the effects of diversity in Asia are speculative, and it is necessary to evaluate them empirically. In order to develop a universal framework, we need systemic theory development and empirical research. If organizations are after all a place where complex interactions occur, only those who can organize and manage diversity well will survive. It is our hope that this chapter will contribute to the understanding of the diversity of human resources in Asia.

NOTES

1. The composition of recent World Cup soccer teams demonstrates how diverse organizations in our society have been globalized. The most important new trend in the 2002 World Cup soccer teams is that many players worked for foreign soccer clubs. These players occupied central positions in their national teams, bringing home new skills they learned from foreign countries. Many countries also hired foreign team managers for their national teams. All three Asian teams had international managers, and the majority of the thirty-two teams that participated in the World Cup games were using or had hired foreign managers. Since players and managers move across national boundaries, soccer techniques and managerial know-how (managers' methods of leadership) are becoming cross-fertilized internationally.
2. Renault Samsung Automobiles combines the technological and managerial capacities of Renault, Samsung, and Nissan. In its meetings, there are no hierarchies among participants in order to induce open discussion. Renault's liberal communication principles have spilled over into Korea. The project team for the new SM3 models is a cross-functional team which consists of members from sales, procurement, production, public relations, finance and so on. Nissan's accurate and meticulous quality control and Samsung's well-organized human-resource system and smooth labor-management relations have all been preserved (Chosun Daily, April 8, 2002, p. 13.).

REFERENCES

Ancona, D.G. and Caldwell, D.F. 1992. Bridging the boundary: External activity and performance in organizational teams. *Administrative Science Quarterly*, 37: 634-665.

Baek, Y., Jung, J. and Choi, S. 2002. The effect of top management team knowledge-base diversity and social category diversity on organizational performance. *Journal of Korean Academy of Management*, 10(2): 1-34.

Bantel, K.A. and Jackson, S.E. 1989. Top management and innovations in banking: Does the composition of the top team make a difference? *Strategic Management Journal*, 10: 107-125.

Barner, R. 1996. The new millennium workplace: Seven changes that will challenge managers and workers. *The Futurist*, 30: 14-18.

Barsade, S.G., Ward, A.J., Turner, J.D.F. and Sonnenfeld, J.A. 2000. To your heart's content: A model of affective diversity in top management teams. *Administrative Science Quarterly*, 45: 802-836.

Cho, B. and Cho, G. 2002. Top management team composition and firm performance: The mediating effect of intra-group conflicts. *Journal of Korean Academy of Management*, 10(2): 119-147.

Deal, T.E. and Kennedy, A.A. 1982. *Corporate Cultures: The Rite and Rituals of Corporate Life* (pp. 107-127). Boston: Addison-Wesley Publishing Co.

DeSanctis, G. and Monge, P. 1999. Introduction to the special issues: Communication processes for virtual organizations. *Organization Science*, 10: 693-703.

Dougherty, D. 1987. New products in old organizations: The myth of the better mousetrap in search of the beaten path. Ph.D. Dissertation, Sloan School of Management, M.I.T.

Glick, W.H., Miller, C.C. and Huber, G.P. 1993. The impact of upper-echelon diversity on organizational performance. In G.H. Huber and W.H. Glick (eds.), *Organizational Change and Redesign: Ideas and Insights for Improving Organizational Performance* (pp. 176-214). NY: Oxford Univ. Press.

Grave, D. 1986. *Corporate Culture: Diagnosis and Change* (pp. 43-47). London: Frances Printer.

Hampden-Turner, C. 1992. *Creating Corporate Culture: From Discord to Harmony* (pp. 16-24). Boston: Addison-Wesley Publishing Co.

Harrison, R. 1986. Understanding your organization's character. *Harvard Business Review*, May-June: 119-128.

Harrison, D.A., Price, K.H. and Bell, M.P. 1998. Beyond relational demography: Time and the effects of surface- and deep-level diversity on work group cohesion. *Academy of Management Journal*, 41: 96-107.

Herriot, P. and Pemberton, C. 1993. *Competitive Advantage through Diversity – Organizational Learning from Difference* (p. 8). London: Sage.

Hofstede, G. 1991. *Cultures and Organizations: Software of the Mind*. UK: McGraw-Hill.

Jackson, S.E., Brett, J.F., Sessa, V.I., Cooper, D.M., Julin, J.A. and Peyronnin, K. 1991. Some differences make a difference: Individual dissimilarity and group heterogeneity as correlates of recruitment, promotions, and turnover. *Journal of Applied Psychology*, 76: 675-690.

Jackson, S.E., May, K.E. and Whitney, K. 1995. Understanding the dynamics of diversity in decision making teams. In R.A. Guzzo and E. Salas (eds.), *Team Effectiveness and Decision Making in Organizations* (pp. 204-261). San Francisco: Jossey-Bass.

Jackson, S.E. and Schuler, R.S. 1985. A meta-analysis and conceptual critique of research on role ambiguity and role conflict in work settings. *Organizational Behavior and Human Decision Processes*, 36: 16-79.

Jehn, K.A. 1997. A qualitative analysis of conflict types and dimensions in organizational groups. *Administrative Science Quarterly*, 42: 530-557.

Jehn, K.A., Northcraft, G.B. and Neale, M.A. 1999. Why differences make a difference: A field study of diversity, conflict, and performance in workgroups. *Administrative Science Quarterly*, 44: 741-763.

Judge, T.A. and Ferris, G.R. 1993. Social context of performance evaluation decisions. *Academy of Management Journal*, 36: 80-106.

Jun, Y.W. and Han, J.H. 1994. *The Road to Super Excellent Company: The Growth and Transformation of Samsung*. Seoul: Kimyoungsa.

Kluttz, L. 2002. SHRM/Fortune Survey on the Changing Face of Diversity, SHRM Research Paper, Sept. 2002.

Korn, H.J., Milliken, F.J. and Lant, T.K. 1992. Top management team change and organizational performance: The influence of succession, composition, and context. *Academy of Management Journal*, 33: 129-150.

Kusunoki, K. and Numagami, T. 1996. Interfunctional transfers of engineers in a Japanese firm: An empirical study on frequency, timing, and pattern. Working paper.

Lawrence, Q. and Lorsch, J. 1969. Differentiation and integration in complex organizations. *Administrative Science Quarterly*, 12: 153-167.

Lee, H.J. 1999. *The Cultural Characteristics of Korean Companies and the Development of New Corporate Culture* (pp. 314-364). Seoul: Parkyoungsa.

Lewin, R. and Regine, B. 2002. *The Soul at Work: Listen, Respond, Let Go*. NY: Ralph M. Vicinanza, Ltd.

McEvily, B. and Zaheer, A. 1999. Bridging ties: A source of firm heterogeneity in competitive capabilities. *Strategic Management Journal*, 20: 1133-1156.

Milliken, F.J. and Martins, L.L. 1996. Searching for common threads: Understanding the multiple effects of diversity of in organizational groups. *Academy of Management Review*, 21: 402-433.

Mowshowitz, A. 1994. Virtual organization: A vision of management in the information age. *The Information Society*, 10: 267-288.

Nohria, N. and Berkley, D. 1994. The virtual organization: Bureaucracy, technology, and the implosion of control. In C. Heckscher and A. Donnelon (eds.), *The Post-Bureaucratic Organization: New Perspectives on Organizational Change* (pp. 108-128). CA: Sage.

Nonaka, I. and Takeuchi, H. 1995. *The Knowledge-Creating Company: How Japanese Companies Create the Dynamics of Innovation* (pp. 166-171). NY: Oxford Univ. Press.

O'Reilly, C.A., Caldwell, D.F. and Barnett, W.P. 1989. Work group demography, social integration, and turnover. *Administrative Science Quarterly*, 34: 21-37.

O'Reilly, C.A. and Flatt, S. 1989. Executive team demography, organizational innovation, and firm performance. Working Paper, Univ. of California, Berkeley.

Park, H.J. and Sung, S.H. 2000. Diversity and knowledge-creating project team performance. *Presented at the Conference of Korean Academy of Management*, 25, March: 207-229.

Park, J.K. 1998. *The Crisis of Asian Value and Search for Solutions*. Seoul, Korea: Samsung Economic Research Institute.

Pelled, L.H. 1996. Democratic diversity, conflict, and work group outcomes: An intervening process theory. *Organization Science*, 7: 615-631.

Pelled, L.H., Eisenhardt, K.M. and Xin, K.R. 1999. Exploring the black box: An analysis of work group diversity, conflict, and performance. *Administrative Science Quarterly*, 44: 1-28.

Simons, T. 1995. Top management team consensus, heterogeneity, and debate as contingent predictors of company performance: The complementarity of group structure and process. *Academy of Management Journal*, 62-66.

Simons, T., Pelled, L.H. and Smith, K.A. 1999. Making use of difference: Diversity, debate, and decision comprehesiveness in top management teams. *Academy of Management Journal*, 42: 662-673.

Smith, K.G., Smith, K.A., Olian, J.D., Sims, H.P., O'Bannon, D.P. and Scully, J.A. 1994. Top management team demography and process: The role of social integration and communication. *Administrative Science Quarterly*, 39: 412-438.

Souder, W.E. 1987. *Managing New Product Innovations*. Lexington, MA: Lexington Books.

Thomas, D.A. 1996. Making differences matter: A new paradigm for managing diversity. *Harvard Business Review*, 74, Sept.-Oct.: 79-91.

Thomas, R. and Woodruff, M.I. 1999. *Building a House for Diversity: How a Fable about a Giraffe and an Elephant Offer New Strategies*. NY: Thomas and Associates Inc.

Tziner, A. and Eden, D. 1985. Effects of crew composition on crew performance: Does the whole equal the sum of its parts? *Journal of Applied Psychology*, 70: 1, 85-93.

Wagner, W.G., Pfeffer, J. and O'Reilly, C.A. 1984. Organizational demography and turnover in top-management groups. *Administrative Science Quarterly*, 29: 74-92.

Watson, W., Kumar, K. and Michaelsen, L.K. 1993. Cultural diversity's impact on interaction process and performance. *Academy of Management Journal*, 36: 590-603.

Webber, S.S. and Donahue, L. 2001. Impact of highly and less job-related diversity on work group cohesion and performance: A meta-analysis. *Journal of Management*, 27: 141-162.

White, S. 2002. Rigor and relevance in Asian management research: Where are we and where can we go? *Asia Pacific Journal of Management*, 19: 287-352.

Zenger, T.R. and Lawrence, B.S. 1989. Organizational demography: The differential effects of age and tenure distributions on technical communication. *Academy of Management Journal*, 32: 353-376.

Chapter 18

HUMAN RESOURCE MANAGEMENT IN ASIA
Understanding Variations in Human Resource Practices Using a Resource Exchange Perspective

K. Yee Ng
Nanyang Technological University, Singapore

Soon Ang
Nayang Technological University, Singapore

INTRODUCTION

"If we divide resources into material (natural and capital) and human resources, the latter are strategic in their interactions with the former as it is man who manipulates material resources through institutions. The unpredictable and sometimes capricious forces of nature can be offset by the diligence and ingenuity of man, which are a function of the human resources embodied in him." – Oshima (1988: S107), in explaining the success of East Asia using a human resource approach.

The impressive economic growth of Asia has aroused much interest in the West to identify an Asian model, be it in the domain of macroeconomics, public policy, or organizational management. In this chapter, our focus is on one particular aspect of management that can have a critical impact on the effective functioning of the firm – human resource management (HRM). Specifically, HRM refers to functions undertaken by organizations to attract, develop, motivate, and retain employees, and comprises broad aspects such as human resource planning, staffing, appraising, rewarding and training (Jackson & Schuler, 1995).

Consequent to the sweeping wave of globalization, HRM research in the last two decades has extended rapidly beyond the boundaries of the United States and Western Europe, where the majority of theoretical and empirical work in HRM began. An Asian focus on HRM first emerged with Japan's economic success in the 1960s, and was sustained through to the 1990s by the "Tigers" and "Dragons" of Asia, which attracted huge foreign investments into the region (Rowley, 1998). More recently, the economic potential of China and India – the most populous countries in the world, continues to provide impetus for both research and practice to acquire a deeper understanding of HRM in Asia.

Yet, despite the extensive amount of research conducted on HRM practices in various Asian countries, it remains elusive what an Asian model of HRM is. Difficulty in pinpointing an Asian model may be attributed to at least two reasons. First, Asia is a continent of great diversity, as evidenced by its myriad economic, political and geographical conditions. Kuruvilla and Venkataratnam (1996), for instance, remark that the region offers examples at both extremes in terms of geographical area, population, gross national product, political ideology, unemployment levels, poverty, literacy and so on. Given that HRM is shaped by the environment to a large extent (Jackson & Schuler, 1995; Jennings, 1994; Morishima, 1995), these diverse contextual factors imply diverse HRM practices across the continent, particularly across sub-regions such as East Asia (e.g., China, Hong Kong, Japan, Taiwan, South Korea), Southeast Asia (e.g., Indonesia, Philippines, Malaysia, Singapore, Thailand) and South Asia (e.g., Bangladesh, India).

The second reason is the lack of a theoretical framework to integrate and synthesize existing findings related to Asian HRM practices. Jackson and Schuler (1995) note that the current dominant focus in international HRM research is on the overwhelming variety of specific practices, rather than on the fundamental, abstract dimensions of HRM systems. We argue that this bias impedes the development of an Asian model because differences are inevitably more likely to emerge when comparing HR practices at a concrete, specific level. However, if we examine the abstract, fundamental dimensions of HRM, we are more likely to find some underlying patterns across Asia. In other words, comparative studies involving specific HRM practices are likely to lose the "forest for the trees," making it easier to find divergence, but harder to identify broad patterns, in the HRM systems within regions.

Hence, it is clear that given the diversity of the region, arguing for total convergence within Asia that culminates in a unique Asian HRM model is untenable. Rather, a more reasonable approach in discussing an "Asian HRM model" is to focus on "soft convergence," which requires only some family resemblances (Warner, 2000). This approach implies that there is variation in HRM within Asia, but such variation is smaller than the variation that exists between regions (e.g., Asia versus North America). Further, research that focuses on the more abstract, fundamental concepts underlying HRM can help identify meaningful differences or similarities amongst HRM systems within a region, as opposed to research that examines specific HRM practices.

Our objectives in this chapter are twofold. The first objective, which is descriptive in nature, aims to provide an overview of the context and HRM practices in Asia. Including a brief description of the environment in Asia is aligned with calls to take into consideration context when examining HRM. Drawing upon Jackson and Schuler's (1995) framework, we describe the context of Asia in terms of its culture, industry characteristics, politics, laws and legislations pertaining to employment, labor markets and unions. We then review practices commonly observed in Asia, classified under five HRM functions: planning, staffing, appraising, rewarding and training.

Our second objective is theoretical in focus, and aims to expound on a fundamental concept underlying HRM – the employment exchange relationship. We argue that surfacing the assumptions concerning the nature of the employment relationship is critical to understanding HRM practices, and also provides a useful approach for comparative HRM research. Specifically, we adopt Foa and Foa's (1974; Foa, 1971) resource typology to describe the nature of the employment exchange, and argue that these expectations in turn affect HRM policies. Further, we advance an integrative framework that illustrates how the context of a country can influence the nature of its employment relationship, and consequently, its HRM practices.

Consistent with our objectives, the remaining of this chapter is organized into three major sections. The first section is a literature review that describes the broader context of Asia and her HRM practices. The second section introduces a theoretical model of HRM that highlights the interplay between external context, the employment relationship, and HRM practices. Finally, we conclude the chapter by relating our theoretical model to Asian HRM practices, and discuss how future HRM research can adopt our framework to examine and compare HRM practices in the international context.

A REVIEW OF THE ASIAN CONTEXT AND HRM PRACTICES

The Asian Context

Considering the broader context in which HRM systems are embedded is imperative for a better understanding of HRM practices, particularly when different cultures are involved (Jackson & Schuler, 1995; Jennings, 1994; Morishima, 1995). Jackson and Schuler (1995), for instance, delineate six dimensions of the external context that HRM models should incorporate. In this section, we describe briefly the Asian context along each of these dimensions, focusing on aspects that are particularly relevant to employment. Specifically, *culture* refers to values and traditions that have been passed from one generation to the next; politics focus on the role of the government in the labor market; *laws and regulations* highlight labor-related legislations that have significant impact on employment; *unions* refer to labor-management relations in general; *labor markets* refer to the demand and supply of workers in the economy; and finally, *industry characteristics* focus on the stage of economic development and the dominant business players in the region.

Culture

Defined as the "collective programming of the mind" (Hofstede, 1984), culture is one contextual aspect in which Asian countries share some degree of similarity. Empirical work has demonstrated that Asian countries tend to cluster together on certain cultural dimensions such as collectivism (i.e., less individualism) and high power distance (e.g., Hofstede, 1984; Smith, Dugan, & Trompenaars, 1996), and subscribe more to particularistic and ascription-based relationships with the organization or group (Smith et al., 1996). This means that Asian countries tend to place greater emphasis on group membership rather than individual identity (collectivism), more likely to accept inequality of power as an acceptable norm in life (high power distance), and have different interactions with people depending on who the other party is (particularism).

One reason for this predominantly collectivistic and hierarchical orientation across most parts of Asia may be attributed to the influence of Confucianism – a philosophy that originated from the teachings of Confucius, a sage in ancient China (551–479 BC). Central to Confucianism is the emphases placed on the moral nature of man, harmony of society, political legitimacy, order and unity, and hierarchy (Chang, 1976). Indeed, an interesting finding emerged in the late 1980s that Asians espouse a unique value termed Confucian work dynamism, a dimension that describes orientation toward the future versus the present and the past (Bond, 1988; CCC, 1987). Some specific beliefs associated with this dimension are persistence, ordering relationships by status, thrift, and having a sense of shame. Not surprisingly, East Asian countries such as Hong Kong, Japan, Taiwan and South Korea score highest on this dimension (i.e., high perseverance and thrift), and to which many have attributed their economic success (e.g., Hofstede & Bond, 1993). India, Singapore, and Thailand have moderate scores, whereas the Philippines scores relatively lower (CCC, 1987).

Industry Characteristics

Economic development has occurred in different time periods across Asia, resulting in different stages of industrialization for different countries. For instance, the four Asian Tigers are at the advanced stage of their export-orientation strategy, which focuses on high value added manufacturing that requires skilled labor. In fact, Singapore and Hong Kong are now shifting toward being more service-oriented. On the other hand, Malaysia and Thailand are becoming advanced export-oriented economies, whereas the Philippines and Indonesia are still presently at the first stage of the low-cost export-orientation phase. China and India have only begun to shift to an export-orientation phase, after having had a heavy and capital-intensive inward-looking import substitution strategy for many years (Kuruvilla & Venkataratnam, 1996).

Another relevant aspect of industrialization is the dominant firm structures of these Asian economies. In general, small to medium-sized family-owned enterprises dominate the scene, particularly in Taiwan, Hong Kong and Southeast Asia. Their organizational structure may be typified by closed family ownership with a simple and informal structure. These firms are personal in nature as they are typically regarded as family possessions, and control is greatly associated with ownership and highly centralized. However, with increasing globalization and the economic challenges posed by the currency crisis in 1997, family businesses in Asia are slowly absorbing more professional managers into their upper echelons. For instance, Tsui-Auch and Lee (2003) argued and found some support that the currency crisis resulted in credit squeeze and national reforms that consequently increased the pressure on family-controlled businesses to relinquish family control and corporate rule.

Large locally-owned enterprises, on the other hand, play a significant role in Japan and South Korea. Known as keiretsus in Japan and chaebols in Korea, these firms account for substantial shares of their respective economies. Both types of organizations have relatively similar internal structures, but a major difference lies with the separation of ownership and management. In Korean chaebols, control is firmly retained by founders and their families, resulting in little managerial independence from dominant shareholders. Japanese keiretsus, in contrast, experience a high degree of managerial autonomy from shareholders because personal authority derived from competence is more valued in Japan than that derived from ownership (Chen, 1995; Whitley, 1990).

State-owned enterprises, where the state acts as the owner and employer, used to dominate the Chinese and Indian economies. However, with economic liberation in China and a push for privatization in India, the role of state-owned enterprises has diminished substantially in both economies over the years. In contrast, foreign multinationals, attracted by the relatively cheap and high-quality labor, are increasing becoming dominant players, particularly in Southeast Asia, and more recently, in China.

Labor Markets

Asia is highly diverse in terms of population figures, with two very small city states (Hong Kong and Singapore) and two highly populous nations (China and India). Most of the remaining Asian countries are medium-sized, with populations ranging from 18 to 60 million (Verma, Kochan, & Lansbury, 1995).

Due in part to differences in population size and different stages of economic development, unemployment rates differ rather substantially across Asia. In the 1980s and early 1990s, most of East Asia and Singapore experienced severe labor shortages, whereas most parts of Southeast and South Asia faced relatively high unemployment rates. In the former case of labor shortages, the problem was sometimes aggravated by other social-political factors, such as the greying population in Japan and Singapore, and the "brain-drain" phenomenon in Hong Kong arising from the political uncertainties associated with China's reunification in 1997. Nonetheless, these countries are currently also facing increased unemployment due to the global economic slowdown.

Politics

Unlike the West, governmental intervention is common and often acceptable in most Asian countries, though the degree and form may vary from country to country. Within East Asia alone, for example, there is considerable variation in political ideology. Although referred to as the Greater China, China, Taiwan and Hong Kong have had very different political leadership in the last three decades. The political history of China in the period after the Communist Party defeated the Nationalist Party (the latter fled to Taiwan) and the 1978 reforms may be characterized as a period of ideological oscillations between moderation/pragmatism and radicalism (Nyaw, 1995). Once under extreme communist rule, China used to be a centrally-planned economy where the political leadership of the Party played a major role in manpower policies. With her transition to a market-driven economy, there is now a shift of responsibility and decision-making from the state to the enterprise.

Hong Kong, on the other extreme, is reputed for her being a bastion of free market capitalism and entrepreneur spirit (Friedman & Friedman, 1980) after its colonization by Britain in 1841 (ceded by China under the Treaty of Nanking). Even after the 1997 reunification with China, Hong Kong continues to enjoy a substantial amount of autonomy under China's "one country, two systems" policy.

The rest of Asia lie somewhere between the two extremes. Although a democratic country, India is inclined toward a centrally planned economy with strong state regulation. For instance, state-owned firms in the public sector, and investment and production restrictions in the private sector, are widespread in India (Kuruvilla, 1996). Korea, Singapore and Taiwan are also known for their state-controlled market economies, albeit to a lesser extent compared to India. Japan's government, in comparison, is more of a coordinator of activity and mediator of conflicting interests, rather than an authoritarian controller.

Labor Unions

Labor-management relationships in Asia are generally less adversarial and more mutually supportive, with varying degree of regulatory restrictions placed on them. Countries like Singapore, China and Indonesia have only one union federation, while most of the other Asian countries have multiple union federations (ranging from two to 155), although none of these has significant influence on national policies (Kuruvilla & Venkataratnam, 1996).

There are several models of unionism in Asia. In the state-employer dominated model, the state plays a strong role and the union has little influence on national policies (Kuruvilla & Venkataratnam, 1996). Worker unions in China may be classified under this model, since they are virtually controlled by the political party and act as the "conveyor belt" between the Party and the workers. Union roles include communicating socialist goals (Goodall & Warner, 1997; Hoffman, 1981; Nyaw, 1995) and administering welfare benefits to the workers (Tan, 1989).

In the politicized multi-union model, trade unions are affiliated with political parties, thus enabling them to participate in national policy-making. Union formation, recognition, and functioning are well protected by law, and bargaining is highly decentralized. India and most of Southeast Asia may be described by this model (Kuruvilla & Venkataratnam, 1996).

The newly democratic transitory model is characteristic of Taiwan and South Korea, where the shift from authoritarian to democratic forms of government has destabilized existing patterns of industrial relations. As a result, employers who had never dealt with unions in the past are now faced with the prospect of labor-management negotiations, which they had little experience in.

The tripartite model, which involves the equal partnership of trade unions, employers and the government, is a critical and unique feature of Singapore. Although many Asian countries have attempted to institutionalize formal tripartism, none has had achieved significant benefits from the model as Singapore has in terms of national policy-making (Kuruvilla & Venkataratnam, 1996).

Another unique model in Asia is enterprise unionism in Japan, where union membership is restricted to a firm's employees. These in-house trade unions not only represent the interests of the employees, but also have the responsibility to protect the interests of the company. Because the well-being of union members is tied to the company's economic success, there is great incentive for unions to work with management to increase productivity and profitability.

With regards to union legislations, one distinctive feature of Asian economies is that there are several administrative restrictions on the right to strike. The most common restriction is the prohibition to strike in essential industries, with some countries having more industries classified under this category than others. Not surprisingly, the number of strikes per year for each country varies within the region. According to the statistics reported by the US Department of Labor, the number of strikes in 1990 ranged from none in Singapore to 1,825 in India. Nonetheless, the region on the whole exhibits a trend of declining number of strikes over the years.

Labor Laws

Although there is remarkable similarity in the labor protection legislation in Asian economies, there is a wide variation in the enforcement of these laws. According to Kuruvilla & Venkataratnam (1996), most of the Asian countries have advanced legislation regulating leave, overtime, working hours, safety and health, terminations, bonus, retirement benefits, and in some cases, even equal employment laws (see also the Forum section in the Asia Business Law Review, volumes 23–26). However, very few countries have enforced these laws in full, with Singapore being one of the few exceptions. In some countries (e.g., the Philippines), labor standards laws have been revised downward because they were too advanced for developing economies. In others (e.g., Taiwan), enactment of the labor standards law has become the basis for increased union activity and the cause of increased labor-management conflicts (Kuruvilla & Venkataratnam, 1996).

As can be seen from the paragraphs above, Asia is far from a region of homogeneity. In addition to diversity in the economic, labor market, political, and legal conditions described here, the region is also heterogeneous in terms of natural endowments, ethnic composition, colonial experiences, and more. This diversity leads to an important question: how homogeneous are Asian HRM practices?

In the next section, we review the literature on Asian HRM and describe dominant practices in the region. However, it should be cautioned that our review below is biased toward East Asia because most of the existing work is conducted there. With perhaps the exception of India, Singapore and Thailand, very few studies have examined countries located elsewhere in Asia. This itself suggests a gap in the Asian HRM literature that should be addressed by future research.

HRM Practices in Asia

Adopting Jackson and Schuler's (1995; see also Schuler, 1988) framework, we describe HRM practices in Asia subsumed under five HRM functions: planning, staffing, appraising, rewarding, and training.

Planning

The functions of human resource planning (HRP) are to anticipate future business and environment demands on an organization in order to meet the personnel requirements dictated by those conditions (Cascio, 1982). Hence, HRP is a critical function particularly for economies with tight labor markets and dynamic business conditions.

Because of the prevalence of small and family-owned businesses in Asia, HRP is generally informal and unsophisticated (e.g., Lawler & Atmiyanandana, 1995). Larger firms such as MNCs or state-owned enterprises are more likely to conduct systematic HRP, such as the computation of current staffing ratio as well as predicted sales order (Kirkbride & Tang, 1989). In addition, explicit job analyses which are part of the HRP function in the West (Schuler, 1988), are less common in Asia.

Government intervention and/or assistance in HRP is quite common in Asia, albeit to varying degrees. At one extreme, virtually all forms of HRP in China under her former mode of central government planning are conducted by the state. Thus, HRP, and even staffing, are relatively new areas of personnel management for Chinese enterprises after China's economic liberation in 1978. In other Asian economies, particularly those with acute labor shortages, government initiatives are often in place to assist organizations in HRP. Singapore, for instance, has established the National Manpower Council to spearhead an integrated national manpower planning approach. This Council sets directions and oversees national manpower planning and development strategies to meet the changing needs of industries in Singapore (The National Human Resources Handbook, 2000).

Staffing

Broadly, staffing encompasses recruitment and selection practices that are aimed at getting the right people to join the company. There are several choices organizations make with respect to staffing, such as using internal versus external sources of recruitment, and adopting explicit versus implicit criteria for selection (Schuler, 1988).

Internal recruitment is generally preferred in Asian organizations, especially for high-level positions. This is not surprising, given the prevalence of family-owned businesses and Asians' emphasis on close relationships. Therefore, top positions in small to large family-owned enterprises in most Asian countries are typically filled by family members and relatives (e.g., Chen, 1998; Farh, 1995; Gopalan & Rivera, 1997; Lawler & Atmiyanandana, 1995; Sinha, 1991). Promotions and rotations within the organization are also common, particularly in large firms that can afford an internal labor market. Japan's flexible staffing practice is one example, where extensive job rotations and employee

reassignments are often implemented to redeploy manpower whenever necessary, thus enabling firms to retain their staff even in times of poor economic
performance (Mroczkowski & Hanaoka, 1989).

Entry-level positions are inevitably less amenable to internal recruitment.
Instead, personal referrals are frequently used by Asian firms, especially for
blue-collar jobs (Chew & Goh, 1997; Farh, 1995; Hsu & Leat, 2000; Kirkbride
& Tang, 1989; Koch et al., 1995; Lawler & Atmiyanandana, 1995). Advertise-
ments are also widely used for all levels of recruiting. Other methods that are
used in varying degrees include external employment agencies/head hunters,
job fairs, and more recently, internet postings.

A unique external recruitment strategy in Asia is the cohort-hiring practice
adopted by Japanese kereitsus and Korean chaebols, where cohorts of fresh
graduates from schools and universities are recruited once or twice a year, as
opposed to all-year hiring that is practiced in other parts of Asia and the US
(Koch et al., 1995; Pucik, 1984). According to Pucik (1984), a major reason for
cohort-hiring is to provide a reference point for the organization to evaluate an
employee's performance and progress, vis-à-vis his/her cohort members'. As
such, social comparison is one mechanism used to gauge performance throughout an employee's tenure under the cohort-hiring system.

Selection criteria in Asia are generally less explicit and objective than the
West. Personal attributes such as loyalty, diligence, and the ability to work with
others (e.g., Chen, 1998; Farh, 1995; Koch et al., 1995) are often important
considerations for selection. In India where the caste system still exists to some
extent, background characteristics based on caste considerations are sometimes
accorded equal importance as work qualifications (Gopalan & Rivera, 1997).
In many Asian countries, having personal connections can also substantially
improve one's chances of being selected (Lawler & Atmiyanandana, 1995).

Nevertheless, one "objective" selection criterion that is commonly emphasized by firms across Asia, especially in East Asia, is educational credentials.
In Japan and South Korea, for instance, graduates from prestigious universities are much more likely to find jobs with large companies than those from
less well-known universities. Some scholars attribute this "credentialism" phenomenon to Confucianism, where possessing a good education is seen as one
means of contributing to the society (e.g., Huang et al., 2000; Sarachek, 1990).

The sophistication of selection techniques varies across countries as well as
firm sizes. In general, interviews and screening of application forms are very
common techniques, whereas psychometric tests and assessment centers are
rarely used by small and local firms. Reference/background checks (especially
for hiring higher-level personnel) and physical examinations have also been
frequently reported (Chew & Goh, 1997; Chen, 1995; Kirkbride & Tang, 1989;
Latham & Napier, 1989; Shaw et al., 1995).

Appraising

Appraisals in Asia can be differentiated from those in the West along two dimensions: the content and the process. Indeed, the term "performance appraisal" reflects the ethnocentrism of the Western practice of appraising, which typically focuses on the performance of employees. In Asia, "performance appraisal" can be a misnomer since appraisal criteria typically extend beyond actual performance results to personal attributes such as moral character, loyalty and effort.

In China for instance, four broad areas are appraised: "de" (good moral practice), "neng" (adequate competence), "qing" (positive attitude), and "jie" (strong performance record), with good moral practice (such as moral integrity and political attitude) being the most important criterion (Child, 1994; Nyaw, 1995; Von Glinow & Chung, 1989). In India, loyalty to and dependence on one's superiors are likely to lead to more positive ratings (Gopalan & Rivera, 1997). In Japan, communication skills, seniority, sense of responsibility, the capability of performing the job (as opposed to the actual ability) and expenditure of good faith effort are important factors to consider in an appraisal (Morishima, 1995; Mroczkowski & Hanaoka, 1989). Likewise, Latham and Napier (1989) report a dominant use of trait-oriented characteristics (e.g., adaptability, attitude, initiative) in appraisals in Singapore and Hong Kong. However, it should be noted that there is a gradual shift in most countries to a more performance-centered appraisal system.

With regards to the process, many appraisal systems in Asia are closed-appraisals, which means that employees do not discuss their evaluations with supervisors who assess them (Latham & Napier, 1989; Lawrence, 1996; Yuen & Yeo, 1995). This one-way appraisal can be largely attributed to the Asian concept of "face," which is an important factor for achieving harmony with others (Fuller & Peterson, 1992). Lawrence (1996), for instance, observes that many Singapore managers dislike open appraisals because they involve confronting people with personal evaluations, which may lead to a loss of "face." Nonetheless, many organizations in Asia are slowly adopting "open" appraisals, since this practice is more amenable to developmental objectives.

The appraisal process in Asia is also likely to be less participative and more directive (Snape, Thompson, Yan, & Redman, 1998). Due to the high power-distance values in the region, appraisal techniques such as the 360-degree feedback system where subordinates' views and perceptions are solicited, may not be as accepted or as effective (Entrekin & Chung, 2001; Latham & Napier, 1989).

Although appraising is universally considered an important HRM function, the purpose underlying the appraisals can differ across countries. In general, appraisals are seen more as evaluative tools (rather than developmental) in Asia than in the West, plausibly due to the nature of the criteria (trait-based versus performance-oriented), as well as the process (closed versus open) used in the appraisal systems.

Rewarding

Given that work is an exchange of labor for money, rewarding is undoubtedly a universal practice. Nonetheless, the basis for rewarding can differ substantially between the West and Asia, and even within Asia itself. The seniority-based system, for instance, is a well-established practice in Asian organizations that is clearly at odds with the Western philosophy of meritocracy. Under this system, tenure, age and educational background are significant determinants in pay and promotion systems (Gopalan & Rivera, 1997; Koch et al., 1995; Lincoln & Nakata, 1997; Ornatowski, 1998). The seniority-based system is seen as a way by management to encourage company loyalty and to maintain social harmony by minimizing competition and protecting face (Milliman, Nason, Von Glinow, Huo, Lowe, & Kim, 1995).

The extent to which seniority-based system is implemented, however, varies among Asian countries, possibly with Japan and Korea being most noted for the practice. In India, seniority-based pay is more prevalent in the public than in the private sector (Venkataratnam, 1995). Due to the influence of foreign organizations in some of the Asian nations (e.g., Singapore, Hong Kong, Taiwan), the seniority-based system is less prevalent. Nonetheless, a common trend across Asia is the gradual shift to a more performance-oriented pay system, even in Japan and Korea (Lincoln & Nakata, 1997; Morishima, 1995).

Another common feature related to Asian pay practices is the relatively egalitarian wage structure. At one extreme is the pay system under the old communist rule of China, where very minimal wage differential existed within the same category of employees, and remuneration was not tied to performance indicators, whether at the enterprise or individual level (Goodall & Warner, 1997). However, Chinese enterprises are beginning to inject performance-related components into their pay systems, such as the use of a "floating-wage" system (Nyaw, 1995). Likewise, seniority-based practices in the Japanese and Korean systems result in a relatively egalitarian wage structure for employees within the same cohort. Even in Hong Kong, Singapore and Taiwan where the culture of pay-for-performance is comparatively stronger (Kirkbride & Tang, 1989), it is likely that the emphasis is more on group performance rather than individual performance, compared to the West (Shaw et al., 1995; White, Luk, Druker, & Chiu, 1998). For instance, in a study comparing Hong Kong and Britain banks, White et al. (1998) conclude that although performance-related pay is a key component in both countries, the emphasis on individual performance is greater in the UK, whereas salary increases tend to be more uniform and determined more by group performance in Hong Kong.

Finally, it is worthy to note that Singapore has a rather unique element in her remuneration system – the involvement of a tripartite body consisting of the government, employers and trade unions. This committee, known as the National Wage Council (NWC), makes annual recommendations to organizations concerning the size of the variable payment in employees' total pay, which is largely determined by the economy's performance. Although not mandatory, the NWC recommendations are adopted by the majority of companies in Singapore (The National Human Resources Handbook, 2000). This feature is characteristic of the active involvement of the Singapore government in ensuring a competitive workforce and a viable economy.

Developing

Belief in, and commitment to, training differs rather substantially across Asia. In Japan and Korea, training and development is viewed as a critical form of employee investment, and is evidenced by the skill grade pay system where pay increments and promotions are tied to skills acquired from training (Hashimoto, 1994; Kalleberg & Lincoln, 1988; Morishima, 1995).

In contrast, training in India is viewed with greater scepticism, in part due to the local cultural belief that change is limited (human nature orientation) (Gopalan & Rivera, 1997), and in part due to financial constraints as well as the possibility of poaching by competitor firms (Sharma, 1992). Likewise in Singapore, Hong Kong, and Taiwan, training is very much deterred by the high employee turnover amidst tight labor markets. For example, Taormina and Bauer (2000) observed that training in Hong Kong is often viewed as a means for personal progression (a stepping stone to a better job elsewhere), thus explaining the reluctance of companies to offer training in these countries.

Unlike the West where training focuses highly on technical aspects of the jobs, training in Asia is typically more broad-based and focuses more on fostering positive attitudes and a fit with the company's philosophy (Koch et al., 1995). For instance, the Japanese training program in the automobile industry begins from orientation sessions in safety and corporate culture, followed by intensive technical training, followed by on-the-job training with experienced workers, job rotations, and through participation in consensus-based decision making, quality control circles and suggestion systems (Hashimoto, 1994). Likewise in Korea, the focus of training is to develop an "all-around man," a generalist (as opposed to a specialist) who understands the organization's goals and exhibits the correct spirit (Koch et al., 1995). In China, worker education used to include political courses aimed at inculcating employees with the correct political ideology, as well as scientific-cultural subjects aimed at equipping employees with basic knowledge of relevance to daily life (Nyaw, 1995). Now, with the influx of MNCs requiring a large pool of skilled workers, China is also emphasizing vocational training to upgrade the skills of the Chinese labor force.

As with the West, on-the-job training (OJT) is more frequent than off-the-job training. Japan in particular, is well-known for her extensive and systematic OJT system that aims at familiarizing employees with the various operations of the organization (Morishima, 1995). Across Asia, large firms are more likely to offer in-house training than small firms, owing to their greater pool of resources. Company-sponsored education leave, a rarely observed practice in the West, is common in China and Taiwan. Such an opportunity is considered a great privilege, and employees who return from the educational training trips are typically given a raise and/or are promoted (Huang & Cullen, 2001; Nyaw, 1995).

Because of the lack of resources in small Asian businesses to offer formal training to employees, governmental intervention is necessary, even in the usually laissez-faire economy of Hong Kong (Poon, 1995). For instance, the Hong Kong government set up the Management Development Center in 1984 to provide training on managerial skills and knowledge (Poon, 1995) upon recognizing the need for supervisory training in the workforce. In Singapore, employers are required by law to contribute 1% of the monthly pay of their workers earning $1500 or less to the Skills Development Fund, which is used by the government to set up training centers, subsidize employers' training costs, and to provide training for retrenched workers (The National Human Resources Handbook, 2000).

How does Asia's investment in training compare to the rest of the world? A study conducted by the American Society for Training and Development (ASTD; see Van Buren & King, 2000) in 1999 concludes that respondents in Asia reported spending the least on training per employee, and respondents in Japan reported spending the least on training as a percentage of total annual payroll (Van Buren & King, 2000), compared to four other regions: Australia/New Zealand, the US, Canada, and Europe. However, the finding concerning Japan merits some qualifications – certain forms of training, such as costs for self-enlightenment programs, formal OJT, and training which employees assume responsibility are not captured in the study's training index. Hence, although the study by ASTD is laudable in terms of its efforts to create a framework for comparing training investments in the world, it also demonstrates the many problems associated with standardizing the definition and operationalizations of training.

To summarize, our review has demonstrated some similarities in the HRM practices within Asia, such as the widespread use of personal referrals for recruitment, the emphasis on educational qualifications and personal background information as selection criteria, the egalitarian wage structures, and performance appraisals that include assessment of seniority and personal values and attitudes.

Yet, there are also substantial variations in the HRM practices observed within Asia, both in terms of the extent as well as the nature, of the practices. For instance, the degree of egalitarianism in the wage structure varies across countries in Asia, with perhaps China being one of the stronger adherents compared to the rest. Certain HRM practices can also be rather unique to a country, such as the cohort-hiring practice, which is observed only in Japan and to some extent, Korea. However, as we noted on the outset, the use of specific HRM practices as the basis of comparison inevitably reduces the "visibility" of some meaningful patterns underlying HRM practices. Next, we shift from a descriptive to a theoretical focus to expound on a conceptual model that can potentially provide a deeper understanding of HRM, and a new perspective for future comparative HRM research.

A MODEL OF THE EMPLOYMENT RELATIONSHIP

In essence, we argue that HRM practices are intricately linked to the employment relationship – to understand the variations in HRM practices across cultures, we need to delve further and understand the nature of the employment relationship in these cultures. The employment relationship, in turn, is influenced by the external context. We elaborate on our conceptual model, illustrated in Figure 1, in greater detail in the ensuing paragraphs, beginning with a discussion of the nature of the employment relationship.

The Nature of the Employment Relationship

Scholars from various disciplines have offered different conceptualizations of the employment relationship. Legal scholars, for instance, view the employment relationship as a set of rights and obligations that can, to a large extent, be spelled out in employment contracts binding both employers and employees. Economists view it in terms of transaction costs that can be minimized through efficient governance structures of organizations (Williamson, 1975, 1985). Sociologists, on the other hand, conceptualize the employment relationship as a set of rules and norms governing the legitimate expectations of employers and employees in a society (Bridges & Villemez, 1995). Psychologists propose the concept of "psychological contracts," which refers to individuals' idiosyncratic beliefs regarding the terms of the exchange agreement between employees and employers (Rousseau, 1995).

In this chapter, we adopt a sociological approach to expound on a fundamental aspect of the employment relationship: the nature of the resources expected to be exchanged in the employment relationship. It is sociological as our focus is on the "social contract" of employment – the collective beliefs of

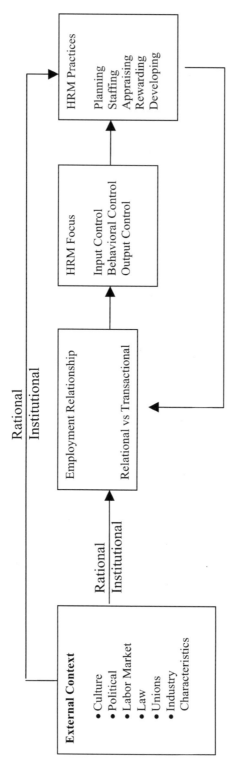

Figure 1. A Model of Employment Relationship and HRM.

a group of people regarding appropriate and legitimate transactions or expectations between employers and employees (e.g., see Rousseau, 1995). Bridges and Villemez (1995: 2), for instance, define the employment relationship as

"The typical set of terms and conditions that regulate the exchange of labor for money between an employer and a given category of employees laboring under his or her auspices. Transcending the specific quantities of work and money (or other material benefits) agreed to by the employee and the employer, the employment relationship most often extends to other matters such as grievance procedures, expectations about promotion chances, and stipulations about procedures for making any change in the relationship that might be desired by either party."

The excerpt above highlights two points concerning the employment relationship. First, the relationship between the employer and employee is one of exchange. The most basic resources transacted are employers' pecuniary remuneration for employees' work (such as time and effort). Second, there is general consensus, at least within a certain group, of what some of the conditions governing the employment relationship are. Indirectly, this implies that the nature of the employment relationship can and does vary from group to group, such as across national boundaries (e.g., see Rousseau & Schalk, 2000).

How then, can we characterize the nature of the employment relationship in a society? Here, we apply Foa's resource exchange theory (1971; Foa & Foa, 1974), which asserts that people involved in a relationship depend on one another for material and psychological resources necessary for their well-being, to the employment context and propose that the employment relationship be viewed as an exchange of resources between the employers and the employees. In other words, the employment relationship may be defined more specifically here as the collective beliefs of a group of people regarding the appropriate and legitimate types of resources to be exchanged between employers and employees.

Foa defines a resource as anything that can be transmitted from person to person, and further develops a typology consisting of six types of resources (love, status, information, money, goods, services) that can be delineated by two underlying dimensions: concreteness and particularism (see Figure 2). Concreteness describes how tangible a resource is. Some behaviors like giving an object or performing an activity are quite concrete. Others are more symbolic, such as language, posture of the body, or a smile. Hence, service and goods are considered concrete since they involve the exchange of some overtly tangible activity or product. Status and information are more symbolic as they are typically conveyed by verbal or paralinguistic behaviors. Love and money are exchanged in both concrete and symbolic forms, and thus occupy intermediate positions on the concreteness continuum (McLean Parks, Conlon, Ang, & Bontempo, 1999).

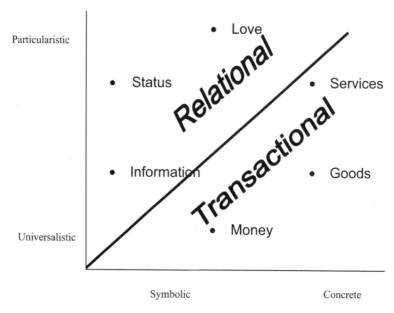

Figure 2. A resource perspective of the employment relationship: Foa and Foa's (1976) Resource Typology mapped onto Transactional vs Relationship Employment Relationship.

Particularism describes the significance of the person who provides the resource. Changing the bank teller will not make much of a difference to the client wishing to cash a cheque, but a change of doctor is less likely to be met with the same level of indifference. Hence, love is very particularistic in nature since it matters who one receives the love from, whereas money is the least particularistic, given that the value of money is unlikely to change according to the relationship between the recipient and the giver. Services and status are less particularistic than love, but more particularistic than goods and information.

Applying Foa's theory, we propose two major forms of employment relationship that can be distinguished by the types of resources expected in the employment exchange – a relational employment relationship versus a transactional employment relationship (see Figure 2). Specifically, a relational employment relationship, represented by the area above the bold diagonal line that runs through the origin, is an exchange dominated by particularistic and symbolic resources, such as love (e.g., loyalty, lifetime employment security), status (membership, seniority-based promotion), and information (e.g., advice, counseling, training). This is similar to the features of a relational contract espoused by MacNeil (1980; see also Rousseau, 1990), illustrated in Figure 3: involvement of the entire person, unique relationships, extensive communication, a large overlap between internal and external reinforcements, diffuse obligations and rights, and an emphasis on relationships. Because of the intangible and particularistic nature of the resources underlying this form of em-

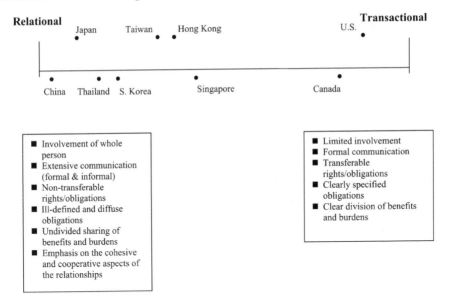

Figure 3. Employment relationships in Asia versus the West.

ployment relationship, the exchange between the employer and employee is not easily replicable or transferable to other parties. In other words, a relational employment relationship is oriented toward building a long-term relationship where employees are deeply embedded in the organization's culture and network.

In contrast, a transactional employment relationship, represented by the area below the bold diagonal line, is characterized by exchanges of concrete and universal resources between the employer and employee, such as money (e.g., wages), goods (for production employees) and services (for service-related employees and professionals). MacNeils' (1980; see also Rousseau (1990)) "discrete" contract is synonymous with a transactional relationship, where there is limited involvement of the person, formal communication, clearly specified obligations and benefits, and an awareness of conflict of interest between the two parties. In other words, a transactional employment relationship is short-termed in focus, and is guided by the goal of optimizing the economic benefits of both employers and employees.

Having expounded on the attributes of the two forms of employment relationship, we move on to discuss their influence on HRM.

Employment Relationship and HRM

While the employment relationship is about the resources employers and employees exchange (Bridges & Villemez, 1995), HR practices are rules that arise from the need to monitor and manage these resources. Given that a transactional employment relationship differs substantially from a relational one, it logically follows that the nature of HR practices will also differ accordingly. In other words, we argue that different HR practices are more appropriate for regulating and controlling different types of employment relationship.

According to Snell's (1992) control theory in strategic HRM, there are three types of control that HRM practices can potentially emphasize: behavioral, output, and input control (Snell, 1992). Behavioral control system emphasizes the regulation of employees' actions displayed on the job, and is initiated top-down in the form of articulated operating procedures (Hitt, Hoskisson, & Ireland, 1990). Output control system focuses on setting goals for employees and monitoring their achievement of these goals (Hill & Hoskisson, 1987). Input control, or clan control (Ouchi, 1979), emphasizes the antecedent conditions of performance, such as employees' knowledge, skills, abilities, values, and motives.

Although the three types of control systems are not mutually exclusive, the relative emphasis placed on each of them depends on knowledge of the cause-effect relationship and how crystallized performance standards are (Ouchi, 1977; Snell, 1992; Thompson, 1967). Behavioral control is ideal when there is complete cause-effect relationship and ambiguous performance standards; output control when there is incomplete causal relationship and crystallized standards; and input control when there is both incomplete causal relationship and vague standards.

Accordingly, we argue that different employment relationships, with the different types of resources, will necessitate different forms of control in the HRM system. For instance, an emphasis on symbolic resources (e.g., loyalty) implies that performance standards should be more difficult to formalize, given their intangible nature. Likewise, an emphasis on particularistic resources (e.g., family ties, guanxi, connections see Bian & Ang, 1997) implies that cause-effect relationships related to work performance are less standardized, since the rules may differ from person to person. Thus, in a relational employment relationship where symbolic and particularistic resources are emphasized, input controls are likely to be more prevalent than output controls given the inherent ambiguity in the performance standards and cause-effect relationships. On the other hand, a transactional employment relationship (where concrete and universal resources are emphasized) should lead to relatively more crystallized performance standards and complete cause-effect relationships, thus resulting in both output and behavioral controls being more commonly in place.

Further, differences in the relative emphases placed on input, behavioral and output control in the HRM system are likely to lead to differences in the HRM practices (Snell, 1992). HRM systems with an input-control focus are typified by rigorous staffing, intensive socialization, training and development. Those with a behavioral focus tend to have standardized and formalized operating procedures, with supervisors closely monitoring and evaluating subordinates' actions over time. Output-focused HRM systems, on the other hand, tend to have elaborate information systems that explicitly link appraisals and rewards to results achieved. One prevalent example of an output-focused HRM practice is "management by objectives" (Snell, 1992).

To summarize, we have argued that that the type of employment relationship (transactional versus relational) will influence the type of control (behavioral, input, output) dominant in that culture's HRM system, which in turn, shapes the specific HRM practices. Next, we examine the role of context in influencing the type of employment relationship that is dominant in a particular culture.

Contextual Influence

Consistent with our focus on the national-level of analysis in this chapter, we examine only the external environment of organizations as characterized by Jackson & Schuler (1995). We acknowledge the importance of incorporating the internal environment (e.g., technology, size, structure, life cycle stage and business strategy) but exclude them in this chapter due to space constraint.

Many theoretical perspectives grounded in various disciplines (e.g., economics, sociology, organizational science, etc.) have been advanced to explain how external macro factors influence HRM (e.g., Jackson & Schuler, 1995; Jennings, 1994). The myriad theories, however, may be broadly classified into two camps: rational versus non-rational (institutional) (e.g., Bridges & Villemez, 1995; Gooderham, Nordhaug, & Ringdal, 1999).

The rational camp comprises normative theories that are based on the assumption that HRM practices that are best for the firm will be implemented. Hence, decisions on what HRM practices to adopt are presumably guided purely by the goal to maximize efficiency and economic outcomes. At one extreme, there are theories that prescribe a universal set of practices that will maximize performance. One example is Harbison and Myers' (1959) economic development model, which argues that for a particular stage of economic development, there is a corresponding management system.

A softer variant of the rational approach is offered by contingency theory, which asserts that optimum performance is achieved through a fit between structural characteristics of the organization and its environment (Lawrence & Lorsch, 1967). Studies adopting this theory examine how the internal and/or external context of the firm will influence the HRM practices, based on the notion of congruence (e.g., Burns & Stalker, 1961). Another example is Williamson's (1975) transaction-cost analysis, which rests on the fundamental assumption that organizational variety exists primarily to economize transaction costs. Hence, the organization of work and labor is governed by efficiency consideration, for labor market transactions, like all other transactions of organizations, have costs that can be minimized by effective organizational arrangement (Bridges & Villemez, 1995).

In response to the widespread criticisms on the "shaky ground" of the rational approach, the second camp of theories focuses on non-rational forces that can influence organizational structures and practices. Institutional theorists view organizations as social entities that seek to gain acceptance and legitimacy from various stakeholders in the environment in order to survive (Meyer & Rowan, 1977; Selznick, 1957). Different types of institutional pressures can drive organizations to adapt to their external environment: coercive, normative, and mimetic (DiMaggio & Powell, 1983). Coercive pressures include the direct pressures of compliance exerted on the organization (e.g., employment regulation from the government), or the indirect persuasion of other actors whom the organization is dependent on (e.g., demands from trade unions). Normative pressures are those that arise from the values and expectations of a group or groups (e.g., the HR profession). Mimetic pressures refer to forces arising from the desire to copy the behavior/practices of other organizations, apart from specific coercive or normative pressures (e.g., HR fads).

The application of institutional theory to HRM research thus presumes that the adoption of specific HR practices centers on one major criterion: whether they are acceptable and legitimate (as opposed to the goal of maximizing performance espoused by the rational approach). In other words, one critical function of the HR unit is to maintain its acceptance by the rest of the firm as a legitimate function with unique insight into employment relationship problems (Jennings & Moore, 1995). Cultural theories and political theories in the field of HRM may be subsumed under this camp, since they operate through at least one of the three forces of normative, coercive, and mimetic pressures (rather than rational approach of maximizing economic benefits).

These two camps of theories arise because of a fundamental difference in one assumption: maximizing economic/performance outcomes versus gaining social acceptance. Both goals, however, exist in reality. Hence, we incorporate both into our model as illustrated in Figure 1, and argue that the external context influences HRM practices via both rational and institutional forces. Further, these forces affect HRM practices in two ways: (1) indirectly by shaping the nature of the employment relationship and the type of control dominant in the HRM system, and (2) directly without affecting the nature of the employment relationship. In the latter case, such practices (when sustained over time) may subsequently alter the employment relationship, thus forming a feedback loop. We elaborate on the indirect and direct influences of the external context on HRM practices below.

Indirect Influence

The external context can influence HRM practices indirectly via the general expectations of what type of resources are desired in the employment exchange relationship. For instance, industrialization/modernization resulting from an economic boom may incline the employment relationship toward a transactional exchange between the employer and employee. From a rational perspective, concrete and universal resources are more conducive to the goal of maximizing profits and minimizing transaction costs. From a non-rational standpoint, the culture of a modernized and industrialized society is likely to be more individualistic in orientation (e.g., Hofstede, 1984), thus favoring a transactional employment relationship over a relational one.

The cultural tradition and values of a society should by definition, exert a substantial amount of normative influence on the type of employment relationship because they shape the societal beliefs about what is good and what is bad. Hence, in individualistic and masculine cultures where individual work achievements and performance results are emphasized (e.g., Hofstede, 1984), transactional, rather than relational employment relationships are likely to dominate the exchange between employers and employees.

As advanced in our earlier arguments, the nature of the employment relationship may in turn influence the type of control (input, output, behavioral) dominant in the HRM system of that culture, thereby shaping the specific HRM practices observed.

Direct Influence

Politics and legislations, on the other hand, are more likely to operate directly on HRM practices. This is because the employment relationship is a "social contract" which is implicitly understood by the society, and hence, not subjected to explicit manipulations by laws or legislations. Nonetheless, a reverse relationship between the employment relationship and HRM may be observed here. Specifically, we argue that when coercive pressures exerted on HRM practices are sustained over time, they may become "internalized" by the society as the norm, thus altering the general expectations of the employment relationship to be more consistent with such practices. This in turn reinforces the HRM practices that were originally instituted by law.

Likewise, mimetic influences from the external context are also likely to influence HRM practices directly. Bandwagons, which refer to diffusion processes in which organizations adopt an innovation because of the sheer number of organizations that have already adopted that particular innovation (Abrahamson, 1991), are common examples of this type of influence. Here, organizations adopt a particular technology or practice not because of efficiency considerations, but because of the mimetic pressure to follow the crowd. When sustained over time, such practices may be gradually internalized, thus altering the nature of the employment relationship.

Other contextual factors can also influence HRM practices directly through the other forces, such as rational considerations and normative pressure. For instance, a tight labor market may directly influence certain HR practices, such as reducing investments in employee training (Ang, Van Dyne, & Begley, 1999). This influence occurs mainly through economic considerations without altering the employment relationship first. However, if reduced investments in employee training persist, the employment relationship is likely to become more transactional over time, which further reinforces organizations' decisions to cut down on training costs.

To recapitulate, we have proposed a model that argues for both direct and indirect influences of the external context on HRM. In either case, the employment relationship remains an important concept underlying HRM practices. In the case of indirect influence, the nature of the employment relationship can affect HRM practices through its impact on the control focus of the HRM system. In the case of direct influence, HRM practices will alter the nature of the employment relationship over time, which will in turn serve to reinforce those HRM practices. In the next and final section, we relate our theoretical model to Asian HRM practices, and conclude with suggestions for future research on comparative HRM.

ASIAN HRM REVISITED

How can our framework explain existing findings on HRM practices in Asia presented in the earlier part of this chapter? To begin, we first speculate on the nature of the employment relationship of Asia in general. Given that Asian countries have generally been found to be more collectivistic than their Western counterparts (e.g., Hofstede, 1984; Smith et al., 1996), we anticipate that the employment relationship in Asia will be based more on expectations for symbolic and intangible resources (e.g., harmony, affection, loyalty, cooperation, etc). In addition, since Asian countries also emphasize more on particularistic obligations and ascription (rather than achievement) (Smith et al., 1996), we also expect the Asian employment relationship to revolve more around particularistic rather than universalistic resources.

Taken together, we argue that the employment relationship should be more relational in Asia than compared to the West. This is consistent with many existing findings. For instance, comparative studies examining work values have reported that Asian employees place a significantly greater emphasis on harmonious relationships, collective welfare, and cooperation, while placing less emphasis on material rewards and individual recognition compared to their counterparts from the West, usually the US (e.g., Elizur, Borg, Hunt, & Beck,

1991; Shenkar & Ronen, 1987; Weldon & Jehn, 1993). Ng and Ilgen (1999) found that Asian teaching assistants generally possessed more relational and less transactional psychological contracts than their US counterparts. Likewise, Hofstede (1993) and Yang (2000) propose that motivation in Southeast Asia and Chinese societies respectively centers on social acceptance rather than individual achievement. This is also aligned with Whiteley, Cheung and Zhang's (2000) proposition that the philosophy of the man at work is different under the Chinese system and the Western system of management. In the former, man is seen as an adaptive, family-oriented, socially responsible being. Rewards based on social approval, family honor and face are likely to be more effective than instituting calculative, individual-driven incentives. In the latter Western system, the man at work is a rational/economic being with a focus on maximizing monetary rewards and efficiency.

However, due to the diverse economic, political, legal, and labor market conditions characterizing the various Asian countries, we expect some degree of divergence in the nature of the employment relationship within the region. For instance, the four NICs (Singapore, Taiwan, Hong Kong and South Korea) are likely to have a more transactional employment relationship than countries such as India, China, Malaysia and Thailand due to their more advanced economic development, tighter labor markets, and greater enforcement of labor laws. The work of Van Dyne & Ang (1998) and Ang, Tan & Ng (2000) for instance, suggest that Singaporean employees expect a mix of relational and transactional elements in their employment relationship. Through a series of interviews with managers, Singapore employees were described as flexible and willing to take on broad and ambiguous roles in their jobs (i.e., relational). At the same time, they had a rather "temporary" outlook toward the employment relationship, preferring to remain employable in the job market rather than remaining loyal to one firm.

China's employment relationship may, at the moment, be the most relational because of her closed-door policy until her economic liberation in 1978. However, we expect this to change rapidly in the next few years to become more transactional in orientation.

Figure 3 presents our speculations of the employment relationship of the various Asian countries with that in the U.S. The figure illustrates that in general, Asian countries are more relational (i.e., symbolic and particularistic resources) in their employment relationship.

According to our theoretical model, this relational orientation in turn influences the type of HRM practices commonly observed in Asia, which may be summarized as having a strong input control focus and a weak output control focus. For instance, selection and appraisal criteria typically focus on achieving person-organization (P-O) fit, with more emphasis given to individuals' attitudes (e.g., attitude to learning, conforming) and traits (e.g., diligence) than to work experience and specialized skills. The seniority-based system common in Asia may be interpreted as another example of an input-control mechanism, since it presumes that selecting the right people who will remain with the firm for a long time is desired. Likewise, the prevalent use of internal recruitment and referrals in external recruitment is consistent with an input-control emphasis, where it matters more who the person is, rather than his/her achievements.

On the other hand, the less widespread use of individual-based incentive plans point to a weaker output-control focus in Asian HRM practices. Another HRM practice that reflects such a weak output control focus is the broad and ambiguous job scope typical in Asia. Unlike the US where poorly-defined jobs may result in legal lawsuits (e.g., Thompson & Thompson, 1982), it is common to have less defined job boundaries in Asia (e.g., Ang et al., 2000; Lincoln, Hanada, & McBride, 1986).

CONCLUSION

This chapter reviews HRM practices in Asia, and highlights the importance of understanding the employment relationship in examining the types of HRM practices in the region. Why is it important to examine the nature of the employment relationship in furthering our understanding of HRM, particularly in a global context? To quote Jackson and Schuler (1995: 264),

"To meet this [global HRM] challenge, those responsible for the design of globally effective HRM must shift their focus away from the almost overwhelming variety of specific practices and policies found around the world and look instead at the more abstract, fundamental dimensions of contexts, HRM systems, and dimensions of employees' reactions."

Thus, by exploring the abstract, and often-time implicit assumptions underlying the HRM practices, research can advance to developing an integrated conceptual base for the field of HRM, which at the moment, is dominated by a disjointed set of employment practices (Snell, 1992). By probing the underlying assumptions of the employment relationship, HRM scholars can offer an overarching construct to examine the (in)consistencies of HRM practices, rather than treat different HR functions and practices independently.

Further, the need to understand the fundamental assumptions of the employment relationship is accentuated by the transcending of cultural boundaries. This is because culture, being the "software of the mind" (Hofstede, 1991), is likely to give rise to a very different set of assumptions in many spheres of life, including the employment relationship. Hence, variations in national HRM systems can be better understood when examined in the context of fundamental assumptions governing the employment relationship.

In this chapter, we have presented a very broad model that attempts to understand cross-national differences in HRM practices, and subsequently applied it to the Asian context. Through our model, we hope to highlight three important general directions that future research in international HRM should aim toward. First, as aptly pointed out by Barrett and Bass (1976) with reference to I/O research, there is no longer a question on whether or not culture really mattered, but how culture matters. In this chapter, we have provided a theoretical model explaining *how* and *why* HRM practices can be shaped by their environmental context. Future international HRM research should move away from the current *what* paradigm and strive toward gaining a deeper understanding of the process and the mechanisms underlying culture and HRM.

Second, Kochan, Batt and Dyer (1992) lamented that much of the existing work on international HRM tends to focus on cultural explanations to the exclusion of the political, economic, institutional, and strategic context. We concur, and have hence included these other critical contextual factors in our model and highlighted their influence on the employment relationship and HRM practices. Future research should take good heed of Kochan et al.'s advice, and build broader sets of research questions that can provide greater insights into international HRM.

Third, we have proposed a dynamic framework that takes into account time. Given the rapid changes taking place in this global economy, it is imperative that future research adopt a dynamic, as opposed to a static, model of international HRM. One application of our model to a current phenomenon is to understand the impact of the recent economic downturn experienced by most Asian countries since 1997. In order to remain viable, Asian firms may retrench employees or drastically reduce their training costs, thus reflecting a direct influence of the economy on HRM practices. According to our model, such practices may alter the nature of the employment relationship in the long run, causing it to become more transactional over time.

Finally, we suggest that future comparative HRM research may take our model as a starting point to formulate more specific and testable hypotheses in cross-national HRM systems. We also urge future research to examine in greater depth, the nature of the employment relationship in making predictions about cross-cultural/national differences HRM systems. We have proposed a transactional-relational framework based on the concreteness and universalism of resources expected in the employment exchange relationship. More conceptual and empirical efforts should be expended to validate this framework, as well as to uncover additional dimensions pertaining to the nature of the employment relationship. These advances will help create overarching constructs for HRM research, and allow more systematic comparisons of HRM systems across the globe. Last but not least, such efforts can facilitate the development of parsimonious theories and the accumulation of knowledge in the field.

REFERENCES

Abrahamson, E. 1991. Fads and fashions: The diffusion and rejection of innovations. *Academy of Management Review*, 16: 586-612.

Ang, S., Van Dyne, L. and Begley, T.M. 1999. Work status and job technology: A field study comparing foreign and local Chinese technicians in Singapore. Paper presented at *Survey Research in Chinese Societies: Methods and Findings*, 27-28 June, Hong Kong University Science and Technology, HKUST.

Ang, S., Tan, M.L. and Ng, K.Y. 2000. Psychological contracts in Singapore. In D.M. Rousseau and R. Schalk (eds.), *Psychological Contracts in Employment: Cross-national Perspectives* (pp. 213-230). Thousand Oaks, CA: Sage.

Barrett, G.V. and Bass, B.M. 1976. Cross-cultural issues in industrial and organizational psychology. In M. Dunnette (ed.), *Handbook of Industrial and Organizational Psychology* (pp. 1639-1686). Chicago: Rand McNally.

Bian, Y. and Ang, S. 1997. Guanxi networks and job mobility in China and Singapore. *Social Forces*, 75: 981-1005.

Bond, M.H. 1988. Finding universal dimensions of individual variation in multicultural studies of values: The Rokeach and Chinese Value Surveys. *Journal of Personality and Social Psychology*, 55: 1009-1015.

Bridges, W.P. and Villemez, W.J. 1995. *The Employment Relationship: Causes and Consequences of Modern Personnel Administration*. New York: Plenum Press.

Burns, T. and Stalker, G.M. 1961. *The Management of Innovation*. London: Tavistock.

Cascio, W.F. 1982. *Applied Psychology in Personnel Management*. Reston, VA: Reston.

Chang, Y.N. 1976. Early Chinese management thought. *California Management Review*, 19(2): 71-76.

Chen, S. 1998. The development of HRM practices in Taiwan. In C. Rowley (ed.), *Human Resource Management in the Asia Pacific Region* (pp. 152-169). London, UK: Frank Cass & Company.

Chen, M. 1995. *Asian Management Systems: Chinese, Japanese, and Korean Styles of Business*. London: Routledge.

Chew, I. and Goh, M. 1997. Some future directions of human resource practices in Singapore. *Career Development International*, 2: 238-244.

Child, J. 1994. *Management in China During the Age of Reform*. Cambridge: Cambridge University Press.

Chinese Culture Connection. 1987. Chinese values and the search for culture-free dimensions of culture. *Journal of Cross-Cultural Psychology*, 18: 143-164.

DiMaggio, P.J. and Powell, W.W. 1983. The iron cage revisited: Institutional isomorphism and collective rationality in organizational fields. *American Sociological Review*, 48: 147-160.

Elizur, D., Borg, I., Hunt, R. and Beck, I.M. 1991. The structure of work values: A cross-cultural comparison. *Journal of Organizational Behavior*, 12: 21-38.

Entrekin, L. and Chung, Y.W. 2001. Attitudes toward different sources of executive appraisal: A comparison of Hong Kong Chinese and American managers in Hong Kong. *International Journal of Human Resource Management*, 12: 965-987.

Farh, J.L. 1995. Human resource management in Taiwan, the Republic of China. In L.F. Moore and P.D. Jennings (eds.), *Human Resource Management on the Pacific Rim: Institutions, Practices and Attitudes* (pp. 265-294). Berlin: Walter de Gruyter.

Foa, U.G. 1971. Interpersonal and economic resources: Their structure and differential properties offer new insight into problems of modern society. *Science*, 171: 345-351.

Foa, U.G. 1976. Resource theory of social exchanges. In J.S. Thibaut, J. Spence and R. Carson (eds.), *Contemporary Topics in Social Psychology*. Morristown, NJ: General Learning Press.

Foa, U.G. and Foa, E.B. 1974. *Societal Structures of the Mind*. Springfield, IL: Charles Thomas.

Friedman, M. and Friedman, R. 1980. *Free to Choose*. Harmondsworth: Penguin Books.

Fuller, E. and Peterson, R.B. 1992. China and Taiwan: Common culture but divergent economic success. *Advances in International Comparative Management*, 7: 185-201.

Goodall, K. and Warner, M. 1997. Human resources in Sino-foreign joint ventures: Selected case studies in Shanghai, compared with Beijing. *The International Journal of Human Resource Management*, 8: 569-594.

Gooderham, P.N., Nordhaug, O. and Ringdal, K. 1999. Institutional and rational determinants of organizational practices: Human resource management in European firms. *Administrative Science Quarterly*, 44: 507-531.

Gopalan, S. and Rivera, J.B. 1997. Gaining a perspective on Indian value orientations: Implications for expatriate managers. *The International Journal of Organizational Analysis*, 5(2): 156-179.

Harbison, F. and Myers, C. 1959. *Management in the Industrial World: An International Study*. New York: McGraw-Hill.

Hashimoto, M. 1994. Employment-based training in Japanese firms in Japan and in the United States: Experiences of automobile manufacturers. In L.M. Lynch (ed.), *Training and the Private Sector: International Comparisons* (pp. 109-148). Chicago, IL: National Bureau of Economic Research.

Hill, C.W.L. and Hoskisson, R.E. 1987. Strategy and structure in multiproduct firms. *Academy of Management Review*, 12: 331-341.

Hitt, M.A., Hoskisson, R.E. and Ireland, R.D. 1990. Mergers and acquisitions and managerial commitment to innovation in M-form firms. *Strategic Management Journal*, 11 (special issue): 29-47.

Hoffman, C. 1981. People's Republic of China. In A.A. Blum (ed.), *International Handbook of Industrial Relations*. Westport, CT: Greenwood Press.

Hofstede, G. 1984. *Culture's Consequences: International Differences in Work-related Values*. Beverly Hills, Sage.

Hofstede, G. 1991. *Cultures and Organizations: Software of the Mind*. New York: McGraw Hill.

Hofstede, G. 1993. The applicability of McGregor's theories in Southeast Asia. In P. Blunt and D. Richards (eds.), *Readings in Management, Organization and Culture in East and Southeast Asia* (pp. 133-142). Darwin, Australia: Northern Territory University.

Hofstede, G. and Bond, M.H. 1993. The Confucius connection: From cultural roots to economic growth. In P. Blunt and D. Richards (eds.), *Readings in Management, Organization and Culture in East and Southeast Asia* (pp. 105-121). Darwin, Australia: Northern Territory University.

Hsu, Y.R. and Leat, M. 2000. A study of HRM and recruitment and selection policies and practices in Taiwan. *International Journal of Human Resource Management*, 11: 413-435.

Huang, H.J. and Cullen, J.B. 2001. Labor flexibility and related HRM practices: A study of large Taiwanese manufacturers. *Canadian Journal of Administrative Sciences*, 18: 33-39.

Huang, H.J., Eveleth, D.M. and Huo, Y.P. 2000. A Chinese work-related value system. In C.M. Lau, K.K.S. Law, D.K. Tse and C.S. Wong (eds.), *Asian Management Matters: Regional Relevance and Global Impact* (pp. 33-46). London: Imperial College Press.

Jackson, S.E. and Schuler, R.S. 1995. Understanding human resource management in the context of organizations and their environment. *Annual Review of Psychology*, 46: 237-264.

Jennings, P.D. 1994. Viewing macro HRM from without: Political and institutional perspectives. In G.R. Ferris and K.M. Rowland (eds.), *Research in Personnel and Human Resources Management* (Vol. 12, pp.1-40). Greenwich, CT: JAI Press.

Jennings, P.D. and Moore, L.F. 1995. Introduction and theoretical rationale. In L.F. Moore and P.D. Jennings (eds.), *Human Resource Management on the Pacific Rim: Institutions, Practices and Attitudes* (pp. 7-27). Berlin: Walter de Gruyter.

Kalleberg, A.L. and Lincoln, J.R. 1988. The structure of earnings inequality in the Untied States and Japan. *American Journal of Sociology*, 94: S121-S153.

Kirkbride, P.S. and Tang, S.F.Y. 1989. *The Present State of Personnel Management in Hong Kong*. Hong Kong: The Management Development Center of Hong Kong.

Kuruvilla, S. 1996. Linkages between industrialization strategies and industrial relations/human resource Polices: Singapore, Malaysia, the Philippines, and India. *Industrial and Labor Relations Review*, 49: 635-657.

Koch, M., Nam, S.H. and Steers, R.M. 1995. Human resource management in South Korea. In L.F. Moore and P.D. Jennings (eds.), *Human Resource Management on the Pacific Rim: Institutions, Practices and Attitudes* (pp. 217-242). Berlin: Walter de Gruyter.

Kochan, T.A., Batt, R. and Dyer, L. 1992. International human resource studies: A framework for future research. In D. Lewin, O.S. Mitchell and P.D. Sherer (eds.), *Research Frontiers in Industrial Relations and Human Resources*. Madison, WI: Industrial Relations Research Association.

Kuruvilla, S. and Venkataratnam, C.S. 1996. Economic development and industrial relations: The case of South and Southeast Asia. *Industrial Relations Journal*, 27: 9-23.

Latham, G.A. and Napier, N.K. 1989. Chinese human resource management practices in Hong Kong and Singapore: An exploratory study. In G.R. Ferris and K.M. Rowland (eds.), *Research in Personnel and Human Resources Management* (supplement 1, pp. 173-199). Greenwich, CT: JAI Press.

Lawler, J.J. and Atmiyanandana, V. 1995. Human resource management in Thailand. In L.F. Moore and P.D. Jennings (eds.), *Human Resource Management on the Pacific Rim: Institutions, Practices and Attitudes* (pp. 295-318). Berlin: Walter de Gruyter.

Lawrence, B. 1996. Performance appraisal. In G. Thong (ed.), *Human Resource Issues in Singapore* (pp. 103-126). Singapore: Addison-Wesley.

Lawrence, P.R. and Lorsch, J.W. 1967. *Organization and Environment: Managing Differentiation and Integration*. Boston: Harvard University Press.

Lincoln, J.R., Hanada, M. and McBride, K. 1986. Organizational structures in Japanese and U.S. manufacturing. *Administrative Science Quarterly*, 31: 338-364.

Lincoln, J.R. and Nakata, Y. 1997. The transformation of the Japanese employment system: Nature, depth, and origins. *Work and Occupations*, 24: 33-55.

MacNeil, I.R. 1980. *The New Social Contract*. NY: Yale University Press.

McLean Parks, J., Conlon, D.E., Ang, S. and Bontempo, R. 1999. The manager Giveth, the manager Taketh away: Variation in distribution/recovery rules due to resource type and cultural orientation, *Journal of Management*, 25: 723-757.

Meyer, J.W. and Rowan, B. 1977. Institutionalized organizations: Formal structure as myth and ceremony. *American Journal of Sociology*, 83: 340-363.

Milliman, J., Nason, S., Von Glinow, M.A., Huo, P., Lowe, K.B. and Kim, N. 1995. In search of "best" strategic pay practices: An exploratory study of Japan, Korea, Taiwan and the United States. *Advances in International Comparative Management*, 10: 227-252.

Morishima, M. 1995. Embedding HRM in a social context. *British Journal of Industrial Relations*, 33: 617-640.

Morishima, M. 1995. The Japanese human resource management system: A learning bureaucracy. In L.F. Moore and P.D. Jennings (eds.), *Human Resource Management on the Pacific Rim: Institutions, Practices and Attitudes* (pp. 119-150). Berlin: Walter de Gruyter.

Mroczkowski, T. and Hanaoka, M. 1989. Continuity and change in Japanese management. *California Management Review*, 31(2): 39-53.

National Human Resources Handbook. 2000. Optimising talent through good human resources practices. Singapore: Ministry of Manpower.

Ng, K.Y. and Ilgen, D.R. 1999. Culture and psychological contract: Effects on job satisfaction and guilt. Paper presented at the 59th Annual Meeting of the Academy of Management, Chicago, Illinois.

Nyaw, M. 1995. Human resource management in the People's Republic of China. In L.F. Moore and P.D. Jennings (eds.), *Human Resource Management on the Pacific Rim: Institutions, Practices and Attitudes* (pp. 187-216). Berlin: Walter de Gruyter.

Ornatowski, G.K. 1998. The end of Japanese-style human resource management? *Sloan Management Review*, 39(3): 73-84.

Oshima, H.T. 1988. Human resources in East Asia's secular growth. *Economic Development and Cultural Change*, 36(3): S103-S122.

Ouchi, W.G. 1977. The relationship between organizational structure and organizational control. *Administrative Science Quarterly*, 20: 95-113.

Ouchi, W.G. 1979. A conceptual framework for the design of organizational and control mechanisms. *Administrative Science Quarterly*, 24: 833-848.

Poon, W.K. 1995. Human resource management in Hong Kong. In L.F. Moore and P.D. Jennings (eds.), *Human Resource Management on the Pacific Rim: Institutions, Practices and Attitudes* (pp. 91-117). Berlin: Walter de Gruyter.

Pucik, V. 1984. White collar human resource management in large Japanese manufacturing firms. *Human Resource Management*, 23: 257-276.

Rousseau, D.M. 1990. New hire perceptions of their own and their employer's obligations: A study of psychological contracts. *Journal of Organizational Behavior*, 11: 389-400.

Rousseau, D.M. 1995. *Psychological Contracts in Organizations*. Thousand Oaks, CA: Sage.

Rousseau, D.M. and Schalk, R. 2000. *Psychological Contracts in Employment: Cross-national Perspectives*. Thousand Oaks, CA: Sage.

Rowley, C. 1998. Introduction: Comparisons and perspectives on HRM in the Asia Pacific. In C. Rowley (ed.), *Human Resource Management in the Asia Pacific Region*. London, UK: Frank Cass & Company.

Sarachek, B. 1990. Chinese administrative thought. *Advances in International Comparative Management*, 5: 149-167.

Schuler, R.S. 1988. Human resource management choices and organizational strategy. In R.S. Schuler, S.A. Youngblood and V.L. Huber (eds.), *Readings in Personnel and Human Resource Management* (pp. 24-39). MN: West Publishing.

Selznick, P. 1957. *Leadership in Administration*. New York: Harper & Row.

Sharma, R.D. 1992. Lack of management training in India: Causes and characteristics. *International Journal of Manpower*, 13(3): 27-34.

Shaw, J.B., Kirkbride, P.S., Fisher, C.D. and Tang, S.F.Y. 1995. Human resource practices in Hong Kong and Singapore: The impact of political forces and imitation processes. *Asia Pacific Journal of Human Resources*, 33: 30-39.

Shenkar, O. and Ronen, S. 1987. Structure and importance of work goals among managers in the PRC. *Academy of Management Journal*, 30: 564-576.

Sinha, D.P. 1991. Indian management: Context, concerns and trends. In J.M. Putti (ed.), *Management: Asian Context* (pp. 95-112). Singapore: McGraw-Hill.

Smith, P.B., Dugan, S. and Trompenaars, F. 1996. National culture and the values of organizational employees: A dimensional analysis across 43 nations. *Journal of Cross Cultural Psychology*, 27: 231-264.

Snape, E., Thompson, D., Yan, F.K. and Redman, T. 1998. Performance appraisal and culture: Practice and attitudes in Hong Kong and Great Britain. *The International Journal of Human Resource Management*, 9: 841-861.

Snell, S.A. 1992. Control theory in strategic human resource management: The mediating effect of administrative information. *Academy of Management Journal*, 35: 292-327.

Tan, C.H. 1989. Human resource management reforms in the People's Republic of China. In G.R. Ferris and K.M. Rowland (eds), *Research in Personnel and Human Resources Management* (supplement 1, pp. 45-58). Greenwich, CT: JAI Press.

Taormina, R.J. and Bauer, T.N. 2000. Organizational socialization in two cultures: Results from the United States and Hong Kong. *The International Journal of Organizational Analysis*, 8: 262-289.

Thompson, J.D. 1967. *Organizations in Action*. New York: McGraw-Hill.

Thompson, D.E. and Thompson, T.A. 1982. Court standards for job analysis in test validation. *Personnel Psychology*, 35: 865-874.

Tsui-Auch, L.S. and Lee, Y.J. (2003). The state matters: Management models of Singaporean Chinese and Korean business groups. *Organization Studies*, 24: 507-534.

Van Buren, M.E. and King, S.B. 2000. ASTD's annual accounting of worldwide patterns in employer-provided training. (pp. 1-24) Training and Development Supplement: The 2000 ASTD International Comparisons Report.

Van Dyne, L. and Ang, S. 1998. Organizational citizenship behavior of contingent workers in Singapore. *Academy of Management Journal*, 41: 692-703.

Venkataratnam, C.S. 1995. Economic liberalization and the transformation of industrial relations policies in India. In A. Verma, T.A. Kochan and R.D. Lansbury (eds.), *Employment Relations in the Growing Asian Economies* (pp. 248-314). London: Routledge.

Verma, A., Kochan, T.A. and Lansbury, R.D. 1995. Lessons from the Asian experience: A summary. In A. Verma, T.A. Kochan and R.D. Lansbury (eds.), *Employment Relations in the Growing Asian Economies* (pp. 336-357). London: Routledge.

Von Glinow, M.A. and Chung, B.J. 1989. Comparative human resource management practices in the United States, Japan, Korea, and the People's Republic of China. In G.R. Ferris and K.M. Rowland (eds.), *Research in Personnel and Human Resources Management* (supplement 1, pp. 153-171). Greenwich, CT: JAI Press.

Warner, M. 2000. Introduction: The Asia-Pacific HRM model revisited. *International Journal of Human Resource Management*, 11: 171-182.

Weldon, E. and Jehn, K.A. 1993. Work goals and work-related beliefs among managers and professionals in the United States and the People's Republic of China. *Asia Pacific Journal of Human Resources*, 31: 55-70.

White, G., Luk, V., Druker, J. and Chiu, R. 1998. Paying their way: A comparison of managerial reward systems in the London and Hong Kong banking industries. *Asia Pacific Journal of Human Resources*, 36: 54-71.

Whitley, R.D. 1990. Eastern Asian enterprise structures and the comparative analysis of forms of business organization. *Organization Studies*, 11: 47-74.

Whiteley, A.M., Cheung, S. and Zhang, S.Q. 2000. *Human Resource Strategies in China*. NJ: World Scientific.

Williamson, O.E. 1975. *Markets and Hierarchies: Analysis and Antitrust Implications*. New York: Free Press.

Williamson, O.E. 1985. *The Economic Institution of Capitalism*. New York: Free Press.

Yang, N. 2000. Cultural relativity of employee motivation: When West meets East. In C.M. Lau, K.K.S. Law, D.K. Tse and C.S. Wong (eds.), *Asian Management Matters: Regional Relevance and Global Impact* (pp. 47-57). London: Imperial College Press.

Yuen, C. and Yeo, K. 1995. Human resource management practices in Singapore. In L.F. Moore and P.D. Jennings (eds.), *Human Resource Management on the Pacific Rim: Institutions, Practices and Attitudes* (pp. 243-264). Berlin: Walter de Gruyter.

BIOGRAPHICAL SKETCHES

Soon Ang is Professor & Chair, Strategy, Management and Organization, at Nanyang Business School, NTU Singapore & Founding Director for the Center for Cultural Intelligence (CCI). Her research includes international management; outsourcing; leadership development; and careers & work. She has published award winning papers in *Academy of Management Journal*, *Management Science*, *Organization Science*, *Social Forces*, *Journal of Organizational Behavior*, *Journal of Management Studies*, *Information Systems Research*, and others. She recently co-authored a book on the theory of Cultural Intelligence (Stanford University Press, 2003) and is working on a follow-up book on the Practice of Cultural Intelligence.

Richard W. Brislin is Professor of Management and Industrial Relations at the College of Business Administration, University of Hawaii. He is the co-developer of materials used in cross-cultural training programs (e.g., *Intercultural Interactions: A Practical Guide* (2nd edn, 1996) and is author of a text in *cross-cultural psychology* (*Understanding Culture's Influence on Behavior*, 2nd edn, 2000). One of his books, *The Art of Getting Things Done: A Practical Guide to the Use of Power*, was a Book of the Month Club Selection in 1992. He is frequently asked to give workshops for American and Asian managers working on international assignments, and the training materials he has prepared are widely used in various international organizations. He writes a weekly newspaper column on understanding cultural differences in the workplace for the Honolulu Star Bulletin. The website for the most recent columns can be found at http://starbulletin.com/columnists/brislin.html.

Susan Brodt is Associate Professor of Organizational Behavior at Queen's School of Business, Queen's University (Canada). She received her Ph.D. in psychology from Stanford University. Her research focuses on negotiation and business relationships with an emphasis on how people construe or interpret their social environment and its effects on conflict, negotiation and interpersonal trust. She has studied attribution processes and trust, trust rebuilding, and the role of psychological attachment in negotiation and problem solving. Most recently, she has researched the interplay between communication technology, conflict and trust, in geographically distributed multi-cultural teams. Her work has appeared in psychology as well as management journals.

Garry D. Bruton is Associate Professor of Management at the M.J. Neeley School of Business at the Texas Christian University, Fort Worth. He specializes in entrepreneurship and strategic management in emerging international markets. His research interests include strategic alliances, corporate restructuring, high technology entrepreneurship, and venture capital. His prior research has appeared in *Academy of Management Journal*, *Strategic Management Journal*, and the *Journal of Business Venturing*, among other publications.

John Butler is Professor at The Hong Kong Polytechnic University. He has also taught at universities in Thailand, Vietnam and Singapore. He served as Chair of the South East Asia Studies Program at the University of Washington, and much of his research relates to this region. Currently, he serves as editor for *Entrepreneurship Theory & Practice* and series editor for *Research in Entrepreneurship and Management*.

Michael Carney is Professor in the Management Department, John Molson School of Business, Concordia University, Montreal, Canada. He received his Ph.D. in 1984 from the University of Bradford, U.K. His research focuses upon the relationship between corporate strategy, restructuring processes and regulatory reform. In the context of Asia, he is interested in the intergenerational development of overseas Chinese Business Groups. His work on strategy and organization structure has been published in *Strategic Management Journal*, *Organization Studies*, *Journal of Management Studies*, and the *Asia Pacific Journal of Management*.

Wai Chamornmarn is Associate Professor of Human Resources and Organization Management, Faculty of Commerce and Accountancy, Thammasat University, Bangkok, Thailand. He has served as the Associate Director of the Institute of East Asian Studies and his research interests are in the area of entrepreneurship, management values, technological innovation, and the historical development of entrepreneurs and entrepreneurial behavior in Thailand.

Nobuyuki Chikudate is currently Associate Professor of Organization studies in the Department of Management Studies, Graduate School of Social Science, Hiroshima University, Japan. He was born in March, 1963. He received his Ph.D. from State University of New York at Buffalo, and completed the postdoctoral training at the Johns Hopkins University. Formerly, he taught at Tokyo University of Foreign Studies, Asia University-Japan, and so on. His specialities include methodological issues, comparative studies, and cultural studies of organizations. His major publications appeared in such journals as *Journal of Applied Behavioral Science*, *Journal of Business Ethics*, and *Journal of Management Studies*.

John Child holds the Chair of Commerce in the Birmingham Business School, University of Birmingham, U.K. His M.A. and Ph.D. are from the University of Cambridge, which also awarded him an ScD for his outstanding scholarly work. In 2002, he was elected a Fellow of the Academy of Management, and in 2003 received the first Distinguished Contribution Award of the International Academy for Chinese Management Research. Professor Child is author or co-author of 17 books and over 120 articles in learned journals. His new book *Organization: Contemporary Principles and Practice* will be published by Blackwell in 2004.

Eric Gedajlovic is Associate Professor in the Management Department at the University of Connecticut. Previously he was the Associate Professor of International Business at Erasmus University and the Rotterdam School of Management. His research interests pertain to the influence of governance, financial and enterprise systems on firm behaviour, capability creation and performance. His research has appeared in *Organization Studies*, *Strategic Management Journal*, *Academy of Management Journal*, *Journal of Management Studies* and the *Asia Pacific Journal of Management*.

Chun Hui received his Ph.D. from Indiana University at Bloomington, U.S.A. and is currently Professor at the Department of Management, the Chinese University of Hong Kong. His research interests include leadership, conflict management, selection, performance appraisal, comparative management and Chinese management. He has published in major management journals, including *Academy of Management Journal*, *Journal of Applied Psychology*, *Organizational Behavior* and *Human Decision Processes*, and *Journal of International Business Studies*.

Stephen Ko is Lecturer of Management and Marketing at the Hong Kong Polytechnic University. He received an MBA from the Chinese University of Hong Kong, and has taught at universities in Hong Kong. His research focuses on entrepreneurship in high technology firms.

Daryl Koehn holds the Cullen Chair in Business Ethics at the University of St. Thomas in Houston. She founded and edits the *Online Journal of Ethics*. Her books include *The Ground of Professional Ethics*, *Rethinking Feminist*

Ethics: Care, Trust, Empathy, and *Local Insights, Global Ethics for Business, Corporate Governance: Ethics Across the Board*, and *Trust: Barriers and Bridges*. In additional to scores of journal articles in several languages, Professor Koehn regularly publishes in business newspapers and journals. She is routinely quoted in *The New York Times* and has been interviewed several times on National Public Radio. She has been profiled in *Time* and *Life* magazines.

Jessica Y. Y. Kwong is Assistant Professor in the Department of Marketing at The Chinese University of Hong Kong. She received her Ph.D. in industrial-organizational psychology at The Chinese University of Hong Kong. She has interests in organizational justice, personality and work performance, and judgment and decision-making processes.

Hailan Lan is Professor of Management and Dean of the School of Business of Southern China University of Technology in Guangzhou, China. He studies competitive dynamics and strategic management in large business groups, and has published extensively in China and in the *Academy of Management Executive*.

Cynthia Lee received her Ph.D. from University of Maryland and is currently Associate Professor at Northeastern University. Her current research focuses on managing change, motivation, performance management, and Chinese management including group processes and effectiveness, understanding the changing nature of psychological contracts, workplace justice, and effects of job insecurity. She has published in major management journals, including *Academy of Management Journal*, *Journal of Applied Psychology*, *Organizational Behavior* and *Human Decision Processes*, and *Journal of Management*.

Alicia S. M. Leung is Assistant Professor in the Department of Management at Hong Kong Baptist University. She holds a Ph.D. in Management Learning from the University of Lancaster, U.K. Her research interests include gender issues and feminist methodology, business ethics, organizational behavior, and strategic management in the Asian context.

Kwok Leung (Ph.D. in Psychology, University of Illinois) is Professor of management, City University of Hong Kong. His research interests include justice, conflict, and culture, and he has published widely in these areas. He is currently the Editor of *Asian Journal of Social Psychology*, an associate editor of *Asia Pacific Journal of Management*, and a departmental editor of *Journal of International Business Studies*. He is on the editorial board of several journals, including *Journal of Applied Psychology*, *Applied Psychology: An International Review*, and *Journal of Cross-Cultural Psychology*.

Brent Mac Nab is a double Fulbright Scholar and is Lecturer on Asia-Pacific strategy and organizational behavior at the University of Hawaii. His professional interests include research within a range of relevant management topics, including ethics management, Asia-Pacific strategy, NAFTA research and motivation. The common element of cross-cultural psychology normally encompasses his work. In addition to his academic endeavors, Brent has worked directly on projects with organizations including BankAmerica Corp., AT&T Wireless and Volkswagen of America, Inc. in aspects of management and promotion. Brent can be reached at bmacnab@cba.hawaii.edu.

Kok Yee Ng is Assistant Professor in Organizational Behavior and Human Resource Management in the Division of Strategy, Management & Organization at the Nanyang Business School. She received her Ph.D. from Michigan State University, with a major in Organizational Behavior and minor in I/O Psychology. Her research interests are in cross cultural I/O psychology and international organizational behavior, focusing in areas such as resource dilemmas, extra-role behavior, leadership and negotiation. She has published in the *Journal of Applied Psychology*, *Organizational Behavior And Human Decision Processes*, and *Management Science*.

Mara Olekalns currently teaches negotiation at the Melbourne Business School. Before joining MBS, Professor Olekalns taught organisational behaviour for the Department of Management at Melbourne University, and the Department of Psychology at the University of Otago (New Zealand). She has also worked for several Australian government departments, in research and management roles. Professor Olekalns' research examines the relationships between how individuals think about negotiation, what they do and say during the negotiation, and their outcomes. The aim of her research is to help negotiators understand and improve the process of negotiating, so that they can create better agreements.

Nitin Pangarkar received his Ph.D. from the University of Michigan in 1993. He teaches strategy and international business courses at the National University of Singapore. Previously, he has held visiting academic positions at the University of Minnesota (USA) and the Helsinki School of Economics (Finland). His research interests lie in the areas of strategic management and international business—specifically cross-border strategic alliances, mode of entry and global strategy. Dr Pangarkar's research has been published in the form of several international journal articles, conference proceedings, cases, and book chapters. He is a co-author of *Business Strategy in Asia: A Casebook (2nd edition)* published by Thomson Learning in 2003/04.

Hun-Joon Park (Ph.D., The Ohio State University) is Professor of Management and Associate Dean at Yonsei School of Business, Seoul, Korea. He was Director at the Korea Research Foundation and Visiting Associate Professor at the Ohio State University and Bowling Green State University. He has also served as Managing Director for the Korea Institute of Management Case Research. He has been actively involved in consulting with many Korean firms in addition to his contributions to the academic community. He has published articles in *Academy of Management Journal, Organizational Behavior and Human Decision Processes, Journal of Business Ethics, Asia Pacific Business Review, International Journal of Entrepreneurship and Innovation Management*, and many other Korean academic journals. His research interests include top management team, corporate governance, leadership, and negotiation.

Oded Shenkar is the Ford Motor Company Chair in Global Business Management at the Fisher College of Business, The Ohio State University. Professor Shenkar, who also holds a degree in East-Asian Studies, has been studying comparative and international management for a quarter of a century and is particularly interested in cross-border alliances. He has published over eighty refereed articles and books with Blackwell, M.E. Sharpe, Prentice-Hall, Routledge and John Wiley & Sons, and is on the editorial board of the *Academy of Management Executive, Human Relations, Management International Review, Organization Studies, International Journal of Cross-Cultural Management* and *Journal of International Business Studies*.

Kulwant Singh is Associate Professor of Business Policy at The National University of Singapore. He studies competition and alliances in technology intensive and rapidly changing industries, as well as strategy and competition in Asia. His research has been published in *Strategic Management Journal, Academy of Management Journal, Organization Science, Journal of Management, Journal of Economic Behavior and Organization*, and *Industrial and Corporate Change*.

Jai B. B. Sinha is Professor of psychology & management in ASSERT Institute of Management Studies, Patna (India). He has taught in India, USA, and Canada. Professor Sinha has been associated with International Association of Applied Psychology, the International Association for Cross Cultural Psychology and World Association for Dynamic Psychiatry. He has published over 150 research articles and half a dozen books, some of which are *Multinationals in India: Managing the Interface of Cultures, Patterns of Work Culture, Cultural Context of Leadership and Power, Work Culture in the Indian Context: The Nurturant Task Leader*, and *Some Problems of Public Sector Organizations*.

Steven Su is Assistant Professor at INSEAD in Fontainebleau, France and Singapore. His work focuses on the intersection between cultural psychology and Organizational Behavior. Steve received his Ph.D. from the Graduate School of Business at Stanford University.

Sang-Hyeon Sung is chief researcher and consultant in the field of HRM and organization at Samsung Economic Research Institute (SERI), Seoul, Korea. He has designed and provided consultancy to HRM architectures in industries of electronics, insurance, investment banking, petrochemical, textiles, and paper. His research interests include group dynamics, diversity, virtual organization, and strategic human resources management. He graduated from Seoul National University (BA) and Yonsei School of Business (MBA), and is currently a Ph.D. candidate (ABD) in management at Yonsei School of Business.

Catherine H. Tinsley is Associate Professor at the McDonough School of Business at Georgetown University, having received her Masters and Ph.D. in Organizational Behavior from J.L. Kellogg Graduate School of Management at Northwestern University. She is a faculty affiliate at the School for Advanced International Studies at John's Hopkins University, the Center for Peace and Securities Studies at the Edmund Walsh School of Foreign Service, and is a Zaeslin fellow at the College of Law and Economics, University of Basel. She studies how factors such as culture, reputations, negotiator mobility, and perceptions of fairness influence how people negotiate and how they manage conflict.

Dean Tjosvold (Ph.D., University of Minnesota) is Chair Professor, Lingnan University, Hong Kong. In 1992, Simon Fraser University awarded him a University Professorship for his research contributions. He has published over 200 articles and fifteen books on managing conflict, cooperation and competition, decision making, power, and other management issues. He is past president of the International Association of Conflict Management and has served on several editorial boards, including the *Academy of Management Review*, *Journal of Management* and *Journal of Organizational Behavior*. He is a partner in his family health care business, which has 600 employees and is based in Minnesota.

Steven White is Assistant Professor of Asian Business and Comparative Management at INSEAD. He studies the dynamics of organizational change, interorganizational relationships, and cross-cultural management issues. His work has appeared in the *Academy of Management Journal*, *Journal of Management Studies*, *Organization Studies*, *Research Policy* and *Asia Pacific Journal of Management*.

Alfred Wong is Associate Professor of Management and Associate BBA Programme Director at Lingnan University in Hong Kong. Before he joined Lingnan in 1991, he had worked in the business field for several years. He earned his Ph.D. from Sheffield Hallam University, UK. Alfred Wong's research interests include supply chain management, quality management, leadership and teamwork. He has published research articles in international journals including *International Journal of Physical Distribution & Logistics Management, International Journal of Quality and Reliability Management, International Journal of Technology Management, Journal of General Management, Logistics Information Management, The Leadership & Organization Development Journal* and *Total Quality Management.*

Zhixing Xiao is Ph.D. candidate at INSEAD and will join CEIBS (China Europe International Business School) in Shanghai as a resident faculty member in 2004. Before he joined the INSEAD Ph.D. program, he worked for a multinational company and a state-owned company in China. His research focuses on comparative management issues, social capital, social networks and guanxi.

Lu Yuan is Professor at Department of Management, Chinese University of Hong Kong, where he teaches strategic management, management of Chinese firms, and general management. Dr. Lu received his Ph.D. degree in 1991 at the University of Aston, Birmingham, the United Kingdom, and then worked as a research associate at School of Management, the University of Lancaster. Prior to joining Chinese University of Hong Kong, he was the Rothmans Research Fellow at the Judge Institute of Management Studies, University of Cambridge (1993–96). His research focuses on strategic decision-making, Chinese management, and international strategic alliances. Dr. Lu Yuan has played a leading role in a number of research projects studying international joint ventures and multinational corporations in China and strategic management in Chinese firms. His current research concerns strategic management in the digital economy, business networks, mergers and acquisitions, diversification and restructuring strategies in China. Dr. Lu Yuan is author of *Management Decision-making in Chinese Enterprises* (1996, by Macmillan) and co-editor of *Management Issues for China in the 1990s: International Enterprises* (1996, Routledge). He has also contributed to publications in *Academy of Management Executives, Organization Studies, Organization Science, Journal of General Management, International Journal of Human Resource Management,* and *Journal of World Business.* Apart from academic research, he also acts as a consultant to multinational corporations and Chinese companies on strategic management and management of joint ventures. He was recently invited to be an external advisor to the Strategy Committee of Guangdong Kelon Electrical Corp.

AUTHOR INDEX

SUBJECT INDEX